Clinical
Neuropsychology

Clinical Neuropsychology

SECOND EDITION

Edited by

KENNETH M. HEILMAN, M.D.

PROFESSOR OF NEUROLOGY AND CLINICAL PSYCHOLOGY
UNIVERSITY OF FLORIDA COLLEGE OF MEDICINE

EDWARD VALENSTEIN, M.D.

PROFESSOR OF NEUROLOGY AND CLINICAL PSYCHOLOGY
UNIVERSITY OF FLORIDA COLLEGE OF MEDICINE

New York   Oxford
OXFORD UNIVERSITY PRESS
1985

Library of Congress Cataloging in Publication Data

Main entry under title:
Clinical neuropsychology.

Includes bibliographies and index.
1. Neuropsychiatry.   2. Neuropsychology.   I. Heilman,
Kenneth M., 1938–   .   II. Valenstein, Edward.   [DNLM:
1. Behavior.   2. Nervous system diseases.   3. Neurologic
manifestations.   4. Psychophysiology.   WL 340 C641]
RC341.C693   1984   616.89   83-23662
ISBN 0-19-503416-3

Printing (last digit):   9 8 7 6 5 4 3 2

Printed in the Unites States of America

Preface to the Second Edition

The information explosion that has affected so many areas of knowledge today has not bypassed neuropsychology. While Broca and Wernicke had to wait years for postmortem examinations to confirm their hypotheses, CT, PET, and NMR scanners now provide much of this information without necessitating the patient's demise. The convergence of many disciplines on the investigation of brain-behavior relationships has greatly enriched our understanding of the mechanisms of brain dysfunction. With increasing interest in this area, many more students are being trained than ever before. Students who were being trained in neuropsychology, behavioral neurology, and related disciplines at the time of our first edition only five years ago have by now contributed importantly to our knowledge. Their contributions and those of others have made it necessary to extensively revise many of the chapters in this volume. Some of these chapters have, unavoidably, gotten longer. We did not think that we could do justice to the large area of developmental and child neuropsychology without making this volume unwieldy: we have therefore not included the chapters on learning disabilities and hyperactivity that concluded the first edition. Readers interested in these areas may now consult one of several volumes devoted entirely to these areas.

The organization and approach of the book have otherwise remained unchanged. We are immensely indebted to our contributing authors, most of whom contributed to the first edition: many rewrote their chapters completely, but nevertheless managed to get them to us promptly. The chapter on agraphia has a new author. With deep regret we note the passing of Professor Henri Hécaen, who co-authored this chapter in the first edition.

As before, we are grateful for the editorial assistance provided by Oxford University Press, and for the indulgence and support of our families.

Gainesville, Florida   K.M.H.
August 1984   E.V.

Preface to the First Edition

The growth of interest in brain-behavior relationships has generated a literature that is both impressive and bewildering. In teaching neuropsychology, we have found that the reading lists necessary for adequate coverage of the subject have been unwieldy, and the information provided in the reading has been difficult to integrate. We therefore set out to provide a text that comprehensively covers the major clinical syndromes. The focus of the text is the *clinical* presentation of human brain dysfunction. The authors who have contributed to this volume have provided clinical descriptions of the major neuropsychological disorders. They have discussed methods of diagnosis, and have described specific tests, often of use at the bedside. They have also commented upon therapy. Since the study of pathophysiological and neuropsychological mechanisms underlying these disorders is inextricably intertwined with the definition and treatment of these disorders, considerable space has been devoted to a discussion of these mechanisms, and to the clinical and experimental evidence which bears on them.

A multi-authored text has the advantage of allowing authorities to write about areas in which they have special expertise. This also exposes the reader to several different approaches to the study of brain-behavior relationships, an advantage in a field in which a variety of theoretical and methodological positions have been fruitful. We therefore have not attempted to impose our own views on the contributing authors, but where there were conflicts in terminology, we have provided synonyms and cross-references. Much of brain activity is integrative, and isolated neuropsychological disturbances are rare. Discussions of alexia or agraphia must necessarily include more than a passing reference to aphasia, and so on. Since we wanted each chapter to stand on its own, with its author's viewpoint intact, we have generally allowed some overlap between chapters.

We wish to thank all of the persons who devoted their time and effort to this book. Professor Arthur Benton not only contributed two outstanding chapters, but was instrumental in advising us about authors and content, and in leading us to Oxford University Press. We are grateful to all the other contributing authors, who promptly provided high quality manuscripts; to our secretary, Ann Tison, who typed our manuscripts so many times; and to the editors at Oxford University Press, who helped to improve our grammar and syntax, and, not infrequently, the clarity of our thought. Not least, we are grateful to our families, who have endured many evenings of work with this volume with patience and understanding.

Gainesville, Florida   K.M.H.
March 1979   E.V.

Contents

Contributors

Martin L. Albert, M.D., Ph.D.
Professor of Neurology
Clinical Director, Aphasia Research Center
Boston University School of Medicine and
Chief, Clinical Neurology Section
Neurology Service
Boston Veterans Administration Hospital, Boston

Russell M. Bauer, Ph.D.
Assistant Professor of Clinical Psychology
University of Florida, Gainesville

D. Frank Benson, M.D.
The Augustus S. Rose Professor of Neurology
University of California, Los Angeles

Arthur Benton, Ph.D., D.Sc.
Professor Emeritus of Neurology and Psychology,
University of Iowa, Iowa City

Joseph E. Bogen, M.D.
Clinical Professor, Department of Neurological Surgery
University of Southern California School of Medicine,
and the White Memorial Medical Center, Los Angeles

Dawn Bowers, Ph.D.
Assistant Professor of Neurology (Neuropsychology)
University of Florida, Gainesville

Nelson Butters, Ph.D.
Chief, Psychology Service, San Diego Veterans Administration Medical Center
Professor,
Department of Psychiatry
University of California, San Diego

Antonio R. Damasio, M.D., D. Med. Sci.
Professor of Neurology
Director, Division of Behavioral Neurology
University of Iowa, Iowa City

Rhonda B. Friedman, Ph.D.
Assistant Professor of Neurology (Neuropsychology)
Boston University School of Medicine, Boston

Leslie J. Gonzalez Rothi, Ph.D.
Speech Pathologist, Gainesville Veterans Administration Medical Center
Adjunct Assistant Professor of Neurology and Speech
University of Florida, Gainesville

Kenneth M. Heilman, M.D.
Professor of Neurology and Clinical Psychology
University of Florida College of Medicine
Gainesville

Robert J. Joynt, M.D., Ph.D.
Professor and Chairman, Department of Neurology,
University of Rochester School of Medicine and Dentistry
Strong Memorial Hospital
Rochester

Andrew Kertesz, M.D., F.R.C.P. (C)
Professor, Department of Clinical Neurological Sciences,
University of Western Ontario,
St. Joseph's Hospital, London, Ontario

Harvey S. Levin, Ph.D.
Professor, Division of Neurosurgery, University of Texas Medical Branch
Galveston

Patti Miliotis, M.A.
Research Associate in Psychology
Boston Veterans Administration Medical Center, Boston

David Roeltgen, M.D.
Assistant Professor of Neurology
School of Medicine, University of Missouri Health Sciences Center
Columbia

Alan B. Rubens, M.D.
Associate Professor of Neurology, University of Minnesota,
Chief, Neurobehavioral Unit, Hennepin County Medical Center, Minneapolis

Ira Shoulson, M.D.
Associate Professor of Neurology, Medicine and Pharmacology and Toxicology
University of Rochester School of Medicine and Dentistry and Strong
Memorial Hospital, Rochester

Paul A. Spiers, M.D.
Behavioral Neurology Unit,
Beth Israel Hospital
Harvard Medical School, Boston.

Edward Valenstein, M.D.
Professor of Neurology and Clinical Psychology
University of Florida College of Medicine
Gainesville

Robert T. Watson, M.D.
Professor of Neurology and Neurosciences
University of Florida College of Medicine
Gainesville

Clinical
Neuropsychology

1
Introduction

KENNETH M. HEILMAN AND EDWARD VALENSTEIN

Aristotle thought that the mind, with the function of thinking, had no relation to the body or the senses and could not be destroyed. The first attempts to localize mental processes to the brain may nevertheless be traced back to antiquity. In the fifth century B.C., Hippocrates of Croton claimed that the brain was the organ of intellect and the heart the organ of the senses. Herophilus, in the third century B.C., studied the structure of the brain and regarded it as the site of intelligence. He believed that the middle ventricle was responsible for the faculty of cognition and the posterior ventricle was the seat of memory. Galen, in the second century B.C., thought that the activities of the mind were performed by the substance of the brain rather than the ventricles, but it was not until the anatomical work of Vesalius in the sixteenth century A.D. that this thesis was accepted. Vesalius, however, thought that the brains of most mammals and birds had similar structures in almost every respect except for size and that the brain attained its greatest dimensions in humans. In the seventeenth century, Descartes suggested that the soul resided in the pineal. He chose the pineal because of its central location: all things must emanate from the soul.

At the end of the eighteenth century, Gall postulated that various human faculties were localized in different organs, or centers, of the brain. He thought that these centers were expansions of lower nervous mechanisms and that, although independent, they were able to interact with one another. Unlike Descartes, Gall conceived brain structures as having successive development, with no central point where all nerves unite. He proposed that the vital forces resided in the brainstem and that intellectual qualities were situated in various parts of the two cerebral hemispheres. The hemispheres were united by the commissures, the largest being the corpus callosum.

Unfortunately, Gall also postulated that measurements of the skull may allow one to deduce moral and intellectual characteristics, since the shape of the skull is modified by the underlying brain. This hypothesis was the foundation of phrenology. When phrenology fell into disrepute, many of Gall's original contributions were blighted. His teachings, however, are the foundation of modern neuropsychology.

Noting that students with good verbal memory had prominent eyes, Gall suggested that memory for words was situated in the frontal lobes. He studied two patients who had lost their memory for words and attributed their disorder to frontal lobe lesions. In 1825, Bouillaud wrote that he also believed cerebral function to be localized. He demonstrated that discrete lesions could produce paralysis in one limb and not others, and cited this as proof of localized function. He also believed that the anterior lobe was the center of speech. He observed that the tongue had many functions other than speech and that one function could be disordered (e.g., speech) while others remained intact (e.g., mastication). This observation suggested to him that an effector can have more than one center that controls its actions.

In 1861, Broca heard Bouillaud's pupil Auburtin speak about the importance of the anterior lobe in speech and asked Auburtin to see a patient suffering from right hemiplegia and loss of speech and writing. The patient was able to understand speech but could articulate only one word, "tan." This patient died, and postmortem inspection of the brain revealed that there was a cavity filled with fluid on the lateral aspect of the left hemisphere. When the fluid was drained, there could be seen a large left-hemisphere lesion that included the first temporal gyrus, the insula and corpus striatum, and the frontal lobe, including the second and third frontal convolutions as well as the inferior portion of the transverse convolution. In 1861, Broca saw another patient who had lost the power of speech and writing but could comprehend spoken language. Autopsy again revealed a left-hemisphere lesion involving the second and third frontal convolutions.

Broca later saw eight patients who had suffered a loss of speech (which he called *aphemia*, but which Trousseau later called *aphasia*). All eight had left-hemisphere lesions. This was the first demonstration of left-hemisphere dominance for language (Broca, 1865).

Broca's observations produced great excitement in the medical world. Despite his clear demonstration of left-hemisphere dominance, medical opinion appeared to split into two camps, one favoring the view that different functions are exercised by the various portions of the cerebral hemisphere and the other denying that psychic functions are or can be localized.

Following Broca's initial observations, there was a flurry of activity. In 1868, Hughlings Jackson noted that there were two types of aphasic patients—fluent and nonfluent—and, in 1869, Bastian argued that there were patients who had deficits not only in the articulation of words but also in the memory for words. Bastian also postulated the presence of a visual and auditory word center and a kinesthetic center for the hand and the tongue. He proposed that these centers were connected and that information, such as language, was processed by the brain in different ways by each of these centers. Lesions in these centers would thus produce distinct syndromes, depending upon which aspect of the processing was disturbed. Bastian thus viewed the brain as a processor. He was the first to describe word deafness and word blindness.

In 1874, Wernicke published his famous *Der Aphasische Symptomenkomplex*. He was familiar with Meynert's work which demonstrated that sensory systems project to the posterior portions of the hemispheres whereas the anterior portions appear to be efferent. Wernicke noted that lesions of the posterior portion of the superior temporal region produced an aphasia in which comprehension was poor. He thought that this auditory center contained sound images while Broca's area contained images for

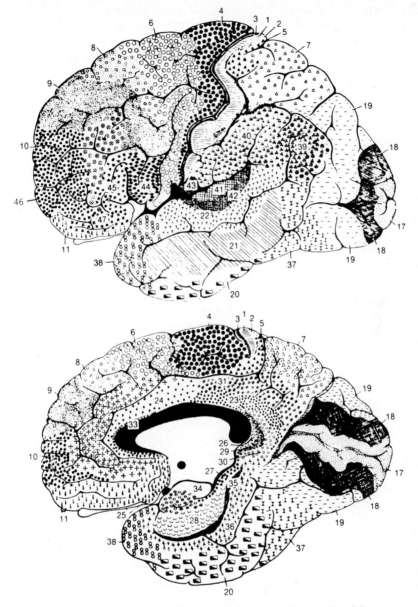

Fig. 1-1. Brodmann's cytoarchitectural map of the human brain. The different areas are defined on the basis of subtle differences in cortical cell structure and organization. Broca's area corresponds roughly to areas 44 and 45 and Wernicke's area to the posterior part of area 22.

movement. He also thought that these areas were connected by a commissure and that a lesion of this commissure would disconnect the area for sound images from the area for images of movement.

Wernicke's scheme could account for motor, conduction, and sensory aphasia with poor repetition. Lichtheim (1885), however, described patients who were nonfluent but repeated normally and sensory aphasics who could not comprehend but could repeat words. Elaborating on Wernicke's ideas, he devised a complex scheme to explain the mechanisms underlying seven types of speech and language disorders.

Following World War I, the localizationist-connectionist approach was abandoned in favor of a holistic approach. Probably there were many factors underlying this change. The localizationist theory was built on the foundation laid by Gall. When phrenology was discredited, other localizationist theorizes became suspect. Lashley (1938), using experimental methods (as opposed to the case reports of the classical neurologists), found that engrams were not localized in the brain but rather appeared to be diffusely represented. From these observations, he proposed a theory of mass action: the behavioral result of a lesion depends on the amount of brain removed more than on the location of the lesion. Head (1926) studied aphasics' linguistic performance and was not satisfied with the classical neurologists' attempts to deduce schemas from clinical observations. Discussing one of Wernicke's case reports, he wrote, "No better example could be chosen of the manner in which the writers of this period were compelled to lop and twist their cases to fit the Procrustean bed of their hypothetical conceptions." Although Freud studied the relationships between brain and behavior early in his career, he later provided the scientific world with psychodynamic theories of behavior that did not rely on an understanding of brain-behavior relationships. The Gestalt psychologists abandoned localizationism and connectionism in favor of the holistic approach.

Social and political influences, however, were perhaps more important in changing neuropsychological thought than were the newer scientific theories. The continental European scientific community was strongly influenced by Kant's *Critique of Pure Reason*, which held that, although knowledge cannot transcend experience, it is nevertheless in part a priori. According to Kant, the outer world produces only the matter of sensation while the mental apparatus (the brain) orders this matter and supplies the concepts by means of which we understand experience. After World War I, the influence of science on the continent waned while in English-speaking countries it bloomed. The American and English political and social systems were strongly influenced by Locke, the seventeenth-century liberal philosopher who, unlike Kant, believed that behavior and ideas were not innate but rather derived from experience.

In the second half of the twentieth century, there has been a reawakening of interest in brain-behavior relationships. Many developments contributed to this. The classical neurologists were rediscovered and their findings replicated. Electronic technology provided researchers with new instruments for observing physiological processes. New statistical procedures enabled them to distinguish random results from significant behavior. New behavioral paradigms, such as dichotic listening and lateral visual half-field viewing, permitted psychologists to explore brain mechanisms in normal individuals as well as in pathological cases. Anatomical studies using new staining methods permitted more detailed mapping of connections, and advances in neurochemistry and neuropharmacology ushered in a new form of neuropsychology in which, in addition to studying behavioral-structural relationships, investigators can study behavioral-chemical relationships.

METHODS AND CONCEPTS

The attempt to relate behavior to the brain rests on the assumptions that all behavior is mediated by physical processes and that the complex behavior of higher animals depends upon physical processes in the central nervous system. Changes in complex behavior must therefore be associated with changes in the physical state of the brain. Conversely, changes in the physical state of the brain (such as these associated with brain damage) affect behavior. The genetically determined organization of the nervous system sets limits on the brain changes that can be caused by experience, and thus sets limits on what can be perceived and learned. This organization also determines to a great extent the nature of the behavioral changes that occur in response to brain injury.

The understanding of brain-behavior relationships is aided most by the study of behaviors that can be clearly defined and that are likely to be related to brain processes that can be directly or indirectly observed. Behaviors that can be selectively affected by focal brain lesions or by specific pharmacological agents are therefore most often chosen for neuropsychological study. Conversely, behaviors that are difficult to define or that appear unlikely to be correlated with *observable* anatomical, physiological, or chemical processes in the brain are poor candidates for study. As techniques for studying the brain improve, more kinds of behavior should become amenable to study.

Explanations of behavior that are not based on an attempt to understand brain-behavior relationships are of limited interest to the neuropsychologist. Thus, while psychodynamic explanations of behavior may be of considerable clinical utility in the evaluation and treatment of certain behavior disorders, they will be of little interest to neuropsychologists until some correlation with underlying brain processes is demonstrated. Furthermore, psychodynamic explanations of the behavior of brain-damaged patients must be examined critically since the brain damage may have impaired normal emotional mechanisms. Depression, for example, can be seen in brain-damaged persons. The obvious psychodyamic explanation is that depression is a "normal" reaction to a loss of function the patient has experienced as a result of the brain injury. Evidence that depression correlates less with the severity of functional loss than with the site of the brain lesion, however, suggests that in some patients depression may be a direct result of the brain injury and that in such cases the psychodynamic explanation may be irrelevant. Similar caveats apply to the better-documented association of apathy and denial of illness with lesions in the frontal lobes or in the right hemisphere.

There are many valid approaches to the study of brain-behavior relationships, and no morally and intellectually sound approach should be neglected. We will briefly consider the major approaches, emphasizing those that have been used to greatest advantage.

The Black Box Approach

Behavior can be studied without any knowledge of the nervous system. Just as the electrical engineer can study the function of an electronic apparatus without taking it apart (by applying different inputs and studying the outputs), the brain can also be approached as a "black box." The object of the black box approach is to determine laws of behavior. These laws can then be used to predict behavior, which of course is one expressed aim of the study of psychology.

To the extent that laws of behavior are determined by the "hard-wiring" of the brain, the black box approach also yields information about brain function. In this regard, the systematic study of any behavior or set of behaviors is relevant to the study of brain function. Psychology, linguistics, sociology, aesthetics, and related disciplines may all reveal a priori principles of behavior. The study of linguistics, for example, has revealed a basic structure that is common to all languages (Chomsky, 1967). Since there is no logical constraint that gives language this structure and since its generality makes environmental influences unlikely, one can assume that the basic structure of language is hard-wired in the brain. However, although the black box approach yields useful behavioral information about brain function, such information is limited because the brain itself is not studied. This approach is therefore peripheral to the study of neuropsychology, which reflects its origins in nineteenth-century medical science by emphasizing brain anatomy, chemistry, and physiology as relevant variables.

Brain Ablation Paradigms

Lesions in specific areas of the brain change behavior in specific ways. Studies correlating these behavioral changes with the site of lesions yield information that can be used to predict from a given behavioral disturbance the site of the lesions, and vice versa. Such information has great clinical utility.

It is another matter, however, to try to deduce from the behavioral effects of an ablative lesion the normal mechanisms of brain function. As Hughlings Jackson pointed out nearly a century ago, the abnormal behavior observed after a brain lesion reflects the functioning of the remaining brain tissue. This remaining brain may react adversely to or compensate for the loss of function caused by the lesion, and thus either add to or minimize the behavioral deficit. Acute lesions often disturb function in other brain areas (termed *diaschisis*); these metabolic and physiological changes may not be detectable by neuropathological methods and may thus contribute to an overestimate of the function of the lesioned area. Lesions may also produce changes in behavior by releasing other brain areas from facilitation or inhibition. Thus it may be difficult to distinguish behavioral effects caused by an interruption of processing normally occurring in the damaged area from effects due to less specific alterations of function in other areas of the brain.

Possible nonspecific effects of a lesion, such as diaschisis, mass action effects, and reactions to disability or discomfort, can be excluded as major determinants of abnormal behavior by the use of "control" lesions. If lesions of comparable size in other brain areas do not produce similar behavioral effects, one cannot ascribe these effects to nonspecific causes. It is especially elegant to be able to demonstrate that such a control lesion has a different behavioral effect. This has been termed "double-dissociation": lesion A produces behavioral change a but not b, while lesion B produces behavioral change b but not a (Teuber, 1955).

Once nonspecific effects have been excluded, one must take into account the various ways in which a lesion may specifically affect behavior. If a lesion in a particular region results in the loss of a behavior, one must not simply ascribe to that region the normal function of performing that behavior. The first step toward making a meaningful statement about brain-behavior relationships is a scrupulous analysis of the behavior in question. If a lesion in a particular area of the brain interferes with writing, that does not mean that the area is the "writing center" of the brain. Writing is a complex process that requires many other functions: sensory and motor control over the limb must be excellent; there must be no praxic disturbances; language function must be intact; the subject must be mentally alert and able to attend to the task, and so on. One must study every aspect of behavior that is directly related to the task of writing in order to define as closely as possible which aspect of the process of writing is disturbed. It may then be possible to make a correlation between the damaged portion of the brain and the aspect of the writing process that has been disrupted. It is important to distinguish between lesions that destroy areas of the brain involved in processing and lesions that disconnect such areas from one another, disrupting processes which require coordination between two or more such areas (Geschwind, 1965). When a person is writing, for example, the language and motor areas must be coordinated. Lesions that disconnect these areas produce agraphia even though there may be no other language or motor deficit. A lesion in the corpus callosum, for example, may disconnect the language areas in the left hemisphere from the right-hemisphere motor area, thus producing agraphia in the left hand.

Partial recovery of function often occurs after brain lesions and can be attributed to many factors, including resolution of edema, increase in blood supply to ischemic areas, and resolution of diaschisis (see Chap. 16). In addition, the brain is capable of a limited amount of reorganization that may enable remaining structures to take over the functions of the damaged portion. Brain plasticity is greatest in the developing organism and probably decreases with increasing age. This clearly complicates the study of behavioral disorders, especially in children.

In addition to these difficulties in interpretation, gross ablations have a further disadvantage in the investigation of brain function. Natural lesions, such as strokes or tumors, do not necessarily respect functional neuroanatomical boundaries. Ischemic strokes occur in the distribution of particular vessels, and the vascular territory often overlaps various anatomical boundaries. The association of two behavioral deficits may thereby result not from a functional relationship but rather from the fact that two brain regions with little anatomical or physiological relation are supplied by the same vessel. The association of a memory disturbance with pure word blindness (alexia without agraphia) merely indicates that the mesial temporal lobe, the occipital lobe, and the splenium of the corpus callosum are all in the distribution of the posterior cerebral artery. Experimental lesions in animals can avoid this problem; even within a specific anatomical region, however, there may be many systems operating, often with contrasting behavioral functions.

Despite all these problems, the study of brain ablations in humans and animals has yielded more information about brain-behavior relationships than other approaches and it has been given renewed impetus by the recent development of powerful methods of neural imaging. Lesions as small as two or three millimeters in diameter can be detected by modern x-ray computerized tomography (CT). Positron emission tomography (PET) has less resolution but can provide images that reflect the metabolic activity of brain regions. Nuclear magnetic resonance (NMR) scanning gives information about brain structure and blood flow and in the future will probably also provide information about metabolic activity. Already it can provide information comparable to a CT scan without exposing the patient to x-irradiation. This lessened risk may further enlarge the population of subjects for whom neural imaging can be justified.

Brain Stimulation Paradigms

Brain stimulation has been used to map connections in the brain and to elicit changes in behavior. One attraction of this method has been that stimulation, as opposed to ablation, is reversible. (Reversible methods of ablation, such as cooling, have been used, however.) The additional claim that stimulation is more like normal physiological function is open to question: it is highly unlikely that gross electrical stimulation of the brain reproduces any normally occurring physiological state. The stimulation techniques that are usually employed cannot selectively affect only one class of neurons. Furthermore, stimulation disrupts ongoing activity, frequently inhibiting it in a way that resembles the effects of ablation. Some of these objections may be overcome by the use of neurotransmitters or drugs with similar properties to stimulate (or inhibit) specific neurotransmitter systems.

Neurochemical Manipulations

Neurochemical and immunological methods have identified groups of neurons in the central nervous system which use specific neurotransmitters. The number of neurotransmitters identified continues to increase: in addition to norepinephrine, dopamine, acetylcholine, and serotonin, the amino acids glycine and gamma-aminobutyric acid (GABA) have been identified as transmitters. Most recently, polypeptide neurotransmitters (the endorphins and enkephalins) that act at receptors that are also stimulated by opiates have been found. Some of these systems can be selectively stimulated by the ontophoresis of neurotransmitters or of drugs with similar properties. Some can be selectively depressed by drugs that block the action of the transmitter (or inhibit its release), and some can be selectively destroyed by drugs that damage the neurons containing a specific transmitter. Brain sections can be analyzed to determine the concentration of transmitters, and the concentrations can be correlated with behavioral data. These and related techniques hold great promise, especially because of their ability to correlate the behavioral effects of pharmacological agents with dysfunction in anatomical areas "redefined" by chemical criteria.

Electrophysiological Studies

THE ELECTROENCEPHALOGRAM

Electrophysiological studies of human behavior have been attempted during brain surgery and depth electrode recording may be justified in the evaluation of a few patients (usually in preparation for epilepsy surgery), but most studies rely on the surface-recorded electroencephalogram (EEG). The raw EEG, however, demonstrates changes in amplitude and frequency that are generally nonspecific and poorly localizing. Computer analysis of EEG frequency and amplitude (power spectra) in different behavioral situations (and from different brain regions) has demonstrated correlations between EEG activity and behavior, but only for certain aspects of behavior (such as arousal) or for broad anatomical fields (e.g., between hemispheres). The use of computer averaging has increased our ability to detect electrical events that are time-locked to stimuli and responses. Thus, cortical evoked potentials to visual, auditory, and somesthetic stimuli have been recorded, as have potentials that precede a response. Certain potentials appear to correlate with expectancy or arousal (the contingent negative variation and the P300 potential). Others correspond to purely mental events, e.g., the nonoccurrence of an expected stimulus. The use of these techniques in behavioral research has been limited by our ignorance of the meaning of the various components of averaged responses and by technical difficulties. The conditions of the experiment must ensure that the stimulus (or the signal to respond) is temporally discrete and reproducible and that extraneous activity does not interfere with the recording of the response. Computers have also been used to trace the spatial and temporal spread of electrical activity associated with specific single events.

SINGLE-UNIT RECORDING

Discrete activity of individual neurons can be recorded by inserting microelectrodes into the brain. Obviously, this is largely limited to animal experiments. Much has been learned (and remains to be learned) from the use of this technique in alert, responding animals. Responses to well-controlled stimuli can be recorded with precision and analyzed quantitatively. Interpretation of single-unit recording presents its own difficulties. The brain activity related to a behavioral event may occur simultaneously in many cells spatially dispersed over a considerable area. Recording from only one cell may not yield a meaningful pattern. In addition, single-unit recording may be difficult to analyze in relation to complex behaviors.

Introspection

At times, patients' observations of their own mental state may be not only helpful but necessary. How else can one learn of many sensory abnormalities, hallucinations, or emotional changes? It is conceivable that people's insights into their own mental processes may be of importance in delineating brain mechanisms. For example, persons with "photographic" memory not surprisingly report that they rely on visual rather than verbal memory, and experiments suggest that visual memory has a greater

capacity than verbal memory. Patients may have similarly useful insights, and clinicians would do well to listen carefully to what their patients say. This does not mean,
however, that they must believe it all. In normal persons, introspection is not always
trustworthy. In brain-damaged patients, it may be even less reliable. This is particularly true when the language centers have been disconnected from the region of the
brain that processes the information the patient is asked about (Geschwind, 1965).
For example, patients with a callosal lesion (separating the left language-dominant
hemisphere from the right hemisphere) cannot name correctly an object placed in
their left hand. Curiously, such patients do not say that they cannot name the object
nor do they explain that their left hand can feel it but they cannot find the right
word. Instead, in nearly every such case recorded, the patient confabulates a name.
It is clear that in this situation the patient's language area, which is providing the
spoken "insight," cannot even appreciate the presence of a deficit (until it is later
brought to its attention), let alone explain the nature of the difficulty. In other situations, it is apparent that patients make incorrect assumptions about their deficits.
Patients with pure word deafness (who can understand no spoken language but who
nevertheless can speak well and can hear) often assume that people are deliberately
being obscure; the result of this introspection is often paranoia. Thus, although a
patient's introspection at times can provide useful clues for the clinician, this information must always be analyzed critically and used with caution.

ANIMAL VERSUS HUMAN EXPERIMENTATION

Many of the techniques mentioned above are either not applicable to humans or can
be applied only with great difficulty. In detailed anatomical studies, for instance, discrete brain lesions are made and the whole brain is studied meticulously soon after
the operation. Other anatomical methods entail the injection of substances into the
brain. Advances in neurochemistry and neurophysiology, like those in neuroanatomy,
rely heavily on animal work. Despite major differences in anatomy between even the
subhuman primates and humans (Fig. 1-2), much of this basic research is of direct
relevance to human neurobiology. Behavioral studies in animals have also yielded a
great deal of information, but the applicability of this information to the study of
complex human behavior is not clear-cut. Nothing in the literature on temporal-lobe
lesions in animals would have led to the prediction that bilateral temporal lobectomy
in humans would result in permanent impairment of memory; only recently, nearly
20 years after its demonstration in humans, have new testing paradigms demonstrated
memory impairment in animals with bitemporal ablations (Mishkin, 1978). Conversely, the applicability of behavioral deficits in animals (and especially in nonhuman primates) to syndromes in humans has also only recently been systematically
investigated, and some parallels are discernable (Oscar-Berman et al., 1982). Studies
of the limbic system and hypothalamus in animals have contributed important information about the relevance of these structures to emotional behavior; however, the
emotional content of behavior is difficult to study in animals because they cannot
report how they feel. Most obviously, animals cannot be used to study behavior that

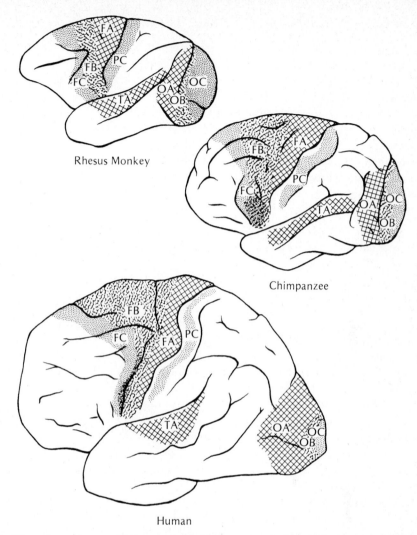

Fig. 1-2. The primary motor (FA) and visual (OC) areas and the association areas of the motor, visual, somatosensory (PC), and auditory (TA) systems are compared in these lateral views of the hemispheres of the monkey, chimpanzee, and human. Note the expansion of the unshaded areas of cortex, particularly in the frontal lobe and in the area between TA and OA, as one progresses from monkey to human. The latter area is important for language development (see Chap. 2). The significance of the frontal lobes is discussed in Chap. 12.

is uniquely human, such as language. Studies of nonlinguistic communication in animals may relate to some aspects of speech in humans but they do not elucidate the neural mechanisms underlying language. Studies of "linguistic" behavior in primates are controversial, and their relevance to the study of language in humans remains unclear.

Problems of Human Experimentation

Human experimentation is therefore necessary, but it presents many problems. The ablation paradigm must rely upon lesions occurring naturally or upon lesions made by neurosurgeons for medical reasons. Obviously, such lesions often are not ideally situated for study of the problem at hand. In addition, considerable labor and some luck are required to collect a series of comparable patients for study. Unlike experimental animals, which are often comparable in both genetic and environmental terms, patients vary widely in premorbid capabilities and backgrounds. Finally, experiments must be designed to avoid putting the patient at any additional risk. Even if the experimental manipulations themselves are harmless, researchers must always be sure that they are not interfering with expeditious medical evaluation and treatment.

Forms of Human Experimentation

STUDIES OF NORMALS

A few of the techniques mentioned above can yield physiological data in normal individuals. EEG studies have revealed hemisphere asymmetries associated with cognitive mode. Evoked response studies have also been fruitful. Dichotic listening (and binocular viewing) techniques have revealed hemisphere asymmetries in the processing of verbal, visuospatial, and musical information. (In this approach, competing [dissimilar] auditory or visual stimuli are presented to the two ears or the two visual half-fields simultaneously and subjects identify what they have heard or seen. Usually more correct responses are made for stimuli presented to the ear or half-field opposite the hemisphere primarily involved in processing the stimulus.)

CASE REPORTS

The careful study of a single patient can provide valuable clues to the mechanisms underlying a behavioral deficit. The advantage of the case report is that an individual patient can be studied in depth and an effort made to relate all the manifestations of the illness to each other and to the pathology identified. The famous studies of Dejerine (1892) and of Liepmann and Maas (1907) were of single patients. The problem with case reports is that it is difficult to generalize from one patient.

SERIES OF PATIENTS

The study of a group of patients increases one's ability to generalize from the data presented. In 1861, finding a single patient with aphasia and a lesion in the left frontal lobe would have been of interest as a case report, but the finding of eight such cases enabled Broca to state that language deficits appeared to be associated specifically with *left* frontal opercular lesions. Precise statistical methods now permit the simultaneous analysis of several variables. The problem with the statistical analysis of a group of patients is that potentially significant data from an individual patient may be lost when averaged with data from the group. For example, a study of a group of patients might demonstrate that language disability is correlated with impairment on nonverbal tests of intelligence. In such a study, the findings on one patient with severe language disability but normal performance on nonverbal cognitive tasks might be neglected. It could be argued, however, that the data on this single patient are more important than all the other data because they indicate that the abilities to make verbal and nonverbal generalizations are likely to be functionally and anatomically discrete. The statistical analysis of the whole group of patients, however, might support the opposite conclusion.

CONCEPTUAL ANALYSIS

We often hear that science proceeds by way of careful observation followed by analysis and then hypothesis on the basis of the observed data (a posteriori hypothesis). In fact, meaningful observations frequently cannot be made without some sort of a priori hypothesis. How else can one decide which observations to make? An observation can be significant only in terms of a conceptual framework.

Some investigators are loathe to put either their a priori or a posteriori hypotheses in print, feeling that they are too tentative. They report observations with a minimum of interpretation. This may be unfortunate because tentative hypotheses are the seeds of further observations and hypotheses. Other investigators speculate extensively on the basis of only a few observations. These speculations may lead to clearly stated hypotheses which generate further observations, but there is a risk that observations may be honestly and inadvertently distorted to fit the hypotheses. For example, investigators always discard "irrelevant" information either intentionally or not; however, an investigator with an alternative hypothesis may find observations presumed irrelevant by others to be of critical importance. It is important to deal with all hypotheses as though they were tentative so that, as Head (1926) warned, we do not invite observations to sleep in the Procrustean bed of our hypotheses.

We are too far from understanding brain-behavior relationships to be able to state hypotheses entirely without the use of metaphorical terms. Metaphor is not to be taken literally. Diagrams, for example, may be used in a metaphorical way to present a hypothesis. The diagrams found in this book are offered in this spirit: they are meant to be not pictures of the brain but sketches of hypotheses.

Similarly, when we speak of the function of different areas of the brain, it often appears that we assume that the area under discussion operates entirely independently from others. Clearly, this is true only to a limited extent. For the purposes of analysis, however, we must often ignore interactions between brain regions in order to discuss the distinguishing features of these areas. We do not deny that consideration of the brain as a functioning whole may at times be of equal value in explaining behavioral data, as it is in explaining the concept of diaschisis.

Thus, we support a flexible approach to the study of brain-behavior relationships. We know too little about the subject to limit our methods of investigation. We must be prepared to analyze data from many sources and make new hypotheses and test them with the best methods available. Similarly, behavioral testing and methods of treatment must be tailored to the individual situation. Inflexible test batteries, although necessary for obtaining normative data, limit our view of the nervous system if used exclusively. Rigid formulations of therapy similarly limit progress. Changes in testing and therapy, however, should be made not capriciously but rather according to our current understanding of brain-behavior relationships. In this book, therefore, we do not emphasize standardized tests or treatment batteries; instead, we present the existing knowledge on brain-behavior relationships, which should form the basis of diagnosis and treatment.

REFERENCES

Bastian, H. C. (1869). On the various forms of loss of speech in cerebral disease. *Br. Foreign Medico-Surg. Rev.* 43:470–492.

Bouillaud, J. B. (1825). Recherches cliniques propres a demontrer que la perte de la parole correspond a la lesion de lobules anterieurs du cerveau, et a confirmer l'opinion de M. Gall sur le siege de l'organe du langage articulé. *Archives Generales de Medecine* 8:25–45.

Broca, P. (1865). Sur la faculté du langage articulé. *Bull. Soc. Anthr. Paris* 6:337–393).

Chomsky, N. (1967). The general properties of language. In *Brain Mechanisms Underlying Speech and Language* (C. H. Millikan and F. L. Darley, eds.) New York: Grune & Stratton.

Dejerine, J. (1892). Contribution a l'etude anatomo-pathologique et clinique des differentes varietes de cecite verbale. *Mem. Soc. Biol.* 4:61–90.

Geschwind, N. (1965). Disconnexion syndrome in animals and men. I and II. *Brain* 88:237–294, 585–644.

Head, H. (1926). *Aphasia and Kindred Disorders of Speech*. Cambridge: Cambridge University Press.

Lashley, K. S. (1938). Factors limiting recovery after central nervous lesions. *J. Nervous Mental Dis.* 888:733–755.

Lichtheim, L. (1885). On aphasia. *Brain* 7:433–484.

Liepmann, H., and Maas, O. (1907). Fall von linksseitiger Agraphie nd Apraxie bei rechtsseitiger Lahmung. *Z. B. Psychol. Neurol.* 10:214–227.

Mishkin, M. (1978). Memory in monkeys severely impaired by combined but not by separate removal of amygdala and hippocampus. *Nature (London)* 273:297–278.

Oscar-Berman, M., Zola-Morgan, S. M., Oberg, R. G. E., and Bonner, R. T. (1982) Comparative neuropsychology and Korsakoff's syndrome. III: Delayed response, delayed alternation and DRL performance. *Neuropsychologia* 20:187–202.

Teuber, H. L. (1955). Physiological psychology. *Ann. Rev. Psychol.* 6:267–296.

Wernicke, C. (1874). *Des Aphasische Symptomenkomplex*. Breslau: Cohn and Weigart.

2

APHASIA

D. FRANK BENSON

Aphasia is a clinical term that denotes the loss or impairment of language following brain damage. By this definition, aphasia is clearly a neurological disorder, but over 50 years ago the British neurologist, Kinnear Wilson (1926), stated that aphasia was unique among neurological disorders in that it demanded understanding from anatomical, physiological, and psychological viewpoints. Now, other disciplines have entered into the study of aphasia, including linguistics, developmental language studies, and aphasia rehabilitation.

Investigations of language encourage cross-disciplinary efforts and this chapter will approach aphasia from three viewpoints: anatomical, neurological, and psychological. A complete review of contemporary neuropsychological investigations of aphasia is not possible here; an attempt will be made to correlate major aspects of current neurological and neuropsychological thinking, drawing on other disciplines where they offer information pertinent to this approach.

The word language demands comment. While the term is used freely in reference to communication, it is difficult to define precisely. Four distinctly different types of language have been described (Ross et al., 1981): gestural, prosodic, semantic, and syntactic. The first two are present widely among animal species, while the latter two are almost or totally unique to humans (depending on the interpretation of symbol communication by higher apes) (Gardner and Gardner, 1969; Premack, 1971). The language loss in aphasia routinely involves all four types but the latter two are of particular importance for human neuropsychology.

HISTORICAL BACKGROUND

The history of thought about aphasia abounds with controversy. Many fascinating historical reviews, invariably slanted toward the author's bias, have been published. Some highlights will be presented here, but for a more complete historical background the reader is referred to the following books and papers: Freud, 1891/1953;

Head, 1926/1964; Weisenburg and McBride, 1935/1964; Benton and Joynt, 1960; Brain, 1961; Hécaen and Albert, 1978; Benson, 1979b.

While most currently recognized varieties of aphasia were described centuries ago, aphasia, as currently recognized, dates from 1861. After several centuries of debate, two views of brain function had polarized. One group, taking their lead from the new "science" of phrenology, maintained that specific mental functions (such as speech) were subserved by separate areas of the brain. Opponents of this "localizationist" viewpoint maintained that mental capability was the product of total brain activity. In 1861, a primitive skull was demonstrated to a French anthropological society meeting to support a direct relationship between mental competence and brain volume. At this time a patient of one physician-member became "speechless" and then died. Postmortem studies revealed a large frontal lesion and the physician, Paul Broca (1861) submitted this as evidence favoring the localizationist viewpoint. Additional cases of speechlessness (aphasia) were presented subsequently, some supporting and others failing to support the localizationist viewpoint. The introduction of human case material and the use of clinical/pathological correlations into medical research opened new vistas and eventually produced much basic knowledge in neurology, including multiple classifications of aphasia.

A major advance in the localizationist viewpoint followed publication of Wernicke's doctoral thesis (1874) describing two types of aphasia, motor and sensory, and postulating others, based on limited clinical/pathological data and a hypothetical diagram of language function in the brain. Both the clinical/pathological localization of varieties of aphasia and the use of diagrams became popular. Within a few years, many schemes of language appeared along with additional case material supporting localization of language functions. Among the early contributors to this approach to aphasia were Lichtheim (1885), Charcot (1889), Bastian (1898), Dejerine (1914), Henschen (1922), Kleist (1934, 1962), and Nielson (1928, 1962). Much of the localizationists' work dates from late nineteenth and early twentieth centuries and corresponded to the flowering of the clinical-pathological approach to medicine. Excesses and errors in these early efforts are now obvious, and many of the correlations would not be accepted at present. The localizationist viewpoint received and deserved considerable criticism and eventually lost credibility.

During this period there were many who advocated a more holistic view of language. One early proponent was John Hughlings Jackson (1868, 1915, 1932), the great English neurologist. Jackson's opinions were neither well understood nor accepted for many years but eventually had considerable influence. Sigmund Freud, in a monograph on aphasia published in 1891, strongly criticized the "diagram makers" but this effort received scant attention. It was not until Pierre Marie's time (1906) that a holistic approach to aphasia reached a wide audience. Another Paris debate, resembling the 1861 discussion, involved Dejerine, a proponent of the classic localizationist view, and Marie. From this time on, the influence of the holistic approach steadily increased and included such significant advocates as Head (1926/1964), Pick (1973), Isserlin (1929, 1931, 1932), Kinnear Wilson (1926), and more recently Weisenburg and McBride (1935/1964), Bay (1964), Wepman (1951), Schuell et al. (1964), J. R. Brown (1968) and Critchley (1970).

Despite the dramatic differences, most serious students of aphasia made observations supportive of both viewpoints; only in theoretical overview was there a clash. Indeed, a number of influential investigators are linked theoretically with one approach but produced meaningful work in the other. For instance, Kurt Goldstein (1948) is best recognized as a staunch proponent of a holistic (organismic) approach to aphasia, but in his writings one finds some of the best descriptions of focal aphasia available in contemporary literature. Similarly, the Russian psychologists, headed by Luria (1970), are often said to have an anti-localizationist bias but their work features superb descriptions of aphasic syndromes, clearly demonstrating distinct localizing features. Thus, while it is accurate to divide the prevailing philosophies into the anatomically based localizing and the more psychologically based holistic approaches, most investigators utilize both to some degree. This is true of contemporary neuropsychology; some investigators are anatomically and clinically oriented while others are far more psychologically and linguistically based. The two approaches are complementary, not exclusive.

Interest in aphasia waned considerably before and immediately after World War II, but the work of many contemporary investigators has altered this situation, both by reviving older localizationist ideas and by developing a better integrated, neuropsychological approach to aphasia. A major impetus came from Geschwind (1965) who emphasized cortical–cortical disconnection as a cause of language disorder. The Italians DeRenzi and Vignolo; the French investigators Lhermitte and Hecaen; the Russians headed by Luria; the Germans Leischner, Bay, and Poeck; and the Americans Goodglass, Kaplan, and Benton have all contributed to the resurgence of interest in aphasia. Many contemporary investigators, some of whom are contributors to this volume, have provided important advances. Research in aphasia continues and while the opposing theoretical stances outlined by the Paris Debates in 1861 remain, it is within the realm of neuropsychology to bridge them.

In his book *Aphasia and Kindred Disorders*, Henry Head (1926/1964) described the investigation of aphasia as "chaos." He then added his own novel approach and seriously compounded the chaos. But Head also introduced a new method to the study of aphasia: the use of a standard repeatable series of tests to probe language competency. Weisenburg and McBride (1932/1964) borrowed this idea and designed a battery of language function tests to study their aphasic subjects. Testing with a standardized battery has become a major tool in the study of aphasia and skill in this function combined with efforts to rehabilitate the aphasic have lead to a new and fruitful approach by language therapists such as Porch (1967), Sarno (1970), Darley (1975), Holland (1980), and Wertz (1981).

CLASSIFICATIONS OF APHASIA

To better understand the "chaos," many individual investigators, representing different theoretical approaches and working in different languages, have subdivided aphasia into separate varieties (syndromes), producing many classifications of aphasia. Probably more than any other factor, this proliferation of classification schemes has led to the difficulty that most students experience when they first encounter aphasia.

The same name (e.g., semantic aphasia) may be used in two classifications to represent strikingly different language disorders. In recent years, the degree of confusion has actually increased as many nonphysicians (linguists, speech pathologists, psychologists) have introduced classifications expressed in their own specialized jargon. A careful study of the classifications of aphasia is almost mandatory for understanding of the subject.

One long-standing problem has been the attempt to describe aphasia as a simple dichotomy. Probably most widely used is the expressive–receptive division of Weisenburg and McBride (1932/1964) which is adequate only as a rough description and is often misleading. Almost no aphasia fails to have expressive abnormality; conversely, a purely expressive aphasia, one with no receptive problem, is extremely rare. The expressive–receptive dichotomy is inadequate for clinical classification.

Another commonly used dichotomy is the motor–sensory division suggested by Wernicke that attempts to link language problems with cortical localization. Most sensory activities are carried out in the posterior cortex and most motor activities are controlled by the anterior or frontal regions. Thus, a division of aphasia into two types, anterior/motor and posterior/sensory can claim some utility, but produces a false simplification that fails to encompass the significant clinical differences that distinguish the varieties of aphasia.

The most complete lumping of categories was that of Marie (1906), who suggested that there was only one type of aphasia, the "sensory" aphasia originally described by Wernicke. In this view there is a single disturbance of language function with variations in clinical features dependent on involvement of neighboring motor or sensory functions. The holistic approach proposed by Marie probably reached its zenith in the studies of Schuell et al. (1964), whose extensive writings suggested "one aphasia" and emphasized severity as the variable factor. The linguist Jakobson (1964) strongly refuted this approach and subsequent neuropsychological studies have tended to emphasize, not minimize, the diversity of the language disorders called aphasia.

Beyond the babel, as Davis Howes (1964) noted, there is considerable agreement on most salient points among those experienced in the field. It would appear that the academic effort to classify the aphasic disturbances has been a roadblock rather than a guide to their understanding. The same clusters of clinical features appear in most classifications and the number of reported combinations is limited.

By focusing on a cluster of symptoms (a syndrome) for each variety of aphasia in a given classification and by noting, when available, the suggested location of pathology, obvious correlations between the various classifications are noted. Table 2-1 presents a number of recognized classifications, beginning with the earlier continental writers and moving to contemporary literature. For each variety of aphasia listed, either the clinical syndromes or the location of pathology (or both) are sufficiently well described by the author to allow correlation with other classifications. Note that four or five types of aphasia are almost constantly reported; syndromes such as those often called Broca's aphasia and Wernicke's aphasia occur in all, and several other syndromes appear in most. In a study of traditional aphasia syndromes, Kertesz and colleagues (1979) have successfully used the methods of taxonomy to prove the reality of the symptom clusters in aphasia. If used abstractly as an aid to clinical separation,

Table 2-1. Classifications of Aphasia

Wernicke Lichtheim (1885)	Head (1926)	Kleist (1934)	Nielsen (1948)	Goldstein (1948)	Brain (1962)	Gloning (1963)	Bay (1964)	Wepman (1964)	Luria (1966)	BVAH (1971)	Hécaen Albert (1977)
Cortical motor	Verbal	Word muteness	Broca's	Central motor	Broca's	Motor	Cortical dysarthria	Syntactic	Efferent motor	Broca's	Motor
Cortical sensory	Syntactic	Word deafness	Wernicke's	Wernicke's sensory	Central	Sensory	Sensory	Jargon Pragmatic	Sensory	Wernicke	Sensory
Conduction		Repetition		Central	Central	Conduction	Sensory		Afferent motor	Conduction	Conduction
				Isolation of speech area						Mixed transcortical	
Transcortical motor			Transcortical motor	Transcortical motor			Echolalia		Dynamic	Transcortical motor	Transcortical motor
Transcortical sensory	Nominal		Transcortical sensory	Transcortical sensory					Acoustic Amnestic	Transcortical sensory	Transcortical sensory
	Semantic	Amnestic	Amnestic	Amnestic	Nominal	Amnestic	Pure	Semantic	Semantic	Anomic	Amnestic
Subcortical motor		Anarthric	Subcortical motor	Peripheral motor	Pure word dumbness					Aphemia	Pure motor
Subcortical sensory		Word sound deafness		Peripheral sensory	Pure word deafness	Pure word deafness				Pure word deafness	Pure word deafness

not as rigid, precise entities, the syndromes of aphasia can enhance the understanding of language disorders.

EXAMINATION FOR APHASIA

One additional source of confusion concerning aphasia stems from the diversity of methods used for evaluation. Observations on language disturbance are dependent on the methods used for testing. As an overview, three different approaches to language evaluation will be discussed. The first will be the clinician's evaluation of language as part of a mental status examination, the second, some of the more widely used standardized aphasia test batteries and, finally, a few of the myriad experimental approaches introduced in recent years by psychologists, linguists, speech pathologists, and others, to probe language function.

Clinical Testing for Aphasia

Clinical testing for aphasia is the oldest, although not necessarily the best established of the examination methods. It is neither exacting nor thorough and is usually performed by evaluating rather gross and fixed language functions (e.g., naming, reading). Unfortunately, most of these functions were selected over a century ago and, in some instances, reflect obsolete concepts. The traditional approach is widely used, however, and remains basic to most discussions of aphasia syndromes. In general, correlation can be made between results of these tests and the portion of the neuroanatomical language area involved (Fig. 2-1).

CONVERSATIONAL SPEECH

Evaluation of aphasia traditionally begins with a description of the spontaneous or conversational verbalization of the patient, which many clinicians attempt to classify as a fluent or nonfluent output. This division was recorded at least as early as 1868 by Jackson and the terms fluent and nonfluent were used by Wernicke in 1874. In recent years, several studies have been performed to probe the validity of this dichotomy and, in general, support the fluent/nonfluent division (Benson, 1967; Poeck, Kerschensteiner, and Hartje, 1972; Wagenaar, Snow, and Prins, 1975). Specific output criteria can be outlined. Nonfluent speech has the following characteristics: sparse output (under 50 words per minute), considerable effort necessary for verbalization, poor articulation, short phrase length (often only a single word), notable dysprosody (disturbance of rhythm, timbre, inflection), and preferential use of substantive, meaningful words. Fluent aphasia is almost a direct opposite: plentiful output (100–200 words per minute), easy production, good articulation, normal phrase length (averaging 5–8 words per phrase) and normal prosodic quality but a tendency to omit words (usually the meaningful, semantically significant words) plus an excessive number of paraphasias in some cases.

Using these criteria, formal studies have demonstrated that most (but not all) aphasics fall into one of the two subtypes. In addition, an anatomical correlation is often

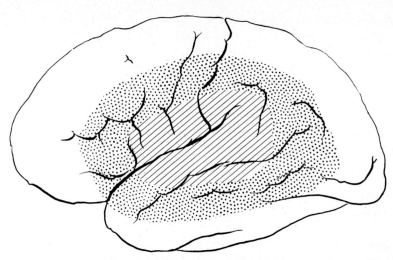

Fig. 2-1. An outline of the left hemisphere cortex suggesting the boundaries of the "language area." The inner, perisylvian region (slanted lines) is a strongly sensitive area so that pathology here almost invariably produces aphasia. The surrounding area (stippled) is a less consistent region, but pathology in this area is also likely to produce an aphasic syndrome. Pathology in other portions of the brain is far less likely to produce a significant language disturbance.

possible; fluent paraphasic aphasia almost invariably indicates pathology located posterior to the major central sulcus (fissure of Rolando) while, with a few well established exceptions, nonfluent aphasia is associated with pathology anterior to this sulcus (Benson, 1967).

Repetition

The ability to repeat, precisely, words presented by the examiner is a language function that received insufficient emphasis until recent years. Repetition is readily tested, starting with simple tasks such as repeating digits or single-syllable words and building to repetition of multisyllabic words, complex sentences and phrases, verbal sequences, etc. Many aphasic patients show inordinate difficulty in repeating. Most often this exists with abnormal verbal output or poor comprehension of spoken language but in some cases the repetition difficulty may be the most pronounced. In sharp contrast, some aphasics are remarkably competent at repetition, despite abnormal output and/or poor comprehension.

In aphasia, both disturbed and normal repetition have important anatomic correlations. Individuals with serious problems in repetition have pathology that involves the perisylvian region, either the posterior-superior temporal lobe (Wernicke's area), the posterior-inferior frontal area (Broca's area), or the superior perisylvian region between these two areas (arcuate fasciculus, supramarginal gyrus, parietal operculum). When an aphasic retains the ability to repeat (sometimes the only remaining language function) the perisylvian area is free of pathology. In such cases the pathology involves cortex surrounding the perisylvian area (the border between the middle cerebral and the anterior and posterior cerebral artery circulations) or subcortical regions. A strong, almost mandatory, tendency to repeat what has been said by the examiner (called *echolalia*) often indicates a border zone location of pathology.

COMPREHENSION OF SPOKEN LANGUAGE

Comprehension is difficult to test. Both clinical evaluations and standardized tests of language comprehension often prove inadequate and can produce downright misleading results. One classic method for probing comprehension is through response to commands. The ability to carry out complex verbal commands, particularly when presented in multiples, is a good indication of intact comprehension. Failure to carry out commands, on the other hand, does not necessarily indicate comprehension disturbance. Both *apraxia* (inability to carry out motor activities on verbal command— see Chap. 7) and difficulty in maintaining sequences may interfere but do not necessarily indicate that the patient cannot comprehend language. To obviate this problem, a second method utilizes tests such as yes-no questions that require less motor activity for response. Unfortunately, some aphasics cannot handle yes and no, and give incomprehensible, perseverative, or combination responses; the examiner cannot be certain that the response is either right or wrong. A third method requests that the patient point to objects about the room or in an array as the examiner gives the name. If the patient can accomplish this pointing task, the requests can be made increasingly complex by offering vague, functional descriptions of the specific objects. Even the simple task of pointing cannot be accurately performed by some apraxic individuals, however, and this test may also fail to reflect the true ability to comprehend language.

Comprehension is not an all-or-none phenomenon. Many aphasic patients comprehend frequently used words but fail to understand words used less often. Other aphasics comprehend concrete real-world names, but do not understand relational or syntactical structures such as prepositions, possessives, verb tenses, etc. Some aphasics succeed with single, simple comprehension tasks but fail when information is offered serially. There is much to be learned about comprehension testing but it is almost never correct to state flatly that comprehension is present or absent. Most aphasics understand some language and almost all have at least some degree of deficiency. Comprehension abnormality should be described in qualitative as well as quantitative terms.

Clinical studies have demonstrated a number of types of comprehension disturbance and suggest a correlation of these variations with localization of the pathology (Luria, 1966; Benson, 1978). These clinical observations are enticing and deserve evaluation by stringent neuropsychological techniques.

WORD FINDING

Almost without exception, every aphasic has difficulty in word finding *(anomia)*, but the degree and circumstances vary considerably. Testing for word-finding difficulty is comparatively easy. Objects, parts of objects, body parts, colors, geometrical figures, and actions are demonstrated and the patient is asked for the name. Failure to produce the name indicates a word-finding defect. Many examiners follow such a failure by offering a multiple-choice list of names including the correct one; this is a good test of comprehension but is easily misinterpreted by the naive observer as proof that the patient actually "knows" the name. It is much better to follow the patient's failure to produce a name with prompting (offering a cue). An initial phoneme (phonetic prompting) or an open-ended statement in which the missing word would be appropriate (contextual prompting) can be presented (Barton et al., 1969).

Clinical studies have demonstrated distinct variations in word-finding problems (Luria, 1966) and a correlation between the variations and the site of aphasia-producing pathology has been suggested (Benson, 1979a). A number of "nonaphasic" disorders including dementia, the confusional states, and others, also cause problems in word finding so word-finding difficulty does not automatically indicate aphasia. Any time anomia is present, however, aphasia must be considered.

Reading

Disturbances of reading ability *(alexia)*, either with or without aphasia, have long been recognized (see Chap. 3). Reading is relatively easy to evaluate and specific test materials are needed only if quantified results are required. Simply offering the written name of a body part or a room object for the patient to identify is one way to begin. Success at this level can be followed by phrases or sentences composed of high- or low-frequency words and by phrases dependent on relational words for interpretation. A more challenging test of reading ability requires understanding of a paragraph from a newspaper or magazine. The most common mistake in testing reading ability is equating the ability to read aloud with the ability to comprehend written material. Many aphasics with output disturbances fail to read aloud but comprehend written material adequately. In contrast, some patients (particularly those with Alzheimer's disease), can read sentences aloud without comprehending the material. The ability to comprehend written language must be abnormal if alexia is to be diagnosed. Distinct varieties of alexia with discrete anatomic correlations have been accepted for nearly a century; these will be discussed in Chapter 3.

Writing

Almost every aphasic suffers some degree of *agraphia*. However, the ability to sign one's name is so ubiquitous that many aphasics with severe writing disturbances can produce their own signature without difficulty. Tests of writing ability must probe further and should include dictated words and sentences plus sentences produced to command (i.e., "Describe your job."). There are numerous qualitative variations in agraphia, some aphasic, others nonaphasic (mechanical), and many mixed. Disorders of writing are discussed in Chapter 4.

In summary, the clinical testing of aphasia is inexact, nonstandardized, and constantly changing. Therein lies both the weakness and the strength of the clinical approach. Many of the techniques used in clinical and research batteries have evolved from the experiences of the clinical examiner. An experienced examiner can evaluate an aphasic patient in minutes and, by focusing on the primary problems, obtain an in-depth view of the type and severity of the aphasia. Even in the best of hands, however, these results are subject to the theoretical bias of the examiner, and in the hands of an inexperienced examiner, clinical evaluation methods can be untrustworthy. The need for exact, standardized testing methods is obvious.

Formal Tests of Aphasia

In the past 25 years many formal tests of aphasia have been devised, standardized to a greater or lesser degree, and widely utilized. While these tests tend to be similar, there are significant differences. There is no consensus as to which tests are best and all of the tests to be mentioned are in use somewhere. Nearly all aphasics entering a formal rehabilitation program are given part or all of one or more of these tests. Some of the currently popular tests will be listed with some of their distinguishing characteristics mentioned.

One of the earliest formal aphasia tests still in use is Eisenson's *Examining for Aphasia* (1954). This is of medium length and divided into two sections, expressive and receptive. Many techniques for formal language evaluation found in subsequent tests were first widely used in the Eisenson test. While no longer generally used, it remains the standard test of some treatment centers.

Two longer, more thorough, and rationally formulated tests came into general use in the 1960's, the *Language Modalities Test for Aphasia* of Wepman (1961) and the *Minnesota Test for the Differential Diagnosis of Aphasia* of Schuell (1957). They are significantly different in composition. The Schuell test is an extensive evaluation of language function that eventually divides aphasic patients into five types based on prognosis for language recovery. The full test is long and somewhat difficult to present but provides considerable information. The Wepman test, on the other hand, was designed along psychological parameters, stressing variations in stimulus and response. Although the Schuell test was devised by an aphasia therapist to guide language therapy and the Wepman test was devised by a psychologist to demonstrate psychological characteristics, findings from the Wepman test prove helpful to the aphasia therapist planning a language program and vice versa. Both tests have proved valuable in evaluating and understanding aphasia.

More recently a rigidly quantified test of language disability, the *Porch Index of Communicative Ability* (PICA) (1967), has become popular. This relatively short test (approximately one hour for administration) is easily repeated with good reliability. While easy to administer, the scoring system is complex and demands special training for accurate use. The PICA offers excellent quantitative but comparatively little qualitative information; its greatest usefulness lies in predicting outcome and recording language recovery through serial administration. Therapy directed toward tasks on the PICA can improve the score without significantly altering the functional use of language. When this trap is avoided the PICA has an important place among current testing methods.

Several diagnostic aphasia batteries have become popular in recent years. The most widely used is the *Boston Diagnostic Aphasia Examination* (BDAE) (Goodglass and Kaplan, 1972) which provides a broad range of evaluation but is so lengthy that it must be administered in separate sessions over several days. The results can be difficult to interpret because they demand understanding of the system of classifying aphasic disturbances used at the Boston Veterans Administration Hospital Aphasia Research Center (see below). The test is far more inclusive than any of its predecessors, however, and when properly interpreted offers much more diagnostic information. A shorter test based on the BDAE, the *Western Aphasia Battery* (WAB) (Kertesz and Poole, 1974), is used at a number of centers and is growing in popularity. A somewhat similar test, also used at a number of centers, is the *Neurosensory Center Test for Aphasia* (NSCTA) (Spreen and Benton, 1969). Excellent normal values (percentiles) are available for each subtest of the NSCTA so that each language function can be rated separately or the disturbance can be rated as a whole. The BDAE, the WAB, and the NSCTA are superior to previous tests for diagnostic purposes and as research tools but, to date, have not proved superior in helping the therapist plan a rehabilitation program.

Finally, several tests have been designed to measure the aphasic's ability to communicate rather than probe the specific language dysfunction. The original test, still widely used, is the *Functional Communication Profile* devised by Taylor-Sarno (1965). Though not standardized, the FCP is helpful for making qualitative judgments and can demonstrate major changes in communication. There is little quantification, with scoring dependent on comparative observations by the evaluator. The observations are easily classed, even by untrained personnel, however, and formal evaluations have demonstrated good interobserver reliability. A more complete evaluation of communication ability is the *Communicative Abilities in Daily Living* (CADL) devised by Holland and colleagues (1980). CADL is being used increasingly as a gauge of the aphasic's ability to cope with real world problems.

Each test mentioned above has some useful features and none has proved clearly superior.

Research Testing Procedures

The most striking change in the approach to aphasia evaluation during the past several decades has been the introduction of psychological experimentation techniques. Since the work of Weisenburg and McBride in the 1930s, the use of psychological evaluation techniques has expanded greatly in language research. Activity is so intense in this field that three current journals are either exclusively or primarily devoted to neuropsychological studies of language and innumerable articles in other journals and many books feature this approach. Even cursory review of this plethora of information reaches far beyond the scope of this chapter and only a few of the more prominent directions can be highlighted.

A number of outstanding early investigators in this field such as Luria, Hécaen, and Zangwill and their co-workers advanced the understanding of language through formal psychological studies of language impairment. DeRenzi and Vignolo of Italy introduced the *Token Test* (1962), considered an excellent probe for subtle comprehension difficulties. In America the leaders in the neuropsychological study of language include Benton, Teuber, and Goodglass, whose investigations feature careful, fully replicable designs. The number of psychologists currently studying language disorders is enormous and the field is advancing accordingly.

Following the initial psychological studies of language, aphasia was investigated by linguists or psychologists who had training in linguistics and could combine linguistic theory with the scientific design of experimental psychology. Some psycholinguists have specialized in phonological problems, others in syntactical or grammatical problems, and still others in semantic disturbances. Most early work centered on normal language and only recently have these specialists discovered the wealth of information available from aphasia. Many psycholinguistic studies now probe normal language by studying aphasic language; the potential for reciprocal understanding is obvious.

Abnormalities of syntax have been investigated in aphasia. Goodglass and Berko (1960) demonstrated consistent defects in the syntactical composition of the output of selected aphasics, a condition called agrammatism. Agrammatic language is characterized by omission of most relational words—the articles, prepositions, conjunctions, and minor modifiers—and is a striking feature of nonfluent aphasia. More recent studies (Zurif et al., 1972; Samuels and Benson, 1979) demonstrate that a comparable comprehension defect, an inability to "understand" these same relational words, coexists with agrammatic output. Agrammatic individuals handle (verbalize and comprehend) substantive, semantically significant, imagable words far better than relational, syntactically significant, functor words (Caramazza and Berndt, 1978). Isolated syntactic disability is strongly correlated with Broca's or other anterior aphasia, implying that grammatical competence depends primarily on frontal language function.

The question of intelligence in aphasia (whether retained or lost) has been widely disputed. Disturbed language function invalidates most of the recognized intelligence assessment techniques, leading to the categorical statement that all aphasics must suffer a disturbance of intellectual capability because we think in words (Bastian, 1898). Aphasia is accepted by many as evidence of decreased intelligence (Goldstein, 1948; Bay, 1962). Many others, however, believe that some aphasics retain an essentially normal intelligence, locked in by the language problem (Kennedy and Wolf, 1936; Orgass et al., 1972). Nonverbal tests such as the Ravens Matrices (Ravens, 1952) and the performance section of the WAIS (Wechsler, 1958) have been used as substitute techniques for gauging intelligence but demand rather unsatisfactory interpolation (Kertesz, 1979). The major problem, of course, is the dilemma of defining intelligence. It is safe to say that most aphasics have more understanding and more intelligence than can be demonstrated by present evaluation techniques (Zangwill, 1969). It can be anticipated that future neuropsychological techniques will overcome at least part of the testing problem and provide a better gauge of the aphasic patient's underlying intellectual competency. This problem becomes more than mere academic controversy when the problem of testamentary capacity for an aphasic is raised (Critchley, 1970; Benson, 1973). Aphasics may be called upon to make important decisions and the clinician is likely to be queried about their competence.

The relationship of language loss to cerebral dominance, handedness, and functional laterality of the hemispheres has long been studied. The unique role of the left hemisphere in language was recognized early (Broca, 1864) and subsequent clinical observations suggest asymmetry of hemispheric influence on a number of higher activities (Gloning et al., 1969; Warrington, 1969; Bogen and Bogen, 1969; Gainotti, 1972; Galin, 1974). Studies of language dysfunction following section of the corpus callosum (Geschwind and Kaplan, 1962; Gazzaniga and Sperry, 1967; Zaidel, 1978), and following hemispherectomy (Smith and Sugar, 1975), of language loss after intra-carotid barbiturate injection (Wada and Rasmussen, 1960), of asymmetrical interference with language by dichotic auditory stimulation (Broadbent, 1971; Sparks and Geschwind, 1968), and of neuroanatomical asymmetries of the hemispheres (Yakovlev and Rakic, 1966; Geschwind and Levitsky, 1968) have all improved knowledge of the role of the two hemispheres in language. Asymmetry of hemispheric function has become a popular topic for psychological research in recent years, stimulated in large part by the dramatic hemispheric lateralization of language function.

In recent years language function and malfunction have both been intensively studied by dichotic listening techniques, the simultaneous presentation of different verbal (and nonverbal) messages to each ear and, hypothetically, to the contralateral hemisphere. After Broadbent's original report (1971), Kimura studied language dominance (1967) and many others have studied individual linguistic functions by this method (Bryden, 1963; Shankweiler and Studdert-Kennedy, 1967; Spellacy, 1970).

Finally, linguists have made elegant studies of the characteristics of aphasic output. These include studies of the phonology of aphasic output, particularly the articulatory disturbances of the anterior aphasias (Lecours and Lhermitte, 1969; Blumstein, 1973), semantic disturbances (Osgood, 1960; Goodglass and Baker, 1976), and syntactical abnormalities (Zurif et al., 1972: Goodglass et al., 1972). The field of linguistic research in aphasia is both wide and active. Several recent books (Goodglass and Blumstein, 1973; Whitaker and Whitaker, 1977; Brown, 1981) and the journal *Brain and Language* provide good sources of information.

VARIETIES OF APHASIA

As noted, despite the proliferation of classifications of aphasia, the actual number of different types of aphasia is limited. A number of aphasic syndromes will now be described, utilizing the terminology originally proposed at the Aphasia Research Center of the Boston Veterans Administration Hospital (Table 2-2). For comparison of this nomenclature with other systems, readers are referred to Table 2-1. The division in Table 2-2 between aphasias in which repetition is seriously disturbed and those in which this ability remains intact is dramatic and clinically useful.

Broca's Aphasia

This syndrome has been given many different names but is almost universally recognized as Broca's aphasia. Clinically, the patient has a nonfluent aphasic output, relatively intact comprehension (almost never fully intact, however), and a serious disorder in repetition similar to, but often not as severe as, the expressive problem.

Naming is usually poor but is aided by contextual or phonetic prompting. Reading comprehension may be intact but most often is not (see Chap. 3). Reading aloud is invariably disturbed and so is writing which shows a combination of mechanical and aphasic abnormalities. Along with the characteristic language syndrome, several neighboring features are noteworthy. Most patients with Broca's aphasia have a right hemiplegia and while they may have some degree of sensory loss or even of visual

Table 2-2. Varieties of Aphasia

Aphasia with abnormal repetition
   Broca's aphasia
   Wernicke's aphasia
   Conduction aphasia
   Global aphasia

Aphasia with preserved repetition
   Mixed transcortical aphasia
   Transcortical motor aphasia
   Transcortical sensory aphasia
   Anomic aphasia

Disturbances of a single language modality
   Aphemia
   Pure word deafness
   Alexia without agraphia

Subcortical aphasia

---

field disturbance, these two findings are less common and less severe than the motor disturbance. In addition, a significant ideomotor apraxia affecting the "good" left side is common (Benson and Geschwind, 1971). Thus, simple actions that can be carried out spontaneously and are easily imitated by the left extremities will be performed clumsily or not at all on verbal command (see Chap. 7). The syndrome was named after Broca and is the most widely recognized variety of aphasia.

Individuals with the clinical symptoms of Broca's aphasia characteristically have pathology involving the posterior, inferior portion of the dominant (usually left) hemisphere (the rontal operculum, often called Broca's area, Fig. 2-2). There may be a considerable variation in the amount of cerebral tissue damaged, however, and evidence suggests that variations in the clinical picture and the degree of recovery in Broca's aphasia reflect this quantitative aspect (Mohr, 1973). However, it has also been contended that at least some of the variation of clinical features depend on whether or not pathology involves neighboring frontal structures.

Wernicke's Aphasia

The second type of disorder in Table 2-2, Wernicke's aphasia, differs dramatically from Broca's aphasia. The verbal output is fluent but almost invariably contaminated with paraphasia, most often semantic substitutions (verbal paraphasia). The key language finding in Wernicke's aphasia, however, is a striking disturbance of comprehension and a matching disturbance of repetition competency. The abilities to repeat and to comprehend run parallel so that comprehension of a few words is likely to be accompanied by a similar level of repetition. Naming ability is usually disturbed in Wernicke's aphasia and, in contrast to Broca's aphasia, prompting rarely helps. Reading is abnormal and, in general, parallels the disturbance of auditory language comprehension. Some investigators (Hécaen and Albert, 1978; Mohr et al., 1978), however, describe two variations of Wernicke's aphasia, one in which reading comprehension is more disturbed than spoken language comprehension (predomi-

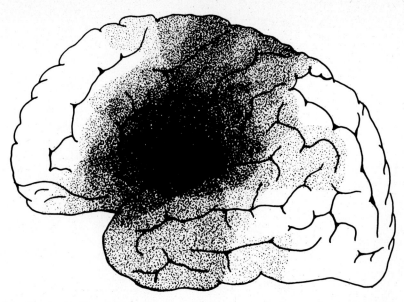

Fig. 2-2. Composite diagram: the areas of abnormality in the brain scans of 14 patients with Broca's aphasia are superimposed. Note the overlapping of lesions in the region of Broca's area. (From Kertesz et al., 1977)

nantly word-blind) and another in which the opposite is true (predominantly word-deaf). If reading ability is relatively intact in the face of serious auditory comprehension defect, the term "pure word deafness" is appropriate (see below). Writing ability is routinely compromised in Wernicke's aphasia and often consists of combinations of real letters with an appearance of words that make little or no sense. Unlike patients with Broca's aphasia, those with Wernicke's aphasia often have no apparent physical or elementary neurologic disability. It is easy to mistake the individual who fails to comprehend, speaks a jargon, and has no visible neurologic defects for a psychiatric problem, and overlook the neurologic etiology. Patients with Wernicke's aphasia are still at risk of being misplaced in no-diagnosis, no-return mental health services.

In most cases of Wernicke's aphasia, tissue pathology is found in the dominant temporal lobe, particularly the auditory association cortex located in the posterior-superior portion of the first temporal gyrus (Wernicke's area, Fig. 2-3). In those cases in which word deafness overshadows reading disturbance, a greater degree of pathology will be found deep in the first temporal gyrus involving the fibers approaching the primary auditory cortex. (See Auerbach et al., 1982, for a discussion of another localization of the pure word deaf syndrome.) On the other hand, when word blindness predominates, the pathology is probably more posterior, involving portions of the angular gyrus as well as the dominant temporal lobe.

Conduction Aphasia

The third variety of aphasia with abnormal repetition is more controversial, but in every clinic where repetition is routinely tested as a language function, conduction

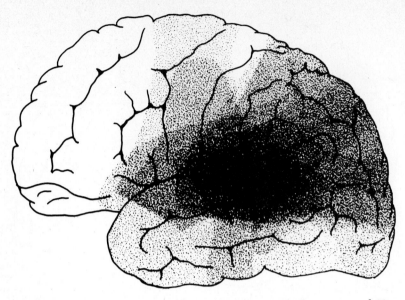

Fig. 2-3. Composite diagram of the areas of abnormality in the brain scans of 13 patients with Wernicke's aphasia. The area of greatest involvement is inferior to the sylvian fissure, in Wernicke's area. (From Kertesz et al., 1977)

Table 2-3. Language Symptomatology in Aphasia

Type of Aphasia	Spontaneous Speech	Paraphasia	Comprehension	Repetition	Naming
Broca's aphasia	Nonfluent	Uncommon	Good	Poor	Poor
Wernicke's aphasia	Fluent	Common (verbal)	Poor	Poor	Poor
Conduction aphasia	Fluent	Common (literal)	Good	Poor	Poor
Global	Nonfluent	Variable	Poor	Poor	Poor
Mixed transcortical	Nonfluent	Uncommon	Poor	Good (echolalia)	Poor
Transcortical motor	Nonfluent	Uncommon	Good	Good (echolalia)	Poor
Transcortical sensory	Fluent	Common	Poor	Good (echolalia)	Poor
Anomic	Fluent	Absent	Good	Good	Poor
Subcortical aphasia	Fluent or nonfluent	Common	Variable	Good	Variable

aphasia has gained acceptance as a distinct entity. As Table 2-3 indicates, the speech characteristics of conduction aphasia include fluent paraphasic output (primarily phonetic substitutions, often called literal paraphasia), relatively normal comprehension of spoken language, and severe disability in repetition. Most individuals with conduction aphasia have difficulty naming, at least partially based on contamination of the correct name with incorrect phonemes, producing a literal paraphasia or a totally unrecognizable word substitution (neologism). Classically, individuals with conduction aphasia read aloud poorly (again because of paraphasic contamination) but can comprehend written material. Problems with writing are common but comparatively mild, usually involving insertion of incorrect letters or reversal of letters or words in a sentence (see Chap. 4).

It has been suggested that the pathology in conduction aphasia damages the white matter, particularly the arcuate fasciculus beneath the supramarginal gyrus. A lesion here could separate an intact language comprehension area in the temporal lobe from an equally intact language output area in the frontal lobe (Geschwind, 1965; Benson et al., 1973). Others contend that the symptom picture derives from damage to or undercutting of the supramarginal gyrus (Damasio and Damasio, 1980). Not all reported cases of conduction aphasia have lesions in this area, however. In fact, conduction aphasia has been reported following damage to a variety of areas in the posterior perisylvian region, including both supra- and subsylvian sites and combinations of the two (Hécaen et al., 1955) (see Fig. 2-4). While conduction aphasia has been reported with purely temporal lesions, with purely suprasylvian lesions, and with callosal disconnections (Mendez and Benson, 1984), the language characteristics remain

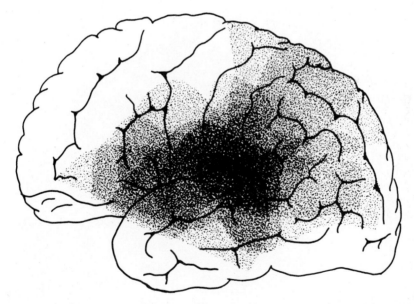

Fig. 2-4. Composite diagram of the areas of abormality in the brain scans of 11 patients with conduction aphasia. Note that there are both supra– and infrasylvian lesions. (From Kertesz et al., 1977)

consistent and usually indicate pathology in the posterior perisylvian region of the dominant hemisphere.

Global Aphasia

Aphasia in which language loss is nearly complete is usually called total or global aphasia. For most investigators, global aphasia includes a severe output disturbance (nonfluent), equally severe disturbance of comprehension, and little or no ability to repeat, read, or write. A more rigid quantitative basis is sometimes used to define global aphasia. Thus, patients who score lower than 6.0 on the PICA or are 1.5 standard deviations or more below normal on the major subtests of the BDAE are considered to have a global aphasia. The degree and localization of pathology varies considerably, however, and both the scores and descriptions fail to reflect the significant variations of global aphasia seen in clinical practice. In general, both Wernicke's and Broca's areas and, to a greater or lesser extent, the remainder of the language territory of the dominant hemisphere are damaged in global aphasia (Fig. 2-5).

Mixed Transcortical Aphasia (isolation of the speech area)

The outstanding characteristic of the transcortical aphasias is an intact or at least relatively good ability to repeat spoken language despite serious aphasia. The most dramatic example is mixed transcortical aphasia, a nonfluent (in fact, speechless unless spoken to), noncomprehending, totally anomic, alexic and agraphic disorder with accurate repetition of what is said by the examiner up to a span level. One charac-

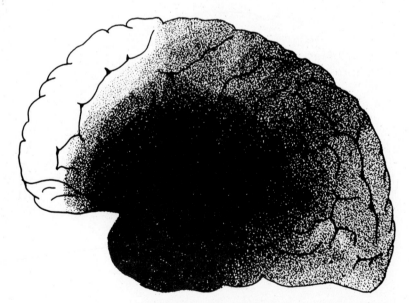

Fig. 2-5. Composite diagram of the areas of abnormality in the brain scans of 12 patients with global aphasia. Note the extensive involvement, which usually involves both Broca's and Wernicke's areas. (From Kertesz et al., 1977)

teristic is *echolalia*, an almost mandatory tendency to repeat what has just been said. As Stengel (1947) demonstrated, such individuals show a remarkable ability to complete sentences. When given an overlearned phrase such as "roses are ____," the patient will complete the phrase and may carry on with the next line. Reports of mixed transcortical aphasia are rare; one published under the title "Isolation of the Speech Area" (Geschwind et al., 1968) described pathology that spared the perisylvian area (Broca's area, Wernicke's area, and the white matter connecting them) but involved the surrounding area, often called the border zone or watershed area. The most common etiology is acute carotid artery occlusion causing insufficient blood flow in the distal tributaries of the middle cerebral artery. The syndrome has also been reported following hypoxic episodes and severe cerebral edema. Here again, it is surmised that the distribution of pathology reflects poor oxygen supply in the outer vascular tributaries.

Transcortical Motor Aphasia

A partial transcortical aphasia in which motor disturbance is predominant is considerably more common (Rubens, 1976). Verbal output is nonfluent except for the ability to echo. Comprehension is relatively well preserved and repetition is excellent. Most such patients have difficulty naming but accept and benefit from cues. Reading comprehension is often preserved but writing is almost invariably abnormal. These cases closely resemble Broca's aphasia except for the incongruously good ability to repeat (Whitaker, 1976). Pathology in transcortical motor aphasia is located in the dominant frontal lobe, either superior or anterior to Broca's area (Rubens, 1975, Freedman et al., 1984). The etiology may be vascular (middle cerebral artery branch occlusion), but trauma and postoperative brain tumor also cause this distinctive type of aphasia.

Transcortical Sensory Aphasia

A less commonly recognized variety of aphasia with intact repetition involves the sensory modalities. The classic description of transcortical sensory aphasia includes a fluent output, frequent repetition (echoing) of what has been said by the examiner with additional, nonrelated verbal material only occasionally contaminated by semantic paraphasia. The total output is a string of real words bearing little relationship to the topic of conversation. Comprehension of spoken language is severely limited and there are equally serious problems in both reading and writing. This disorder is not commonly diagnosed (again, it is easy to misinterpret these findings as evidence of psychosis) and few pathological correlations have been reported. Kertesz and associates (1982) recently reported the CT scan findings of 12 individuals with transcortical sensory aphasia and suggested a posterior parietal-occipital junction location of pathology (Fig. 2-6.)

Anomic Aphasia

Anomic (amnestic, nominal) aphasia is very common but is the most difficult to localize. Following recovery from any type of aphasia, some residual word-finding diffi-

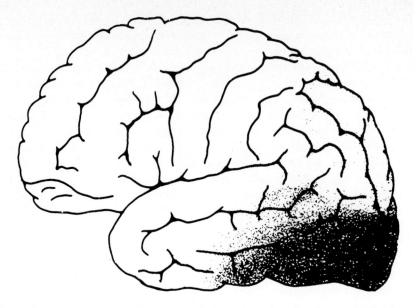

Fig. 2-6. Composite diagram of the areas of abnormality in the radioisotope brain scans of 12 patients with transcortical sensory aphasia. (From Kertesz et al., 1982.)

culty is almost always present (see Chap. 16). Almost all aphasics have some degree of anomia (Goodglass and Geschwind, 1976) and there is little agreement as to which variations deserve the title of anomic aphasia. Certain language characteristics, however, characterize the diagnosis (See Table 2-3). These include a fluent output with little or no paraphasia, relatively normal ability to comprehend spoken language, and an excellent ability to repeat words coupled with a notable deficiency in word finding. Naming problems may be apparent on evaluation of conversational speech: a wordy, lengthy output lacking specificity, often called "empty speech," is produced. The patient may try to substitute for a missing word; if a phrase used in the substitution also demands a specific but unobtainable word, yet another substitute phrase is needed, producing a convoluted output called *circumlocution*. An incorrect substitution, a semantic paraphasia, may be presented but literal paraphasias and neologisms are not characteristic of "pure" anomic aphasia. Empty speech is characterized by multiple pauses at points where a semantically significant word is needed. While not necessarily involved, reading and writing are frequently abnormal. In fact, the combination of alexia with agraphia (see Chap. 3), anomic aphasia, and the Gerstmann syndrome is common and strongly suggests pathology involving the dominant angular gyrus (Benson et al., 1982). Anomia alone does not necessarily indicate angular gyrus pathology, however. In fact, pathology involving almost any part of the language area, and even parts of the nondominant hemisphere, can cause word-finding problems. Anomia alone is not a useful indication of the site of pathology, and localization of anomic aphasia is treacherous unless accompanied by clear neighborhood signs.

an excellent ability to repeat words coupled with a notable deficiency in word finding. Naming problems may be apparent on evaluation of conversational speech: a wordy, lengthy output lacking specificity, often called *empty speech*, is produced. The patient may try to substitute for a missing word; if a phrase used in the substitution also demands a specific but unobtainable word, yet another substitute phrase is needed, producing a convoluted output called *circumlocution*. An incorrect substitution, a semantic paraphasia, may be presented but literal paraphasias and neologisms are not characteristic of "pure" anomic aphasia. Empty speech is characterized by multiple pauses at points where a semantically significant word is needed. While not necessarily involved, reading and writing are frequently abnormal. In fact, the combination of alexia with agraphia (see Chap. 3), anomic aphasia, and the Gerstmann syndrome is common and strongly suggests pathology involving the dominant angular gyrus (Benson et al., 1982). Anomia alone does not necessarily indicate angular gyrus pathology, however. In fact, pathology involving almost any part of the language area, and even parts of the nondominant hemisphere, can cause word-finding problems. Anomia alone is not a useful indication of the site of pathology, and localization of anomic aphasia is treacherous unless accompanied by clear neighborhood signs.

Subcortical Aphasia

With the widespread use of x-ray CT scanning, it has been realized that aphasic findings could occur with subcortical pathology. As this evidence accumulates, the aphasia following subcortical lesions appears to have sufficiently unique characteristics to warrant identification as a specific subtype of aphasia. Paradoxically, some investigators question whether it may not be distant effects, not the subcortically located lesion itself, that underlie this aphasic symptom cluster. Characteristically, a state of mutism occurs acutely, with or without neighborhood neurologic disturbances such as hemiplegia. This is followed by a return to an abnormal verbal output, usually hypophonic and paraphasic but either fluent or nonfluent. The output defects, most particularly the paraphasias, are greatly improved or even disappear completely, when the patient is asked to repeat. Comprehension, naming, reading, and writing may or may not be involved. In many instances, the output abnormality recovers to an essentially normal state but in some instances there is a residual aphasic and/or speech output abnormality. The transient nature of the severe language disturbance present in the early stages of subcortical aphasia is a unique feature.

The neuroanatomic localization and pathology underlying the so-called subcortical aphasias has been remarkably diverse. The syndrome has been reported with thalamic pathology, both hemorrhagic and occlusive (Mohr et al., 1975; Cappa and Vignolo, 1979; Alexander and LoVerme, 1980), with putaminal pathology (Naeser, et al., 1982), and caudate lesions (Damasio et al., 1982). While a number of investigators have suggested that thalamic pathology alone can produce aphasia (Ojemann and Ward, 1971; Van Buren, 1975), there is also evidence that it does not (Brown, 1974). The fact that a major lesion that causes permanent scarring or cyst formation in the thalamus causes only a transient aphasia (Ciemans, 1970) suggests that the subcortical influence is nonspecific for language. Two theories have been proposed (Benson,

1979b). One is that the subcortical structures (particularly the thalamus) function as activators for the cortex and that with the passage of time alternate sources of activation become available. The second theory states that intracranial swelling secondary to the acute process can produce a vascular insufficiency that primarily effects the border-zone territory (producing a syndrome resembling the transcortical aphasias). In both instances the aphasia is transient unless cortical infarction also occurs. Recent information from metabolic studies with positron isotope CT can be used to support both views and, to date, the issue has not been settled (Metter et al., 1981). Nonetheless, the diagnosis of a subcortical aphasia can be made by the characteristic clinical features and confirmed by x-ray CT.

Disturbances of a Single Language Modality

There are three conditions in which only a single modality of language input or output is disrupted. Legitimately, these should not be called aphasia, since basic language function remains intact. Nonetheless, they closely resemble the varieties of aphasia just mentioned and must be considered when examining for aphasia.

The first has been given a number of different names such as *aphemia*, pure-word dumbness, anarthria, and subcortical motor aphasia, none of which has gained general acceptance. The patient with this disorder becomes acutely mute. With recovery, a severe hypophonia gradually improves to a soft, slow but grammatically and syntactically intact verbal output. During the entire period, comprehension of spoken language and the ability to read and write are basically normal. In neither verbal nor written output does the patient show signs of either agrammatism or anomia. This disorder involves only speech output and is not truly an impairment of language (aphasia). But it resembles several of the aphasias and deserves a place in the differential diagnosis of aphasia. In the few cases that have come to autopsy, lesions have been found to either involve Broca's area itself or the tissues immediately under it (Bastian, 1898; Mohr, 1973). Nearly identical syndromes can result from pathology in other locations, however. In particular, acute involvement of the dominant supplementary motor area or one of the subcortical areas just discussed can produce mutism followed by hypophonic but grammatically correct language. In these disorders, however, there is paraphasic contamination that is not seen in the aphemia syndrome. Facial apraxia may accompany aphemia (Benson, 1979b) but is not a consistent finding. Recovery often leaves the patient with a severely dysprosodic output, the so-called foreign accent syndrome (Monrad-Krohn, 1947).

An isolated defect of the reception of spoken language is traditionally called *pure word deafness*. Clinically, the individual with pure word deafness does not understand spoken language although adequate hearing competency can be demonstrated by the identification of nonverbal sounds (e.g., clicks, whistle, telephone ring). Verbal output may be entirely normal but paraphasia is usually present in the acute stage. In long-standing cases of pure word deafness, however, fully normal verbal output with almost no comprehension of spoken language may be seen. These patients cannot repeat spoken language but read without difficulty and write adequately. Pathology in autopsied cases has been found in two different locations (Weisenburg and McBride, 1932/1964). About half of the cases reported have had subcortical lesions of the dominant superior temporal region, with destruction of the primary auditory cortex (Heschl's gyrus) and/or the pathways from the medial geniculate nucleus. Other clinically similar cases, however, have had bilateral pathology affecting the superior temporal gyrus, particularly the mid-portion of the first temporal gyrus, of both hemispheres (Auerbach et al., 1982). Again, pure word deafness should not be considered a true aphasia because language production and comprehension of written language are not disturbed. Only the ability to understand spoken language is impaired (see Chap. 9).

A similar disorder involving reading is called *alexia without agraphia* or pure word blindness, and will be discussed in Chapter 3. In this condition the patient is unable to read but has no other language disturbance. As in pure word deafness, the pathology involves a primary sensory modality and prevents information from reaching the intact language area.

Acquired Stuttering and Palilalia

Stuttering and palilalia are nonaphasic disorders of speech involving repetitive utterances. Stuttering entails repetition of phonemes or syllables, most often at the beginning of words. Palilalia refers to repetition of syllables, words, or phrases, most often at the ends of phrases or sentences. When there is no associated aphasia, utterances are linguistically normal when the repetitions are deleted.

Acquired stuttering has been described following unilateral or bilateral hemisphere damage involving the frontal, parietal, or temporal lobes. With unilateral lesions the left hemisphere is more often affected, but unilateral right-hemipshere lesions have been reported (Rosenbek et al., 1978; Horner and Massey, 1983). Bilateral lesions are more likely to be associated with persistent stuttering (Helm et al., 1978).

Palilalia is associated with bilateral lesions, most often of frontal lobes or subcortical structures. It has been described in association with postencephalitic Parkinson's disease, pseudobulbar palsy, Alzheimer's disease, general paresis (tertiary syphilis), and head trauma, among other conditions (Boller et al., 1973). Typically, palilalic speech becomes more rapid and less loud with repeated utterances, trailing off into an indistinguishable mutter. These features may be more prominent in patients with parkinsonian symptoms, since rapid speech and hypophonia are seen in Parkinson's patients without palilalia.

The speech of patients with acquired stuttering or palilalia may be difficult to understand, and confusion with aphasic disorders may therefore occur. The lesions responsible for these disorders, however, are not as well delineated as those responsible for aphasia and often occur outside the classical language areas.

Finally, a note of caution must be voiced concerning the correlation of language symptoms with neuropathology. Most of the syndromes discussed above were described long ago and the clinical-pathological correlations have been confirmed many times and by many techniques through the years. In the past decade good correlations between these syndromes and the location of pathology have been demonstrated by radioisotope brain scans (Benson and Patten, 1967; Kertesz et al., 1977, x-ray CT scans (Naeser and Hayward, 1976; Kertesz, et al., 1979), and isotope CT's

Since a greater or lesser degree of spontaneous recovery occurs in most aphasic patients, assessment of the efficacy of speech therapy has proved difficult. One recent study suggests a meaningful benefit from therapy (Basso et al., 1975) but others suggest the benefit might well accrue from the emotional support of therapy, rather than the specific therapeutic methods. Recovery of function and therapy for aphasia are considered in more detail in Chapter 16.

Most "traditional" aphasia therapy represents variations on techniques used in speech training and education, particularly rote practice and selective stimulation (Darley, 1975). A number of innovations in aphasia therapy have been made in the past few years, and many more can be expected. Melodic intonation therapy (MIT) (Albert et al., 1973) has met with some success in the treatment of aphasics with severe expressive difficulty, poor repetition, and good comprehension. Attempts to use sign language as a substitute for verbal communication have met with minimal success (Chen, 1971; Skelly et al., 1974), because it appears that most sign languages demand as much language competency as spoken language. One happy exception is *Amerind*, a manual communication system that is not a complete language. Aphasics with severe comprehension disability often respond to Amerind, which reintroduces them to interpersonal communication leading toward more formal language therapy (Skelly et al., 1974).

A variety of speaking machines have been devised to aid the aphasic in communication but have met with little success. Even aphasics who master operation of the apparatus usually believe they can communicate better without the machine. The successful teaching of a symbol system for communication to chimpanzees (Gardner and Gardner, 1969; Premack, 1971) was followed by an attempt to use a similar system with aphasic adults (Gardner et al., 1976). While improvement has not been striking, a system of symbols—a visual communication system (VIC)—has been shown to help some global aphasics (Baker et al., 1975). A variation, visual action therapy (VAT) has proved successful for some aphasics (Helm-Estabrooks et al., 1982), primarily those with severe comprehension problems.

While traditional therapy is rather broad and does not promise specific treatment for a specific type of aphasia, some of the newer methods of therapy appear to be more directed. MIT has proved effective for a limited group with output problems and Amerind, VIC and VAT appear particularly suited to patients with poor comprehension. It seems likely that future therapies will be devised to treat specific language problems, not aphasia as a single problem.

Finally, some attention should be given to the important part played by emotional support in aphasia therapy. The loss of language is a severe blow at any age and aphasia often strikes individuals near their prime. Both employment and economic status are drastically altered and, in addition, position in the family, regular recreation activities, and even sexual functioning are threatened (Benson, 1973). Frustration and depression often complicate the picture of aphasia. Careful attention to these emotional factors is mandatory for any aphasia therapy program. The loss, real or threatened, of position in the family must be faced, particularly if the individual has been the breadwinner and leader in the family. Careful counseling of the family, helping them to understand the situation and to aid the patient in maintaining as much of his or her prior status as possible, is important.

Similarly, many aphasics have serious physical problems such as hemiplegia and visual disturbance. Full-scale rehabilitation programs should be carried out in conjunction with language therapy. Success in a physical rehabilitation program is often reflected by improvement in language therapy programs and vice versa. The aphasic gets considerable support from working with someone who understands aphasia and is dedicated to the improvement of the patient's language function. Thus, the therapist as a person becomes an important factor in the patient's improvement. Similarly, many aphasics benefit from group interaction. Either observing or actively participating with others who share the disorder offers a form of psychic support.

Finally, it must always be remembered that aphasia almost never occurs in isolation. Damage to the brain sufficient to produce aphasia almost invariably causes other, often significant, behavioral abnormalities (Benson, 1979b). The presence of hemiplegia or hemiparesis is obvious; pseudobulbar changes may be less so. Equally disabling but largely hidden and frequently overlooked are the sensory disturbances, hemisensory loss, visual field loss, and unilateral inattention. Multiple speech disturbances such as varieties of dysarthria (Darley et al., 1975), scanning speech (Kremer et al., 1947), acquired stutter (Helm et al., 1978), palilalia, and logoclonia can occur. Generalized mental disturbances such as confusional state (Strub, 1982), dementia (Cummings, 1982), and amnesia (Benson and Blumer, 1982) as well as specialized problems, agnosia (see Chap. 9), apraxia (see Chap. 7), Gerstmann syndrome (Gerstmann, 1931), constructional disturbance (see Chap. 8), and many others may be present. Both the clinician and the investigator must be aware of these common complications. The success of any therapy program will depend on recognizing and handling these problems. In addition, research on language may be totally invalid if performed on an aphasic with serious neurobehavioral complications.

The loss of language (aphasia) is a complex clinical problem, often obscured by both emotional and physical problems. While almost every case of aphasia is different, the study of recurrent patterns of language disturbance offers great aid in understanding both the afflicted patient and the brain's activities in the function of language. Mastery of the syndromes of aphasia is a valuable accomplishment for any student of language.

REFERENCES

Albert, M. L., Sparks, R. W., and Helm, N. A. (1973). Melodic intonation therapy for aphasia. *Arch. Neurol. 29*:130–131.

Alexander, M. P. and LoVerme, S. R. Jr. (1980). Aphasia after left hemispheric intracerebral hemorrhage. *Neurology 30*:1193–1202.

Appell, J., Kertesz, A., and Fisman, M. (1982). A study of language functioning in Alzheimer patients. *Brain and Lang. 17*:73–91.

Auerbach, S. H., Alland, T., Naeser, M., Alexander, M. P., and Albert, M. L. (1982). Pure word deafness: analysis of a case with bilateral lesions and a defect at the prephonemic level. *Brain 105*:271–300.

Baker, E., Berry. T., Gardner, H., Zurif, E., Davis, L., and Veroff, A. (1975). Can linguistic competence be dissociated from natural language functions? *Nature* 254:509–510.

Barton, M., Maruszeqski, M., and Urrea, D. (1969). Variation of stimulus context and its effect on word-finding ability in aphasics. *Cortex* 5:351–365.

Basso, A., Faglioni, P., and Vignolo, L. A. (1975). Etude controlle de la reeducation du langage dous l'aphasie: comparison entre aphasiques traites et nontraites. *Rev. Neurol.* 131:607–614.

Bastian, H. C. (1898). *Aphasia and Other Speech Defects*. London: H. K. Lewis.

Bay, E. (1962). Aphasia and nonverbal disorders of language. *Brain* 85:411–426.

Bay, E. (1964). Principles of classification and their influence on our concepts of aphasia. In *Disorders of Language*, A. V. S. DeReuk and M. O'Connor (eds). Boston: Little, Brown.

Benson, D. F. (1967). Fluency in aphasia: correlation with radioactive scan localization. *Cortex* 3:373–394.

Benson, D. F. (1973). Psychiatric aspects of aphasia. *Br. J. Psychiat.* 123:555–566.

Benson, D. F. (1978). Neurologic correlates of aphasia and apraxia. In *Recent Advances in Neurology*, W. B. Matthews and G. Glaser (eds). London: Churchill Livingstone.

Benson, D. F. (1979a). Neurologic correlates of anomia. In *Studies in Neurolinguistics*, Vol. 4, H. Whitaker and H. Whitaker (eds). New York: Academic Press.

Benson, D. F. (1979b). *Aphasia, Alexia, and Agraphia*. New York: Churchill Livingstone.

Benson, D. F. and Blumer, D. (1982). Amnesia: a clinical approach to memory. In *Psychiatric Aspects of Neurologic Disease*, Vol. 2, D. F. Benson and D. Blumer (eds). New York: Grune & Stratton.

Benson, D. F., Cummings, J. L., and Tsai, S. Y. (1982). Angular gyrus syndrome simulating Alzheimer's disease. *Arch. Neurol.* 39:612–620.

Benson, D. F. and Geschwind, N. (1971). Aphasia and related cortical disturbances. In *Clinical Neurology*. A. B. Baker and L. H. Baker (eds). New York: Harper & Row.

Benson, D. F. and Patten, D. H. (1967). The use of radioactive isotopes in the localization of aphasia-producing lesions. *Cortex* 3:258–271.

Benson, D. F., Sheremata, W. A., Buchard, R., Segarra, J., Price, D., and Geschwind, N. 1973). Conduction aphasia. *Arch. Neurol.* 28: 339–346.

Benton, A. L. (1964). Developmental aphasia and brain damage. *Cortex* 1:40–52.

Benton, A. L. and Joynt, R. J. (1960). Early descriptions of aphasia. *Arch. Neurol.* 3:205–222.

Blumstein, S. E. (1973). *A Phonological Investigation of Aphasic Speech*. The Hague: Mouton.

Bogen, J. E. and Bogen, G. M. (1969). The other side of the brain III: The corpus callosum and creativity. *Bull. Los Angeles Neurol. Soc.* 34:191–220.

Boller, F., Boller, M., Denes, F., Timberlake, W. H., Zieper, I., and Albert, M. (1973). Familial palilalia. *Neurology* 23:1117–1125.

Brain, R. (1961). *Speech Disorders—Aphasia, Apraxia and Agnosia*. London: Butterworths.

Broadbent, D. E. (1971). *Decision and Stress*. New York: Academic Press.

Broca, P. (1861). Remarques sur le siège de la faculté du langage articulé, suives d'une observation d'aphemie. *Bull. Soc. Anat.* 2:330–357.

Broca, P. (1864). Deux cas d'aphemie tramatique, produite par des lesions de la troisieme circonvolution frontale gauche. *Bull. d. l. Soc. d. Chiurg.* V:51–54.

Brown, J. R. (1968). A model for central and peripheral behavior in aphasia. Paper presented at Annual Meeting, Academy of Aphasia, Rochester, Minn.

Brown, J. W. (1974). Language, cognition and the thalamus. *Confin. Neurol.* 36:33–60.

Brown, J. W. (ed) (1981). *Jargonaphasia*. New York: Academic.

Bryden, M. P. (1963). Ear perferences in auditory perception. *J. Exp. Psychol.* 65:103–105.

Cappa, S. F. and Vignolo, L. A. (1979). "Transcortical" features of aphasia following left thalamic hemorrhage. *Cortex 15*:121–130.

Caramazza, A. and Berndt, R. S. (1978). Semantic and syntactic processes in aphasia: a review of the literature. *Psychol. Bull. 85*:898–918.

Charcot, J. M. (1889). *Clinical Lectures on Diseases of the Nervous System*, Vol. 3. London: New Sydenham Society.

Chen, L. C. (1971). Manual communication by combined alphabet and gestures. *Arch. Phys. Med. Rehab. 52*:381–384.

Ciemins, V. A. (1970). Localized thalamic hemorrhage: a cause of aphasia. *Neurology 20*:776–782.

Critchley, M. (1970). *Aphasiology*. London: Edward Arnold Ltd.

Cummings, J. L. (1982). Cortical dementias. In *Psychiatric Aspects of Neurologic Disease*, Vol. 2, D. F. Benson and D. Blumer (eds). New York: Grune & Stratton.

Damasio, A. R., Damasio, H., Rizzo, M., Varney, N., and Gersh, F. (1982). Aphasia with nonhemorrhagic lesions in the basal ganglia and internal capsule. *Arch. Neurol. 39*:15–20.

Damasio, H. and Damasio, A. (1980). The anatomical basis of conduction aphasia. *Brain 103*:337–350.

Darley, F. L. (1975). Treatment of acquired aphasia. In *Advances in Neurology*, Vol. 7, W. J. Friedlander (ed). New York: Raven.

Darley, F. L., Aronson, A. E., and Brown, J. R. (1975).*Motor Speech Disorders*. Philadalphia: Saunders.

Dejerine, J. (1914). *Semiologie des Affections du Systeme Nerveaux*. Paris: Masson.

DeRenzi, E. and Vignolo, L. A. (1962). The token test: a sensitive test to detect receptive disturbances in aphasics. *Brain 85*:665–678.

Eisenson, J. (1954). *Examining for Aphasia*. New York: Psychological Corp.

Freedman, M., Alexander, M. P., and Naeser, M. A. (1984). Anatomic basis of transcortical motor aphasia. *Neurology 34*:409–417.

Freud, S. (1891/1953). *On aphasia*. Trans. E. Stengl. New York: Int. Univ. Press.

Gainotti, G. (1972). Emotional behavior and hemispheric side of the lesion. *Cortex 8*:41–55.

Galin, D. (1974). Implications for psychiatry of left and right cerebral specialization. *Arch. Gen. Psychol. 31*:572–583.

Gardner, H., Zurif, E., Berry. T., and Baker, E. (1976). Visual communication in aphasia. *Neuropsychologia 14*:275–292.

Gardner, R. A. and Gardner, B. (1969). Teaching sign language to a chimpanzee. *Science 165*:664–672.

Gazzaniga, M. S. and Sperry, R. W. (1967). Language after section of the cerebral commissures. *Brain 90*:131–148.

Gerstmann, J. (1931). Zur symptomatologie der Hirnlasionen im Uebergangsgebiet der unteren Parietal und mitterleren Occipital- windung. *Nervenarzt. 3*:691–695.

Geschwind, N. (1965). Disconnexion syndromes in animals and man. *Brain 88*:Part II, 237–294; Part III, 585–644.

Geschwind, N. and Kaplan, E. F. (1962). A human cerebral deconnection sundrome. *Neurology 12*:675–685.

Geschwind, N. and Levitsky, W. (1968). Human brain: Left-right asymmetries in temporal speech region. *Science 161*:186–187.

Geschwind, N., Quadfasel, F. A., and Segarra, J. (1968). Isolation of the speech area. *Neuropsychologia 6*:327–340.

Gloning, I., Gloning, K., Haub, C., and Quatember, R. (1969). Comparison of verbal behavior in right-handed and non-right-handed patients with anatomically verified lesion of one hemisphere. *Cortex* 5:43–52.

Goldstein, K. (1948). *Language and Language Disturbances*. New York: Grune & Stratton.

Goodglass, H. and Baker, E. (1976). Semantic field naming and auditory comprehension in aphasia. *Brain and Lang*. 3:359–374.

Goodglass, H. and Berko, J. (1960). Agrammatism and inflectional morphology in English. *J. Speech Hearing Res*. 3:257–267.

Goodglass, H. and Blumstein, S. (1973). *Psycholinguistics and Aphasia*. Baltimore: Johns Hopkins.

Goodglass, H. and Geschwind, N. (1976). Language disturbance (aphasia). In *Handbook of Perception*, Vol. 7, E. C. Carterette and M. P. Friedman (eds). New York: Academic Press.

Goodglass, H., Gleason, J. B., Bernholtz, N. A., and Hyde, M. (1972). Some linguistic structures in the speech of Broca's aphasia. *Cortex* 8:191–192.

Goodglass, H. and Kaplan, E. (1972). *The Assessment of Aphasia and Related Disorders*. Philadelphia: Lea & Febiger.

Head, H. (1926). *Aphasia and Kindred Disorders* (2 volumes). London: Cambridge University Press.

Hécaen, H. and Albert, M. (1978). *Human Neuropsychology*. New York: Wiley.

Hécaen, H. and Angelergues, R. (1965). *Pathologie du Langage*. Paris: Larousse.

Hécaen, H., Dell, M. B., and Roger, A. (1955). L'Aphasia de Conduction. *L'Encephale* 2:170–195.

Helm, N. A., Butler, R. B., and Benson, D. F. (1978). Acquired stuttering. *Neurology* 28:1159–1165.

Helm, N. A., Fitzpatrick, P. M., and Barresi, B. (1982). Visual action therapy for global aphasia. *J. Speech Hearing Dis*. 47:385–389, 1982.

Henschen, S. E. (1922). *Klinische und Anatomische Bertrage zur Pathologie der Gehirms*. Stockholm: Almquist and Wiksell.

Holland, A. L. (1980). *Communicative Abilities in Daily Living*. Baltimore: University Park press.

Horner, J., and Massey, E. W. (1983). Progressive dysfluency associated with right hemisphere disease. *Brain and Language* 18:71–85.

Howes, D. (1964). Application of the word fluency concept to aphasia. In *Disorders of Language: A Ciba Foundation Symposium*, A. V. S. DeReuk and M. O'Connor (eds). London: Churchill.

Isserlin, M. (1929, 1931, 1932). Die pathologische Physiologie der Sprache. *Eigebn. Physiol*. 29:129–249; 33:1–202; 34:1065–1144.

Jackson, J. H. (1864). Clinical remarks on cases of defects of expression by words, writing, signs, etc.) in diseases of the nervous system. *Lancet* 1:604–605.

Jackson, J. H. (1932). (J. Taylor, ed). *Selected Writings*. London: Hodder & Stoughton.

Jackson, J. H. (1868). On the physiology of language. *Medical Times and Gazette* 2:275 (1915). Reprinted in *Brain* 38:59–64.

Jakobson, R. (1964). Towards a linguistic typology of aphasic impairments. In *Disorders of Language*, A. V. S. ReReuk and M. O'Connor (eds). Boston: Little, Brown.

Kennedy, F. and Wolf, A. (1936). The relationship of intellect to speech defect in aphasic patients. *J. Nervous Mental Dis*. 84: 125–145, 293–311.

Kertesz, A. (1979), *Aphasia and Associated Disorders*. New York: Grune & Stratton.

Kertesz, A., Harlock, W., and Coates, R. (1979). Computer tomographic localization and prognosis in aphasia and nonverbal impairment. *Brain* 8:34–50.

Kertesz, A., Lesk, D., and McCabe, P. (1977). Isotope localization of infarcts in aphasia. *Arch. Neurol. 34*:590–601.

Kertesz, A. and Poole, E. (1974). The aphasia quotient: the taxonomic approach to measurement of aphasic disability. *Can. J. Neurol. Sci. 1*:7–16.

Kertesz, A., Sheppard, A., and MacKenzie, R. (1982). Localization in transcortical sensory aphasia. *Arch. Neurol. 39*:475–478.

Kimura, D. (1967). Functional asymmetry of the brain in dichotic listening. *Cortex 3*:163–178.

Kleist, K. (1934). *Gehirnpathologie*. Leipzig: Barth.

Kleist, K. (1962). *Sensory Aphasia and Amusia—The Myeloarchitectunic Basis*. London: Pergammon Press.

Kremer, M., Russell, W. R., and Smyth, G. E. (1947). A mid-brain syndrome following head injury. *J. Neurol. Neurosurg. Psychiat. 10:* 49–60.

Lecours, A. R. and Lhermitte, F. (1969). Phonemic paraphasias: linguistic structures and tentative hypotheses. *Cortex 5*:193–228.

Leischner, A. (1957). *Die Storungen der Schriftsprache (Agraphie und Alexie)*. Stuttgart: Georg Thiem Verlag.

Lhermitte, F. and Gautier, J. C. (1969). Aphasia. In *Handbook of Clinical Neurology*, Vol. 4, P. J. Vinken and G. W. Bruyn (eds). Amsterdam: North Holland.

Lichtheim, L. (1885) On aphasia. *Brain 7*:433–484.

Luria, A. R. (1966). *Higher Cortical Functions in Man*. New York: Basic Books.

Luria, A. R. (1970). *Traumatic Aphasia*. The Hague: Mouton.

Marie, P. (1906). Revision de la question de l'aphasie: l'aphasie de 1801 a 1866; essai de critique historique sur la genese de la doctrine de Broca. *Semaine Medicale 48*:565–571.

Mendez, M. F. and Benson, D. F. Conduction aphasia without apraxia. Paper in preparation.

Metter, E. J., Wasterlain, C. G., Kuhl, D. E., Hanson, W. R., and Phelps, M. E. (1981). [18]FDG positron emission computed tomography in a study of aphasia. *Ann. Neurol. 10*:173–183.

Mohr, J. P. (1973). Rapid amelioration of motor aphasia. *Arch. Neurol. 28:* 77–82.

Mohr, J. P., Hier, D. B., and Kirshner, H. S. (1978). Modality bias in Wernicke aphasia. Presented at the annual meeting, American Academy of Neurology, Los Angeles, April 1978.

Mohr, J. P., Wattes, W.C., and Duncan, G. W. (1975). Thalamic hemorrhage and aphasia. *Brain and Lang. 2*:3–18.

Monrad-Krohn, G. H. (1947). Dysprosody or altered melody of language. *Brain 70*:405–415.

Naeser, M. A., Alexander, M. P., Helm-Estabrooks, N., Levine, H., Laughlin, S. A., and Geschwind, N. (1982). Aphasia with predominately subcortical lesion sites. *Arch. Neurol. 39*:2–14.

Naeser, M. A. and Hayward, R. W. (1976). The evolving stroke and aphasia: a case study with computed tomography. Presented at the Academy of Aphasia Meeting, Miami, Florida.

Nielson, J. M. (1940). The unsolved problems in aphasia—Part III. Amnesic aphasia. *Bull. L.A. Neurol. Soc. 5*:78–84.

Nielsen, J. M. (1962). *Agnosia, Apraxia and Aphasia: Their Value in Cerebral Localization*, 2nd ed. New York: Hafner.

Ojemann, G. and Ward, A. (1971). Speech representation in ventrolateral thalamus. *Brain 94*:669–680.

Orgass, B., Hartje, W., Kerschensteiner, M., and Poeck, K. (1972). Aphasie and nichtsprachliche Intelligenz. *Nervenarzt 43*:623–627.

Osgood, C. E. (1960). *Method and Theory in Experimental Psychology*. New York: Oxford.

Pick, A. (1973). *Aphasia*. Springfield, Ill.: C. C. Thomas.

Poeck, K., Kerschensteiner, M., and Hartje, W. (1972). A quantitative study on language understanding in fluent and nonfluent aphasia. *Cortex* 8:299–305.

Porch, B. (1967) *Porch Index of Communicative Ability*. Palo Alto: Consulting Psychologists.

Premack, D. (1971). Language in the Chimpanzee. *Science* 172:808– 822.

Ravens, J. C. (1952). *Human Nature: Its Development, Variations and Assessment*. London: H. K. Lewis.

Rosenbek, J. C., Messert, B., Collins, M., and Wertz, R. T. (1978). Stuttering following brain damage. *Brain and language* 6:82–96.

Ross, E. D., Harner, J. H., de la Corte-Utamsing, C., and Pardy, P. D. (1981). How the brain integrates affective and propositional language into a unified behavioral function. *Arch. Neurol.* 38:745–748.

Rothi, L. J., McFarling, D., and Heilman, K. M. (1982). Conduction aphasia, syntactic alexia and the anatomy of syntactic comprehension. *Arch. Neurol.* 39:272–275.

Rubens, A. B. (1975). Aphasia with infarction in the territory of the anterior cerebral artery. *Cortex* 11:239–250.

Rubens, A. B. (1976). Transcortical motor aphasia. In *Studies in Neurolinguistics*, Vol. 1, H. Whitaker and H. Whitaker (eds). New York: Academic.

Samuels, J. and Benson, D. F. (1979). Observations on anterior alexia. *Brain and Lang.* 8:275–280.

Sarno, M. T., Silverman, M. and Sands, E. (1970). Speech and language recovery in servere aphasia. *J. Speech Hearing Res.* 13:607–623.

Schuell, H. (1957). *Minnesota Test for the Differential Diagnosis of Aphasia*. Minneapolis: University of Minnesota Press.

Schuell, H. Jenkins, J., and Jiminez-Pabon, E. (1964). *Aphasia in Adults—Diagnosis, Prognosis and Treatment*. New York: Harper & Row.

Shankweiler, D. and Studdert-Kennedy, M. (1967). Identification of consonants and vowels presented to the left and right ears. *Quart. J. Exp. Psychol.* 19:59–63.

Skelly, M., Schinsky, L., Smith, R., and Fust, R. (1974). American Indian sign (Amerind) as a facilitator of verbalization for the oral verbal apraxic. *J. Speech Hearing Disorders* 39:445–446.

Smith, A. and Sugar, O. (1975). Development of above-normal language and inelligence 21 years after left hemispherectomy. *Neurology* 25: 813–818.

Sparks, R. and Geschwind, N. (1968). Dichotic listening in man after section of neocortical commissures. *Cortex* 4:3–16.

Spellacy, F. (1970). Lateral preferences in the identification of patterned stimuli. *J. Acoust. Soc. Am.* 47:574–578.

Spreen, O. and Benton, A. (1969). *Neurosensory Center Comprehensive Examination for Aphasia*. Victoria: Neurosychoogy Laboratory, University of Victoria.

Stengl, E. (1947). A clinical and psychological study of echo reactions. *J. Mental Sci.* 93:598–612.

Strub, R. L. (1982). Acute confusional state. In *Psychiatric Aspects of Neurologic Disease*, Vol. 2, D. F. Benson and D. Blumer (eds).New York: Grune & Stratton.

Taylor, M. L. (1965). A measurement of functional communication in aphasia *Arch. Phys. Med. Rehab.* 46:101–107.

Taylor-Sarno, M. T., Silverman, M., and Sands, E. (1970). Speech therapy and language recovery in severe aphasia. *J. Speech Hearing Res.* 13:607–623.

Van Buren, J. M. (1975). The question of thalamic participation in speech mechanisms. *Brain and Lang.* 2:31–44.

Wade, J. and Rasmussen, T. (1960). Intracarotid injection of sodium amytal for the lateralization of cerebral speech dominance: experimental and clinical observations. *J. Neurosurg.* 17:266–282.

Wagenaar, E., Snow, C., and Prins, R. (1975). Spontaneous speech of aphasic patients: a psycholinguistic analysis. *Brain and Lang.* 3: 281–303.

Warrington, E. W. (1969). Constructional apraxia. In *Handbook of Clinical Neurology.* Vol. 4, P. J. Vinken and G. W. Bruyn (eds). Amsterdam: North Holland.

Wechsler, D. (1958). *The Measurement and Appraisal of Adult Intelligence.* Baltimore: Williams and Wilkins.

Weisenburg, T. S. and McBride, K. L. (1964). *Aphasia.* New York: Hafner.

Wepman, J. (1951). *Recovery from Aphasia.* New York: Ronald.

Wepman, J. 1961). *Language Modalities Test for Aphasia.* Chicago: Education Industry Service.

Wernicke, C. (1874). *Der Aphasiche Symptomencomplex.* Breslau: Cohn & Weigart.

Wertz, R. T. (1981). Aphasia management: the speech pathologist's role. *Seminars in Speech, Language and Hearing* 2:315–331.

Whitaker, H. (1976). A case of isolation of the language function. In *Studies in Neuolinguistics,* Vol. 2, H. Whitaker and H. Whitaker (eds). New York: Academic Press.

Whitaker, H. and Whitaker H. A. (1977). *Studies in Neurolinguistics,* Vol. 3. New York: Academic Press.

Wilson, S. A. K. (1926). *Aphasia.* London: Kegan Paul.

Yakovlev, P. I. and Rakic, P. (1966). Patterns of decussation of bulbar pyramids and distribution of pyramidal tracts on two sides of the spinal cord. *Trans. Am. Neurol. Assoc.* 91:366–367.

Zaidel, E. (1978). Lexical organization in the right hemisphere. In *Cerebral Correlates of Conscious Experience,* INSERM symposium #6, P. Buser and A. Rougel-Buser (eds). Elsevier: North Holland.

Zangwill, O. (1946). Some qualitative observations on verbal memory in cases of cerebral lesion. *Br. J. Psychol.* 37:8–19.

Zangwill, O. (1969) Intellectual status in aphasia. In *Handbook of Clinical Neurology,* Vol. 4, P. J. Vinken and G. W. Bruyn (eds). Amsterdam: North Holland.

Zurif, E. B., Caramazza, A., and Myerson, R. (1972). Grammatical judgements of agrammatic aphasics. *Neuropsychologia* 10:405–417.

3

Alexia

RHONDA B. FRIEDMAN AND MARTIN L. ALBERT

Alexia may be defined as an acquired inability to comprehend written language as a consequence of brain damage. The term *acquired dyslexia* is used by some authors synonymously with alexia. Acquired dyslexia occurs in the individual who has already learned to read in a normal fashion; in contrast, developmental dyslexia refers to an inability to learn to read normally from childhood. In the definition of alexia, emphasis is placed on the impairment of comprehension. Inability to read aloud may, as we shall see, form part of an alexic syndrome, but this deficit is neither necessary nor sufficient for the diagnosis of alexia. The term "word blindness" is a classical expression for alexia, and is still occasionally used, especially in continental Europe.

This chapter begins with a discussion of the traditional classifications of alexia. We present the clinical syndromes of alexia as they have been described over the past several decades, and we discuss the anatomy of these syndromes. The classical alexic syndromes have been defined on the basis of patterns of observations made by clinical neurologists. Their descriptions tend to center around the presence of a reading disturbance and the accompanying neurological symptoms—e.g., visual field defect, aphasia, agraphia, color anomia, acalculia, etc.

In the second part of this chapter we discuss a newer approach to the study of alexia, one that has been gaining in popularity in the past few years. This approach, which we call "psycholinguistic", has been developed chiefly by cognitive psychologists and neuropsychologists. Their goal is to tie together our understanding of the normal reading process with studies of the ways in which reading can break down in the brain-damaged person. This type of investigation focuses chiefly on the neuropsychological mechanisms underlying reading. The descriptions and classifications of alexia derived from this mode of research concern the components of normal reading that have been disturbed and the mechanisms that account for the abnormal reading behavior that results.

THE TRADITIONAL APPROACH

Classification of the Alexias

The alexias have been classified differently by various authors depending on the emphasis each wanted to give to description or interpretation.

LITERAL ALEXIA AND VERBAL ALEXIA

One standard practice has been to divide the alexias into major clinical types with respect to the reading deficit: literal alexia, the inability to read letters, with relative preservation of ability to read words; verbal alexia, the inability to read words, with relative preservation of ability to read letters; and global alexia, the inability to read letters or words. (See, for example, Benson et al., 1971, for a contemporary statement of this position.)

The distinction between literal alexia and verbal alexia dates back to the classic 1900 book by Hinshelwood entitled *Letter-, Word- and Mind-Blindness*. In this book Hinshelwood discusses two syndromes that he considers to be distinct: "letter-without-word-blindness" (pure letter blindness; literal alexia) and "word-without-letter-blindness" (pure word blindness; verbal alexia). In letter-without-word-blindness, words can be read but the individual letters that compose the word cannot be read. Hinshelwood describes a patient who could not name letters, could not write letters to dictation, and could not point to any named letters except "t". This same patient could read "almost every word presented to him." In what is taken to be the opposite condition, word-without-letter-blindness, individual letters are recognized and named but words are not apprehended as wholes.

The concept of pure letter blindness is ambiguous, since it is not clear what is meant by "reading" letters. Inability to read letters may refer to inability to name letters. This difficulty has little to do with reading; it is a naming problem (Benson and Geschwind, 1969). Alternatively, the inability to read letters may refer to the inability to recognize individual letters, i.e., to comprehend the significance of the letters, regardless of the ability to name them. In this case, the patient would experience difficulty in reading all but the most familiar words, which are recognized as ideographs (single units). Words are, after all, differentiated from each other solely on the basis of their differing constituent letters. Referring to patients with so-called "pure letter blindness," Benson and Geschwind (1969) state that "in fact, only a few words are actually identified by these patients who thus can be considered 'word blind' as well as 'letter blind'" (p. 119).

Benson and Geschwind (1969) note that many authors consider verbal and literal alexia to be points on a continuum rather than discrete entities. In an article whose purpose was to illustrate the verbal alexia/literal alexia dichotomy, Benson et al. (1971) admit that "it would not be correct to state that these patients were either word-blind or letter-blind exclusively (p. 955)." Most so-called word-blind patients can, in fact, recognize certain highly familiar words without relying upon a letter-by-letter analysis. And, these patients usually have at least some difficulty identifying individual letters as well as words.

Thus, the traditional distinction between letter blindness and word blindness is not useful for the neuropsychologist. Nevertheless, there is a distinction of a related nature that is important. Reading can be accomplished by translating a word's letters (graphemes) into their corresponding sounds (phonemes) and combining these sounds to arrive at the phonological representation of a word. Or, reading can be accomplished by direct recognition of the word, without resorting to phonological mediation. This distinction does have significant implications for the ways in which reading disorders might present themselves. We will return to this issue.

ALEXIA WITH AGRAPHIA AND ALEXIA WITHOUT AGRAPHIA

Another approach to classification has been to speak of the alexias with reference to the presence or absence of writing disorders. Thus we have alexia without agraphia (pure alexia, pure word blindness) versus alexia with agraphia (Déjerine, 1891, 1892). This dichotomy has anatomic implications, and, accepting the same clinical distinctions, Wernicke (1874) and Kleist (1934) spoke of cortical alexia (alexia with agraphia) versus subcortical alexia (pure alexia): Hermann and Poetzl (1926) spoke of parietal alexia-agraphia versus pure word blindness.

VISUAL PROBLEMS AND LANGUAGE PROBLEMS

A third approach has been to consider reading disorders in terms of the general locus of the deficit—primarily within the visual system or primarily within the language system. According to this formulation we have agnosic alexia versus aphasic alexia (e.g., Misch and Frankl, 1929; Alajouanine et al., 1960). It should be stressed that regardless of the labels and interpretations of the phenomena, these two syndromes are identical to the clinical syndromes of pure alexia (agnosic alexia) and alexia with agraphia (aphasic alexia). Using different terminology, Goldstein (1948), Brain (1961), and Luria (1966) spoke of the same two clinical syndromes: for agnosic versus aphasic alexia, Goldstein spoke of primary versus secondary alexias; Brain, of agnosic alexia versus visual asymbolia; and Luria, of visual alexia versus aphasic alexia.

Thus, for all that has been written on the subject, there is a general consensus that there are two principal varieties of alexia: alexia without agraphia and alexia with agraphia. Each of these varieties is clinically distinct, each has subtypes, each may have a different anatomic basis, and each has a different theoretical explanation. In the section on clinical syndromes of alexia which follows, we use this major clinical dichotomy: alexia without agraphia versus alexia with agraphia.

Clinical Syndromes of Alexia

ALEXIA WITHOUT AGRAPHIA

The clinical syndrome. In pure alexia, comprehension of written language is greatly impaired. In addition, one often finds (1) impairment of ability to copy and (2) written acalculia. By contrast, oral language is normal or nearly normal, although there may be a mild anomia. Writing and spelling are close to normal. Color anomia is frequently found. Much less common is visual agnosia for objects and/or colors. Right homonymous hemianopia is almost always present. Hemiplegia is rare and, if present at all, is mild.

Pure alexia is an accepted clinical syndrome, although the mechanisms underlying the syndrome are still disputed. For Déjerine (1891, 1892), and many of his followers,

it represented a specialized form of aphasia. For Marie (1906), Poetzl (1928), Alajouanine et al. (1960), and others it represented a specialized form of visual agnosia.
For Goldstein (1948) and Conrad (1948), it represented the clinical expression of a
more general disturbance: the loss of "structuration of forms" and the loss of abstract
attitude. Hécaen and Kremin (1977) considered it an incorrect application of the rules
of recoding from the written to the spoken language.

The anatomy of alexia without agraphia.

A *disconnection syndrome.*   Déjerine (1891, 1892) described two varieties of
alexia for which he proposed two different anatomic lesions. One type, alexia with
agraphia, will be discussed later. The other type, pure word blindness, results from
destruction of fibers connecting the calcarine region to the angular gyrus, with the
central site of damage being in the white matter of the lingual lobule. Déjerine
referred to a lesion of the corpus callosum in his report of 1892, but did not ascribe
any role to it in the pathogenesis of alexia. Brissaud (1900) and Redlich (1895) pointed
out that two lesions, one involving the left primary visual area and the other destroying the corpus callosum, might prevent the arrival of visual impulses from the intact
hemisphere. It was Quensel (1931) who stressed the necessity of the callosal lesion,
and emphasized the "disconnection" aspect of the syndrome.

According to this theory, the lesion in the left visual area prevents visual stimuli
entering the left hemisphere from reaching the angular gyrus, which is necessary for
reading, while visual stimuli that enter the intact right hemisphere are prevented
from reaching the left hemisphere because the splenium of the corpus callosum is
destroyed. This theory, that the significant factors in pure alexia are a combination of
lesions in the lingual and fusiform gyri of the dominant occipital lobe and in the
splenium of the corpus callosum, has been stressed by most authors (Vincent et al.,
1930; Geschwind, 1962, 1965; Geschwind and Fusillo, 1966; Sperry and Gazzaniga,
1967; Mouren et al., 1967; Cumming, 1970; Yamadori, 1980). Credit for renewing
current interest in the disconnection theory is usually given to Geschwind (1965).

Most, but not all, cases of pure alexia result from cerebrovascular lesions. Foix and
Hillemand (1925) indicated that pure alexia followed disturbances in the territory of
the posterior cerebral artery, rather than of the middle cerebral artery, which had
been found to be the territory responsible for oral language disorders. Subsequent
studies have confirmed these observations.

Arguments for and against the disconnection theory.   Implicit in the disconnection theory of pure alexia, as originally stated, were certain conditions: (1) in pure
alexia, a deficit in verbalization exists only for graphic symbols; (2) a right homonymous hemianopia is present, and (3) the splenium of the corpus callosum is destroyed.
As to the first factor, Hécaen and Kremin (1977) ask how can objects be named, and
words not named, if there is a posterior callosal disconnection? As to the second factor,
they ask, how can one explain those cases of pure alexia with no right homonymous
hemianopia? (e.g., Hinshelwood, 1900; Peron and Goutner, 1944; Alajouanine et al.,
1960; Ajax, 1967; Goldstein et al., 1971; Greenblatt, 1973). Finally, in some cases of
pure alexia the splenium may be intact (e.g., Hécaen and Gruner, 1975). How can
these cases be explained?

Geschwind (1965) tried to overcome the first problem by suggesting that the visual input relating to objects can evoke sensory associations other than visual ones, and this nonvisual information may cross the corpus callosum in the intact anterior portions. Alternatively, Oxbury et al. (1969) proposed that the posterior callosal lesion may not be complete, and that degraded visual information may traverse the corpus callosum sufficiently to allow gross visual recognition (e.g. for objects) but not fine visual recognition (e.g., for reading).

Studies by Greenblatt (1973, 1976), Ajax et al. (1977), and Vincent et al. (1977) deal directly with the second and third problems. In two cases of alexia without agraphia and without hemianopia, Greenblatt described and interpreted the anatomic findings. His interpretation is consistent with Déjerine's hypothesis of a lesion deep in the white matter of the left occipitoparietal region disconnecting visual cortex from angular gyrus. Greenblatt proposed four types of pure alexia and the anatomic lesions causing them: splenio-occipital alexia with and without hemianopia; and subangular alexia with and without hemianopia.

Splenio-occipital alexia with hemianopia is the usual type of pure alexia and is caused by a combination of lesions in the left lingual and fusiform gyrus of the occipital lobe and in the posterior third (splenium) of the corpus callosum. Splenio-occipital alexia without hemianopia (Ajax, 1967; Greenblatt, 1973) is rare, and is caused by a combination of lesions in the splenium and in the afferent pathways from the left calcarine cortex. In this situation, both calcarine areas are intact, but are disconnected from the left angular gyrus. Alexia but no hemianopia occurs.

The subangular alexias, according to Greenblatt, are caused by lesions located in the white matter beneath the angular gyrus, undercutting the angular gyrus and isolating it from visual stimuli. Subangular alexia with hemianopia (Wechsler et al., 1972; Sroka et al., 1973) would result from a subangular lesion located more dorsally and medially, affecting the optic radiations. Subangular alexia without hemianopia would occur if the lesion were more ventrally located, sparing the optic radiations.

The case reports by Vincent et al. (1977), Ajax et al. (1977) and Johansson and Fahlgren (1979) support Greenblatt's suggestions. They indicate that the angular gyrus receives dorsal and ventral inputs from the splenium of the corpus callosum as well as medial and lateral inputs from the visual cortex. Selective lesions in corpus callosum or occipital lobe or both may interrupt different sets of inputs to the angular gyrus, thereby producing pure alexia, with or without hemianopia, with or without a callosal lesion. Some form of disconnection theory thus seems to explain all forms of pure alexia.

ALEXIA WITH AGRAPHIA

It seems reasonable on the basis of clinical, anatomic and neuropsychological data to subdivide this condition into two separate syndromes: one, consisting of alexia with agraphia in relative isolation from disorders of oral language; the other, a form of alexia which accompanies aphasia.

Agraphic alexia
The clinical syndrome. The syndrome of alexia with agraphia in the absence of obvious or significant aphasia has been called "parietal alexia" by some authors (e.g.

Hermann and Poetzl, 1926; Quensel, 1931; Hoff, et al., 1954). Clinically, the reading disorder appears as letter blindness plus word blindness (Benson, 1977). Disorders of writing are severe, and appear in all aspects of writing (spontaneous, to dictation, etc.).

Associated findings are as follows: Apraxia is often present. Disorders of spoken language are either absent or quite mild, although an anomia is usually found. The ability to spell is affected. Often, but not always, one may see elements of the Gerstmann syndrome: agraphia, acalculia, right–left spatial disorientation, and impairment in the ability to identify fingers. One of these, acalculia, is almost always found. Hemianopia is not necessarily present.

The anatomy of agraphic alexia. Much less controversy surrounds the anatomic basis of alexia with agraphia. In 1891, Déjerine discussed the anatomy of a syndrome of impaired ability to read and write with minimal disturbances in oral language. He found a cortical-subcortical lesion affecting the left angular gyrus. Since then, most authors have agreed that a dominant angular gyrus lesion is the antomic correlate of this syndrome (Wolpert, 1930; Nielsen and Raney, 1938; Alajouanine et al., 1960; Hécaen, 1967; Benson and Geschwind, 1969; Hécaen and Kremin, 1977).

Aphasic alexia. The term aphasic alexia has been applied to situations in which alexia is seen as part of a larger picture of a substantial aphasic disturbance. The term has typically been applied to alexia accompanying sensory aphasia caused by lesions extending into the dominant posterior temporal lobe. Another form of aphasic alexia has been discussed, i.e., the alexia that accompanies Broca's aphasia, associated with lesions of the dominant frontal lobe (Benson, 1977; Benson et al., 1971; Déjerine and Mirallié, 1893). The characteristics of these two alexic classifications differ significantly. The reading disorders tend to parallel the disorders of language.

The factors that affect reading in Broca's aphasia are similar to the factors that affect speech in Broca's aphasia. For example, concrete nouns are most likely to be produced in speech, and they are also more likely to be read correctly than abstract nouns or grammatical words (Gardner and Zurif, 1975). Benson (1977; Benson et al., 1971) observes that "anterior alexia" is typified by "pure letter blindness." Words that are read correctly are read as wholes; they are not broken down letter-by-letter. These features of the alexia of Broca's aphasia look much like the features of the syndrome of "deep dyslexia," as we shall see in a later section of this chapter.

In Wernicke's aphasia, part of speech is not an important predictor of either speech production or reading. Wernicke's aphasics may use function words in their speech, and do not experience any particular difficulty reading function words compared with other words. The speech of Wernicke's aphasics contains paraphasias, and their reading tends to be paralexic as well. It had been generally agreed that the reading impairment seen in Wernicke's aphasia is consistent with the degree of auditory comprehension impairment (Benson and Geschwind, 1969; Wernicke, 1874). However, recent studies suggest that the degree of reading impairment relative to auditory comprehension impairment is variable in Wernicke's aphasia (Hécaen and Albert, 1978; Heilman et al., 1979; Hier and Mohr, 1977; Mohr et al., 1978).

A PSYCHOLINGUISTIC APPROACH

In 1973, Marshall and Newcombe published an article entitled "Patterns of Paralexia: A Psycholinguistic Approach." Since then there has been a proliferation of articles in which alexia is studied from the point of view of disturbances of underlying psycholinguistic mechanisms. The nature of paralexic errors (reading errors) is now examined carefully. The interaction of various factors, such as part of speech, with reading disability is explored. The results are interpreted in terms of the breakdown of hypothesized components of the normal reading process.

On the following pages, we use the psycholinguistic approach to explore three major issues in alexia research: (1) the cause of the reading disturbance; (2) the nature of the resultant reading behavior; and (3) the source of the resultant reading behavior.

The first issue concerns the precise locus of the reading deficit. Is the patient suffering from a purely perceptual problem? Is the problem specific to reading or does it extend to other visually presented stimuli? Can the problem be attributed to a more general language deficit?

The second issue concerns the nature of the current reading behavior. In delineating the characteristics of the current reading performance, we note the types of reading errors that the patient produces. Are they related to the target word visually, semantically, or phonologically? Does the patient tend to make more errors on certain types of words? For example, is there an effect of word length, word frequency, or part of speech?

The third issue to be considered is the reason that a particular reading behavior becomes manifest. One possibility is that the behavior represents the residual normal reading abilities of an impaired reading system. A second possibility is that the reading behavior reflects a compensatory strategy discovered by the patient to help overcome his/her diffculties. A third possibility is that an alternative, normally subordinate or latent, reading system has taken over. The presence of such a system in the right hemisphere has been put forth as an explanation of the reading behavior seen in the syndrome known as deep dyslexia (Saffran et al., 1980; Coltheart, 1980b).

These three major questions to be asked about alexic patients will be discussed in greater detail. In order to facilitate an understanding of the many issues to be raised, we will first present a simple model of reading to which we can then refer.

A Simple Working Model of Reading

A main objective when examining a patient with an acquired disorder of reading is to discover which components of the reading process have broken down. This query presupposes that we know how reading normally proceeds. Models of reading have been proposed, modified, and refined for decades; consensus on details has yet to be reached. Nevertheless certain assumptions regarding the reading process are generally agreed upon and appear in most current models.

It is generally agreed that subsequent to initial perceptual analysis there is a stage at which letters are identified (e.g., Estes, 1975; McClelland, 1976), prior to word recognition. Identification of letters occurs rapidly, automatically, and can occur simultaneously for several letters at a time (LaBerge and Samuels, 1974). Following letter identification, reading may proceed along two paths, one considered "direct," the other "indirect."

In direct reading, following letter identification the written word is matched to a visual word in memory—i.e., it is recognized. Once the word has been recognized, its meaning can be retrieved from the lexicon; the word's pronunciation may also be retrieved, but not necessarily, unless the task demands it. Ideographic languages such as Chinese rely upon the direct reading route, since there is no correspondence between the sounds of words and the characters of which words are composed. While alphabetic languages need not rely upon direct reading, in that the indirect route detailed below would serve as well, most reading theorists agree that the direct route is normally used (Smith, 1971; Baron, 1977). English and other languages with many homophonic words (e.g., him-hymn; blue-blew) must rely upon direct access reading at least some of the time.

The indirect route makes use of the relationship of reading to speech. The written word is transformed into a spoken word, and the meaning of the spoken word is then attained just as when comprehending speech. The precise nature of the transformation process is still under debate (Baron, 1977; Marcel, 1980). It may be based on grapheme-to-phoneme correspondence rules (Marshall and Newcombe, 1973; Morton and Patterson, 1980; Patterson and Marcel, 1977) or on analogy to words whose pronunciations are known (Baron, 1977; Glushko, 1979; Marcel, 1980). In any case, the existence of a mechanism for translating letter sequences into sounds is not under debate. Without this route we would be unable to pronounce such pseudowords as *pome, rithy,* and *pentrithamulous.*[°]

These two paths represent ways of attaining the meanings of individual written words. It is assumed that written sentence comprehension utilizes the same mechanisms used for oral sentence comprehension. A syntactic processor specific to written material is not postulated.

How Reading Might Become Disturbed

In this section, we describe many different disturbances that have been described in the literature, all of which, it is claimed, can cause alexia. Some of these disturbances have been taken to be the single cause of a particular alexic disturbance. Others are observed neurologic deficits of which alexia may be one of several possible effects. In describing these postulated disturbances we do not wish to imply that we accept their explanatory powers with regard to alexia; nor do we necessarily agree that they exist. They are presented with the intent to stimulate the reader to consider all conceivable factors when evaluating the patient with alexia.

VISUAL PROBLEMS

Reading problems may occur at any stage between perceptual analysis and paragraph comprehension. One visual problem that has been described in relation to alexic dis-

---

[°]It is also possible that a word's phonological representation can be retrieved directly—without benefit of a set of intermediate rules (Schwartz et al., 1980)—yet prior to the accessing of meaning. Meaning could then be attained on the basis of this phonological representation, i.e., in an indirect fashion. There is currently no convincing evidence that this occurs in normal reading. Hence we will not include such a mechanism in our model.

turbance is simultanagnosia (Levine and Calvanio, 1978; Luria, 1966; Kinsbourne and Warrington, 1962). This is a problem with the simultaneous perception of multiple elements in a visual display. The patient with simultanagnosia can recognize individual items within a visual display such as a picture, but cannot determine how the items relate to one another; that is, the picture as a whole cannot be interpreted. Kinsbourne and Warrington (1962) described four patients with this sort of difficulty with picture interpretation who also had a severe deficit in reading whole words. Words were read slowly, one letter at a time. This form of alexia was taken to reflect a difficulty with "simultaneous form perception." (See Chap. 9 for more about simultanagnosia.)

Optic aphasia may contribute to alexia. In optic aphasia, visually presented items may be recognized and their functions demonstrated, but they cannot be named. Tactile examination of the same items results in correct naming. Luria considered literal alexia to be a form of optic aphasia, while verbal alexia was said to be an instance of simultanagnosia.

Visual agnosia is another possible source of reading disorder (see, for example, Caplan and Hedley-White, 1974). The agnosic patient has trouble recognizing visually presented items, despite adequate perception of those items (see Chap. 9). That is, although the patient can describe what he sees, he can neither name it nor indicate its function. This agnosia may extend to written words. Recognition need not be totally destroyed; the recognition process may be impaired just enough so that the time required to recognize each visual item is increased. This could have a particularly devastating effect on reading, in which so many visual items (letters) must be identified rapidly in order to read at a normal pace (Friedman and Alexander, 1984).

Another possible cause of reading disturbance specific to the visual system has been described as "failure in oculomotor adjustment secondary to a complete right homonymous hemianopia" (Warrington and Zangwill, 1957). That is, visual stimuli that fall to the right of fixation, in the hemianopic field, fail to elicit normal saccadic eye movements. The impaired reading that results is characterized by a relative difficulty in reading long words and phrases, the errors occurring at the ends of words.

PROBLEMS OF VISUAL–VERBAL CONNECTIONS

A written word that has been accurately perceived may not be comprehended despite an intact lexicon and the absence of visual perceptual problems or visual agnosia. The trouble may arise in the transmission of visual information to the lexicon. Language areas, including those specific to reading, remain intact but inaccessible through the visual modality. Therefore no aphasia or agraphia is expected; a "pure" alexia should result. An example of this type of transmission failure is provided by Warrington and Shallice (1979). They describe a patient with pure alexia who has relative difficulty accessing the exact meanings of written words compared with spoken words. Partial semantic information may be transmitted, allowing for the correct categorization into subordinate and superordinate classes of written words that cannot be named or identified. Warrington and Shallice have called this disturbance "semantic access dyslexia."

Warrington and Shallice (1980) outlined another possible cause of reading disorder that can occur in the absence of aphasia, agnosia, or early perceptual deficits. They describe two patients who read in a letter-by-letter fashion. These patients could be classified as pure alexics, although one of the patients actually read fairly well. His difficulty was in the decreased rate of his reading and in his dependence on letter-by-letter reading. The authors rule out perceptual causes of the reading deficit and conclude that the deficit occurs at a stage of processing that follows early visual analysis but precedes phonological and semantic processing—at a stage "which parses (multiply and in parallel) letter strings into ordered familiar units and categorizes these units visually" (Warrington and Shallice, 1980, p. 109).

PROBLEMS OF ORTHOGRAPHIC MEMORY

Reading disorders may result from disturbances of orthographic memory. These disturbances may take two forms, one related to the direct reading route, the other to the indirect route.

The direct reading route makes use of visual word memories, i.e., memories of the compositions of written words. When a written word is found to correspond to a visual word in memory, the word is recognized as a familiar one. In 1891, Déjerine spoke of a theoretical center in which word memories are stored, the "visual memory center for words." If the neurologic regions responsible for the storage of visual memories for words were destroyed, written words would not be recognized via the direct route. In addition, spelling and writing difficulties might be expected to occur, particularly for words with irregular spellings which cannot be spelled accurately by applying phoneme-to-grapheme correspondence rules. Thus, a disturbance of visual word memories would be manifest as alexia with agraphia. This syndrome, as mentioned earlier, has been linked with the angular gyrus (Déjerine, 1892: Geschwind, 1965).

The indirect reading route may be disturbed by a loss of knowledge of the correspondence between graphemes (letters) and phonemes (sounds). Provided that the direct route to reading remains intact, this difficulty produces a relatively severe impairment in reading pseudowords compared with real words. In addition, words that tend to rely on the indirect reading route—perhaps low frequency words or very long words (Friedman, 1982)—would be relatively impaired.

READING PROBLEMS CAUSED BY LANGUAGE PROBLEMS

Reading is the comprehension of language through the visual modality. As a type of language comprehension system, reading is ultimately dependent on intact language mechanisms. Thus, when evaluating reading deficits, one should be careful to consider the possible role of disturbances of language.

At the single word level, reading will be affected by disturbances of phonology or disruption of the lexicon. For example, if the phonological representations of words have been disturbed, then the indirect reading route will suffer. Even if grapheme-to-phoneme correspondence rules remain intact, the product of their application, i.e., the phonological representation of the word, will be useless in accessing the meaning of the word. If direct-access reading remains preserved at all, then reading comprehension may be possible to some extent and may be better preserved than speech comprehension. In such a circumstance words that normally do not rely on the indirect route (e.g., many function words, which typically do not abide by grapheme-to-phoneme rules) may be more likely to be read correctly than other words.

If a patient's semantic lexicon is disturbed such that objects and concepts are no longer well defined (cf. Caramazza et al., 1982), or are no longer represented in the lexicon, then the reading of the written words corresponding to these objects and concepts will probably be impaired. If there is a problem matching words with the appropriate concepts, then it will likely affect written words as well as spoken words. Friedman and Perlman (1982) discuss the case of a patient who was unable to match certain common written words with their referents. Oral presentation of the same words on a different day yielded similar results. It was argued that the "dyslexia" seen in this patient might reflect a general language disturbance rather than a specific reading disorder.

PROBLEMS OF SENTENCE COMPREHENSION

Beyond the single word level, a reading disturbance may be manifest only at the sentence level. A deficit specific to written sentence comprehension is improbable. A disturbance in the comprehension of written sentences is likely to reflect a larger deficit of language or cognitive processing. One possible source of difficulty with sentence comprehension is difficulty with syntactic processing (Rothi et al., 1982), often found in patients with left hemisphere damage (Berndt and Caramazza, 1980; Zurif and Caramazza, 1976).

Written sentences comprehension may also be affected by short-term memory deficits. It has been claimed that the ability to process the syntactic as well as semantic meaning of written sentences depends on the ability to keep the initial part of the sentence in memory while the rest of the sentence is read (Kleiman, 1975). Inability to hold the initial words in memory, then, would have an effect on comprehension.

Specifically, it has been proposed that during the processing of a written sentence, words are held in memory in an acoustic format (Levy, 1975). Thus direct access to the meanings of written words, in the absence of access to their phonological representations, may result in comprehension difficulties at the sentence and paragraph level. Single word comprehension may be relatively less impaired.

The Resultant Reading Behaviors—A Psycholinguistic Classification System

There has been a recent trend in the literature to describe reading disorders by the characteristic types of reading errors, or "paralexias" that are produced and/or by the types of words that are likely to be misread.

PHONOLOGICAL ALEXIA AND VISUAL ALEXIA

In one such disorder the probability of reading a word correctly is related to word frequency. High-frequency words are more likely to be read correctly than low-frequency words, while pseudowords (which can be thought of as a special subset of low-

frequency words—i.e., zero frequency words) are rarely read correctly. It is presumed that patients exhibiting this reading pattern are suffering from an inability to make use of the spelling-to-sound correspondence rules of the language. This disturbance has been labeled "phonological alexia" (Beauvois and Dérouesné, 1979).

The patient with phonological alexia typically complains of difficulty reading books or newspapers. But the nature of the reading disturbance may not be readily apparent to the examiner, since the patient's reading of real words, particularly high-frequency substantives, may remain relatively intact. The specific nature of the reading problem becomes obvious, however, when the patient is asked to read a pseudoword such as *bome*. This will present a great deal of difficulty to the patient with phonological alexia.

The paralexias produced by patients with phonological alexia tend to be visual errors (i.e., visual paralexias); read words are misread as other real words that are visually similar to the target. Even pseudowords are often misread as real words that share visual characteristics. These paralexias may be the natural result of the inability to check the pronunciations of written letter strings.

The term visual paralexia, as used above, is actually misleading. Some visual paralexias, e.g., *lop* → "slob" and *mild* → "slid" (Marshall and Newcombe, 1973), are not really visually similar. The grossest measures of visual similarity—global word shape and length—are not even compatible in many of these examples. Rather, the similarity is orthographic—i.e., the target word and the paralexic error have many letters in common. Perhaps a better term for this type of reading error is orthographic paralexia.

In 1973, Marshall and Newcombe described two patients with "visual alexia," i.e., whose reading was characterized by visual paralexic errors. Their patients were not described as suffering from an inability to use grapheme-to-phoneme correspondence rules. However, it appears that their patients were not asked to read pseudowords. It may, in fact, be reasonable to infer that at least one of their patients did indeed have such difficulty. He was noted to have misread 14 words whose letters he read aloud correctly (e.g., *rut* → "tug, r-u-t"). Given that he did perceive and identify all of the letters of the word correctly, and in the correct order, an intact ability to make use of grapheme-to-phoneme correspondence rules should have insured that he read the word correctly.

Phonological alexia may be accompanied by impaired spelling, as in the cases reported by Shallice and Warrington (1980), or it may be found in patients who can spell aloud by using phoneme-to-grapheme rules, as in the cases of Beauvois and Dérouesné (1979) and Friedman (1982). The impairment in the phonological decoding of words and pseudowords may be restricted to visually presented items, as in Beauvois and Dérouesné's patient, who could use grapheme-to-phoneme rules in deciphering orally spelled words. The impairment may be more general, extending to orally spelled words, as in Friedman's patient. Aphasia may be absent. When neither aphasia nor a substantial writing disturbance is present, the patient with phonological alexia may be seen as a pure alexic—i.e., reading disturbance in the absence of writing or language disturbance.

DEEP DYSLEXIA

The cardinal feature of deep dyslexia is the occurrence of semantic paralexias in oral reading (Coltheart, 1980a). Semantic paralexias are reading errors that are semantically related to the target word in some way. The error may be synonymous with the target, it may be an associate of the target, it may be an antonym of the target, or it may be a subordinate of the target.

Other features characteristic of deep dyslexia are the presence of visual paralexias and of derivational errors in oral reading. A derivational error is a word derived from the same base morpheme as the target word (e.g., *twist* → "twisted"; *buy* → "bought"). A disproportionate amount of difficulty reading function words is also seen. Function words may be substituted for one another, but rarely are they read correctly. Other effects of word class or type are evident as well. Verbs present more difficulty than adjectives, which in turn present more difficulty than nouns. In addition, like patients with phonological dyslexia, deep dyslexics cannot make use of grapheme-to-phoneme conversion rules in oral reading; thus, pseudowords cannot be read.

SURFACE DYSLEXIA

The pattern of reading characterized by paralexias that appear to be caused by the "inadequate application of grapheme-to-phoneme conversion rules" (Deloche et al., 1982) has been called "surface dyslexia." Unlike patients with phonological alexia, who cannot even attempt to use grapheme-to-phoneme conversion rules, patients with surface dyslexia appear to rely very heavily on these rules, although the results are often less than satisfactory. Words and nonwords whose pronunciations are unambiguous according to the grapheme-to-phoneme correspondence rules of the language are read well. Words with irregular or ambiguous orthographies are likely to be mispronounced. Comprehension appears to be tied to success at pronunciation; if a word is mispronounced as another real word, meaning will be assigned in accordance with the incorrect pronunciation, e.g., *begin*—"beggin ... collecting money" (Marshall and Newcombe,1973).

The cases of surface dyslexia reported in the literature (Deloche et al., 1982; Marcel, 1980; Marshall and Newcombe, 1973; Shallice and Warrington, 1980) are all poor spellers as well as poor readers. Most are mildly aphasic.

LETTER-BY-LETTER READING

One type of abnormal reading performance is characterized not by type of reading error but by the manner in which written words are read. In *letter-by-letter reading*, each letter of a written word is named (often aloud) before the word is identified. This type of reading has also been called *spelling dyslexia* (Kinsbourne and Warrington, 1962) because words are spelled aloud during reading. We feel that the term "spelling dyslexia" is misleading, since it implies that there is a disorder of spelling.

There have been recent attempts to equate letter-by-letter reading with pure alexia (Coltheart, 1982; Patterson and Kay, 1982), thus associating it with an entire syndrome of reading behaviors. In describing this syndrome, Patterson and Kay mention right homonymous hemianopia, anomia, and color naming impairment as symptoms frequently observed. It is not clear, however, that all pure alexic patients read in a letter-by-letter fashion, or that *only* pure alexic patients read in this manner. Whether or not letter-by-letter reading and pure alexia are equivalent, the defining features of the two syndromes are different. In letter-by-letter reading, the effect of word length on the time needed to read a word is taken as a principal feature of the syndrome. Word class effects are not typically found. Letter identification is usually good but rarely perfect in patients who read in a letter-by-letter fashion.

INTERRELATIONSHIP OF ALEXIC SYNDROMES

The alexias discussed above should not be viewed as clear-cut unambiguous syndromes. As they are described, they represent the theoretical extremes. In fact, Beauvois and Dérouesné (1979), in discussing phonological alexia, call it "a theoretical construct" rather than "a clinical entity." In reality, most patients will exhibit reading abnormalities such as paralexias on only a subset of the reading opportunities afforded them. Many words will be read correctly. There will be large variations among patients.

Furthermore, the reading behaviors described above are not mutually exclusive. Letter-by-letter strategy does not define a syndrome apart from surface dyslexia, for example. A patient seen by one of us recently produced the following responses when asked to read a list of words aloud:

    gloss— "g-l-o-s-s. I don't know that one. I do, but I don't know it now . . . glōsse."

    marine— "marin m-a-r-i-n-e . . . I don't know what it is."

These are examples of the use of a letter-by-letter strategy of reading combined with a surface dyslexia result. Marshall and Newcombe (1973) report a similar pattern in one of their patients, as do Patterson and Kay (1982).

Causes of the Alexic Symptoms

All of the various forms of alexia that we have discussed reflect disturbances of the normal reading process. We now ask the question: What is the source of the abnormal reading behavior that appears when normal reading has been disturbed? We consider three possibilities: a compromised normal reading system, an alternative reading system, and the development of new reading strategies.

COMPROMISED NORMAL READING SYSTEM

If only part of the normal reading process is disturbed, if only certain cognitive abilities have been impaired, if only a small number of reading mechanisms have broken down, then the reading performance exhibited by the alexic patient may reflect the operation of the normal reading process in its compromised state.

Phonological alexia is one rather obvious pattern of abnormal reading that appears to represent the residual reading capabilities of a partially disturbed reading system. In this disorder one of the two postulated major routes to reading has been disturbed.

The ability to use grapheme-to-phoneme correspondence rules is lost; words can no longer be "decoded" into their phonological representations. What remains is the direct route to written word comprehension, the route that is not mediated by covert speech. It appears that the use of this route results in better performance on high than low frequency words. Reading comprehension is still possible, but at a greatly reduced rate.

Surface alexia may be thought of as the opposite of phonological alexia. In surface alexia it is the direct route from the written word to word comprehension that is said to be impaired. The reading that remains reflects the use of the pathway to meaning that is mediated by speech. Through the application of orthographic spelling-to-sound rules the phonological representations of words are obtained; these representations are used to access the internal lexicon. One problem with this explanation of surface alexia is that many paralexias occur which appear to be caused by the "misapplication" or "partial failure" of grapheme-to-phoneme rules (Deloche et al., 1982; Marshall and Newcombe, 1973; Morton and Patterson, 1980). In a recent study of a surface alexic patient, Bub et al. (1982) demonstrated that their patient's reading errors were actually predictable according to the orthographic rules enunciated by Venezky (1970). It is possible that he variation found among patients with surface alexia may reflect differing degrees of prior knowledge of spelling rules. Alternatively, surface alexia may reflect two disturbances: one of direct whole-word access to meaning, and the second of orthographic knowledge.

The cases of surface alexia reported to date have all been shown to have disturbances of spelling which are usually more severe with words that have irregular spellings. These words tend to be spelled phonetically (e.g. *does* → d-u-z) (Deloche et al., 1982; Marshall and Newcombe, 1973; Shallice and Warrington, 1980). Thus surface alexia fits into the classification of alexia with agraphia. The necessity of using the indirect route in spelling as well as in reading suggests that the problem may be more than one of visual access to the visual word memories of the direct route. The problem may be a disturbance of the visual word memories themselves.

Visual alexia, the presence of visual paralexias in reading, may indicate a perceptual problem in the presence of an intact reading system, particularly if all the errors bear a strong visual resemblance to their targets. Alternatively, visual errors that do not bear close resemblance to their targets in number of letters or overall word shape—those errors that we have called orthographic errors—may actually be symptomatic of a disturbance in accessing the lexicon. If a sequence of letters making up a word fails to access that word in the lexicon, then another word of higher frequency composed of similar letters may be accessed instead. For example, the word *lice*, a low frequency word, may not be recognized; instead it may be misread as *ice* or *like*, high-frequency words that are more readily accessible in the internal lexicon. These were, in fact, the responses given by one of our alexic patients to the written word *lice*. She knew that her responses were incorrect, but could not correct her errors. In a study by Patterson (1978), one of her two patients often knew when he had responded with a visual paralexia. The fact that these patients are aware of their errors is consistent with the notion that the problem is not a perceptual one. Like surface alexia and phonological alexia, visual alexia appears to reflect the residual operation of the normal reading system which has been compromised in some way.

ALTERNATIVE READING SYSTEM

Abnormal reading performance following brain damage need not represent the vestiges of the reading process as it normally occurs. There has been much discussion recently about the possibility of another reading system, one that remains dormant under normal circumstances. This alternative reading system is postulated to reside in the right hemisphere (Coltheart, 1980b). It has been hypothesized that right hemisphere reading becomes manifest only if a good deal of the left hemisphere of the brain has been destroyed. Such is generally the case for people presenting with the syndrome of deep dyslexia.

The mechanism underlying deep dyslexia is still a much-debated issue. (Much of the debate can be found in a single volume, *Deep Dyslexia*, edited by Coltheart, Patterson, and Marshall, 1980.) There are those who claim that deep dyslexia represents the dissolution of the indirect route to meaning (as in phonological alexia) plus a partial disturbance of the direct reading route. The reading behavior that is manifest represents the operation of the defective remaining route to reading (Shallice and Warrington, 1980). Yet others who have studied deep dyslexic patients argue that the unusual pattern of reading behaviors (e.g., the concreteness effect and the word class effect) and the fact that so many features occur together with such great reliability (given the cardinal feature of semantic paralexias) are strong suggestions that a different reading system is implicated, one with different characteristics from the normal system (Saffran et al., 1980). This argument is bolstered by pointing to similarities between deep dyslexic reading and features of reading attributed to the right hemisphere on the basis of split-brain studies and tachistoscopic studies of hemispheric processing asymmetries in normals (Coltheart, 1980b).

DEVELOPMENT OF NEW STRATEGIES

There is yet another potential source of abnormal reading behavior following brain injury, one that reflects neither the residual operation of the normal system nor the expression of an existing but normally dormant second reading system. This alternative source is the development of an entirely new mechanism or strategy for understanding the printed word.

Letter-by-letter reading is an example of the development of a new strategy for reading. Certainly the normal reader is capable of naming the letters of a word one by one, but this is not how normal reading proceeds. The reading-impaired patient who uses this strategy is calling upon a skill from outside the normal reading system to circumvent an impairment somewhere within the normal reading system.

This strategy may be used to overcome more than one type of reading disturbance. It seems quite reasonable that the patient with simultanagnosia, who can only process one letter at a time, should name the letters of a word one at a time when reading. The patient with word form dyslexia can perceive more than one letter simultaneously, but cannot match these simultaneously-perceived letters with a visual word form in memory. This patient may use the sequential naming of letters to circumvent the need to access visual word forms, reaching the lexicon instead by making use of prior knowledge of how words are spelled.

Patients who cannot recognize words or letters presented visually have been observed using another alternative reading strategy, that of letter tracing (see, for example, Karanth, 1981). In letter tracing, the patient moves his finger directly over the outline of the letter, or he moves his finger in the air in the shape of the letter that he sees. It is believed that patients using this strategy are relying upon kinesthetic feedback to recognize letters and subsequently words, thereby circumventing the difficulty that exists within the visual processing system (Déjerine, 1892: Luria, 1966).

HOW PSYCHOLINGUISTIC DESCRIPTIONS OF ALEXIA RELATE TO CLASSICAL ALEXIC SYNDROMES

In our discussions of the psycholinguistically based descriptions of alexic syndromes we have tried to note, where appropriate, the relationship of these syndromes to the classical categorization of the alexias. This is not an easy task. The number of alexic patients who have been studied within the psycholinguistic framework are still relatively few. Anatomic information on these patients is not always given in sufficient detail. We attempt here to draw some very tentative conclusions about the relationship between these two systems of classification.

Letter-by-letter reading is the easiest of the four varieties of alexia to compare with the classical syndromes. As we observed earlier, letter-by-letter reading resembles alexia without agraphia. The two "syndromes" may actually be the same entity. Yet the different emphases and defining characteristics of these syndromes may lead to specific instances in which a patient may qualify as a pure alexic but not as a letter-by-letter reader, or vice versa.

Deep dyslexia is always accompanied by agraphia and aphasia. It must, then, be considered a form of aphasic alexia. From the evidence we have at this time, it appears that deep dyslexia most closely resembles the alexia that accompanies Broca's aphasia. A concrete/abstract effect and the inability to use spelling-to-sound translation rules in reading are common to both deep dyslexia and the alexia of Broca's aphasia. Semantic paralexias have not typically been reported in cases of Broca's aphasia. However, this may be due to the limited output of Broca's aphasics. It is also true that the *types* of reading errors made by Broca's aphasics have not been recorded systematically in the past. Further studies may reveal that deep dyslexia and the alexia of Broca's aphasia are quite similar. Still, the infrequency of the syndrome of deep dyslexia suggests that it may very well be a unique entity, dissociable from the alexia of Broca's aphasia.

Surface alexia may be most closely compared with agraphic alexia. Patients with surface alexia (Marshall and Newcombe, 1973; Shallice and Warrington, 1980) show poor performance on both spelling and reading. Object naming difficulties and word finding difficulties are usually present. Speech is otherwise normal. Letter naming is frequently impaired. Disorders of calculation and left–right orientation may be observed. All of these characteristics of surface alexia are also true of agraphic alexia.

However, not all patients with surface alexia fit the definition of agraphic alexia. The patient with surface alexia described by Deloche et al. (1982), for example, was clearly aphasic. His alexia would fit into the category of aphasic alexia. His lesion appeared to be confined to the temporal lobe; the patients of Marshall and Newcombe had temporoparietal lesions. We can be reasonably sure that surface alexia is not related to the syndrome of pure alexia, since spelling disturbances are always present. Beyond this, our understanding of its relationship to classical alexic syndromes awaits further studies.

Phonological alexia is the most difficult of the psycholinguistic varieties of alexia to relate to the classical syndromes. Some patients with this type of alexia resemble pure alexics—i.e., they have no substantial spelling disorder or aphasia (Beauvois and Dérouesné, 1979; Friedman, 1982). Others may have markedly impaired spelling (Shallice and Warrington, 1980, Case Report 2) and substantial aphasia (Shallice and Warrington, 1980, Case Report 3). At present, then, there is no obvious relationship between phonological alexia and any of the classical alexia syndromes.

ASSESSMENT

When examining the patient with a reading problem, one must distinguish between problems of reading aloud and problems of reading comprehension. Oral reading problems may be present for a number of reasons. The patient may know the name of the word, but may have articulatory difficulties, which would also be exhibited in spontaneous speech, or in object naming tasks. Alternatively, the patient may have a naming deficit; the patient knows what the written word refers to but does not have access to its name. This, too, would be apparent in an object naming task. Another possibility is that the patient knows the name of the word but produces literal paraphasias when pronouncing it. This problem should result in literal paraphasias in other spoken tasks as well.

The patient who cannot read aloud may still be able to comprehend what he has read. Reading comprehension must be tested independently from oral reading. One method of testing word recognition is to use a word–picture matching test. This procedure allows for testing fine semantic discriminations by using semantically similar foils. Individual word recognition can also be tested with an "odd word out" test (Albert et al., 1973.) In this test the patient is presented with five words. Four of the words belong to one semantic category. The task is to pick the word that "does not belong." This test may be useful in testing abstract words that are not readily depicted in pictures. Sentence comprehension can be tested by asking the patient to follow written commands, by asking the patient to point to the picture that corresponds to a written sentence, by asking the patient to decide which sentences are true and which are false, or with a "fill-in-the-blank" procedure. Paragraph comprehension is tested by asking the patient to answer questions about a written paragraph.

Many tests of alexia include a test of upper-to-lower-case single letter matching. Since most alexic patients can perform this task, patients who fail tend to be severely alexic. However, we urge caution in interpreting the results. We do not agree that failure on this task indicates that letters have totally lost their meanings. Friedman (1981) found that patients who failed a letter matching task were still able to use their knowledge of letter identities to separate real words and potentially real nonwords from letter strings that violated the rules of English orthography. Preservation of letter recognition may thus be revealed under the right conditions.

Once a reading problem is uncovered, the next step is determining which aspects of the normal reading process have broken down. To evaluate the integrity of the rule-guided phonological decoding system, the patient should be asked to read aloud a list of "pseudowords," e.g., *bape, stog.* If there is an oral production problem, a forced choice task may be used in which a pseudoword is to be matched to the word that sounds the same (e.g., chare–chair), or to another pseudoword that sounds the same (e.g. poat–pote).

To evaluate the integrity of the direct route to the orthographic lexicon, the patient should be asked to read a list of "exception" words, i.e., words whose pronunciations cannot be determined directly from the orthography (e.g., pint, sew). Compare performance on this task with performance on a list of words matched for frequency and similar in orthography, but with regular spellings (e.g., mint, dew). If production is impaired, a written homophone matching task (e.g., sew—so) may be employed.

The integrity of the direct route to meaning—the route that bypasses any phonological representation at all—can be tested by having the patient indicate the meanings of words that have homophones, e.g., *blue, son,* using one of the reading comprehenion tests outlined above.

Discovering the properties of words that affect a patient's reading performance can be an important diagnostic tool. One such property is word class. Patients' reading should be examined for words of all classes, from concrete nouns to abstract nouns, verbs, adjectives, and function words (prepositions, pronouns, conjunctions, modal verbs). Care must be exercised to avoid confounding word frequency and word length with word class. Differential performance on words of different class suggests a problem related to the lexicon.

Another revealing property of words is length. Words of the same word class and frequency but differing in number of letters should be presented to the patient for reading. A patient with pure alexia will have greater difficulty as the word becomes longer; other patients will not be affected by increasing length (although extremely long words may present some difficulty).

When assessing reading behavior, record not only the number of errors produced by the patient, but the types of errors as well. The proportion of paralexias that are semantic, visual, orthographic, and derivational will aid substantially in diagnosing the patient's reading disturbance.

PROGNOSIS, RECOVERY, TREATMENT

Prognosis

Little research has been conducted in the area of recovery from alexia. Some of the many potential factors that may contribute to the rate and likelihood of recovery include: the age of the patient, the patient's handedness, the sex of the patient, the patient's premorbid intelligence and premorbid reading ability, the size of the lesion, the precise location of the lesion, the severity of the reading deficit, the nature of the reading deficit, and the motivation of the patient to resume reading. Until studies of these factors are carried out, our ability to predict the recovery of an alexic patient will continue to be greatly deficient.

Recovery Patterns

Our inability to predict speed and extent of recovery from alexia is paralleled by our lack of knowledge of the patterns or stages of recovery from alexia that we can expect. To eliminate this problem, many more studies like that conducted by Newcombe and Marshall(1973) are needed. They analyzed the stages in recovery from alexia in a patient with a left occipital abscess. They wanted to see if a "lawful" description of stages in recovery could be determined. A pattern of recovery did emerge during the three-month period of evaluation. They found a parallel between language reacquis-ition and the initial stages of language acquisition.

Treatment

In their review of the alexias, Benson and Geschwind (1969) were pessimistic about treatment and prognosis. "The therapy of alexia," they stated, "must be individual-ized, demands arduous labor on the part of both the patient and the therapist plus considerable ingenuity on the part of the therapist and in many cases an end result far below normal levels must be accepted" (p. 137). With respect to current therapy, little has changed since that statement in 1969. And yet, the contemporary work of behavioral neurologists and neuropsychologists has provided insights into the direction that the needed therapeutic ingenuity might take.

One currently popular approach is to retrain alexic patients to read using what has been called "right hemisphere strategies" of reading (Carmon et al., 1977; Heilman et al., 1979). The right hemisphere is said to possess a system of reading not unlike the "direct" reading route discussed earlier. (See Coltheart, 1980b, for a review of the literature pertaining to this issue.) With this notion in mind, Carmon et al. (1977) successfully retrained a patient suffering from alexia with agraphia to memorize the visual configurations of 800 words. The patient never learned to break down these words in any way, i.e., to read deviations of any kind. But direct access reading was clearly a viable alternative. The significance of this case is that the treatment was adapted to the abilities and limitations of the patient.

The treatment plan that Moyer (1979) devised for her pure alexic patient was designed to deal with the patient's most pressing reading problem, decreased reading speed. She had the patient read and reread the same paragraphs from a child's ency-clopedia. Moyer hoped that the patient would learn to use the syntactic and semantic constraints provided by the structure of the sentences and the paragraph to facilitate his reading of the words composing the sentences. She found that the patient's reading speed on new paragraphs increased with this treatment plan. It is difficult to know the effect that the treatment itself had on the patient's improved reading, since he was a highly motivated, intelligent man who had shown signs of progressive improve-ment prior to initiation of the program. Once again, the important point is the way the treatment was designed with the specific abilities and disabilities of the patient in mind.

Larger studies with adequate controls are clearly needed before general treatment plans can be recommended. For the present, the best strategy is to carefully delineate the individual patient's current deficits—*and abilities*—and to devise a rehabilitative program appropriate to those abilities.

REFERENCES

Ajax, E. T. (1967). Dyslexia without agraphia. *Arch. Neurol. 17:* 645–652.

Ajax, E. T., Schenkenberg, T., and Kasteljanetz, M. (1977). Alexia without agraphia and the inferior splenium. *Neurology 27:* 685–688.

Alajouanine, T., Lhermitte, F., and Ribaucourt-Ducarne, B. (1960). Les alexies agnosiques et aphasiques. In *Les Grandes Activites du Lobe Occipital*, T. Alajouanine (ed). Paris: Masson, pp.235–265.

Albert, M., Yamadori, A., Gardner, H. and Howes, D. (1973). Comprehension in alexia. *Brain 96:* 317–328.

Baron, J. (1977). Mechanisms for pronouncing printed words: use and acquisition. In *Basic Processes in Reading: Perception and Comprehension*, D. LaBerge and S. J. Samuels (eds). Hillsdale, N.J.: Lawrence Erlbaum Associates.

Beauvois, M. F. and Dérouesné, J. (1979). Phonological alexia: three dissociations. *J. Neurol. Neurosurg. Psychiat. 42:* 1115–1124.

Benson, D. F. (1977). The third alexia. *Arch. Neurol. 34:* 327–331.

Benson, D. F., Brown, J., and Tomlinson, E. B. (1971). Varieties of alexia. *Neurology 21:* 951–957.

Benson, D. F. and Geschwind, N. (1969). The alexias. In *Handbook of Clinical Neurology: Disorders of Speech, Perception, and Symbolic Behavior*, Vol. 4, P. J. Vinken and G. W. Bruyn (eds). Amsterdam: North-Holland.

Berndt, R. S., and Caramazza, A. (1980). A redefinition of the syndrome of Broca's aphasia: implications for a neuropsychological model of language. *J. Appl. Psycholing. 1:* 225–278.

Brain, R. (1961). *Speech Disorders*. London: Butterworths.

Brissaud, E. (1900). Cecite verbale sans aphasie ni agraphie. *Rev. Neurol. 8:* 757.

Bub, D. N., Cancelliere, A., and Kertesz, A. (1982). The orthographic reading route: evidence for algorithmic grapheme-phoneme conversion in a surface dyslexic. Paper presented at the 20th Annual Meeting of the Academy of Aphasia, New Paltz, N.Y.

Caplan, L. and Hedley-White, T. (1974). Cuing and memory dysfunction in alexia without agraphia: a case report. *Brain 97:* 251–262.

Caramazza, A., Berndt, R. S., and Brownell, H. (1982). The semantic deficit hypothesis: perceptual parsing and object classification by aphasic patients. *Brain and Lang. 15:* 161–189.

Carmon, A., Gordon, H. W., Bental, E., and Harness, B. Z. (1977). Retraining in literal alexia: substitution of a right hemisphere perceptual strategy for impaired left hemispheric processing. *Bull. L.A. Neurol. Soc. 42:* 41–50.

Coltheart, M. (1980a). Deep dyslexia: a review of the syndrome. In *Deep Dyslexia*, M. Coltheart, K. Patterson, and J. C. Marshall (eds). London: Routledge and Kegan Paul.

Coltheart, M. (1980b). Deep dyslexia: a right hemisphere hypothesis. In *Deep Dyslexia*, M. Coltheart, K. Patterson, and J. C. Marshall (eds). London: Routledge and Kegan Paul.

Coltheart, M. (1982). The acquired dyslexias. Academy Address. Presented at the 20th Annual Meeting of the Academy of Aphasia, New Paltz, N.Y.

Coltheart, M., Patterson, K., and Marshall, J. C. (1980). *Deep Dyslexia*. London: Routledge and Kegan Paul.

Conrad, K. (1948). Beitrag zum Problem der parietalen Alexie. *Arch. Psychol. 181:* 398–420.

Cumming, W. J. (1970). Anatomical findings in a case of alexia without agraphia. *J. Anatomy 106:* 170.

Déjerine, J. (1891). Sur un cas de cecite verbal avec agraphie suivi d'autopsie. *Memoires de la Societe de Biologie 3:* 197–201.

Déjerine, J. (1892). Contribution a l'etude anatomo–pathologique et clinique des differentes varietes de cecite verbale. *Memoires de la Societe de Biologie 4:* 61–90.

Déjerine, J. and Mirallié, C. (1895). Sur les alterations de la lecture mentale chez les aphasiques moteurs corticaux. *C. R. Soc. Biol. (Paris), 47:* 523–527.

Deloche, G., Andreewsky, E., and Desi, M. (1982). Surface dyslexia: a case report and some theoretical implications to reading models. *Brain and Lang. 15:* 12–31.

Estes, W. K. (1975). The locus of inferential and perceptual processes in letter identification. *J. Exp. Psychol.: Gen. 1:* 122–145.

Foix, C. and Hillemand, P. (1925). Role vraisemblable du splenium dans la pathologenie de l'alexie pure par lesion de la cerebrale posterieure. *Bull. et Mem. de la Soc. Med. des Hopitaux de Paris 49:* 393–395.

Friedman, R. B. (1981). Preservation of orthographic knowledge in aphasia. *Brain and Lang. 14:* 307–314.

Friedman, R. B. (1982). Mechanisms of reading and spelling in a case of alexia without agraphia. *Neuropsychologia 20:* 533–545.

Friedman, R. B., and Alexander, M. P. (1984). Pictures, images, and pure alexia: a case study. *Cognitive Neuropsychology, 1:* 9–23.

Friedman, R. B. and Perlman, M. B. (1982). On the underlying causes of semantic paralexias in a patient with deep dyslexia. *Neuropsychologia 20:* 559–568.

Gardner, H. and Zurif, E. B. (1975). Bee but not Be: Oral reading of single words in aphasia and alexia. *Neuropsychologia 13:* 181–190.

Geschwind, N. (1962). The anatomy of acquired disorders of reading. In *Reading Disability*, J. Money (ed). Baltimore: Johns Hopkins Press, pp. 115.-128.

Geschwind, N. (1965). Disconnexion syndromes in animals and man, I and II. *Brain 88:* 237–294, 585–644.

Geschwind, N. and Fusillo, M. (1966). Color naming defects in association with alexia. *Arch. Neurol. 15:* 137–146.

Glushko, R. (1979). The organization and activation of orthographic knowledge in reading aloud. *J. Exp. Psychol.: Human Perception and Performance 5:* 674–691.

Goldstein, J., Joynt, R., and Goldblatt, D. (1971). Word blindness with intact central visual fields. *Neurology 21:* 873–876.

Goldstein, K. (1948). *Language and Language Disturbances*. New York: Grune & Stratton.

Greenblatt, S. (1973). Alexia without agraphia or hemianopia: anatomical analysis of an autopsied case. *Brain 96:* 307–316.

Greenblatt, S. (1976). Subangular alexia without agraphia or hemianopia. *Brain and Lang. 3:* 229–245.

Hécaen, H. (1967). Aspects des troubles de la lecture (alexie) au cours des lesions cerebrales en foyer. *Word 23:* 265–287.

Hécaen, H. and Albert, M. L. (1978). *Human Neuropsychology*. New York: Wiley

Hécaen, H. and Gruner, J. (1975). Alexie "pure" avec integrite du corps calleux. In *Les Syndromes de Disconnexion Calleuse Chez L'Homme*, F. Michel and B. Schott (eds). Lyon: Hospital Neurologique, pp. 347–361.

Hécaen, H. and Kremin, H. (1977). Reading disorders resulting from left hemisphere lesions: aphasic and "pure" alexias. In *Studies in Neurolinguistics*, Vol. 2, H. Whitaker and H. A. Whitaker (eds). New York: Academic Press.

Heilman, K. M., Rothi, L., Campanella, D., and Wolfson, S. (1979). Wernicke's and global aphasia without alexia. *Arch. Neurol. 36:* 129–133.

Hermann, G. and Poetzl, O. (1926). *Uber die Agraphie und ihre Lokaldiagnostischen Beziehungen*. Berlin: Karger.

Hier, D. B. and Mohr, J. P. (1977). Incongruous oral and written naming: evidence for a subdivision of the syndrome of Wernicke's aphasia. *Brain and Lang. 4:* 115–126.

Hinshelwood, J. (1900). *Letter, Word, and Mind-Blindness*. London: H. K. Lewis.

Hoff, H., Gloning, I., and Gloning, K. (1954). Ueber Alexie. *Wiener Zeitshrift für Nervenheilkunde 10:* 149–162.

Johansson, T. and Fahlgren, H. (1979). Alexia without agraphia: lateral and medial infarction of left occipital lobe. *Neurology 29:* 390–393.

Karanth, P. (1981). Pure alexia in a Kannada-English bilingual. *Cortex 17:* 187–198.

Kinsbourne, M. and Warrington, E. K. (1962). A variety of reading disability associated with right hemisphere lesions. *J. Neurol. Neurosurg. Psychiat. 25:* 339–344.

Kleiman, G. M. (1975). Speech recoding in reading. *J. Verbal Learn. Verbal Behav. 14:* 323–339.

Kleist, K. (1934). *Gehirnpathologie*. Leipzig: Barth.

LaBerge, D. and Samuels, S. J. (1974). Toward a theory of automatic information processing in reading. *Cog. Psychol. 6:* 293–322.

Levine, D. N. and Calvanio, R. (1978). A study of the visual defect in verbal alexia-simultanagnosia. *Brain 101:* 65–81.

Levy, B. A. (1975). Vocalization and suppression effects in sentence memory. *J. Verbal Learn. Verbal Behav. 14:* 304–316.

Luria, A. R. (1966). *Higher Cortical Functions in Man*. New York: Basic Books.

Marcel, T. (1980). Surface dyslexia and beginning reading: a revised hypothesis of the pronunciation of print and its impairments. In *Deep Dyslexia*, M. Coltheart, K. Patterson and J. C. Marshall (eds). London: Routledge and Kegan Paul.

Marie, P. (1906). Revision de la question de l'aphasie. *Semaine Medicale (Paris) 42:* 493–500.

Marshall, J. C. and Newcombe, F. (1973). Patterns of paralexia: a psycholinguistic approach. *J. Psycholing. Res. 2:* 175–199.

McClelland, J. L. (1976). Preliminary letter identification in the perception of words and nonwords. *J. Exp. Psychol.: Human Perception and Performance 2:* 80–91.

Misch, W. and Frankl, K. (1929). Beitrag zur Alexielehre. *Monatschrift für Psychiatrie und Neurologie 71:* 1–47.

Mohr, J. P., Hier, D. B., and Kirshner, H. (1978). Modality bias in Wernicke's aphasia. *Neurology 28:* 395 (abstract).

Morton, J. and Patterson, K. (1980). A new attempt at an interpretation, or, an attempt at a new interpretation. In *Deep Dyslexia*, M. Coltheart, K. Patterson, and J. C. Marshall (eds). London: Routledge and Kegan Paul.

Mouren, P., Tatossian, A., Trupheme, R., Giudicelli, S., and Fresco, R. (1967). Alexia due to visual-verbal disconnection (Geschwind). Apropos of a case of pure verbal blindness without agraphia but with disorders of designation of colors, or names and of images. *Encephale 56:* 112–137.

Moyer, S. B. (1979). Rehabilitation of alexia: a case study. *Cortex 15:* 139–144.

Newcombe, F. and Marshall, J. C. (1973). Stages in recovery from dyslexia following a left cerebral abscess. *Cortex 9:* 329–332.

Nielson, J. M. and Raney, R. B. (1938). Symptoms following surgical removal of major (left) angular gyrus. *Bull. L.A. Neurol. Soc. 3:* 42–46.

Oxbury, J. M., Oxbury, S. M., and Humphrey, N. K. (1969). Varieties of colour anomia. *Brain 92:* 847–860.

Patterson, K. E. (1978). Phonemic dyslexia: errors of meaning and the meaning of errors. *Quart. J. Exp. Psychol. 30:* 587–601.

Patterson, K. E. and Kay, J. (1982). Letter-by-letter reading: psychological descriptions of a neurological syndrome. *Quart. J. Exp. Psychol. 34:* 411–442.

Patterson, K. E. and Marcel, A. J. (1977). Aphasia, dyslexia, and the phonological coding of written words. *Quart. J. Exp. Psychol. 29:* 307–318.

Peron, N. and Goutner, V. (1944). Alexie pure sans hemianopsie. *Rev. Neurol. 76: 81–82.*

Poetzl, O. (1928). *Die Optisch-Agnostischen Storungen.* Vienna: Deuticke.

Quensel, F. (1931). Die Alexie. In *Kurzes Handbuch der Ophtalmologie.* Berlin: Springer.

Redlich, E. (1895). Ueber die sogenannte subcorticale Alexie. *Jahrbucher für Psychiatrie und Neurologie 13:* 1–60.

Rothi, L. J., McFarling, D., and Heilman, K. M. (1982). Conduction aphasia, syntactic alexia, and the anatomy of syntactic comprehension. *Arch. Neurol. 39:* 272–275.

Saffran, E. M., Bogyo. L. C., Schwartz, M. F., and Marin, O.S.M. (1980). Does deep dyslexia reflect right hemispere reading? In *Deep Dyslexia,* M. Coltheart, K. Patterson, and J. C. Marshall (eds). London: Routledge and Kegan Paul.

Shallice, T. and Warrington, E. K. (1980). Single and multiple component central dyslexic syndromes. In *Deep Dyslexia,* M. Coltheart, K. Patterson and J. C. Marshall (eds). London: Routledge and Kegan Paul.

Smith, F. (1971). *Understanding Reading.* New York: Holt, Rinehart and Winston.

Sperry, R. W. and Gazzaniga, M. S. (1967). Language following surgical disconnection of the hemispheres. In *Brain Mechanisms Underlying Speech and Language,* C. H. Millikan and F. L. Darley (eds). New York: Grune and Stratton.

Sroka, H., Solsi, P., and Bornstein, B. (1973). Alexia without agraphia with complete recovery. *Confin. Neurology 35:* 167–176.

Venezky, R. L. (1970). *The Structure of English Orthography.* The Hague: Mouton.

Vincent, C., David, M. and Puech, P. (1930). Sur l'alexie. Production du phenomene a la suite de l'extirpation de la corne occipitale du ventricule lateral gauche. *Rev. Neurol. 1:* 262–272.

Vincent, F. M., Sadowsky, C. H., Saunders, R. L., and Reeves, A. G. (1977). Alexia without agraphia, hemianopia, or color, naming defect: a disconnection syndrome. *Neurology 27:* 689–691.

Warrington, E. K. and Shallice, T. (1979). Semantic access dyslexia. *Brain 102:* 43–63.

Warrington, E. K. and Shallice, T. (1980). Word-form dyslexia. *Brain 103:* 99–112.

Warrington, E. K. and Zangwill, O. L. (1957). A study of dyslexia. *J. Neurol. Neurosurg. Psychiat. 20:* 208–215.

Wechsler, A. F., Weinstein, E. A. and Antin, S. P. (1972). Alexia without agraphia. *Bull. L.A. Neurol. Soc. 37:* 1–11.

Wernicke, C. (1874). *Der aphasische Symptomencomplex.* Breslau: Frank und Weigert.

Wolpert, I. (1930). Ueber das Wesen der literalen Alexie. *Monatschrift für Psychiatrie und Neurologie 75:* 207–266.

Yamadori, A. (1980). Right unilateral dyscopia of letters in alexia without agraphia. *Neurology 30:* 991–994.

Zurif, E. and Caramazza, A. (1976). Psycholinguistic structures in aphasia: studies in syntax and semantics. In *Studies in Neurolinguistics*, Vol. 1, H. Whitaker and H. A. Whitaker (eds). New York: Academic Press.

4
Agraphia

DAVID ROELTGEN

Ogle (1867) applied the term "agraphia" to disorders of writing. He was one of the first to describe the relationship of agraphia to aphasia and to classify the agraphias. He found that although aphasia and agraphia usually occurred together they were occasionally separable. He described one patient who was aphasic but not agraphic and a second who was agraphic but not aphasic. Therefore, he concluded that there were distinct cerebral centers for writing and for speaking. Because agraphia and aphasia usually occurred together, he concluded that these centers were close together. Ogle's classification of agraphia included amnemonic agraphia and atactica agraphia. Patients with the former wrote well-formed, but incorrect letters. Patients with the latter made poorly formed letters but usually had an element of amnemonic agraphia as well.

In contrast to Ogle, Lichtheim (1885) proposed that disorders of writing usually were the same as disorders of speech. The exception was agraphia due to disruption of the "center from which the organs of writing are innervated." Clinically, this agraphia was similar to Ogle's atactica agraphia. Lichtheim proposed that agraphia and aphasia were similar because the acquisition of writing (and spelling) was superimposed on speech, and therefore utilized the previously acquired speech centers.

Head's position (1926) was similar to Lichtheim's. He stressed that the capacity to write was associated with internal speech because writing development was superimposed on speech. Therefore, his classification of the agraphias was the same as his classification of the aphasias. With verbal aphasia the production of language was disturbed and therefore these patients had severe agraphia. Syntactical aphasia led to disruption of phrase structure. Nominal aphasia led to poor word choice and to poor letter choice (misspellings). Semantic aphasia led to the production of incoherent phrases.

Nielson's classification (1946) reflected his view that writing is closely associated with speech but separable from it (a view similar to Ogle's). Nielson described three types of agraphia: apractic (apraxic), aphasic, and isolated. Apractic agraphia was characterized by poorly formed letters and was associated with the various apraxias. Aphasic agraphia was associated with the various aphasias and the patients' written

errors reflected the aphasic disturbance. Agraphia without associated neuropsychological signs (isolated agraphia) resulted from a lesion of the frontal writing center
(Exner's area) or of the angular gyrus. Neilson thought that isolated agraphias were
rare. He theorized that Exner's area, the foot of the second frontal convolution (Fig.
4-1), worked in close association with the angular gyrus and Wernicke's area to produce writing. He also proposed that the fibers carrying information from the angular
gyrus to Exner's area passed close to Broca's speech area. Nielson suggested that these
functional and anatomic connections accounted for the frequent association of
agraphia and aphasia.

Goldstein (1948) took the position that agraphia is often but not always associated
with aphasia. Thus, he described two general types of agraphia: primary, due to
impairment of the motor act of writing, and secondary, due to disturbances of speech.
The primary agraphias were divided into five types: (1) poor impulse for writing
(with transcortical aphasias); (2) impairment of the abstract attitude, leading to trouble using small words with better production of concrete words; (3) ideatoric agraphia
characterized by loss of the idea of letter form; (4) pure or motor agraphia characterized by production of incorrect letters; and (5) agraphia associated with apraxia of
the minor hand. In secondary agraphias the letter form is unimpaired but words are
misspelled. He described five types of secondary agraphia, corresponding to the five
types of aphasia: motor aphasia, central aphasia, pure sensory aphasia, cortical sensory
aphasia, and the transcortical aphasias. In most of these the agraphia was thought to
parallel the aphasia.

TESTING FOR AGRAPHIA

As discussed above, most investigators have agreed that there are two major components of writing: linguistic and motor. In the evaluation of a patient with agraphia,

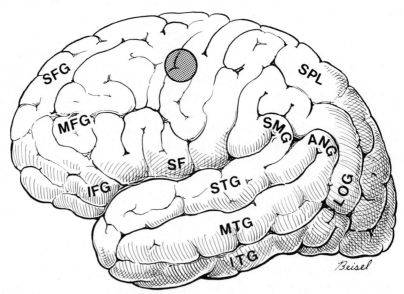

Fig. 4-1. The location of Exner's area.

both components must be evaluated. The linguistic component includes the choice of the correct letter (spelling) and the choice of the correct word (meaning). The motor component includes those neuropsychologic functions necessary for producing the correct letter form and correct word form. In order to evaluate these features it is convenient to divide the tests into three types: spontaneous writing, writing to dictation, and copying.

To test spontaneous writing the patient is asked to write sentences or words about a familiar topic. For maximum value the topic should be standard from patient to patient, and controlled. Therefore we recommend having the patient write about a picture. The same picture can then be used with different patients and at different times with the same patient in order to compare performance. From this spontaneous writing sample it is possible to judge in a general way both the content and form of the patient's writing.

Having the patient write to dictation gives the examiner better stimulus control. This enables the examiner to evaluate some of the specific features of writing. To evaluate the effects of particular variables on writing, the type of word may be varied (e.g., long versus short, common versus uncommon). The word type can also be varied to test specific hypotheses based on models of agraphia such as those presented later in this chapter. These models may predict, for example, that certain patients would have more difficulty with nouns, functors, imageable words, abstract words, or non-words. The type of patient response may also be varied: the patient can be asked to spell orally, type, or spell using anagram letters (blocks with single letters written on them). This enables the examiner to determine if the disorder is only within the writing mechanism, or if it is part of a more fundamental linguistic disorder, encompassing not only letter production, but also letter choice.

The third group of writing tests evaluates copying. Depending on the goals of the examination, the task may include copying single letters, words, sentences and/or paragraphs. When one asks a patient to copy, it is important, but not always possible, to distinguish slavish or "stroke by stroke" copying from transcribing. Transcribing is characterized by reading the material, and then writing it in an almost spontaneous fashion. It may be possible to distinguish these copying methods by: (1) varying the length of material to be copied (increased length usually decreases slavish copying), (2) increasing the distance between the stimulus and the response (it is difficult to slavishly copy material from across the room), and (3) having the patient copy nonsense figures (figures which have no symbolic meaning) since it is very difficult to transcribe nonsense symbols.

In addition to these detailed tests of writing, it is important to evaluate the patient for neurologic disorders that may interfere with writing, oral spelling, or copying. These include disorders of speech, reading, ideomotor praxis, visuoperceptual, visuospatial and constructional abilities, and elementary motor and sensory functions.

CURRENT CLASSIFICATIONS OF AGRAPHIA

Recent classifications of agraphia have included those by Leischner (1969), Hécaen and Albert (1978), Benson (1979), and Kaplan and Goodglass (1981). These classifications, derived from clinical valuations of agraphic patients, have usually included five general types of agraphia (Table 4-1): pure agraphia, aphasic agraphia, agraphia with alexia (also called parietal agraphia) (Kaplan and Goodglass, 1981), apraxic agraphia, and spatial agraphia.

Pure agraphia is characterized by the presence of agraphia in the absence of any other significant language disturbance. Pure agraphia may be due to a focal lesion or to an acute confusional state. Patients with the former are described as making well-formed graphemes (written letters) with spelling errors that vary in type, depending on the lesion location. Pure agraphia has been reported from focal lesions in the second frontal convolution (Exner's area) (Aimard, et al., 1975; Hécaen and Albert, 1978; Marcie and Hécaen, 1979; Kaplan and Goodglass, 1981), superior parietal lobule (Basso et al., 1978), the posterior perisylvian region (Rosati and De Bastiani, 1979; Auerbach and Alexander, 1981), and the region of the left caudate and internal capsule (Laine and Martilla, 1981). Pure agraphia due to an acute confusional state (Chedru and Geschwind, 1972) is characterized by poorly formed graphemes, inability to write on a line, and writing over the model when copying. When the letters are well formed, spelling errors may be recognized.

Aphasic agraphia has been described with Broca's aphasia, conduction aphasia, Wernicke's aphasia, and transcortical sensory aphasia (Marcie and Hécaen, 1979; Benson, 1979; Kaplan and Goodglass, 1981; Grossfeld and Clark, 1983). Two distinct subtypes of agraphia have been described in patients with Broca's aphasia. One agraphia is characterized by a difficulty in graphemic production and the second by agrammatism (Marcie and Hécaen, 1979; Kaplan and Goodglass, 1981). Patients with the former make poorly formed graphemes and have severe difficulty spelling. Patients with the latter make well-formed graphemes but produce agrammatic sentence structure. Agraphia with conduction aphasia is characterized by misspellings and overwriting (Marcie and Hécaen, 1979). Wernicke's aphasics make severe spelling errors that are similar to the phonemic and semantic jargon typically heard in their speech (Marcie and Hécaen, 1979; Kaplan and Goodglass, 1981). The lesions causing the aphasic agraphias are usually not different from the lesions that typically cause the associated aphasic disorder.

Agraphia with alexia has also been called parietal agraphia because these two symptoms, in the absence of significant aphasia, usually occur together in patients with parietal lesions (Kaplan and Goodglass, 1981). These patients typically make poorly formed graphemes when writing. When spelling aloud they pronounce letters correctly but have difficulty spelling.

Apraxic agraphia is characterized by difficulty in forming graphemes when writing spontaneously and to dictation (Leischner, 1969; Hécaen and Albert, 1978; Marcie and Hécaen, 1979). Frequently, copying and oral spelling are disturbed as well.

Table 4-1. Present Classification of Agraphia

Pure agraphia
Aphasic agraphia
Agraphia with alexia (parietal agraphia)
Apractic agraphia
Spatial agraphia

"Writing" frequently improves with the use of anagram letters. The lesions causing apraxic agraphia are in the parietal lobe opposite the preferred hand.

Lesions in the nondominant parietal lobe may cause spatial agraphia. Patients with this type of agraphia typically duplicate strokes, have trouble writing on a horizontal line, write on only the right side of the paper, and have intrusion of blank spaces between graphemes. It is frequently associated with the neglect syndrome (Hécaen and Albert, 1978; Marcie and Hécaen, 1979; Benson, 1979).

Although we have attempted to classify agraphia into five well-defined groups, detailed analysis of agraphic patients reveals difficulty in classifying many of them. For example, some patients with Broca's aphasia have agraphias that more closely resemble the agraphias of patients with Wernicke's aphasia than the agraphias of other patients with Broca's aphasia. Also, parietal lesions may cause parietal agraphia (agraphia with alexia) but may also cause apraxic agraphia. In some discussions it is not clear whether or not these two syndromes represent the same abnormality seen from two different perspectives. One way that these difficulties may be resolved is by using an alternative approach to classifying the agraphias. Rather than base classification on clinical descriptions of agraphic patients, the classification can be based on the neuropsychological mechanism within the writing system that is presumed to be disturbed.

A NEUROPSYCHOLOGICAL MODEL OF WRITING AND SPELLING

In order to develop such a classification it is necessary first to appreciate what neuropsychological mechanisms are necessary for writing. Clinical analysis of agraphic patients has enabled us to begin to understand these mechanisms and to construct a neuropsychological model of writing.

Goldstein (1948) delineated two general categories of functions necessary for writing. He described mechanisms that were associated with language and mechanisms associated with the motor output necessary for writing. We may term the former group the linguistic components of writing and the latter the motor components. In addition, the integrity of certain visuospatial skills appears necessary for successful writing.

The model of writing that we have developed (Fig. 4-2) defines many of the linguistic and motor components. It also addresses the mode of interaction between motor components and visuospatial skills. Among the linguistic components, there are at least two parallel systems available for spelling and a mechanism by which semantics (meaning) interacts with these systems. This interaction enables one to write with meaning.

The motor components include mechanisms by which words can be spelled or written. It appears that the parallel spelling systems converge prior to motor output as drawn in Fig. 4-2. A detailed discussion of this model follows.

Linguistic Components

LEXICAL AGRAPHIA

There are at least two systems available to adults for spelling words: one lexical and one phonological (Beauvois and Dérouesné, 1981; Shallice, 1981; Ellis, 1982; Roeltgen

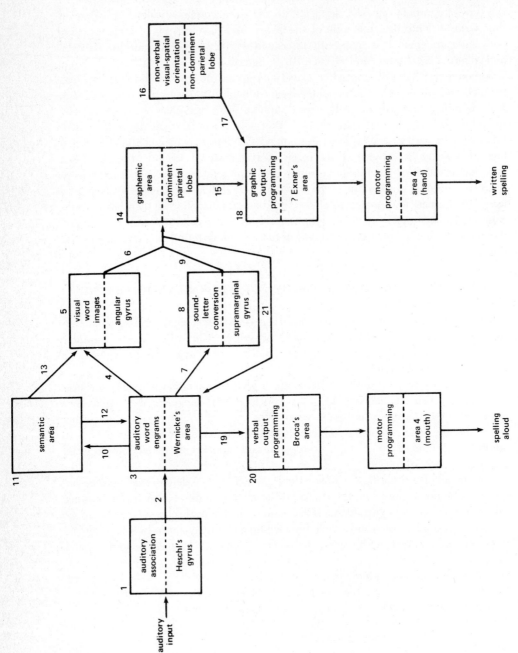

Fig. 4-2. Neuropsychological model for writing and oral spelling. The neuropsychological component is noted in the upper portion of each box. The lower portion contains a probable anatomic substrate for that function.

et al., 1983a; Roeltgen et al., 1982a; Roeltgen and Heilman, in press; Hatfield and Patterson, 1983). Probably the most important is the lexical system (components 4–5–6 in Fig. 4-2). This system appears to utilize a whole-word retrieval process that incorporates visual word images. It is thought that these visual word images arise from word engrams that are visual rather than phonological. The lexical strategy is necessary for spelling familiar orthographically irregular words (words that cannot be spelled utilizing direct sound-to-letter correspondence rules, e.g., "comb") and ambiguous words (words with sounds that may be represented by multiple letters or letter clusters, e.g., "phone"). The lexical system can also be used for spelling familiar orthographically regular words (words with direct sound-to-letter correspondence, e.g., "animal") that the phonological system can also handle (see below).

Dysfunction of the lexical system is called lexical agraphia (Beauvois and Dérouesné, 1981; Roeltgen and Heilman, in press). It has also been called phonological spelling (Hatfield and Patterson, 1983). This disorder is characterized by impaired ability to spell irregular and ambiguous words with preserved ability to spell regular words and nonwords. These patients usually make errors that are phonologically correct (e.g., "gelosy" for "jealousy").

We have attempted to delineate the anatomy underlying the syndrome of lexical agraphia (Roeltgen and Heilman, in press). We studied the computerized tomograms (CT) of four patients with lexical agraphia by plotting the lesions seen on CT on a lateral view of the left hemisphere. Overlap of these plots revealed that the junction of the posterior angular gyrus and the parieto-occipital lobule was lesioned in each patient (Fig. 4-3). This suggests that this area is an important anatomic substrate for lexical agraphia.

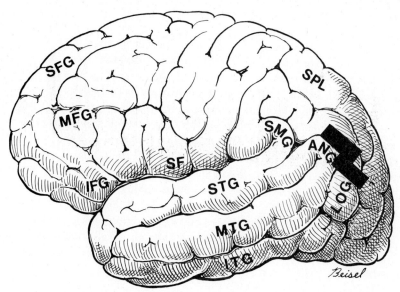

Fig. 4-3. Lateral view of the left hemisphere demonstrating the region damaged in four patients with lexical agraphia. (Reprinted with permission from Roeltgen and Heilman, in press)

Fig. 4-4. Example of visual similarity of errors made by patients with phonological agraphia. Above, "wallet" written correctly; below, "wallet" written incorrectly. (Reprinted with permission from Roeltgen, D. P. and Heilman, K. M., Phonological agraphia—writing by the lexical-semantic route. *Neurology*, in press)

PHONOLOGICAL AGRAPHIA

The alternative parallel spelling system is the phonological system (components 7–8–9 in Fig. 4-2). Speech sounds are initially phonologically decoded (Roeltgen and Heilman, 1983). These phonemes are then converted into letters. This conversion has been termed sound-letter or phoneme-grapheme conversion. In order to spell phonologically, two components are probably necessary: segmentation, and sound-letter conversion. The former parses the phoneme string into separate phonemes and the latter converts the single phonemes into letters. The phonological system is used for spelling unfamiliar orthographically regular words and pronouncible nonwords (e.g., "flig"). It is probable that this system is used to spell familiar regular words only when the lexical system is dysfunctional or when there is no available engram for the word that is to be spelled (an unfamiliar word).

Dysfunction of the phonological system causes what is called phonological agraphia (Shallice, 1981; Roeltgen et al., 1983a). This disorder is characterized by impaired ability to spell nonwords and preserved ability to write familiar words, both regular and irregular. Spelling errors by patients with phonological agraphia are usually not phonologically correct but may have a high degree of visual resemblance (Fig. 4-4).

We have investigated the anatomic basis of phonological agraphia in the same way that we investigated the anatomic basis of lexical agraphia (Roeltgen et al., 1983a). The lesion site common to eight patients with phonological agraphia was the supramarginal gyrus or the insula medial to it (Fig. 4-5). In addition, one patient with isolated phonological agraphia (that is, with no additional language deficits) had a small lesion confined to the insula or possibly extending to the surface of the supramarginal gyrus as revealed by CT scan. We concluded that lesions of the supramarginal gyrus or the insula medial to it (or both) are the critical anatomic loci for inducing phonological agraphia. Consistent with this hypothesis, all other reported patients with phonological agraphia have had lesions that included this area (Shallice, 1981; Bub and Kertesz, 1982; Nolan and Caramazza, 1982).

DEEP AGRAPHIA

Bub and Kertesz (1982) and Hatfield (1982) have used the term "deep agraphia" to describe a syndrome of phonological agraphia with a group of associated findings.

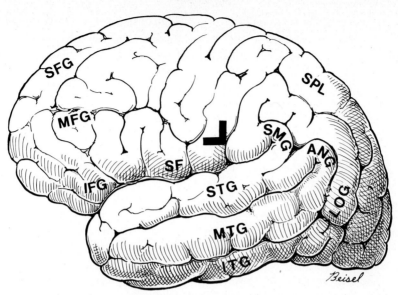

Fig. 4-5. A lateral view of the left hemisphere demonstrating the region damaged in eight patients with phonological agraphia. (Reprinted with permission from Roeltgen and Heilman, in press)

Their patients, as well as two others (Roeltgen et al., 1983a), had trouble spelling nonwords but also had trouble spelling function words (conjunctions, prepositions, adverbs) and spelled nouns of high imageability better than nouns of low imageability. For example, they might spell "arm" correctly, but "law" incorrectly. These patients also made semantic paragraphias. These are spelling errors that consist of real words related in meaning to the target word, but with little phonological or visual resemblance to the target. For example, they might spell "flight" when asked to spell "propeller."

All reported cases of deep agraphia have had phonological agraphia as well, and have had lesions of the supramarginal gyrus or insula (Roeltgen et al., 1983a; Bub and Kertesz, 1982; Nolan and Caramazza, 1982). But their lesions have been large, extending well beyond the circumscribed area thought to be important for phonological agraphia. It is possible that "deep agraphia" reflects right hemisphere writing processes. This hypothesis is similar to a proposed explanation for "deep dyslexia," a reading disorder that is clinically similar to deep agraphia. Patients with deep dyslexia have trouble reading nonwords and make frequent semantic errors. Also, their reading ability is affected by word class and imageability (Coltheart, 1980; Saffran et al., 1980). The alternative hypothesis is that residual left hemisphere mechanisms are important for the residual abilities in patients with deep agraphia (Roeltgen and Heilman, 1982). A possible anatomic correlate of this hypothesis is that the left posterior angular gyrus is spared in patients with deep agraphia.

SEMANTIC INFLUENCE ON WRITING

The incorporation of meaning into what is written is termed the semantic influence on writing. The classical view of the interaction between semantics and language is that semantics interacts with auditory word images (Heilman et al., 1981; Heilman et al., 1976) (Fig. 4-2, pathway 12). Such an interaction would enable a writer to incorporate meaning into words utilizing both the lexical strategy and the phonological strategy. With this arrangement the incorporation of meaning into spelling is indirect: it must come through auditory word images. There is evidence to suggest, however, that semantics may directly influence the lexical strategy (Roeltgen, et al., 1983a; Shallice, 1981; Hier and Mohr, 1977; Brown and McNeill, 1966; Morton, 1980) (Fig. 4-2, pathway 13).

Semantic agraphia.   There are three clinical disorders that exemplify the interactions of semantics and spelling. A disruption of semantic ability (Fig. 4-2, component 11) or a disconnection of semantics from spelling (disruption of pathways 12, and 13, Fig. 4-2) has been termed semantic agraphia (Roeltgen et al., 1982b). Patients with semantic agraphia lose their ability to spell and write with meaning. They write sentences that they do not comprehend, either aurally or visually. Also, they spell and write semantically incorrect but correctly spelled dictated homophones (words that are pronounced the same, but have different meanings dependent on the spelling, such as "doe" and "dough"). For example, when asked to "spell doe as in the *doe* ran through the forest," these patients may spell "dough." They spell irregular words and nonwords correctly, demonstrating intact lexical and phonological systems (Fig. 4-2, pathways 4–5–6 and 7–8–9). The pathology of the reported patients with semantic agraphia has one common feature: they all involved anatomic substrates important for assessing meaning in speech (Roeltgen et al., 1982b). These anatomic areas are diverse, and included (1) a subcortical lesion involving the caudate, internal capsule, and frontal subcortical region; (2) the medial frontal and parietal areas, (3) hemispheric cortical watershed areas, and (4) the thalamus. Lesions in these areas typically cause transcortical aphasia with impaired comprehension. Therefore, the anatomic substrates of semantic agraphia may be the same as those responsible for speech comprehension.

Phonological agraphia and Wernicke's aphasia.   The second clinical disorder exemplifying the interaction of semantics and spelling involves disruption of both the phonological system for writing (phonological agraphia) and of auditory word images (Wernicke's aphasia). Some patients with phonological agraphia and Wernicke's aphasia are nevertheless able to spell meaningful words (and thus may write with more meaning than they speak). Thus semantics may directly influence the lexical system, even though auditory decoding is not possible. Spelling in such patients therefore occurs through components 11–13–5–6 (Fig. 4-2).

Lexical agraphia with semantic paragraphia.   The third disorder involving semantic interaction with spelling is a part of the syndrome of lexical agraphia. Many patients with lexical agraphia have difficulty utilizing semantic information when writing (Hatfield and Patterson, 1983; Roeltgen and Heilman, personal observation). These patients, when asked to spell dictated homophones, frequently spell the semantically incorrect homophone (as do patients with semantic agraphia). They differ from patients with semantic agraphia in that they are able to comprehend the meaning of the words when they read or hear them. Therefore, general semantic knowledge (Fig.

4-2, component 11) is preserved, but interacts poorly with spelling. This is presumably because there is a disturbance of the direct semantic influence on spelling (through the lexical route).

Transition from Linguistic Information to Motor Output

Potential spellings produced by the phonological and lexical systems converge prior to motor output, whether it be oral (oral spelling) or graphic (writing). This convergence is evident clinically, since patients with disorders of either spelling system produce substantially the same errors in oral spelling as in writing.

Since the lexical and semantic systems need not come up with the same spellings, there must be some way of choosing which spelling is to be produced. For example, in attempting to spell "comb," the lexical system, if familiar with the word, will produce "c-o-m-b." The phonological system, however, may produce "k-o-m" or "c-o-m," since the silent "b" does not conform to the rules of English orthography. These alternative spellings will converge on the motor system, which must choose the correct output. Since the lexical system produces only one response that is dependent on prior experience (visual word images can be developed only by prior experience), while the phonological system has the potential to produce multiple letter sequences for a single phonetic sequence, it is only reasonable to assume that under normal circumstances the output of the lexical system is preferentially incorporated into oral or written spelling. Data from patients with semantic agraphia support this contention (Roeltgen et al., 1982b): patterns of responses obtained from these patients suggest that the phonological system is probably only used for spelling nonwords and unfamiliar regular words.

Rarely, normal writers produce "slips of the pen" that are phonologically correct (Hotopf, 1980). These errors (responses such as "k-o-m" for "comb") suggest that although most normal spelling (and writing) utilizes the lexical system, the phonological system continues to function in the background.

A lesion affecting the transitional phase of writing (from linguistic to motor components) should cause a patient to make particular types of errors. We believe that we have seen one such patient (Roeltgen and Heilman, personal observation). This patient made spelling errors on words and nonwords when writing and spelling aloud. Some errors were phonologically correct and some were not. The errors consisted of substitutions (letters substituted for other letters), omissions (letters left out), and insertions (extra letters added). He was able to recognize his incorrect spellings but was unable to correct them. However, he was not tested for the ability to distinguish correct from incorrect aurally perceived spelled words. If he had been able to perform correctly on that task, it would have further confirmed the preservation of phonological and lexical systems with disturbed writing and spelling. Because disturbances of the transitional phase of writing have not been well studied, the anatomic substrate is not defined. Although our patient had a lesion in the second frontal convolution (Exner's area), we cannot draw definite conclusions from only one case.

Motor Components

Motor output of spelled words may be either manual (writing letters or graphemes) or oral (oral spelling). Writing may be performed by the dominant or nondominant hand. Writing is not a unitary process, but includes motor and visuospatial skills, as well as knowledge of graphemes. Although there is some understanding of the neuropsychological bases of these skills, less is known about the components underlying oral spelling. Oral spelling and writing, however, do appear to be functionally dissociable.

DISORDERS OF WRITING WITH PRESERVED ORAL SPELLING

Apraxic agraphia.   In order to write, motor functions are necessary. In addition to the pyramidal and extrapyramidal motor systems (which will not be discussed here), praxis is necessary for writing (see Chap. 7). Praxis includes the ability to properly hold a pen or pencil as well as the ability to perform the other learned fine finger movements necessary for forming written letters (graphemes). Apraxia usually results from lesions in the hemisphere opposite the preferred hand. In most right-handers, this is also the hemisphere dominant for language, and consequently apraxia is often associated with aphasia. In aphasic apraxic patients, it may not be possible to separate clearly the aphasic from the apraxic elements of agraphia. Several patients have been described who have had language in the hemisphere ipsilateral to the preferred hand. When the hemisphere opposite the preferred hand was damaged, they developed idieomotor apraxia without aphasia (Heilman et al., 1974; Heilman et al., 1973; Valenstein and Heilman, 1979). These patients have illegible writing, both spontaneously and to dictation. Their oral spelling is preserved. Their writing typically improves with copying. They should be able to type or use anagram letters (Valenstein and Heilman, 1979). This syndrome may be termed apraxic agraphia with ideomotor apraxia and without aphasia. Lesions in the parietal lobe opposite the hand dominant for writing may be the most common etiology for this disorder.

Apraxic agraphia without apraxia.   The areas of the brain that perform skilled movement must have knowledge of the features of letters. The area or areas that store this information have been termed graphemic areas (Rothi and Heilman, 1981) (Fig. 4-2, number 14). These space-time or visuokinesthetic-motor engrams for letters may be a subset of the engrams necessary to program other skilled movements. Alternatively, letter engrams may be separate from other motor engrams. A syndrome of abnormal grapheme formation with normal praxis has been described, and is called apraxic agraphia with normal praxis (Roeltgen and Heilman, 1983b; Margolin and Binder, in press). It is characterized by the production of illegibly formed graphemes in spontaneous writing and writing to dictation (Fig. 4-6), with preserved oral spelling. Grapheme production improved with copying (Fig. 4-7), however, the patients also had disturbed visuospatial skills and therefore copying was moderately impaired. The patients were able to read and pronounce words spelled to them. Despite poorly formed graphemes, they had normal praxis, including the ability to imitate holding a pen or pencil. The anatomic substrate for this syndrome appears to be in the parietal lobe. In one case (Margolin and Binder in press) the lesion was in the hemisphere contralateral to the hand used for writing, while in another (Roeltgen and Heilman, 1983b) it was in the ipsilateral hemisphere.

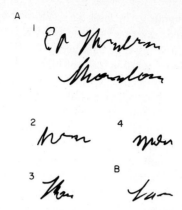

Fig. 4-6. (A) A patient's attempt to write his name (1), the dictated letter "b" (2), the dictated word "cat" (3) and "comb" when shown the object (4). **(B)** The patient's attempt to write "dog" to dictation. There is one scrawl for each letter. (Reprinted with permission from Roeltgen and Heilman, 1983b)

Fig. 4-7. Examples of words copied by the patient in Fig. 4-6. The examiner's samples are on top. (Reprinted with permission from Roeltgen and Heilman, 1983b)

Spatial agraphia.   Visuospatial skills are also necessary for the proper formation of letters and words. Spatial orientation must interact with graphic output in order that letter components (strokes) can be properly formed by the system of graphic output programming (Fig. 4-2, pathway 16–17–18). Disruption of this ability has been termed visuospatial agraphia or constructional agraphia. It is characterized by the following three features: (1) reiteration of strokes; (2) inability to write on a straight horizontal line; and (3) insertion of blank spaces between graphemes. In patients with this disorder the ability to copy is usually disturbed, but ability to spell orally and pronounce aurally perceived words is preserved. This syndrome is usually due to non-dominant parietal lobe lesions. For this reason, it is also frequently associated with the syndrome of unilateral neglect, where the patient's writing may be confined to only one side of the paper, ispilateral to the lesion (see Chap. 10).

Unilateral (callosal) agraphia.   In most agraphias the dominant and nondominant hands are equally affected, except when one hand is paretic. The spelling and graphemic systems of the left hemisphere have access via the neocommissures to the right hemisphere motor system responsible for controlling the nondominant hand. Patients may have this interhemispheric transfer disrupted, resulting in unilateral agraphia (Liepmann and Maas, 1907; Geschwind and Kaplan, 1962; Yamadori, et al., 1980; Gersh and Damasio, 1981; Bogen, 1969; Rubens et al., 1977; Levy et al., 1971; Sugishita et al., 1980; Watson and Heilman, 1983). Most of these patients make unintelligible scrawl when they attempt to write with their left hands. Most improve with copying and are able to spell orally and read. Watson and Heilman (1983) have described a patient with left unilateral agraphia who was able to type with her left hand. They termed this syndrome unilateral apraxic agraphia, limited to the left hand. Their patient had a lesion affecting the body of the corpus callosum, sparing the genu and the splenium. Geschwind and Kaplan (1962) described a patient with an acquired callosal lesion and unilateral left agraphia who was unable to type or use anagram letters with his left hand. This patient's lesion affected the entire anterior four-fifths of the corpus callosum. Watson and Heilman (1983) suggested that the difference between their patient and that of Geschwind and Kaplan (1962) was that the genu of the corpus collosum was spared in Watson and Heilman's patient. They hypothesized that the genu is important for the transmission of verbal-motor programs from the left to the right hemisphere. They also hypothesized that the body of the corpus callosum is important for the transmission of visuokinesthetic (space-time) engrams. These engrams are thought to "command the motor systems to adopt the appropriate spatial positions of the relevant body parts over time" (Watson and Heilman, 1983). The disruption of transmission of these engrams was thought to account for the ideomotor apraxia that was also observed in Watson and Heilman's patient.

Some patients with left-sided unilateral agraphia do not have ideomotor apraxia (Sugishita et al., 1980; Yamadori et al., 1980; Gersh and Damasio, 1981). The agraphia of these patients consists of illegible scrawls as well as incorrect letters. The patient of Gersh and Damasio was unable to write using anagram letters. This syndrome has been called unilateral aphasic agraphia (Watson and Heilman, 1983). The lesions in these patients were confined to the posterior portion of the corpus callosum. Gersh and Damasio suggested that the pathways for ideomotor praxis were more anterior in the callosum than those for writing. Watson and Heilman (1983) further suggested that although the body of the callosum was important for the transfer of visuokinesthetic engrams (ideomotor praxis for writing and other motor tasks), the posterior callosum (especially the splenium) was important for the transmission of linguistic information. This explanation, they felt, accounted for the apraxic agraphia in their patient and the aphasic agraphia in Gersh and Damasio's patient (Fig. 4-8).

DISORDERS OF ORAL SPELLING

The mechanisms for oral spelling are not as well defined as those for writing. Two possible systems exist. One would utilize the area of auditory word engrams (Wernicke's area) to guide the anterior perisylvian speech regions (e.g., Broca's area) to

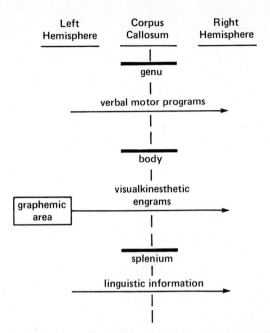

Fig. 4-8. Transfer of information across corpus callosum. Evidence suggest that there are at least three separable components necessary for writing and they cross at different levels of the callosum. Verbal motor programs cross in the genu, visuokinesthetic engrams cross in the body, and linguistic information in the splenium.

produce oral letters (Fig. 4-2, pathway 3–19–20). The other would utilize an independent area of oral motor engrams for letters to guide or program Broca's area. Evidence at this time supports the former mechanism. One patient with relatively spared writing but disturbed oral spelling has been well described (Kinsbourne and Warrington, 1965). This patient also had difficulty saying words spelled to him. This finding suggests that the first mechanism is correct and that the system of auditory word images (Wernicke's area) is necessary for both perception of aurally perceived spelled words and the production of oral letters. Alternatively, there may be a close anatomic proximity between the area of auditory word images and the area of oral motor engrams for letters. If this hypothesis is correct, both systems were damaged in the patient of Kinsbourne and Warrington. Also, this hypothesis would predict that patients with destruction of auditory word images (Wernicke's aphasia) could retain preserved oral spelling. Although patients with Wernicke's aphasia and preserved written spelling have been described (Hier and Mohr, 1977; Roeltgen et al., 1983a), no patients with preserved oral spelling have been described.

Patients and normal subjects produce only one response when spelling orally, similar to what is found with written spelling. Therefore, the outputs from the lexical and phonological systems (Fig. 4-2, pathways 6 and 9) converge prior to programming of verbal output, in a way similar to their convergence prior to programming of graphic output.

THE RELATIONSHIPS OF THE LINGUISTIC AND MOTOR AGRAPHIAS WITH OTHER NEUROPSYCHOLOGICAL DISORDERS

As discussed, some classifications of agraphia are based on associated findings. Although they are not classified in this manner, the agraphias discussed in this chapter are associated with other neuropsychological disorders, such as aphasia, alexia, the Gerstmann syndrome, and ideomotor apraxia. Although not specific, many of the associations between agraphias and other neuropsychological disorders may have an anatomic or physiologic basis. These anatomic and physiologic mechanisms may also provide a means of understanding why these associations are nonspecific.

Phonological Agraphia

Eighteen patients with phonological agraphia have been described (Roeltgen et al., 1983a; Roeltgen, 1983; Roeltgen and Heilman, in press; Shallice, 1981; Bub and Kertesz, 1982; Hatfield, 1982). Seventeen of these patients had aphasia: six Wernicke's, five Broca's, two conduction, two anomic, one global, and one transcortical motor. Except for transcortical motor aphasia, each of these aphasias is typically induced by a perisylvian lesion (Benson, 1979). Phonological agraphia is also due to a perisylvian lesion (the insula or supramarginal gyrus). This shared anatomic relationship rather than the specific type of aphasia may account for the associations between phonological agraphia and the aphasias.

Not only may phonological agraphia be dissociated from aphasia but also in aphasic patients, writing may be dissociated from speech. Two patients with phonological agraphia (Roeltgen et al., 1983a) wrote better than they spoke. This type of dissociation has been previously described in aphasic patients (Weisenberg and McBride, 1964; Mohr et al., 1973; Hier and Mohr, 1977; Assal et al., 1981). Our evaluation suggested that this dissociation occurs because speech depends on the left hemisphere phonological systems, whereas writing may be performed nonphonologically by a lexical system using structures outside the left perisylvian area.

Similarly, disorders of writing and disorders of reading are sometimes dissociable. Neuropsychological models have been proposed for reading, similar to the model for writing discussed here (Beauvois and Dérouesné, 1981; Shallice and Warrington, 1980). The reading models usually contain both a phonological system and a lexical system. Disruption of the phonological system, phonological alexia (dyslexia), is similar in many ways to phonological agraphia. In each of these disorders there is an inability to transcode nonwords. Also, each of these disorders may be accompanied by effects due to imageability and word class with production of semantic paralexias and paragraphias resulting in the syndromes of "deep dyslexia" and "deep dysgraphia." Most patients with phonological agraphia who have alexia, have phonological alexia (Roeltgen, 1983). However, at least one has had no alexia, and one had lexical (or surface) alexia (preserved ability to read nonwords with impaired ability to read irregular words). These findings indicate that phonological agraphia and phonological alexia are dissociable. There are two possible explanations for this dissociation. First, the neuropsychological mechanisms for phonological spelling and phonological reading may represent the same function in opposite directions. The first, phoneme-grapheme conversion, proceeds from sound to sight, and the second, graph-eme-phoneme conversion, from sight to sound. This hypothesis suggests that a single lesion affecting the basic phonological system would disrupt both phonological spelling and reading. One of these systems could become dysfunctional in isolation by disruption of information either as it exits the system or enters the system (Fig. 4-9A). Alternatively, each system may be dissociable from the other and the association or lack of association between phonological agraphia and the alexias might relate to the anatomic pathology of agraphia and alexia (Fig. 4-9B). The anatomic substrate of phonological agraphia appears to be the supramarginal gyrus or insula. It is possible that structures close to this area play an important role in phonological alexia.

In our reported series of 14 patients with phonological agraphia (Roeltgen, 1983) three had other elements of the Gerstmann syndrome (right–left confusion, finger agnosia, or dyscalculia) in addition to agraphia. Also, seven of them had mild or severe ideomotor apraxia. The Gerstmann syndrome has been attributed to lesions in the

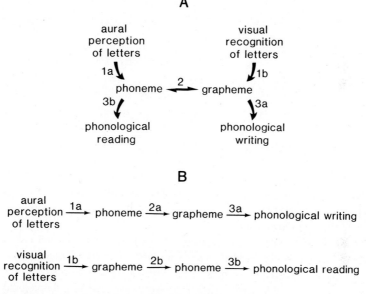

Fig. 4-9. Possible relationships of phonological reading and writing
A. A common phonological system for both reading and writing

Lesion site	Syndrome
1	Phonological agraphia and alexia
2a or 2b	Phonological agraphia
3a or 3b	Phonological alexia

B. Two separate phonological systems, one for reading and one for writing

Lesion site	Syndrome
Any combination of one "a" lesion and one "b" lesion	Phonological agraphia and alexia
1a, 2a, or 3a	Phonological agraphia
1b, 2b, or 3b	Phonological alexia

angular gyrus (Nielson, 1938; Gerstmann, 1940; Roeltgen et al., 1983b) and ideomotor apraxia is frequently attributed to lesions in the dominant parietal lobe (Heilman, 1979). The association of phonological agraphia with these disorders also appears to depend on the anatomic pathology of the lesions. It is probable that phonological agraphia is accompanied by the Gertsmann syndrome and/or ideomotor apraxia when the extent of the lesion is sufficient to involve the anatomic substrates of the Gerstmann functions and praxis.

Eleven of our fourteen patients with phonological agraphia had a presumed ischemic cerebral infarction in the distribution of the middle cerebral artery. The perisylvian aphasias, as well as the Gerstmann syndrome and ideomotor apraxia, also frequently but not invariably follow ischemic disease in the distribution of the middle cerebral artery. Therefore, although these syndromes may have different pathological anatomies, they frequently have a common pathology.

Lexical Agraphia

Six patients with lexical agraphia have been described (Beauvois and Dérouesné, 1981; Roeltgen and Heilman, 1983a; Hatfield and Patterson, 1983). Each of these patients had aphasia. However, the frequency of aphasia types differs from that found in phonological agraphia. Two patients had transcortical sensory aphasia, two had Wernicke's aphasia, and two had anomia. Similar to phonological agraphia, the associations of lexical agraphia with aphasia appear to depend on the underlying pathological anatomy of the syndromes. Transcortical sensory aphasia may be caused by lesions of the posterior parietal region (Heilman et al., 1981; Benson, 1979; Roeltgen et al., 1982b) and Wernicke's aphasia is typically caused by lesions in the posterior superior temporal gyrus (Benson, 1979). Anomia may also be caused by lesions of the angular gyrus (Benson, 1979). Therefore, lexical agraphia, a disorder that can be caused by an angular gyrus lesion, is associated with aphasias caused by lesions in and adjacent to the angular gyrus.

Of the six patients with lexical agraphia, three had lexical (surface) alexia and had difficulty reading as well as writing irregular words. The other three had phonological alexia and had relatively preserved ability to read irregular words but difficulty reading nonwords plus trouble writing irregular words. Similar to phonological agraphia, there are at least two explanations for the dissociation between lexical agraphia and lexial alexia. Either the two lexical systems are subserved by two separate mechanisms or one mechanism common to reading and spelling is disrupted at different levels causing disruption of spelling or reading.

Information about the occurrence of the Gerstmann syndrome and ideomotor apraxia in patients with lexical agraphia is available in only five and four patients, respectively. However, they occur sufficiently often (four of five and three of four) to conclude that these syndromes probably frequently occur together. Given the aforementioned anatomic pathology underlying the Gerstmann syndrome and ideomotor apraxia, it is not unexpected that lexical agraphia, a disorder commonly due to angular gyrus lesions, occurs with them.

Of the six patients described with lexical agraphia, only one had ischemic cerebral vascular disease, and that patient's lesion appeared to be in the distribution of the vascular watershed between the internal carotid and posterior cerebral arteries. Three had cerebral hemorrhages, and two of these had surgical removal of an angioma. The fifth patient had a neoplasm and the sixth had demyelinating disease. In contrast to those patients with phonological agraphia, patients with lexical agraphia have varying etiologies. This, and the relative infrequency of lexical agraphia (probably only one-third as common as phonological agraphia) may be explained by the anatomic locus. Unlike the insula and supramarginal gyrus which are in the center of the area supplied by the middle cerebral artery, the posterior angular gyrus is not in the distribution of any one primary cerebral vessel. Therefore, we might expect that disorders other than occlusive cerebral vascular disease will be the primary etiologies of lexical agraphia.

Semantic Agraphia

Semantic agraphia, in the four patients studied, was associated with transcortical aphasia and poor comprehension (three patients had mixed transcortical aphasia and one had transcortical sensory aphasia). This relationship is not surprising given that the lesions causing semantic agraphia disrupt the semantic system. It is also not surprising that two patients developed what we termed "semantic alexia": fluent, preserved oral reading with absent comprehension (Roeltgen, 1982b). Again this would appear to be secondary to a general disruption of semantics. The alexia in the other two patients is not as easily understood. These patients had trouble reading nonwords and could be classified as having phonological alexia. Since the anatomic substrate of phonological alexia is not known, we cannot be certain as to the relationship between semantic agraphia and phonological alexia.

Other elements of the Gerstmann syndrome, as well as ideomotor apraxia, were noted in the patients with semantic agraphia. However, because of the severe comprehension disturbance in these patients, it is difficult to interpret these results.

Apraxic Agraphia

Apraxic agraphia with ideomotor apraxia is typically associated with aphasia as well as alexia and other elements of the Gerstmann syndrome. However, other associations are not constant because ideomotor apraxia, and therefore agraphia with ideomotor apraxia, may be due to dominant parietal lesions or to lesions anterior to this region (Heilman et al., 1982). In those rare patients with crossed dominance (language in one hemisphere and motor in the other) apraxic agraphia with ideomotor apraxia may occur without aphasia (Heilman et al., 1973; Heilman et al., 1974; Valenstein and Heilman, 1979.)

Agraphia in patients without apraxia has been well described in only two patients (Roeltgen and Heilman, 1983b; Margolin and Binder, in press). Therefore, it is difficult to draw any conclusions regarding the associations of this syndrome with disorders of other neuropsychological functions.

CONCLUSIONS

As can be seen from the small number of cases cited, the neuropsychological classification of the agraphias offer a tentative but promising method of dealing with these
disorders. It complements, rather than supplants, the traditional classifications that
rely on associated neurological findings, such as aphasia, apraxia, or visuospatial disorders, rather than on the strict analysis of writing itself. Neuropsychological analysis
may be of use not only in classifying agraphias, but also in clarifying the brain mechanisms underlying them and perhaps also in pointing toward rational methods of
therapy.

REFERENCES

Aimard, G., Devick, M. Lebel, M., Trouillas, P., and Boisson, D. (1975). Agraphie pure
    (Dynamique?) D'origine Frontale. *Rev. Neurol. 131*:505–512.
Auerbach, S. H. and Alexander, M. P. (1981). Pure agraphia and unilateral optic ataxia asso-
    ciated with a left superior lobule lesion. *J. Neurol. Neurosurg. Psychiat. 44*:430–432.
Assal, G., Buttet, J., and Jolivet, R. (1981). Dissociations in aphasia: a case report. *Brain and
    Lang. 13*:223–240.
Basso, A., Taborelli, A., and Vignollo, L. A. (1978). Dissociated disorders of speaking and
    writing in aphasia. *J. Neurol. Neurosurg. Psychiat. 41*:556–563.
Beauvois, M. F. and Dérouesné, J. (1979). Phonological alexia: three dissociations. *J. Neurol.
    Neursurg. Psychiat. 42*:1115–1124.
Beauvois, M. F. and Dérouesné, J. (1981). Lexical or orthographic agraphia. *Brain. 104*:2–49.
Benson, D. F. (1979). Aphasia, alexia and agraphia. New York: Churchill Livingston.
Bogen, J. E. (1969). The other side of the brain. I. Disgraphia and dyscopia following cerebral
    commissurotomy. *Bull. L.A. Neurol. Soc. 34*:3–105.
Brown, R. and McNeill, D. (1966). The "tip of the tongue" phenomenon. *J. Verbal Learning
    and Verbal Behavior. 5*:325–337.
Bub, D. and Kertesz, A. (1982). Deep agraphia. *Brain and Lang. 17*:146–165.
Chedru, F. and Geschwind N. (1972). Writing disturbances in acute confusional states. *Neu-
    ropsychologia 10*:343–354.
Coltheart, M. (1980). Deep dyslexia: a review of the syndrome. In *Deep Dyslexia*, M. Col-
    theart, K. Patterson, and J. C. Marshall (Eds). London: Rutledge and Kegan Paul.
Ellis, A. W. (1982). Spelling and writing (and reading and speaking). *Normality and Pathol-
    ogy in Cognitive Functions*, A. W. Ellis (Ed). London: Academic Press.
Gersh, F. and Damasio, A. R. (1981). Praxis and writing of the left hand may be served by
    different callosal pathways. *Arch. Neurology 38*:634–636.
Gerstmann, J. (1940). Syndrome of finger agnosia, disorientation for right and left, agraphia
    and acalculia. *Arch. Neurol. Psychia. 44*:398–408.
Geshwind, N. and Kaplan, E. (1962). A human cerebral disconnection syndrome. *Neurology
    12*:675–685.
Goldstein, K. (1948). *Language and language disturbances*. New York: Grune and Stratton.
Grossfeld, M. L. and Clark, L. W. (1983) Nature of spelling errors in transcortical sensory
    aphasia: a case study. *Brain and Lang. 18*:47–56.
Hatfield, F. M. (1982). Visual and phonological factors in acquired dysgraphia. Paper pre-
    sented as a poster to International Neuropsychological Society Symposium, Deauville,
    France.

Hatfield, F. M. and Patterson, K. E. (1983). Phonological spelling. *Quarterly Journal of Experimental Psychology.* 35:451–468.

Head, H. (1926). *Aphasia and Kindred Disorders of Speech.* Cambridge: Cambridge University Press.

Hécaen H. and Albert, M. L. (1978). *Human Neuropsychology.* New York: Wiley.

Heilman, K. M. (1979). Apraxia. In *Clinical Neuropsychology,* K. M. Heilman and Valenstein (Eds) New York: Oxford University Press.

Heilman, K. M., Coyle, J. M., Gonyea, E. F., and Geschwind, N. (1973). Apraxia and agraphia in the left hander. *Brain 96:21–28.*

Heilman, K. M., Gonyea, E. F., and Geschwind, N. (1974). Apraxia and agraphia in a right hander. *Cortex 10:284–288.*

Heilman, K. M., Rothi, L., McFarling, D., and Rottmann, A. L. (1981). Transcortical sensory aphasia with relatively spared spontaneous speech and naming. *Arch. Neurol.* 38:236–239.

Heilman, K. M., Rothi, L., and Valenstein, E. (1982). Two forms of ideomotor apraxia. *Neurology.* 4:342–346.

Heilman, K. M., Tucker, D. M., and Valenstein, E. (1976). A case of mixed transcortical aphasia with intact naming. *Brain 99:415–426.*

Hier, D. B., and Mohr, J. P. (1977). Incongruous oral and written naming. *Brain and Lang.* 4:115–126.

Hotopf, N. (1980). Slips of the pen. In *Cognitive processes in spelling,* U. Frith (Ed). London: Academic Press.

Kaplan, E. and Goodglass, H. (1981). Aphasia-related disorders. In *Acquired Aphasia,* M. T. Sarno (Ed). New York: Academic Press.

Kinsbourne, M. and Warrington, E. K. (1965). A case showing selectively impaired oral spelling. *J. Neurol. Neurosurg. Psychiat.* 28:563–566.

Laine, T. and Marttila R. J. (1981). Pure agraphia: a case study. *Neuropsychologia 19:311–316.*

Leischner. A. (1969). The agraphias. In *Disorders of Speech, Perception and Symbolic Behavior,* P. J. Vinken and G. W. Bruyn (Eds). Amsterdam: North-Holland.

Levy, J., Nebes, R. D., and Sperry, R. W. (1971). Expressive language in the surgically separated minor hemisphere. *Cortex 71:49–58.*

Lichtheim, L. (1885). On aphasia. *Brain 7:433–484.*

Leipmann, H. and Maas. O. (1907). Fall von Linksseitger agraphie und apraxie bei rechtsseitiger lahmung, translated by C. Wirsig and R. T. Watson. *Journal fur psychologie und Neurologie 10:214–227.*

Marcie, P. and Hécaen. (1979). Agraphia, *Clinical Neuropsychology,* 1st ed, K. M. Heilman and E. Valenstein (Eds). New York: Oxford University Press.

Margolin, D. I. and Binder, L. (in press). Multiple component agraphia in a patient with atypical cerebral dominance: on error analysis. *Brain and Lang.*

Mohr, J. P., Sidman, M., Stoddard, L. T., Leichester J., and Rosenberger, P. B. (1973). Evaluation of the defect in total aphasia. *Neurology 23:1302–1312.*

Morton, J. (1980). The logogen model and or orthographic structure. In *Cognitive processes in spelling,* U. Frith (Ed). London: Academic Press.

Nielson, J. M. (1938). Gerstmann syndrome: finger agnosia, agraphia, confusion of right and left and acalculia. *Arch. Neurol. Psychiatry 39:536–559.*

Nielson, J. M. (1946). *Agnosia, Apraxia, Aphasia: Their Value in Cerebral Localization.* New York: Hoeber.

Nolan, K. A. and Caramazza, A (1982). Modality-independent impairments in word processing in a deep dyslexic patient. *Brain and Lang. 16:237–264.*

Ogle, J. W. (1867). Aphasia and agraphia. In Report of the Medical Research Counsel of Saint George's Hospital. London. 2:83–122.

Roeltgen, D. P. (1983). The neurolinguistics of writing: anatomic and neurologic correlates. Paper presented at International Neuropsychological Society Symposium, Mexico City, Mexico.

Roeltgen, D. P. and Heilman, K. M. (1982). Global aphasia with spared lexical writing. Paper presented as poster to International Neuropsychological Society, Pittsburgh, Pa.

Roeltgen, D. P. and Heilman, K. M., (in press). Lexical agraphia, further support for the two-strategy hypothesis of linguistic agraphia *Brain*.

Roeltgen, D. P. and Heilman, K. M. (1983a). The functions of "Wernicke's area." Paper presented at the International Neuropsychological Society, Mexico City, Mexico.

Roeltgen, D. P., and Heilman, K. M., (1983b). Apractic agraphia in a patient with normal praxis. *Brain and Lang. 18:* 35–46.

Roeltgen, D. P., Rothi L., and Heilman, K. M., (1982a). Isolated phonological agraphia from a focal lesion. Paper presented at the Academy of Aphasia, New Paltz, N.Y.

Roeltgen, D. P., Rothi L., and Heilman, K. M., (1982b). Semantic agraphia. Poster presented at the American Neurological Association, Washington, D.C.

Roeltgen, D. P., Sevush S., and Heilman, K. M., (1983a). Phonological agraphia, writing by the lexical-semantic route. *Neurology. 33:*755–765.

Roeltgen, D. P., Sevush S. and Heilman, K. M., (1983b). Pure Gerstmann syndrome from a focal lesion. *Arch Neurol. 40:*46–47.

Rosati, G. and De Bastiani, P. (1979). Pure agraphia: a discreet form of aphasia. *J. Neurol. Neurosurg. Psychiat. 42:*266–269.

Rothi, L. and Heilman, K. M. (1981). Alexia and agraphia with spared spelling and letter recognition abilities. *Brain and Lang. 12:*1–13.

Rubens A. B., Geschwind, N., Mahowald, M. W., and Mastri, A. (1977). Posttraumatic cerebral hemispheric disconnection syndrome. *Arch. Neurol. 34:*750–755.

Saffran, E. M., Bogeyo, L. C., Schwartz, M. F. and Marin, O. S. M. (1980). Does deep dyslexia reflect right-hemispheric reading? In *Deep Dyslexia*, M. Coltheart. K. Patterson and J. C. Marshall. London: Routledge and Kegan Paul.

Shallice, T. (1981). Phonological agraphia and the lexical route in writing. *Brain 104:*412–429.

Shallice, T. and Warrington, E. K. (1980). Single and multiple component central dyslexic syndromes. In *Deep Dyslexia*, M. Coltheart, K. E. Patterson, and J. C. Marshall (Eds). London: Routledge and Kegan Paul.

Sugishita, M., Toyokura, Y., Yoshioka, M., and Yamada, R. (1980). Unilateral agraphia after section of the posterior half of the truncus of the corpus callosum. *Brain and Lang. 9:*212–225.

Valenstein, E. and Heilman K. M. (1979). Apraxic agraphia with neglect-induced paragraphia. *Arch. Neurol. 36:*506–508.

Watson, R. T. and Heilman, K. M. (1983). Callosal apraxia. *Brain. 106:*391–404.

Weisenberg, T. and McBride. K. E. (1964). Types of aphasia: the expressive. In *Aphasia, a Clinical and Psychological Study*, T. Weisenburg and K. E. McBride (Eds). New York: Haffner.

Yamadori, A., Osumi, Y., Ikeda, H., and Kanazawa, Y. (1980). Left unilateral agraphia and tactile anomia. Disturbances seen after occlusion of the anterior cerebral artery. *Arch. Neurol. 37:*88–91.

5
Acalculia

HARVEY S. LEVIN AND PAUL A. SPIERS

HISTORICAL BACKGROUND AND CLASSIFICATION

In 1920 Henschen coined the term "Akalkulia" to describe disturbances in computation following brain damage. Although his report was the first statistical compilation
of a large number of cases, interest in the relationship between calculating ability and
the brain was already a century old by the time Henschen's monograph appeared. In
1808 Gall and Spurzheim postulated the existence of a "calculation centre" in the
brain which they depicted in their phrenological atlas. Based on the examination of
mathematical prodigies, mathematicians, and cases of dementia or retardation where
calculation was preserved, these authors came to the conclusion that "man has an
organ which permits him to come into contact with the laws of mathematics" and
that this organ is located "in a convolution on the most lateral portion of the external,
orbital surface of the anterior lobes." It was not until Broca's work on language in the
1860's that phrenology fell into disfavor and the new methodology emerging at that
time for the study of brain–behavior relationships was extended to include research
on mathematical ability.

Aphasiologists in the second half of the 19th century recognized that their patients
often suffered impaired ability to perform numerical operations and they interpreted
this as an expression of a pervasive linguistic disorder. Lewandowsky and Stadelman
(1908) published the first detailed report of calculation disorder resulting from focal
brain damage in a patient who had a right homonymous hemianopia. They attributed
the difficulties in written and mental calculation to "gaps" in number reading and to
problems in the "optic representation" of numbers, respectively. Lewandowsky and
Stadelman proposed a "specific type of alexia for numbers in which the form and

Preparation of this chapter was supported in part by NS 07377-13, Center for the Study of Nervous
System Injury (first author), and by a Doctoral Fellowship from the Humanities and Social Sciences Coun-
cil (Canada) while the second author was a visiting researcher at the Unite de Recherches Neuropsychologiques et Neurolinguistiques (U.111-INSERM). The inspiration and encouragement for this work were
provided by Dr. Edith Kaplan in Boston, Professor Henry Hécaen in Paris, and Gail Hochanadel. We
are indebted to Professor A. L. Benton for his review of the manuscript and helpful suggestions.

significance of isolated digits are perceived but that at the stage where synthesis is
required for the comprehension of several digits the patient fails." This failure was
apparently related to an inability to apply the learned rules of the positional system.
In the same paper these authors reported that the patient was often unable to recognize arithmetic symbols, though he could still follow the correct procedure for
effecting a computation.

These observations are notable for focusing primarily on disturbances in calculation
ability as distinct from aphasia. Similarly, the authors' description of a specific form
of number alexia departed from the popular conception that alexia and agraphia for
numbers were simply variants of alexia and agraphia for linguistic material. Their
paper was the first to suggest that calculation disorders should be considered the result
of a specific cerebral lesion different from those proposed to account for aphasia. Consistent with their emphasis on visual factors, and their patient's right hemianopia,
Lewandowsky and Stadelman situated the "centre for arithmetic faculties" in the left
occipital region. Henschen (1920) distinguished "akalkulia" from disturbances in
reading and writing numbers, "cipher alexia" and "cipher agraphia," respectively.
Upon reviewing 305 brain-damaged cases of calculation disturbance reported in the
literature and 67 of his own patients, Henschen identified a subgroup of nonaphasic
or mildly aphasic patients in whom calculation disorder was the predominant deficit.
He inferred the existence of a cerebral substrate for arithmetic operations that is anatomically distinct from but proximal to the neural organization of speech and musical
capacity. Although Henschen's analysis of a large series provided convincing evidence
that acalculia can occur independently of aphasia, he neglected to differentiate
defects in oral as opposed to written arithmetic skills and studied only addition and
subtraction.

Hans Berger (1926) proposed a distinction between primary and secondary acalculia on the basis of his observations that certain abilities such as short-term memory
and capacity for sustained attention are necessary to perform calculation problems.
He asserted that primary acalculia cannot be attributed to a more pervasive impairment, though it may occur in association with other deficits which are not sufficiently
severe to disrupt calculation. Secondary acalculia, as he defined it, is an expression of
a severe general disturbance of memory, language, attention, or cognition. Berger
reported that the secondary type is the more common of the acalculias, and is often
among the neuropsychological defects found in patients with diffuse cerebral disease
and in left-hemisphere-damaged patients with receptive aphasia. Mild word-finding
difficulty and paraphasic errors were the main concomitant neuropsychological symptoms in the patients Berger described as manifesting primary acalculia.

More recently, Hécaen et al. (1961) proposed a classification of acquired calculation
disorder based on the mechanism presumed to be responsible for the acalculia.
Although they elucidated the neuropsychological deficits which frequently accompany but do not necessarily produce the various types of acalculia, it is important to
recognize that there is considerable overlap with respect to the associated symptoms.
As will become apparent, exceptional cases of acalculia have been reported that do
not conform to this classification. While recognizing that these categories of acalculia
are not mutually exclusive and that forthcoming research may produce a more useful
classification, we have organized this review according to the categories of acalculia

proposed by Hécaen and his associates for heuristic purposes. Their classification includes:

1. Acalculia associated with alexia and agraphia for numbers which may or may not be accompanied by verbal alexia and agraphia or other aphasic defects.

2. Impaired spatial organization of numbers frequently reflected by misalignment of digits, visual neglect, inversion (e.g., 9 and 6), and reversal errors (e.g., 12 interpreted as 21), and inability to maintain the decimal place. Hécaen et al. designated this disorder as "acalculia of the spatial type."

3. Anarithmetria, i.e., impairment of calculation per se. Of the three types of acalculia, this category corresponds most closely to Berger's primary acalculia. The concept of anarithmetria does not imply an isolated deficit but excludes alexia and agraphia for numbers and spatial disorganization as causes of acalculia.

Nonspecific acalculia contributing to the symptom complex of dementia and developmental disturbance of calculation are not encompassed by this scheme, nor is reduced rate of calculation as a consequence of closed head trauma (Gronwall and Wrightson, 1974).

VARIETIES OF ACALCULIA

Alexia and/or Agraphia for Numbers

Although the acalculia arising from alexia and agraphia for numbers has been referred to as "aphasic acalculia" (Benson and Weir, 1972), Hécaen et al. (1961) found that an aphasic disorder was neither a necessary nor sufficient condition for this type of acalculia. The relationship between alexia for numbers and impaired reading of words was systematically investigated by Henschen (1919, 1925) who found a dissociation in more than 50% of his cases (Table 5-1). Hécaen et al. later confirmed this dissociation and observed a greater frequency of number alexia than in Henschen's material. Table 5-1 shows that agraphia confined to words or numbers was also common to both series of patients, though agraphia for numbers with preserved ability to

Table 5-1. The Relationship Between Alexia and Agraphia for Numbers and Impaired Reading and Writing of Words

Type of Disorder	Henschen, 1919		Hécaen et al., 1961	
	Number	%	Number	%
	$n = 132$		$n = 101$	
Verbal alexia	71	54	23	23
Number alexia	4	3	20	20
Mixed alexia	57	43	58	57
	$n = 105$		$n = 108$	
Verbal agraphia	33	31	24	22
Number agraphia	21	20	13	12
Mixed agraphia	51	49	71	66

write words was more frequent in Henschen's study. The explanation for the disparity between the Henschen and Hécaen findings remains unclear.

Many investigators of acalculia have presumed a unitary expression of number alexia and agraphia, but few studies have addressed this issue by analyzing the pattern of errors. Based on his case material and review of the literature, Kleist (1934) distinguished two forms of number alexia. The first type was the inability to read numbers per se, analogous to literal alexia. In contrast, the second form of number alexia was confined to multidigit numbers which had positional errors (e.g., 205,678 read as "two million, five hundred sixty thousand and seventy eight"). Similarly, he identified two forms of number agraphia. Kleist labeled the first type "ideopraxic," since the patient was totally unable to write numbers or he wrote them in a distorted form. He referred to the second form of agraphia as "constructive" because the patient had positional or grouping errors (e.g., 54 38 instead of 5,438) when writing multidigit numbers. Although confirmation of Kleist's subtypes of number alexia and agraphia awaits future research, the dissociation between written and oral calculation secondary to number alexia has been corroborated (cf. Lindquist, 1936).

The chief neuropsychological correlates of alexia for number (n = 63) found by Hécaen et al. (1961) were aphasia (in 84% of patients), verbal alexia (79%), ideational or ideomotor apraxia (36.5%), visuoconstructive deficit (68%), and general somatognosia (26%). The latter deficit refers to a basic impairment in the appreciation of body schema. It should be noted that aphasia was not confined to the alexic type of acalculia. Visual-field and oculomotor defect and somatosensory impairment were frequent neurological abnormalities though these often accompanied all three types of acalculia. Hécaen et al. characterized the aphasic disorder associated with alexia for numbers as a general disturbance in verbal formulation, though other authors have emphasized the receptive impairment in patients with acalculia (Head, 1926). Paraphasic or paragraphic substitution of numbers may contaminate the calculations by patients with fluent aphasia (Benson and Denckla, 1969) and obscure their relatively preserved capacity for arithmetic operations. Benson and Denckla described a patient with suspected left parietal disease who responded orally to the written problem "4 + 5" with the answer "8"; his written answer was "5," and he chose the correct answer when given a multiple-choice format. Clinicopathological correlation has established that either a lesion of the left hemisphere or bilateral cerebral disease may be responsible for number alexia and agraphia (Hécaen, 1962).

The association between alexia/agraphia for numbers and left hemisphere disease received ample confirmation in a study of patients manifesting this type of acalculia (Hécaen et al., 1961). In a subsequent study, Hécaen (1962) reported that in a series of unselected cases of left hemisphere damage, 37% were alexic and agraphic for numbers as compared to 2% of patients with right hemisphere disease. Figure alexia and aphasia were often found to coexist in patients with bilateral cerebral disease. Acquired aphasia and acalculia were also closely associated in children with left hemisphere damage (Hécaen, 1976). In a seres of 17 left-hemisphere-damaged children of whom 15 were aphasic, 11 patients had a definite acalculia while equivocal acalculia was noted in 3 other aphasic children. Although Hécaen emphasized the persistence of acalculia in these children, he did not elaborate on its qualitative aspects. No child with right hemisphere damage (n = 6) in Hécaen's study showed acalculia.

Alexic acalculia can also result from inability to read arithmetical signs despite relatively preserved comprehension of written numbers. Ferro and Bothelho (1982) described two aphasic patients (anomic and conduction, respectively) with left hemisphere lesions who misnamed arithmetical signs and could neither read nor write them to dictation. Although both patients could copy the signs, neither could match them to corresponding words. In contrast, number reading, writing, and naming were relatively spared as was simple oral calculation. The authors suggested that arithmetic signs are similar to ideographic notation because both consist of signs which have unique and universal value and neither combines into more complex symbols.

Acalculia of the Spatial Type

Manifestations of the "spatial" type of acalculia include improper arrangements of numbers during the initial stage of computation or while summing the partial products of multiplication. However, the principle of calculation is retained as reflected by the relatively preserved calculation of numbers presented orally (Benton, 1963, 1966). Of the 48 cases of spatial acalculia studied by Hécaen et al. (1961), visuoconstructive impairment was present in 94% of the patients, directional confusion in 78%, oculomotor disturbance in 70%, unilateral spatial agnosia in 69%, general spatial agnosia in 62.5%, reading deficit arising from spatial problems in 58%, general cognitive deterioration in 46%, apraxia for dressing in 41.5%, and visual-field defect in 56%. These correlates of the spatial type of acalculia were corroborated in a smaller series of patients (including four cases of unilateral right hemisphere disease) described by Cohn (1961) who observed errors in written multiplication resulting from difficulty in horizontal positioning, vertical alignment, and transposition of numbers (e.g., "31" instead of "13") even in patients who retained multiplication values. Leleux et al. (1979) described similar errors in a mathematics teacher who exhibited impairment of advanced quantitative skills (e.g., algebra, geometry) after he developed a right frontoparietal hematoma. The patient's failure to displace an intermediate multiplication, which was associated with neglect of the left visual field, produced incorrect columnar alignment. Selecting patients with the spatial type of acalculia, Hécaen et al. implicated the role of right hemisphere disease, since this disorder was shown to be rare in patients with lesions confined to the left hemisphere. Bilateral brain disease produced the spatial type of acalculia with a frequency comparable to that of right hemisphere lesions.

Spatial deficit of another type may contribute to disorders of calculation in aphasic patients. Dahmen and colleagues (1982) postulated that patients with Wernicke's aphasia associated with lesions in the left temporoparietal region would exhibit a disproportionately severe impairment on calculation tasks emphasizing spatial capacity (e.g., pointing to an array of circles which corresponds to the numerical value of a set of geometric symbols) as compared to numeric-symbolic tasks (e.g., matching an array of circles to number words or digits). The authors found that patients with Wernicke's aphasia were markedly impaired across all calculation tasks as compared to Broca's aphasics and deviated maximally from normal subjects on those calculation tasks which stressed spatial ability. In contrast, there was only a slight, nonsignificant trend for the performance of patients with Broca's aphasia and control subjects to decline on the spatial calculation tasks. By limiting the arithmetic computation to two-digit numbers and omitting presentation of examples in the usual vertical arrangement, Dahmen et al. were unable to differentiate subtypes of acalculia in their series according to Hécaen's classification. While they did not describe the types of errors produced by their patients, the strategy they employed to study the spatial aspects of calculation warrants further study.

There is general agreement that the spatial type of acalculia, which occurs in patients with unilateral right hemisphere disease and in cases with bilateral lesions, is frequently associated with visuoconstructive impairment and directional confusion. Although the association of specific visuospatial deficit in patients with the spatial type of acalculia is firmly established, Collignon et al. (1977) found that spatial problems were common in a series of 26 cases of acalculia irrespective of the lateralization of lesion. Furthermore, the authors concluded that spatial deficit (e.g., poor visualization) and visuoconstructive impairment were two of the three "instrumental problems" (aphasia being a third) that could cause acalculia. Consequently, the presence of visuospatial deficit per se may not differentiate types of acalculia unless it is a prominent or isolated finding with otherwise minor or absent neuropsychological deficit.

Anarithmetria

Hécaen's definition of anarithmetria excludes impairments in calculation secondary to alexia and agraphia for numbers or spatial disorganization of numbers. Anarithmetria is compatible, however, with other associated neuropsychological deficits which may directly affect calculation. Hécaen et al. (1961) studied 72 cases of anarithmetria and found a pattern similar to that of patients with acalculia secondary to alexia and agraphia for numbers. The correlates and the corresponding percent of patients affected were: aphasia (62.5%), visuoconstructive impairment (61%), general cognitive deterioration (50%), verbal alexia (39%), and directional confusion (37%). Deficits found on neurological examination included visual-field defect (54.5%), oculomotor disturbance (33%), and sensory impairment (37%). Left-sided lesions and bilateral brain disease predominated in the cases of anarithmetria; for every patient with a lesion confined to the minor hemisphere, there were four patients with unilateral left hemisphere damage. This pattern of hemispheric involvement is compatible with the principal concomitant deficts found in patients with anarithmetria.

Consistent with the findings of Hécaen et al. demonstrating the presence of general cognitive deterioration in half of their patients with anarithmetria, Cohn (1961) and Grewel (1952) implicated the role of memory impairment in rendering patients unable to carry numbers or retrieve previously learned muliplication-table values. Although Benson and Weir (1972) considered the possibility that disruption of memory was responsible for the posttraumatic anarithmetria which they described in a case report, there was no quantitative assessment of memory other than digit span (which was intact). The patient of Benson and Weir was mildly alexic and agraphic for words, but neither number nor calculation symbols (e.g., "+") were affected. Conversational speech was nonaphasic, though naming of visually presented objects was hesitant. Counting both forward and backward was preserved, as was counting in series (e.g., by 3's) and in discontinuous groups. Judgment of quantities was mildly impaired (e.g., "36 ft. in a yard"). Both oral and written presentation of computational problems disclosed preservation of addition and subtraction, but the patient was unable to perform multiplication or division regardless of the format used for presentation or the mode of response. Although the patient of Benson and Weir produced individual errors at various points of the multiplication process, the most impressive deficit was observed when he attempted to "carry over" from one column to the other in multidigit multiplication. This aspect of calculation was impaired despite intact spatial organization of the numbers in their appropriate columns. Neurological findings included a right homonymous visual field cut confined to the temporal area; subtle sensory and motor deficits were present over the right extremities and face. Serial radioisotope brain scans indicated focal left parietal brain damage.

LOCALIZATION OF LESION IN THE ACALCULIAS

Clinicoanatomical correlations by Henschen (1919) disclosed that acalculia associated with alexia and agraphia for numbers frequently accompanied global aphasia in patients with extensive left hemisphere disease. Henschen implicated left angular gyrus lesions in patients with alexia and agraphia for numbers who were not globally aphasic. Consistent with the evidence for behavioral dissociation of alexia and agraphia for numbers as opposed to words, Hécaen et al. found that left parietal lesions predominated in the former while left temporal and occipital lesions were primarily involved in the latter. Of the patients with alexia and agraphia for numbers studied by Hécaen, bilateral parietal lobe disease was present nearly as often as lesions confined to the dominant hemisphere. Consequently, inability to read and/or write numbers that is not an artifact of presenting figures to the neglected visual field strongly suggests a left parietal lesion but does not exclude involvement of the right hemisphere.

Similarly, alexia for arithmetical signs with preserved reading of numbers and otherwise intact visual recognition is also associated with a focal left hemisphere lesion (parietal, temporal-occipital). Although the strong association between posterior left hemisphere lesions and an anarithmetria has been corroborated, calculation disorder without spatial deficit has also been reported in rare cases of right hemisphere damage (Collignon et al., 1977; Grafman et al., 1982). Although the localization of lesions in patients with anarithmetria resembles that of alexia and agraphia for numbers, an important distinction may be drawn.

Parietal disease confined to the right hemisphere is a definite, albeit improbable, etiology of anarithmetria, whereas this circumstance is extremely unlikely to produce figure alexia or agraphia (Hécaen et al., 1961). Hécaen et al. found that focal temporal or occipital lesions of the dominant hemisphere were sufficient to cause anarithmetria, whereas this disorder was not present in patients with right hemisphere disease unless the parietal lobe was involved.

The localizing findings for anarithmetria reported by Hécaen were corroborated by Luria (1973) who described qualitative features of calculation disorder in relation to intrahemispheric locus of lesion. Luria found that patients with parieto-occipital lesions were unable to perform arithmetic word problems because of both calculation disorder and difficulty in processing complex grammatical or numerical features. He reported that patients with temporal lobe lesions had difficulty in retaining the elements of the problem and could not use intermediate speech components in reasoning out the solution. However, they were aided by written presentation of the problems because their ability to calculate was intact. Luria observed that patients with frontal lobe damage were unable to solve arithmetic word problems because they frequently failed to perceive the task as a problem and tended to give impulsive responses despite their preserved understanding of the logical-grammatical equations and arithmetical operations. Luria noted that written presentation did not necessarily facilitate performance of patients with frontal lobe lesions. Although he did not specifically investigate the effects of lateralization of injury, the majority of the patients Luria described as exhibiting calculation disturbance had left hemisphere lesions.

Further support for the contribution of left posterior lesions to calculation disorder was provided by a study of patients with focal brain damage who were initially screened to verify that they could read and write numbers (Grafman et al., 1982). Analysis of the number of correct answers and the number of qualitative errors on a written test of all four arithmetic operations disclosed that patients with left posterior lesions were impaired relative to left anterior or right hemisphere lesions even when the test scores were adjusted for differences in language comprehension performance (Token Test scores). The authors concluded that the calculation disturbance of the patients with posterior left hemisphere lesions could not be attributed to linguistic deficit. Unfortunately, they did not assess the presence of spatial acalculia. Warrington (1982) reported a specific decline in efficiency of calculation in a physician with a left parietal intracerebral hematoma.

The spatial type of acalculia suggests a post-Rolandic lesion of the right hemisphere but does not exclude the possibility of bilateral disease (Hécaen et al., 1961). However, spatial acalculia in a patient without evidence of linguistic defect or general cognitive deterioration most likely indicates the presence of a lesion confined to the right hemisphere (Hécaen et al., 1961).

The aggregate of symptoms including agraphia, finger agnosia, and right–left disorientation in addition to acalculia was interpreted by Gerstmann (1940) as a syndrome characterized by disturbance of body schema arising from left parietal lobe disease. The Gerstmann syndrome was subsequently recognized by neurologists as a clinical entity with localizing significance for the posterior parietal region of the dominant hemisphere. However, there has been no consensus with respect to the type of acalculia manifested by patients with the syndrome. Gerstmann (1940) claimed that anarithmetria was a component of the syndrome, whereas the spatial type of acalculia has been implicated by other authors (Critchley, 1953). The clinical features of patients with finger agnosia described by Kinsbourne and Warrington (1963) suggest that they include both patients with acalculia related to alexia and agraphia for numbers and patients with acalculia of the spatial type. That no specific form of acalculia appears to be consistently associated with the Gerstmann syndrome is understandable in view of systematic studies which have shown that the syndrome is part of a constellation of symptoms predominated by aphasia, impaired visuoconstructive capacity, and general cognitive deterioration (Benton, 1977; Poeck and Orgass, 1966).

Although calculation disturbance without aphasia had been reported by Strub and Geschwind (1974), their patient was diagnosed as having presenile dementia and, without the benefit of standardized intellectual assessment, it is difficult to assess the contribution of general cognitive decline. In a more recent report, however, Roeltgen et al. (1983) described a patient whose initial confusion resolved to Gerstmann's tetrad of symptoms. A discrete cortical lesion was demonstrated on CT scan in the superior angular gyrus extending into the superior parietal lobe. Although the authors administered tests which showed that the patient had neither a constructional apraxia nor aphasia, they neither characterized his acalculia nor reported his intellectual functioning.

The debate over the validity of Gerstmann's syndrome is likely to continue so long as patient populations remain unselected in terms of the criteria defining the syndrome and until clearly defined testing procedures are adopted to assess each of the component deficits and to rule out more generalized impairment. More careful analysis and reporting of the calculation disorders in patients supposedly suffering from this syndrome are clearly needed. Similarly, systematic investigations of the other deficits in the Gerstmann tetrad may eventually decide the issue of whether any specific set of symptoms can be associated with a discrete lesion in the dominant angular gyrus.

HEMISPHERIC SPECIALIZATION FOR CALCULATION

An implication of the foregoing localization studies for hemispheric functional asymmetry is that calculation is primarily subserved by the left hemisphere. This possibility was confirmed by Sperry (1968) who demonstrated in commissurotomized patients that computation of groups of pegs presented in sequence was far superior on the right hand as compared to the left hand. Calculation based on inputs to the left hand was limited to addition of sums less than five. Consistent with these findings, electroencephalographic (EEG) recordings in normal subjects performing calculations have shown greater activation of the left hemisphere than the right hemisphere. Shepherd and Gale (1982) found that cortical arousal, as reflected by the relative abundance of alpha and theta activity, was more strongly related to calculation performance when analysis was confined to the left hemisphere recordings as compared to the activity of the nondominant hemisphere. In conformity with these EEG findings, Papanicolaou et al. (in press) showed that evoked potentials recorded from parietal and temporal areas reflected greater activation of the left hemisphere (as compared to a control condition) than the homotopic region of the right hemisphere while dextral adults were engaged in an arithmetic task. These electrophysiological studies lend support to the concept that the left hemisphere is specialized for performing calculation. Further research is necessary to explore regional cerebral activation during a wider range of calculation and mathematical operations.

DEVELOPMENTAL DYSCALCULIA

In comparison with the extensive body of research on developmental dyslexia, relatively few investigators have studied developmental dyscalculia. In fact, there are no widely accepted criteria for the diagnosis of developmental dyscalculia and there is a dearth of information concerning epidemiology, genetic factors, the presence of congenital or postnatal brain injury, and neuropsychological correlates. Guttman (1936) described neuropsychological findings in four children with dyscalculia, including two children of normal intelligence whose condition he referred to as "pure arithmetical disability." One child, a ten-year-old boy, could perform simple addition and subtraction but had no concept of division. He was unable to divide a group of objects into equal portions and he was also deficient in multiplication. The second child, a nine-year-old girl, confused the place values of numbers greater than 100, had difficulty counting in groups greater than 20, and could not accurately estimate the number of objects in a group. Guttman also described other children with calculation disorder who had concomitant neuropsychological and intellectual impairment. He postulated that specific arithmetic disability in children arises from "structural or functional anomalies of the brain."

Since publication of Guttman's findings, investigators have proposed various criteria for diagnosing developmental dyscalculia. The criteria have included the appearance of difficulty in counting and arithmetic at an early age, a profile of psychological test findings which shows a specific disturbance of calculation, but otherwise normal intelligence. Slade and Russell (1971) described four adolescents who had long-standing difficulties in all four arithmetic operations, although impaired multiplication was the most prominent defect. The authors found that these patients had a faulty grasp of the multiplication table. They attempted to compensate for this by breaking down problems into simpler units, gradually approximating the answer or drawing groups of dots which they counted.

Benson and Geschwind (1970) described two children (ages 12 and 13) whose calculation was effortful, hesitant, and uncertain. One of the patients had superior verbal ability in contrast to his average level of visuospatial capacity. He could perform only simple calculations, exhibiting difficulty in column placement in both addition and multiplication. The second patient, who was of borderline-defective intelligence, could not write multidigit numbers to dictation and could calculate only simple addition problems. Both children exhibited elements of the Gerstmann syndrome in addition to constructional deficit.

Guidelines for identification of dyscalculia in children were advanced by Spellacy and Peter (1978) who reviewed their findings in 430 children referred for assessment of learning disability. They defined dyscalculia on the basis of a score on the arithmetic subtest of the Wide Range Achievement Test which fell below the 20th percentile for age in a child who had a Full Scale Wechsler IQ above 80 and no disabling emotional disturbance. Applying this definition, the authors accrued 14 dyscalculics whom they subdivided according to the presence of associated reading disability. They found that dyscalculics who were good readers had poor right–left orientation, whereas dyscalculics who were poor readers evidenced dysgraphia and difficulty in word retrieval (oral word association test). Both groups performed below expectation for age on three-dimensional block construction, drawing designs, perception of embedded figures, and finger identification. Interestingly, none of the children showed deficits confined to the four elements of the Gerstmann syndrome nor did the presence of all four elements "describe a behaviorally homogeneous group" (Spellacy and Peter, 1978, p. 202). Although both groups were within the normal range of intelligence, they fell below the median intellectual level for the schools from which they were drawn. This finding, in combination with other features of these children, led the authors to suggest that developmental dyscalculia may indicate "undiagnosed cerebral impairment."

Saxe and Shaheen (1981) described two nine-year-old boys of normal intelligence who were dyscalculic. Neither child could count adequately to compare the number of objects in two arrays nor could they perform "Piagetian concrete operational tasks" such as liquid conservation and serial ordering of sticks according to their length.

In summary, prospective longitudinal research is necessary to confirm and extend the findings of these studies which implicate a specific developmental disturbance of calculation. The results of case reports and retrospective studies suggest that more than a single type of developmental dyscalculia exists, but a definitive classification and analysis of associated deficits await further research.

CLINICAL ASSESSMENT OF NUMBER OPERATIONS

An important contribution to our understanding and clinical assessment of acalculia was made in 1933 by Singer and Low who reported a detailed study of a case of calculation disorder following carbon monoxide poisoning. Their procedures for elucidating the patient's acalculia, which are still relevant to investigators and clinicians, are reviewed here. Despite six months of remediation and generally well-preserved speech and reading, the patient described by Singer and Low was persistently agraphic for all written material and could not perform oral calculations other than addition of single-digit numbers and rote retrieval of multiplication-table values. Subtraction and division were totally impaired, as the patient failed to enter the digits in proper columnar arrangement. The authors analyzed the pattern of errors in this patient and inferred the presence of several mechanisms contributing to the acalculia:

1. Substitution of one operation for another, e.g., $2 + 3 = 6$, $4 + 2 = 8$. The converse error, i.e., substitution of addition for multiplication, was also observed. Subtraction was spontaneously substituted for addition (e.g., $8 + 2 = 6$), whereas the patient could not perform subtraction on request.
2. Substitution of counting for calculation as shown by $15 + 6 = 16$ and $4 + 7 = 8$.
3. Perseveration of the last digit presented, as in $5 \times 4 = 24$.
4. Giving a reversal of a presented number as an answer, e.g., $13 + 6 = 31$.
5. Impaired immediate retention of components of the problem was inferred when the patient failed to repeat it, i.e., "$2 + 6$" was reported as "2×6." Further testing indicated that defective repetition could not be attributed entirely to decreased digit span; the context of a calculation problem appeared to accentuate repetition errors. Memory for words exceeded that for numbers.

The patient of Singer and Low could count in forward sequence, whereas backward counting was defective. Counting objects arranged in equal groups (e.g., 5 groups of 4 pills) surpassed counting objects in a discontinuous series (e.g., groups of 3, 6, 6, and 5 pills of different color) where the sum exceeded 10 objects. However, the patient was unable to utilize multiplication (e.g., 5×4) instead of counting objects in the continuous series. Reading and writing figures were limited to two-digit numbers. Number concept was relatively preserved, i.e., the patient could correctly state which of two numbers was greater, 304 or 403. However, he could not integrate orally presented single digits (e.g., 1,4,3 into 143) because of spatial errors in "place value."

In contrast to the nonspecific calculation disturbance exhibited by the patient of Singer and Low, the format for presentation of computational problems and mode of response used may determine whether acalculia is detected in some patients. Oral presentation may be expected to facilitate the performance of a patient with spatial acalculia, whereas utilization of a multiple-choice format would reduce the opportunity for paraphasic errors to contaminate the performance of an aphasic patient with intact computational skill. Benton (1963) found that noteworthy inferiority of written as compared to oral calculation occurred in 2% of patients with no brain damage with at least an eighth grade education; 4.5% of patients with left hemisphere disease showed that discrepancy, whereas the pattern was observed in 21% of patients with right hemisphere lesions.

Systematic comparison of oral and written modes of presentation and responding is afforded by the examination of number operations devised by Benton (1963). It consists of 12 brief tests:

1. Appreciation of number values: the patient is asked to state which of two numbers is greater.
2. The patient is asked the value of numbers presented visually and the response is either oral or pointing to the larger of the two numbers.
3. The patient is asked to read numbers aloud.
4. The patient is required to point to written numbers which are named by the examiner.
5. Writing numbers to dictation.
6. Writing numbers from copy.

The preliminary six tests serve to estimate the patient's comprehension of numbers when presented in auditory or visual form in order to evaluate the aphasic component in number operations. Two tests assess counting ability, a prerequisite of arithmetic calculation:

7. The patient is required to count out loud from 1 to 20 from 20 to 1, and to count in 2's from 1 to 20.
8. The patient is required to estimate the number of items in a series of continuous dots and again in a discontinuous series of dots (e.g., four groups of five dots each arranged horizontally).

It is important to note on Test 8 whether the patient utilizes a multiplication strategy in the discontinuous series instead of counting all the dots. Errors on these tests may result from severe memory impairment or unilateral visual inattention in which the errors on Test 8 are lateralized to one side of the page.

9. Oral arithmetic calculation in which simple examples are given using each of the four basic operations.
10. Written arithmetic calculation in which the examples are similar to those given orally.
11. Arithmetic reasoning ability; the Arithmetic Reasoning subtest of the WAIS-R is given.
12. Immediate memory for calculation problems. (This test is a component of Test 9 and serves as a control to ascertain whether a memory deficit is responsible for inability to perform calculation problems given orally.)

Assessment of the aphasic component of acalculia is provided by the tests which require the patient to read, aurally comprehend, and write numbers.

However, number alexia and agraphia may be present without major language deficit. Analysis of the patient's errors in written calculation can show misidentification of arithmetical signs as the primary source of calculation errors. Inability to read, name, or write arithmetic signs to dictation may be present despite preserved reading and writing of words and numbers (Ferro and Botelho, 1980). Spatial aspects of acalculia are reflected by reversals in reading or pointing to numbers (e.g., "12" instead of "21"); columns of numbers are frequently misaligned. Numbers appearing in an area of visual neglect may be omitted by the patient. Patients with parietal disease may produce numbers which drift vertically across the lines and they may find writing the digits difficult. A suggested modification of Tests 9 and 10 is providing the patient with a multiple-choice format for half of the questions in each test, as well as distinguishing between problems which require computation (like $42 - 25$) and those which depend solely on the retrieval of basic number facts (e.g., $8 - 3$) or table values (4×7, $28/4$).

Warrington (1982) found that response speed (e.g., percent of long-latency responses) and accuracy of oral calculation were sensitive measures of subclinical or mild calculation disorder, particularly when she related these measures to the manipulation required to solve the arithmetic problems (e.g., difference between the whole and remainder or subtrahend). She also tested rapid estimation of two- and three-digit calculation problems and obtained numeric cognitive estimates (e.g., How tall is the average woman?). These procedures can disclose laborious and inaccurate calculations in patients who retain quantitative concepts and knowledge of individual numbers.

Individually administered tests of achievement in mathematics, which have been standardized for children and adolescents according to age and grade, are available. The Wide Range Achievement Test or WRAT (Jastak and Jastak, 1965) and the Peabody Individual Achievement Test or PIAT (Dunn and Markwardt, 1970) are useful if the pattern of errors is examined qualitatively for indications of a particular type of acalculia. The WRAT includes preliminary questions to assess counting, number concept, and written calculation problems ranging in difficulty from simple addition to college-level mathematics. In contrast, the PIAT utilizes a multiple-choice format to evaluate number concept, counting (e.g., "point to the number which comes just before 100") and number operations presented in a mixture of verbal problems and examples using numbers. Problems on the PIAT appear in large print and may be presented concurrently in both written and oral modes. Although the PIAT is less likely to reflect paraphasic errors, it is important to consider any systematic neglect of answers given in one or the other visual half-field and to concurrently obtain oral responses from nonaphasic patients.

Administration of either the WRAT or PIAT permits direct comparison of arithmetic calculation with proficiency in reading and spelling. The standardized tests are used for screening purposes but more qualitative individualized assessment (both written and oral) is necessary to differentiate various types of errors.

RECENT FORMULATIONS OF CALCULATION DISORDER

While Hécaen and colleagues' (1961) categories provide a useful schema around which to organize our current knowledge of calculation disorders, they are neither mutually exclusive and exhaustive nor do they represent the only attempt at classification in this field. Grewel (1952, 1969) postulated that disorders of calculation result from disruption of a symbolic-semantic system, the components and principles of which are clearly definable. As such, errors in calculation depend on both the method of calculation and its notation system, as well as on the location and extent of injury to the neural substrate. Grewel, therefore, adopted Berger's (1926) overall classification of primary and secondary acalculia but expanded on the former category by postulating asymbolic (inability to use numbers reliably) and asyntactic (inability to combine numbers correctly according to the computational rules governing calculation) forms of primary acalculia. He did not link these to a specific localization. Grewel's formulation emphasizes the contribution of the calculation system itself to the deficits manifested by patients and implies that there is no unitary concept of acalculia or single localization of a cortical lesion which is responsible for calculation disorders.

More recently, Mazzuchi and colleagues (1976) proposed a functional hierarchy for calculation abilities. The foundation of the hierarchy is provided by counting and knowledge of basic mathematical table values. Next are the four elementary calculation operations which are divided into two levels: (1) addition and subtraction, (2) multiplication and division. Following this is the level of fixed algebraic and geometric rules which are independent of elementary calculation, and at the highest level is the ability to analyze and program mathematical data in order to solve problems. The authors refer to this hierarchy in their analysis of a residual calculation disorder in a patient who had partially recovered from global aphasia. Because their patient experienced frequent errors in number reading and writing and exhibited difficulty in retrieving basic number facts and calculations, Mazzuchi et al. inferred the presence of deficits at several levels of the hierarchy. Further study is necessary to characterize the relationship among the levels of function in this hierarchy and to determine whether the deficits exhibited by other thoroughly examined patients may be successfully classified within its categories.

In another recent study, Collignon and colleagues (1977) concluded that acalculia does not exist as a distinctive deficit in the sense implied by Grewel's (1969) primary category or Hécaen and colleagues' (1961) anarithmetria. Based on an analysis of the calculation abilities of patients with lateralized lesions and the frequency with which they had associated cognitive deficits, Collignon et al. proposed that acalculia is always a secondary problem and falls into three categories. The first is acalculia secondary to one of three "instrumental problems" that include aphasia, spatial disorders, and constructional apraxia. Second is acalculia as a result of some combination of these three problems, and third is acalculia due to generalized intellectual deterioration. In effect, then, the classification of Collignon's group challenges the notion that calculation is a separate cognitive function and reduces it to the level of a skilled performance based on the efficient use of more fundamental, presumably localizable functions.

Bresson et al. (1972) embraced a similar strategy in their categorization of calculation errors according to lesion lateralization. They found that errors in number facts and incorrect carrying or borrowing were characteristic of patients with left hemisphere lesions, whereas errors in place value and misalignment of columns or intermediate product errors in multiplication were most common in cases of right hemisphere lesions. They found that most other calculation errors occurred with similar frequency in left and right unilateral lesion groups.

Clearly, there is no unitary deficit that warrants the diagnosis of acalculia and which can be specifically lateralized and localized. However, it is probably the case that the calculation system may be disrupted in various ways for which there will be corresponding specifiable lesions. By this definition, calculation is as much a "function" as language. Certainly, there is no unitary aphasia or lesion localization that produces a generalized language disturbance. Rather, this function is differentially disrupted by compromise in its various neural substrates which produce different patterns of language errors. Recent studies where patients' performances and patterns of error on calculation tasks have been analyzed in greater detail (Bresson et al., 1972; Benson and Denckla, 1969; Benson and Weir, 1972; Leleux et al., 1979; Warrington, 1982) suggest that such a perspective is also correct for understanding the status of calculation as a higher cognitive function. Most encouraging in this respect is a recent study by Warrington which deserves to be discussed in some detail.

Warrington (1982) studied a physician whose language fully recovered within one month of a left posterior parieto-occipital intracerebral hematoma which had produced an acute aphasia. The patient exhibited a residual decline in efficiency and accuracy of calculation for all oral and written arithmetical operations, whereas his capacity to follow procedural rules (e.g., borrowing) in solutions to mathematical problems, provide numerical cognitive estimates (e.g., how tall is the average English woman?), and select the larger of two numbers were relatively well preserved. Whenever the patient produced errors, they closely approximated the correct response. Warrington concluded that her patient demonstrated a "dissociation between arithmetical processing in general and accurate arithmetical computations (p. 46)." Furthermore, she suggested that this patient had a specific reduction in the accessibility of arithmetical facts despite his use of a processing strategy similar to that of a normal adult.

In her discussion, Warrington refutes any notion that this patient's calculation disorder could be attributed to deficits in language, constructional ability, or fundamental number knowledge. Furthermore, the rules of the calculation operations per se were intact. According to Warrington, then, this case demonstrates several points. First, it is possible to demonstrate a dissociation between arithmetical processing in general and accurate retrieval of specific computational values. Second, numeracy (calculation) represents a major category of semantic knowledge within which it is possible to identify various subcategories that may become inoperative. Warrington's report adds to the evidence that the left hemisphere is preferentially involved in mediating the fundamental calculation process.

In summary, recent contributions to the classification of acalculia show a trend toward more detailed analysis of errors. When combined with improved methods of lesion localization by CT and new techniques to measure regional cerebral blood flow and metabolism, the cerebral organization of calculation may be better understood.

SUMMARY

Acquired disorders of calculation may be divided into three categories: acalculia secondary to alexia and agraphia for numbers, acalculia resulting from spatial disorganization of numbers, and anarithmetria or impaired calculation in the strict sense. Review of the literature provides empirical confirmation of the dissociation between alexia for words as compared to numbers and shows that the three types of acalculia are often associated with distinct patterns of cerebral lesions. Further study of anarithmetria is necessary to elucidate its mechanisms and localization. Cerebral activation techniques are beginning to elucidate hemispheric dominance for calculation in normal persons.

REFERENCES

Benson, D. F. and Denckla, M. B. (1969). Verbal paraphasia as a source of calculation disturbance. *Arch. Neurol.* 21:96–102.

Benson, D. F. and Geschwind, N. (1970). Developmental Gerstmann syndrome. *Neurology* 20:293–298.

Benson, D. F. and Weir, W. F. (1972). Acalculia: acquired anarithmetria. *Cortex* 8:465–472.

Benton, A. L. (1963) *Assessment of Number Operations.* Iowa City: University of Iowa Hospitals, Department of Neurology.

Benton, A. L. (1966). *Problemi di Neuropsicologia.* Firenze: Editrice Universitaria.

Benton, A. L. (1977). Reflections on the Gerstmann syndrome. *Brain and Lang.* 4:45–62.

Berger, H. (1926). Ueber rechenstorungen bei herderkrankungen des Grosshirns. *Archive fuer Psychiatrie und Nervenkrankheiten* 78:238–263.

Bresson, F., DeSchonen, S., and Tzortzis, C. (1972). Étude des perturbations dans des performances logico-arithmétiques chez des sujets atteints de diverses lesions cérébrales. *Langages* 7:108–122.

Cohn, R. (1961). Dyscalculia. *Arch. Neurol.* 4:301–307.

Collignon, R., Leclerq, C., and Mahy, J. (1977). Etude de la sémiologie des troubles du calcul observés au cours des lesions corticales. *Acta Neurologique Belgique* 77: 257–275.

Critchley, M. (1953). *The Parietal Lobes*. London: Arnold.

Dahmen, W., Hartje, W., Bussing, A., and Sturm, W. (1982). Disorders of calculation in aphasic patients—spatial and verbal components. *Neuropsychologia 20:* 145–153.

Dunn, L. M. and Markwardt, F. C. (1970). *Manual for the Peabody Individual Achievement Test*, Circle Pines, Minnesota: American Guidance Service.

Ferro, J. M. and Botelho, M. A. S. (1980). Alexia for arithmetical signs. A cause of disturbed calculation. *Cortex 16:*175–180.

Gall, F. J. and Spurzheim, J. C. (1967). [Recherches sur le système nerveux en général et sur celui du cerveau en particulier. Amsterdam: E. J. Bonset (originally published 1808).

Gerstmann, J. (1940). Syndrome of finger agnosia, disorientation for right and left, agraphia and acalculia. *Arch Neurol. Psychiat.* 44:398–408.

Grafman, J., Passafiume, D., Faglioni, P., and Boller, F. (1982). Calculation disturbances in adults with focal hemispheric damage. *Cortex 18:*37–50.

Grewel, F. (1952), Acalculia. *Brain* 75:397–407.

Grewel, F. (1969). The acalculias. In *Handbook of Clinical Neurology*, (Vol. 3, P. J. Vinken and G. Bruyn (eds). Amsterdam: North Holland.

Gronwall, D. and Wrightson, P. (1974). Delayed recovery of intellectual function after minor head injury. *Lancet* 2:7881, 606–609.

Guttman, E. (1936). Congenital arithmetic disability and acalculia. *Br J. Med. Psychol.* 16:16–365.

Head, H. (1926). *Aphasia and the Kindred Disorders of Speech*. Cambridge: Cambridge University Press.

Hécaen, H. (1962). Clinical symptomatology in right and left hemispheric lesions. In *Inter-hemispheric Relations and Cerebral Dominance*, V. B. Mountcastle (Ed). Baltimore: Johns Hopkins Press.

Hécaen, H. (1976). Acquired aphasia in children and the ontogenesis of hemispheric functional specialization. *Brain and Lang.* 3:114–134.

Hécaen, H., Angelergues, R., and Houillier, S. (1961). Les varietes cliniques des acalculies au cours des lesions retrorolandiques: approche statistique du probleme. *Revue Neurologique 105:*85–103.

Henschen, S. E. (1925). Clinical and anatomical contributions on brain pathology *Arch. Neurol. Psychiat.* W. F. Schaller (trans). 13:226–249 (originally published 1919).

Jastak, J. F. and Jastak, S. R. (1965). *Manual for the Wide Range Achievement Test*. Wilmington, Del.: Guidance Associates of Delaware.

Kinsbourne, M. and Warrington, E. K. (1963). The developmental Gerstmann syndrome. *Arch. Neurol.* 8:490–501.

Kleist, K. (1934) *Gehrinpathologie*. Leipzig: J. Barth.

Leleux, C., Kaiser, G., and LeBrun, Y. (1979). Dyscalculia in a right-handed teacher of mathematics with right cerebral damage. In *Problems of Aphasia. Neurolinguistics*, Vol. 9, R. Hoops and Y. LeBrun (eds). Lisse: Swets and Zeitlinger.

Lewandowsky, M. and Stadelmann, E. (1908). Ueber einen bemerkenswerten Fall von Hirnblutung und über Rechenstörungen bei Herderkrankung des Gehirns. *Zeit. f. Neurol. Psychiat.*, 2:249–65.

Lindquist, T. (1936). De L'acalculie. *Acta Medica Scandinavica* 38:217–277.

Luria, A. R. (1973). *The Working Brain: An Introduction to Neuropsychology*, London: Penguin-Allen Lane.

Mazzuchi, A., Manzoni, G. C., Mainini, P., and Parma, M. (1976). Il problema dell'acalculia: studio di un caso. *Rivista Neurologica 46*:2, 102–115.

Papanicolaou, A. C., Schmidt, A. L., Moore, B. D., and Eisenberg, H. M. (1983) Cerebral activation patterns in an arithmetic and a visuospatial processing task. *Intern. J. Neurosci. 20*:283–288.

Poeck, K. and Orgass, B. (1966). Gerstmann's syndrome and aphasia. *Cortex 2*:421–437.

Roeltgen, D. P., Sevush, S., and Heilman, K. M. (1983). Pure Gerstmann's syndrome from a focal lesion. *Arch. Neurol. 40*:46–47.

Saxe, G. B. and Shaheen, S. (1981). Piagetian theory and the atypical case: an analysis of the developmental Gerstmann syndrome. *J. Learn. Disabil. 14*:131–135.

Shepherd, R. and Gale, A. (1982). EEG correlates of hemisphere differences during a rapid calculation task. *J. Psychol. 73*:73–84.

Singer, H. D. and Low, A. A. (1933). Acalculia. *Arch. Neurol. Psychiat. 29*:467–498.

Slade, P. D. and Russell, G. F. M. (1971). Developmental dyscalculia: brief report on four cases. *Psychol. Med. 1*:292–298.

Spellacy, F. and Peter, B. (1978). Dyscalculia and elements of the developmental Gerstmann syndrome in school children. *Cortex 14*:197–206.

Sperry, R. W. (1968). Mental unity following surgical disconnection of the cerebral hemispheres. *The Harvey Lecture Series 62*:293–323.

Spiers, P. A. (1983). *Acalculia: Review and Reformulation*. Unpublished doctoral dissertation, Clark University.

Strub, R. and Geschwind, N. (1974). Gerstmann Syndrome without aphasia. *Cortex 10*:378–387.

Warrington, E. K. (1982). The fractionation of arithmetical skills: single case study. *Quart. J. Exp. Psychol. 34A*:31–51.

6

Body Schema Disturbances: Finger Agnosia and Right–Left Disorientation

ARTHUR BENTON

The behavioral deficits discussed in this chapter are conventionally classified as disorders of the "body schema" (or "body image"). This concept arose out of diverse neurological and psychiatric observations that seemed to be most readily explained by hypothesizing the existence of a long-standing spatially organized model of one's body that provided a framework within which perceptual, motor, and judgmental reactions directed toward one's body occur. The phantom-limb phenomenon, for example, was interpreted as reflecting the determining influence of the amputee's schema of an intact body on his perceptual responses. Conversely, impairment of the body schema resulting from brain disease was hypothesized by Pick (1908) to explain the gross errors made by some patients in pointing to parts of their body on verbal command (termed autotopagnosia). Head (1920) explained normal and defective somatosensory localization on the basis of organized representational models of one's body which he called "schemata."

> Such schemata modify the impressions produced by incoming sensory impulses in such a way that the final sensations of position, or of locality, rise into consciousness charged with a relation to something that has happened before. Destruction of such "schemata" by a lesion of the cortex renders impossible all recognition of posture or of the locality of a stimulated spot in the affected part of the body. (Head, 1920, pp. 607–8)

Head postulated the existence of a number of different types of schemata, the main ones being (1) postural schemata that underlie position sense and appreciation of the direction of movement and (2) body surface schemata that furnish the background for tactile point localization and two-point discrimination.

The "body schema" has never been defined in a standard way: each author presents his own view of what he means by it. To some the concept represents the conscious awareness of the body, but to others it is a form of unconscious memory or representation. To some authors (Pick, for example) it was essentially a visual representation. but Head thought primarily in terms of a constantly changing somatosensory organization against which the character of current stimulation was judged.

Nor is it clear that the concept possesses any real explanatory value. Decades ago, Oldfield and Zangwill (1942–43) discussed the many points that were ambiguous and obscure in Head's formulation. Subsequently, the topic was critically evaluated by Benton (1959) and Poeck (1963, 1969; Poeck and Orgass, 1967) who concluded that the "body schema" is merely a label for perceptual and localizing responses related to one's body. Indeed, Poeck (1975) has placed disturbances of the body schema in a category of "neuropsychological symptoms without specific significance."

However, the "body schema" is a useful label. Dissociation in level of performance with respect to one's body as compared to objects in external space is often observed. For example, many patients with visuospatial defects, such as inaccurate object localization, show intact capacity to localize the parts of their own body, including the fingers (Hécaen and Angelergues 1963). Similarly, most patients with impaired right–left discrimination or finger localization show intact orientation to objects in external space (Benton, 1959; De Renzi, 1982). Aphasic patients may show a more severe disability in understanding the names of body parts as compared to their understanding of the names of other classes of objects (Goodglass, et al., 1966; Yamadori and Albert, 1973). Thus a distinction between performances relating to the body and those relating to external space is justified.

FINGER AGNOSIA

This term was coined by Gerstmann (1924) to denote impairment in the ability to identify the fingers of either one's own hand or those of another person. He regarded the disability as the behavioral expression of a partial dissolution of the body schema and he made it the core symptom in the aggregate of deficits (finger agnosia, agraphia, acalculia, right–left disorientation) that has come to be known as the Gerstmann syndrome.

There is ample evidence that finger agnosia is not a unitary disability but rather a collective term for diverse types of defective performances relating to identification of the fingers (cf. Schilder, 1931; Benton, 1959; Ettlinger, 1963; Critchley, 1966). These performances can be classified along a number of dimensions, e.g., whether the stimulus to be responded to is verbal, visual, or tactile, whether the required response is verbal or nonverbal, whether the task involves localizing fingers on one's own hand or their representation on a two-dimensional model of the hand. It is also important to differentiate between bilateral and unilateral disturbances of finger recognition. Gerstmann meant by "finger agnosia" an impairment in finger identification on both hands. However, defective localization of tactile stimulation of the fingers of one hand in association with other types of samatosensory impairment in that hand is a recognized sign of unilateral brain disease (cf. Head, 1920; Gainotti and Tiacci, 1973).

There is also some doubt about the validity of Gerstmann's assumption that finger agnosia represents a partial dissolution of the body schema. As De Renzi (1982) has pointed out, autotopagnosic patients, who cannot point to their body parts (e.g., nose, mouth, eyes) on verbal command and who presumably suffer from a gross dissolution of the body schema, may still be able to localize their fingers accurately.

Developmental Aspects

The development of finger recognition in preschool children has been studied in detail by Lefford et al. (1974) who demonstrated that performance level was a function of the stimulus characteristics and response requirements of the specific tasks that were presented and that, within the age range of three to five years, performance on each task showed a regular developmental course.

The easiest task was pointing to fingers that the examiner touched as the child watched him: 73% of the three-year-old children, 93% of the four-year-olds, and 99% of the five-year-olds showed successful performance. Localizing fingers which the examiner pointed to (but did not touch) was about as easy (63, 98, and 99% success at three, four, and five years, respectively). But purely tactile recognition (i.e., identifying touched fingers without the aid of vision) was more difficult for the children (24, 63, and 72% success at three, four, and five years, respectively). Still more difficult was tactile localization of touched fingers on a schematic representation of the hand instead of the child's own hand (Fig. 6-1). Only 11% of the three-year-old children, 28% of the four-year-olds, and 52% of the five-year-olds succeeded on this task.

Lefford et al. analyzed the performances of the children in terms of intrasensory differentiation (tactile-visual localization), intersensory integration (tactile localization), and the capacity for representational thinking (localization on a model). Their findings made it evident that different tasks present different age-related cognitive demands.

Fig. 6-1. Arrangement for tactile localization of fingers on a schematic representation of the hand.

The normative observations of Benton (1955, 1959) on school children may be viewed as an extension of those of Lefford et al.

Three tasks were presented to children in the age range of six to nine: (1) with the hand visible, identification of single fingers touched by the examiner; (2) with the hand hidden from view, identification of single fingers touched by the examiner; (3) with the hand hidden from view, identification of pairs of fingers simultaneously touched by the examiner. In the purely tactile tasks, an outline drawing of the right or left hand, with the thumb and fingers numbered from 1 to 5, was placed before the child who could identify the stimulated finger or fingers by naming them, pointing to them, or calling out their number (Fig. 6-1).

Virtually all six-year-olds performed adequately on the tactile-visual task. The other two types of finger localization involving identification of touched fingers on a model showed a progressive development with age. The more difficult task was, of course, the identification of simultaneously stimulated pairs of fingers, a task which a substantial proportion of nine-year-old children performed inaccurately. The studies of Wake (cf. Benton et al., 1983) extended these normative observations with the finding that at the age of 12 years, the tactile localization of simultaneously stimulated pairs of fingers had not yet reached the level of performance of adults.

Clearly there are aspects of finger recognition that call on cognitive skills which reach maturity only after the age of 12 years. One of these skills appears to be visuospatial representational thinking, as reflected in making localizations on an external schematic model in place of one's own hand. There are also indications that the verbal encoding of sensory information may play a significant role in the performances of young school children (cf. Stone and Robinson, 1968; Lindgren, 1978).

Behavioral Correlates

Since different tasks having to do with the identification of the fingers make demands on different cognitive capacities, it is evident that there is no such entity as a unitary "finger agnosia." Consequently, in discussing the clinical or pathological correlates of impairment in finger recognition, it is necessary to specify the particular tasks employed to assess the capacity.

Utilizing a nonverbal task in which mentally retarded subjects identified touched fingers (with their hand hidden from view) by pointing to them with the contralateral hand, Matthews et al. (1966) found a closer association between performance level and Wechsler-Bellevue Performance Scale IQ than Verbal Scale IQ. This relationship was confirmed in patients with brain disease by Poeck and Orgass (1969) who assessed diverse aspects of finger recognition with verbal and nonverbal tests. The correlation coefficient of nonverbal tactile localization on a schematic model with the WAIS Performance Scale IQ was .53 while the corresponding correlation coefficient for the WAIS Verbal Scale IQ was .34. On the other hand, performance on verbal tests of finger recognition (identification on verbal command, visual naming, tactile naming) correlated somewhat more closely with the WAIS Verbal Scale IQ (mean $r = .58$) than with the WAIS Performance Scale IQ (mean $r = .52$). Poeck and Orgass found further that the verbal tests of finger recognition formed a highly intercorrelated cluster (mean r = .72) while nonverbal test performance showed a more modest association with these verbal tests (mean r = .47).

Poeck and Orgass also assessed the relationship between finger recognition performance and scores on other verbal (rote memory, Token Test) and nonverbal (recognition memory for designs) tests. The mean correlation coefficient between verbal finger recognition and the verbal tests was .48, while the correlation coefficient between verbal finger recognition and the nonverbal test was .36. Nonverbal finger recognition did not show this differential relationship with verbal and nonverbal abilities, the correlation coefficient with the verbal tests being .31 and that with the visual memory test being .32.

Studying nine patients with impairment in finger recognition as assessed by nonverbal tests, Kinsbourne and Warrington (1962) found that every patient showed some degree of visuoconstructive disability. Only two patients in the group were clinically aphasic. However, eight of the nine patients were judged to show mild to severe general mental impairment.

Thus the available correlational data indicate that it is useful to distinguish between defects in finger recognition elicited by tasks requiring naming of fingers or their identification when the name is given and those elicited by tasks requiring manual localization of fingers subjected to sensory stimulation. Both types of disability show a significant association with both linguistic and visuoperceptive impairment. But the verbal disability is somewhat more closely correlated with linguistic impairment and the nonverbal disability is somewhat more closely associated with visuoperceptive impairment.

Defective finger recognition may be shown by deviant children in different diagnostic categories. Some mental retardates are grossly defective, performing far below the level that would be predicted from their mental ages (cf. Strauss and Werner, 1938; Benton, 1955b, 1959). Giving a finger localization test to small samples of brain-injured, emotionally disturbed and normal children who had been matched for age and WISC IQ, Clawson (1962) found that 80% of the brain-injured children performed at a level exceeded by 90% of the normal and emotionally disturbed children.

Finger Agnosia and Reading Disability

The empirical evidence on the question of a relationship between finger recognition and reading achievement in children is conflicting (cf. Benton, 1975). To the degree that there is a concurrent association, it is more likely to be stronger among younger school-age children than among older ones (Benton, 1962; Fletcher et al., 1982; Sparrow and Satz, 1970). It is also possible that lateral differences in finger recognition are related to reading achievement (Fletcher et al., 1982; Reed, 1967). However, there are indications that the finger localization performances of kindergarten children are a significant predictor of their subsequent reading achievement, particularly in the early school grades (Fletcher et al., 1982; Lindgren, 1978). It is not clear why finger recognition should possess this predictive significance and specifically whether it is the body schema component of performance that is the important variable (cf. Benton, 1979). As has been pointed out, "finger recognition" is only a collective name for a series of tasks having to do with the identification of the fingers, each of which may make specific demands on different abilities such as intrasensory discrimination, inter-sensory integration, perceptual-representational processes, and verbal coding. The analysis of Fletcher et al., (1982) indicates that these different task performances load on different factors and that each may make a specific contribution to the prediction of reading achievement at different grade levels.

Anatomical Correlates

When Gerstmann first described finger agnosia, he placed the causative lesion for the disability at the parieto-occipital junction around the angular gyrus of the left hemi-sphere. It was in this area that visual and somatosensory information was integrated to provide the basis for an intact and well-integrated body image. Subsequent study indicated that this localization was much more precise than was warranted by the facts: finger agnosia, in one form or another, was encountered in patients with lesions in the temporal and frontal lobes as well as in the posterior parietal area. At the same time, Gerstmann's localization of the responsible lesion in the left hemisphere was generally supported. For example, studying diverse performances in patients with unilateral brain disease, Hécaen (1962) found that finger agnosia was shown by 20% of patients with left hemisphere lesions, but by only 3% of those with right hemi-sphere lesions.

However, more recent investigative work has cast considerable doubt on the assumption of a specific correlation between the disability and left hemisphere dis-ease. The association of finger agnosia with side-of-lesion seems to be dependent, first, on whether the disability is manifested in verbal or nonverbal form and, second, on the presence or absence of aphasia and general mental impairment. The findings of two studies that explored these relationships in detail will be described.

Sauguet et al. (1971) assessed both verbal and nonverbal finger recognition in patients with unilateral brain disease. The three verbal tests were naming the fingers, pointing to fingers named by the examiner, and pointing to fingers which the exam-iner had designated by number. The two nonverbal tests were indicating the fingers touched by the examiner and the inter-digital object identification test of Kinsbourne and Warrington (1962). Three groups of right-handed patients were studied: nona-phasic with right hemisphere lesions; nonaphasic (or only expressive speech disorder without oral comprehension difficulties) with left hemisphere lesions, aphasic (with oral comprehension difficulties) with left-hemisphere lesions. Of an original sample of 94 patients, 14 (15%) were excluded from consideration either because they appeared confused or they showed clinical and/or psychometric evidence of signifi-cant general mental impairment.

The results of the study may be summarized as follows: (1) naming of the fingers and their identification by pointing when their name was called out were closely asso-ciated with receptive aphasic disorder; about two-thirds of the patients with receptive language impairment showed defective verbal finger recognition, as compared to about 10% of patients in the other groups; (2) impaired performance on nonverbal tests of finger recognition was shown only by patients with receptive aphasic disorder, the frequency of failure ranging from 20 to 30%. Thus the predominant influence of linguistic impairment on performance in patients who are free from general mental impairment was evident.

Gainotti et al. (1972) studied nonverbal finger recognition in right-handed patients with unilateral brain disease. The relative frequency of bilateral impairment was about equal in the patients with left hemisphere (18%) and right hemisphere (16%) lesions. Further analysis showed that most of the left hemisphere patients who performed defectively were aphasic and that the right hemisphere patients who performed defectively showed clinical and/or psychometric evidence of general mental impairment (Table 6-1).

A number of conclusions emerge when the findings of these two studies are considered together. Impairment in finger recognition is closely associated with aphasic disorder or general mental impairment in patients with left hemisphere disease. Impairment in finger recognition is closely associated with general mental impairment in patients with right hemisphere disease. Since patients with general mental impairment were excluded from consideration in the study of Sauguet et al., this relationship was not evident in that study but it is quite clear in the results of Gainotti et al. Finally, neither aphasic disorder nor general mental impairment can be considered to be solely responsible for the occurrence of impairment in finger recognition. Many aphasic patients showed intact finger recognition, even on the task of finger naming, as did many mentally deteriorated patients.

Summary

Thus it appears that, imbedded as it is within a setting of either aphasic disorder or general mental impairment, finger agnosia does not represent a specific cognitive deficit or have a specific localizing significance. The question remains as to why some aphasic and mentally impaired patients show the disability in one or another form and others do not. One proposed explanation is that somatosensory defect, interacting with aphasic or mental impairment, plays a role in the production of the disability (cf. Benton, 1959; Selecki and Herron, 1965; Gainotti et al., 1972). This possibility deserves to be explored.

Table 6-1. Finger Agnosia in Patients with Unilateral Lesions

Left hemisphere lesions (n = 88)	*16 (18%)*
Mentally deteriorated (n = 30)	10 (33%)
Not mentally deteriorated (n = 58)	6 (10%)
Aphasic (n = 34)	13 (38%)
Not aphasic (n = 54)	3 (6%)
Right hemisphere lesions (n = 74)	*12 (16%)*
Mentally deteriorated (n = 22)	10 (45%)
Not mentally deteriorated (n = 52)	2 (4%)

°Adapted from Gainotti et al. (1972).

RIGHT–LEFT DISORIENTATION

Inability to identify the right and left sides of one's body or that of the confronting examiner is a familiar symptom to neurologists. First described as one aspect of the picture of general mental impairment associated with diffuse disease, the disability attracted greater interest from a diagnostic and theoretical standpoint when Head (1926), Bonhoeffer (1923), and Gerstmann (1924, 1930) showed that it could also occur as a consequence of disease of the left hemisphere.

"Right–left disorientation" is a very broad concept, even broader than "finger agnosia." It refers not to one ability, but to a number of performances on different levels of complexity, each making demands on different cognitive abilities and types of response. Naming, executing movements to verbal command, or imitation of movements may be called for. The execution of commands involving the identification of a single lateral body part or of commands involving the identification of more than one lateral body part may be required. The patients may be requested to identify his own body parts, those of the confronting examiner, or a combination of the two. Hence, meaningful assessment of "right–left orientation" requires that it be analyzed into operationally defined components or levels.

An example of such an analysis is presented in Table 6-2. Some of the types of performance listed in the table stand in a rather definite hierarchical relationship to

Table 6-2. Components of Right–Left Orientation

I. ORIENTATION TOWARD ONE'S OWN BODY
  A. Naming single lateral body parts touched by examiner
  B. Pointing to single lateral body parts on verbal command
  C. Executing double *uncrossed* movements on verbal command (e.g., touching *left* ear with *left* hand)
  D. Executing double *crossed* movements on verbal command (e.g., touching *right* ear with *left* hand)

II. ORIENTATION TOWARD ONE'S OWN BODY WITHOUT VISUAL GUIDANCE (BLIND-FOLDED OR EYES CLOSED)
  A. Naming single lateral body parts touched by examiner
  B. Pointing to single lateral body parts on verbal command
  C. Executing double *uncrossed* movements on verbal command (e.g., touching *left* ear with *left* hand)
  D. Executing double *crossed* movements on verbal command (e.g., touching *right* ear with *left* hand)

III. ORIENTATION TOWARD CONFRONTING EXAMINER OR PICTURE
  A. Naming single lateral body parts
  B. Pointing to single lateral body parts on verbal command
  C. Imitating uncrossed movements of examiner (e.g., *left* hand on *left* ear)
  D. Imitating crossed movements of examiner (e.g., *left* hand on *right* ear)

IV. COMBINED ORIENTATION TOWARD ONE'S OWN BODY AND CONFRONTING PERSON
  A. Placing either left or right hand on specified part of confronting person on verbal command (e.g., placing right hand on confronting person's left ear)

each other. The ability to point to single lateral body parts (IB) is prerequisite for success in the execution of double commands (IC, D). The ability to execute double uncrossed commands (IC) is prerequisite for success on crossed commands (ID). The ability to point correctly to the body parts of the confronting examiner (IIIB) is prerequisite for successful combined orientation (IVA). Other performances are qualitatively different from each other and patients may show dissociation, failing in naming but not in pointing or imitation or vice versa (cf. Sauguet et al., 1971; Dennis, 1976).

Developmental Aspects

Many five-year-old children and the majority of six-year-olds are able to identify single lateral parts of their body in terms of "right" and "left," (Terman, 1916; Benton, 1959; Belmont and Birch, 1963). However, they are likely to make errors in the execution of double commands, particularly "crossed" commands. In the latter instance, failure to cross the midline is the most frequent type of error (e.g., the child touches his left ear with his left hand in response to the command to touch his right ear with his left hand). Some children perform decidedly less well with their eyes closed than with their eyes open. Most of them fail to make the necessary 180 degrees reversal in orientation in pointing to lateral body parts of the confronting examiner.

The ability to execute double commands develops rapidly after the age of six years and it is unusual to encounter a nine-year-old who has difficulty in executing these commands. The difference in level of performance under the "eyes open" and "eyes closed" conditions also disappears with advancing age. However, some nine-year-old children evidently are not aware of the relativistic nature of the right–left concept, for they fail to make the necessary 180 degrees reorientation in pointing to the lateral body parts of the confronting examiner. Moreover, a majority of them still make errors in executing tasks involving both the "own body" and "confronting persons" systems of orientation, i.e., placing their right (or left) hand on a specified lateral body part of the confronting examiner (cf. Benton and Kemble, 1960). By the age of 12 years, practically all normal children perform successfully in identifying body parts of the confronting examiner and in combined orientation tasks.

Occasionally a child who shows a systematic reversal in response to instructions will be encountered. Such a child will show his left hand when asked to show his right hand and touch his right ear with his left hand when asked to touch his left ear with his right hand. The consistency of his responses indicates that the child is quite capable of discriminating between the two sides of his body. At the same time, it is clear that he has attached the wrong verbal labels to the two sides. Not surprisingly, many of these children prove to be relatively deficient in the development of language skills (Benton, 1958; Benton and Kemble, 1960).

Basis of Right–Left Orientation

When one considers the nature of these right–left discrimination tasks, it is evident that they make demands on a number of cognitive abilities. There is a verbal element in performance since the child must understand the verbal labels of "right" and "left" before he can apply them to the sides of his body and he must retain these labels in mind long enough to execute double commands. Of course, right–left orientation can be assessed by nonverbal performances, such as imitation tasks, as well as verbal performance.

[Another form of nonverbal "right–left orientation" is operationally expressed in the localization of stimulation to the right or left side of the body. Disturbances in this capacity, particularly lateral mislocalization of tactile stimulation (allesthesia, allochiria), have been described and a variety of explanations have been proposed to account for them (cf. Bender, 1952; Benton, 1959). However, the relationship between these disturbances and right–left disorientation, as conventionally defined, is a tenuous one. It is true that a few brain-diseased or hysterical patients who showed both types of impairment have been described (Jones, 1907; Seidemann, 1932; Bender, 1952; Hécaen and Ajuriaguerra, 1952). But most patients who show right–left disorientation do not show allesthesia; conversely, allesthesia, particularly when it appears in the context of spinal cord or brainstem disease, is not accompanied by right–left disorientation.]

A second component is sensory in nature. The labels of "right" and "left" are applied (or misapplied, as in systematic reversal) to a distinction between the sides of the body which necessarily involves a sensory discrimination. The basis for this distinction is not immediately obvious. The supposition is that it is primarily of a somesthetic nature, consisting of a continuous asymmetric pattern of sensory excitation from the muscles and joints of the two sides of the body (Benton, 1959; Benton and Kemble, 1960). Presumably this difference in excitation between the two sides of the body provides a right–left gradient of excitation which forms the basis for the intuitive awareness of a difference between the sides which most (but not all) normal persons possess. This awareness is often verbalized in terms of the right side being felt as larger, heavier, and stronger than the left.

When this gradient develops in young children is not known. It is probably related to some degree to the establishment of unilateral manual preference (cf. Elze, 1924; Benton and Menefee, 1957). However, there are normal right-handed adults who admit to having difficulty in the immediate discrimination between right and left and who report a lack of any intuitive feeling of a difference between the two sides of the body. The study of Wolf (1973), in which physicians and their spouses were asked how often they experienced difficulty when they had to identify right and left quickly, provides data on sex differences in "right–left blindness," as Elze (1924) called it. Two percent of the men and 5% of the women reported that they experienced such difficulty "all the time." Another 7% of the men and 13% of the women reported "frequent" difficulty. Similar findings have been reported by Harris and Gitterman (1978).

A third component is of a conceptual nature. Correct identification of the lateral body parts of a confronting person and simultaneous manipulation of the "own body" and "confronting person" orientational systems requires thorough understanding of the relativistic nature of the right–left concept.

Finally, a fourth element is the visuospatial component which is brought into play when pointing to lateral body parts of a confronting person or to objects on the left or right. Some of the more complex tests of right–left orientation, such as those of

Thurstone (1938), Culver (1969), Kao and Li (1939), and Money (1965) make strong demands on visuospatial abilities.

Impairment in Patients with Brain Disease

Apart from the earliest observations of defective performance in demented patients, right–left disorientation has been traditionally associated with the presence of disease of the left hemisphere and aphasic disorders. A particularly important early contribution was that of Bonhoeffer (1923) who described a patient with a left temporoparietal lesion who showed marked right–left disorientation. He was aphasic and showed some impairment in oral language understanding, but his disability in right–left performances was disproportionally severe. However, he also showed a variety of somesthetic disturbances in the right arm and hand—impaired tactile localization, position sense, stereognosis, barognosis, and graphesthesis—raising the question of whether his right–left disorientation might be the product of an interaction between his sensory and linguistic impairments.

Head (1926) found that defective performance was so frequent in his aphasic patients that he incorporated both verbal and nonverbal tests of right–left orientation as measures of "symbolic formulation and expression" in his aphasia examination. Later confirmation of the association between left hemisphere disease and right–left disorientation is found in the observations of Gerstmann (1939) and McFie and Zangwill (1960). Gerstmann related the disability (along with finger agnosia) to dysfunction of the left parieto-occipital region. McFie and Zangwill found defective right–left orientation in five of eight patients with left hemisphere lesions; in contrast, not a single patient in the group of 21 with right hemisphere lesions showed the disability.

Sauguet et al. (1971) investigated the relationship of various forms of right–left disorientation to side-of-lesion and the presence of aphasic disorder in patients with unilateral lesions. The major findings were:

1. With respect to orientation to their own body, nonaphasic patients with lesions in either hemisphere performed adequately while two-thirds of those patients with left hemisphere disease who had impaired language understanding performed defectively, primarily in the execution of double commands.
2. Identification of single body parts of the confronting examiner was performed defectively by about 50% of the patients with left hemisphere disease who had impaired language understanding but also by 13% of the nonaphasic patients with right hemisphere disease; all nonaphasic patients with left hemisphere disease performed adequately.
3. The imitation of lateral movements (the head-eye-ear items of Head's battery) was performed defectively by aphasic patients with left hemisphere disease (48%) and by nonaphasic patients with right hemisphere disease (32%); 14% of the nonaphasic patients with left hemisphere disease also performed defectively.

Thus the findings indicated that the hemispheric contribution to right–left orientation depends on what aspect of it is assessed. Impairment in "own body" performances is shown by aphasic patients with left hemisphere disease, but is rarely seen in nonaphasic patients. On the other hand, nonaphasic patients with right hemisphere lesions, as well as aphasic patients, may show defects both in "confronting person" performances and in imitating right–left movements.

"Right–left disorientation" in patients with the syndrome of lateral neglect also needs to be considered. Many of these patients show a unilateral disability, so to speak, in that they will consistently fail to point to body parts on the neglected side or to point to parts of the confronting examiner corresponding spatially to the neglected side of their body.

Concluding Comments

It is clear that, in general, right–left disorientation is closely connected with impairment of language comprehension in patients with unilateral brain disease. This holds for nonverbal performances, such as imitation, as well as for performances that clearly demand understanding of the labels "right" and "left." Thus is appears that Head (1926) was correct in his assumption that even the imitation of lateralized movements involves verbal mediation.

It is equally clear that some forms of right–left disorientation are associated with the presence of right hemisphere disease. The tasks on which these patients fail are the identification of the body parts of a confronting person and the imitation of lateralized movements. It seems likely that visuospatial disability is the essential basis for failing performance in these nonaphasic patients. This is best regarded as a hypothesis for empirical test.

With the exception of severe dements, nonaphasic patients with general mental impairment typically perform adequately when identifying their own body parts but fail on "confronting person" and "combined orientation" tasks. Here one suspects that the conceptual demands of these tasks, rather than the linguistic or visuospatial, pose particular difficulties for the patient.

There remains the question of why some aphasic patients show failure on relatively simple right–left orientation tasks, while others with equally severe linguistic defects do not. As Bonhoeffer (1923) intimated and as Benton (1959) and Selecki and Herron (1965) have proposed, the observed failure perhaps reflects the outcome of aphasic disorder combined with sensory disturbances, the latter having the effect of attenuating the asymmetric pattern of somesthetic excitation that underlies the discrimination of right and left.

REFERENCES

Belmont, L. and Birch, H. G. (1963). Lateral dominance and right–left awareness in normal children. *Child Dev.* 34:257–270.

Bender, M. B. (1952). *Disorders in Perception*. Springfield, Ill.: C. C. Thomas.

Benton, A. L. (1955a). Development of finger-localization capacity in school children. *Child Dev.* 26:225–230.

Benton, A. L. (1955b). Right–left discrimination and finger localization in defective children. *Arch. Neurol. Psychiat.* 74:583–589.

Benton, A. L. (1958). Significance of systematic reversal in right–left discrimination. *Acta Psychiat. Neurol. Scand.* 33:129–137.

Benton, A. L. (1959). *Right–Left Discrimination and Finger Localization: Development and Pathology.* New York: Hoeber-Harper.

Benton, A. L. and Kemble, J. D. (1960). Right–left orientation and reading ability. *P sychiat. Neurol. (Basel)* 139:49–60.

Benton, A. L. (1962). Dyslexia in relation to form perception and directional sense. In *Reading Disability*, J. Money (ed). Baltimore: Johns Hopkins Press.

Benton, A. L. (1975). Developmental dyslexia: neurological aspects. In *Advances in Neurology*, Vol. 7, W. Friedlander (ed). New York: Raven Press.

Benton, A. L., Hamsher, K., Varney, N. R., and Spreen, O. (1983). Contributions to Neuropsychological Assessment. New York: Oxford University Press.

Benton, A. L. and Menefee, F. L. (1957). Handedness and right–left discrimination. *Child Dev.* 28:237–242.

Bonhoeffer, K. (1923). Zur Klinik und Lokalization des Agrammatismus und der Rechts-Links-Desorientierung. *Monatsschr. f. Psychiat. u. Neurol.* 54:11–42.

Clawson, A. (1962). Relationship of psychological tests to cerebral disorders in children. *Psychol. Rep.* 10:187–190.

Critchley, M. (1966). The enigma of Gerstmann's syndrome. *Brain* 89:183–198.

Culver, C. M. (1969). Test of right–left discrimination. *Percept. Motor Skills* 29:863–867.

Dennis, M. (1976). Dissociated naming and locating of body parts after left temporal lobe resection. *Brain and Lang.* 3:147–163.

De Renzi, E. (1982). *Disorders of Space Exploration and Cognition.* New York: Wiley.

Elze, C. (1924). Rechtslinksempfinden und Rechtslinksblindheit. *Zeitschrift für angewandte Psychologie* 24:129–135.

Ettlinger, G. (1963). Defective identification of fingers. *Neuropsychologia* 1:39–45.

Fletcher, J. M., Taylor, H. G., Morris, R., and Satz, P. (1982). Finger recognition skills and reading achievement: a developmental neuropsychological perspective. *Dev. Psychol.* 18:124–132.

Gainotti, G., Cianchetti, C., and Tiacci, C. (1972). The influence of hemispheric side of lesion on nonverbal tests of finger localization. *Cortex* 8:364–381.

Gainotti. G. and Tiacci, C. (1973). The unilateral forms of finger agnosia. *Confinia Neurol.* 35:271–284.

Gerstmann, J. (1924). Fingeragnosie: cine umschriebene Störung der Orientierung am eigenen Körper. *Wiener Klinische Wochenschrift* 37:1010–1012.

Gerstmann, J. (1930). Zur Symptomatologie der Hirnläsionen im Uebergangsgebiet der unteren parietal-und mittleren. Occipitalwindung. *Nervenarzt* 3:691–695.

Goodglass, H., Klein, B., Carey, P., and Jones, K. (1966). Specific semantic word categories in aphasia. *Cortex* 2:74–89.

Harris, L. J. and Gitterman, S. R. (1978). University professors' self-descriptions of left–right confusability: sex and handedness differences. *Percept. Motor Skills* 47:819–823.

Head, H. (1920). *Studies in Neurology.* London: Oxford University Press.

Head, H. (1926). *Aphasia and Kindred Disorders of Speech.* Cambridge, England: Cambridge University Press.

Hécaen, H. (1962). Clinical symptomatology in right and left hemispheric lesions. In *Interhemispheric Relations and Cerebral Dominance*, V. B. Mountcastle (ed). Baltimore: Johns Hopkins Press.

Hécaen, H. and de Ajuriaguerra, J. (1952). *Méconnaissances et Hallucinations Corporelles.* Paris: Masson.

Hécaen, H. and Angelergues, R. (1963). *La Cécité Psychique.* Paris: Masson.

Jones, E. (1907). The precise diagnostic value of allochiria. *Brain* 30:490–532.

Kao, C. C. and Li, M. Y. (1939). Tests of finger orientation: methods for testing right–left differentiation and finger identification. In *Neuropsychiatry in China*, R. S. Lyman (ed). Peking: Henri Vetch.

Kinsbourne, M. and Warrington, E. K. (1962). A study of finger agnosia. *Brain* 85:47–66.

Lefford, A., Birch, H. G., and Green, G. (1974). The perceptual and cognitive bases for finger localization and selection finger movement in preschool children. *Child Dev.* 45:335–343.

Lindgren, S. (1978). Finger localization and the prediction of reading disability. *Cortex* 14:87–101.

Matthews, C. G., Folk, E. G., and Zerfas, P. G. (1966). Lateralized finger localization deficits and differential Wechsler-Bellevue results in retardates. *Am. J. Mental Deficiency* 70:695–702.

McFie, J. and Zangwill, O. L. (1960). Visual-constructive disabilities associated with lesions of the left hemisphere. *Brain* 83:243–260.

Money, J. (1965). *A Standardized Road-Map Test of Directional Sense*. Baltimore: Johns Hopkins Press.

Oldfield, R. C. and Zangwill, O. L. (1942–43). Head's concept of the schema and its application in contemporary British psychology. *Br. J. Psychol.* 32:267–286; 33:58–64, 113–129, 143–149.

Pick, A. (1908). Ueber Störungen der Orientierung am eigenen Körper. *Arbeiten aus den Deutschen Psychiatrischen Universitäts-Klinik in Prag*. Berlin: Karger.

Poeck, K. (1963). Die Modellvorstellung des Körperschemas. *Deutsche Zeitschrift fur Nervenheilkunde* 187:472–477.

Poeck, K. (1969). Modern trends in neuropsychology. In *Contributions to Clinical Neuropsychology*, A. L. Benton (ed). Chicago: Aldine.

Poeck, K. (1975). Neuropsychologische Symptomen ohne eigenstaendliche Bedeutung. *Aktuelle Neurologie* 2:199–208.

Poeck, K. and Orgass, B. (1967). *Ueber Störungen der Rechts-Links Oreintierung*. *Nervenarzt* 28:285–291.

Poeck, K. and Orgass, B. (1969). An experimental investigation of finger agnosia. *Neurology* 19:801–807.

Reed, J. C. (1967). Lateralized finger agnosia and reading achievement at ages 6 and 10. *Child Dev.* 38:213–220.

Sauguet, J., Benton, A. L., and Hécaen, H. (1971). Disturbances of the body schema in relation to language impairment and hemispheric locus of lesion. *J. Neurol. Nuerosurg. Psychiat.* 34:496–501.

Schilder, P. (1931). Fingeragnosie, Fingerapraxie, Fingeraphasie. *Nervenarzi* 4:625–629.

Seidemann, H. (1932). Cerebrale Luftemboilie mach Pneumothoraxfüllung. (Rechts-Links-Störung. Fingeragnosie, Rechenstörung). *Zentralblatt für Neurologie und Psychiatrie* 63:729–731.

Selecki, B. R. and Herron, J. T. (1965). Disturbances of the verbal body image: a particular form of sensory aphasia. *J. Nerv. Ment. Dis.* 141:42–52.

Sparrow, S. and Satz (1970). Dyslexia, laterality and neuropsychological development. In *Specific Reading Disability*, D. J. Bakker and P. Satz (eds). Rotterdam: Rotterdam University Press.

Stone, F. B. and Robinson, D. (1968). The effect of response mode on finger localization errors. *Cortex* 4:233–244.

Strauss, A. A. and Werner, H. (1938). Deficiency in the finger schema in relation to arithmetic disability. *Am. J. Orthopsychiat.* 8:719–725.

Terman, L. M. (1916). *The Measurement of Intelligence*. Boston: Houghton Mifflin.

Thurstone, L. L. (1938). *Primary Mental Abilities*. Chicago: University of Chicago Press.

Wolf, S. M. (1973). Difficulties in right–left discrimination in a normal population. *Arch. Neurol.* 29:128–129.

Yamadori, A. and Albert, M. L. (1973). Word category aphasia. *Cortex* 9:112–125.

7

Apraxia

KENNETH M. HEILMAN AND LESLIE J. GONZALEZ ROTHI

DEFINITION

The relation of apraxia to more elementary disorders of skilled movement is similar to the relation of aphasia to more elementary disorders of speech (such as dysarthria). But the definition of apraxic disturbances is more difficult even than the definition of aphasia, since the distinguishing features of movement have not been adequately described. Whereas the aphasic's linguistic errors can be quite precisely described, the abnormalities of movement of the apraxic patient cannot be similarly noted or described. Operationally, therefore, apraxia has been defined by exclusion. It is a disorder of skilled movement not caused by weakness, akinesia, deafferentation, abnormal tone or posture, movement disorders (such as tremors or chorea), intellectual deterioration, poor comprehension, or uncooperativeness. A variety of errors may characterize the apraxic patient's performance and these errors help define the variety of apraxias seen in the clinic. This chapter will be limited to descriptions of limb-kinetic apraxia, ideomotor apraxia, disconnection and disassociation apraxias, ideational apraxia, and buccofacial apraxia. Constructional and dressing apraxia are discussed in Chap. 8, and apraxic agraphia is discussed in Chap. 4. Gait apraxia is not discussed.

EXAMINATION AND TESTING

Differential Diagnosis

Since apraxia is defined by excluding other disorders of movement, a thorough neurological examination is required. This examination will serve to exclude weakness or deafferentation (sensory loss) as a cause of abnormal movements. In addition, diseases that affect either the basal ganglia or the cerebellum (that typically do not cause weakness or sensory change) can be associated with nonapraxic disorders of movement. But disorders of the basal ganglia and cerebellum are also manifested by

131

changes in posture and tone, and by tremors, dysmetria, or stereotypic movements, that are evident on neurological examination. If motor, sensory, basal ganglia, or cerebellar signs are limited to one side, the normal side can still be tested for apraxia. If the abnormality is mild enough to permit use of the affected extremity, it should also be tested. In this case, the examiner will make allowance for the underlying disorder in judging whether apraxia is present.

Many apraxic patients are also aphasic, and language disorders are sometimes difficult to distinguish from apraxic disorders. Patients may be thought to be apraxic when they fail to make an appropriate movement in response to a command. However, a patient who also cannot correctly answer yes/no questions or pointing commands probably has a language comprehension disturbance. Conversely, apraxic patients with aphasia are occasionally mistakenly thought to have a comprehension disorder. It is important to test aphasic patients not only with commands such as "stick out your tongue" or "show me how you would throw a ball," but also with questions that can be answered by pointing or with yes/no responses such as "point to the ceiling," or "are you in the hospital." If a patient performs poorly when given limb or buccofacial commands but can answer questions that require yes/no responses or can accurately describe the movement task he was asked to perform the patient may not have a comprehension disturbance but may be apraxic. Athough a portion of the aphasic's abnormal performance may be attributed to aphasia, the clinician should remember that a comprehension disturbance does not preclude the possibility that the patient also has an apraxic disturbance, since both symptoms frequently coexist.

Typically, apraxic patients use body parts as objects or make spatial errors, but these movements can be recognized as having the correct intent. If a patient with a mild language comprehension disturbance uses a body part as the object or makes a clumsy but recognizable movement in response to a command, then the errors are of movement formation and are not language related, and should not be attributed to comprehension disturbance.

Methods

It is rare for patients to spontaneously complain of apraxic disturbances. There are several possible explanations for this. Apraxic patients may be anosognosic. They are frequently also aphasic and have a right hemiparesis, and they may therefore attribute their clumsiness to use of their nondominant hand (i.e., they think their left hand is clumsy because they are not accustomed to using it). Furthermore, apraxia is usually mildest when a patient uses actual objects and most severe with pantomime. Since patients at home are rarely called upon to use pantomime, they and their families are often not aware of this disorder. Therefore, in diagnosing apraxia, one cannot rely on history but must test patients.

In testing for apraxia, there are four ways to assess patient performance: (1) gesture ("Show me how you would ———."), (2) imitation of gesture ("Watch how I ———, then you do it."), (3) use of an actual object ("Here is a ———, show me how you would use it."). and (4) imitation of examiner using the object. The act may be performed by either the limb (e.g., hand) or face (buccofacial). The movement may be either an emblem (an arbitrarily coded nonverbal communicative hand move-

such as "OK") or pantomime (the pretended manipulation of an object). It may be an isolated act (i.e., "blow out a match") or a series of acts. Table 7-1 is a list of apraxia tests.

Frequently, when patients perform pantomimed tasks, they use a body part as the object. They may perform in this manner either because they do not understand that they are supposed to pantomime (i.e., they are using the body part as a symbol of the object) or because they cannot perform the task even though they understand it. If a patient uses a body part as the object, his performance should be corrected (e.g., "Do not use your finger as a key. Make believe you are really holding a key."). If verbal instructions do not help, the examiner should demonstrate the correct pantomime. If the patient still uses body part as object, this is strongly suggestive of apraxia.

The examiner should test both hands when possible. If one hand is severely paretic, the nonparetic hand should be tested. The type of errors made by the patient should be noted (e.g., body part as object, spatial orientation error, sequencing error, wrong movement, imprecision, or other).

Goodglass and Kaplan (1972) recommended testing movements with real objects only if patients failed to command (pantomime). Since some forms of apraxia are defined by an isolated difficulty with the use of actual objects, we recommend testing the use of actual objects even when pantomime is performed correctly. Normal adults should not have difficulty with any of the acts listed in Table 7-1.

Comprehension of movement commands may also be tested by (1) asking the patient to describe what he was asked to do, (2) having the patient point to the object (from an array of objects) which he would use to perform a specific action, and (3) having the examiner perform a series of actions and having the patient pick out the correct act. Not infrequently, patients with severe language comprehension disturbances have a defect in language decoding but still comprehend gestures and pictures.

In addition to observing a patient's performance, the clinician should ascertain if a patient is disturbed by his own errors or if he even can recognize these as errors. In addition, the examiner should determine if a patient who is making apraxic errors can distinguish (when the examiner performs) incorrect from correct movements

Table 7-1

Limb gesture	Buccofacial gesture
1. Wave goodbye	1. Stick out tongue
2. Hitchhike	2. Blow a kiss
3. Salute	Buccofacial manipulation
4. Beckon "come here"	1. Blow out a match
5. Stop	2. Suck on a straw
6. Go	Serial acts
Limb manipulation	1. Clean pipe, put in tobacco, and light pipe
1. Open a door with a key	2. Fold letter, put it in envelope, seal
2. Flip a coin	envelope, and place stamp on it
3. Open a catsup bottle	
4. Use a screwdriver	
5. Use a hammer	
6. Use scissors	

(e.g., the examiner asks, "Am I flipping a coin?" while pantomiming opening a door with a key). The patient should also be tested to see if he can distinguish well-executed movements from poorly executed movements (e.g., the patient uses his finger as a screwdriver and the examiner asks, "Is this the way to use a screwdriver?").

VARIETIES OF LIMB APRAXIA

Because of the diverse nature of the apraxias, each will be discussed separately.

Limb-Kinetic Apraxia

Patients with limb-kinetic apraxia are incapable of making fine precise movements with the limb contralateral to a central nervous system lesion. The disorder is more obvious when testing distal movements (finger movements) than proximal movements and is especially evident when the patient makes rapid finger movements such as tapping. The movement abnormality can be seen when the patient pantomimes, imitates, or uses objects. In the clinic we ask patients to pick up a dime from a flat surface. Patients with limb-kinetic apraxia may not be able to perform the necessary pinching movement with their thumb and index finger and instead will slip the dime off the table and grasp the coin between their fingers and their palm. When asked to gesture, the patient makes movements that, although lacking precision, are accurately selected sequences correctly oriented in space.

The neuroanatomic correlates of limb-kinetic apraxia are unclear. Liepmann (1920) postulated that lesions in the sensory motor cortex may induce this disorder. It has been demonstrated, however, that pyramidal lesions in monkeys can cause clumsiness that is not completely accounted for by weakness or by change in tone or posture (Lawrence and Kuypers, 1968). This suggests, therefore, that the clumsiness seen in patients with limb-kinetic apraxia may be induced by pyramidal lesions. The role of the premotor regions in the pathogenesis of limb-kinetic apraxia is also unclear. Unfortunately, many patients with lesions of premotor and motor cortex have tone and posture changes that make testing for limb-kinetic apraxia difficult.

Ideomotor Apraxia

Unlike patients with limb-kinetic apraxia, patients with ideomotor apraxia have difficulty with the selection, sequencing, and spatial orientation of movements involved in gestures including emblems and pantomimes. They have greatest difficulty when asked to make believe they are using a tool or instrument (Haaland, personal communication). They may improve their performance by imitating, but frequently gesture to imitation is defective. Similarly, improvement may be noted when the actual object is used but often performance remains defective.

The types of errors made by patients with ideomotor apraxia are difficult to classify. Often these patients use a body part as the object, in spite of repeatedly being reminded to act as if they were actually holding and using the object. They occasionally make errors in sequencing the various movements required for the complete act.

Lastly, they make spatial errors such as orienting their fingers and hands incorrectly in space or in relation to other parts of the body.

Although in 1866 Hughlings Jackson (cited by Taylor, 1932) described patients with normal strength who were unable to perform voluntary skilled movements, it was primarily Liepmann (Liepmann and Maas, 1907; Liepmann, 1905) who initiated interest in ideomotor apraxia.

CALLOSAL LESIONS (INTERHEMISPHERIC)

Liepmann and Maas (1907) studied a patient with right hemiplegia who performed poorly when attempting to carry out verbal commands with his left hand. On post-mortem examination he was found to have a lesion in the left basis pontis, which accounted for his right hemiplegia, and an infarction of the corpus callosum, which spared the splenium. The callosal lesion could produce abnormalities of skilled movement by disconnecting the language areas in the left hemisphere (Wernicke, 1874) from the motor areas in the right hemisphere that control fine movements of the left hand. It was apparent to Liepmann and Maas, however, that their patient's deficit could not be fully explained by a language-motor disconnection since their patient also failed both to imitate skilled movements and to properly manipulate actual objects. Because this patient's primary visual, visual association, primary somesthetic, somesthetic association, and premotor and motor areas in the right hemisphere were all intact he should still have been able to use an object correctly and to imitate. Since he could not imitate or use an object, Liepmann and Maas concluded that the left hemisphere contains not only language but also motor engrams that control purposeful skilled movements. Liepmann (1920) called these motor engrams "movement formulas" containing the "time-space-form picture of the movement" (See Kimura, 1979). We refer to them as visuokinesthetic motor engrams (Heilman, 1979).

In order to perform a skilled learned act, one must place particular body parts in certain spatial positions in a specific order at specific times. The spatial positions assumed by the relevant body parts depend not only on the nature of the act but also on the position and size of an external object with which the body parts must interact if an external object is present. Skilled acts also require orderly changes in the spatial positions of the body parts over time. These visuokinesthetic engrams command the motor systems to adopt the appropriate spatial positions of the relevant body parts over time.

Lesions of the corpus callosum therefore not only disconnect the language hemisphere from the hemisphere controlling the left hand but also separate these left hemisphere visuokinesthetic motor engrams from the motor areas in the right hemispheres. According to Liepmann's postulate, a callosal lesion in a right-handed patient who has both motor and language engrams in his left hemisphere would not interfere with the ability of the patient to carry out commands, imitate, and use actual objects correctly with his right hand, but would result in the patient having difficulty with all these tasks when using his left hand.

Until recently there has been little support for this hypothesis. Geschwind and Kaplan (1962) described a patient with a left hemisphere glioblastoma and a post-operative left anterior cerebral artery infarction that had caused destruction of the anterior four-fifths of the corpus callosum. That patient could not follow commands with his left hand but could correctly imitate and could use actual objects. He was agraphic with the left hand and could not type or use anagram letters with the left hand but performed flawlessly with the right hand. He followed commands with his right hand but not with his left. The aphasic agraphia was interpreted as resulting from a disconnection of the right hemisphere from left hemisphere language areas, and the apraxic difficulties were attributed to the separation of stimulus (verbal or nonverbal) and response across hemispheres. Similarly, surgical lesions of the corpus callosum (Gazzaniga et al., 1967) were not associated with the type of apraxias proposed by Liepmann and Maas (1907).

Watson and Heilman (1983) recently reported a patient with an acute naturally occurring callosal lesion who, unlike the patient of Geschwind and Kaplan (1962), had severe apraxia with imitation and object usage, thereby providing support for Liepmann's hypothesis. In addition, Haaland (personal communication) described a case of a partial anterior surgical disconnection that also demonstrated apraxia of the left hand to imitation.

We do not know why these cases differed from previously reported cases of callosal disconnection. In Watson and Heilman's (1983) case, the CT scan did not show any extra-callosal damage. Many of the patients who had surgical callosal lesions had prior seizures and brain injury which may have induced brain reorganization. However, Geschwind and Kaplan's (1962) patient did not have long-standing injury, suggesting that the absence of a left-hand ideomotor apraxia cannot be entirely explained by brain reorganization. In right-handers, right hemispheric lesions almost never produce apraxia; however, left hemisphere lesions in areas known to induce both aphasia and apraxia more often induce aphasia. In one study only 57% (20 of 35) of aphasic patients were also apraxic (Heilman, 1975). The discrepancy between the incidence of aphasia and apraxia suggests that although in right-handers visuokinesthetic motor engrams for skilled movements are localized in the left hemisphere, the right hemisphere in many of these persons can substitute for the left (Heilman, 1979). Kertesz (personal communication), using CT scans, studied anatomic asymmetries in right-handed patients who had left hemisphere lesions. Nonapraxic patients had less hemispheric asymmetry (i.e., the left occipital pole was not larger than the right) than apraxic patients. If anatomic asymmetry correlates with lateralization of motor engrams, then persons with less asymmetry would be expected to have bilateral motor engrams and therefore would not become apraxic with unilateral lesions. Because patients with large left hemisphere lesions in regions known to induce apraxia sometimes have aphasia without apraxia, it should not be surprising that callosal damage does not induce apraxia in all patients.

Geschwind (1965) remarked that the independence of the right hemisphere in nonlanguage function manifested by his patient was unusual and may have been an exception. The patient of Liepmann and Maas probably had language and visuokinesthetic motor engrams restricted to the left hemisphere, which might represent a more common pattern. The patients reported by Gazzaniga et al. (1967) and Geschwind and Kaplan (1962) were left-hemisphere dominant for language but probably had bilateral visuokinesthetic motor engrams.

The nature of the apraxic deficit seen with callosal lesions depends on the pattern of language and motor dominance in the individual patient. For example, we have seen two left-handed patients who had right hemisphere lesions and were apraxic (Heilman et al., 1973; Valenstein and Heilman, 1979). Motor engrams in these two patients were stored in the right hemisphere while language was mediated by the left hemisphere. We can speculate that if, prior to their right hemisphere lesion, these patients had a lesion of their corpus callosum, the right hand, deprived of visuokinesthetic motor engrams, should perform poorly to command, imitation, and with the use of the actual object. Their left hand, deprived of language, should perform poorly to gestural command but perform well with imitation and with an actual object.

LEFT HEMISPHERIC LESIONS (INTRAHEMISPHERIC)

Defect in symbolization versus motor defects.   In right-handed patients, almost all cases of apraxia are associated with left hemispheric lesions (Geschwind, 1965; Goodglass and Kaplan, 1963; Hécaen and Ajuriaguerra, 1964; Hécaen and Sanguet, 1971). In right-handers, the left hemisphere is also dominant for language. Apraxia therefore is commonly associated with aphasia. This has led to the suggestion that apraxia and aphasia may both be manifestations of a primary defect in symbolization: aphasia is a disturbance of verbal symbolization, while apraxia is a defect of nonverbal symbolization (e.g., emblem and pantomime) (Goldstein, 1948). The observation that patients with apraxia perform poorly to command and imitation but improve with the use of the actual object (Goodglass and Kaplan, 1963) lends support to Goldstein's postulate. In addition, Dee et al. (1970) and Kertesz and Hooper (1982) found a close relationship between language impairment and apraxia. However, several studies lend support to Liepmann's hypothesis that the left hemisphere controls skilled movements and that destruction of the engrams or separation of these engrams from the motor areas controlling the extremity causes abnormalities of skilled movement. Goodglass and Kaplan (1963) tested apraxic aphasic patients and control aphasic subjects with the Weschler Adult Intelligence Scale and used the performance-scaled score as a measure of intellectual ability. They also tested their subject's ability to gesture and perform simple and complex pantomimes. Although the apraxic aphasics performed less well on these motor skills than did their intellectual counterparts in the control groups, no clear relationship emerged between the severity of aphasia and the degree of gestural deficiency; the apraxic aphasic patients were also less able to imitate than were the nonapraxic controls.

Although Goodglass and Kaplan believed that their results supported Liepmann's hypothesis, they noted that their apraxic subjects did not have any difficulty in handling objects. Liepmann, however, thought apraxic patients were clumsy with objects and Geschwind (1965) noted that although such patients may improve after actually handling objects, their actions nevertheless remain clumsy. Clumsiness of the left hand is difficult to quantify and, if apraxia is in part a disconnection from or destruction of the area containing motor memories, then brain-damaged apraxic patients should differ in movement quality from nonapraxic patients. Apraxic aphasics and nonapraxic aphasics were given a rapid finger-tapping task with the left hand (Heilman, 1975). The apraxic-aphasic group performed significantly worse than the non-apraxic aphasic group. Similar results were reported by Wyke (1967) who, although she did not test for apraxia, used a repetitive nonsymbolic movement to test patients with disease of either the right or the left hemisphere. She demonstrated that patients with left hemisphere disease performed more poorly with their ipsilateral hand than did those with right hemisphere disease. Wyke concluded that "ipsilateral control does not exist for the right hemisphere"; however, her results also support Liepmann's hypothesis that the left hemisphere contains the motor memories that help control the right hemisphere via the corpus callosum. Kimura and Archibald (1974) studied the ability of left-hemisphere impaired aphasics and right-hemisphere impaired controls to imitate unfamiliar, meaningless motor sequences. The performance of aphasic apraxic patients with left hemisphere impairment was poorer than that of the controls, again supporting Liepmann's hypothesis. In contrast, Haaland et al. (1977) were not able to replicate Heilman's (1975) finding that apraxics tap more slowly with their left hand than do controls. In addition, Pieczuro and Vignolo (1967) tested the manual dexterity of 35 patients with lesions of the right hemisphere and 70 patients with lesions of the left hemisphere. These patients' performance was impaired by lesions in either hemisphere and the severity of the apraxia was independent of manual dexterity. Although it is not clear why there is a discrepancy between these studies contributing factors might be that the criteria for subject selection may have been different and in some of the studies the tasks were different.

The strongest support for the postulate that apraxia is a disorder of skilled movement rather than a symbolic defect comes from Liepmann's own observations that only 14 out of 20 apraxic patients were aphasic. Goodglass and Kaplan (1963), Heilman et al. (1973), and Heilman et al. (1974) have also described similar patients. In addition, aphasic patients are often not apraxic (Heilman, 1975). In summary, because there is a poor correlation between the severity of symbolic disorders (aphasia) and disorders of skilled movements and because even nonsymbolic movements are poorly performed by apraxics, there is little evidence to support the hypothesis that apraxia is a disorder of symbolic behavior.

Destruction of motor engrams and disconnection of motor engrams from motor areas.   Geschwind (1965) proposed that language elicits motor behavior by using a neural substrate similar to that proposed by Wernicke (1874) to explain language processing (see Fig. 7-1). Auditory stimuli travel along auditory pathways and reach Heschl's gyrus (primary auditory cortex). From Heschl's gyrus, the auditory message is relayed to the posterior superior portion of the temporal lobe (auditory association cortex). On the left side, this area is called Wernicke's area and appears to be important in language comprehension. Wernicke's area is connected to the premotor areas (motor association cortex) by the arcuate fasciculus and the motor association area on the left is connected to the primary motor area on the left. When someone is told to carry out a command with his right hand, he uses this pathway. To carry out a verbal command with the left hand, information must be carried to the right premotor cortex (Geschwind, 1965) and, since it is rare to find fibers that run obliquely in the corpus callosum, fibers either cross from Wernicke's area to the auditory association area on the other side or cross from the premotor area on the left side to the premotor

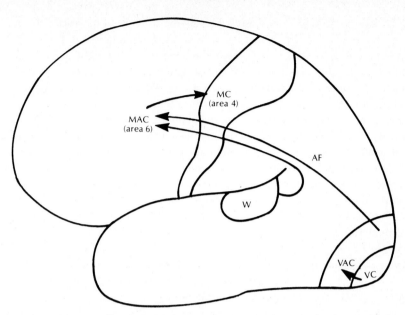

Fig. 7-1. Geshwind's schema. Lateral view of left side of brain. AF = arcuate fasciculus, MAC = motor association cortex, MC = motor cortex, VAC = visual association cortex, VC = visual cortex. The arrows indicate major connections of the areas shown.

area on the right side. The information is then conveyed to the motor areas on the right side. Geschwind (1965) postulated that the connections between the motor association areas are the active pathway. He believed that disruptions in these pathways explain most apraxic disturbances.

It is not clear, however, that lesions in Geschwind's schema can indeed explain the variety of apraxic disturbances. Lesions in Heschl's gyrus, Wernicke's area, or the connections between Herschl's gyrus and Wernicke's area cause defects in language comprehension. When these patients fail to carry out commands, their defect is not in the ability to perform skilled movements but rather in comprehending language.

We have already discussed callosal lesions which produce unilateral ideomotor apraxia. Lesions that destroy the left motor association cortex (premotor areas) would also destroy association neurons including the cell bodies of neurons that cross the corpus callosum. Therefore, a lesion in the left motor association cortex would induce a defect similar to that induced by a lesion in the body of the corpus callosum (sympathetic dyspraxia). Lesions of the left motor association cortex are often associated with right hemiplegia, so the right limb can frequently not be tested. If, however, these patients were not hemiparetic, they would probably be apraxic on the right. According to Geschwind's (1965) schema, lesions of the acuate fasciculus should disconnect the posterior language areas which are important in comprehension from the motor association cortex which is important in encoding motor engrams. According to this schema, patients with parietal lesions (or arcuate fasciculus lesions) that spare motor association cortex should be able to comprehend commands but not perform skilled movements in response to command. Although these patients should theoretically be able to imitate, they cannot. Geschwind attempted to explain this discrepancy by noting that fibers passing from visual association cortex to premotor cortex also pass anteriorly via the arcuate fasciculus. He proposed that the arcuate fasciculus of the left hemisphere is dominant for these visuomotor connections, but there is no evidence to support this hypothesis. Even if one assumes that the left arcuate fasciculus is dominant for visuomotor connections and interruption of this dominant pathway explains why patients cannot imitate, it could not explain why these patients are clumsy when they use objects or perform other somesthestic motor tasks. One would have to assume that the arcuate fasciculus also carries somesthetic-motor impulses and that the left arcuate fasciculus is also dominant for this function.

An alternative hypothesis that may explain why patients with parietal lesions cannot properly imitate or use an object is that visuokinesthetic motor engrams are stored in the dominant parietal cortex (Heilman, 1979; Kimura, 1979). These engrams help program the motor association cortex for the necessary movements, and the motor association cortex programs the motor cortex, which innervates the specific muscle motor neuron pools needed to carry out the skilled act (Asanuma, 1975) (Fig. 7-2).

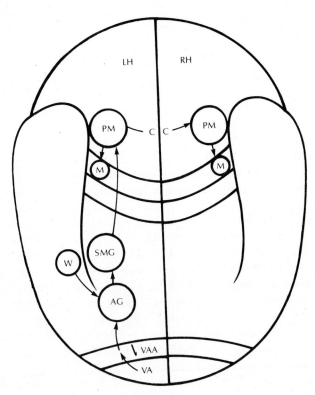

Fig. 7-2. Author's schema. View from top of brain. W = Wernicke's area, VA = primary visual area, VAA = visual association area, AG = angular gyrus, SMG = supramarginal gyrus, PM = premotor area (motor association cortex), M = motor cortex, CC = corpus callosum, LH = left hemisphere, RH = right hemisphere. The arrows indicate major connections of the areas shown.

Theoretically, it is possible to distinguish between dysfunction caused by destruction of parietal areas where acts are programmed (the visuokinesthetic motor engrams) and the apraxia which results from disconnection of this parietal area from motor association areas. Although patients with either disorder should experience difficulty in performing a skilled act in response to command, imitating, and using an object, patients whose engrams for skilled acts are retained but whose motor association areas are disconnected (or motor association cortex is destroyed) should be able to differentiate a correctly performed skilled act from an incorrectly performed one because they still have visuokinesthetic motor engrams. They therefore have the information characterizing distinctive features of movement or movement formula. Patients with parietal lesions that destroy visuokinesthetic motor engrams should not be able to perform this analysis.

To test the postulates that the visuokinesthetic motor engrams are stored in the dominant parietal lobe and that destruction of these engrams induces a discrimination deficit, we (Heilman et al., 1982) gave a gestural recognition and discrimination task to apraxic and nonapraxic patients with anterior lesions or nonfluent aphasia and to patients with posterior lesions or fluent aphasia. In the discrimination task the subject was to select a correctly performed act from a poorly performed act (e.g., using a body part as an object). In the comprehension task all acts were executed correctly. The subject was asked to select the requested (target) act from two foils (e.g., if the target was flipping a coin, the foils were using a screwdriver and brushing teeth). On both the discrimination and recognition task the posterior/fluent patients performed worse than the other subjects. In addition, we performed a similar task in a patient who had ideomotor apraxia of the left hand resulting from a lesion of the corpus callosum (Rothi, Heilman and Watson, in preparation) and this patient's performance was flawless.

Agnosia is a failure of recognition not induced by deafferentation or a naming disorder. The discrimination and recognition disorders associated with apraxia from posterior lesions may be considered by some to be a form of agnosia (agnosia for gesture). To explain our subjects' impaired ability to perform or to recognize well-performed acts, we postulate that posterior lesions destroy the visuokinesthetic motor engrams. However, some patients might have a disconnection between the visual areas and these engrams. These patients should correctly use objects and perform to command but not imitate or recognize gestures. Such patients might be considered agnosic for gesture. We have seen one patient with a left occipitotemporal lesion who had alexia without agraphia and was not aphasic, but was agnostic for pantomimes and gestures.

Patients with posterior dominant-hemisphere lesions who have difficulty comprehending language also often have difficulty comprehending gesture. Although a conceptual or semantic disorder might underlie both defects, an inability to perform an auditory or phonemic analysis could account for their inability to comprehend language, whereas their inability to comprehend gestures could be related to destruction of, or disconnection from, visuokinesthetic motor engrams.

Based on our observations, we believe there are at least two forms of ideomotor apraxia. One is induced by lesions of the supramarginal or angular gyrus. The patients perform poorly to command and imitation, and also cannot discriminate poorly performed from well performed acts. The other is induced by lesions anterior to the supramarginal gyrus that disconnect the visuokinesthetic motor engrams from the premotor and motor areas important in programming movements. These patients cannot perform well to command or imitation, but can discriminate between well-performed and poorly performed acts. This disconnection form of ideomotor apraxia may be subdivided into two forms—one induced by callosal lesions and the other by lesions of the hemisphere containing visuokinesthetic motor engrams. Patients with disconnection ideomotor apraxia induced by callosal lesions fail to perform correctly with the hand ipsilateral to the hemisphere containing the engrams, but should perform normally with the hand contralateral to these engrams. Patients with disconnection ideomotor apraxia induced by lesions of the hemisphere containing visuokinesthetic motor engrams, if not hemiparetic, should fail to perform correctly with either hand.

Memory defects.   If ideomotor apraxia results from destruction of visuokinesthetic motor engrams (time/space engrams) patients with the disorder should have difficulty acquiring new motor skills and retaining new gestures in memory. In regard to the former, Heilman et al. (1975) studied nine right-handed hemiparetic patients with apraxia and aphasia and eight right-handed hemiparetic controls with aphasia but without apraxia. These subjects were given six trials on a rotary pursuit apparatus (five acquisition trials and one retention trial). All subjects used their left, nonparetic hand. The performance of the control group on the sixth trial was significantly better than on the first trial; however, there was no significant difference between the first and sixth trials in the apraxic group, suggesting that these patients had a defect in motor learning. The defect appeared to be caused by a combined impairment of both acquisition and retention. Wyke (1971), studying patients with either right or left hemisphere disease, gave her subjects a motor acquisition task that required bimanual coordination. Atlhough patients with left hemisphere disease demonstrated acquisition, it was below the level of skill in those with right hemisphere disease. Since Wyke did not separate her left hemisphere group into apraxic and nonapraxic patients, one could not be certain whether apraxic patients would have demonstrated poorer learning than the nonapraxic patients with left hemisphere impairment.

   Rothi and Heilman (in preparation A) studied the ability of apraxic patients (with parietal lesions) to learn a list of gestures by using a modified Buschke paradigm. In this paradigm (Buschke, 1973; Buschke and Fuld, 1974) a series of 12 gestures are presented to the patient who is asked to reproduce as many as possible. On subsequent trials the subjects are reminded only of those gestures they have never produced or failed to produce on two consecutive occasions. A gesture that contained apraxic errors was not considered an error if the intent could be recognized. Apraxic subjects may fail to reproduce a gesture because of a performance deficit related to their apraxia or because they cannot encode or retrieve a gesture. However, if a subject can demonstrate that they can produce a gesture on one trial and fail to perform the gesture on a subsequent trial, the failure may be attributed to either a consolidation or retrieval failure rather than a performance deficit since they have already shown that they are capable of producing the movement. When a subject failed to recall a gesture on two consecutive trials we assumed that the patient had either a failure to consolidate the gesture (information was lost from memory) or a retrieval failure (a momentary lapse in retrieval from an intact store). We found that apraxics made more recall errors than did the normal nonapraxic controls. If a subject failed to recall a gesture but subsequently recalled the gesture without being reminded, we considered the initial recall failure a retrieval error. If a subject failed to recall a gesture for two consecutive trials and recalled the gesture only after being reminded, we considered the initial recall failure a consolidation error. There were no significant differences between the three groups in the number of retrieval errors. However, we did note significantly more consolidation errors in the apraxic groups, suggesting a memory consolidation deficit.

A person may use at least two strategies for consolidating gestures in memory—a linguistic-verbal strategy and a sensory-motor strategy (visuokinesthetic). Failure to consolidate gestures may thus be due to an inability to form an engram either from the sensory perceptual trace or from the verbal linguistic trace or both. The Buschke paradigm cannot differentiate between these two alternatives. To address this issue, Rothi and Heilman (in preparation B) used a Brown-Peterson (Brown 1958; Peterson and Peterson, 1959) paradigm. Normal, apraxic, and nonapraxic aphasic subjects were presented with multiple sets of three gestures and either immediately or after an 18-second delay were asked to recall (reproduce) the gestures. During the delay interval there was either no distraction, a verbal distractor (counting), or a movement distractor (finger movements). With a delay and no distraction none of the groups (apraxic, nonapraxic aphasic, normal) lost information. We found that the verbal distractors caused forgetting in all groups, suggesting that all groups use verbal rehearsal. The finger movement distractor did not cause forgetting in any group. This finding suggests that gestural information may be directly consolidated into secondary memory (engram consolidation) or that the visuospatial-kinesthetic code is not used for rehearsal in primary memory or both.

The finding that apraxics with parietal lesions have more difficulty consolidating memory for gesture supports the hypothesis that visuokinesthetic motor engrams are stored in the parietal lobe. Destruction of these engrams not only produces a performance deficit (apraxia) but also comprehension and memory deficits.

Disconnection and Disassociation Apraxias

VERBAL-MOTOR DISASSOCIATION APRAXIA

Heilman (1973) described three apraxic patients who, when asked to gesture, performed differently than patients with ideomotor apraxia. Unlike the patients with ideomotor apraxia who make spatial-temporal errors and use body parts as objects, these patients hesitated to make any movements and often appeared as if they did not understand the command. They could, however, demonstrate both verbally and by picking out the correct act (from several performed by the examiner) that they understood the command. Unlike patients with ideomotor apraxia, these patients were able to imitate and use actual objects flawlessly. Because imitation and actual object use was performed well, it would seem that their engrams for motor skills were intact. What seemed to be defective in these patients was the ability to elicit the correct motor sequences in response to language. Unfortunately, we never learned the exact location of the left hemisphere lesion that induced this apraxia. However, we hypothesized that the lesions were in, or deep to, the parietal region (angular gyrus).

The patients with callosal lesions described by Geschwind and Kaplan (1962) and Gazzaniga et al. (1967) could not perform with their left hand in response to command, but they could imitate and use objects. Performance with their left hand was similar to the performance with both hands of patients with left-hemisphere inferior parietal lobule lesions (Heilman, 1973). If normal performance on imitation and use-of-object suggests that visuokinesthetic motor engrams are intact and connected to premotor and primary motor areas, then patients with callosal lesions and patients with angular gyrus or subcortical lesions deep in the parietal lobe must have a disassociation between language areas and the area where visuokinesthetic motor engrams are stored. In patients with callosal lesions, these engrams were presumed to be in both hemispheres, whereas comprehension of commands was being mediated by the left hemisphere. In patients with angular gyrus lesions or deep lesions, both comprehension of the commands and the visuokinesthetic engrams were being mediated by the left hemisphere and the lesion disassociated language areas from these engrams so that language was not able to elicit retrieval of these engrams. An alternative hypothesis is that in patients with angular gyrus lesions the right hemisphere was mediating language comprehension, the left hemisphere contained the visuokinesthetic engrams, and the lesions disconnected the language areas from these engrams.

VISUOMOTOR AND TACTILE-MOTOR DISASSOCIATION APRAXIA

DeRenzi et al. (1982) not only replicated Heilman's (1973) observations but also described a patient who performed in the opposite manner. The patient failed to perform with visual stimuli but performed well to verbal command. Although most patients performed better with tactile stimuli than command, the authors also described two patients who performed better with visual and verbal stimuli than tactile stimuli. The mechanism proposed by DeRenzi et al. to explain these modality-specific apraxias was similar to that proposed by Heilman (1973), namely a disconnection between modality-specific pathways and the center where movements are programmed.

Ideational Apraxia

Unfortunately, there has been much confusion about this term. Several of the disassociation apraxias discussed above were unfortunately termed ideational apraxia (Heilman, 1973; DeRenzi et al., 1968). The inability to carry out a series of acts has also been called ideational apraxia (Marcuse, 1904; Pick, 1905; Liepmann 1920). When given a goal that requires a series of acts, these apraxic patients have difficulty with sequencing the acts (for example, instead of cleaning the pipe, putting tobacco in, lighting it and smoking it, the patient might light it, put tobacco in, and then clean it). Most of the patients described in the literature with this type of ideational apraxia have had dementing diseases (such as Alzheimer's disease). As their disease progresses they may demonstrate profound conceptual defects so that they do not even know the intended use of objects.

Although most patients with this latter severe form of ideational apraxia do not have focal lesions, the patient of Watson and Heilman (1983) who had an infarction in her corpus callosum, initially appeared to have ideational apraxia. When asked to pantomime skilled acts with her left hand, she looked at her left hand and alternately pronated and supinated her hand or flexed and extended her fingers. She could not even attempt the requested pantomime. Unlike patients with verbal-motor disconnection apraxia who could imitate and use actual objects flawlessly (Heilman, 1973) this patient's performance during imitation or with actual object was precisely the same as it was to command. Some aphasics with profound comprehension disorders cannot pantomime to verbal commands but can hold the actual object and accurately pretend to use it. These observations suggest that verbal comprehension and knowledge of object use are dissociable. The failure of this patient to use actual objects with her left hand therefore cannot be entirely explained by an inability of her right hemisphere to understand a command (either directly or via the corpus callosum). Similarly, although severely apraxic patients with left hemisphere lesions may have difficulty with the spatial and temporal dimensions of their movements when using actual objects, these patients demonstrate that they know the intended use of the objects. Our patient's inability to demonstrate the intended use of an object or even to attempt to use actual objects cannot therefore be explained by a verbal-motor disconnection or by a disconnection of visuokinesthetic motor engrams from the right hemisphere motor areas. When she first held objects in her left hand, her performance was as if she had never seen or worked with these objects and did not know their intended use. We therefore suspect that initially there was a conceptual disorder. The disconnected right hemisphere did not know what the object was used for or even that it was to be used. Ideational apraxia perhaps best describes the left-hand performance of this patient. However, because the right hand performed normally, the concepts of what objects are used for were not destroyed but were disconnected from the right hemisphere.

BUCCOFACIAL APRAXIA (ORAL APRAXIA)

Hughlings Jackson (cited by Taylor, 1932) was the first to describe buccofacial or oral apraxia (nonprotrusion of the tongue). Patients with oral apraxia have difficulty performing learned skilled movements with their face, lips, tongue, cheeks, larynx, and pharynx on command. For example, when they are asked to pretend to blow out a match, suck on a straw, lick a sucker, or blow a kiss, they will make incorrect movements. Poeck and Kerschensteiner (1975) found several types of errors. Verbal descriptions may be substituted for the movement: the oral apraxic asked to pantomime blowing out a match may respond by saying "blow." Other error types include movement substitutions and perserverations.

Mateer and Kimura (1977) demonstrated that imitation of meaningless movements was also impaired, providing evidence that oral apraxia is not a form of asymbolia. Although many of these patients do not improve with imitation, they consistently improve dramatically when seeing or using an actual object (e.g., a lit match). The ability to discriminate and comprehend oral gestures has not been tested in these patients.

Tognola and Vignolo (1980) studied patients who were unable to imitate oral gestures. The critical areas for lesions included the frontal and central opercula, anterior insula and a small area of the first temporal gyrus (adjacent to the frontal and central opercula). Tognola and Vignolo (1980) and Kolb and Milner (1981) found parietal lesions were not associated with oral apraxia, but they did not test performance to command. Benson et al. (1973), however, described patients with parietal lesions who exhibited oral apraxia to command. Although Kleist (1934) proposed that the oral apraxia induced by anterior perisylvian lesion was different from that induced by posterior (parietal) perisylvian lesions, we do not currently have sufficient information to present a model of oral apraxia.

Some authors have classified the phonological selection and sequencing deficit of nonfluent aphasia as "apraxia of speech" (Johns and Darley, 1970, Deal and Darley, 1972). Although Pieczuro and Vignolo (1967) noted that 90% of Broca's aphasics have oral apraxia, it would seem unlikely that buccofacial apraxia causes this phonological disturbance because there are patients with nonfluent aphasia who do not have oral apraxia. It can be argued, however, that oral and verbal apraxias are points along a continuum, sharing a common underlying mechanism. It could by hypothesized that speech requires finer coordination than does response to a command such as "blow out a match," and therefore the effortful, phonologically inaccurate speech of the nonfluent aphasic may still be caused by an apraxic disturbance affecting speech more than oral, nonverbal movement. Oral apraxia and Broca's aphasia often coexist, but they can also be completely dissociated (Heilman et al., 1974), suggesting that the association cortex that mediates facial praxis is not the same as the mechanism that mediates the organization of movements important in speech. Furthermore, because patients may have conduction aphasia with or without oral apraxia (Benson et al., 1973) oral apraxia may coexist with fluent speech. If one attributes the nonfluent disorders of speech in Broca's aphasics to a generalized oral motor programming deficit, one cannot explain how oral apraxia may be associated with the fluent speech seen in conduction aphasia. In addition, we have examined two patients with aphemia (nonfluent speech with intact writing skills) who did not have oral apraxia. If the speech deficits exhibited by left hemisphere impaired patients is induced by a motor defect, this motor programming defect is strongly linked to the language and phonological systems and is not a generalized oral motor programming deficit. Without proposing a separate motor programming system for speech, the dependence on the language system and lack of oral motor programming dysfunction call into question the appropriateness of the term apraxia as used in "apraxia of speech."

NEUROPATHOLOGY OF APRAXIA

Ideomotor apraxia in right-handers is most commonly associated with focal lesions of the left hemisphere. In left-handers, apraxia may be associated with right hemisphere lesions. Heilman et al., 1973; Valenstein and Heilman, 1979). The most common etiology is infarction in the distribution of the middle cerebral artery. These infarctions may be caused by thrombosis or emboli. Other pathological processes (e.g., trauma, tumor) may also cause apraxia. Ideomotor apraxia may also be seen in primary degenerative dementias.

The callosal form of ideomotor apraxia may be iatrogenic (surgical) or induced by infarction in the distribution of the anterior cerebral artery. The infarction may be related to spasm induced by an aneurysm. Trauma and tumors may also cause callosal disconnection.

Ideomotor apraxia is also often associated with severe primary dementias (such as Alzheimer's disease).

RECOVERY FROM APRAXIA AND TREATMENT

Although it has been proposed that in right-handers motor engrams are stored in the left hemisphere, some right-handed left-hemisphere damaged patients are not apraxic. Possibly in some of these patients the lesion was small and missed a critical area. However, some patients with large lesions are not apraxic, while others with small lesions are severely apraxic. Of patients who have lesions in the same area, some are apraxic and some are not. Therefore, although the size and locus of a lesion may in part determine the presence or absence of apraxia as well as its severity, they appear not to be only determinants. Perhaps patients with large left hemisphere lesions who have aphasia and hemiplegia are not apraxic because their right hemisphere is capable of supporting skilled motor movement programming. This hypothesis is similar to the one first proposed by Kleist (1916) to explain why certain patients with lesions of the left hemisphere recover language function.

Nowhere is the ability to pantomime more appreciated than in patients who suffer communication impairments that preclude interactions with their world. When these patients are able to learn and use a gestural system in lieu of spoken language, it is referred to as an alternate communicative mode. However, gesture has also been used as a reorganizing agent (Skelly et al., 1974): when gesture is used in conjunction with spoken attempts, patients are shown to improve verbal expressive skills. Therefore, praxis ability plays a critical role in treating aphasia or neurological disorders of speech.

No information is presently available on methods or efficacy of treatment of apraxia. However, information from animal recovery models (Rothi and Horner, 1983) suggests that therapy should be initially aimed at restitution of function: treating the underlying disorder so that maximum function can be achieved within the limits set by the recovery process. Then other therapeutic measures can be attempted to institute substitute strategies. Apraxic patients should be taught alternative strategies for performing tasks which pose difficulty for them. For example, the body part-as-object error commonly seen in the performance of ideomotor apraxics may actually be a compensatory strategy spontaneously generated by the patient. We believe these errors represent an attempt to provide an external representation for a lost or impaired internal reference from which to generate a skilled movement.

Because it does not impair communicative intent, these strategies should be encouraged in those who spontaneously use them and instituted in those who do not.

REFERENCES

Asanuma, H. (1975). Recent developments in the study of columnar arrangement of neurons within the motor cortex. *Physiol. Rev.* 55, 143–156.

Benson, D. F. and Geschwind, N. (1969) The alexias. In *Handbook of Clinical Neurology: Disorders of Speech Perception and Symbolic Behavior*, P. J. Vinken, and G. W. Bruyn (Eds), pp. 112–140. New York: American Elsevier.

Benson, F., Sheremata, W., Bouchard, R., Segarra, J., Prie, D., and Geschwind, N. (1973). Conduction aphasia. A clinicopatholological study. *Arch. Neurol.* 28:339–346.

Brown, J. (1958). Some tests of the decay theory of immediate memory. *Quart. J. Exp. Psychol.* 10:12–21, 1958.

Buschke, H. (1973). Selective reminding for analysis of memory and learning. *J. Verbal Learning Verbal Behav.* 12:543–550.

Buschke, H. and Fuld, P A. (1974). Evaluating storage, retention, and retrieval in disordered memory and learning. *Neurology* 24:1019–1025.

De Renzi, E., Pieczuro, A., and Vignolo, L. (1968). Ideational apraxia: a quantitative study. *Neuropsychologia* 6:41–52.

De Renzi, E., Faglioni, P., and Sorgato, P. (1982). Modality–specific and supramodal mechanisms of apraxia. *Brain* 105:301–312.

Deal, J. L. and Darley, F. L. (1972). The influence of linguistic and situational variables on phonemic accuracy in apraxia of speech. *J. Speech Hearing Res.* 15:639–653.

Dee, H. L., Benton, A., and Van Allen, M. W. (1970). Apraxia in relation to hemisphere locus of lesion, and aphasia. *Trans. Am. Neurol. Assoc.* 95:147–150.

Duffy, J. and Pearson, K. (1975). Pantomime in aphasic patients. *J. Speech Hearing Res.* 18:115–132.

Gazzaniga, M., Bogen, J., and Sperry, R. (1967). Dyspraxia following diversion of the cerebral commissures. *Arch. Neurol.* 16:606–612.

Geschwind, N . (1965). Disconnexion syndromes in animals and man. *Brain* 88:237–294, 585–644.

Geschwind, N., and Kaplan, E. (1962). A human cerebral disconnection syndrome. *Neurology* 12:675–685.

Goldstein, K. (1948). *Language and Language Disturbances*. New York: Grune and Stratton.

Goodglass, H. and Kaplan E., (1963). Disturbance of gesture and pantomime in aphasia. *Brain* 86:703–720.

Goodglass, H. and Kaplan, E. (1972). *The Assessment of Aphasia and Related Disorders*. Philadelphia: Lea and Febiger.

Greenblatt, S. (1962). Subangular alexia without agraphia or hemianopia. *Brain and Lang.* 3:229–245.

Haaland, K. Y., Cleeland, C. S., and Carr, D. (1977). Motor performance after unilateral hemisphere damage in patients with tumor. *Arch. Neurol.* 34:556–559.

Hécaen, H. and de Ajuriaguerra, J. (1964). *Left-Handedness*. New York: Grune & Stratton.

Hécaen, H., and Sanguet, J. (1971). Cerebral dominance in left-handed subjects. *Cortex* 7:19–48.

Heilman, K. M. (1973). Ideational apraxia—a re-definition. *Brain* 96:861–864.

Heilman, K. M. 1975). A tapping test in apraxia. *Cortex* 11:259–263.

Heilman, K. M. (1979). Apraxia. In *Clinical Neuropsychology*, K. M. Heilman, and E. Valenstein (Eds). New York: Oxford University Press.

Heilman, K. M., Coyle, J. M., Gonyea, E. F., and Geschwind, N. (1973). Apraxia and agraphia in a left-hander. *Brain 96*:21–28.

Heilman, K. M., Gonyea, E. F., and Geschwind, N. (1974). Apraxia and agraphia in a right hander. *Brain 96*:21–28.

Heilman, K. M., Schwartz, H. D., and Geschwind, N. (1975). Defective motor learning in ideomotor apraxia. *Neurology 25*:1018–1020.

Heilman, K. M., Rothi, L. J., and Valenstein, E. (1982). Two forms of ideomotor apraxia. *Neurology 32*:342–346.

Hines, D. (1977). Differences in tachistoscopic recognition between abstract and concrete words as a function of visual half-field frequency. *Cortex 13*:66–73.

Johns, D. F. and Darley, F. L. (1970). Phonemic variability in apraxia of speech. *J. Speech Hearing Res. 13*:556–583.

Kertesz, A. and Hooper, P. (1982). Praxis and language: the extent and variety of apraxia in aphasia. *Neuropsychologia 20*:275–286.

Kimura, D. and Archibald, Y. (1974). Motor functions of the left hemisphere. *Brain 97*:337–350.

Kimura, D. (1979). Neuromotor mechanisms in the evolution of human communication. In *Neurobiology of Social Communication in Primates: an Evolutionary Perspective*, H. D. Steklis and M. J. Raleigh (Eds). New York: Academic Press.

Kleist, K. (1916). Uber Leitungsaphasie und grammatische Storungen. *Monatsschr. f. Psychiatr. u. Neurol. 40*:118–121.

Kleist, K. (1934). *Gehirnpathologie*. Barth, Leipzig.

Kolb, B. and Milner, B. (1981). Performance of complex arm and facial movements after focal brain lesions. *Neuropsychologia 19*:491–503, 1981.

Lawrence, D. G. and Kuypers, H. G. J. M. (1968). The functional organization of the motor system in the monkey. *Brain 91*:1–36

Liepmann, H. Dulinke hemisphare und das handelin. *Munch. Med. Wschr. 49*:2375–2378.

Liepmann, H. and Maas, O. (1907) Fall von linksseitiger agraphie und apraxie bei rechsseitiger lahmung. Z.L. Psychologie u. Neurol 10:214–227.

Liepmann, H. (1920). Apraxia. *Erbgn. der ges Med. 1*:516–543.

Marcuse, H. (1904). Apraktiscke symotome bei linem fall von seniler demenz. *Zetble Mervheik Psychiat. 27*:737–751.

Mateer, K. and Kimura, D. (1977). Impairment of nonverbal movements in aphasia. *Brain and Lang. 4*:262–276.

Paivio, A., Yuile J. C., and Madigan, S. (1968). Concreteness, imagery, and meaningfulness values for 925 nouns. *J. Exp. Psychol. Mono. Supp. 76*.

Peterson, L. R. and Peterson, M. J. (1959). Short-term retention of individual verbal items. *J. Exp. Psychol. 58*:193–198.

Pick, A. (1905). *Studien uber Motorische Apraxia und ihre Mahestenhende Erscheinungen*, Leipzig: Deuticke.

Pieczuro, A. and Vignolo, L. A. (1967). Studio sperimentale sull'aprassia ideomotoria. *Sistema Nervoso 19*:131–143.

Poeck, K. and Kerschensteiner, M. (1975). Analysis of the sequential motor events in oral apraxia. In *Otfried Foerster Symposium*. K. Zulch, O. Kreutzfeld, and G. Galbraith (Eds). Springer, Berlin pp. 98–109.

Roland, P. E., Skinhoj, N., Lassen, N. A., and Larsen, B. (1980). Different cortical areas in man in organization of voluntary movements in extrapersonal space. *J. Neurophysiol. 43*:137–150.

Rothi, L. J. and Heilman, K. M: in preparation A. Acquisition and retention of gestures by apraxic patients.

Rothi, L. J. and Heilman, K. M.: in preparation B. Retention of gestural information, memory encoding and ideomotor apraxia.

Rothi, L. J. and Horner, J. (1983). Restitution and substitution: two theories of recovery with application to neurobehavioral treatment. *J Clin. Neuropsychol.* 5:73–82.

Skelly, M., Sehinsky, L., Smith, R., and Fust, R. (1974). American Indian Sign (AMERIND) as a facilitator of verbalization for the oral-verbal apractic. *J. Speech Hearing Dis.* 39:445–456.

Taylor, J. (1932). *Selected Writings*, London, Hodder and Stoughton.

Tognola, G. and Vignolo, L. A. (1980). Brain lesions associated with oral apraxia in stroke patients: a cliniconeuroradiological investigation with the CT scan. *Neuropsychologia*, 18:257–272 (1980).

Valenstein, E. and Heilman, K. M. (1979). Apraxic agraphia with neglect induced paragraphia. *Arch. Neurol.* 36;506–508.

Varney, N. R. (1978). Linguistic correlates of pantomime recognition in aphasic patients. *J. Neurol. Neurosurg. Psychol.* 41:564–568.

Varney, N. R (1982). Pantomime recognition defect in aphasia: implications for the concept of asymbolia. *Brain and Lang.* 15:32–39.

Watson, R. T. and Heilman, K. M. (1983) Callosal apraxia. *Brain 106*:391–403.

Wernicke, C. (1874). *Der Aphasische Symptomenkomplex*, Breslau: Cohn and Weigart.

Wyke, M. (1969). Effect of brain lesions on the rapidity of arm movement. *Neurology* 17:1113–1130.

Wyke, M. (1971). The effects of brain lesions on the learning performance of a bimanual coordination task. *Cortex 7*:59–71.

8

Visuoperceptual, Visuospatial, and Visuoconstructive Disorders

ARTHUR BENTON

The perceptual and perceptuomotor disabilities discussed in this chapter are reflected behaviorally in a variety of performance deficits: in failure to identify (or discriminate between) objects, pictorial representations, and faces; in defective discrimination of complex stimulus configuration (e.g., nonsense figures, combinations of forms); in faulty localization of objects in space and defective topographical orientation; and in impaired capacity to organize elements in correct spatial relationships so that they form an entity, as in drawing a house or building a block model. In traditional neurological terminology, most of these deficits are described as one or another form of visual agnosia. The visuoconstructional deficits are usually designated as constructional apraxia or apractagnosia.

There has always been considerable controversy about the fundamental nature of the agnosic disorders. According to one point of view, they represent impairment in either perceptual-integrative or associative processes within the context of adequate sensory capacity; the assumption here is that the patient cannot achieve recognition in spite of having received sufficient sensory information to do so. A competing explanation has been that the agnosic disorders result from sensory defects, often coupled with general mental impairment, so that the patient has only incomplete information as a basis for achieving perceptual recognition.

Whether one considers agnosia to be a "higher-level" disorder or thinks of it in terms of sensory deficit, it is clear that the neurological mechanisms involved in the agnosic disorders are not the same as those underlying perceptual deficits that are a direct consequence of impaired visual acuity, color blindness, or visual field defect. Thus, in either case, these perceptual and perceptuomotor disabilities need to be considered separately from "simple" sensory or motor deficits because of their distinctive neurological implications.

Over the years, a large number of specific performance deficits indicative of visuoperceptual, visuospatial, or visuoconstructive disorder have been described. The exact nature of the relationships among these performance deficits has yet to be worked out and a definitive classification of neurologically meaningful types of disability remains an unfinished task. However, some fundamental distinctions can be

made. For example, it is clear that there is a difference between defects in the identification of the formal characteristics of objects and defects in the localization of these
objects in space. Many patients show dissociated impairment in this regard, i.e., they
are defective in one type of performance but not in the other. An early study by
Newcombe and Russell (1969) will be cited to illustrate both the fact of dissociation
and its differential neurological implications.

Newcombe and Russell gave two visual tasks to right-handed patients with penetrating brain wounds and to control subjects. One task was the "faces" test of Mooney
(1957), in which the subject is requested to identify drawings of human faces with
exaggerated shadows and highlights as being that of a boy, girl, man, woman, old
man, or old woman. An earlier study by Lansdell (1968) had shown that defective
performance on this "closure" task, in which the subject must achieve a configurational percept from fragmentary information, is associated with right temporal-lobe
injury. The second task was a visual maze test in which the subject was required to
learn a 20-element path over trials. Impairment on this type of spatial learning problem has also been shown to be associated with disease of the right hemisphere (Reitan
and Tarshes, 1959; Benton et al., 1963; Milner, 1965; Corkin, 1965).

Separate groups of patients with well-localized focal wounds of the left or right
hemisphere, as well as control groups matched with the brain-diseased patients for
age and vocabulary level, were studied. The performance of the patients with right
hemisphere lesions on both tasks was significantly inferior to that of the left-hemisphere-damaged patients, who were not different in this respect from the controls.
However, although both the "closure" and "spatial" task performances proved once
again to be associated with right hemisphere disease, more detailed analysis showed
that their relations to locus-of-lesion within the hemisphere and to visual field defect
were quite different.

The perceptual and spatial task performances were not significantly correlated in
either the right-hemisphere or the left-hemisphere group and this lack of correlation
was reflected in many instances of dissociation in the right hemisphere patients. None
of the patients with markedly defective "closure" performance showed correspondingly defective "spatial" performance. They were found to have posterior temporal-
lobe lesions with an associated left upper quadrantic field defect. (Curiously, the men
with complete left hemianopia were not particularly severely impaired on this task.)
In contrast, the patients with markedly defective spatial performances proved to have
high posterior parietal injuries with an associated left hemianopia. Those with an
upper quadrantic defect performed quite well, while those with a lower quadrantic
defect tended to perform defectively.

This dissociation in performance level on spatial and nonspatial visual tasks on the
part of patients with brain disease has been documented in a number of studies in
addition to the one by Newcombe and Russell. This finding provides an empirical
basis for a broad division of visuoperceptive performances into spatial and nonspatial
types.

A second distinction that can be made is between the loss of ability to identify
familiar faces (prosopagnosia or facial agnosia) and impairment in the discrimination
of unfamiliar faces. These two deficits, which on first encounter might seem to rep-

resent the same underlying disability, are behaviorally dissociable and are produced by the derangement of different anatomic systems.

In all probability, there are other types of defect, each with its more-or-less specific neurological implications, that need to be identifed. A provisional classification of clinically differentiated forms of visuoperceptive, visuospatial, and visuoconstructive disorders is presented in Table 8-1.

HISTORICAL BACKGROUND

Perhaps the earliest explicit description of visuoperceptive defects associated with brain disease was that of Quaglino and Borelli (1867). Their patient showed four persisting symptoms after a stroke: left homonymous hemianopia; inability to recognize family and friends; impairment in color vision; and defective spatial orientation. The authors' diagnosis was hemorrhage in the right hemisphere but the fact that the patient was aphasic and apparently blind directly after his stroke suggests that there was bilateral disease.

Hughlings Jackson (1876) was the first neurologist to call special attention to the occurrence of visuoperceptive and visuopractic disabilities in patients with brain disease. Advancing the idea that the posterior region of the right hemisphere played a crucial role in visual recognition and memory, he described a patient with a tumor in this area who showed what he called "imperception"—lack of recognition of familiar persons and places, losing one's way in familiar surroundings, and inability to dress oneself. Jackson's observations had little immediate influence. The animal experimentation of Munk made a greater impact on clinical thinking (cf. Benton, 1978).

In 1878, Munk described a condition which he designated as "mindblindness." Following limited bilateral ablation of the upper convex surface of their occipital lobes, his dogs showed a peculiar disturbance in visual behavior. Although they could ambu-

Table 8-1. Classification of Visuoperceptual, Visuospatial, and Visuoconstructive Disorders

I. VISUOPERCEPTUAL
    A. Visual object agnosia
    B. Defective visual analysis and synthesis
    C. Impairment in facial recognition
        1. Facial agnosia (prosopagnosia)
        2. Defective discrimination of unfamiliar faces
    D. Impairment in color recognition

II. VISUOSPATIAL
    A. Defective localization of points in space
    B. Defective judgment of direction and distance
    C. Defective topographical orientation
    D. Unilateral visual neglect

III. VISUOCONSTRUCTIVE
    A. Defective assembling performance
    B. Defective graphomotor performance

late freely both indoors and in the garden, avoiding or climbing over obstacles, they seemed to have lost the ability to appreciate the meaning of many visual stimuli. For example, they would merely gaze at a piece of meat instead of snapping at it as would a normal dog. If a threatening gesture was made, they would neither cringe nor bark and they showed no signs of special recognition of their master or other familiar persons as compared to strangers. Munk's explanation of the condition was that the ablation had destroyed their "memory images" of earlier visual experience. As a consequence, they could not relate current perceptions to past experience and hence failed to grasp the meaning of visually perceived stimuli.

"Mindblindness" in patients who did not recognize objects or persons despite seemingly adequate visual acuity was then the subject of many clinical reports. Wilbrand (1887) followed Munk in attributing the disability to a loss of visual memory images and he postulated the existence of a "visual memory center" in the occipital cortex. Lissauer's (1890) classic case report included a penetrating discussion of the mechanisms underlying mindblindness. According to his formulation, visual recognition involves two processes: accurate perception of an object and association of that perception with past experince. A defect in the first mechanism could lead to an "apperceptive" type of mindblindness, a defect in the second to an "associative" type of disorder (cf. Chap. 9).

But other clinicians and experimentalists, while acknowledging the empirical reality of the condition described by Munk, interpreted it as the product of visuosensory defect. Their position was well expressed by Pavlov (1927) who suggested that the classical formula for mindblindness, "the dog sees but does not understand" in fact should read "the dog understands but does not see sufficiently well."

Nomenclature in the field changed with the introduction by Freud (1891) of the concept of agnosia to denote disorders of recognition in contrast to disorders of naming and "visual agnosia" gradually supplanted "mindblindness" as the preferred term for a range of disabilities having to do with the visual apprehension of objects, events, and spatial relations. Various forms of defect were then described. The mindblindness of Munk, Wilbrand, and Lissauer, in which the patient fails to recognize even common objects, was designated as visual object agnosia. Impairment in the discrimination of forms or complex figures with preserved recognition of common objects came to be known as visual form agnosia or geometric form agnosia. The inability to recognize familiar persons on the basis of facial characteristics was described as a specific entity, as was symbol agnosia and color agnosia. The inability to grasp the import of a complex pictorial presentation with preserved recognition of its constituent elements was given the designation of simultanagnosia.

Hughlings Jackson's concept of "imperception" involved disturbances in visual orientation as well as lack of recognition of familiar persons and places. Visuospatial disability became a topic of much clinical investigation and discussion in the 1880's, particularly among ophthalmologists (cf. Benton, 1982). An important early contribution was the detailed case report of Badal (1888) describing a patient with preserved central visual acuity who showed spatial disorientation. She could not find her way about the house or the immediate neighborhood and had difficulty in locating objects. She could read letters, numbers, and familiar words, but serial reading was grossly impaired because of directional impairment as she scanned printed material.

She recognized objects, but could not estimate their size, distance, or location. Like Jackson' s patient, she could not dress herself. Since her disorientation extended to the auditory and somesthetic realms, Badal interpreted her defects as a reflection of a supramodal disability of the "sense of space."

Rather similar cases were described by Foerster (1890), Dunn (1895), and Meyer (1900). The motoric element of "psychic paralysis of gaze" was added to the clinical picture by Balint (1909). On the basis of his observations on younger patients with penetrating brain wounds, Gordon Holmes (1918; Holmes and Horrax, 1919) divided visuospatial disabilities into two major types: (1) disturbances in orientation and in size and distance estimation, and (2) disturbances in ocular fixation with consequent inability to "find" objects.

The neurological interest of these early observations came from the demonstration that visuospatial disabilities of the types described were produced by focal posterior brain disease. For example, autopsy examination (Sachs, 1895) of Foerster's case disclosed bilateral softening confined to the occipital and temporal lobes and the brain of Balint's patient showed essentially the same picture. In his cases, Holmes found bilateral lesions involving the angular and surpamarginal gyri and extending into adjacent occipital and temporal areas.

Visuoconstructive disabilities were first described under the broader heading of optic apraxia, a term used to designate virtually any disturbance in action referable to defective visual guidance of action. For example, Poppelreuter (1917) described awkwardness in the execution of acts requiring manual dexterity, inability to maintain one's balance in tests of locomotion, and defective imitation of movements, as well as visuoconstructive disabilities, as forms of optic apraxia. Kleist (1923; Strauss, 1924) then singled out constructional apraxia as a separate disorder because of his observation that it could occur independently of other forms of apraxia and his conviction that it possessed a distinctive neuropathological significance. He conceived of it as a particular type of visuoconstructive impairment that reflected an inability to translate an adequate visual perception into appropriate action. It was a perceptuomotor, rather than purely visuoperceptual, disability that occurred as a consequence of a break in the connections between visual and kinesthetic processes. Thus, in Kleist's view, constructional apraxia was essentially a disconnection symptom and he placed the locus of the causative lesion in the posterior area of the dominant hemisphere. Yet, at the same time, he emphasized the spatial nature of the disability, defining it as a disturbance "in formative activities such as assembling, building, and drawing, in which the spatial form of the product proves to be unsuccessful, without there being an apraxia of single movements."

After Kleist's description, constructional apraxia was recognized as a form of behavioral disability associated with brain disease. However, his precise formulation that it was neither perceptual nor motor but rather "perceptuomotor" and "executive" in nature was generally ignored and the term was used to designate any visuoconstructive disability, whether or not it appeared within a context of visuoperceptive impairment. Later, Duensing (1953) made a distinction between an "ideational-apractic" type of constructional disability, comparable to Kleist's constructional apraxia, and a "spatio-agnostic" type resulting from visuoperceptive impairment.

DEFECTIVE VISUAL ANALYSIS AND SYNTHESIS

There is a huge literature on this topic describing performance deficits on tasks that make demands on various capacities such as making fine visual discriminations, separating figure from ground in complex configurations, achieving recognition on the basis of incomplete information, and synthesizing disparate elements into a meaningful unity as, for example, when viewing a picture depicting action. Selected aspects of this literature will be reviewed.

VISUAL DISCRIMINATION

The question of the frequency with which patients with brain disease show defects in simple visual discrimination, i.e., in altered thresholds for the discrimination of single attributes of a stimulus such as size, brightness, or length, has been the subject of study. Two examples will be cited.

Taylor and Warrington (1973) assessed the discrimination of size, length, shading, and curvature in groups of patients with focal lesions confined to the left or right hemisphere and a comparable group of control patients. The mean error score of the controls over all tasks was 1.6. Neither the mean error score (1.8) of the left-hemisphere-damaged patients nor that (2.4) of the right-hemisphere-damaged patients was significantly higher than that of the controls. The poorest performances were made by the subgroup of patients with posterior parietal disease of the right hemisphere; however, even their mean score of 3.7 was not significantly higher than that of the controls. That this failure to find between-group differences was not due to sampling bias is indicated by the fact that the patients with right hemisphere lesions were inferior to the controls on two other tasks (dot localization, block designs) that were part of the test battery.

A study by Bisiach et al. (1976) approached the problem from the standpoint of signal detection theory and showed that the performances of patients with brain disease were not differentially affected by response biases. Patients with unilateral disease of either hemisphere generally performed at a lower level than controls in the discrimination of length, size, curvature, and brightness. Patients with right hemisphere disease and with visual field defects showed the most marked impairment. However, in only one test (discrimination of length) were between-group differences significant.

Thus the indications are that impairment in simple visual discrimination is not a particularly frequent occurrence in patients with brain disease. Of all groups of patients, those with posterior parietal disease of the right hemisphere are most likely to show defects of this type. Analogous somesthetic performance presents an interesting contrast in this respect. Raised thresholds for light pressure and passive movement, and impairment in tactile two-point discrimination on the side of the body ipsilateral to the side of lesion have been reported by some investigators to occur with notable frequency in patients with unilateral brain disease (Semmes et al., 1960; Vaughan and Costa, 1962; Carmon, 1971). Similarly, in the field of audition, Milner (1962) found that patients with right temporal-lobe excisions were inferior to both control patients and those with left temporal-lobe excisions in the discrimination of loudness, duration, and pitch. Moreover, the observations of Bertoloni et al. (1978) of a left field (i.e., right hemisphere) superiority in the visual discrimination of velocity in normal subjects suggest that there are other types of "simple" visual discrimination which might be explored with profit in patients with brain lesions.

More impressive between-group differences are found when patients are required to discriminate between complex visual stimulus-configurations that differ in one or another subtle characteristic, if the task presented is sufficiently difficult that relatively few subjects make perfect performances. Two examples will be cited to illustrate the point.

Meier and French (1965) studied the visual discrimination of complex figures in patients who had undergone resection of either the right or the left temporal lobe for relief of psychomotor seizures. The two groups were equated for mean age (31–33 years), mean WAIS IQ (96–97), and mean Porteus Maze performance level (13.3–13.5 years). The tasks that were presented assessed the ability to discriminate between fragmented concentric circular patterns on the basis of either a rotational or a structural cue that differentiated one pattern from three other identical patterns. The patients with right hemisphere lesions were clearly inferior to those with left hemisphere excisions, their mean error score being 46% higher and the between-groups difference in mean error score being significant at the .01 level. Both brain-diseased groups performed at levels significantly below that of normal subjects.

Benton et al. (1983) assessed the performances of control and brain-diseased patients on a standardized test of complex form discrimination. A remarkably high proportion of the patients with brain lesions performed defectively (as defined by a score exceeded by 98% of the controls). The overall frequency of failure was 53% painets with right hemisphere lesions showing a somewhat higher frequency (58%) than those with lesions of the left hemisphere (47%). Within the right hemisphere group, the patients with posterior lesions showed the highest frequency of failure (78%). A high proportion (71%) of patients with bilateral disease also performed defectively.

The findings of both studies showed that impairment in complex form discrimination is quite frequent in brain-diseased patients, independent of the side of lesion; however, there is a trend toward a higher frequency in patients with lesions of the right hemisphere. The fact that tasks of this type make demands on the capacity for sustained attention suggests that failing performance in some cases may be due to an attention-concentration disturbance rather than to a specific visuoperceptual defect. The clinical examiner should be able to evaluate this possibility by determining whether defective attention-concentration is evident in other performances.

Figure–Ground Differentiation

Impairment in the ability to separate figure from ground in the visual perception of complex stimulus-configurations has long been considered a prominent feature of higher-level visuoperceptive defect in patients with brain disease. The ability is typically assessed by tasks requiring the detection of "imbedded" or "mixed" figures. The *Embedded Figure Test* developed by Gottschaldt to investigate the determinants of figure–ground differentiation has been utilized in a number of clinical neuropsychological studies (Teuber and Weinstein, 1956; Weinstein, 1964; Russo and Vignolo, 1967; Orgass et al., 1972). The findings of these studies indicate that: (1) impaired performance is found in a significant proportion of patients with focal brain disease, independently of locus of lesion; (2) among nonaphasic patients with focal brain disease, those with parieto-occipital lesions of the right hemisphere show the most severe impairment; (3) the performance level of aphasic patients with left hemisphere disease is inferior to that of nonaphasic patients with left hemisphere disease and comparable to that of nonaphasic patients with posterior right-hemisphere disease; (4) performance level is not significantly associated with the presence or absence of visual field defect.

The reasons for the observed association between aphasic disorder and defective performance on this nonverbal visuoperceptive task have not been clearly identified. One possibility is that the aphasic patients have more extensive lesions than their nonaphasic counterparts with left hemisphere disease and that their defective imbedded-figure-test performances reflect general mental impairment associated with a relatively large loss of neuronal tissue. Although no empirical findings have been marshalled to support this possibility, it cannot be ruled out. An argument against it is that, as will be seen, there are other types of visuoperceptive performance that are not related to the presence of aphasia in patients with left hemisphere disease. A second possibility is that performance on the Gottschaldt test is language dependent in the sense that detection of the target figure imbedded in a distracting background is facilitated by implicit verbal mediation processes, i.e., the visual information is verbally coded. If this is so, it would be expected that aphasic patients with disturbances in verbal thinking would perform on a subnormal level. It is perhaps relevant to note that dyslexic children have been found to be deficient on the Gottschaldt test as compared to normal readers with whom they were matched for age and IQ (cf. Goetzinger et al., 1960; Lovell et al., 1964).

Visual Synthesis

Some patients who can identify and name single stimuli are unable to grasp the interrelations among a number of simultaneously presented stimuli and to integrate the separate elements into a meaningful whole. For example, when presented with an action picture, a patient may enumerate the persons and objects in it but not describe what action is taking place or interpret the implications of the action. A task of this type was introduced by Binet in his intelligence scale and found a place in versions of the Binet Scale developed in different countries. Three levels of performance are typically distinguished: enumeration of elements; depiction of action; interpretation of the central meaning of the picture.

Binet considered the task to be an appropriate measure of "intelligence" and defective performance by patients with brain disease was at first interpreted as an expression of general mental impairment. However, Wolpert (1924) advanced the view that failure could reflect a modality-specific deficit in visual "integrated apprehension" (Gesamtauffassung) which prevented the patient from grasping the import of a complex stimulus situation even though each detail in it was recognized. He regarded the deficit as a form of visual agnosia for which he coined the term "simultaneous agnosia" (Simultanagnosie).

The nature and localizing significance of this defect have been the subject of many studies (Brain, 1941; Luria, 1959; Ettlinger, 1960; McFie and Zangwill, 1960; Kinsbourne and Warrington, 1962, 1963; Weigl, 1964; Fogel, 1967). Failure on picture description and interpretation tasks in patients with brain disease is certainly not rare. Fogel found that 25% of a heterogeneous group of 100 brain-damaged patients performed defectively in the sense that their description of a picture did not go beyond describing elements in it. Fogel also found that failing performance was associated with, but not completely determined by, general mental impairment. When "general mental impairment" was defined as a WAIS IQ score significantly below expectations for the patient's educational background, 32% of the impaired cases showed defective performance as compared to 21% of the unimpaired cases. Some investigators (e.g., Luria; Kinsburne and Warrington) have related the deficit to either left-sided or bilateral occipital lobe disease, but the findings of others suggest that failure may be associated with lesions in diverse areas. Fogel, in fact, found in his sample that patients with frontal lobe disease made the poorest performances. Nor have comparisons of patients with left and right hemisphere lesions shown consistent differences. This rather confused assemblage of results is understandable when one considers that the task of interpreting a complex meaningful picture makes demands not only on visual integration but also on ideational-associative capacity, verbal encoding, and verbal fluency. Thus a task such as this may be failed by different patients for different reasons. In the light of these considerations, Weigl (1964) questioned the validity of the concept of "simultaneous agnosia" itself, although he did not deny the potential usefulness of picture description tests in the assessment of brain-diseased patients.

The identification of incomplete and mutilated figures and "closure" tasks such as Mooney's (1957) faces and the figure completion test of Street (1931) furnish rather purer measures of the ability to synthesize visual information. As has already been noted, defective performance on the Mooney test is associated with right hemisphere disease (Lansdell, 1968; Newcombe and Russell, 1969). Impaired perception of incomplete figures has also been related to right hemisphere lesions. Presenting such a task to patients with unilateral brain disease, Warrington and James (1967) found that patients with right hemisphere lesions performed significantly worse than either controls or patients with left hemisphere lesions. Within the right hemisphere group, those patients with lesions involving the posterior parietal region performed most defectively. In contrast, both aphasic and nonaphasic patients with left hemisphere disease performed on a level comparable to that of controls. Poor performance on the Street test has also been found in patients with right hemisphere disease, particularly those with lesions involving the occipital lobe or with visual-field defects (Orgass et al., 1972).

IMPAIRMENT IN FACIAL RECOGNITION

There are at least two reasons why the identification and discrimination of faces have been singled out for particular study in the field of neuropsychology. First, there are patients who present as their primary complaint a loss in the ability to identify familiar persons, a defect that has come to be known as prosopagnosia or facial agnosia. Thus, facial recognition possesses an inherent clinical interest. Secondly, as Meadows (1974a) and Benton (1980) have pointed out, facial recognition does occupy a special place in visual experience. Over the course of a lifetime one learns to identify thousands of different faces. Even the faces of persons whom one has met on only one occasion may be recognized instantly at a second encounter years later. There is no other category of nonverbal visual stimulus remotely like it in this respect. It is true that thousands of words can be discriminated but these are phonologically analyzable and encodable.

There are two types of impairment of facial recognition that are essentially independent of each other and that have different neurological implications. The first is facial agnosia or the inability to identify the faces of familiar persons. The second is defective discrimination or matching of unfamiliar faces which makes no demands on memory or past experience.

Facial Agnosia (Prosopagnosia)

The primary disability in facial agnosia is a patient's incapacity to recognize persons familiar to him, even the members of his family, on the basis of visual perception of their faces. He may succeed in identifying another person on the basis of stature, a distinctive coiffure, facial mark, type of clothing, voice, or gait. He may be able to give an adequate verbal description of the face of a familiar person and at the same time to be unable to identify it on confrontation. Such patients have no difficulty in recognizing objects.

A number of other disabilities are frequently (but not invariably) associated with facial agnosia. The patient may fail to recognize the meaning of such graphic symbols as a red cross or a swastika, even though he perceives them clearly. And, while he readily recognizes objects, he may be unable to identify a specific object, such as a particular building or automobile. He may show spatial disorientation, defective perception of colors, loss of topographic memory, or constructional apraxia. Defects in the left visual field are the rule. So-called dyspraxia for dressing has been observed in some patients. Thus, in general, facial agnosia is seen in combination with the constellation of behavioral defects associated with right hemisphere disease, leading to the conclusion on clinical grounds that it also is a "right hemisphere" phenomenon. In support of this conclusion, Hécaen and Angelergues (1963) found in a study of 22 cases of facial agnosia that 16 had right-hemisphere lesions, 4 had bilateral disease, and 2 had left hemisphere lesions.

However, although clinical evidence favors an association between facial agnosia and right hemisphere disease, the analyses by Rondot and Tzavaras (1969), Lhermitte et al. (1972), Meadows (1974a), and Damasio et al. (1982) of the anatomic findings in these cases strongly suggest that bilateral lesions are necessary for the appearance of the deficit. Table 8-2 reproduces the listing of autopsied cases presented by Lhermitte et al. (1972), augmented by the case studies of Benson et al. (1974) and Cohn et al. (1977). As will be seen, bilateral lesions were found in all instances.

Table 8-2. Autopsy Findings in Facial Agnosia

Author	Etiology	Sites of Lesion
1. Wilbrand (1892)	Encephalomalacia	Right occipital lobe extending to calcarine fissure; left occipital lobe (smaller lesion)
2. Heidenhain (1927)	Encephalomalacia	Right and left occipital lobes extending to lower aspect of calcarine fissures
3. Arseni et al. (1958)	Spongioblastoma	Left temporal lobe; right tapetum corporis callosi
4. Hécaen and Angelergues (1962)	Glioblastoma	Right parieto-occipital tumor infiltrating splenium and extending to left hemisphere
5. Pevzner et al. (1962)	Encephalomalacia	Left angular gyrus extending to parieto-occipital fissure; inferior lip of right striate cortex
6. Bornstein (1965)	Glioblastoma	Left temporoparieto-occipital tumor infiltrating splenium
7. Gloning et al. (1970)	Encephalomalacia	Left frontal lobe, insula and fusiform gyrus; right frontal lobe, insula, supramarginal gyrus, and fusiform gyrus
8. Lhermitte et al. (1972)	Encephalomalacia	Left fusiform gyrus; white matter of right fusiform and lingual gyri
9. Benson et al. (1974)	Encephalomalacia	Left medial occipital area; splenium and right inferior longitudinal fasciculus
10. Cohn et al. (1977)	Encephalomalacia	Right precuneus, cingulate, fusiform, and hippocampal gyri, pericalcarine area; left fusiform and lingual gyri, pericalcarine area
11. Cohn et al. (1977)	Encephalomalacia	"Bilateral symmetrical vascular lesions in the distribution of the posterior cerebral arteries, more extensive on the left"

CT scan findings, although less consistent in their indications, also support the inference that bilateral occipital disease is the basis for prosopagnosia. Of the three cases described by Whitely and Warrington (1977), one had bilateral infarctions, but only right occipitoparietal changes were evident in the other two cases. However, at 9 months followup the deficit was no longer present in one unilateral case and was apparently less severe in the other. In contrast, the patient with bilateral disease showed no change in his symptoms. The three prosopagnosic patients reported by Damasio et al. (1982) had bilateral lesions after stroke with persistence of the deficit for more than one year.

Thus there is convincing evidence that bilateral occipital disease is the context in which persisting prosopagnosia appears. No doubt this circumstance accounts for the fact that it occurs so rarely as a primary complaint. If posterior right-hemisphere disease involving the lingual and fusiform gyri were a sufficient condition, the deficit would be encountered far more frequently than it is. Moreover, clinical symptomatology in these cases has not proved to be a reliable indication of the unilateral nature of the lesion. As Lhermitte et al. (1972) pointed out, the cases of Hécaen and Angelergues (1962) and Pevzner, et al (1962), that are listed in Table 8-2, were judged on clinical grounds to have lesions confined to the right hemisphere but autopsy study showed bilateral involvement. Conversely, Lhermitte et al. (1972) and Damasio et al. (1982) cite patients with lesions directly compromising the right lingual and fusiform gyri and hippocampus who were not prosopagnosic.

Yet clinical evidence suggests that, within the context of bilateral disease, a lesion in the inferior occipital area of the right hemisphere may be a crucial factor. Many years ago, Faust (1955) emphasized the association between left superior quadrantanopia and facial agnosia and this point has been documented by Meadows (1974a) whose tabulation of the field defects found in prosopagnosic patients shows that a left upper quadrantic defect was observed in 33 of 34 patients who presented with either a bilateral or left field defect. As Table 8-2 shows, this indication of right inferior occipital involvement is substantiated by autopsy findings. Meadows points out that the possible functional effect of lesions so situated is to prevent visual information from reaching nonoccipital areas, primarily the temporal lobe. Still, as Damasio et al. (1982) have insisted, anatomic evidence indicates that homologous lesions in the left hemisphere are no less crucial.

The nature of the basic disability that underlies facial agnosia has been the topic of much discussion (cf. Benton, 1980; Damasio et al., 1982). This striking failure in recognition can scarcely be explained in terms of a general incapacity to discriminate between complex visual configurations. On the one hand, most prosopagnosic patients can identify and discriminate unfamiliar faces quite adequately, an achievement that significant visuoperceptive disability would render impossible. On the other hand, patients with demonstrably severe defects in visuoanalytic and visuosynthetic capacity—as reflected in failure on discrimination, figure–ground, fragmented figure, and feature detection tasks—generally are not prosopagnosic.

One proposed explanation is that the patient with facial agnosia has lost the capacity to recognize individuality within a single class of objects such as faces, buildings, automobiles or one or another category of animal (cf. Lhermitte and Pillon, 1975; Whitely and Warrington, 1977; Damasio et al. 1982). According to this view, prosopagnosia does not represent a defect that is specific to faces but one that affects performance on any task requiring the identification of a particular object such as one's own car, cat, or dog. Other theorists favor the concept that prosopagnosia is a highly specific impairment restricted to the recognition of faces (cf. Bodamer, 1941; Tzavaras et al., 1970). To date, the empirical evidence marshalled in favor of either interpretation is sparse and fragmentary.

Defective Discrimination of Unfamiliar Faces

Studies of the capacity of patients to discriminate and identify unfamiliar faces were originally undertaken on the assumption that the abilities which would be assessed were the same as those underlying the identification of familiar faces and with the expectation that the results would elucidate the nature of facial agnosia. Subsequent experience showed that the assumption was unfounded. If the assumption were correct, then prosopagnosic patients would be expected to show defective discrimination of unfamiliar faces and patients who failed to discriminate unfamiliar faces should have difficulty in identifying familiar persons. In fact, a number of case reports have described prosopagnosic patients who performed adequately on tests requiring the discrimination of unfamiliar faces (cf. Rondot and Tzavaras 1969; Assal, 1969; Benton and Van Allen, 1972; Tzavaras et al., 1973). Conversely, failure in the discrimination of unfamiliar faces is not at all rare among brain-diseased patients who show no evidence of prosopagnosia.

Studies of facial discrimination in nonaphasic patients with unilateral brain disease have consistently shown an association between failing performance and the presence of right hemisphere lesions (De Renzi and Spinnler, 1966; Warrington and James, 1967; Benton and Van Allen, 1968; De Renzi et al., 1968; Tzavaras et al., 1970; Bentin and Gordon, 1979; Hamsher et al., 1979). The observed frequency of defective performance varies from one sample to another, but all studies have found that the relative frequency of defect is more than twice as high in patients with right hemisphere disease than in those with left hemisphere lesions. The highest frequency of failure is found in patients with right hemisphere disease and visual field defect, the latter pointing to the importance of the retrorolandic localization of the lesion. (That visual field defect per se is not an important determinant of performance level is indicated by the finding that left-hemisphere-damaged patients with field defects do not perform less well than those without field defects). Among aphasic patients with left hemisphere disease, those with posterior lesions and significant impairment in oral language understanding are most likely to show defective performance. Indeed, the frequency of failure in this group of patients is almost as high as that in patients with right posterior lesions (cf. Hamsher, et al., 1979).

In summary, studies of facial discrimination in patients with unilateral lesions indicate that failure is prominent in two categories: nonaphasic patients with right posterior lesions and linguistically impaired patients (as reflected in poor oral verbal comprehension) with left hemisphere lesions. Tachistoscopic visual field studies of normal subjects have found a significant left field superiority in the accuracy and speed of identification of unfamiliar faces (cf. Rizzolati et al., 1971; Hilliard, 1973; Patterson and Bradshaw, 1975; Hannay and Rogers, 1979; St. John, 1981). Yet it is possible to reconcile these results with the clinical findings for it is generally the case that a minority of normal right-handed subjects show either no difference between the visual fields or a right field superiority. The performances of these exceptional subjects can be interpreted as reflecting the participation, or even the preferential use, of left hemisphere mechanisms in the mediation of facial discrimination. The differential association of holistic and analytical modes of information processing to hemispheric function provides one clue to understanding of the basis of these individual differences (cf. Galper and Costa, 1980; Sergent and Bindra, 1981).

IMPAIRMENT IN COLOR RECOGNITION

A variety of performance deficits are subsumed under this heading as well as under the terms, "color imperception," "achromatopsia," "color agnosia," "color anomia," and "amnesia for colors" found in the clinical literature. A patient may be unable to name colors correctly, but not show a correspondingly severe impairment in object naming. He may be unable to point to colors named by the examiner. He may not be able to give the characteristic colors of common objects, e.g., "red" for blood, "white" for snow, etc. Presented with uncolored line drawings of common objects (e.g., a banana or a fork) and a display of different colors, he may make gross errors in matching colors to the drawings, choosing blue for the banana or black for the fork. Presented with a large display of different colors, for example, the Holmgren woolen skeins, he may not achieve an adequate sorting of the colors into categories on the basis of hue. He may perform defectively on tests for color blindness, such as the Ishihara plates. Finally, he may show a visual field defect for colored targets but not for a white target. These deficits may or may not be the subject of complaint by the patient.

It is obvious that there is no unitary impairment in color recognition. Instead, these diverse performance defects point to the presence of distinctive underlying disabilities of a sensory, perceptual, associative, or linguistic nature, each of which has a different neurological basis. The major forms of deficit are described below.

Impaired Perception of Colors (Achromatopsia)

It has long been known that defects in the discrimination of colors, roughly analogous to congenital weakness in color discrimination, may occur as a consequence of brain disease. Central or acquired achromatopsia, dyschromatopsia, color blindness, and color imperception are some of the names that have been employed to designate these defects. The defect may be present in the whole visual field or in one half-field (hemiachromatopsia). Its presence is assessed by the same tests, such as the Ishihara plates and the Farnsworth-Munsell 100 Hue test, utilized to probe for congenital color weakness.

The first large-scale study of color imperception in patients with brain disease was undertaken by De Renzi and Spinnler (1967). The capacity was assessed by two tests, the Ishihara plates and a color matching task in which the patients had to abstract pairs of identical colors from two sets of colored squares. Failing performance on the color matching test was shown by 17% of the brain-diseased patients, with a decidedly higher frequency in those with right hemisphere lesions (23%) than in those with left hemisphere lesions (12%). Essentially the same findings were obtained for the Ishihara test where failing performance was shown by 9% of the total group, 14% of right-hemisphere-damaged patients, and 6% of left-hemisphere-damaged patients. Further analysis showed that failure was particularly frequent among patients with visual field defects. In the patients with left hemisphere disease, aphasics showed a higher frequency of failure than nonaphasics, but it is not clear whether the aphasic patients also had visual field defects.

A second large-scale study (Scotti and Spinnler, 1970) utilized the Farnsworth-Munsell 100 Hue test to determine whether the observed effects of side-of-lesion and visual field defect could be confirmed and also to investigate performance along the color spectrum in brain-diseased and control patients. The salient findings were that patients with right hemisphere disease and visual field defect performed most poorly and patients with left hemisphere disease but without visual field defect performed at a normal level. All groups, including the control patients, showed the same performance profile characterized by a relatively high number of errors in the green-blue section of the spectrum. Essentially similar findings indicating a higher frequency of color imperception in patients with right hemisphere disease have also been reported by Lhermitte et al. (1969) and Assal et al. (1969). In the latter study, however, the observed between-hemispheres difference was small and nonsignificant.

It should be noted that these large-scale studies defined "color imperception" on a statistical basis as a performance level below that of the great majority of normal subjects and not in terms of gross disability, as reflected in a patient's spontaneous complaints or evident loss of function. In contrast, anatomic investigations have dealt with cases in which loss of color perception was a prominent, if not the primary, complaint.

Anatomic study of cases of color imperception or "central achromatopsia" has a long history dating back to the 1880's (cf. Meadows, 1974b; Damasio et al., 1980). All the reports, the most recent of which are those of Green and Lessell (1977), Pearlman et al. (1979) and Damasio et al. (1980), are in agreement that bilateral lesions in the region of the occipitotemporal junction are the basis for full achromatopsia and that a unilateral lesion in the same territory will produce hemiachromatopsia in the contralateral visual half-field. Although the defect usually appears in association with other types of visuoperceptual impairment (e.g., facial agnosia, defective visuospatial judgment), it can occur in remarkably pure form. Thus it appears that a specialized neural mechanism in visual association cortex subserves human color perception (cf. Pearlman et al., 1979; Damasio et al., 1980).

Impairment in Color Association

Failure in tasks requiring a patient to indicate the characteristic colors of familiar objects, within the context of intact color perception, is the primary performance deficit covered by this concept. Provided that the patient understands and can produce the names of colors and familiar objects, an appropriate method to probe for the presence of the defect is to ask him what the usual color of an object, such as salt, peas, or a banana, is. Having him match colors to uncolored line drawings of objects either by actually coloring the drawing or pointing to the appropriate color in a display, is a more desirable procedure since it circumvents overt language activity.

The inability of some patients with brain disease to link colors (or their names) to objects with which they are characteristically associated was noted as early as the 1880's by ophthalmologists and neurologists and was the topic of considerable discussion over the course of subsequent decades. Wilbrand and Saenger (1904–1906) postulated a disconnection between the cortical visual center and the speech area in the left hemisphere as the essential basis for the disability. However, Lewandowsky (1908) pointed out that the failure of these patients on nonverbal coloring tasks (sometimes with preserved ability to give the name of the colors associated with objects) indicated a deficit beyond color anomia. Instead, Lewandowsky advanced the idea that the basic deficit consisted of a "splitting" between the concept of form and that of color, leading to a loss of associations between objects and their characteristic colors. All authors acknowledged the close relationship of the disability to aphasic disorder and Sittig (1921) emphasized the crucial role of verbal associative functions in performance.

De Renzi and Spinnler (1967) included both verbal and nonverbal color association tests in their study of color imperception. The verbal task consisted of asking the patient to name the characteristic color of familiar objects. In the nonverbal task, the patient was given a choice of 10 colored pencils and instructed to color a number of line drawings. Predictably, most of the failures on the verbal color association task were made by aphasic patients. However, a few nonaphasic patients with right hemisphere disease (about 10%) also failed; most of these showed defects in color perception (Ishihara plates and color matching). No such relationship was evident in the patients with left hemisphere disease. The results for the nonverbal coloring task were most interesting. About 50% of the aphasics failed the task, i.e., made a score below that of the poorest control. Performance level within the aphasic group showed a modest correlation ($r = .48$) with assessed severity of aphasic disorder. A few nonaphasic patients (11% of those with right hemisphere disease; 7% of those with left hemisphere disease) also performed defectively, failure here being closely associated with defective color perception.

A second study by De Renzi et al. (1972) also demonstrated a close relationship between impaired performance on a nonverbal coloring task and aphasic disorder. When attention was restricted to the 18 poorest performances in a sample of 166 patients with unilateral brain disease (60 of whom were aphasic), it was found that 17 of these were made by aphasic patients. Stated in another way, gross failure on the task was shown by 28% of the aphasic but only 1% of the nonaphasic patients.

Varney (1982) found that impaired reading comprehension was closely correlated with defective color-object maching. In a sample of 50 aphasic patients, 15 (30%) performed defectively (below the level of 96% of control patients) on a test requiring the subject to point to the characteristic color of objects depicted in line drawings. All 15 patients also showed defective reading comprehension, while only 10 of the 15 showed impaired oral verbal comprehension as assessed by standardized aphasia tests. Thus it appeared that whatever cognitive disability underlies defective color-object matching also impairs reading comprehension. Other relevant studies are those of Lhermitte et al. (1969) and Tzavaras et al. (1971).

The remarkable frequency with which aphasic patients fail the nonverbal task of matching colors to line drawings is often interpreted as implying that verbal mediational processes must underlie the matching performance. This is a reasonable conclusion but, as De Renzi and his co-workers have pointed out, it has not been securely established. Another possibility is that defective performance reflects impairment in a cognitive function subserved by left hemisphere mechanisms and hence is likely to be associated with (but not dependent on) aphasic disorder. De Renzi et al. identified the functional impairment as a "general disorder in conceptualisation," while Varney suggested that the color-form matching disability is an expression of "a relatively specific visual information processing disorder."

Impairment in the Verbal Identification of Colors

The inability to name colors on visual confrontation or to point to them when their names are supplied by the examiner are the major performance deficits subsumed under this heading. Other tasks that have been used to probe for defective verbal identification of colors are the completion of sentences calling for the name of a color (e.g., "The color of an apple is __") and controlled word association in which the patient is asked to name as many different colors as he can (cf. Wyke and Holgate, 1973).

It is to be expected that aphasic patients will perform defectively on these tasks, the degree of defect being proportional to the severity of their linguistic disabilities. It is also to be expected that patients with impairment in color perception will perform defectively on visuoverbal tasks. In line with these expectations, De Renzi and Spinnler (1967) found that 42% of their group of aphasic patients failed a combined test of color naming and identifying colors when the names were supplied, as compared to 10% of nonaphasic patients. Moreover, five of the six nonaphasic patients with right hemisphere disease who failed the verbal tests were found to have defective color perception as well. There remained five nonaphasic patients with left hemisphere disease who failed the verbal tests and who did not show impairment in color perception. These patients showed an apparently specific "color anomia" and/or "color name amnesia" not attributable to either linguistic impairment or perceptual deficit.

The most striking examples of specific visuoverbal color disability are seen in alexic patients who fail color naming tasks and at the same time show intact (or only mildly impaired) ability to name objects and pictures. This association of incorrect color verbalization with acquired alexia is highly frequent and is often included in the syndrome of pure alexia (i.e., without agraphia) and right hemianopia (see Chap. 3). Gloning et al. (1968) found evidence of "color agnosia" in 19 of 27 patients with pure alexia. Some insight into the neural mechanisms underlying visuoverbal color disabilities has been gained from clinicopathological studies of individual alexic patients. The findings and implications of two detailed case reports, one dealing with an alexic patient with impairment in verbal color identification and the other with an alexic patient without such impairment, will be considered.

Geschwind and Fusillo (1964, 1966) described a 58-year-old man who, following a vascular accident, manifested pure alexia and right hemianopia as permanent defects after the acute episode. He could not read words aloud or match them to corresponding pictures. He could read a few single letters and some two-digit numbers. He could write to dictation but was not able to read his handwriting. He was able both to spell orally and to identify words spelled to him orally. Speech production, understanding of oral speech, and object naming were intact, as were right–left orientation, finger naming, and oral arithmetic calculation. The single remarkable nonverbal disability was a severe disturbance in topographical orientation, reflected in his inability to give the location of his home or to describe routes in traveling from one place to another.

He was totally unable to name colors (including black, white, and gray) correctly, to identify the colors of pictures of objects where there was no inherent association between the color and the object (e.g., necktie, dress), and even to identify the colors of objects that are associated with specific colors (e.g., white writing paper, red bricks). Nor could he point to colors when their names were supplied by the examiner. In contrast, his performance on nonverbal color tasks was quite adequate. He could match and sort colors and correctly matched colors to uncolored line drawings (e.g., yellow to a banana). His performance on pseudoisochromatic tests of color vision was normal. He was able to state the usual colors of familiar objects such as an apple or the sky.

Postmortem examination disclosed areas of infarction in the left calcarine cortex, the splenium of the corpus callosum, and the left hippocampus, all within the territory of the left posterior cerebral artery.

Geschwind and Fusillo interpret this syndrome of alexia, impaired color cognition, and right hemianopia as the functional outcome of a disconnection between the right occipital cortex and the language area of the left hemisphere. The interpretation follows the classic explanation that the failure in naming (and identification) of colors as well as the alexia are due to a break in the connections between the visual cortex and the language area. Thus color anomia comes about because visual information cannot reach the language zone of the left hemisphere to be encoded. Faulty identification of colors named by the examiner comes about because verbal information cannot reach the visual cortex to be decoded.

A persisting problem has been how to explain the retained capacity for object naming and object identification by name shown by patients with alexia and color anomia since these sensory-verbal performances also would seem to depend on the same visual mechanisms that are invoked to explain color naming and identification performances. A number of possible explanations have been advanced, none with great confidence. One possibility is that visually presented objects or pictures arouse tactile associative activity in the brain leading to excitation of anterior areas in the right hemisphere which is then transmitted to the language zone of the left hemisphere through callosal fibers anterior to the splenium. Letters, words, and colors do not arouse such tactile associative activity (cf. Geschwind, 1962). Another possibility is that the naming of familiar objects is such an elementary and automatized performance that (assuming that the splenial fibers have not been completely destroyed) it can be sustained by meager interhemispheric connections (cf. Howes, 1962). This explanation implies that the patient with alexia and color anomia should have difficulty in naming less familiar objects. The clinical observation that the majority of alexic patients do in fact exhibit mild word-finding difficulties can be cited to support the implication. Still another possibility is that object naming is observed by neural mechanisms that are different from those involved in color naming or reading.

As has been noted, color anomia and alexia do not invariably appear in combination. The case report of Greenblatt (1973) describing an alexic patient without agraphia, hemianopia, or color anomia is instructive because it points to the possible neural mechanisms underlying each of the two performances. Autopsy study of this patient disclosed a neoplasm that had invaded the splenium and inferior part of the left occipital lobe, leaving the left calcarine cortex and optic radiation intact. Thus there was an interruption in the connection between the left angular gyrus and the right visual cortex, and a partial interruption between the left angular gyrus and the left visual cortex, involving the inferior or ventral connections. Greenblatt suggests that this disconnection was responsible for the patient's isolated alexia and that the remaining intact dorsal connection from the occipital cortex to the angular gyrus accounts for the preservation of color naming.

Thus the indications are that specific impairment in verbal operations with colors is explainable in terms of derangement of specific neural mechanisms and that some progress has been made in the identification of these mechanisms. Advances in knowledge depend on the continued accumulation of detailed clinicopathological correlational data.

VISUOSPATIAL DEFECTS

Patients with brain disease may show any of a variety of performance deficits indicative of faulty appreciation of the spatial aspects of visual experience. Some of the more prominent deficits and their correlates and interrelations are described below.

Defective Localization of Points in Space

This disability has long been familiar to clinicians who observed that patients with parieto-occipital injuries exhibited it in particularly severe form (cf. Benton, 1969). In addition, some large-scale studies have assessed its frequency and its association with locus-of-lesion.

Warrington and Rabin (1970) presented two cards containing single dots in a vertical array to patients who were required to state whether or not the position of the dots was the same on the two cards. Both simultaneous and successive presentations were given. The task proved to be rather easy, all groups of patients making relatively low error scores. Nevertheless, it could be shown that the performance of patients with right parietal lesions was significantly poorer than that of patients with left hemisphere disease or control patients; the latter two groups did not differ from each other.

However, Ratcliffe and Davies-Jones (1972; Ratcliff, 1982), using a different procedure for assessing accuracy of visual localization, obtained rather different results. In their study, patients were required to touch point stimuli on a projection perimeter while maintaining fixation of gaze. Defective localization was defined in terms of an average error greater than that made by any control subject. The essential findings were that patients with posterior parietotemporo-occipital lesions in either hemisphere performed defectively while none of the patients with anterior lesions showed defective localization. Visual field defect was not a significant correlate of performance level.

Thus the results of the two studies were in agreement about the importance of parieto-occipital disease in the production of the deficit but differed in their implications about the role of the right hemisphere in the mediation of visual localization performances. However, a subsequent investigation by Hannay et al. (1976) generated strong evidence of a difference in the performances of patients with right and left hemisphere lesions on a visual localization task. In this study the level of difficulty of the task was deliberately augmented by reducing the exposure time and requiring the patient to identify the locations of simultaneously exposed pairs of dots as well as single dots. Under these experimental conditions, 45% of a group of 22 patients with right hemisphere lesions performed defectively (i.e., below the level of the poorest control patient). None of the 22 patients with left hemisphere disease performed defectively and the mean score of this group was practically the same as that of the control patient group. In contrast to the Warrington-Rabin findings, visual field defect was associated with defective performance in this study. And, in contrast to the results of both of the earlier studies, patients with perirolandic lesions of the right hemisphere were found to be impaired as frequently as those with posterior lesions. All three studies were in agreement that patients with unilateral frontal lesions are likely to perform normally.

Possible reasons for the inconsistency of these findings may be considered. Some clinicians have differentiated between the localization of stimuli within "grasping distance" (thus permitting a reaching or pointing response) and those beyond arm's reach that require a verbal judgment (cf. Brain, 1941; Birkmayer, 1951). In addition, a distinction is somtimes made between the "absolute" localization of a single stimulus in relation to the observer and "relative" localization involving the spatial relationship between two stimuli as seen by the observer (cf. Kleist, 1923). The pointing responses made by the patients in the study of Ratcliff and Davies-Jones assessed "absolute" localization of stimuli within grasping distance. In contrast, the judgmental and matching responses called for in the Warrington-Rabin and Hannay-Varney-Benton studies assessed "relative" localization of stimuli which could not be touched. Thus it may be that the right hemisphere plays a distinctively important role in the mediation of "relative" but not "absolute" localization performances. A study in which both types of localization tasks are given to the same group of patients could be done to test the congency of this hypothesis as well as to assess whether the unexpectedly high frequency of defect in the patients with right perirolandic lesions found in the Hannay-Varney-Benton study was a chance finding in a small sample of cases.

Defective Judgment of Direction and Distance

Appreciation of the directional orientation of lines presented as either tactile or visual stimuli has been the subject of a number of experimental and clinical studies designed to determine whether there is a differential hemispheric contribution in the mediation of this spatial performance (Carmon and Benton, 1969; Newcombe and Russell, 1969; Warrington and Rabin, 1970; Fontenot and Benton, 1971, 1972; Benton et al., 1973; Benton et al., 1975; Benton et al., 1978 a,b; Sasanuma and Koboyashi, 1978; Benton et al., 1983). The results of all these studies have been consistent in indicating that perception of directional orientation is mediated primarily by the right hemisphere in right-handed subjects.

The findings of Benton et al. (1983) provide a clear demonstration of this hemispheric asymmetry, as reflected in the high frequency of severe defect in patients with right hemisphere disease. A test requiring identification of the directional orientation of lines was given to right-handed patients with focal brain disease and a group of control patients. The procedure consisted of presenting pairs of lines in different orientations to the patient and requesting him to point to them (or call their number) on a visual display (Fig. 8-1). Scores on this 30-item test were corrected for age and sex on the basis of normative observations. The distributions of these corrected scores in the control and brain-diseased groups are shown in Table 8-3. Severe disability (defined as a performance poorer than that of 98.5% of the controls) was shown by 36% of the patients with right hemisphere disease but by only 2% of those with left hemisphere disease, the majority of whom were aphasic. Analysis of the relationship of performance level to intrahemispheric locus of lesion in the patients with right hemisphere disease indicated that failure was particularly frequent in those with posterior lesions.

As was noted, tasks assessing the tactile perception of line direction have generated similar results showing hemispheric asymmetry in the mediation of performance. Thus the indications are that the right hemisphere plays a more important role than the left in subserving behavior requiring the apprehension of spatial relations independently of sensory modality. However, this conclusion does not imply that performances in both the tactile and visual modalities are necessarily mediated by the same neural mechanism in the right hemisphere.

DEPTH PERCEPTION AND DISTANCE JUDGMENT

A distinction between two types of depth perception can be made: real depth perception of objects in space and the perception of apparent depth produced by binocular disparity in stereoscopic presentation. Impairment in both types of depth perception and concomitant inaccuracy in judging distances have been described in the clinical literature as sequelae of bain injury (cf. Holmes and Horrax, 1919; Paterson and Zangwill, 1944; Critchley, 1953; De Renzi, 1982).

A further distinction can be made between two types of stereoscopic perception of apparent depth (Julesz, 1971; Hamsher, 1978; Ratcliff, 1982). Local stereopsis, or stereoacuity, is defined as the ability to detect small differences in depth through point-to-point matching of disparate points in the two retinas and it is presumably mediated by the activation of disparity-detecting neurons in the visual cortex. As assessed by performance with stereograms with well-defined forms, impairment in stereoacuity has been found in some patients with lesions of either the right or left hemisphere (Rothstein and Sacks, 1972; Lehmann and Walchli, 1975; Danta, Hilton and O'Boyle, 1978).

The other type of apparent depth perception is called global stereopsis (Julesz, 1971). The term refers to the capacity to achieve depth perception in the absence of well-defined stimulus forms and is presumed to be mediated by neural mechanisms other than those involved in stereoacuity. Assessed by the random-dot (or random-letter) stereograms of Julesz (1964, 1971), impairment in global stereopsis appears to be specifically associated with disease of the right hemisphere. This relationship was first demonstrated by Carmon and Bechtoldt (1969), who found that some patients with right hemisphere lesions showed strikingly defective global stereopsis, while patients with left hemisphere lesions performed on the same level as control patients. Carmon and Bechtoldt interpreted their results as supporting the hypothesis that, in the absence of monocular cues of form and depth, the right hemisphere is "dominant"

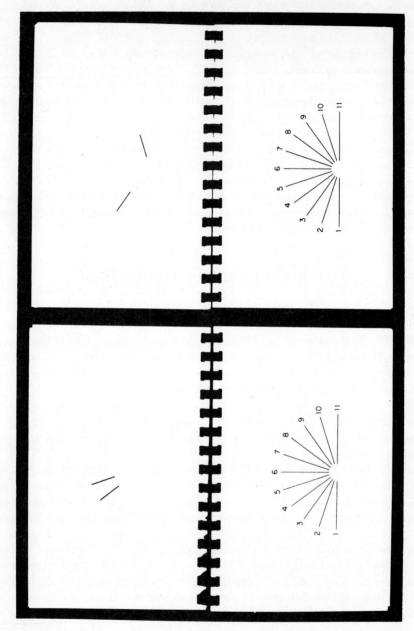

Fig. 8-1. Items in test of visuospatial judgment (Benton et al., 1983).

Table 8-3. Score Distributions of Control and Brain-Diseased Patients on Test of Judgment of Line Orientation (Benton et al., 1983).

Score	Normative Sample (N = 137)	Left Hemisphere Lesions (N = 50)	Right Hemisphere Lesions (N = 50)
29–30	38	6	2
27–28	22	11	5
25–26	22	8	3
23–24	25	7	3
21–22	18	9	8
19–20	7	4	6
17–18	3	4	5
>17	2	1	18

for stereopsis in right-handed subjects. Their findings were confirmed by Benton and Hécaen (1970) and Hamsher (1978). Both of the latter studies found that many patients who failed the random-letter stereoscopic task were able to perform adequately on a conventional test of stereoscopic vision involving defined forms. Thus it seemed evident that the technique devised by Julesz, in which monocular cues are completely excluded, is required to demonstrate the presence of the defect.

The frequency of impairment in real depth perception in patients with brain disease and the relationship of such impairment to locus of lesion have not been systematically investigated. A comparative study of both types of depth perception would be informative and, in fact, is necessary for further understanding of the underlying neural mechanisms.

Defective Topographical Orientation

A variety of performance defects have been placed under this heading. Some, such as inability to describe the spatial arrangement of the rooms in one's house or the disposition of buildings in a public square, to tell how one would travel from one point to another in one's home town, or to indicate the location of cities on a map, implicate failure in representational processes and memory. In these instances the patient is apparently unable to call up the detailed visual schema necessary to describe routes or make localizations. Other defects, such as failure to follow familiar routes, or to learn to do so in a new setting (e.g., a hospital), seem to be on a perceptual or attention level. Unilateral visual neglect is not only a demonstrably important determinant of failure in following routes but also can be a factor in failure on representational and memory tasks (cf. De Renzi, 1982). The findings of some pertinent clinical studies are summarized below.

Hécaen and Angelergues (1963) assessed "topographical memory" by requiring the patient to describe familiar routes, the arrangement of rooms in his house, the street on which the house is located, or the main square of the city. Studying large samples of patients with unilateral or bilateral retrorolandic disease, they found that loss of topographical memory, as refelcted in poor performance on these tasks, was shown only by patients with either bilateral or right hemisphere disease; even in these groups the deficit occurred rather infrequently. The highest incidence of failure (8%) was found in the bilateral cases. The patients with right hemisphere disease showed a 6%

and those with left hemisphere disease a 1% incidence. Control patients were not studied and it is not made clear how defective performance was defined.

Hécaen and Angelergues also studied geographic orientation (under the heading of "topographical concepts") by having their patients identify the principal cities, regions, and rivers of France on a map. Again, the criteria for judging whether a performance was defective are not explicitly stated. Here the authors found that no less than 21% of the patients with retrorolandic lesions of the right hemisphere performed defectively, as compared to 4% of left hemisphere cases and 6% of bilateral cases. It is clear from the descriptions in the monograph that failure on this map test was often associated with visual neglect of (i.e., failure to attend to) the left half of the map.

Benton et al. (1974) assessed geographic orientation both with a verbal test (requiring the patient to state the direction he would travel in going from one city or state to another) and with a nonverbal test in which he localized cities and states on a large map of the United States. Since educational background is an obvious determinant of performance level on these tasks, normative data were collected on two separate groups of control patients, one with 12 or more years and the other with fewer than 12 years of education. Defective performance was defined as a score 3 or more standard deviations below the respective group mean on each task. Defective performance on the verbal directions test occurred with equally low frequency (about 5%) in patients with right or left hemisphere disease. The frequency of failure on the map localization test was somewhat higher (22%) with only a slight difference between the right and left hemisphere groups (25% versus 20%). However, a "vector" score for the map test, which provided a measure of directional bias in localization, clearly differentiated between the two unilateral groups. The mean "vector" score of the patients with left hemisphere disease was −3.2, reflecting a systematic shift in localization toward the left or "western" half of the map. The mean "vector" score of the patients with right hemisphere disease was +4.4, reflecting an even greater systematic shift in localization toward the right or "eastern" half of the map. For the most part, defective performance was shown only by patients with less than a twelfth-grade education.

The ability of patients with penetrating brain wounds to follow routes on the basis of maps showing the path to be taken was investigated by Semmes et al. (1955, 1963). Patients with left parietal injury or bilateral parietal injury performed defectively, while the performances of those with lesions in other sites (including the right posterior parietal area) were comparable to that of control subjects. Among the patients with left hemisphere disease, those with aphasic disorder performed most defectively. Employing the same procedure, Ratcliff and Newcombe (1973) found that only patients with bilateral posterior injury performed defectively on the task.

Our knowledge of the determinants, correlates, and interrelations of defective topographical orientation, in the sense in which the term has been used in this section, is still rather scanty. From the anatomic standpoint, it is not clear that there is an unequal hemispheric contribution to the mediation of these performances. As has been noted, neglect of the left or right visual field may distort performance and lead to failure on some tasks. Visual neglect is shown more frequently by patients with right-hemisphere disease than those with left hemisphere lesions, thus creating a bias toward a higher incidence of failure in the first group, as Hécaen and Angelergues found. These authors also reported an association between impaired topographical orientation and a number of other defects associated with right hemisphere disease, such as constructional apraxia, dressing dyspraxia, and a "spatial" type of dyslexia.

VISUOCONSTRUCTIVE DISABILITIES

"Constructional praxis" refers to any type of performance in which parts are put together or articulated to form a single entity or object, for example, assembling blocks to form a design or drawing four lines to form a square or diamond. Thus it implies organizing activity in which the spatial relations among the component parts must be accurately perceived if these parts are to be synthesized into the desired unity. Following the designation of Kleist (1923), the pathological counterpart of constructional praxis, i.e., a specific defect in spatial-organizational performances, usually has been referred to as "constructional apraxia." However, as the historical sketch presented earlier in this chapter indicates, Kleist had a specific idea of what he meant by "constructional apraxia" and did not think that all forms of constructional failure belonged in that category. For this reason, the neutral and more inclusive term "visuoconstructive disability" is now more often used to refer to failing performances of this type.

Given the very broad definition of the disability as a disturbance in "organizing" or "constructional" activity, it is inevitable that a variety of tasks should have been employed to probe for its presence. The types of tasks that have been used in clinical and investigative work are listed below:

1. Building in the vertical dimension. An illustrative example of some historical interest is shown in Fig. 8-2. It appears in Poppelreuter's monograph published in 1917 and is probably the first pictorial representation of defective block construction by a brain-injured patient.
2. Building in the horizontal dimension, as in block design and stick constructions (see Critchley, 1953 for illustrative examples).
3. Three-dimensional block construction, either from a block model or a photograph (see Warrington, 1969, and Benton et al., 1983, for illustrative examples).
4. Copying line drawings (see Benton, 1962, for illustrative examples).
5. Drawing to verbal command, e.g., a house or a man (see Critchley, 1953 and Warrington, 1969, for illustrative examples).

In practice the level of difficulty of each type of task varies widely. With respect to copying, for example, a patient may be required to reproduce a few single figures, a design comprising several figures in a specific spatial relationship, or an extremely complicated figure containing innumerable details, such as Rey's complex figure (cf. Lezak, 1983). The actual block model may be presented to him for block design construction or he may have to proceed on the basis of a reduced schematic representation, as in the WAIS block design subtest. The stimulus for a three-dimensional block construction may be either the actual model or a two-dimensional representation of

Fig. 8-2. Defective vertical block building (Poppelreuter, 1917).

it. Clearly these diverse tasks are not equivalent in their demands on sustained attention, the capacity for deliberation, perceptual acuity, the apprehension of spatial relationships, judgment of perspective, and motor skill. Yet all are considered to be measures of "constructional praxis."

As has been mentioned, Kleist localized the causative lesion of "constructional apraxia" in the posterior parietal area of the left hemisphere. Subsequent clinical observation supported this localization, in particular, the frequent association of constructional apraxia with other symptoms referable to posterior left hemisphere disease, such as aphasic disorder, finger agnosia, and right–left disorientation. However, the fact that patients with right hemisphere disease also showed visuoconstructive disabilities became increasingly evident and, indeed, the indications were that these patients were likely to be more frequently and more severely impaired than those with left hemisphere lesions.

Systematic studies generally have supported these indications of a hemispheric difference in the direction of more frequent and more severe constructional disability in patients with right hemisphere disease (e.g., Piercy et al., 1960; Benton, 1962; Benton and Fogel, 1962; Piercy and Smyth, 1962; Arrigoni and De Renzi, 1964; Benton, 1967; De Renzi and Faglioni, 1967; Benton, 1968). However, a substantial number of studies have not found important differences between hemispheres (e.g., Warrington et al., 1966; Benson and Barton, 1970; Benton, 1973; Black and Strub, 1976; Colombo et al., 1976). This inconsistency is only to be expected when one considers the several factors that may determine level of performance on constructional tasks; for the most part, these were not controlled in the studies above.

An important factor is the task used to assess constructional ability. Benton (1967) found that impairment in three-dimensional block building and in copying designs was more than twice as frequent in patients with right hemisphere lesions than in those with left hemisphere disease; but an approximately equal proportion of patients in the two unilateral groups performed defectively on the WAIS block design subtest. Similarly, Benson and Barton (1970) found differences in the direction of poorer performance by patients with right hemisphere lesions on a template matching test and the "token-pattern" test of Arrigoni and De Renzi (1964) but not for three other constructional tasks.

Another factor is intrahemispheric locus of lesion, the general (but not invariable) rule being a trend toward poorer performance on the part of patients with posterior lesions. For example, Black and Strub (1976), investigating performance on three constructional tests in patients with prerolandic and retrorolandic unilateral penetrating brain wounds, found significant between-hemispheres differences in the direction of more defective performance by the patients with right hemisphere wounds on two of the three tests and a nonsignificant difference in the same direction on the third test. However, more impressive differences were shown in anterior–posterior comparisons, the patients with retrorolandic wounds being consistently poorer than those with prerolandic lesions. Moreover, some studies suggest an interactive effect of side and intrahemispheric locus of lesion on performance. In the Black-Strub study, the patients with right retrorolandic lesions consistently performed less well than did the patients in the other three "quadrant" groups. Benson and Barton (1970) noted a tendency for patients with either left retroroandic or right prerolandic lesions to perform most defectively. However, their groups were very small, and this may have been a chance finding.

Still another important correlate of performance level is the presence of sensory aphasic disorder. Benton (1973) compared the performances of nonaphasic patients with right hemisphere disease on a three-dimensonal block construction test with the performances of three discrete groups of patients with left hemisphere disease: (1) nonaphasics, (2) expressive aphasics with no significant receptive language impairment, and (3) aphasics with significant receptive language impairment. The highest frequency of defect (50%) was shown by the aphasic patients with receptive impairment. The right-hemisphere-damaged patients showed a 36% frequency of defect. The other two groups of patients with left hemisphere disease (nonaphasics or expressive aphasics only) showed a relatively low frequency of defect (13%).

The study by Arena and Gainotti (1978) of the performances of patients with unilateral lesions on a design-copying task generated similar findings. There was no overall difference in the frequency of defective performance (37% in both the right hemisphere and left hemisphere groups). However, within the left hemisphere group, the frequency of defective performance was 57% in the aphasic patients but only 15% in the nonaphasic patients. Moreover, a highly significant correlation of moderate degree

(r = .59) was found between scores on the Token Test and the constructional praxis test in the aphasic patients.

Still another variable that needs to be considered as a determinant of performance level is the size of the brain lesion. This factor has been invoked to explain between-hemispheric differences in constructional task performance, the argument being that since patients with right hemisphere disease have more extensive lesions, their performance is generally poorer than that of left-hemisphere-damaged patients. In fact, no empirical evidence has been added to support the contention. In the study of Benson and Barton (1970), the size of lesion was estimated by brain scan in 19 of the 25 cases. The left frontal group showed the largest mean (and median) size and the right frontal group the smallest. But the left frontal patients were superior to the other three "quadrant" groups on all the constructional tasks and, as has been noted, there was a tendency for the right frontal patients to perform particularly poorly.

The fact that such a wide diversity of tasks has been utilized and the observation that different tasks appear to interact in different ways with other factors to determine performance level had led some researchers to conclude that the visuoconstructive disability concept is too broad to be optimally useful in clinical or investigative work (cf. Benton, 1967; Benson and Barton, 1970). Instead, a classification in terms of types of constructional tasks differing in their demands on visuoperceptive, motor, and linguistic capacities offers greater promise of relating performance to cerebral function.

An initial distinction might be made between assembling performances (such as block building and stick construction) and graphomotor performances (such as drawing from a model or to verbal command). Dissociation in performance level on the two types of tasks, with a patient failing one and not the other, is often encountered in clinical evaluation and large-scale studies also provide justification for the distinction. In a study by Dee (1970), a group of 86 patients with unilateral brain disease were given both a three-dimensional block-construction test and a test of copying designs. Forty-six patients failed one or both tests. Of these 46 patients, 34 (74%) performed defectively on both tests. Thus 26% of the patients performed defectively on one test but not the other.

The differentiation first made by Duensing (1935) between an "ideational-apractic" form of constructional disability and a "spatioagnostic" form has been utilized by some theorists to explain the fact that defective performance may be shown by patients with lesions of either hemisphere. Following Kleist's original formulation, it is assumed that a perceptuomotor integrative mechanism in the left hemisphere mediates the motor aspect of constructional activity and that a lesion impairing this mechanism will disrupt performance even in the absence of visuospatial disability. On the other hand, impairment in visuospatial abilities resulting from right hemisphere disease will also be reflected in defective constructional performance as well as in failure on nonmotor tasks making demands on spatial thinking. If the theory is correct, defective constructional performance should be more closely related to perceptual impairment in patients with right hemisphere disease than in those with left hemisphere lesions. But empirical tests of this hypothesis have not confirmed it. The studies of Piercy and Smyth (1962), Dee (1970), and Arena and Gainotti (1978) indicate that visuoconstructional disability is closely associated with visuoperceptive impairment in patients with lesions of either hemisphere.

One or another form of constructional disability is shown by a remarkably high proportion of patients with brain disease. One study (Benton, 1967) found that in a sample of 100 patients, the majority of whom had unilateral lesions, 47 showed defective performance on one or more of four constructional tests (copying designs, three-dimensional block construction, stick construction, WAIS block designs). Twenty-two patients performed defectively on at least two tests. Of the 35 patients with right hemisphere lesions, 54% were defective on at least one test and 29% on two or more tests. Of the 43 patients with left hemisphere lesions, 35% were defective on at least one test but only 12% on two or more tests. The proportions of patients with bilateral or diffuse disease (bifrontal tumor or degenerative disease) who performed defectively were about the same as in the right hemisphere group, 55% failing at least one test and 36% failing two or more. Thus these tests may be diagnostically useful in that they often disclose disabilities related to brain disease which are only rarely the subject of complaint on the part of patients.

REFERENCES

Albert, M. L. (1973). A simple test of visual neglect. *Neurology* 23:658–664.

Arena, R. and Gainotti, G. (1978). Constructional apraxia and visuoperceptive disabilities in relation to laterality of cerebral lesions. *Cortex* 14:463–473.

Arrigoni, G. and De Renzi, E. (1964). Constructional apraxia and hemispheric locus of lesion. *Cortex* 1:180–197.

Assal, G. (1969). Régression des troubles de la reconnaissance des physionomies et de la mémoire topographique chez un malade opéré dún hématome intracérébral pariéto-temporal droite. *Rev. Neurol.* 121:184–185.

Assal, G., Eisert, H. G., and Hécaen, H. (1969). Analyse des résultats du Farnsworth D15 chez 155 malades atteints de lésions hémisphériques droites ou gauches. *Acta Neurol. Psychiat. Belgica* 69:705–717.

Badal, J. (1888). Contribution à l'étude des cécités psychiques: alexie, agraphie, hémianopsie inférieure, trouble du sens de l'espace. *Archives d'Ophtalmologie* 8:97–117.

Balint, R. (1909). Seelenlähmung des "Schauens," optische Ataxie, räumliche Störung der Aufmerksamkeit. *Monatsschr. f. Psychiat. u. Neurol.* 25:51–81.

Benson, D. F. and Barton, M. I. (1970). Disturbances in constructional ability. *Cortex* 6:19–46.

Benson, D. F., Segarra, J., and Albert, M. L. (1974). Visual agnosia-prosopagnosia. *Arch. Neurol.* 30:307–310.

Bentin, S. and Gordon, H. W. (1979). Assessment of cognitive asymmetries in brain damaged and normal subjects: validation of a test battery. *J. Neurol. Neurosurg. Psychiat.* 41:715–723.

Benton, A. L. (1962). The visual retention test as a constructional praxis task. *Confinia Neurologica* 22:141–155.

Benton, A. L. (1967). Constructional apraxia and the minor hemisphere. *Confinia Neurologica* 29:1–16.

Benton, A. L. (1968). Differential behavioral effects in frontal lobe disease. *Neuropsychologia* 6:53–60.

Benton, A. L. (1969). Disorders of spatial orientation. In *Handbook of Clinical Neurology*, Vol. 3, P. J. Vinken and G. W. Bruyn (eds). Amsterdam: North-Holland.

Benton, A. L. (1973). Visuoconstructive disability in patients with cerebral disease: its relationship to side of lesion and aphasic disorder. *Documenta Ophthal.* 34:67–76.

Benton, A. L. (1978). The interplay of experimental and clinical approaches in brain lesion research. In *Recovery from Brain Damage*, S. Finger (ed). New York: Plenum Press.

Benton, A. L. (1980), The neuropsychology of facial recognition. *Am. Psychol.* 35:176–186.

Benton. A. L. (1982). Spatial thinking in neurological patients: historical aspects. In *Spatial Abilities: Development and Physiological Foundations*, M. Potegal (ed). New York: Academic Press.

Benton, A. L. and Fogel, M. L. (1962). Three-dimensional constructional praxis. *Arch. Neurol.* 7:347–354.

Benton, A. L. and Hécaen, H. (1970). Stereoscopic vision in patients with unilteral cerebral disease. *Neurology* 20:1084–1088.

Benton, A. L. and Van Allen, M. W. (1968). Impairment in facial recognition in patients with cerebral disease. *Cortex* 4:344–358.

Benton, A. L. and Van Allen, M. W. (1972). Prosopagnosia and facial discrimination. *J. Neurol. Sci.* 15:167–172.

Benton, A. L. Elithorn, A., Fogel, M. L., and Kerr, M. (1963). A perceptual maze test sensitive to brain damage. *J. Neurol. Neurosurg. Psychiat.* 26:540–543.

Benton, A. L., Levin, H. S., and Varney, N. R. (1973). Tactile perception of direction in normal subjects. *Neurology* 23:1248–1250.

Benton, A. L., Levin, H. S., and Van Allen, M. W. (1974). Geographic orientation in patients with unilateral cerebral disease. *Neuropsychologia* 12:183–191.

Benton, A. L., Hannay, J., and Varney, N. R. (1975). Visual perception of line direction in patients with unilateral brain disease. *Neurology* 25:907–910.

Benton, A. L., Varney, N. R., and Hamsher, K. (1978a). Visuospatial judgment: a clinical test. *Arch. Neurol.* 35:364–367.

Benton, A. L., Varney, N. R., and Hamsher, K. (1978b). Lateral differences in tactile directional perception. *Neuropsychologia* 16:109–114.

Benton, A. L., Hamsher, K., Varney, N. R., and Spreen, O. (1983). *Contributions to Neuropsychological Assessment*. New York: Oxford University Press.

Bertoloni, G., Anzola, G. P., Buchtel, H. A., and Rizzolati, G. (1978). Hemispheric differences in the discrimination of the velocity and duration of a simple visual stimulus. *Neuropsychologia* 16:213–220.

Birkmayer, W. (1951). *Hirnverletzungen*. Wien: Springer-Verlag.

Bisiach, E., Nichelli, P., and Spinnler, H. (1976). Hemispheric functional asymmetry in visual discrimination between univariate stimuli: an analysis of sensitivity and response criterion. *Neuropsychologia* 14:335–342.

Black, F. W. and Strub, R. L. (1976). Constructional apraxia in patients with discrete missile wounds of the brain. *Cortex* 12:212–220.

Bodamer, J. (1941). Die Prosop-Agnosie (die Agnosie des Physiognomieerkennens). *Arch. f. Psychiat. u. Nervenkrankheit* 179:6–53.

Brain, W. R. (1941). Visual disorientation with special reference to lesions of the right cerebral hemisphere. *Brain* 64:224–272.

Carmon, A. (1971). Disturbances in tactile sensitivity in patients with cerebral lesions. *Cortex* 7:83–97.

Carmon, A. and Bechtoldt, H. P. (1969). Dominance of the right cerebral hemisphere for stereopsis. *Neuropsychologia* 7:29–39.

Carmon, A. and Benton, A. L. (1969). Tactile perception of direction and number in patients with unilateral cerebral disease. *Neurology* 19:525–532.

Cohn, R., Neumann, M. S., and Wood, D. H. (1977). Prosopagnosia: a clinicopathological study. *Ann. Neurol.* 1:177–182.

Colombo, A., De Renzi, E., and Faglioni, P. (1976). The occurrence of visual neglect in patients with unilateral cerebral disease. *Cortex* 12:221–231.

Corkin, S. (1965). Tactually-guided maze learning in man: effects of unilateral cortical excisions and bilateral hippocampal lesions. *Neuropsycholigia* 3:339–351

Critchley, M. (1953). *The Parietal Lobes*. London: Edward Arnold.

Damasio, A. R., Damasio, H., and Van Hoesen, G. W. (1982). Prosopagnosia: anatomic basis and behavioral mechanisms. *Neurology* 32:331–341.

Damasio, A. R., Yamada, T., Damasio, H., Corbett, J., and McKee, J. (1980). Central achromatopsia: behavioral, anatomic and physiologic aspects. *Neurology* 30:1064–1071.

Danta, G., Hilton, R. C., and O'Boyle, D. J. (1978). Hemisphere function and binocular depth perception. *Brain* 101:569–590.

Dee, H. L. (1970). Visuoconstructive and visuoperceptive deficits in patients with unilateral cerebral lesions. *Neuropsychologia* 3:305–314.

Denny-Brown, D. (1963). The physiological basis of perception and speech. In *Problems of Dynamic Neurology*, L. Halpern (ed). Jerusalem: Hebrew University Medical School.

De Renzi, E. (1982). *Disorders of Space Exploration and Cognition*. New York: Wiley.

De Renzi, E. and Faglioni, P. (1967). The relationship between visuospatial impairment and constructional apraxia. *Cortex* 3:327–342.

De Renzi, E. and Spinnler, H. (1966). Facial recognition in brain-damaged patients. *Neurology* 16:144–152.

De Renzi, E. and Spinnler, H. (1967). Impaired performance on color tasks in patients with hemispheric damage. *Cortex* 3:194–216.

De Renzi, E., Faglioni, P., and Spinnler, H. (1968). The performance of patients with unilateral brain damage on face recognition tasks. *Cortex* 4:17–34.

De Renzi, E., Faglioni, P., and Scotti, G. (1970). Hemispheric contribution to exploration of space through the visual tactile modality. *Cortex* 6:191–203.

De Renzi, E., Faglioni, P., Scotti, G., and Spinnler, H. (1972). Impairment of color sorting behavior after hemispheric damage: an experimental study with the Holmgren skein test. *Cortex* 8:147–163.

Duensing, F. (1935). Raumagnostische und ideatorisch-apraktische Störung des gestaltenden Handelns. *Deutsche Z. F. Nervenheilkunde* 170:72–94.

Dunn, T. D. (1895). Double hemiplegia with double hemianopsia and loss of geographic centre. *Transactions of the College of Physicians of Philadelphia* 17:45–56.

Ettlinger, G. (1960). The description and interpretation of pictures in cases of brain lesion. *J. Mental Sci.* 106:1337–1346.

Faust, C. (1955). *Die Zerebralen Herdstörungen bei Hinterhauptsverletzungen und ihre Beurteilung*. Stuttgart: Thieme.

Foerster, R. (1890). Ueber Rindenblindheit. *Graefes Archiv für Ophthalmologie* 36:94–108.

Fogel, M. L. (1967). Picture description and interpretation in brain-damaged patients. *Cortex* 3:433–448.

Fontenot, D. J. and Benton, A. L. (1971). Tactile perception of direction in relation to hemispheric locus of lesion. *Neuropsychologia* 9:83–88.

Fontenot, D. J. and Benton, A. L. (1972). Perception of direction in the right and left visual fields. *Neuropsychologia* 10:447–452.

Freud, S . (1891). *Zur Auffassung der Aphasien*. Deuticke: Leipzig und Wien. English Translation by E. Stengel (1953). New York: International Universities Press.

Gainotti, G., Messerli, P., and Tissot, R. (1972). Qualitative analysis of unilateral neglect in relation to laterality of cerebral lesions. *J. Neurol. Neurosurg. Psychiat.* 35:545–550.

Galper, R. E. and Costa, L. (1980). Hemispheric superiority for recognizing faces depends upon how they are learned. *Cortex 16*:21–38.

Geschwind, N. (1962). The anatomy of acquired disorders in reading. In *Reading Disability*. J. Money (ed). Baltimore: Johns Hopkins Press.

Geschwind, N. and Fusillo, M. (1964). Color-naming defects in association with alexia. *Trans. Am. Neurol. Associ. 89*:172–176.

Geschwind, N. and Fusillo, M. (1966). Color-naming defects in association with alexia. *Arch. Neurol. 15*:137–146.

Gloning, I., Gloning, K., and Hoff, H. (1968). *Neuropsychological Symptoms and Syndromes in Lesions of the Occipital Lobe and the Adjacent Areas*. Paris: Gauthier-Villars.

Goetzinger, C. P., Dirks, D. D., and Baer, C. J. (1960). Auditory discrimination and visual perception in good and poor readers. *Ann. Otol. Rhinol. Laryngol. 69*:121–136.

Green, G. J. and Lessell, S. (1977). Acquired cerebral dyschromatopsia. *Arch. Ophthalmol. 95*:121–128.

Greenblatt, S. H. (1973). Alexia without agraphia or hemianopsia. *Brain 96*:307–316.

Hamsher, K. DeS. (1978). Stereopsis and unilateral brain disease. *Invest. Ophthalmol. 4*:336–343.

Hamsher, K., Levin, H. S., and Benton, A. L. (1979). Facial recognition in patients with focal brain lesions. *Arch. Neurol. 36*:837–839.

Hannay, H. J. and Rogers, J. P. (1979). Individual differences and asymmetry effects in memory for unfamiliar faces. *Cortex 15*:257–267.

Hannay, H. J., Varney, N. R., and Benton, A. L. (1976). Visual localization in patients with unilateral brain disease. *J. Neurol. Neurosurg. Psychiat. 39*:307–313.

Hécaen, H. and Angelergues, R. (1962). Agnosia for faces (prosopagnosia). *Arch. Neurol. 7*:92–100.

Hécaen, H. and Angelergues, R. (1963). *La Cécité Psychique*. Paris: Masson.

Heilman, K. M. and Valenstein, E. (1972a). Frontal lobe neglect in man. *Neurology 22*:660–664.

Heilman, K. M. and Valenstein, E. (1972b). Auditory neglect in man. *Arch. Neurol. 26*:32–35.

Heilman, K. M., Watson, R. S., and Schulman, H. M. (1974). A unilateral memory defect. *J. Neurol. Neurosurg. Psychiat. 37*:790–793.

Hilliard, R. D. (1973). Hemispheric laterality effects on a facial recognition task in normal subjects. *Cortex 9*:246–258.

Holmes G. (1918). Disturbances of visual orientation. *Br. J. Ophthalmol. 2*:449–486, 506–516.

Holmes, G. and Horrax, G. (1919). Disturbances of spatial orientation and visual attention, with loss of stereoscopic vision. *Arch. Neurol. Psychiat. 1*:385–407.

Howes, D. H. (1962). A quantitative approach to word blindness. In *Reading Disability*, J. Money (ed). Baltimore: Johns Hopkins Press.

Jackson, J. H. (1876). Case of large cerebral tumour without optic neuritis and with left hemiplegia and imperception. *Royal Ophthalmological Hospital Reports 8*:434–444.

Julesz, B. (1964). Binocular depth perception without familiarity cues. *Science 145*:356.

Julesz, B. (1971). *Foundations of Cyclopean Perception*. Chicago: University of Chicago Press.

Kinsbourne, M. and Warrington, E. (1962). A disorder of simultaneous form perception. *Brain 85*:461–486.

Kinsbourne, M. and Warrington, E. (1963). The localizing significance of limited simultaneous form perception. *Brain 86*:699–702.

Kleist, K. (1923). Kriegsverletzungen des Gehirns in ihrer Bedeutung für die Hirnlokalisation und Hirnpathologie, in *Handbuch der Arztlichen Erfahrung im Weltkriege, 1914/ 1918*, Vol. 4, O. von Schjerning (ed). Leipzig: Barth.

Lansdell, H. C. (1968). Effect of extent of temporal lobe ablations on two lateralized deficits. *Physiol. Behav.* 3:271–273.

Lehmann, D. and Walchi, P. (1975). Depth perception and location of brain lesions. *J. Neurol.* 209:157–164.

Lewandowsky, M. (1908). Ueber abspaltung des Farbensinnes. *Montasschr. f. Psychiat. Neurol.* 23:488–510.

Lezak, M. D. (1983). *Neuropsychological Assessment*, 2nd ed. New York: Oxford University Press.

Lhermitte, F. and Pillon, B. (1975). La prosopagnosie: rôle de hémisphère droit dans la perception visuelle. *Rev. Neurol.* 131:791–812.

Lhermitte, F., Chain, F., Aron, D., Leblanc, M., and Jouty, O. (1969). Les troubles de la vision des couleurs dans les lésions postérieures du cerveau. *Rev. Neurol.* 121:5–29.

Lhermitte, J., Chain, F., Escourolle, R., Ducarne, B., and Pillon, B. (1972). Étude anatomoclinique d'un cas de prosopagnosie. *Rev. Neurol.* 126:329–346.

Lissauer, H. (1890). Ein fall von Seelenblindheit nebst einem Beitrag zur Theorie derselben. *Archiv für Psychiatrie und Nervenkrankheiten* 21:22–70.

Lovell, K., Gray, E. A., and Oliver, D. E. (1964). A further study of some cognitive and other disabilities in backward readers of average nonverbal reasoning scores. *Br. J. Educ. Psychol.* 34:275–279.

Luria, A. R. (1959). Disorders of simultaneous perception in a case of bilateral occipito-parietal brain injury. *Brain* 82:437–449.

McFie, J. and Zangwill, O. L. (1960). Visuo-constructive disabilities associated with lesions of the right cerebral hemisphere. *Brain* 82:243–259.

Meadows, J.C. (1974a). The anatomical basis of prosopagnosia. *J. Neurol. Neurosurg. Psychiat.* 37:489–501.

Meadows, J. C. (1974b). Disturbed perception of colors associated with localized cerebral lesions. *Brain* 97:615–632.

Meier, M. J. and French, L. A. (1965). Lateralized deficits in complex visual discrimination and bilateral transfer of reminiscence following unilateral temporal lobectomy. *Neuropsychologia* 3:261–272.

Meyer, O. (1900). Ein-und doppelseitige homonyme Hemianopsie mit Orientierungsstörungen. *Monatsschr. f. Psychiat. u. Neurol.* 8:440–456.

Milner, B. (1962). Laterality effects in audition. In *Interhemispheric Relations and Cerebral Dominance*, V. B. Mountcastle (ed). Baltimore: Johns Hopkins Press.

Milner, B. (1965). Visually-guided maze learning in man: effects of bilateral hippocampal, bilateral frontal, and unilateral cerebral lesions. *Neuropsychologia* 3:317–338.

Mooney, C. M. (1957). Closure as affected by configural clarity and contextual consistency. *Can. J. Psychol.* 11:80–88.

Munk, H. (1878). Weitere Mittheilungen zur Physiologie der Grosshirnrinde. *Arch. f. Anatomie u. Physiologie* 2:161–178.

Newcombe, F. and Russell, W. R. (1969). Dissociated visual perceptual and spatial deficits in focal lesions of the right hemisphere. *J. Neurol. Neurosurg. Psychiat.* 32:73–81.

Orgass, B., Poeck, K., Kerschensteiner, M. and Hartje, W. (1972). Visuocognitive performances in patients with unilateral hemispheric lesions. *Z. Neurol.* 202:177–195.

Paterson, A. and Zangwill, O. L. (1944). Disorders of visual space perception associated with lesions of the right cerebral hemisphere. *Brain* 67:331–358.

Patterson, K. and Bradshaw, J. L. (1975). Differential hemispheric mediation of nonverbal stimuli. *J. Exp. Psychol.: Human Perception and Performance* 1:246–252.

Pavlov, I. P. (1927). *Conditioned Reflexes.* London: Oxford University Press.

Pearlman, A. L., Birch, J., and Meadows, J. C. (1978). Cerebral color blindness: an acquired defect in hue discrimination. *Ann Neurol.* 5:153–261.

Pevzner, S., Bornstein, B., and Loewenthal, M. (1962). Prosopagnosia. *J. Neurol. Neurosurg. Psychiat.* 25:336–338.

Piercy, M. and Smyth, V. O. G. (1962). Right hemisphere dominance for certain nonverbal intellectual skills. *Brain* 85:775–790.

Piercy, M., Hécaen, H., and de Ajuriaguerra, J. (1960). Constructional apraxia associated with cerebral lesions: left and right cases compared. *Brain* 83:225–242.

Poppelreuter, W. (1917). *Die psychischen Schädigungen durch Kopfschuss im Kriege 1914–1916: die Störungen der neideren und höheren Sehleistungen durch Verletzungen des Okzipitalhirns.* Leipzig: Voss.

Quaglino, A. and Borelli, G. (1867). Emiplegia sinistra con amaurosi; guaragione; perdita totale della percezione dei colori e della memoria della configurazione degli oggetti. *Giornale d'Oftalmologia Italiano* 10:106–117.

Ratcliff, G. (1982). Disturbances of spatial orientation associated with cerebral lesions. In *Spatial Abilities: Development and Physiological Foundations,* M. Potegal (ed). New York: Academic Press.

Ratcliff, G. and Davies-Jones, G. A. B. (1972). Defective visual localization in focal brain wounds. *Brain* 95:49–60.

Ratcliff, G. and Newcombe, F. (1973). Spatial orientation in man: effects of left, right and bilateral posterior lesions. *J. Neurol. Neurosurg. Psychiat.* 36:448–454.

Reitan, R. M. and Tarshes, E. L. (1959). Differential effects of lateralized brain lesions on the trail making test. *J. Nerv. Mental Dis.* 129:257–262.

Rizzolati, G., Umiltà, C., and Berlucchi, G. (1971). Opposite superiorities of the right and left cerebral hemispheres in discrimintive reaction time of physiognomic and alphabetical material. *Brain* 94:431–442.

Rondot, P. and Tzavaras, A. (1969). La prosopagnosie après vingt années d'études cliniques et neuropsychologiques. *J. Psychologie Normale et Pathologique* 2:133–165.

Rothstein, T. B. and Sacks, J. (1972). Defective stereopsis in lesions of the parietal lobe. *Am. J. Ophthalmol.* 73:281–284.

Russo, M. and Vignolo, L. A. (1967). Visual figure-ground discrimination in patients with unilateral cerebral disease. *Cortex* 3:113–127.

Sachs, H. (1895). Das gehirn des Förster'schen Rindenblinden. *Arbeiten der Psychiatrischen Klinik Breslau* 2:55–104.

St. John, R. C. (1981). Lateral asymmetry in face perception. *Can. J. Psychol.* 35:213–223.

Sasanuma, S. and Koboyashi, Y. (1978). Tachistoscopic recognition of line orientation. *Neuropsychologia* 16:239–242.

Scotti, G. and Spinnler, H. (1970). Colour imperception in unilateral hemisphere-damaged patients. *J. Neurol. Neuosurg. Psychiat.* 33:22–28.

Semmes, J., Weinstein, S., Ghent, L., and Teuber, H.-L. (1955). Spatial orientation in man: I. Analyses by locus of lesion. *J. Psychol.* 39:227–244.

Semmes, J., Weinstein, S., Ghent, L., and Teuber, H.-L. (1960). *Somatosensory Changes after Penetrating Brain Wounds in Man.* Cambridge: Harvard University Press.

Semmes, J., Weinstein, S., Ghent, L., and Teuber, H.-L. (1963). Correlates of impaired orientation in personal and extrapersonal space. *Brain* 86:742–772.

Sergent, J. and Bindra, D. (1981). Differential hemispheric processing of faces: methodological considerations and reinterpretation. *Psychol. Bull.* 89:541–554.

Sittig, O. (1921). Störungen im Verhalten gegenüber Farben bei Aphasischen. *Monatsschr. f. Psychiat. u. Neurol. 49:*63–68, 169–187.

Strauss, H. (1924). Ueber konstruktiv Apraxie. *Monatsschr. f. Psychiat. u. Neurol. 56:*65–124.

Street, R. F. (1931). *A Gestalt Completion Test.* New York: Bureau of Publications, Teachers College.

Taylor, A. M. and Warrington, E . (1973). Visual discrimination in patients with localized brain lesions. *Cortex 9:*82–93.

Teuber, H.-L. and Weinstein, S. (1956). Ability to discover hidden figures after cerebral lesions. *Arch. Neurol. Psychiat. 76:*369–379.

Tzavaras, A., Hécaen, H., and LeBras, H. (1970). Le problème de la spécificité du déficit de la reconnaissance du visage humain lors les lésions hémisphériques unilatérales. *Neuropsychologia 8:*403–416.

Tzavaras, A., Hécaen, H., and LeBras, H. (1971). Troubles de la vision des couleurs après lésions corticules unilatérales. *Rev. Neurol. 124:*396–402.

Varney, N. R. (1982). Colour association and "colour amnesia" in aphasia. *J. Neurol. Neurosurg. Psychiat. 45:*248–252.

Vaughan, H. G. and Costa, L. D. (1962). Performances of patients with lateralized cerebral lesions. *J. Nerv. Mental Dis. 134:*237–243.

Warrington, E. K. (1969). Constructional apraxia. In *Handbook of Clinical Neurology,* Vol. 4, P. J. Vinken and G. W. Bruyn (eds). Amsterdam: North-Holland.

Warrington, E. K. and James, M. (1967). An experimental investigation of facial recognition in patients with unilateral lesions. *Cortex 3:*317–326.

Warrington, E. K. and Rabin, P. (1970). Perceptual matching in patients with cerebral lesions. *Neuropsychologia 8:*475–487.

Warrington, E. K., James, M., and Kinsbourne, M. (1966). Drawing disability in relation to laterality of cerebral lesion. *Brain 89:*53–82.

Watson, R. T., Heilman, K. M, Cauthen, J. C., and King, F. A. (1973). Neglect after cingulectomy. *Neurology 23:*1003–1007.

Weigl, E. (1964). Some critical remarks concerning the problem of socalled simultanagnosia. *Neuropsychologia 2:*189–207.

Weinstein, S. (1964). Deficits concomitant with aphasia or lesions of either cerebral hemisphere. *Cortex 1:*151–169.

Whitely, A. M. and Warrington, E. K. (1977). Prosopagnosia: a clinical, psychological and anatomical study of three patients. *J. Neurol. Neurosurg. Psychiat. 40:*395–403.

Wilbrand, H. (1887). *Die Seelenblindheit als Herderscheinung und ihre Beziehungen zur Homonymen Hemianopsie.* Wiesbaden: Bergmann.

Wilbrand, H. and Saenger, A. (1906). *Die Neurologie des Auges,* Vol. 3. Wiesbaden: Bergmann.

Wolpert, I. (1924). Die Simultanagnosie: Störung der Gesamtauffassung. *Z. f. d. gesamte Neurol. u. Psychiatr. 93:*397–425.

Wyke, M. and Holgate, D. (1973). Colour-naming defects in dysphasic patients: a qualitative analysis. *Neuropsychologia 1:*457–461.

9

Agnosia

RUSSELL M. BAUER AND ALAN B. RUBENS

Agnosia is a relatively rare neuropsychological symptom defined in the classical literature as a failure of recognition. The impairment cannot be reduced to sensory defects, mental deterioration, attentional disturbances, aphasic misnaming, or unfamiliarity with sensorially presented stimuli (Frederiks, 1969). In Teuber's (1968) words, "two limiting sets of conditions, failure of processing and failure of naming, thus bracket, so to speak, the alleged disorder of recognition per se, which would appear in its purest form as a normal percept that has somehow been stripped of its meaning." The notion that there actually exists a separate neuropsychological disturbance of recognition ("gnosis") fitting Teuber's narrow definition has come under attack in the modern literature from two directions. On the one hand, critics have claimed that agnosic failures can be understood as the combined result of a primary sensory processing disturbance and generalized mental deteriortion (Bay, 1953; Bender and Feldman, 1972) or as a complex mixture of disturbed perception and faulty sensory-motor exploration (Luria, 1959; Luria et al., 1963). More recently, Geschwind (1965) has stated that recognition is not a unitary process and has suggested that agnosic errors result from disconnection of intact cortical sensory regions from an intact speech area. In his scheme, the accuracy of the patient's report of sensory stimuli varies inversely with the extent of disconnection. These views are discussed more fully in the section on visual agnosia.

The first demonstration of agnosic phenomena was not in humans but in dogs with partial bilateral occipital lobe excisions. Munk (1881) observed that such animals neatly avoided obstacles placed in their paths but failed to recognize (react appropriately) to objects that previously had frightened or attracted them. Similar observations have been made more recently by Horel and Keating (1969, 1972) in macaques with lesions of the occipital lobe and its efferent connections to temporal regions. Munk attributed the failure to recognize without blindness to a loss of mem-

Preparation of this chapter was supported in part by a grant from the Division of Sponsored Research, The Graduate School, University of Florida. The authors wish to thank Mieke Verfaellie for translating some of the foreign language references and Maggie Dardis for help in preparing the manuscript.

ory images of previous visual experience and termed the condition "Seelenblindheit" (mind, psychic, or soul blindness). Lissauer (1889) was the first to provide a detailed report of a recognition disturbance in humans, and his views on varieties of the disturbance survive to this day (see below). The term "agnosia" was introduced by Freud (1891) and eventually replaced "mind blindness" and terms such as "asymbolia" (Finkelnburg, 1870) and "imperception" (Jackson, 1876). Liepmann (1900) was the first to clearly distinguish between agnosic and apractic disturbances.

The concept of agnosia has had a controversial, at times stormy, legacy. Historically, there has been heated debate concerning the underlying neuropsychological mechanism(s) responsible for disturbances in recognition. Not surprisingly, interpretation of available cases has varied according to the *zeitgeist* prevailing at the time. Benson and Greenberg (1969) remarked that the number of putative mechanisms has nearly equaled the number of well-documented cases. For example, in the early twentieth century, when Gestalt psychology provided the guiding structure of perceptual theory, published cases of agnosia were clinically evaluated with Gestalt concepts in mind (cf. Goldstein and Gelb, 1918 and Goldstein, 1943, with Poppelreuter, 1923, and Brain, 1941). More recently, with the reascendency of disconnection theory (Geschwind, 1965), agnosic defects have been largely interpreted as sensory-verbal or sensory-limbic disconnections. It is important to recognize that there is an intimate relationship between the clinical study of recognition disturbances and the experimental analysis of normal perceptual processes. Theories of perception must be able to account for dissolutions in perception observable in the clinic. Conversely, the specific clinical phenomena that receive attention are, to a large extent, dependent upon prevailing views of the nature of the perceptual apparatus.

Agnosia is most often modality-specific; the patient who fails to recognize material presented through a particular sensory channel (e.g., vision) is successful when allowed to handle it or to hear its characteristic sound. Visual, auditory, and tactile agnosias have received the most attention and are reviewed in this chapter. Visual and auditory agnosia continue to be by far the most thoroughly studied in the contemporary literature.

THE NATURE OF RECOGNITION

Before reviewing the varieties of agnosia, some comments about the nature of recognition processes are warranted. Some of the earliest neuropsychological theories of recognition were stage models that held that the cortex builds up a percept from elementary sensory impressions. Lissauer (1889) proposed that recognition is comprised of two stages, apperception and association, and outlined a theoretical separation of agnosias resulting from disturbance at each of these stages. By apperception, Lissauer meant the final conscious perception of a sensory impression, the piecing together of separate visual attributes into a whole. By association, Lissauer meant the imparting of meaning to the content of perception by matching and linking it to a previous experience, a process that requires the participation of association cortex. Lissauer felt that patients with a defect at the apperceptive level would not be able to match or copy a misidentified object or picture whereas patients with an associative deficit would be able to copy because they perceive normally.

Lissauer's distinction has been criticized by those who believe that a simple two-stage model is inadequate to the task of explaining perception. While a review of these criticisms is beyond the scope of this chapter, it is important to note that there are several fundamental difficulties with such a model and, in fact, with any theory that suggests that perception occurs exclusively from "the outside in" (from sensation to perception to cognition; cf. Weimer, 1978). Several studies (e.g., Brandt, 1971; Bradshaw et al., 1979) have shown that subjects can make cognitive (i.e., lexical) decisions about verbal stimuli presented too quickly to result in conscious perception. Furthermore, the conscious experience of perceptual data seems to depend not only upon the nature and quality of visual input but also on the efferent motor commands (e.g., oculomotor and exploratory behaviors) generated by sensory input (Festinger et al., 1967). Perception is an active process involving not only input from the ambient stimulus array but also coordinated motor and attentional mechanisms resident in "non-sensory" neuronal systems.

Clinically, several criteria are used to indicate that sensorially presented stimuli have been recognized: (1) naming the stimulus, (2) demonstrating its use, and (3) choosing from an array the stimulus named by the examiner. In many cases, these criteria allow the examiner to decide whether stimuli are adequately recognized. In other cases, however, the situation is more complex. The patient who fails to recognize according to these criteria may be observed to behave appropriately toward the stimulus once formal testing has ended. The problem results from the fact that these are criteria of stimulus *identification*, not of recognition in the broader sense of the word.

This issue led Geschwind (1965) to propose that recognition is not a unitary phenomenon. He states,

> There is no single faculty of "recognition.". . . The term covers the totality of all the associations aroused by any object. Phrased another way, we "manifest recognition" by responding appropriately; to the extent that any appropriate response occurs, we have shown "recognition." . . . There are multiple parallel processes of appropriate response to a stimulus.

Damasio et al. (1982), echoing this basic thesis, state that recognition is the "combined evocation of pertinent multi-modal memories that permit the experience of familiarity." We are in fundamental agreement with these views.

From these considerations, three general sets of performance criteria can be clinically utilized to index recognition. First, the patient's ability to *overtly identify the stimulus* can be assessed. This category subsumes the conventional criteria of naming, pointing, and object use mentioned above. Second, *subjective familiarity with the stimulus* (Pallis, 1955) may be formally determined by self-report. Third, the presence or absence of *responses adequate to the stimulus* (e.g., nonverbal, undirected discrimination of the object from others, or spontaneous object use) can be assessed. These tasks are arranged (roughly) in order of decreasing difficulty, although there may be exceptions to this in the individual patient. Noting the pattern of spared and impaired performance according to these three sets of performance criteria may be a useful way of understanding each patient's unique deficit.

VISUAL AGNOSIA

The patient with visual agnosia does not respond appropriately to visually presented material even though visual sensory processing, language, and general intellectual functions are preserved at sufficient levels so that their impairment cannot account individually or in combination for the failure to recognize. Poor recognition is usually limited to the visual sphere, and appropriate responses occur when the patient is allowed to handle the object or hear it in use.

When the patient fails to name but can indicate visual recognition by other means (description, gesture, etc.), the failure is considered to be "anomic" in nature and part of a more general aphasic disturbance. Unlike the agnosic patient the anomic patient does not improve when the material is presented through another sensory modality (Spreen et al., 1966; Goodglass et al., 1968) and is less apt to improve when asked to produce lists of words in specific categories, to complete open-ended sentences, or to respond to definitions. In contrast to the spontaneous speech of the nonaphasic agnosic patient, the conversational speech of the anomic patient may alert the examiner to the possibility of difficulty on visual confrontation naming because it contains word-finding pauses, circumlocutions, semantic paraphasias, and a general lack of substantives (see Chap. 2).

There is no general classification of visual agnosia that has met with universal acceptance. Lissauer's distinction between apperceptive and associative forms of agnosia remains, despite its problems, the most clinically useful scheme, at least as a starting point in the description of visual agnosia. Several subsequent classifications are quite similar to that of Lissauer. For example, Kliest (1934) distinguished between "Formblindheit" (a disorder of the early stages of perceptual discrimination) and "Dingblindheit" ("true" agnosia).

Visual agnosia has also been classified according to the specific category of visual material that cannot be recognized. Impairment in the recognition of faces (prosopagnosia), colors (color agnosia), or objects (object agnosia) and an agnosic inability to read (agnosic alexia) are found in various combinations and in isolation. The co-occurrence of associative visual object agnosia with alexia, color agnosia, and prosopagnosia is common, though not invariant.

From recent cases and literature reviews (Damasio et al., 1982; Bauer and Trobe, in press), another classification scheme has emerged. Some agnosias (e.g., visual object agnosia) involve a defect that prevents the recognition not only of the specific identity of an object but also of the general *semantic class* to which it belongs. Other forms of agnosia (e.g., prosopagnosia) are characterized by an ability to recognize the general nature of the object (e.g., a face) but a profound inability to appreciate its *individual identity*. Further well-documented cases are needed to support this distinction. It remains to be determined whether the distinction between "agnosia for object classes" versus "agnosia for specific identities" is a variant of the content-related schemes outlined above or whether it sheds light on a fundamental difference between various forms of recognition defect.

Apperceptive Visual Agnosia

Well-documented cases of apperceptive visual agnosia are rare. Most published cases have been criticized as examples of primary sensory failure and/or faulty visual exploration. No two patients present with exactly the same set of spared and impaired visual skills. The vast majority of cases have been associated with such pathological processes as carbon monoxide poisoning (Von Hagen, 1941; Adler, 1944; Benson and Greenberg, 1969), mercury intoxication (Landis et al., 1982), cardiac arrest (Brown, Case 11, 1972), bilateral cerebrovascular accidents (Stauffenberg, 1914), basilar artery occlusion (Caplan, 1980), or an atrophic process that produces bilateral posterior hemispheric lesions. The behavior of these patients suggests severe visual difficulties. Many are recovering from cortical blindness. Because of their helplessness in the visual environment, many are considered blind until they report that they can see, but not clearly. Standard testing then reveals normal or near-normal acuity in the spared portion of the visual field. Preservation of sufficient visual field and acuity to allow for recognition distinguishes the apperceptive agnosic deficit from that of Anton's (1899) syndrome, denial of cerebral blindness. Like Munk's dogs, these patients may appear blind until they can be seen avoiding obstacles with ease (cf. Benson and Greenberg, 1969).

Patients with apperceptive visual agnosia generally fail at recognition tasks because they cannot perceive clearly. They cannot draw misidentified items accurately or match them to sample. They are generally unable to point to objects named by the examiner. The impairment most often involves elements of the visual environment that require shape and pattern perception (faces, objects, letters). The recognition of even the simplest of line drawings may be impossible. However, bright and highly saturated colors may be more easily recognized. Again, there is tremendous variability in the pattern of spared and impaired skills, both across patients and across testing sessions.

Some patients are able to trace the outlines of letters, objects, or drawings (Goldstein and Gelb, 1918; Landis et al., 1982) but often retrace them over and over because they have lost the starting point. The patient of Benson and Greenberg (1969) was able to distingush small differences in the luminance (0.1 log unit) and wavelength (7 to 10 microns) of a test aperture subtending a visual angle of approximately 2 degrees. Many patients behave as if they are unaware of and unconcerned about their deficit until they are confronted with a visual recognition task. They then acknowledge that they do not see clearly. Others are aware of their difficulty but try to conceal it. A typical example is the patient of Landis et al. (1982), who stated, "People are easy to fool. They want to believe that I see. If my wife points to an airplane and asks me if I see it, I hear it and know it's an airplane, turn my head in that direction and say yes and she believes I have seen it."

Many patients complain that their visual environment changes or disappears as they try to scrutinize it (Riddoch, 1935). Recognition may improve when visual stimuli are moved (Botez,1975; cf. Riddoch, 1917). Patients may attribute their problems to a need for new glasses, to poor lighting, or to the fact that they have not had much prior experience with the particular kind of visual material they are being asked to identify. One of our patients, a retired architect, condescendingly remarked about the poor quality of the artwork making up line drawings of objects.

It has always been difficult to analyze and describe the visual performance of these patients, in part because of the tremendous variability in performance. The problem resides in determining whether, in these patients, the visual system is able to construct a sensory representation adequate to the task of identification. In most cases, the deficit does not fit the narrow definition of "a normal percept stripped of its meaning," thus calling into question the accuracy of the term "agnosia" as a descriptive label for these disorders. According to Bay (1953), there exists neither a specific gnostic function nor a specific disorder of gnosis, agnosia. Apparent cases of agnosia are actually disorders of primary sensory function due to lesions of the primary sensory fields or their connections. According to Bay, the presence of a generalized dementing process further complicates the interpretation of faulty primary sensory data. Bay reported abnormalities in sensation time (the minimal exposure time sufficient for recognition of portions of the visual field) and in local adaptation time (the elapsed time needed for a visual stimulus to fade from portions of the field) in patients with otherwise normal visual acuity and field. In these patients, visual stimuli tend to drop out of awareness because of abnormal fatiguability, particularly at the periphery. This time-dependent lability is referred to as "Funktionswandel" after the Heidelbeg school of psychology. Bay applied his tests to a patient with visual agnosia and, finding an abnormality of Funktionswandel, attributed the recognition deficit to primary visual sensory impairment.

Bay's findings cannot be generalized to all agnosics, however. His argument has been weakened by Ettlinger's (1956) findings of similar abnormalities in patients who presented with various combinations of visual field defects, perceptual derangement, and dementia but were not agnosic. One patient with prosopagnosia performed at a higher level on these tests than most of the nonagnosic patients. Recent studies by Levine and Calvanio (1978) suggest that patients with agnosia do not differ from normal people in sensation time or susceptibility to "backward masking." It is evident, therefore, that visual sensory abnormalities as measured by tests of sensation time and local adaptation time are not, even in the presence of dementia, sufficient in themselves to produce an agnosia-like recognition defect. It is true, however, that many patients with visual agnosia have elements of this type of disturbance and many also have abnormalities in visual attention, search, and exploration (see below). It may be that such defects represent a continuum on which impairment is a necessary but not sufficient characteristic of agnosia.

Bender and Feldman (1972) reasserted the claim that visual agnosias represent nothing more than a complex interaction among primary visual sensory abnormalities, various degrees of inattention, ocular fixation disturbance, and an organic mental syndrome (dementia). In their opinion, previously reported cases of visual agnosia were insufficiently examined. As evidence, they presented data from a retrospective review of patients who had been diagnosed as agnosic. Perceptuo-motor defects and significant organic mental syndromes were found in all cases, which led them to conclude that "visual agnosia is a result of a disorder of the total cerebral activity which renders performance of vision and/or other sensory functions inadequate." However, it is apparent that Bender and Feldman adopted unusually stringent criteria for ascribing a true agnosia, i.e., that the recognition defect must exist in the absence of *any* mental, aphasic, or perceptual deficits. Strictly speaking, this is neither necessary nor accurate; the concurrent presence of a visual sensory defect and visual agnosia cannot by itself be used as evidence that in the individual patient the visual defect is *sufficient* to result in the failure of recognition. It is important when examining such patients to investigate and report not only deficits but also islands of preserved ability in order to gain a fuller understanding of the complex dynamics of the problem.

Luria and his associates (Luria, 1959; Luria et al., 1963) have suggested that the phenomenon of simultanagnosia may be the basic underlying disturbance in visual agnosia. The term "simultanagnosia" was introduced by Wolpert (1924) to refer to a condition in which the patient is unable to recognize or abstract the meaning of the whole (picture or picture series) even though the details are correctly appreciated. Luria uses the term in a more literal sense: the patient actually perceives only one thing at a time. Luria equates simultanagnosia with a perceptual defect often found as part of Balint's (1909) syndrome, which is composed of three defects: (1) psychic paralysis of fixation with an inability to voluntarily look into the peripheral field (Tyler, 1968; Karpov et al. 1979), (2) optic ataxia, manifested by clumsiness or inability to respond manually to visual stimuli, with mislocation in space when pointing to visual targets (Holmes, 1918; Boller et al., 1975; Haaxma and Kuypers, 1975; Levine et al., 1978; Damasio and Benton, 1979), and (3) a disturbance of visual attention affecting mainly the periphery of the visual field and resulting in a dynamic, concentric narrowing of the effective field (Hecaen and de Ajuriaguerra, 1954; Levine and Calvanio, 1978). Balint's syndrome is almost invariably associated with large biparietal lesions and is especially severe when frontal lobe lesions are also found (Hecaen and de Ajuriaguerra, 1954). Frontal lobe involvement may lead to particularly severe psychic paralysis and optic ataxia, presumably because of disruption in visual-motor mechanisms.

Visual fields may be normal by standard perimetric testing but shrink to "shaft vision" when the patient concentrates on the visual environment. Performance may be worse in one hemifield, more often the left. A striking example of narrowing of the effective visual field is given by Hecaen and de Ajuriaguerra (1954, Case 1). While their patient's attention was focused on the tip of a cigarette held between his lips, he failed to see a match flame offered him and held several inches away. Levine and Calvanio (1978) found that patients with simultanagnosia reported only one or two letters when presented with three letters simultaneously. If told in advance which letter to name, they successfully reported any single letter; if told after the exposure which letter to name, they performed poorly. The authors interpreted the defect as a deficit in the perceptual analysis of compound visual arrays. Patients with Balint's syndrome and its minor forms thus do not perceive more than one object or part of an object at a time. It is as though they had bilateral visual neglect with macular sparing. Their problem is compounded by an inability to relate small portions of what they see to the remainder of the stimulus by scanning. Our own observations are that the severity of this problem exceeds the basic oculomotor disturbance, suggesting an immediate memory defect. Based on the study of such patients, Luria (1959; Luria et al., 1963) concluded that visual agnosia represents a complex perceptuo-motor breakdown of the active, serial, feature-by-feature analysis necessary for processing elements of a visual scene or pattern. In the most severe cases, prominent features available in the stimulus array may themselves be fragmented and distorted.

Kinsbourne and Warrington (1962) described patients with a mild form of this defect which they termed a disorder of "simultaneous form perception" and which they believed accounted for the reading disturbance usually present (see also Levine and Calvanio, 1978; Warrington and Shallice, 1980). Botez (1975) identified a group of patients with elements of Balint's syndrome who failed to recognize static objects but could recognize objects or letters slowly drawn in their view. There seems to be a range of effective drawing speeds that lead to recognition; if the stimulus is drawn too quickly or too slowly, it is not identified (Botez and Serbanescu, 1967). Botez attributes the deficit, which he calls visual static agnosia, to impairment in the geniculo-striate visual system and the spared ability to localize and use movement for recognition to spared function within the more primitive tectopulvinar nonstriate system (Zihl and Von Cramon, 1979; Celesia et al., 1980).

We have described Balint's syndrome and its variants in some detail because it is probable that elements of this disorder were present in most published cases of apperceptive visual agnosia (e.g., Goldstein and Gelb, 1918; Adler, 1944). For that reason, it may be helpful to compare a recent detailed case report of Balint's syndrome (Tyler, 1968) with that of a patient considered to have apperceptive visual agnosia (Efron, 1968; Benson and Greenberg, 1969). Whether the two are qualitatively different or simply represent different degrees of severity of the same deficit is unsettled.

> A 66-year-old woman (Tyler, 1968) suddenly developed visual difficulties associated with segmental basilar artery occlusion (see also Caplan, 1980). Visual acuity was 20/30 with glasses. Visual fields were at first considered normal, but careful retesting showed that, while the left field was normal to movement of large objects, these objects faded from awareness in one or two seconds. With continued testing in that field, awareness of even the movement of large objects was lost. In the right visual field, the central 2 degrees around fixation was always normal, the surrounding outer 20 degrees fatigued rapidly, and beyond 20 degrees, movement was recognized but objects faded rapidly. The patient could see only one object or part of one object at a time with her central 2 to 4 degrees of vision. She scanned normally when looking at predictable objects, such as a circle or a square, but frequently lost her place when viewing objects and pictures. Slight movement of the page made her lose her place. She reported seeing bits and fragments. For instance, when shown a picture of a U.S. flag, she said, "I see a lot of lines. Now I see some stars." When shown a dollar bill, she saw a picture of George Washington. Moments later, when shown a cup, she said, "A cup with a picture of Washington on it." Eye movement studies revealed a normal number of visual fixations per unit of time and a normal pattern of fixation for small saccades, or visual steps. However, there were very few, if any, long saccades, or leaps, which relate one part of a picture to another. The patient, therefore, looked for abnormally long periods of time at small portions of the picture.

The verbal reports of Tyler's patient are similar to those of the patient reported by Adler (1944), who was considered to have apperceptive visual agnosia.

When shown a picture of a boy admiring a sailboat in a toy shop followed by a picture of the boy bending down and playing with the same boat in a pool, she pointed to each picture and said simply, "A boy." She then pointed to the boat in each picture and identified it but did not recognize that it was the same boat because of its "different color." However, when referring to the color of the boat, she was actually pointing to the blue water.

In contrast to the two patients described above, whose impaired visual recognition is attributable to the combined effects of narrowed effective visual field and failure to adequately compensate for this by visual exploration, the patient reported by Benson and Greenberg (1969) and also by Efron (1968) appears to demonstrate an isolated failure of visual shape discrimination.

The patient was a 25-year-old man who was the victim of accidental carbon monoxide poisoning. He remained in coma for several days and gradually improved. For several months he was thought to be blind and yet was seen one day navigating the corridor successfully in his wheelchair. He was able to name colors and could often follow moving visual stimuli, but yet could not identify by vision alone objects placed before him. He could occasionally identify the letters "X" and "O" if allowed to see them drawn (Botez, 1975) or if they were moved slowly before his eyes. Visual acuity was at least 20/100 measured by his ability to indicate the orientation of the letter "E," to detect the movement of small objects at standard distances, and to reach for fine threads on a piece of paper. Optokinetic nystagmus was elicited bilaterally with fine ⅛-inch marks on a tape. Visual fields were normal to 3-millimeter-wide objects with minimal inferior constriction bilaterally to 3-millimeter red and green objects. There was an impersistence of gaze with quasi-random searching movements particularly noticeable when he was inspecting an object. His recognition deficit included objects, pictures of objects, body parts, letters, and numbers but not colors. He could tell which of two objects was the larger and could detect very small movements of small targets. He easily identified and named objects tactually and auditorily. He guessed at the names of objects utilizing color, size, and reflectance cues. He was totally unable to match or copy material which he could not identify. However, he was taught to apply a name to each object in a small group of objects which were presented to him one at a time on a piece of white paper. For instance, after he was repeatedly shown the back of a red and white playing card and informed of its identity, he was able on later exposures to identify it. He was thus able to use color and size cues to learn and remember the names of various objects in a closed set. However, when these objects were placed out of context, he was no longer able to name them. His recent memory, spontaneous speech, comprehension of spoken speech, and repetition were intact. On psychophysical testing he was able to distinguish small differences in luminance and wavelength. However, he was unable to distinguish between two objects of the same luminance, wavelength, and area when the only difference between them was shape.

The deficit in this patient, therefore, was a low specificity for the attribute of shape while the specificity for the awareness of other stimulus attributes was retained (Efron, 1968). Benson and Greenberg (1969) referred to the patient's defect as a "visual form agnosia" of the apperceptive type.

It has occasionally been reported that such patients can achieve remarkable compensations for their profound recognition defect. A recent patient reported by Landis et al. (1982) developed an apperceptive visual agnosia secondary to mercury intoxication and presented with a clinical picture similar to that of the famous patient *Schn.* (Goldstein and Gelb, 1918). The patient showed a concentric restriction of the visual field to 0.5 degrees with normal stereoscopic and color vision in the restricted visual field. Recognition of real objects was poor but better than recognition of pictures, which, in turn, was better than recognition of line drawings. Late in the course of the illness, the patient developed a strategy whereby he would trace letters, parts of letters, or words with the left hand alone or with both hands. He could trace simple geometric figures if the point of departure for tracing was unimportant. With more complex figures he was misled by unimportant lines. He could use color and size cues to aid recognition. He developed a sophisticated system of codes that aided in the identification of individual letters. Goldstein and Gelb's (1918) patient *Schn.* also developed a tracing strategy by using both his head and his hand. In both patients, recognition abilities deteriorated instantly if they were prevented from using kinaesthetic feedback.

It would be impossible with our present level of knowledge of visual perceptual physiology to finely localize the lesions responsible for what has been called apperceptive visual agnosia. We have seen that there is actually a spectrum of attentional, perceptual, oculomotor, and mnemonic defects here, and the relative contribution of each probably varies greatly from case to case. There is no singular entity called apperceptive visual agnosia, and there is no single defect that appears in constant form across all patients. From clinical analysis of these patients and from experimental research (Sprague et al., 1977; Perenin and Jeannerod, 1978; Berkley and Sprague, 1979), it now seems that complex visual processes should be viewed as composed of dissociable qualities and abilities, including visual acuity, form discrimination, color perception, luminescence, size, movement, and spatial localization. It is now well established that these abilities can be impaired in isolation or in combination. For example, Weiskrantz et al. (1974) reported a patient with hemianopia resulting from the excision of an arteriovenous malformation limited to striate cortex. In his hemianopic field, the patient could discriminate the large letters "X" and "O," could reach fairly accurately for stimuli, and could differentiate between horizontal, diagonal, and vertical lines. This patient, unlike the patient of Benson and Greenberg (1969) who "saw" but could not recognize, claimed that he did not see targets to which he responded correctly. The term "blindsight" has been applied to this phenomenon. Its existence illustrates the hazards of adopting a unitary concept of recognition.

As noted earlier, bilateral subtotal lesions of striate and peristriate areas have been incriminated in apperceptive visual agnosia. In some patients, clinical evidence suggests additional involvement of area 39 (Von Hagen, 1941, Case 2). It is interesting to note that monkeys with complete bilateral excisions of striate cortex can learn to discriminate simple patterns (Pasik and Pasik, 1971), suggesting that visual association cortex areas (areas 18 and 19) are capable of sustaining these functions. On the other hand, Denny-Brown and Chambers (1976) and Denny-Brown and Fischer (1976) reported that, with either complete removal of corticomesencephalic fibers and the colliculus or bilateral excisions of area 17 with preservation of areas 18 and 19, there is a loss of visual recogition of still objects but sparing of visual-spatial orientation, reaching for moving targets, and appreciation of edges, walls, and depth. Selective excision of areas 18 and 19, however, is associated with no loss of recognition of objects and of individuals. It is clear that the distinction between sensation, perception, and recognition (in its various aspects) and the relative participation of striate and extra-striate visual systems in each of these processes is far from settled.

Associative Visual Agnosia

The major distinguishing feature of associative visual agnosia is that patients can copy and/or match to sample items that they fail to identify visually. In the past decade, a number of well-documented cases of adequate visual perception have appeared in the literature, leaving no doubt about the existence of this form of agnosia (Rubens and Benson, 1971; Taylor and Warrington, 1971; Lhermitte et al., 1973; Benson et al., 1974; Hecaen et al., 1974; Newcombe and Ratcliff, 1974; Albert et al., 1975a, 1975b, 1979; Mack and Boller, 1977; Pillon et al., 1981). The patients of Rubens and Benson, Taylor and Warrington, and Newcombe and Ratcliff [Case 1] matched to sample and produced strikingly accurate drawings of pictures and objects they could not identify (Fig. 9-1). The patient of Lhermitte et al. performed normally on careful tests of ocular motility and scanning. The patients of Rubens and Benson and of Taylor and Warrington were able to find hidden figures in figure-ground tests. Case 1 of Newcombe and Ratcliff showed no deficits on psychophysical tests of visual function. This disturbance, therefore, cannot be attributed to primary sensory or sensory-motor impairment and fits the narrow definition of agnosia as "perception stripped of its meaning."

The core feature of associative visual agnosia is the inability to identify objects or pictures despite adequate demonstrations that the stimulus has been perceived with sufficient resolution or detail to allow for identification. Picture identification is typically more difficult than is object identification, and identification of line drawings is more difficult than either of these. A disturbance in the identification of line drawings or pictures may be the only residual after the acute disturbance has cleared. This dissociation is not seen in the naming performance of aphasics (Corlew and Nation, 1975; Hatfield and Howard, 1977) and may mark the presence of agnosia in naming tasks. The "complexity" (presence of fine-grained visual information) and the presence in the stimulus of "compound" (multiple) information both appear to contribute to ease of identification (Levine and Calvanio, 1978).

Prosopagnosia, color agnosia, and alexia are usually but not invariably found with object agnosia. Object agnosia is rarer than these other conditions, each of which may occur in isolation or in various combinations. For example, the patients of Hecaen and de Ajuriaguerra (1956), and Lhermitte and Beauvois (1973) had no impairment in facial recognition, and reading was spared in the patients of Davidenkov (1956), Newcombe and Ratcliff (1974), Mack and Boller (1977), and Albert et al., (1975a). Levine's patient and Case 1 of Newcombe and Ratcliff had no color agnosia or alexia. Alexia is commonly found alone or with color agnosia (Geschwind and Fusillo, 1966); prosopagnosia is frequently an isolated recognition disturbance (Pallis, 1955; Bauer, 1982) but is often associated with acquired achromatopsia (Critchley, 1965). Much

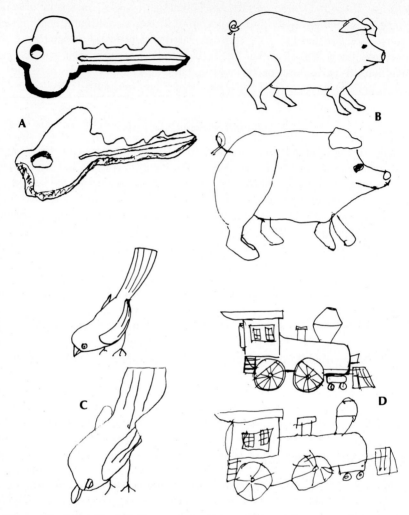

Fig. 9-1. Copies of line drawings by patient with associative visual agnosia. After copies were made, the patient still misidentified drawings as follows:

(A) "I still don't know."
(B) "Could be a dog or any other animal."
(C) "Could be a beach stump."
(D) "A wagon or a car of some kind. The larger vehicle is being pulled by the smaller one."

(From Rubens and Benson, 1971).

debate has centered around the coexistence of these various signs. Some authors believe that, in the individual patient, the coexistence of signs provides a clue about the basic underlying mechanism of agnosia. In this view, disturbances in two or more such functions (e.g. object agnosia and prosopagnosia) reflect task and processing similarities between the recognition of objects and faces. Others believe that the coincidence of these various forms of recognition disturbance reflects a "neighborhood sign" and results from the fact that the different functions are resident in adjacent cortical and subcortical structures. This issue has not been sufficiently resolved.

Tactile and auditory recognition are typically intact. However, two patients of Newcombe and Ratcliff and the patient of Taylor and Warrington were not able to identify objects by touch or by vision. Impairment in short-term verbal memory, particularly as measured by paired-associate word learning, has been present in every patient in whom such testing has been reported. Paradoxically, intact short-term non-verbal memory has been documented in many of these same patients. Modality-specific memory (e.g., visual versus auditory versus tactile) has not been adequately assessed in most patients (Ross, 1980a).

The most common visual field defect is a dense right homonymous hemianopia. In the patient of Albert et al. (1975a), the right visual field defect was confined to the upper quadrant. Two left-handed patients with left homonymous hemianopias have been reported (Newcombe and Ratcliff, 1974, Case 2; Levine, 1978). Interestingly, reading was spared in all three of these patients. Normal visual fields have also been reported (Davidenkov, 1956; Taylor and Warrington, 1971; Newcombe and Ratcliff, 1974, Case 1).

The clinical picture is one of a patient who fails to name or to describe verbally or by gesture the nature of visually presented material but is able to draw or to match the misidentified material with identical or similar samples. Pointing to objects named by the examiner is typically better than identifying objects verbally or by gesture, although in most patients this skill is subnormal. As recovery progresses, pointing may return to normal while other signs of object identification remain impaired. This may reflect the fact that pointing takes place in the context of a closed set whereas naming an object involves a search through an almost infinite list of potential names. However, it is possible that pointing to a named object is an easier task because it does not involve speaking and therefore reduces the chances that an incorrect verbal response will adversely affect parallel, nonverbal aspects of stimulus recognition (see below).

Incorrect responses usually are morphological confusions or perseverations. Semantic confusions, however, are not uncommon. Perseverations may represent previously viewed objects or, more commonly, the verbal response to them. Lhermitte and Beauvois (1973) distinguished between horizontal errors, in which incorrect names occur for the stimulus being viewed, and vertical errors, in which a semantic relationship was found between a given name and a previously presented item. Stimulus complexity (e.g., presence of color, morphological similarity between items) appears to exert a strong effect on the frequency of semantic and morphological errors. The frequency of perseverations is less affected by changes in the quality and complexity of visual stimui (Lhermitte and Beauvois, 1973).

It has been claimed that, in some instances, perseverations are verbal reports of a lingering visual sensory experience of previously viewed material, so-called palinopsia (Critchley, 1964; Cummings et al., 1982). However, the drawings of patients who have perseverated the wrong name in a series of visual presentations are those of the items they are viewing, not the items whose name they have incorrectly perseverated (Rubens and Benson, 1971; Lhermitte and Beauvois, 1973). Successfully copying a misidentified picture does not facilitate identification of that picture (but patients of Goldstein and Gelb [1918] and of Landis et al. [1982] could recognize *only* by kinaesthetic mediation). This general finding indicates that the motor system does not have the ability to cue the visual identification process in most patients. Viewing an object in use or otherwise in context aids recognition. Partially covering an item or placing it in unusual context hinders identification.

There is much evidence that the initial verbalized response to visual presentation affects otherwise intact abilities, often adversely. The strong perseverative tendency and the disrupting influence of visual naming on tactile identification are examples of this. One might expect that patients who have demonstrated adequate blindfolded tactile naming will perform at least as well when they simultaneously inspect and handle the same objects. However, the otherwise superior tactile identification of the patients of Ettlinger and Wyke (1961) and Rubens et al. (1978, cited in Rubens, 1979) fell to the (much lower) level of visual identification alone when the patients were allowed to simultaneously view and handle objects. Ettlinger and Wyke's patient, when given two exposures of each of 21 items (42 total responses), made 26 errors with vision alone, only 9 with touch alone, but 16 with vision and touch.

Requiring the patient to write the name (Lhermitte and Beauvois, 1973) or to supply a description (Newcombe and Ratcliff, 1974) instead of naming aloud normalized recognition in the former case and enhanced it in the latter. Many patients however, insist on speaking despite strict instructions to remain silent. Case 1 of Oxbury et al. (1969), who was instructed to demonstrate in silence the use of objects shown to her, continued to name them aloud and then to produce an incorrect gesture corresponding to her verbal misidentification. This same patient, when asked to match a line drawing to one of three real objects, would misname the drawing and then search vainly for an object corresponding to her incorrect name. One of us (ABR) recently saw a patient who consistently misidentified objects and pictures only when naming preceded demonstration of use; when instructed to first silently (with tongue held between teeth) demonstrate function, he supplied the proper gesture and then followed with the correct name. This patient was also unable to group pictures into categories unless strictly instructed to remain silent. These examples illustrate some of the many ways patients develop and utilize self-cuing strategies to aid visual recognition failures and reinforce the notion that not only afferent input, but also the patient's behavior itself, may provide information about the nature and identity of stimuli.

We have described these behaviors in detail in order to emphasize the importance of controlling for the confabulation factor when examining various cognitive and gnostic functions (Geschwind, 1965). Many authors have commented on the erratic performance of these patients in the test situation and particularly in everyday life (e.g., Critchley, 1964). It is not uncommon for patients to function well in their visual environment in everyday life but then fail miserably on recognition when formally tested in the controlled conditions of the neuropsychology laboratory. Much of the variability, of course, is attributable to the facilitatory effects of context and redundancy inherent in a familiar environment and to the effects of multimodal cross-cuing.

The failure to sort objects and pictures into categories or to match nonmorphologically identical representations of the same object (e.g., a small line drawing of a wrist watch with a real wrist watch) is a common finding. This feature is sometimes so prominent that Hecaen et al. (1974) suggested that the basic disorder underlying visual object agnosia is a specific categorization defect for visual inputs (Pillon et al., 1981). However, this is likely not accurate since this disability is found with varying severity in patients with roughly equal impairments. Some agnosics, for example, can identify and sort to the general semantic class to which a stimulus belongs (e.g., prosopagnosics); their defect is in identifying individuality within that class. Others can identify neither the general class nor the individual within a class. The neuroanatomic basis for this distinction is not clear at present but may involve differences in lesion localization in the inferior-superior plane (Damasio and Damasio, 1982; Damasio et al., 1982; Bauer, in press).

The marked variability of performance of patients in the natural setting as opposed to the test setting has been noted by Geschwind (1965), who proposed that agnosia is not a defect of a unitary process of recognition but rather a special form of a modality-specific naming defect. He views the misidentifications as confabulated responses elaborated by the intact speech area pathologically disconnected from intact sensory area. Failure to supply the correct gesture results from concomitant disconnection between motor and sensory areas. (Incidentally, in the more severe forms of sensory-motor disconnection, copying tasks may be invalid as an index of recognition because of the strong motor component). The common association of visual object agnosia with right homonymous hemianopia, alexia, and color agnosia, a triad known to occur in the context of damage to mesial left occipital lobe and nearby posterior callosal fibers, supports the visual-verbal disconnection hypothesis. Authors arguing against the disconnection hypothesis cite (1) the occasional finding of normal visual fields or left homonymous hemianopia (Cambier et al., 1980), (2) the occasional absence of color agnosia and alexia in the same patient (Newcombe and Ratcliff, 1974, Case 1; Levine, 1978), and (3) the question of why a left occipital-splenial lesion produces the syndrome of alexia without agraphia commonly but object agnosia only rarely. Also, in some cases, there seems to be some (albeit subtle) visual-verbal connectivity present. For example, Levine's (1978) patient was able to verbally code some visually presented stimuli with remarkable accuracy (e.g., "something with 'U' in it," when looking at a padlock). Interestingly, Levine's case was not alexic and had only a unilateral (nondominant) occipital lobe resection.

Strictly speaking, the imperfect correlation between color agnosia, alexia, and visual object agnosia does not by itself invalidate the visual-verbal disconnection hypothesis. It remains possible that there may be highly specific forms of visual-verbal disconnection and that unilateral or bilateral intrahemisphere disconnection and/or selective destruction of independent pathways mediating various elements of visual recognition play a role (Ratcliff and Ross, 1981). There is, for example, evidence for the specificity of neural pathways for color (Meadows, 1974a; Zeki, 1973, 1977). This kind of specificity is also implicit in the classical work of Hubel and Wiesel (1968).

Neuropathological data suggest that sufficient (if not always necessary) pathology for the production of visual object agnosia includes either extensive left mesial occipital lobe destruction with callosal and mesial temporal-limbic involvement (Hahn, 1895 [autopsy of Lissauer's patient]) or bilateral cortical-subcortical occipital lobe lesions with disconnection of visual areas from both the left speech area and the limbic system (Benson et al., 1974 [autopsy of the case of Rubens and Benson]). A combined visual-speech and visual-limbic disconnection is suggested by this material. We discuss the clinical and theoretical significance of visual-limbic disconnection in a later section. There is some debate regarding the relative significance of cortical and white matter lesions (Albert et al., 1979; Ross, 1980b). It seems possible, even likely, that there are multiple forms of associative visual agnosia representing impairment at different levels of processing. Patients such as those of Taylor and Warrington (1971) and Newcombe and Ratcliff (1974, Cases 1 and 2) with diffuse bilateral disease processes, tactile agnosia, and normal visual fields probably form a separate group from those with right homonymous hemianopia associated with infarction in the territory of the left posterior cerebral artery. The relative capability of various disease processes, and of their structural and metabolic sequelae, to produce agnosic syndromes is a relatively uncharted research area.

The nature of pathological processes that affect the posterior part of the brain dictates that many patients with posterior cerebral lesions will have bilateral involvement. For that reason, it is common to see elements of apperceptive and sensory-motor scanning defects in patients with associative visual agnosia. It is rare to find an associative agnosic who does not show signs of piecemeal perception or who does not have to resort on occasion to a feature-by-feature analysis of visual stimuli. The interaction between these levels of impairment makes analysis of visual behavior extremely difficult and often confounds attempts at classification. Pending further knowledge and more refined taxonomies, several patients must be regarded as mixed forms. The recently reported cases of Kertesz (1979) and Wapner et al. (1978) illustrate this problem. Kertesz' patient is extremely difficult to evaluate, since she had elements of Balint's syndrome, visual static agnosia, simultanagnosia, alexia without agraphia, prosopagnosia, and amnestic syndrome. The patient performed poorly on copying tasks (her reproductions were poorly executed and contained only fragmented elements of the associated target stimuli) but matched real objects, line drawings, colors, letters, and geometric figures better than she named or pointed to them. Verbal responses were marked by perseverations and form confusions. The patient had 20/20 acuity (open E method) and a spiraling visual field defect. CT scan revealed right frontal and deep left occipital lobe lesions.

Wapner et al. presented a case report of visual agnosia in an artist in which drawing skills were specifically assessed. Their patient suffered a cerebrovascular accident with resulting right hemianopia, visual recognition defect, and amnestic syndrome. Brain scan revealed bilateral medial occipital infarctions. Visual acuity was 20/70, and again there was a variable visual field defect. The patient showed poor visual recognition of objects and drawings in the context of moderately impaired design copying. Interestingly, the patient showed a striking dissociation in qualitative drawing performance between objects he could and could not recognize. With unrecognized objects, his drawings revealed piecemeal, slavish reproduction of recognized elements. Describing his drawing of a telephone dial, he said, "A circle, another circle, a square ... things keep coming out ... and this is as though it hooks into something." In contrast, when drawing an object he could identify, the patient relied on preserved knowledge of the essential components of the object, producing a sketch that was faithful to the specific target as well as to the general class of objects to which the target belonged. He remarked, "Can't help but use your natural knowledge in drawing the thing." Wapner et al. do not stipulate whether their patient's defect is apperceptive or associative (they designate it as agnosia-like) but indicate that, "were this artistically trained patient experiencing a complete stimulus 'stripped of its meaning,' his ability to copy complex objects [and] line drawings . . . should have been more fully preserved."

The cases of Kertesz and Wapner et al. are important for two reasons. First, they both showed *dissociations* among various tests classically used to tap the apperceptive level. Second, their combined defects at the levels of perception and recognition underscore the exquisite complexity and variability with which many agnosic patients present.

Optic Aphasia

The term "optic aphasia" was introduced by Freund (1889) to describe the deficit of one of his patients with a right homonymous hemianopia and aphasia due to a left parieto-occipital tumor; the patient's naming ability was impaired primarily for objects presented visually. The case report is of little value because of its incompleteness, but Freund's speculations are pertinent. He hypothesized a left speech area–right occipital disconnection as the basis for the visual naming deficit in the intact visual field. In current usage, "optic aphasia" refers to the condition in which patients are unable to name visually presented objects and yet are able to show that they recognize the object either by indicating its use or by pointing to it when it is named. Tactile and auditory naming are preserved. Certain authors have emphasized the distinction between optic aphasia and visual agnosia, the former representing a naming disorder, the latter a disturbance of recognition. As we shall see, a similar distinction has been made in the literature on color agnosia. It is probable, however, that the difference is one of severity, not quality. The patient of Lhermitte and Beauvois (1973), whom the authors classified as an optic aphasic (because he could point to objects on command and indicate the use of objects shown to him but could not utter the name of verbally presented objects), could name when requested to do so in writing. One of us (ABR) has personally observed two patients evolve from classical associative visual agnosia to optic aphasia in the chronic period. The fact that certain patients can be made to oscillate between optic aphasia and visual agnosia by varying the instructions on a particular task blurs the distinction between a naming disorder and a disturbance of recognition and supports Geschwind's contention that at least some forms of visual agnosia represent modality-specific naming disorders in which confabulated verbal misnaming interferes with otherwise intact cognitive and gnostic capacities.

Color Agnosia

Patients with color agnosia are, by classic definition, unable to name colors shown or to point to a color named by the examiner, yet perform normally on tasks of color perception. One of the earliest cases was reported by Wilbrand (1887), who referred to the defect as "amnestic color blindness." Wilbrand observed that his patient could not find the appropriate word for a color displayed, that he frequently perseverated names across trials, and that naming the color of a familiar out-of-sight object was impaired. Wilbrand invoked an "amnestic" disorder because the patient frequently excused himself by saying that he had forgotten the name of the color shown to him.

Since Wilbrand's case, several others have been reported in the literature, each with slightly different deficits and spared skills. At present, there is disagreement in the literature about whether color agnosia (using the narrow sense of that term) exists at all. Most, if not all, of the available cases can be explained as defects in either the perceptual or linguistic spheres that bracket the agnosia concept (Critchley, 1965; De Renzi and Spinnler, 1967, 1968; Bowers, 1981).

The term "color agnosia" itself presents several methodological and conceptual difficulties. Unlike objects, colors cannot be heard or palpated; they can be known only through vision or visual representation (imagery). Therefore it is impossible to devise a clinical tool to assess color recognition in other modalities and thus to establish the modality-specificity of the deficit. Conceptually, the term "color agnosia" implies a distinction between color *perception* on the one hand and color *recognition* (gnosis) on the other. We know of no patient whose clinical data support this distinction. In fact, it is hard to conceive of a set of clinical tests that could demonstrate it.

Still, acquired anomalies of color vision and color performance do occur as a result of lesions to the posterior cortex. In reviews of this literature, Bowers (1981) and Meadows (1974a) discussed four syndromes of color disturbance: (1) central achromatopsia/dyschromatopsia (MacKay and Dunlop, 1899; Meadows, 1974a; Green and Lessell, 1977; Pearlman et al., 1979; Damasio et al., 1980; Young and Fishman, 1980); (2) color anomia, found in association with pure alexia and right homonymous hemianopia, and attributable to visual-verbal disconnection (Stengel, 1948; Geschwind and Fusillo, 1966; Oxbury et al., 1969, Case 1; Meadows, 1974a); (3) a "specific color aphasia" in which the patient has linguistic defects but the impairment in utilizing color names is disproportionately severe (Kinsbourne and Warrington, 1964; Oxbury et al., 1969, Case 2) and (4) color naming and color association defects concomitant with aphasia (De Renzi et al., 1972, 1973; Wyke and Holgate, 1973; Cohen and Kelter, 1979). We shall review the first three of these defects below. The reader is referred to the original literature for a review of the performance of aphasics on color tasks. A summary of performance defects in patients with these various syndromes is presented in Table 9-1 (from Bowers, 1981).

CENTRAL ACHROMATOPSIA/DYSCHROMATOPSIA

Central achromatopsia refers to a loss of color vision due to disease of the central nervous system. The causative lesions can be in the optic nerve, in the chiasm, or in one or both of the cerebral hemispheres (Green and Lessell, 1977). The disorder can be hemianopic (Albert et al., 1975b) or can exist throughout the visual fields. We shall concentrate on the clinical and anatomic aspects of achromatopsia caused by cerebral lesions.

Patients with achromatopsia generally complain about their loss of color vision and describe their visual world as "black and white," "all grey," "washed out," or "dirty." One of the patients of Damasio et al. (1980) had every drapery in her house laundered because they appeared to need cleaning. Such patients generally perform poorly on strictly visual tasks of color perception (Ishihara plates, Munsell Farnsworth 100-Hue

Table 9.1 Summary of Color Performance Defects in Patients With Various Syndromes

Tasks		Achromatopsia	Color Anomia A (visual-verbal d/c)	Color Anomia B (specific color aphasia)	Aphasic Patients
Visual-visual	Ishihara	±°	+	+	+
	Hue discrimination	−	+	+	+
	Color matching	±°	+	+	+
	Coloring pictures	±	+#	−	−
	Color absurdities	±°	+#	+	±@
	Color sorting	±°	+	−	−
Verbal-verbal	Color naming				
	Blood is ———	+	+	−	−
	What color is grass?	+	+	−	−
	Color fluency	+	+	NT	−
	Naming items of				
	specific colors	+	+	−	NT
Visual-verbal	Color naming	±°	−	−	−
	Color pointing	±°	−	−	−
	Color-object naming	±°	−	−	−
	Color-object pointing	±°	−	−	−

Note: The symbol + refers to intact performance and − refers to impaired performance.
°Performance depends upon severity of achromatopsia. In mild cases, only hue discrimination is impaired.
#Performance on these tasks is unimpaired as long as patient does not attempt to verbalize answers. If patient does attempt to do so, then verbalizations can interfere with performance.
@Global and Wernike's aphasics are impaired; all other aphasics ok.

Test, hue discrimination, color matching) but do well on verbal-verbal tasks (e.g., "What color is blood?," "Bananas are . . . ," "Name three blue things," "Name as many colors as possible"). Performance on visual-verbal tasks (naming, pointing, color-object naming and pointing) varies with the severity of the disorder.

Achromatopsia may be partial, affecting one color more than others. Critchley (1965) described a patient with "xanthopsia" who suddenly felt as if all objects around him were covered with gold paint. Red seems most resilient to loss; blue is most vulnerable.

There is agreement in the literature that unilateral or bilateral lesions in the inferior ventromedial sector of the occipital lobe, involving the lingual and fusiform gyri, underlie achromatopsia (Meadows, 1974a; Green and Lessell, 1977; Damasio et al., 1980). Superior field defects are the rule. Prosopagnosia and topographical memory loss are found in the bilateral but not the unilateral cases (Damasio et al., 1980). Two patients (Green and Lessell, 1977, Case 4; Pearlman et al., 1979) each had two separate unilateral posterior cerebral artery infarctions and did not become achromatopsic until their second stroke. Visually evoked responses to alternating green and red checkerboard patterns may be abnormal (Damasio et al., 1980).

The physiological work of Zeki (1973, 1977) has revealed that there exist in rhesus monkeys specialized areas (V-4 complex and an additional region in the superior temporal sulcus) containing "color-coded" cells that selectively respond to specific wavelengths of light. Damasio et al. (1980) speculate that the lingual and fusiform gyri in humans may be the homologues of area V-4, although the exact location is not currently known. What does seem clear from clinical data is that one single area in each hemisphere (eccentrically located in the lower visual association cortex) controls color processing for the entire hemifield (Damasio et al., 1980). This organization is strikingly at variance with the classic notion that inferior cortex subserves superior quadrant processing, and vice versa.

COLOR ANOMIA

Patients with this form of disturbance can adequately perform visual-visual and verbal-verbal tasks but are unable to process in the visual-verbal mode. The disorder is usually associated with the syndrome of alexia without agraphia (Geschwind and Fusillo, 1966) and frequently exists in the context of right homonymous hemianopia. The underlying neuroanatomical mechanism is a visual-verbal disconnection resulting from infarction in the region of the left posterior cerebral artery. The patients of Geschwind and Fusillo (1966) and Oxbury et al. (1969, Case 1) are classic examples of this syndrome.

These patients may occasionally show impairment on some tasks related to color perception, such as coloring pictures or detecting errors in wrongly colored stimuli. This impairment is exacerbated if the patient attempts to verbalize answers (Bowers, 1981). Damasio et al. (1979) suggest that the type of stimuli, the demands of the task, and the patient's problem-solving approach can strongly influence the extent of visual-verbal dissociation. In their analysis, visual-verbal dissociation is maximized when, at the perceptual level, stimuli are purely visual (such as color) or structurally low in association value. At the verbal end, visual-verbal dissociation is maximized when a specific name rather than the name of a broad category is involved. In addition, the confabulation factor mentioned earlier may help explain why some patients have difficulty in coloring. Incorrect verbalizations about the stimulus may interfere with a patient's attempts to assign it the correct color.

SPECIFIC COLOR APHASIA

Although superficially resembling patients with color anomia, patients with specific color aphasia are distinguished from color anomics by their poor performance on verbal-verbal tasks. The patients of Oxbury et al. (1969, Case 2) and of Kinsbourne and Warrington (1964) are the best-documented cases of this variety. The syndrome is usually seen in the context of at least minimal aphasia, but the difficulty with color names and other color-associative skills is disproportionately severe. The patient of Oxbury et al. had head trauma (and therefore probably bilateral lesions) with complete right homonymous hemianopia and mild right hemiparesis. Kinsbourne and Warrington's patient had a subdural hematoma over the left posterior parietal lobe. Although such patients can sort colors categorically and according to hue and can appropriately match colors, they may fail at other visual-visual tasks in a fashion akin to the color anomic. These deficits are similar to those reported in aphasic patients by De Renzi et al. (1972).

Prosopagnosia

The term "prosopagnosia" was formally introduced by Bodamer (1947) to describe the inability to recognize familiar faces. Patients with this disorder may at the same time be able to discriminate and match faces normally (Tzavaras et al., 1970; Benton and Van Allen, 1972). They almost invariably recognize faces as faces; their defect is in identifying whose face they are viewing. In some cases, the impairment of facial recognition is so severe that patients are unable to recognize their own face in a mirror. One of us (RMB) recently saw a patient bump into a mirror and excuse himself, thinking it was someone else. The defect often prevents the recognition of famous personalities by their facial features. Patients learn to identify people by using extra-facial cues, including clothing, gait, length of hair, height, or distinguishing birthmark. The inability to recognize family members, friends, and hospital staff may lead to the mistaken conclusion that the patient is suffering from a severe memory defect or a generalized dementia. The disorder should be differentiated from Capgras syndrome, a psychiatric disturbance in which the patient believes that familiar persons have been replaced by imposters (Synodinou et al., 1978; Alexander et al., 1979; Shraberg and Weitzel, 1979).

The disorder is frequently associated with central achromatopsia, constructional disability, topographical memory loss and dressing apraxia and may exist as part of a more generalized object agnosia (Hecaen and Angelergues, 1962). Some patients (e.g., Macrae and Trolle, 1956; Gloning et al., 1970; Levine, 1978; Nardelli et al., 1982, Case 2) appear to have apperceptive forms of the defect, whereas others (Pallis, 1955; Benton & Van Allen, 1972; Bauer and Trobe, in press) suffer from a clear associative deficit.

From the beginning, prosopagnosia has been surrounded with much fascination because it superficially appears to represent a recognition defect limited to an individual class of stimuli. Several theories have been advanced to explain the nature of the deficit. Some writers have considered the disorder an attenuated form of general object agnosia specific to facial material (Gloning et al., 1970; Beyn and Knyazeva, 1962). Others have implicated a limited form of the amnestic syndrome (Warrington and James, 1967; Benton and Van Allen, 1972; Shuttleworth et al., 1982). A third view has been that the defect involves identifying individuality within a class of objects (Faust, 1955; Whiteley and Warrington, 1977). A final hypothesis is that facial recognition is mediated by a special perceptual process (Overman and Doty, 1982) and that prosopagnosia is a defect of this system (Tzavaras et al., 1970; Yin, 1970; Cohn et al., 1977; Kay and Levin, 1982).

The material-specific agnosia view is disproved by recent reports of prosopagnosic patients who have concurrently lost the ability to recognize specific chairs (Faust, 1955) or automobiles (Lhermitte and Pillon, 1975). Bornstein and associates (Bornstein and Kidron, 1959; Bornstein, 1963; Bornstein et al., 1969) have reported two prosopagnosic patients, one a birdwatcher, the other a farmer, who, in addition to their face agnosia, lost the ability to recognize individual birds or cows, respectively. The defect is not specific to faces, but involves the identification of individuals within semantic classes whose members are visually similar (Damasio et al., 1982).

The limited amnestic syndrome hypothesis is generally supported by the dissociation between these patients' performance on facial matching and on facial memory tests. Prosopagnosic patients can match pictures of faces, even at different photographic angles, but fail in any test that requires recent or remote memory for faces (Meadows, 1974b). Classically stated, this view is that ongoing facial percepts cannot be matched with stored visual representations of faces built up from past experience. There is much clinical support for this hypothesis, including the inability of many prosopagnosic patients to learn new faces (anterograde defect), the presence of recent memory impairment for other complex nonverbal(izable) stimuli, and the poor performance of many amnestic patients on famous-face recognition tasks (Meadows, 1974b; Ross, 1980a, Case 1; Bauer and Trobe, in press). However, there are two problems with viewing prosopagnosia as exclusively a memory disorder. First, patients with full-blown amnesia (e.g., Korsakoff's syndrome) are rarely prosopagnosic. Second, in classical amnestic syndrome there is a relative preservation of remote memory, whereas in prosopagnosia the recognition of remotely learned faces is particularly impaired (Meadows, 1974b).

Damasio et al. (1982), drawing on autopsy cases, CT findings, and the work of Benton (1980), suggest that both a visual categorization defect and a material-specific memory defect are necessary for the production of prosopagnosia. They point out that, since patients are able to immediately recognize others on the basis of voice or other extrafacial characteristics, the storage of "context is not affected, i.e., the memories pertinent to a given face . . . are intact and are retrievable from all the multimodal sensory storage sites, including the visual one. The disturbance resides in that the usual visual trigger cannot activate these multimodal memories." They suggest that the defect is one of evoking the context of a particular stimulus. The reason that faces are so strongly affected is that they belong to a category in which differences between category members are so visually subtle and complex. This view supports the notion that prosopagnosia is not specific to faces but involves any class of visually ambiguous stimuli.

There is now widespread agreement that the lesions causing prosopagnosia are bilateral and involve the cortex and white matter in the occipitotemporal gyrus, similar to the localization discussed previously for achromatopsia. In his review of the anatomical literture, Meadows (1974b) found that superior field defects were frequent and that the typical finding was a right occipitotemporal lesion coupled with a more variably placed, but usually symmetric, lesion in the left hemisphere. In their review of postmortem findings, Damasio et al. (1982) found that all lesions bilaterally involved the mesial occipitotemporal region and were functionally symmetric.

The inferior longitudinal fasciculus (ILF), the principal white matter pathway linking visual association cortex and temporal lobe, has been particularly implicated in prosopagnosia (Benson et al., 1974; Meadows, 1974b; Bauer, 1982). The regions of the temporal lobe in which the ILF terminates subsequently project to the limbic system. Accordingly, prosopagnosia has been interpreted as a visual-limbic disconnection syndrome (Benson et al., 1974; Bauer, 1982). However, the situation seems more complex because ILF lesions anterior to the occipitotemporal area (which, if complete, also produce visual-limbic disconnection) do not typically result in prosopagnosia (Meadows, 1974b). Intrinsic damage to the occipitotemporal area thus seems important. There are two lines of thinking about this. First, it is possible that intrinsic damage to the occipitotemporal region destroys association cortex in which visual representations of faces (or at least the "hardware" for activating such representations) reside (Damasio et al., 1982). Second, occipitotemporal lesions involving the ILF are posterior enough to disconnect ongoing facial perceptions from inferotemporal cortex, a region that seems particularly critical in the ability to make fine visual discriminations and visual categorizations (Iversen and Weiskrantz, 1964, 1967; Kuypers et al., 1965; Gross et al., 1972). This may contribute to the underspecification of visual detail that recent authors (Levine, 1978; Shuttleworth et al., 1982) have considered important in the production of the defect.

Visual-Spatial Agnosia

Several cases bearing the names visual-spatial agnosia (McFie et al., 1950; Ettlinger et al., 1957), visuospatial dysgnosia (Cogan, 1979), disorders of visual space perception (Patterson and Zangwill, 1944), and unilateral spatial agnosia (Battersby et al., 1956; Caltagirone et al., 1977) have been interpreted with reference to the agnosia concept. These syndromes are included here for technical completeness but are better understood in the context of visuospatial disorders and the syndrome of hemispatial neglect. The reader is referred to Chaps. 8 and 10 for a review of these entities.

AUDITORY AGNOSIA

The term "auditory agnosia" refers to impaired capacity to recognize sounds in the presence of otherwise adequate hearing as measured by standard audiometry. The literature is somewhat confusing because the term has been sometimes used in a broad sense to refer to impaired capacity to recognize both speech and nonspeech sounds and in a narrow sense to refer to a selective deficit in the recognition of nonverbal sounds only. If one uses the term to refer to the broad spectrum of all auditory recognition disorders associated with cerebral auditory dysfunction, then the disorder is further subdivided into auditory sound agnosia, auditory verbal agnosia, and a mixed group with deficits in both speech and nonspeech sounds. Using the narrower definition, one speaks of auditory agnosia (selective impairment of nonspeech sound recognition) and pure word deafness (selective impairment of speech sound recognition). The term "cortical deafness" generally has been applied to those patients whose daily activities and auditory behavior indicate an extreme lack of awareness of auditory stimuli of any kind and whose audiometric pure tone thresholds are markedly abnormal. The dividing line between cortical deafness and mixed auditory agnosia is poorly defined. "Receptive (sensory) amusia" refers to loss of the ability to appreciate various characteristics of heard music.

Pure Word Deafness

Patients with pure word deafness (auditory agnosia for speech, auditory verbal agnosia) are unable to comprehend and discriminate spoken language although they can read, write, and speak in a relatively normal manner. Comprehension of nonverbal sounds is, by definition, relatively spared. The syndrome is pure only in the sense that it is *relatively* free of the aphasic symptoms found with other disorders affecting language comprehension, particularly Wernicke's and transcortical sensory aphasia. The disorder was first described by Kussmaul (1877), who used the term "reinen Worttaubheit" to refer to patients who were unable to understand spoken words but whose speech and hearing were normal. Lichteim (1885) defined the disorder as "the inability to understand spoken words as an isolated deficit unaccompanied by disturbance of spontaneous speech or by severe disturbance in writing or understanding of the printed word." He used the term "subcortical sensory aphasia" and postulated a subcortical interruption of fibers from both ascending auditory projections to the left "auditory word center." With few exceptions, pure word deafness has been associated with bilateral, rather symmetric cortical-subcortical lesions involving the anterior part of the superior temporal gyri with some sparing of Heschl's gyrus, particularly on the left. Several patients were found to have unilateral lesions located subcortically in the temporal lobe, destroying the left auditory radiation as well as the callosal fibers from the opposite auditory region (Liepmann and Storch, 1902; Schuster and Taterka, 1926). The neuroanatomical substrate is generally conceived, from a functional point of view, as a bilateral disconnection of Wernicke's area from auditory input (Geschwind, 1965; Hécaen and Albert, 1978). The very low incidence of pure word deafness is attributable to the fact that it takes an unusually placed, very circumscribed lesion of the superior temporal gyrus to involve Heschl's gyrus or its connections and still selectively spare Wernicke's area.

Cerebrovascular disease is the most common cause of pure word deafness. The patient, when first seen, is often recovering from a full-blown Wernicke's aphasia; occasionally the picture of pure word deafness may give way to a Wernicke's aphasia (Ziegler, 1952; Klein and Harper, 1956; Gazzaniga et al., 1973; Albert and Bear, 1974). As the paraphasias and writing and reading disturbances disappear, the patient still does not comprehend spoken languge but can easily communicate by writing. Deafness can be ruled out by normal pure-tone thresholds on audiometry. At this stage, the patient may experience auditory hallucinations or exhibit transient euphoric (Shoumaker et al., 1977) or paranoid (Reinhold, 1950) ideation. The inability to repeat speech stimuli that are not comprehended distinguishes pure word deafness, which is a disturbance at the perceptual-discriminative level (Jerger et al., 1969; Kanshepolsky et al., 1973), from transcortical sensory aphasia, in which word sounds are perceived normally but there is an estrangement of sound from meaning. The absence of florid paraphasia and of reading and writing disruption distinguishes the disorder from Wernicke's aphasia. It should be emphasized, however, that in clinical practice there is frequently substantial overlap between aspects of these "distinct" entities.

The patient with pure word deafness complains that speech is muffled or sounds like a foreign language. Hemphill and Stengel's patient (1940) stated that "voices come but no words." The patient of Klein and Harper (1956) described speech as "an undifferentiated continuous humming noise without any rhythm" and "like foreigners speaking in the distance." Albert and Bear's (1974) patient said "words come too quickly" and "they sound like a foreign language." The speech of these patients may contain occasional word-finding pauses and paraphasias and is often slightly louder than normal. Performance on speech perception tests is very inconsistent and highly dependent upon context (Caplan, 1978) and the linguistic structure of the material (Auerbach et al., 1982). Patients do much better when they are aware of the category under discussion or when they can lip-read. Comprehension often drops suddenly when the topic is changed. Words embedded in sentences are more easily identified than isolated words. Lowering the presentation rate of words in sentences also aids in comprehension. This improvement with lower speech rates may be due to the reduced adverse effects of abnormally slow temporal analysis of auditory stimuli or to the fact that the processing of words and their meaning involves an act of constructive synthesis carried on by the listener (Neisser, 1967, 1976) and the lower rate of presentation allows the patient more time to make educated guesses.

Recent studies on pure word deafness have emphasized the role of auditory processing in the genesis of the disorder (Kanshepolsky et al., 1973; Albert and Bear, 1974; Gordon and Naeser, 1977; Jerger et al., 1979; Auerbach et al., 1982). Temporal resolution (Albert and Bear, 1974), and phonemic discrimination (Denes and Semenza, 1975; Chocholle et al., 1975; Saffran et al., 1976; von Stockert, 1982) have also received attention. In an exceptionally detailed case report and literature review, Auerbach et al. (1982) suggest that the disorder may take two forms: one a prephonemic temporal auditory acuity disturbance associated with bilateral temporal lesions, the other a disorder of phonemic discrimination attributable to left temporal lesions.

Albert and Bear (1974) suggested that the problem in pure word deafness is one of temporal resolution of auditory stimuli rather than specific phonetic impairment (Auerbach et al.'s first type). Their patient demonstrated abnormally long auditory fusion thresholds for clicks (time taken to perceive two clicks as one) and observed improvement in auditory comprehension when speech was presented slower. Saffran et al. (1976), on the other hand, showed that informing their patient of the nature of the topic under discussion—indicating the category of words to be presented or giving the patient a multiple-choice array just before presentation of words—significantly facilitated comprehension. Words embedded in a sentence were better recognized, particularly when they occurred in the latter part of the sentence. Whereas a temporal auditory acuity disorder was likely present in Albert and Bear's (1974) patient, the patient of Saffran et al. (1976) displayed linguistic discrimination deficits that appeared to be independent of a disorder in temporal auditory acuity.

Several studies have reported brainstem and cortical auditory evoked responses in patients with pure word deafness (see Michel et al., 1980, for review). Brainstem EP's are almost universally reported as normal, suggesting normal processing up to the level of the auditory radiations (Albert and Bear, 1974; Stockard and Rossiter, 1977; Auerbach et al., 1982). Results from studies of cortical AEP's are more variable, probably consistent with variable pathology (Auerbach et al., 1982). For example, the patient of Jerger et al. (1969) had no appreciable AEP, yet heard sounds. The patient of Auerbach et al. (1982) showed normal P_1, N_1, and P_2 to right ear stimulation but minimal response over either hemisphere to left ear stimulation.

Phonemic discrimination has been studied in five patients with pure word deafness. Those with bilateral lesions tend to show distinctive deficits for the feature of place of articulation (Naeser, 1974; Chocholle et al., 1975; Auerbach et al., 1982). Those with presumed unilateral left hemisphere disease showed either impaired discrimination for voicing (Saffran et al., 1976) or no distinctive pattern (Denes and Semenza, 1976).

Dichotic listening studies have been performed on three patients. The extreme suppression of right ear perception in the patients of Albert and Bear (1974) and Saffran et al. (1976) suggests the inaccessibility of the left hemisphere phonetic decoding areas (Wernicke's area) to auditory material that has already been acoustically processed by the right hemisphere. However, the patient of Auerbach et al. (1982) showed marked left ear extinction, which the authors attribute to spared auditory cortical processing in the left temporal lobe.

Patients with pure word deafness perform relatively well with environmental sounds, although the appreciation of music is frequently more disturbed. Some may recognize foreign languages by the characteristic prosody inherent in them. Some case reports indicate that patients can recognize *who* is speaking but not what is said, again suggesting preserved ability to comprehend the paralinguistic aspects of speech. In a recently reported case (Coslett et al., in press), a word deaf patient showed a remarkable dissociation between the comprehension of neutral and affectively intoned sentences. He was asked to point to pictures of males and females depicting various emotional expressions. When verbal instructions were given in a neutral voice, he performed poorly. When instructions were given with affective intonations appropriate to the target face, he performed significantly better and at a level commensurate with his performance with written instructions. This patient had bilateral destruction of primary auditory cortex with some sparing of auditory association cortex, suggesting at least some direct contribution of the auditory radiations association to the cortex latter without initial decoding in Heschl's gyrus (Coslett et al., in press). These authors speculate that one reason patients with pure word deafness improve their auditory comprehension with lip-reading is that face-to-face contact allows them to take advantage of gesture and facial expression present in the communicative act. An alternative explanation is that lip-reading provides essential information in place of articulation, a linguistic feature that is markedly impaired at least in the bilateral cases (Auerbach et al., 1982). Whatever the case, the finding of preserved comprehension of paralinguistic aspects of speech further reinforces the notion that comprehension of speech and nonspeech sounds involves different neuropsychological processes.

There is evidence that unilateral left side lesions, particularly those producing Wernicke's aphasia with impaired auditory comprehension, are also associated with impaired ability to match nonverbal sounds with pictures (Vignolo, 1969). These errors, however, are almost exclusively semantic, not acoustic, and thus do not suggest that unilateral left hemisphere temporal lobe damage produces a perceptual-discriminative sound recognition disturbance. For that reason, the finding of impaired ability to discriminate nonverbal speech sounds in a patient with pure word deafness suggests bilateral disease, even in the absence of other neurological findings of bilaterality. Since many of these patients have, by history, successive strokes, the primary and secondary side of damage may be important in producing a picture dominated either by pure word deafness or by auditory sound agnosia (Ulrich, 1978).

Auditory Sound Agnosia

Auditory agnosia restricted to the recognition of nonspeech sounds is a rarely reported entity, more uncommon by far than pure word deafness. This may be because such patients are less likely to seek medical advice than are those with a disorder of speech comprehension and also because nonspecific auditory complaints are often discounted when pure tone audiometric and speech discrimination thresholds are normal. This is unfortunate because normal or near-normal audiometric evaluation does not rule out the possible role played by primary auditory perceptual defects (Goldstein, 1974).

Vignolo (1969) made the case for dividing auditory sound agnosia into a perceptual-discriminative form associated mainly with lesions of the right hemisphere and an associative-semantic type associated with lesions of the left hemisphere and closely linked to Wernicke's aphasia. The former type make predominantly acoustic (e.g., "man whistling" for birdsong) errors on picture-sound matching tasks, whereas the latter group makes predominantly semantic (e.g., "train" for automobile engine) errors. This division follows the original classification of Kliest (1928), who distinguished between the ability to perceive isolated sounds or noises (perceptive Gerauschtaubheit) and the inability to understand the meaning of sounds (Gerauschinntaubheit). It resembles also the apperceptive/associative dichotomy made by Lissauer (1889). In the verbal sphere, the analogous comparison is between pure word deafness (perceptual-discriminative) and transcortical sensory aphasia (semantic-associative).

Two well-studied cases of auditory sound agnosia have been reported in the recent literature (Spreen et al., 1965; Albert et al., 1972). The patient of Spreen et al. was a 65-year-old right-handed male whose major complaint when seen three years after a left hemiparetic episode was that of "nerves" and headache. Audiometric testing demonstrated moderate bilateral high-frequency loss and speech reception thresholds of 12 decibels for both ears. There was no aphasia. The outstanding abnormality was the inability to recognize common sounds; understanding of language was fully retained and there were no other agnosic defects. Sound localization was normal. Scores on the pitch subtest of the Seashore Tests of Musical Talent were at chance level. The patient claimed no experience or talent with music and refused, as many such patients do, to cooperate with further testing of musical ability. The patient was able to match previously heard but misidentified sounds with one of four tape recorded choices, suggesting an associative defect. Postmortem examination revealed a sharply demarcated old infarct of the right hemisphere centering around the parietal lobe and involving the superior temporal and angular gyri, as well as a large portion of the inferior parietal, inferior and middle frontal, and long and short gyri of the insula. This case represents the only example of auditory sound agnosia with unilateral pathology. The lesion was too large to allow for precise anatomicoclinical correlation by comparison to cases of mixed auditory agnosia (cortical auditory disorder).

A more recent case report (Albert et al., 1972) described a patient with auditory sound agnosia with minimal dysphasia. Clinical evidence suggested bilateral involvement. The patient was able to attach meaning to word sounds but not to nonverbal sounds. Albert et al. also demonstrated marked extinction of the left ear to dichotic listening; impaired perception of pitch, loudness, rhythm, and time; and abnormally delayed and attenuated cortical AEP's, worse on the right. They concluded that the nature of the sound agnosia in their patient resided in "an inability to establish the correspondence between the perceived sound and its sensory or motor associations" (associative defect) and suggested that the dissociation between verbal and nonverbal sound recognition reflected different processing mechanisms for linguistic and nonlinguistic aspects of acoustic input.

In the large majority of cases, impairment of nonverbal sound recognition is accompanied by impaired recognition of speech sounds. The relative severity of these impairments may reflect premorbid lateralization of linguistic and nonlinguistic processes in the individual patient and may depend upon which hemisphere is more seriously, or primarily, damaged (Ulrich, 1978). Terminological confusion has arisen with regard to these mixed forms, with such terms as "cortical auditory disorder" (Kanshepolsky et al., 1973; Miceli, 1982) "auditory agnosia" (Oppenheimer and New-combe, 1978; Rosati et al., 1982), "auditory agnosia and word deafness" (Goldstein et al., 1975), and "congenital aphasia" (Laudau et al., 1960) all being used to describe similar phenomena. We shall refer to these mixed forms as "cortical auditory disorders" and discuss them together with cortical deafness. Cortical auditory disorders frequently evolve from a state of cortical deafness, and, as we shall see, it is often difficult to define a clear separation between the two entities.

Cortical Auditory Disorder and Cortical Deafness

Patients with these disorders have difficulty recognizing auditory stimuli of all kinds, verbal and nonverbal (Vignolo, 1969; Lhermitte et al., 1971). Most have absent or minimal signs of aphasia and can typically deal effectively with incoming information provided audition is not required. Difficulties in temporal auditory analysis and localization of sounds in space are freqeuntly encountered in both. These disorders are rare, and their underlying neuroanatomical basis is poorly understood (Rosati et al., 1982). Recent case reports have questioned the distinctive nature of true cortical deafness (Vignolo, 1969; Lhermitte et al., 1971; Kanshepolsky et al., 1973).

Distinguishing between cortical auditory disorders and cortical deafness continues to be problematic. One distinction frequently cited is that the cortically deaf patient feels deaf and seems to be so, whereas the auditory agnosic insists that she or he is not deaf (Michel et al., 1980). This turns out to be a poor criterion. Although it was originally believed that bilateral cortical lesions involving the primary auditory cortex result in total hearing loss, recent evidence from animal experiments (Neff, 1961; Massopoust and Wolin, 1967; Dewson et al., 1969), cortical mapping of the auditory area (Celesia, 1976), and clinicopathological studies in humans (Wohlfart et al., 1952; Mahoudeau et al., 1956) indicate that complete destruction of primary auditory cortex does not lead to substantial permanent loss of audiometric sensitivity (see also patient of Coslett et al., in press). It is common, however, for an asymptomatic patient with old unilateral temporal lobe pathology to become suddenly totally deaf with the occurrence of a second contralateral lesion in the auditory region.

A neuroanatomical distinction between cortical deafness and auditory cortical disorders has been tentatively offered by Michel et al. (1980). Recognizing the hazards of such a dichotomy, they distinguish between lesions of auditory koniocortex (areas 41 to 52 of Brodmann) and lesions of pro- and para-koniocortex (areas 22 and 52 of Brodmann). While this distinction may prove useful, it is unfortunate that naturally occurring lesions "obviously will not match precisely our cytoarchitectonic maps."

In their paper on cortical deafness, Michel et al. (1980) considered the possibility that the two syndromes could be differentiated on the basis of auditory evoked potentials. Several studies (Jerger et al., 1969; Michel et al., 1980) have found either totally absent AEP's or absent late components of AEP in patients with cortical auditory disorders. However, AEP's have been found in other cases (Albert et al., 1972 [pure word deafness]; Assal and Despland (1973) [auditory agnosia]), and normal late AEP's were found in at least one case of cortical deafness (Adams et al., 1977). While results to date are conflicting, this remains a promising area of research. Variability may be due in part to differing pathologies and recording methods. Michel et al. (1980) argue that, to provide data that are comprehensive and comparable to the data for other patients, AEP's must be recorded all over the brain, from one mastoid to the other, in a coronal chain of electrodes.

Cortical deafness is most commonly seen in cerebrovascular disease, where the course is commonly biphasic with a transient deficit (often aphasia and hemiparesis) related to unilateral damage followed by a second deficit associated with sudden but transient total deafness (Jerger et al., 1969, 1972; Earnest et al., 1977; Leicester, 1980). A biphasic course is also typical of cases of auditory cortical disorder. Some patients (Oppenheimer and Newcombe, 1978; Rosati et al., 1982) had left hemisphere lesions; the opposite pattern was seen in the patient of Miceli (1982).

In cortical deafness, bilateral destruction of the auditory radiations or the primary auditory cortex has been a constant finding (Leicester, 1980). The anatomical basis of auditory cortical disorder is more variable. Although lesions can be quite extensive (Oppenheimer and Newcombe, 1978), the superior temporal gyrus (i.e., efferent connections of Heschl's gyrus) is frequently involved. However, it is not possible to tell from the pathology whether an auditory cortical disorder was present or not (Leicester, 1980), since some patients with small lesions do have these problems while others with similarly placed large lesions do not.

The distinction between auditory cortical disorder (mixed sound agnosia) and cortical deafness is similar conceptually to the apperceptive/associative distinction, which is more clearly understood in the context of vision. Auditory perceptual defects, such as impairments in sound localization (e.g., Albert et al., 1972) and disturbances in physical versus temporal parameters of auditory input (Rosati et al., 1982), need to be more precisely understood as they relate to this distinction. One of the lingering problems, of course, is that the nature of auditory recognition is more poorly understood than that of vision. Any generalized theory of agnosia that encompasses both modalities must take into account the intrinsic functional and anatomical differences between the two.

Auditory Agnosias in Childhood

In the recent literature, a diverse population of children with acquired languge disability whose loss of expressive speech is overshadowed by profound impairment in auditory comprehension has been identified and related to the syndrome of pure word deafness in adults (Landau and Kleffner, 1957; Gascon et al., 1973; Shoumaker et al., 1974; Rapin et al., 1977; Cooper and Ferry, 1978; Frumkin and Rapin, 1980). A characteristic feature of these children is that their EEGs show bilateral paroxysmal abnormalities thought to result in physiological interference with auditory sensory processing. Generalized seizures are sometimes, but not invariably, present. Prognosis is variable but not as good as in acquired aphasia, which is usually associated with unilateral hemispheric impairment.

Two studies have assessed recognition of nonverbal sounds in language-impaired retarded subjects (Heffner, 1977; Lamberts, 1980). Heffner found that his subjects were impaired on a task that required them to match sounds with pictures of sound sources and interpreted these findings as evidence that language impairment in these children may have been due to an agnosia-like defect. Using similar procedures, Lamberts found that developmental age was the critical factor in performance on these tests and suggested that the severely retarded achieved the requisite auditory-perceptual knowledge base for language too late, after the critical age for spontaneous and efficient language learning has passed. A detailed review of these syndromes is beyond the scope of this chapter; the reader is referred to the original references for further information.

Sensory (Receptive) Amusia

Amusia has been reviewed in detail by Wertheim (1969), Critchley and Henson (1977), and Gates and Bradshaw (1977). Sensory, or receptive, amusia refers to an inability to appreciate various characteristics of heard music. It occurs to some extent in all cases of auditory sound agnosia and in the majority of cases of aphasia and pure word deafness. As is the case with auditory sound agnosia, the loss of musical perceptual ability is underreported because a specific musical disorder rarely interferes with everyday life. A major obstacle to systematic study of the disorder is the extreme variability of premorbid musical abilities, interests, and skills. It was Wertheim's (1969) conclusion that receptive amusia corresponds more frequently with a lesion of the left hemisphere whereas expressive musical disabilities are more apt to be associated with right hemisphere dysfunction. Recent evidence indicates that cerebral organization of musical ability differs depending on degree of skill and musical sophistication. Musically skilled and trained individuals are more likely to perceive music in a more analytical manner and to rely more heavily on the dominant hemisphere. Dichotic listening studies show that the right hemisphere plays a more important role than the left in the processing of musical and nonlinguistic sound patterns (Blumstein and Cooper, 1974; Gordon, 1974). However, the left hemisphere appears to be of major importance in the processing of sequential (temporally organized) material of any kind, including musical series. In fact, it may be conjectured that what is "spatial" to the right hemisphere is "temporal" to the left. According to Gordon (1974), melody recognition becomes less of a right hemisphere task as the time and rhythm factors become more important for distinguishing tone patterns (see also Mavlov, 1980). These factors contribute to a lack of definition of the entity of receptive amusia and to the difficulty of localizing the deficit to a particular brain region. Further complicating the picture is the fact that pitch, harmony, timbre, intensity, and rhythm may be affected to different degrees and in various combinations in the individual patient. Furthermore, there is recent evidence that aspects of musical denotation (the so-called real-world events referred to in lyrics) and musical connotation (the formal expressive patterns indicted by pitch, timbre, and intensity) are selectively vulnerable to focal brain lesions (Gardner et al., 1977). For instance, on tests of musical denotation, right hemisphere damaged patients perform well on items where acquaintence with lyrics is required; in contrast, aphasics with anterior lesions are superior to both right hemisphere patients and asphasics with posterior lesions on items where knowledge of lyrics is unnecessary. (Incidentally, Benton [1980] reports that aphasics with posterior lesions and comprehension disturbance are also most impaired among aphasics on tests of face recognition, another ostensibly configurational task.) On tests of musical connotation, right hemisphere patients do better in matching sound patterns to temporally sequenced designs than to simultaneous gestalten. Aphasics with posterior lesions perform relatively well on tests of musical connotation.

Auditory Affective Agnosia

Heilman et al. (1975) showed that patients with right temporoparietal lesions and the neglect syndrome were impaired in the comprehension of affectively intoned speech, though they were flawless in the comprehension of speech content. Patients with left temporoparietal lesions and fluent aphasia comprehended both affective (paralinguistic) and content (linguistic) aspects of speech quite well. Whether this defect represents a true agnosia remains to be determined, since auditory sensory and perceptual skills were not assessed. However, the discovery of a specific defect in the comprehension of affectively intoned speech is important in light of the fact that such abilities are frequently spared in cases of pure word deafness (Coslett et al., in press). Although not specifically addressed in many case studies, patients with pure word deafness frequently report that they are able to recognize the speaker of the message and, less frequently, the language in which it is transmitted. These observations, and the finding of an isolated "auditory affective agnosia," lend further support to the speculation by Albert et al. (1972) that linguistic and nonlinguistic processing of auditory signals are based on different neuropsychological processes. Further research is needed to provide more precise neuroanatomical correlates of auditory affective agnosia.

SOMATOSENSORY AGNOSIA

The problem of tactile agnosia has been less well studied, even though loss of higher-order tactual recognition in the absence of elementary somatosensory loss is probably at least as common as visual or auditory agnosia. Several distinct disorders have been identified, and many classifications of somatosensory agnosia have been offered. A commonly accepted framework is that of Delay (1935), who identified (1) impaired recognition of the size and shape of objects (amorphognosia), (2) impaired discrimination of the distinctive qualities of objects, such as density, weight, texture, and thermal properties (ahylognosia), and (3) impaired recognition of the identity of objects in the absence of amorphognosia and ahylognosia (tactile asymboly). Delay's scheme is similar to that of Wernicke (1895), who distinguished between primary agnosia and secondary agnosia, or asymboly. For Wernicke, primary agnosia involved a loss of primary identification because of a destruction of "tactile images." In contrast, secondary agnosia resulted from the inability to associate intact tactile images with other sensory representations, resulting in a loss of appreciation of the object's significance.

The systematic study of tactile recognition disturbances has been beset by terminological confusion. The terms "tactile agnosia" and "astereognosis" have been used interchangeably by some authors, while others draw a sharp distinction between them. "Astereognosis" has been used to denote (1) loss of the ability to distinguish three-dimensional forms (Hoffman, 1885), (2) inability to make shape or size discriminations (Roland, 1976), and (3) inability to identify objects by touch (Delay, 1935). This is confusing, since Hoffman and Roland use the term to describe *discrimination* defects whereas Delay and others use the term to denote defects of object *identification*. It is clear that defects in two-point discrimination, point localization, and position sense can impair tactile form perception, and thus object identification, without producing concomitant defects in sensitivity to light, touch, temperature, or pain (Gans, 1916; Campora, 1925; Corkin, 1978). However, significant defects in discriminative ability need not accompany disorders of tactual identification (Corkin, 1978). Thus, clinical data suggest that discriminative and identificatory tactual defects are dissociable. Unfortunately, the vast majority of the physiological and anatomical data on somatosensory agnosia (astereognosis) have, for obvious reasons, come from animal research almost exclusively, using discrimination rather than identification paradigms. Still, it should be theoretically possible, as it has been with vision and audition, to separate the apperceptive from the associative components of touch. With these considerations in mind, we shall use the term "cortical tactile disorders" to refer to a diverse spectrum of defects in somatosensory discrimination or recognition of distinct object qualities and reserve the term "pure astereognosis" for those rare cases in which there is an inability to identify the nature of tactually presented objects despite adequate sensory, attentional, intellectual, and linguistic capacities.

Before discussing disorders of tactile recognition, some brief anatomical and functional comments about the somatosensory systems are necessary. An exhaustive review of this vast literature is beyond the scope of this chapter; the interested reader is referred to the excellent reviews by Werner and Whitsel (1968, 1973), Corkin (1978), and Hécaen and Albert (1978). In most neuropsychological batteries, simple measures of tactile object identification, fingertip writing (graphesthesia), and bimanual tactile discrimination are used as markers of lateralized sensory function. The reader should note that such measures are overly simplistic in view of the enormous complexity of somatosensory representation. In what immediately follows, we shall discuss those aspects of anatomical and functional organization most relevant to disorders of tactual recognition.

Anatomically, two relatively distinct somatosensory systems have been identified. One is the spinothalamic system: cutaneous nerve endings → spinothalamic tract → reticular formation → intrinsic thalamic nuclei → superior bank of Sylvian fissure [S II] (Hécaen and Albert, 1978; Brodal, 1981). This system is primarily responsible for the less precise aspects of somesthetic perception and seems especially important in nociception and perception of thermal properties. The other system is centered on the medial lemniscus: cutaneous and subcutaneous receptors → medial lemniscal tract → ventroposterolateral thalamic nuclei → postcentral gyrus [S I]. The postcentral gyrus corresponds to Brodmann areas 3, 1, and 2. This system appears responsible for the discriminative aspects of touch and carries information regarding form, position, and temporal change (Mountcastle, 1961).

The two cortical somatosensory "receiving areas" (S I, S II) contain complex "representations" (homunculi) of body parts, with S I strongly arranged somatotopically and S II less so. The postcentral gyrus (S I) receives innervation from contralateral body parts, and S II receives bilateral input. Only in the strict sense are these two regions to be considered as the exclusive receiving areas of thalamic sensory input, since other areas of cortex, including supplementary motor area and superior parietal lobe (areas 5 and 7), also receive direct input from somatosensory thalamus (Brodal, 1981).

In the sections on visual agnosia, we emphasized the strong motor-exploratory components of visuoperceptual activity. This motor theme is also a striking characteristic of the somatosensory system. In a report of the results of cortical stimulation during craniotomy, Penfield (1958) found significant overlap between sensory and motor regions, such that 25 per cent of stimulation points giving rise to sensory experiences were located in the precentral region. Woolsey (1964) found similar results in his evoked potential and stimulation studies of the alert monkey. Because of these and related findings, it has become common to speak of the sensorimotor cortex.

Anatomical interconnections of S I and S II attest to the sensorimotor nature of these regions. Both S I and S II have reciprocal connections with thalamic nuclei, supplementary motor cortex, area 4, and each other (Hécaen and Albert, 1978; Brodal, 1981). In addition, S I projects heavily to area 5 [superior parietal lobule] (Jones and Powell, 1969; Duffy and Burchfiel, 1971; Corkin, 1978), important for arm and leg movement in pursuit of motivationally relevant targets (Mountcastle et al., 1975).

Thus, the functional interconnections of cortical somatosensory areas involve regions which, from numerous other studies, have been found to subserve motor, proprioceptive, and spatial functions. The existence of such a complex system in the human brain is important for intentional, spatially guided motor movements that bring the organism into contact with tactile stimuli. Reciprocal connections between somatosensory, motor, proprioceptive, and spatial components of the system provide the mechanisms whereby regulation of the perceptual act can be achieved. The complex functional organization of the somatosensory systems emphasizes the fact that there is more to perception, and more to perceptual identification, than passive processing of environmental input.

Data from electrophysiological and behavioral studies suggest that primary somatosensory cortex is already more organized for higher functions than are its auditory or visual counterparts. This implies, of course, that primary somatic sensibility is displaced to lower, subcortical (e.g., thalamic) regions (Rose and Woolsey, 1949). Though patients with lesions of the afferent somatosensory pathways frequently cannot identify tactually presented objects, this is due to a severe sensory loss and is referred to as stereoanaesthesia. Lesions of the primary visual and auditory areas produce specific disorders of sensation which can vary in severity depending on the extent and location of the lesion. Total ablation of primary visual and auditory areas results in cortical blindness or deafness, respectively. In contrast, disorders of sensation for touch, temperature, pain, and vibration are rare following cortical lesions (Hécaen and Albert, 1978). The notion that somatosensory cortex is more complexly organized is bolstered by electrophysiological and behavioral data. For example, Paul et al. (1972) explored units in anatomical subdivisions of S I and found multiple representations of the monkey's hand, one in each subdivision (Powell and Montcastle, 1959; Mountcastle and Powell, 1959a, 1959b). Randolph and Semmes (1974) selectively ablated each of these regions (3b, 2, 1). Area 3b excisions resulted in impairment of all aspects of tactile discrimination learning. Lesions of area 1 produced loss of hard-soft and rough-smooth (texture) discrimination but spared convex-concave and square-diamond (shape) discrimination. The opposite pattern was seen in area 2 lesions. Thus, in contrast to the point-to-point representation of the visual fields in area 17 for vision, the hand is represented and re-represented within appropriate subdivisions of somatosensory cortex according to sensory "submodality."

Finally, the notion of sensory submodality has been worked out to a far greater extent for somatosensory function than for vision or audition. Submodality conceptions date back at least to von Frey (1885), who divided the tactile sense into light touch, pressure, temperature, and pain sensitivity. Head (1918) divided sensory functions into three categories: (1) recognition of spatial relations (passive movement, two-point discrimination, and point localization), (2) relative sensitivity to touch, temperature, and pain, and (3) recognition of similarity and difference (size, shape, weight, and texture). Submodalities may be selectively impaired, while others are spared, by circumscribed cortical lesions. Head's (1918) framework, for example, suggests that discriminatory defects (Roland's [1976] astereognosis) are accompanied by defects in the discrimination of texture and weight but not by impaired perception of spatial relations, touch, temperature, or pain (Corkin, 1978). Head et al. (1905), based on studies of recovery from peripheral nerve injuries, distinguished between "protopathic" and "epicritic" sensation. For Head et al., the epicritic system subserved local point sensibility and the protopathic system was more diffuse. The protopathic-epicritic distinction has been widely accepted by anatomists and physiologists (Rose and Woolsey, 1949; Mountcastle, 1961), but unlike Head et al., these authors have emphasized the anatomical implications of this distinction at the cortical and thalamic rather than at the peripheral level (Hécaen and Albert, 1978, p. 279ff). As implied previously, the epicritic aspects of touch are more directly subserved by the medial lemniscal–S I system while the protopathic dimension relates more closely to the functions of the bilaterally represented S II system, though there is considerable functional overlap between the two systems.

Cortical Tactile Disorders

This brief review of the somatosensory systems emphasizes the complexity of this sensory modality and should enable the reader to anticipate the enormous variability with which patients suffering from tactile recognition and identification disorders present. Historically, there have been two views regarding the nature and functional localization of disorders of tactile sensation. The first, more traditional, view is that sensory defects are associated with the contralateral primary somatosensory projection area in the postcentral gyrus (Head, 1920). The other, more recent, perspective is that more diffuse aspects of cortex (e.g., posterior parietal lobe) are involved in somatosensory perception (Semmes et al., 1960). In a series of studies, Corkin and colleagues (Corkin, 1964; Corkin et al., 1970, 1973) administered quantitative tasks similar to those used by Semmes et al. (1960) to patients who had been operated on for relief of focal epileptic seizures. Tests of pressure sensitivity, two-point discrimination, point localization, position sense, and tactual object recognition were used. Two main results emerged from these extensive studies. First, the most severe disorders of cortical tactile sensation were produced by lesions in the contralateral postcentral gyrus. Second, clear demonstration was made of the existence of bilateral sensory defects associated with a unilateral cortical lesion, as had been previously reported by Semmes et al. (1960), Oppenheim (1906), and others.

Corkin found the most severe defects in patients whose lesions encroached on the hand area. This is consistent with the findings of Roland (1976) in his studies of tactual shape and size discrimination impairment with focal cortical lesions. Corkin et al. (1970) also found that disorders of tactile object recognition were restricted to the contralateral hand in patients with lesions that involved the hand area in S I. Importantly, defects of tactile object recognition were always associated with significant defects in pressure sensitivity, two-point discrimination, and other elementary sensory functions. Patients with parietal lobe lesions sparing S I did not show object identification disturbances.

Of 50 patients with involvement of the parietal lobe, 20 showed additional sensory defects ipsilateral to the damaged hemisphere (Corkin et al., 1970). This effect was found equally frequently after left and right hemisphere excisions, in contrast to previous studies that found the incidence of ipsilateral sensory impairment to be much more frequent following left hemisphere damage (Semmes et al., 1960). Differences in the extent of lesions in the samples used by Corkin et al. (circumscribed cortical excisions) and Semmes et al. (penetrating missile wounds) may account for some of these discrepancies. An important anatomical fact is that, in patients with bilateral sensory defects of the hand, the postcentral hand area need not be involved (Corkin et al., 1973). The area of damage implicated in these patients was tentatively offered as S II. In summarizing these data, Corkin (1978) suggested that unilateral S I hand area lesions produce severe contralateral sensory defects and unilateral S II lesions may produce milder defects that affect both hands.

Also relevant to the relationship between unilateral hemispheric lesions and somatosensory loss is growing evidence of hemispheric specialization for certain higher somesthetic functions. Data on this issue can be found in cerebral laterality studies, in examinations of patients following brain bisection, and in studies of performance on complex somatosensory tasks after unilateral hemispheric lesions (Corkin, 1978; Hécaen and Albert, 1978). Laterality studies have failed to show hemispheric specialization for elementary somesthetic functions, such as pressure sensitivity (Fennell et al., 1967), vibration sensitivity (Seiler and Ricker, 1971, cited in Corkin, 1978), two-point discrimination (McCall and Cunningham, 1971), or point localization (Semmes et al., 1960; Weinstein, 1968). In contrast, complex sensory testing, such as tasks requiring spatial exploration of figures or fine temporal analysis, reveals evidence of hemispheric specialization. The left hand–right hemisphere combination appears especially proficient at tasks in which a spatial factor is important, such as in ciphering braille (Rudel et al., 1974) and in perceiving the spatial orientation of tactually presented rods (Benton et al., 1973). Results from studies of split brain patients (reviewed in detail by Corkin, 1978) are remarkably consistent with these conclusions; the left hand–right hemisphere combination is better able to perform complex patterned discriminations, although the right hand–left hemisphere can succeed if familiar stimuli are presented, if a small array of objects is involved, or in other situations in which linguistic processing can be effectively used.

Patients with right hemisphere disease do worse than left hemisphere damaged patients in tasks requiring the perception of complexly organized spatial stimuli, though any patient with elementary somatosensory dysfunction, regardless of hand, can be expected to do poorly in that hand (Corkin, 1978). Semmes (1965) has identified a group of patients without primary sensory tactile impairment who fail in tests of object shape discrimination. These patients, who suffered from lesions of the superior parietal lobe, were unimpaired in roughness, texture, and size discrimination but showed profound impairment on tests of spatial orientation and route finding. Semmes concluded that there is a nontactual factor in these discriminative defects that transcends sensory modality. According to her view, what is spatial for vision is represented in touch by the temporal exploration of object qualities. Teuber (1965a, 1965b) interprets the difficulty as a special form of spatial disorientation rather than one of agnosia for shape.

To summarize, there has been widespread disagreement regarding the neuroanatomical loci subserving somatosensory function. No hemispheric specialization appears to exist for elementary somatosensory function, though there is growing evidence that the right hemisphere is more strongly involved in processing the highly spatial character of some tactile discrimination and identification tasks (Milner and Taylor, 1972). Postcentral gyrus lesions frequently result in severe and long-lasting defects in the contralateral hand, whereas lesions of S II result more frequently in less severe, bilateral defects. A general conclusion from this extensive and complex literature is that the central regions (sensorimotor cortex) are more directly involved in elementary somatosensory function while complex somatosensory tasks possessing strong spatial or motor exploratory components involve additional structures posterior or anterior to the sensorimotor region (Corkin, 1978). This distinction makes it possible to see a higher somatosensory disorder in the absence of elementary sensory loss. Whether this higher disorder deserves to be called an agnosia is a subject to which we now turn.

Pure Astereognosia

The patient with pure astereognosia cannot appreciate the nature or significance of objects placed in the hand despite elementary somatosensory function, intellectual ability, attentional capacity, and linguistic skill adequate to the task of object identification. Because the term "astereognosis" has been applied to discrimination as well as identification disturbances, it is difficult to ascertain the prevalence of this form of agnosia. Clinical case reports of pure astereognosia are rare (Raymond and Egger, 1906; Bonhoeffer, 1918; Campora, 1925; Hecaen and David, 1945; Newcombe and Ratcliff, 1974). Frequently, sensory defects do appear at some point in the clinical course of these patients but not necessarily coincident with the identification disturbance. The astereognosic patient frequently has defects limited to one hand, usually the left, though there are reports of patients with defects limited to the right hand (Hécaen and David, 1945). In some cases, the asymbolic hand can eventually achieve recognition of the object, though only after protracted linguistic analysis of the separate features. For example, the patient of Hécaen and David (1945), when palpating a key in the affected hand, said, "It is a long object, round, an empty circle of metal (long hesitation), a key!" This patient could draw an accurate picture of an object placed in the hand and could then subsequently name the picture. Other patients could tactually match to sample objects they could not identify (Newcombe and Ratcliff, 1974). These defects are obviously at the associative level of recognition.

An important feature is that these patients do not appear to normally palpate the object when it is placed in the hand for identification (Oppenheim, 1906, 1911). This suggests a defect in the mechanism whereby tactile impressions are collected to form an integrated percept of the whole object. Motor and sensory information is highly integrated in the act of palpating an object; motor commands that direct the hand in exploration are issued. Roland and Larsen (1976), in a series of experiments using regional cerebral blood flow (rCBF) during astereognostic testing in humans, showed that local rCBF increases occur most strongly in the contralateral sensorimotor hand area and the premotor region. Though sensorimotor integration and proprioception are crucial components in tactile identification, it should be noted that the motor component probably has a complex role and is not obligatory in any simple sense. This conclusion is warranted by two clinical facts: (1) motor paralysis does not cause tactile identification disturbances and (2) objects can often be identified if they are passively moved across the subject's hand, independent of active manipulation. Still, the fact that true astereognosic patients do not palpate objects may provide a clue into the mechanism underlying the associative defect: although elementary sensory function is intact, it is not actively brought to bear, nor is it adequately integrated with motor information, in the perceptual processing of the stimulus.

As is the case with other forms of agnosia, there is significant debate regarding the existence of pure astereognosia. Three general disclaimers have been proposed. The first, also prevalent in the writings of those opposing visual and auditory agnosia, is that all disturbances of tactile object identification can ultimately be reduced to defects of elementary somatosensory dysfunction. The second states that the defect is not an agnosia but instead represents a modality-specific anomia. Third, there are those who do not deny the existence of higher defects of tactile identification in the context of normal elementary somatosensory function but say that the defect of function in astereognosis is spatial and supramodal, involving both tactile and visual disturbances. Because one of the hallmarks of the agnosia concept is its modality specificity, this third view rejects the notion that astereognosia is agnosic in nature. We shall briefly examine the status of each of these arguments.

The possible role of subtle somatosensory defects in producing disorders of tactile identification has been raised by several authors (Head and Holmes, 1911; Bay, 1944; Corkin et al., 1970). In a fashion similar to his criticism of visual agnosia, Bay stated that most cases of pure astereognosis had been inadequately tested for elementary somatosensory dysfunction. He specifically pointed to labile thresholds and defects in discrimination as essential sensory problems in the "so-called agnosic." Head and Holmes stressed the importance of inconstant thresholds and also found that rapid local fatigue and abnormal persistence of sensations frequently accompanied defects of object identification. These points have been made by other authors as well, most of whom have stressed that longitudinal study of elementary somatosensory function is necessary to reveal the defect. Semmes (1953) mentioned the possible contributory role of tactile extinction revealed by the method of double simultaneous stimulation and states, "If one stimulus 'extinguishes' or 'obscures' the perception of another, or displaces the subjective position, the resultant impression might be sufficiently different from normal perception to make recognition impossible" (p. 144).

It is difficult to fully counter the sensory argument, since historical acceptance of the notion of pure astereognosis has been sufficiently great to cause some authors to be sloppy with respect to evaluations of elementary somatosensory function. In a small number of cases (e.g., Hécaen, 1972), careful attention was paid to somatosensory function, revealing neither lability of threshold nor sensory perseveration. Although only one hand was astereognosic in Hécaen's patient, tactile discrimination, touch, and thickness discrimination were equal in both hands. There did appear to be a subtle defect in shape discrimination in the affected hand, as the patient could not accurately judge a series of objects on a continuum from ovoid to sphere. Delay (1935) found no differences between the hands for pain, temperature, pressure, kinesthesis, or vibration sense, though tactile localization and position sense were poorer in the affected hand (cf. Hécaen and Albert, 1978). In these cases at least, it appears that defects in elementary somatosensory function cannot fully account for the observed defects in object identification.

The possibility that a modality-specific anomia might account for pure astereognosis is raised by the remarkable patient of Geschwind and Kaplan (1962). This patient had a left hemisphere glioblastoma and post-operatively developed a left anterior cerebral artery distribution infarction involving the anterior four fifths of the corpus callosum. He was unable to name or to supply verbal description of items placed in the left hand but could draw misidentified objects with the left hand and could choose a previously presented object tactually from a group of other objects. Because of these spared nonverbal recognition abilities, and because of the intact quality of tactual exploratory movements (active touch), this patient was not a true astereognosic but suffered a disconnection of right hemisphere (left hand) tactual identification mechanisms from the speech area in the left hemisphere.

Although a modality-specific naming defect might account for some alleged cases of astereognosis, there are two reasons this is insufficient as an explanation for all cases. First, several cases exist in which bilateral astereognosis has resulted from unilateral lesions insufficient in size or location to cause a complete tactile-verbal disconnection syndrome (e.g., Oppenheim, 1906; Goldstein, 1916; Lhermitte and deAjuriaguerra, 1938). Second, there are striking differences between pure astereognosic patients and the patient of Geschwind and Kaplan in tactile exploratory behavior. Patients with pure astereognosis show deficient palpation of objects, characterized either by a reluctance to manipulate the object or by a stereotypic pattern of manipulation that is independent of specific object qualities. Patients with tactile-verbal disconnection palpate the object normally, which might be expected given that the hand area and its interconnections with premotor cortex are intact.

Before leaving the topic of tactile-verbal disconnection, it is important to note that most patients with this disorder exhibit tactual identification disturbances that are confined to the left hand (Gazzaniga et al., 1963; Geschwind and Kaplan, 1962; Gazzaniga and Sperry, 1967; Lhermitte et al., 1976; Watson and Heilman, 1983). In contrast, a patient reported by Beauvois et al. (1978) had object-naming deficits when objects were placed in either hand but not when the objects were presented visually. This patient had a left parieto-occipital angioma that was surgically removed. Postoperative CT scan revealed a lesion involving the left angular gyrus, inferior longitudinal fasciculus, thalamic radiations, and the posterior part of the middle temporal gyrus. Although the patient was unable to name objects presented to either hand, he could, when blindfolded, demonstrate the use of tactually presented objects. The defect was not restricted to the name of the object; the patient was unable to describe, without making dysphasic errors, the morphology or use of objects presented tactually. Naming errors were frequently semantic confusions. The authors interpreted the deficit as a "bilateral tactile aphasia" and suggested that it represents the tactile analogue of optic aphasia (Lhermitte and Beauvois, 1973). Unimodal sensory-verbal disconnection appears responsible for the clinical picture in patients who cannot verbally identify tactually or visually presented objects but can demonstrate recognition by nonverbal means and by verbal identification when an alternate sense is used.

A third argument against the existence of pure astereognosis has cited evidence that patients with tactile recognition disorders also have profound defects in spatial localization, route finding, and other visuospatial tasks (Semmes, 1965; Corkin, 1978). In concluding her review of somatosensory function, Corkin (1978) states that it is "possible to observe an impairment of high tactile functions in an individual whose elementary sensory status is preserved. It is inappropriate, however, to call this impairment an agnosia because the higher-order deficits seen are not specific to somesthesis" (p. 145). Although this is a persuasive and important argument, the anatomical lesions leading to tactile identification defects in humans involve primary somatosensory projection areas (S I) and not those portions of posterior parietal cortex known to be involved in complex spatial functions. The reader will also recall Roland and Larsen's (1976) studies of regional cerebral blood flow during astereognostic testing in humans. Focal rCBF increases were seen in somatosensory hand area and in premotor cortex *but not in posterior parietal cortex.*

Although the anatomical and clinical evidence is far from clear, we believe that pure astereognosis exists and that it is primarily caused by a lesion in the complex functional system subserved by the middle third of the postcentral gyrus (the hand area) and its cortical and subcortical connections. Consideration of the complex function of these regions requires a systematic neuropsychological evaluation of the task of tactual object identification. Certainly there are data to suggest that these areas subserve functions that are both sensory and motor. In palpating an object for identification, sensory and proprioceptive cues received by postcentral gyrus interact with premotor region to direct a series of coordinated movements necessary to construct a tactile image of the object. The task contains components that could be described as sensory, spatial, proprioceptive, and motor. The functional interconnections between S I, premotor region, and more posterior portions of the parietal cortex, as well as the enormous confusion that exists in the literature on high tactile disturbances, highlight the hazards of considering these components of stereognosis as separate and distinct aspects of a single complex function.

The reader will note that, with one exception, we have not used the apperceptive—associative dichotomy of Lissauer in discussing somatosensory agnosia. This terminology has been avoided because the clinical, physiological, and anatomical data on somatosensory function are far too complex to be handled by a linear two-step process of recognition. Although it remains the best shorthand system for classifying clinical data, it is clear that this model of the recognition process will eventually have to be discarded in favor of a model that can better account for the relationship between elementary and higher sensory function and for the active, exploratory, motor aspects of higher perceptual processes.

EXAMINATION OF THE PATIENT WITH AGNOSIA

The examination of the agnosic patient has already been discussed in some detail. In distinguishing between agnosic and aphasic errors, it is important to remember that agnosic recognition failures are most often modality-specific. The agnosic patient without associated aphasia will not manifest word-finding difficulty in spontaneous speech, in generating lists of words in specific categories, in completing open-ended sentences, and in supplying words that correspond with defintions. Except in the rare case of optic aphasia, the agnosic patient will not be able to identify the misnamed objects by means of circumlocution or by indicating function. It is important to determine whether the patient is able to demonstrate the use of unseen objects and to follow commands not requiring objects (e.g., salute, wave goodbye, make a fist). Failures of this type in the presence of otherwise intact auditory comprehension indicate *apraxia;* subsequent failure to demonstrate the use of objects presented on visual confrontation may therefore be apractic, not agnosic.

In pointing and naming tasks, it is important to be certain that the patient is visually fixating on the objects to be identified and that pointing errors are not due to the mislocation in space (optic ataxia) found with Balint's syndrome and its minor forms. Recognition should be examined both in the context of normal surroundings and in the formal test setting.

In the visual sphere, the recognition of objects, colors, words, geometric forms, faces, emblems, and signs should be evaluated. In the event of failure to recognize, the patient should be allowed to match misidentified items to sample and to produce drawings of objects not identified. Correct matching and accurate drawing suggest intact perceptual processing and a failure at the associative level. It should be kept in mind that poor drawing does not necessarily implicate an apperceptive defect, since visuomotor or constructional defects may also be present. For this reason, it is important to use tasks in addition to drawing to document intact perception. Cross-modal matching should also be evaluated. It is important to keep in mind that matching a visually presented object to one of four objects presented tactually is different from first presenting an object for palpation and then asking that it be chosen from one of four objects presented visually. Line drawings to be copied should contain sufficient detail so that the slavish, slow tracing of an outline can be distinguished from the more detailed drawings of patients with normal perceptuomotor function.

Other perceptual functions, such as figure-ground perception (hidden figures), closure and synthetic ability, topographical orientation, route finding, and visual counting (counting dots on a white paper, picking up pennies spread over a table top) should also be evaluated. Visual memory for designs, objects, faces, and colors should be assessed by delayed drawing and delayed multiple choice tasks. The ability to categorize, sort misidentified objects, and pair similar objects that are not morphologically identical should be tested.

The patient should be asked to identify pictures of well-known people and to identify hospital staff by face. If recognition does not occur, the patient should be asked to determine whether the face is of a male or female or of a human or animal. Ability to recognize visiting family should also be assessed, preferably by dressing the family member in a white coat or other appropriate hospital garb to reduce extrafacial differences between family member and hospital personnel. Patients with visual agnosia often fail to learn the names of new people and places but are able to demonstrate recognition by other means, such as "That's my doctor." Failure to name a particular face should therefore be further examined by asking for additional information about persons not named. The ability to discriminate identical and morphologically different representations of faces should be evaluated by matching tasks (e.g., Benton Facial Recognition Test).

Color perception should be tested with pseudoisochromatic plates and with the Munsell-Farnsworth 100 Hue Test (visual color tasks). The patient should be asked to respond to verbal tasks, such as listing as many colors as possible in one minute, naming as many items as possible of a certain color, or answering questions like "What is the color of a banana?" Other visual tasks, including coloring line drawings with crayons, should be given. Finally, visual-verbal color tasks, such as naming colors pointed out by the examiner or pointing to named colors, should be routinely presented.

The possibility of confabulation interfering with cognitive and gnostic performance should be kept in mind. Therefore, test performance when patients are allowed to verbalize should be compared with performance when they are prohibited from verbalizing either by being asked to count backwards or by having them place tongue between teeth. Comparisons should also be made between naming with tactile presentation alone and naming with simultaneous visual and tactile presentation.

Careful visual field and visual acuity measurements are crucial. It may be necessary, in testing patients who cannot read, to construct tests of acuity that use nonverbal targets, such as the orientation of lines of various lengths and distances from the viewer or the detection of two points at variable distances from each other and from the patient. If equipment is available, detailed psychophysical tests should be used, including absolute threshold determination, local adaptation time, flicker fusion, movement aftereffect, and tachistoscopic presentation of single and multiple items. In patients with associated alexia without agraphia, tachistoscopic presentation of words and letters, as well as a neurobehaviorally oriented reading battery, should be given. Depth perception using Julesz figures should be tested. Luminance discrimination should also be assessed. The use of an eye-movement monitor is helpful in describing visual scanning behavior. Where such sophisticated equipment is not available, there should be careful observation of visual exploratory behavior, manifested in eye movements, head-turning, and step-by-step feature comparisons.

In the auditory sphere, standard audiometric testing using speech reception and pure tone audiometry should be conducted. The ability to locate sounds in space should be examined using both absolute and relative locating tasks. It should be remembered that patients with acquired auditory sound agnosia do not ordinarily complain about their problem. Recognition of nonverbal sounds should be tested, preferably with a series of tape-recorded sounds, which are now available commercially. Musical ability should be tested, and the Seashore Tests of Musical Talent may be used with the understanding that, in the absence of history of proven musical ability and interest, findings from such tests are difficult to interpret.

In the tactile sphere, each hand should be assessed separately with verbal, pointing, and matching tasks. It is important to allow the patient to draw misidentified objects or to afterselect them from a group tactually. Tactual exploratory behavior should also be carefully observed.

Special Evaluative Procedures

As indicated in the review of various forms of agnosia, several investigators have evaluated the electrophysiological correlates of sensory processing in agnosic patients. Although the results from these studies have been inconclusive, the use of electrophysiological indices or recognition represents a move away from exclusive reliance on overt identification tasks. This represents a conceptual and procedural advance, since identification is only one aspect of recognition (Geschwind, 1965; Bauer, in press). Continued use of cortical and brainsteam evoked potentials, for example, seems warranted as a method for better understanding the relationship between performance and electrophysiological correlates of information processing in agnosic patients. As indicated by Michel et al. (1980), electrodes should be placed over various cortical areas, and both magnitude and latency measures should be derived.

Recognition can also be studied at the psychophysiological level. Peripheral measures of sympathetic nervous system activity (e.g., skin conductance, heart rate, pulse volume) have been used extensively as indices of recognition in the cognitive psychology literature and particularly in perceptual research (Lazarus and McCleary, 1951; Block and Reiser, 1962). Several studies have shown that autonomic discrimination of stimuli can occur even though the stimuli themselves are not overtly recognized (Lazarus and McCleary, 1951; Corteen and Wood, 1972). Skin conductance was recently used to index covert recognition processes in a prosopagnosic patient (Bauer, in press). It was shown that, when differential skin conductance responses were used as the index of recognition, a profoundly prosopagnosic patient could respond correctly to 60 percent of faces, none of which were overtly recognized. This underscores the importance of viewing recognition as a complex entity comprising several components. Answers to the question, "Did the patient recognize?" will vary depending upon the response system used to index recognition (Geschwind, 1965).

CONCLUSION

During the past few decades, significant advances have been made toward an understanding of the complex components of recognition. It is now clear that recognition is not a unitary process that, like the action potential, is either present or absent. Much of the problem of agnosia can be reduced to the problem of fractionated recognition abilities. The concept of recognition encompasses a broad range of behaviors, including attention, feature extraction, exploratory behavior, pattern and form perception, temporal resolution, and memory. New data on sensory and perceptual systems have revealed the exquisite complexity of the cortical and subcortical systems that support sensory and perceptual activities. Because of these advances, we have transcended the notion of a two-stage recognition process made up of apperception and association. Instead, recognition of sensorially presented stimuli is now understood as a complex outcome of parallel processing occurring simultaneously at the cortical and subcortical levels. Awareness of this complexity does not, however, invalidate the agnosias as meaningful neurobehavioral entities, though it does not seem likely that a single underlying mechanism responsible for all the agnosias will be found. It may be more fruitful to specify the conditions under which stimuli can and cannot be recognized (Geschwind, 1965; Ammon, 1979) and to more precisely specify the input, processing, and output requirements of specific tasks of identification and recognition. By doing this, and by correlating the emerging clinical findings with available neuropathological data, a more precise understanding of the spectrum of agnosic deficits, and by extension, of normal recognition abilities, may eventually be achieved.

REFERENCES

Adams, A. E., Rosenberg, K., Winter, H., and Zollner, C. (1977). A case of cortical deafness. *Archiv. Psychiatrie Nervenkrankheiten* 224:213–220.

Adler, A. (1944). Disintegration and restoration of optic recognition in visual agnosia. *Arch Neurol Psychiat* 51:243–259.

Albert, M. L., and Bear, D. (1974). Time to understand: A case study of word deafness with reference to the role of time in auditory comprehension. *Brain* 97:373–384.

Albert, M. L., Reches, A., and Silverberg, R. (1975a). Associative visual agnosia without alexia. *Neurology* 25:322–326.

Albert M. L., Reches, A., and Silverberg, R. (1975b). Hemianopic colour blindness. *J Neurol. Neurosurg. Psychiat.* 38:546–549.

Albert, M. L., Soffer, D., Silverberg, R., and Reches, A. (1979). The anatomic basis of visual agnosia. *Neurol. (Minneap.)* 29:876–879.

Albert, M. L., Sparks, R., von Stockert, T., and Sax, D. (1972). A case study of auditory agnosia: Linguistic and nonlingusitic processing. *Cortex* 8:427–433.

Alexander, M. P., Stuss, D. T., and Benson, D. F. (1979). Capgras syndrome: A reduplicative phenomenon. *Neurology* 29:334–339.

Ammon, K. H. (1979). Common dimensions of visual and auditory agnosia and an explanation of the auditory recognition deficit in aphasia. *Int. J. Neurosci.* 9:11–15.

Anton, G. (1899). Ueber die Selbstwahrnehmungen der Herderkrankungen des Gehirns durch den Kranken bei Rindenblindheit und Rindentaubheit. *Arch. Psychiat.* 32:86–127.

Assal, G., and Despland, P. A. (1973). Presentation d'un cas d'agnosie auditive. *Oto-Neuro-Ophtalmologie* 45:353–355.

Auerbach, S. H., Allard, T., Naeser, M., et al. (1982). Pure word deafness: Analysis of a case with bilateral lesions and a defect at the prehonemic level. *Brain* 105:271–300.

Balint, R. (1909). Seelenlahmung des "Schauens," optische Ataxie, raumliche Storung der Aufmerksamkeit. *Montasschr. Psychiat. Neurol.* 25:57–71.

Battersby, W. S., Bender, M. B., Pollack, M., and Kahn, R. L. (1956). Unilateral "spatial agnosia" (inattention) in patients with cerebral lesions. *Brain* 93:68–93.

Bauer, R. M. (1982). Visual hypoemotionality as a symptom of visual-limbic disconnection in man. *Arch. Neurol.* 39:702–708.

Bauer, R. M. (in press). Autonomic recognition of names and faces in prosopagnosia: A neuropsychological application of the Guilty Knowledge Test. *Neuropsychologia.*

Bauer, R. M., and Trobe, J. (in press). Visual memory and perceptual impairments in prosopagnosia. *J. Clin. Neuro-Ophthalmol.*

Bay, E. (1944). Zum problem der taktilen Agnosie. *D. Ztschr. Nervenk.* 156:1–3, 64–96.

Bay, E. (1953). Disturbances of visual perception and their examination. *Brain* 76:515–550.

Beauvois, M. F., Saillant, B., Meininger, V., and Lhermitte, F. (1978). Bilateral tactile aphasia: A tacto-verbal dysfunction. *Brain* 101:381–401.

Bender, M. D., and Feldman, M. (1972). The so-called "visual agnosias." *Brain* 95:173–186.

Benson, D. F., and Greenberg, J. P. (1969). Visual form agnosia. *Arch. Neurol.* 20:82–89.

Benson, D. F., Segarra, J., and Albert, M. L. (1974). Visual agnosia-prosopagnosia. *Arch. Neurol.* 30:307–310.

Benton, A. L. (1980). The neuropsychology of face recognition. *Am. Psychol.* 35:176–186.

Benton, A. L., and Van Allen, M. W. (1972). Prosopagnosia and facial discrimination. *J. Neurol. Sci.* 15:167–172.

Benton, A. L., Levin, A., and Varney, N. (1973). Tactile perception of direction in normal subjects. *Neurology* 23:1248–1250.

Berkeley, M. A., and Sprague, J. M. (1979). Striate cortex and visual acuity functions in the cat. *J. Compl. Neurol.* 187:679–702.

Beyn, E. S., and Knyazeva, G. R. (1962). The problem of prosopagnosia. *J. Neurol. Neurosurg. Psychiat.* 25:154–158.

Block, J. D., and Reiser, M. F. (1962). Discrimination and recognition of weak stimuli. I: Psychological and physiological relationships. *Arch. Gen. Psychiat.* 6:25–36.

Blumstein, S., and Cooper, W. (1974). Hemispheric processing of intonation contours. *Cortex* 10:146–158.

Bodamer, J. (1947). Prosopagnosie. *Arch. Psychiatr. Nervenkr.* 179:6–54.

Boller, F., and Spinnler, H. (1967). Visual memory for colors in patients with unilateral brain damage. *Cortex* 3:395–405.

Boller, F., Cole, M., Kim, Y., et al. (1975). Optic ataxia: Clinical-radiological correlations with the EMI scan. *J. Neurol. Neurosurg. Psychiat.* 38:954–958.

Bonhoeffer, K. (1918). Partielle reine Tastlahmung. *Mtschr. Psychiat. Neurol.* 43:141–145.

Bornstein, B. (1963). Prosopagnosia. In *Problems of Dynamic Neurology* (L. Halpern. ed.). New York: Grune and Stratton.

Bornstein, B., and Kidron, D. P. (1959). Prosopagnosia. *J. Neurol. Neurosurg. Psychiat.* 22:124–131.

Bornstein, B., Sroka, H., and Munitz, H. (1969). Prosopganosia with animal face agnosia. *Cortex* 5:164–169.

Botez, M. I. (1975). Two visual systems in clinical neurology: Readaptive role of the primitive system in visual agnosic patients. *Eur. Neurol.* 13:101–122.

Botez, M. I., and Serbanescu, T. (1967). Course and outcome of visual static agnosia. *J. Neurol. Sci.* 4:289–297.

Bowers, D. (1981). Acquired color disturbances due to cerebral lesions. Paper presented at seventh annual course in behavior neurology and neuropsychology, Florida Society of Neurology, St. Petersburg Beach, December 1981.

Bradshaw, G. J., Hicks, R. E., and Rose, B. (1979). Lexical discrimination and letter string identification in the two visual fields. *Brain Lang.* 8:10–18.

Brain, W. R. (1941). Visual object agnosia with special reference to the gestalt theory. *Brain* 64:43–62.

Brandt, J. (1971). Classification without identification in visual search. *Q.J. Exp. Psychol.* 23:178–186.

Brodal, A. (1981). *Neurological Anatomy in Relation to Clinical Medicine* (3rd edn.). New York: Oxford University Press.

Brown, J. W. (1972). *Aphasia, Apraxia, and Agnosia—Clinical and Theoretical Aspects.* Springfield, Ill.: Charles C. Thomas.

Caltagirone, C., Miceli, G., and Gianotti, G. (1977). Distinctive features of unilateral spatial agnosia in right and left brain-damaged patients. *Eur. Neurol.* 16:121–126.

Cambier, J., Masson, M., Elghozi, D., et al. (1980). Agnosie visuelle sans hemianopsie droite chez un sujet droitier. *Rev. Neurol. (Paris)* 136:727–740.

Campora, G. (1925). Astereognosis: Its causes and mechanism. *Brain* 18:65–71.

Caplan, L. R. (1978). Variability of perceptual function: The sensory cortex as a "categorizer" and "deducer." *Brain Lang.* 6:1–13.

Caplan, L. R. (1980). "Top of the basilar" syndrome. *Neurology* 30:72–79.

Celesia, G. G. (1976). Organization of auditory cortical areas in man. *Brain* 99:403–414.

Celesia, G. G., Archer, C. R., Kuroiwa, Y., and Goldfader, P. R. (1980). Visual function of the extrageniculo-calcarine system in man. *Arch. Neurol.* 37:704–706.

Chocholle, R., Chedru, F., Bolte, M. C., et al. (1975). Etude psychoacoustique d'un cas de "surdite corticlae." *Neuropsychologia* 13:163–172.

Cogan, D. G. (1979). Visuospatial dysgnosia. *Am.J. Ophthalmol.* 88:361–368.

Cohen, R., and Kelter, S. (1979). Cognitive impairment of aphasics in color to picture matching tasks. *Cortex* 15:235–245.

Cohn, R., Neumann, M. A., and Wood, D. H. (1977). Prosopagnosia: A clinicopathological study. *Ann. Neurol.* 1:177–182.

Cooper, J. A., and Ferry, P. C. (1978). Acquired auditory verbal agnosia and seizures in childhood. *J. Speech Hear. Disor.* 43:176–184.

Corkin, S. (1964). *Somesthetic function after focal cerebral damage in man*. Unpublished doctoral dissertation, McGill University.

Corkin, S. (1978). The role of different cerebral structures in somesthetic perception. In *Handbook of Perception* (vol. ViB) (C. E. Carterette and M. P. Friedman, eds.). New York: Academic Press, pp. 105–155.

Corkin, S., Milner, B., and Rasmussen, T. (1970). Somatosensory thresholds: Contrasting effects of postcentral-gyrus and posterior parietal-lobe excision. *Arch. Neurol.* 23:41–58.

Corkin, S., Milner, B., and Taylor, L. (1973). *Bilateral sensory loss after unilateral cerebral lesions in man*. Paper presented at joint meeting of American Neurological Association and Canadian Congress of Neurological Sciences, Montreal.

Corlew, M. M., and Nation, J. E. (1975). Characteristics of visual stimuli and naming performance in aphasic adults. *Cortex* 11:186–191.

Corteen, R. S., and Wood, B. (1972). Autonomic responses to shock-associated words in an unattended channel. *J. Exp. Psychol.* 94:308–313.

Coslett, H. B., Brashear, H. R., and Heilman, K. M. (in press). Functional anatomy of the human auditory cortex: Evidence from pure word deafness. *Neurology*.

Critchley, M. M. (1964). The problem of visual agnosia. *J. Neurol. Sci.* 1:274–290.

Critchley, M. M. (1965). Acquired anomalies of colour perception of central origin. *Brain* 88:711–724.

Critchley, M. M., and Henson, R. A. (1977). *Music and the Brain: Studies in the Neurology of Music*. Springfield, Ill.: Charles C Thomas.

Cummings, J. L., Syndulko, K., Goldberg, Z., and Treiman, D. M. (1982). Palinopsia reconsidered. *Neurol. (NY)* 32:444–447.

Damasio, A. R., and Benton, A. L. (1979). Impairment of hand movements under visual guidance. *Neurol. (Minneap.)* 29:170–174.

Damasio, A. R., and Damasio, H. (1982). Cerebral localization of complex visual manifestations: Clinical and physiological significance (abst). *Neurology 32:* A96 (suppl.).

Damasio, A. R., Damasio, H., and Van Hoesen, G. W. (1982). Prosopagnosia: Anatomic basis and behavioral mechanisms. *Neurol. (NY)* 32:331–341.

Damasio, H., McKee, H., and Damasio, A. R. (1979). Determinants of performance in color anomia. *Brain Lang.* 7:74–85.

Damasio, A. R., Yamada, T., Damasio, H., et al. (1980). Central achromatopsia: Behavioral, anatomic, and physiologic aspects. *Neurology 30:*1064–1071.

Davidenkov, S. (1956). Impairments of higher nervous activity: Lecture 8, visual agnosias. In *Clinical Lectures on Nervous Diseases*. Leningrad: State Publishing House of Medical Literature.

Delay, J. (1935). *Les Astereognosies. Pathologie due Toucher. Clinique, Physiologie, Topographie*. Paris: Masson.

Denes, G., and Semenza, C. (1975). Auditory modality-specific anomia: Evidence from a case of pure word deafness. *Cortex* 11:401–411.

Denny-Brown, D., and Chambers, R. A. (1976). Physiological aspects of visual perception. I: Functional aspects of visual cortex. *Arch. Neurol.* 33:219–227.

Denny-Brown, D., and Fischer, E. G. (1976). Physiological aspects of visual perception. II: The subcortical visual direction of behavior. *Arch. Neurol.* 33:228–242.

De Renzi, E., and Spinnler, H. (1967). Impaired performance on color tasks in patients with hemispheric damage. *Cortex* 3:194–217.

DeRenzi, E., and Spinnler, H. (1968). Visual recognition in patients with unilateral cerebral disease. *J. Nerv. Ment. Dis.* 142: 515–525.

De Renzi, E., Faglioni, P., Scotti, G., and Spinnler, H. (1972). Impairment in associating colour to form, concomitant with aphasia. *Brain* 95:293–304.

De Renzi, E., Faglioni, P., Scotti, G., and Spinnler, H. (1973). Impairment of color sorting: An experimental study with the Holmgren Skein Test. *Cortex 9*:147–163.

De Renzi, E., Scotti, G., and Spinnler, H. (1969). Perceptual and associative disorders of visual recognition. *Neurology 19*:634–642.

Dewson, J. H., Pribram, K. H., and Lynch, J. C. (1969). Effects of ablation of temporal cortex upon speech sound discrimination in the monkey. *Exp. Neurol. 24*:279–291.

Duffy, F. L., and Burchfiel, J. L. (1971). Somatosensory system: Organizational hierarchy from single units in monkey area 5. *Science 172*:273–275.

Earnest, M. P., Monroe, P. A., and Yarnell, P. A. (1977). Cortical deafness: Demonstration of the pathologic anatomy by CT scan. *Neurology 27*:1175–1175.

Efron, R. (1968). What is perception? In *Boston Studies in the Philosophy of Science* (vol. 4). New York: Humanities Press.

Endtz, L. J., and Frenay, J. J. (1980). Studies on astereognosis and amyotrophy of the hand in brainstem syndromes: Relation to the symptomatology of tumors at the spinocranial junction. *J. Neurol. Sci. 44*:241–246.

Ettlinger, G. (1956). Sensory deficits in visual agnosia. *J. Neurol. Neurosurg. Psychiat. 19*:297–307.

Ettlinger, G., and Wyke, M. (1961). Defects in identifying objects visually in a patient with cerebrovascular disease. *J. Neurol. Neurosurg. Psychiat. 24*:254–259.

Ettlinger, G., Warrington, E. K., and Zangwill, O. L. (1957). A further study of visual-spatial agnosia. *Brain 80*:335–361.

Evans, J. P. (1935). A study of the sensory defects resulting from excision of cerebral substance in humans. *Res. Publ. Assoc. Nerv. Ment. Dis. 15*:331–365.

Faust, C. (1955). *Die zerebralen Herderscheinungen bei Hinterhauptsverletzungen und ihre Beurteilung.* Stuttgart: Thieme Verlag.

Fennell, E., Satz, P. and Wise, R. (1967). Laterality differences in the perception of pressure. *J. Neurol. Neurosurg. Psychiat. 30*:337–340.

Festinger, L., Burnham, C. A., Ono, H., and Bamber, D. (1967). Efference and the conscious experience of perception. *J. Exp. Psychol. 74*:1–36 (monogr. suppl).

Finkelnburg, F. C. (1870). Niederrheinische Gesellschaft in Bonn. Medicinische Section. *Berliner klinische Woch. 7*:449–450, 460–461.

Frederiks, J. A. M. (1969). The agnosias. In *Handbook of Clinical Neurology* (vol. 4) (P. J. Vinken and G. W. Bruyn, eds.). Amsterdam: North Holland.

Freud, S. (1891). *Zur Auffasun der Aphasien: Eine Kritische Studie.* Vienna: Franz Deuticke.

Freund, D. C. (1889). Ueber optische Aphasie und Seelenblindheit. *Arch. Psychiat. Nervenkr 20*:276–297, 371–416.

Frumkin, B., and Rapin, I. (1980). Perception of vowels and consonant-vowels of varying duration in language impaired children. *Neuropsychologia 18*:443–454.

Gans, A. (1916). Uber Tastblinheit und uber Storungen der raumlichen Wahrenhmungen der Sensibilitat. *Z. gesamte Neurol. Psychiatrie 31*:303–428.

Gardner, H., Silverman, H., Denes, G., et al. (1977). Sensitivity to musical denotation and connotation in organic patients. *Cortex 13*:242–256.

Gascon, G., Victor, D., Lombroso, C., and Goodglass, D. (1973). Language disorder, convulsive disorder, and electroencephalographic abnormalities. *Arch. Neurol. 28*:156–162.

Gates, A., and Bradshaw, J. L .(1977). The role of the cerebral hemispheres in music. *Brain Lang. 4*:403–431.

Gazzaniga, M. A., and Sperry, R. W. (1967). Language after section of the cerebral commisures. *Brain 90*:131–148.

Gazzaniga, M. S., Bogen, J. E., and Sperry, R. W. (1963). Laterality effects in somesthesis following cerebral commisurotomy in man. *Neuropsychologia 1*:209–215.

Gazzaniga, M., Glass, A. V., and Sarno, M. T. (1973). Pure word deafness and hemispheric dynamics: A case history. *Cortex* 9:136–143.

Geschwind, N. (1965). Disconnexion syndromes in animals and man. *Brain* 88:237–294, 585–644.

Geschwind, N., and Fusillo, M. (1966). Color-naming defects in association with alexia. *Arch. Neurol.* 15:137–146.

Geschwind, N., and Kaplan, E. F. (1962). A human disconnection syndrome. *Neurol. (Minneap.)* 12:675–685.

Gloning, I., Gloning, K., Jellinger, K., and Quatember, R. (1970). A case of "prosopagnosia" with necropsy findings. *Neurospychologia* 8:199–204.

Goldstein, K. (1916). Uber kortikale Sensibilitsstorungen. *Neurol. Zblt.* 19:825–827.

Goldstein, K. (1943). Some remarks on Russell Brain's article concerning visual object-agnosia. *J. Nerv. Ment. Dis.* 98:148–153.

Goldstein, K., and Gelb, A. (1918). Psychologische Analysen hirnpathologischer Falle auf Grund von Untersuchungen Hirnverletzter. *Z. gesamte Neurol. Psychiatrie* 41:1–142.

Goldstein, M. N. (1974). Auditory agnosia for speech ("pure word deafness"): A historical review with current implications. *Brain Lang.* 1:195–204.

Goldstein, M. N., Brown, M., and Holander, J. (1975). Auditory agnosia and word deafness: Analysis of a case with three-year follow up. *Brain Lang.* 2:324–332.

Goodglass, H., Barton, M. I., and Kaplan, E. F. (1968). Sensory modality and object-naming in aphasia. *J. Speech Hear. Res* 11:488–496.

Gordon, H. W. (1974). Auditory specialization of the right and left hemispheres. In *Hemispheric Disconnection and Cerebral Function* (M. Kinsbourne and W. L. Smith, eds.), Springfield, Ill.: Charles C Thomas.

Gordon, W. P., and Naeser, M. (1977). Frequency discrimination deficits in three word-deaf patients with bilateral temporal lobe lesions. Paper presented at the meetings of the Academy of Aphasia, Montreal.

Green, G. L., and Lessell, S. (1977). Acquired cerebral dyschromatopsia. *Arch. Ophthalmol.* 95:121–128.

Gross, C. G., Rocha-Miranda, C. E., and Bender, D. B. (1972). Visual properties of neurons in inferotemporal cortex of the macaque. *J. Neurophysiol.* 35:96–111.

Haaxma, R., and Kuypers, H. G. J. M. (1975). Intrahemispheric cortical connections and visual guidance of hand and finger movements in the rhesus monkey. *Brain* 98:239–260.

Hahn, E. (1895). Pathologische-anatomische Untersuchung en de Lissauer'schen Falles von Seelenblindheit. *Arbeiten aus dem Psychiatrischen Klinik in Breslau.*

Hatfield, F. M., and Howard, D. (1977). Object naming in aphasia: The lack of effect of context or realism. *Neuropsychologia* 15:717–727.

Head, H. (1918). Sensation and the cerebral cortex. *Brain* 41:57–253.

Head, H. (1920). *Studies in Neurology* (vol. 2). London: Oxford University Press.

Head, H., and Holmes, G. (1911). Sensory disturbances from cerebral lesions. *Brain* 34:102–254.

Head, H., Rivers, W. H. R., and Sherren, J. (1905). The afferent system from a new aspect. *Brain* 28:99.

Hécaen, H. (1972). *Introduction a la neuropsychologie.* Paris: Lasousse.

Hécaen, H., and Albert, M. L. (1978). *Human Neuropsychology.* New York: Wiley.

Hécaen, H., and Angelergues, R. (1962). Agnosia for faces (prosopagnosia). *Arch. Neurol.* 7:92–100.

Hécaen, H., and David, M. (1945). Syndrome parietale traumatique: Asymbolie tactile et hemiasomatognosie paroxystique et douloureuse. *Rev. Neurol.* 77:113–123.

Hécaen, H., and de Ajuriaguerra, J. (1954). Balint's syndrome (psychic paralysis of visual fixation) and its minor forms. *Brain* 77:373–400.

Hécaen, H., and de Ajuriaguerra, J. (1956). Agnosie visuelle pour les objets inanimes par lesion unilaterale gauche. *Rev. Neurol.* 94:222–233.

Hécaen, H., Goldblum, M. C., Masure, M. C., and Ramier, A. M. (1974). Une nouvelle observation d'agnosie d'objet: Deficit de l'association ou de la categorisation, specifique de la modalite visuell? *Neuropsychologia* 12:447–464.

Heffner, R. S. (1977). Developmental auditory agnosia in retarded adolescents: A preliminary investigation. *Brain Lang.* 4:521–536.

Heilman, K. M., Scholes, R., and Watson, R. T. (1975). Auditory affective agnosia: Disturbed comprehension of affective speech. *J. Neurol. Neurosurg. Psychiat.* 38:69–72.

Hemphill, R. C., and Stengel, E. (1940). A study of pure word deafness. *J. Neurol. Psychiat.* 3:251–262.

Holmes, G. (1918). Disturbances of visual orientation. *Br. J. Ophthalmol.* 2:449–468.

Horel, J. A., and Keating, E. G. (1969). Partial Kluver-Bucy syndrome produced by cortical disconnection. *Brain Res.* 16:281–284.

Horel, J. A., and Keating, E. G. (1972). Recovery from a partial Kluver-Bucy syndrome induced by disconnection. *J. Compar. Physiol. Psychol.* 79:105–114.

Hubel, D. H., and Wiesel, T. N. (1968). Receptive fields and functional architecture of monkey striate cortex. *J. Physiol.* 195:215–243.

Iversen, S. D., and Weiskrantz, L. (1964). Temporal lobe lesions and memory in the monkey. *Nature* 201:740–742.

Iversen, S. D., and Weiskrantz, L. (1967). Perception of redundant cues by monkeys with inferotemporal lesions. *Nature* 214:241–243.

Jackson, J. H. (1876). Case of large cerebral tumour without optic neuritis and with left hemiplegia and imperception. *R. Lond. Ophthal. Hosp. Rep.* 8:434. Reprinted (1932) *Selected Writings of John Hughlings Jackson*, Vol. 2 (J. Taylor, ed.). London: Hodder and Stoughton.

Jerger, J., Lovering, L., and Wertz, M. (1972). Auditory disorder following bilateral temporal lobe insult: Report of a case. *J. Speech Hear. Dis.* 37:523–535.

Jerger, J., Weikers, N., Sharbrough, F., and Jerger, S. (1969). Bilateral lesions of the temporal lobe: A case study. *Acta Oto-Laryngologica* (suppl.) 258:1–51.

Jones, E. G., and Powell, T. P. S. (1969). Connections of the somatic sensory cortex of the rhesus monkey. I: Ipsilateral cortical connections. *Brain* 92:477–502. II: Contralateral connections. *Brain* 92:717–730.

Kanshepolsky, J., Kelley, J., and Waggener, J. (1973). A cortical auditory disorder. *Neurology* 23:699–705.

Karpov, B. A., Meerson, Y. A., and Tonkonogii, I. M. (1979). On some peculiarities of the visuomotor system in visual agnosia. *Neuropsychologia* 17:231–294.

Kay, M. C., and Levin, H. S. (1982). Prosopagnosia. *Am. J. Ophthalmol.* 94:75–80.

Kertesz, A. (1979). Visual agnosia: The dual deficit of perception and recognition. *Cortex* 15:403–419.

Kinsbourne, M., and Warrington, E. K. (1962). A disorder of simultaneous form perception. *Brain* 85:461–486.

Kinsbourne, M., and Warrington, E. K. (1964). Observations on color agnosia. *J. Neurol. Neurosurg. Psychiat.* 27:296–299.

Klein, R., and Harper, J. (1956). The problem of agnosia in the light of a case of pure word deafness. *J. Mental Sci.* 102:112–120.

Kliest, K. (1928). Gehirnpathologische und lokalisatorische Ergebnisse uber Horstorungen, Geruschtaubheiten und Amusien. *Monatssche. Psychiat. Neurol.* 68:853–860.

Kliest, K. (1934). *Gelurnpathologie Vornehinlich auf Grund der Kriegerfahrungen*. Leipzig: Barth.

Kussmaul, A. (1877). Disturbances of speech. *Cyclopedia of the Practice of Medicine* (H. von Ziemssien, ed.). New York: William Wood.

Kuypers, H. G. J. M., Szwarcbart, M. K., Mishkin, M., and Rosvold, H. E. (1965). Occipito-temporal corticocortical connections in the rhesus monkey. *Exp. Neurol.* 11:245–262.

Lamberts, F. (1980). Developmental auditory agnosia in the severely retarded: A further investigation. *Brain Lang.* 11:106–118.

Landau, W. U., and Kleffner, F. R. (1957). Syndrome of acquired aphasia with convulsive disorder in children. *Neurology* 7:523–530.

Landau, W. U., Goldstein, R., and Kleffner, F. R. (1960). Congenital aphasia: A clinicopathologic study. *Neurology* 10:915–921.

Landis, T., Graves, R., Benson, D. F., and Hebben, N. (1982). Visual recognition through kinaesthetic mediation. *Psychol. Med.* 12:515–531.

Lazarus, R. S., and McCleary, R. A. (1951). Autonomic discrimination without awareness: A study of subception. *Psy. Rev.* 58:113–122.

Leicester, J. (1980). Central deafness and subcortical motor aphasia. *Brain Lang.* 10:224–242.

Levine, D. N. (1978). Prosopagnosia and visual object agnosia: A behavioral study. *Brain Lang.* 5:341–365.

Levine, D. N., and Calvanio, R. (1978). A study of the visual defect in verbal alexia-simultanagnosia. *Brain* 101:65–81.

Levine, D. N., Kaufman, K. J., and Mohr, J. P. (1978). Inaccurate reaching associated with a superior parietal lobe tumor. *Neurology* 28:556–561.

Lhermitte, F., and Beauvois, M. F. (1973). A visual-speech disconnection syndrome. *Brain* 96:695–714.

Lhermitte, F., and de Ajuriaguerra, J. (1938). Asymbolie tactile et hallucinations du toucher: Etude anatomiclinique. *Rev. Neurol.* 70:492–495.

Lhermitte, F., and Pillon, B. (1975). La prosopagnosie: Role de l'hemisphere droit dans la perception visuelle. *Rev. Neurol.* 131:791–812.

Lhermitte, F., Chain, F., Chedru, J., and Penet, C. (1976). A study of visual process in a case of interhemispheric disconnexion. *J. Neurol. Sci.* 25:317–330.

Lhermitte, F., Chain, F., Escourolle, R., et al. (1971). Etude des troubles perceptifs auditifs dans les lesions temporales bilaterales. *Rev. Neurol.* 128:329–351.

Lhermitte, F., Chedru, F., and Chain, F. (1973). A propos d'une cas d'agnosie visuelle. *Rev. Neurol.* 128:301–322.

Lichteim, L. (1885). On aphasia. *Brain* 7:433–484.

Liepmann, H. (1900). Das Krankheitsbild der Apraxia ("motorischen asymbolie"). *Monatsschr. Psychiat. Neurol.* 8:15–44, 102–132, 181–197.

Lipemann, H., and Storch, E. (1902). Der mikroskopische Gehirnberfund bei dem Fall Gorstelle. *Monatsschr. Psychiat Neurol.* 11:115–120.

Lissauer, H. (1889). Ein Fall von Seelenblindheit nebst conem Beitrage zur Theorie derselben. *Archiv. Psychiatrie* 21:222–270.

Luria, A.R. (1959). Disorders of "simultaneous perception" in a case of bilateral occipitoparietal brain injury. *Brain* 83:437–449.

Luria, A. R., Pravdina-Vinarskaya, E. N., and Yarbus, A. L. (1963). Disorders of ocular movement in a case of simultanagnosia. *Brain* 86:219–228.

Mack, J. L,. and Boller, F. (1977). Associative visual agnosia and its related deficits: The role of the minor hemisphere in assigning meaning to visual perceptions. *Neuropsychologia* 15:345–349.

MacKay, G., and Dunlop, J. C. (1899). The cerebral lesions in a case of complete acquired colour-blindness. *Scot. Med. Surg. J.* 5:503–512.

Macrae, D., and Trolle, E. (1956). The defect of function in visual agnosia. *Brain* 79:94–110.

Mahoudeau, D., Lemoyne, J., Dubrisay, J., and Caraes, J. (1956). Sur un cas d'agnosie auditive. *Rev. Neurol.* 95:57.

Massopoust, L. C., and Wolin, L. R. (1967). Changes in auditory frequency discrimination thresholds after temporal cortex ablation. *Exp. Neurol.* 19:245–251.

Mavlov, L. (1980). Amusia due to rhythm agnosia in a musician with left hemisphere damage: A non-auditory supramodal defect. *Cortex* 16:331–338.

McCall, G. N., and Cunningham, N. M. (1971). Two-point discrimination: Asymmetry in spatial discrimination on the two sides of the tongue, a preliminary report. *Percep. Mot. Skills* 32:368–370.

McFie, J., Piercy, M. F., and Zangwill, O. A. (1950). Visual-spatial agnosia associated with lesions of the right cerebral hemisphere. *Brain* 73:167–190.

Meadows, J. C. (1974a). Disturbed perception of colours associated with localized cerebral lesions. *Brain* 97:615–632.

Meadows, J. C. (1974b). The anatomical basis of prosopganosia. *J. Neurol. Neurosurg. Psychiat.* 37:489–501.

Miceli, G. (1982). The processing of speech sounds in a patient with cortical auditory disorder. *Neuropsychologia* 20:5–20.

Michel, J., Peronnet, F., and Schott, B. (1980). A case of cortical deafness: Clinical and electrophysiological data. *Brain Lang.* 10:367–377.

Milner, B., and Taylor, L. B. (1972). Right-hemisphere superiority in tactile pattern recognition after cerebral commisurotomy: Evidence for nonverbal memory. *Neuropsychologia* 10:1–15.

Mountcastle, V. B. (1961). Some functional properties of the somatic afferent system. In *Sensory Communication* (W. A. Rosenblith, ed.) Cambridge, Mass.: MIT Press, pp. 403–436.

Mountcastle, V. B., and Powell, T. P. S. (1959a). Neural mechanisms subserving cutaneous sensibility, with special reference to the role of afferent inhibition in sensory perception and discrimination. *Bull. Johns Hopkins Hosp.* 105:201–232.

Mountcastle, V. B., and Powell, T. P. S. (1959b). Central nervous mechanisms subserving position sense and kinesthesis. *Bull. Johns Hopkins Hosp.* 105:173–200.

Mountcastle, V. B., Lynch, J. C., Georgopoulos, A., Sakata, H., and Acuna, C. (1975). Posterior parietal association cortex of the monkey: Command functions for operations within extrapersonal space. *J. Neurophysiol.* 38:871–908.

Munk, H. (1881). Ueber die Functionen der Grosshirnrinde. *Gesammelte Mittheilungen aus den Jahren 1877–80.* Berlin: Hirschwald.

Nardelli, E., Buonanno, F., Coccia, G., et al. (1982). Prosopagnosia: Report of four cases. *Eur. Neurol.* 21:289–297.

Neff, W. D. (1961). Neuronal mechanisms of auditory discrimination. In *Sensory Communication* (N. A. Rosenblith, ed.). Cambridge, Mass.: MIT Press.

Neisser, U. (1967). *Cognitive Psychology.* New York: Appleton-Century-Crofts.

Neisser, U. (1976). *Cognition and Reality.* San Francisco: Freeman.

Newcombe, F., and Ratcliff, G. (1974). Agnosia: A disorder of object recognition. In *Les Syndromes de Disconnexion Calleuse chez L'homme* (F. Michel and B. Schott, eds.), Colloque International de Lyon.

Oppenheim, H. (1906). Uber einen bemerkenswerten Fall. von Tumor cerebri. *Berlin Klin. Wschr.* 43:1001–1004.

Oppenheim, H. (1911). *Textbook of Nervous Diseases for Physicians and Students*. Edinburgh: Darien Press.

Oppenheimer, D. R.,and Newcombe, F. (1978). Clinical and anatomic findings in a case of auditory agnosia. *Arch. Neurol.* 35:712–719.

Overman, W. H., and Doty, R. W. (1982). Hemispheric specialization displayed by man but not macaque for analysis of faces. *Neuropsychologia 20*:113–128.

Oxbury, J., Oxbury, S., and Humphrey, N. (1969). Varieties of color anomia. *Brain 92*:847–860.

Pallis, C. A. (1955). Impaired identification of faces and places with agnosia for colors. *J. Neurol. Neurosurg. Psychiat. 18*:218–224.

Pasik, T., and Pasik, P. (1971). The visual world of monkeys deprived of striate cortex: Effective stimulus parameters and the importance of the accessory optic system. *Vision Res. Suppl. 3*:419–435.

Paterson, A., and Zangwill, O. L. (1944). Disorders of visual space perception associated with lesions of the right cerebral hemisphere. *Brain 67*:331–358.

Paul, R. L., Merzenich, M., and Goodman, H. (1972). Representation of slowly and rapidly adapting cutaneous mechanorceptors of the hand in Brodman's areas 3 and 1 of *Macaca mulatta. Brain Res. 36*:229–249.

Pearlman, A. L., Birch, J., and Meadows, J. C. (1979). Cerebral color blindness: An acquired defect in hue discrimination. *Ann. Neurol. 5*:253–261.

Penfield, W. (1958). *The excitable cortex in conscious man*. Springfield, Ill.: Charles C Thomas.

Perenin, M. T., and Jeannerod, M. (1978). Visual function within the hemianopic field following early cerebral hemidecortication in man. I: Spatial localization. *Neuropsychologia 16*:1–13.

Pillon, B., Signoret, J. L., and Lhermitte, F. (1981). Agnosie visuelle associative: Role del'hemisphere gauche dans la perception visuelle. *Rev. Neurol. 137*:831–842.

Poppelreuter, W. (1923). Zur Psychologie und Pathologie der optischen Wahrehmung. *Aschr gesamte Neurol. Psychiat. 83*:26–152.

Powell, T. P. S., and Mountcastle, V. B. (1959). Some aspects of the functional organization of the cortex of the postcentral gyrus of the monkey: A correlation of findings obtained in a single unit analysis with cytoarchitecture. *Bull. Johns Hopkins Hosp. 105*:123–162.

Randolph, M., and Semmes, J. (1974). Behavioral consequences of selective subtotal ablations in the postcentral gyrus of *Macaca mulatta. Brain Res. 70*:55–70.

Rapin, I., Mattis, S., Rowan, A. J., and Golden, G. G. (1977). Verbal auditory agnosia in children. *Dev. Med. Child Neurol. 19*:192–207.

Ratcliff, G., and Ross, J. E. (1981). Visual perception and perceptual disorder. *Br. Med. Bull.* 37:181–186.

Raymond, F., and Egger, M. (1906). Un cas d'aphasie tactile. *Rev. Neurol. 14*:371–375.

Reinhold, M. (1950). A case of auditory agnosia. *Brain 73*:203–223.

Riddoch, G. (1917). Dissociation of visual perception due to occipital injuries with special reference to appreciation of movement. *Brain 40*:15–57.

Riddoch, G. (1935). Visual disorientation in homonymous half-fields. *Brain 58*:376–382.

Roland, P. E. (1976). Astereognosis. *Arch. Neurol. 33*:543–550.

Roland, P. E., and Larsen, B. (1976). Focal increase of cerebral blood flow during stereognostic testing in man. *Arch. Neurol. 33*:551–558.

Rosati, G., DeBastiani, P., Paolino, E., et al. (1982). Clinical and audiological findings in a case of auditory agnosia. *J. Neurol. 227*:21–27.

Rose, J. E., and Woolsey, C. N. (1949). Organization of the mammalian thalamus and its relationship to the cerebral cortex. *E.E.G. Clin. Neurophysiol. 1*:391–400.

Ross, E. D. (1980). Sensory-specific and fractional disorders of recent memory in man. I: Isolated loss of visual recent memory. *Arch. Neurol.* 37:193–200.

Rubens, A. B., and Benson, D. F. (1971). Associative visual agnosia. *Arch. Neurol.* 24:304–316.

Rudel, R. G., Denckla, M. B., and Spalten, E. (1974). The functional asymmetry of Braille letter learning in normal, sighted children. *Neurology* 24:733–738.

Saffran, E. B., Marin, O. S. M., and Yeni-Komshian, G. H. (1976). An analysis of speech perception in word deafness. *Brain Lang.* 3:255–256.

Schuster, P., and Taterka, H. (1926). Beitrag zur Anatomie und Klinik der reinen Worttaubbeit. *Ztschr. gesamte Neurol. Psychiat.* 105:494.

Seiler, J., and Ricker, K. (1971). Das Vibrationsempfinden: Eine apparative Schwellenbestimmung. *Z. Neurol.* 200:70–79.

Semmes, J. (1953). Agnosia in animal and man. *Psy. Rev.* 60:140–147.

Semmes, J. (1965). A non-tactual factor in astereognosis. *Neuropsychologia* 3:295–314.

Semmes, J., Weinstein, S., Ghent, L., and Teuber, H.-L. (1960). *Somatosensory Changes After Penetrating Brain Wounds in Man.* Cambridge, Mass.: Harvard University Press.

Shoumaker, R. D., Ajax, E. T., and Schenkenberg, T. (1977). Pure word deafness (auditory verbal agnosia). *Dis. Nerv. Sys.* 38:293–299.

Shoumaker, R. D., Bennett, D. R., Bray, P. F., and Curless, R. G. (1974). Clinical and EEG manifestations of an unusual aphasic syndrome in children. *Neurology* 24:10–16.

Shraberg, D., and Weitzel, W. D. (1979). Prosopagnosia and the Capgras syndrome. *J. Clin. Psychiat.* 40:313–316.

Shuttleworth, E. C., Syring, V., and Allen, N. (1982). Further observations on the nature of prosopagnosia. *Brain Cog.* 1:307–322.

Sprague, J. M., Levy, J. D., and Berlucci, C. (1977). Visual cortical areas mediating form discrimination in the rat. *J. Comp. Neurol.* 172:441–488.

Spreen, O., Benton, A. L., and Fincham, R. (1965). Auditory agnosia without aphasia. *Arch. Neurol.* 13:84–92.

Spreen, O., Benton, A. L., and Van Allen, M. W. (1966). Dissociation of visual and tactile naming in amnesic aphasia. *Neurol. (Minneapl.)* 16:807–814.

Stauffenburg, V. (1914). Uber Seelenblindheit. *Arbeiten aus dem Hirnanatomischen Institut in Zurich*, Heft 8. Wiesbaden: Bergman.

Stengel, E. (1948). The syndrome of visual alexia with color agnosia *J. Ment. Sci.* 94:46–58.

Stockard, J. J., and Rossiter, V. S. (1977). Clinical and pathologic correlates of brainstem auditory response abnormalities. *Neurol. (Minneap.)* 27:316–325.

Synodinou, C., Christodoulou, G. N., and Tzavaras, A. (1978). Capgras' syndrome and prosopagnosia (letter). *Br. J. Psychiat.* 132:413–414.

Taylor, A., and Warrington, E. K. (1971). Visual agnosia: A single case report. *Cortex* 7:152–164.

Teuber, H.-L. (1965a). Somatosensory disorders due to cortical lesions. *Neuropsychologia* 3:287–294.

Teuber, H.-L. (1965b). Postscript: Some needed revisions of the classical views of agnosia. *Neuropsychologia* 3:371–378.

Teuber, H.-L. (1968). Alteration of perception and memory in man. In *Analysis of Behavioral Change* (L. Weiskrantz, ed.). New York: Harper and Row.

Tyler, H. R. (1968). Abnormalities of perception with defective eye movements (Balint's syndrome). *Cortex* 4:154–171.

Tzavaras, A., Hecaen, H., and LeBras, H. (1970). Le probleme de la specificite du deficit de la reconnaisance du visage humans lors des lesions hemispheriques unilaterales. *Neuropsychologia* 8:403–416.

Ulrich, G. (1978). Interhemispheric functional relationships in auditory agnosia: An analysis of the preconditions and a conceptual model. *Brain Lang.* 5:286–300.

Vignolo, L. A. (1969). Auditory agnosia: A review and report of recent evidence. In *Contributions to Clinical Neuropsychology* (A. L. Benton, ed.). Chicago: Aldine.

Von Frey, M. (1895). Bietrage zur Sinnes physiologie der Haut Berichle u.d. Verhandlungen d.k. Sachs. *Gesellschaft Wissensch.* 2 S:166.

Von Hagen, K. O. (1941). Two cases of mind blindness (visual agnosia), one due to carbon monoxide intoxication, one due to a diffuse degenerative process. *Bull. L.A. Neurol. Soc.* 6:191–194.

Von Stockert, T. R. (1982). On the structure of word deafness and mechanisms underlying the fluctuations of disturbances of higher cortical functions. *Brain Lang.* 16:133–146.

Wapner, W., Judd, T., and Gardner, H. (1978). Visual agnosia in an artist. *Cortex* 14:343–364.

Warrington, E. K., and James, M. (1967). An experimental investigation of facial recognition in patients with unilateral cerebral lesions. *Cortex* 3:317–326.

Warrington, E. K., and Shallice, T. (1980). Word-form dyxlexia. *Brain* 103:99–112.

Watson, R. T., and Heilman, K. M. (1983). Callosal apraxia. *Brain* 106:391–403.

Weimer, W. (1978). A conceptual framework for cognitive psychology: Motor theories of the mind. In *Perceiving, Acting, and Knowing* (M. Shaw and J. Bransford, eds.). Hillsdale, N.J.: Lawrence Erlbaum.

Weinstein, S. (1968). Intensive and extensive aspects of tactile sensitivity as a function of body part, sex, and laterality. In *The Skin Senses* (D. R. Kenshalo, ed.). Springfield, Ill:. Charles C Thomas, pp. 195–222.

Weiskrantz, L., Warrington, E. K., Sanders, M. D., and Marshall, J. (1974). Visual capacity in the hemianopic field following a restricted occipital ablation. *Brain* 97:709–728.

Werner, G., and Whitsel, B. (1968). Topology of the body representation in somatosensory area 1 of primates. *J. Neurophysiol.* 31:856–869.

Werner, G., and Whitsel B. L. (1973). Functional organization of the sematosensory cortex. In A. Iggo (Ed.). *Somatosensory Systems, Handbook of Sensory Physiology* (Vol. 2). New York: Springer-Verlag, pp. 621–700.

Wernicke, C. (1895). Swei Falle von Rindenlasion. *Arb. Psychiat. klin. Breslau* 11:35.

Wertheim, N. (1969).The amusias. In *Handbook of Clinical Neurology*, Vol. 4 (P. J. Vinken and G. W. Bruyn, eds.). Amsterdam: North-Holland.

Whiteley, A. M., and Warrington, E. K. (1977). Prosopagnosia: A clinical, psychological, and anatomical study of three patients. *J. Neurol. Neurosurg. Psychiat.* 40:395–403.

Wilbrand, H. (1887). *Die Seelenblindheit als Herderscheinung.* Wiesbaden: Bergmann.

Wohlfart, G., Lindgren, A., and Jernelius, B. (1952). Clinical picture and mobid anatomy in a case of "pure word deafness." *J. Nerv. Ment. Dis.* 116:818–827.

Wolpert, I. (1924). Die Simultanagnosie: storung der gesamtauffassung. *Z. gesamte Neurol. Psychiat.* 93:397–413.

Woolsey, C. N. (1964). Cortical localization as defined by evoked potential and electrical stimulation studies. In *Cerebral localization and organization* (G. Schaltenbrand and C. N. Woolsey, eds.). Madison, Wis.: University of Wisconsin Press, pp. 17–26.

Wyke, M., and Holgate, D. (1973). Color naming defects in dysphasic patients: A qualitative analysis. *Neuropsychologia* 8:451–461.

Yin, R. K. (1970). Face recognition by brain-injured patients: A dissociable ability? *Neuropsychologia* 8:395–402.

Young, R. S., and Fishman, G. A. (1980). Loss of color vision and Stiles II, mechanism in a patient with cerebral infarction. *J. Opt. Soc. Am.* 170:1301–1305.

Zeki, S. M. (1973). Colour coding in rhesus monkey prestriate cortex. *Brain Res.* 53:422–427.

Zeki, S. M. (1977). Colour coding in the superior temporal sulcus of rhesus monkey visual cortex. *Proc. R. Soc. Lond. [Biol.]* 197:195–223.

Ziegler, D. K. (1952). Word deafness and Wernicke's aphasia: Report of cases and discussion of the syndrome. *Arch. Neurol. Psychiat.* 67:323–331.

Zihl, J., and Von Cramon, D. (1979). The contribution of the "second" visual system to directed visual attention in man. *Brain* 102:835–856.

10
Neglect and Related Disorders

KENNETH M. HEILMAN, ROBERT T. WATSON,
AND EDWARD VALENSTEIN

DEFINITIONS

An individual with the neglect syndrome fails to report, respond, or orient to novel or meaningful stimuli presented to the side opposite a brain lesion (Heilman, 1979). The individual is not considered to have the neglect syndrome if this failure can be attributed to either sensory or motor defects. The signs and symptoms of the syndrome may be present under a variety of stimulus and performance conditions. Different behavioral manifestations may occur at different times and in some patients certain behavioral manifestations are never seen. In this chapter we will describe the major behavioral manifestations of the neglect syndrome and the tests that can be administered at the bedside to detect the syndrome, and then we will discuss in detail what we understand of the pathophysiology of this syndrome.

The major behavioral manifestations of the neglect syndrome are: (1) hemi-inattention, (2) extinction to simultaneous stimuli, (3) hemiakinesia, (4) allesthesia, and (5) hemispatial neglect. Anosognosia and anisodiaphoria are other signs often associated with the neglect syndrome.

Hemi-inattention

Although sensory loss may be the most common cause of a failure to report or respond to stimuli presented contralateral to a hemispheric lesion, patients and animals with lesions in locations other than a primary sensory area or the sensory projection system may also fail to report or respond to stimuli presented contralaterally. This has been termed *hemi-inattention*. Without knowing the site of the lesion, one may be unable to distinguish hemianesthesia or hemianopia from severe somesthetic and visual hemi-inattention. Unlike the patient with hemianesthesia or hemianopia, however, the patient with hemi-inattention may be able to detect the stimulus if his attention is directed to that side.

While hemianesthesia and hemianopia are fairly common manifestations of central nervous system lesions, unilateral hearing loss is almost always due to a disturbance in the peripheral hearing mechanisms or in the auditory nerve. This is because the auditory pathways that ascend from the brainstem to the cortex are bilateral: each ear projects to both hemispheres. A unilateral central nervous system lesion will therefore not produce unilateral hearing loss. Patients without peripheral hearing loss who fail to report unilateral auditory stimulation, therefore, usually do have hemi-inattention. Furthermore, since sound presented on one side of the body projects to both ears, patients with unilateral hearing loss from a perhipheral lesion usually do not fail to respond to unilateral auditory stimulation, unless the stimulus is very close to the ear. Therefore, patients who neglect or orient incorrectly to unilateral auditory stimuli most often have unilateral neglect.

Patients with profound hemi-inattention may even fail to recognize that their contralesional extremities are their own. They may complain that someone else's arm or leg is in bed with them. When confronted with objective evidence, they may still deny that their own extremities belong to them. Patients with milder neglect may be aware that their extremities belong to them (because they are attached), but still refer to their extremities as though they were objects.

Patients with unilateral neglect are most inattentive to stimuli contralateral to their lesion, but it is not unusual for them also to be inattentive to ipsilateral stimuli, although ipsilateral neglect is not as severe.

Sensory Extinction to Simultaneous Stimulation

Most patients who initially have hemi-inattention from a stable lesion later improve. Whereas initially they ignore stimuli presented to the side opposite their lesion, they eventually become able to correctly detect and lateralize these stimuli. When given bilateral simultaneous stimulation, however, they often fail to report the stimulus presented to the contralesional side. This phenomenon was first noted by Loeb (1885) and Oppenheim (1885) in the tactile modality and by Anton (1899) and Poppelreuter (1917) in the visual modality; it has been termed *extinction to double simultaneous stimulation*. It may also be seen in the auditory modality (Bender 1952, Heilman et al., 1970). A patient may have extinction in several modalities (multimodal extinction) or in one modality. Extinction is usually mildest in the auditory modality.

Hemiakinesia, Motor Extinction, and Impersistence

Patients who have neglect from lesions not affecting either primary motor areas or their projections may fail spontaneously to use the extremity contralateral to the cerebral lesion. When attention is focused on the extremity the patient may show good strength (Critchley, 1966).

Patients with unilateral neglect may also fail to orient their head and eyes to the side opposite the lesion. It can be shown that this behavior is not being induced by a simple sensory defect or sensory inattention by asking them to look toward the side opposite the one being touched. These patients will usually have less difficulty looking toward the side of the lesion in response to contralateral stimuli than they will have looking toward the side opposite the lesion in response to ipsilateral stimuli. That this defect is not induced by a brainstem oculomotor disorder can be demonstrated by using doll's eye or caloric maneuvers (Heilman, 1979), since these brainstem reflex eye movements will be intact.

Although patients usually have severe akinesia of the extremities contralateral to their lesion, even their ipsilateral extremities may be slow to respond (Howes and Boller, 1975).

Some patients demonstrate increased contralateral limb akinesia when they must simultaneously use their ipsilateral extremities. This has been termed motor extinction (Valenstein and Heilman, 1980).

Patients with neglect from right hemisphere lesions often have difficulty sustaining movements or postures. For example they may not be able to keep their eyes closed or tongue protuded for more than a few seconds. This has been termed motor impersistence.

Allesthesia

Patients touched on the side opposite their lesion may report that they were touched on the extremity ipsilateral to their lesion (Obersteiner, 1882). This has been called *allesthesia*. A similar defect may be seen in other sensory modalities and in other response modes. For example, a patient addressed from the side opposite a lesion may orient his head and eyes to the wrong (ipsilesional) side. When a patient is asked to move the extremity touched by the examiner and is then stimulated on the side opposite his lesion, he may respond with the ipsilesional extremity.

Hemispatial Neglect

When patients with hemispatial neglect are asked to perform a variety of behavioral tasks in space, they neglect the hemispace contralateral to their lesion. For example, when they are asked to draw a picture of a flower, they may draw only half of the flower (Fig. 10-1). When asked to bisect a line, they may quarter it instead (Fig. 10-2) or may fail to cross out lines distributed over a page (Fig. 10-3). The patients appear to be neglecting one-half of visual space. This has been variously termed hemispatial neglect, visuospatial agnosia, hemispatial agnosia, visuospatial neglect, and unilateral spatial neglect.

Although several authors (Gianotti et al., 1972; Battersby et al., 1956) have attributed the original description of this disorder to Holmes (1918), Holmes actually reported six patients with disturbed visual orientation from bilateral lesions. It was Riddoch (1935) who reported two patients without any disturbance of central vision who had visual disorientation limited to homonymous half-fields. Brain (1941) also described three patients who had visual disorientation limited to homonymous half-fields not caused by defects in visual acuity. Brain attributed this disorder to inattention of the left half of external space and thought it was similar to the "amnesia" for the left half of the body which may follow a lesion of the right parietal lobe. Paterson

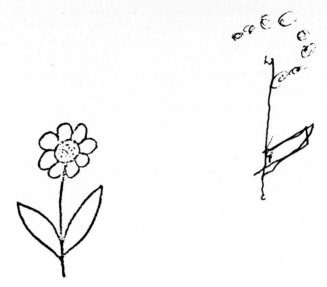

Fig. 10-1. An example of hemispatial neglect (visuospatial agnosia). Drawing on left performed by examiner. Drawing on right performed by patient.

and Zangwill (1944); McFie et al., (1950), and Denny-Brown and Banker (1954) demonstrated that patients with unilateral inattention (hemispatial neglect) not only had visual disorientation limited to a half-field but also omitted material on one side of drawings and failed to eat from one side of their plates.

Frequently, patients with this disorder also fail to dress or groom the abnormal side. Although this may be considered a form of dressing apraxia, the pathophysiology may be different from that seen with other forms of apraxia (see Chap. 7) or that seen in patients with profound visuospatial disorders (see Chap. 8).

Patients with neglect may also fail to read part of a word or a portion of a sentence (i.e., they may read the word "cowboy" as "boy"). This has been termed paralexia (Benson and Geschwind, 1969). Patients may write on only one side of a page (see Chap. 4 on agraphia), or when using a typewriter they may fail to type letters correctly which are on the side of the keyboard contralateral to their lesion (Fig. 10-4). This has been termed paragraphia (Valenstein and Heilman, 1978).

Anosognosia and Anosodiaphoria

Patients with the neglect syndrome may be unaware of or deny their hemiparesis. They may also deny that their paretic extremity belongs to them. This phenomenon has been termed *anosognosia* (Babinski, 1914). Patients may also deny sensory loss or

Fig. 10-2. Performance of patient with hemispatial neglect on line bisection task.

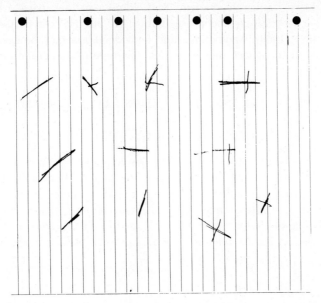

Fig. 10-3. Performance by patient with hemispatial neglect on crossing out task.

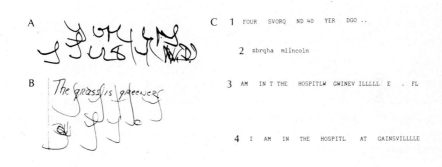

C 1 FOUR   SVORQ   ND 40   YER   DGO ..

2 zbrqha mlincoln

3 AM   IN T THE   HOSPITLW GWINEV ILLLLL E   . FL

4 I   AM   IN   THE   HOSPITL   AT   GAINSVILLLLE

D   Q W E R T Y U I O P °
    A S D F G H J K L ; "
    Z X C V B N M , . ?

Fig. 10-4.

A. Attempting to write, "You are a doctor."

B. Copying.

C. Typing. (1–3) Typewriter directly in front of patient, (4) typewriter moved to patient's right.

D. The typewriter keyboard. Note that the letters missed (A, S, E) are at the left of the keyboard.

hemianopia. More frequently, patients may admit that they have a neurological impairment but they appear unconcerned about it. This has been termed *anosodia-phoria* (Critchley, 1969). Anosognosia and anosodiaphoria may be associated with conditions other than neglect, such as cortical blindness (Anton's syndrome).

TESTING FOR NEGLECT AND RELATED DISORDERS

Mechanism of Stimulation

Various aspects of neglect are detected by observing abnormal responses to sensory stimuli. Stimuli should be given in at least three modalities: (1) somesthetic, (2) visual, and (3) auditory; however, other stimuli (e.g., gustatory and olfactory) may also be used. Examiners most often request an immediate response; however, delaying the response and using distractor techniques may amplify the symptoms of neglect since patients with neglect have a unilateral memory defect (Heilman et al., 1974).

SOMESTHETIC

Although the intensity of a tactile stimulus may be controlled by elaborate equipment, Von Frei hairs, fingers, or cotton applicators are adequate for bedside testing. Other cutaneous stimuli (e.g., pins) can be used.

AUDITORY

Audiometry may be used; however, for bedside testing we use sounds made by rubbing or snapping the fingers.

VISUAL

For testing visual fields, perimetry and tangent screen should be used when possible; however, for bedside testing we use confrontation techniques. Either a cotton-tipped applicator or a finger can be used as the stimulus. For simultaneous testing, finger movements are excellent stimuli. A modified Poppelreuter diagram or words and sentences may also be used.

TECHNIQUES OF ADMINISTRATION

These somesthetic, auditory, and visual stimuli should be presented to the abnormal (contralesional) side and to the normal side of the body in random order. If the patient responds normally to unilateral stimulation, bilateral simultaneous stimulation may be used. Unilateral stimuli should be interspersed with bilateral simultaneous stimuli. Bender (1952) noted that normal subjects may show extinction to simultaneous stimulation when the stimuli are delivered to two different (asymmetrical) parts of the body (simultaneous bilateral heterologous stimulation). For example, if the right side of the face and the left hand are stimulated simultaneously, normal subjects sometimes report only the stimulus on the face. Normal subjects do not extinguish symmetrical simultaneous stimuli (simultaneous bilateral homologous stimulation). Simultaneous bilateral heterologous stimulation can sometimes be used to test for milder defects in patients with neglect. For example, when the right face and left hand are stimulated, the patient with left-sided neglect does not report the stimulus on the left hand, but when the left face and right hand are stimulated he reports both stimuli.

Response Mode

ORIENTING HEAD AND EYES

Prior to stimulation, any head or eye deviation should be noted. Tests for head and eye orientation may be given without verbal instructions and therefore may be used in aphasics with comprehension disorders. They may also be used in patients who have a hemiparesis. Two examiners are needed. One examiner stands behind the patient and presents the stimuli: the examiner may touch the patient on the shoulder, snap his fingers, or move his hand into the patient's field of vision. The other examiner stands in front of the patient and notes any asymmetries of the orienting response: does the patient turn or orient to stimuli on one side better than he orients to stimuli on the other? If the patient does not orient to stimuli or if he habituates to stimuli before a definite response bias can be detected, the examiner may then use stronger stimuli (for example, pin or calling the patient's name) or he may vary the nature of the stimulus.

VERBAL REPORT

The patient is asked where he is being stimulated—right, left, or both (which side he hears fingers snapping or sees fingers moving).

EXTREMITY MOVEMENT

The subject is instructed verbally or nonverbally (by gesture) to move the extremity or extremities the examiner has touched. To demonstrate unilateral akinesia, the examiner requires the patient to use the extremity on the side opposite to that stimulated. Commands for sustained bilateral action may also help demonstrate unilateral akinesia. For example, the patient may demonstrate good strength when he is asked to move only one arm, since his attention is focused on that arm, but when asked to raise both arms he may only raise one, or he may raise both and then let one of them drop.

SPATIAL OPERATIONS

Several tests have been designed to determine if a patient has hemispatial neglect. (a) In the *cancellation test* devised by Horenstein (personal communication), lines are drawn at random on an 8 × 11-inch page (see Fig. 10-3). The patient is asked to cross out all the lines. Failure to cross out lines on one side of the page suggests the presence of hemispatial neglect. (b) In the *line bisection task*, a 4- to 8-inch line is placed before the patient and the patient is asked to bisect the line ("Cross the line out in the middle"). Patients with hemispatial neglect will usually make their mark to the side of the midline ipsilateral to their lesion. Placing the stimuli in left hemispace may enhance this deficit (Fig. 10-2). (c) Having the patient draw a picture is perhaps one of the best ways to demonstrate hemispatial neglect because the drawing task, unlike the crossing out task, does not require afferent stimuli. Patients with unilateral spatial neglect will draw only half of an object (see Fig. 10-1). (d). Since patients with right hemisphere lesions commonly have visuospatial defects and associated constructional apraxia, they may have difficulty with spontaneous drawing. An alternative test is to have patients place numbers on a clock. Frequently, patients with neglect will write only on one side of the clock: they may write in only the numbers which belong on that side, or they may write all 12 numbers on one side.

ANOSOGNOSIA

It is important to observe the position of neglected limbs. For example, the patient may lie on his left arm or hold it in a grotesque position. The examiner should make systematic formal observations as to whether the patient spontaneously complains about deficits such as weakness, sensory loss, or hemianopia. If the patient does not spontaneously complain, the examiner should ask if he recognizes his disability and if he has an emotional response to the deficit. The patient should be asked if his limbs belong to him and if they are weak or numb. The manner in which he refers to his limbs should also be noted: for example, does he refer to them in the third person ("It doesn't want to move.")? Disturbances of mood should also be noted (see Chap. 13).

MECHANISMS UNDERLYING NEGLECT

As can be seen from the above description, unilateral neglect can be a dramatic clinical syndrome, every bit as impressive to the examiner, and every bit as disabling to the patient, as severe aphasia. But whereas the mechanisms underlying many cortical deficits have been relatively easy to conceptualize, at least in broad terms, the mechanisms underlying the neglect syndrome have been difficult to define. For example, it is clear that hemianopia results from unilateral damage to the post-chiasmal visual system, and that aphasia results from interference with systems that mediate language. But it is difficult to make an equivalent statement summarizing the neglect syndrome. There is much evidence, however, to suggest that the neglect syndrome is due to a unilateral disturbance of arousal and attentional mechanisms. In this section, we will summarize the theories that have been proposed to explain neglect, and we will describe in considerable detail the evidence that suggests that neglect is related to dysfunction of arousal and attentional mechanisms.

In our discussion of the symptoms and signs of the neglect syndrome, we have distinguished several of its aspects. Although these aspects of neglect often coexist, they are behaviorally distinct, and therefore must have distinct, although probably related, mechanisms. Furthermore, not every patient with neglect manifests all of these deficits, and in some there are dramatic dissociations. For example, patients have been described with hemiakinesia who do not manifest hemi-inattention (Valenstein and Heilman, 1981). It will therefore be helpful to discuss the mechanisms of hemi-inattention, extinction, hemiakinesia, and hemispatial neglect separately.

Mechanisms Underlying Hemi-inattention

As noted above, patients with neglect may fail to report, respond, or orient to novel or meaningful stimuli. This has been attributed to disorders of sensation, to abnormalities of the "body schema" or to other complex perceptual deficits, and to disorders of attention.

SENSORY HYPOTHESES

Battersby and associates (1956) thought that neglect in humans resulted from decreased sensory input superimposed on a background of decreased mental function. Sprague and colleagues (1961) concluded that neglect was caused by loss of patterned sensory input to the forebrain, particularly to the neocortex. Eidelberg and Schwartz (1971) similarly proposed that neglect (extinction) was a passive phenomenon due to quantitatively asymmetrical sensory input to the two hemispheres. They based this conclusion on the finding that neglect resulted from neospinothalamic lesions but not from medial lemniscal lesions. They claimed that the neospinothalamic tract carries more tactile information to the hemisphere than does the medial lemniscus. However, since lesions in primary and secondary sensory cortex could also produce neglect, they postulated that the syndrome could also be caused by a reduced functional mass of one cortical area concerned with somatic sensation relative to another.

BODY SCHEMA

Brain (1941) believed that the parietal lobes contained the body schema and also mediated spatial perception. Parietal lesions therefore caused a patient to fail to recognize not only half of his body but also half of space. Brain thought that allesthesia resulted from severe damage to the schema for one half of the body causing events occurring on that half, if perceived at all, to be related in consciousness to the surviving schema representing the normal half.

AMORPHOSYNTHESIS

Denny-Brown and Banker (1954) proposed that the parietal lobes were important in cortical sensation and that the phenomenon of inattention belonged to the whole class of cortical disorders of sensation: " . . . a loss of fine discrimination . . . an inability to synthesize more than a few properties of a sensory stimulus and a disturbance of synthesis of multiple sensory stimuli." The neglect syndrome was ascribed to a defect in spatial summation that they called amorphosynthesis.

ATTENTIONAL HYPOTHESES

Some of the first references in the neglect syndrome literature referred to defects of attention. Poppelreuter (1917) introduced the word inattention. Brain (1941) and Critchley (1966) were also strong proponents of this view. However, Bender and Furlow (1944, 1945) challenged the attentional theory: they felt that inattention could not be important in the pathophysiology of the syndrome because neglect could not be overcome by having the patient "concentrate" on the neglected side.

Heilman and Valenstein (1972) and Watson and associates (1973, 1974) again postulated an attention-arousal hypothesis. These authors argued that the sensory and perceptual hypotheses could not explain all cases of neglect, since neglect was often produced by lesions outside the traditional sensory pathways (see below). Evoked potential studies in animals with unilateral neglect have demonstrated a change in late waves (that are known to be influenced by changes in attention and stimulus significance) but no change in the early (sensory) waves (Watson et al., 1977). Furthermore, neglect is often multimodal and therefore cannot be explained by a defect in any one sensory modality.

Unilateral neglect in humans and monkeys can be induced by lesions in many different brain regions. These include cortical areas such as the temporoparietal-occipital junction (Critchley, 1966; Heilman et al., 1970; Heilman et al., 1983) (Fig. 10-5), limbic areas such as the cingulate gyrus (Heilman and Valenstein, 1972; Watson et al., 1973), and subcortical areas such as the thalamus (Fig. 10-6) and mesencephalic reticular formation (Fig. 10-7) (Watson et al., 1974). As we will discuss below, these subcortical areas have been shown to be important in mediating arousal and attention, and the cortical areas are regions which are probably specifically involved in the anal-

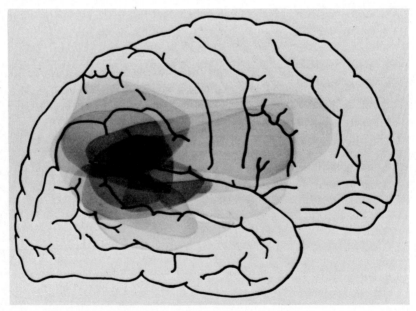

Fig. 10-5. Lateral view of the right hemisphere. Lesions (as determined by CT scan) of 10 patients with the neglect syndrome are superimposed.

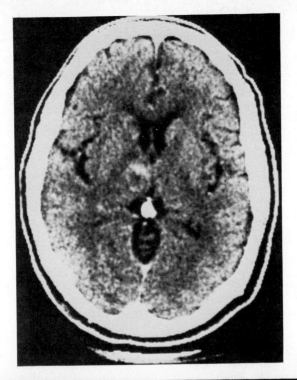

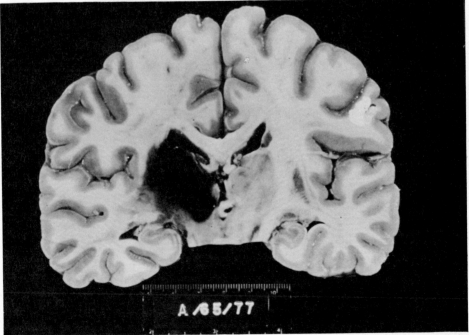

Fig. 10-6. (a) CT scan demonstrating a contrast-enhancing right thalamic infarction in a patient with the neglect syndrome. (b) Right thalamic hemorrhage as determined by post-mortem examination in a patient who had the neglect syndrome.

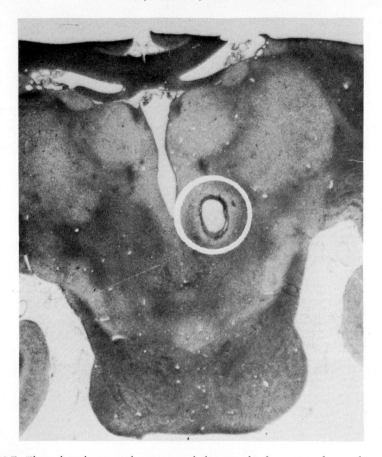

Fig. 10-7. Electrolytic lesion in the mesencephalic reticular formation of a monkey who had developed unilateral neglect after the lesion was made.

ysis of the behavioral significance of stimuli. We have proposed that sensory neglect is an attentional-arousal disorder induced by dysfunction in a corticolimbic reticular formation loop (Heilman and Valenstein, 1972; Watson et al., 1973; Watson et al., 1981). We will review the evidence for this view, and develop a model or schema to explain the neglect syndrome (Fig. 10-8).

Mesencephalic reticular formation (MRF).   In monkeys and cats, profound sensory neglect results from discrete lesions of the mesencephalic reticular formation (MRF) (Reeves and Hagaman, 1971; Watson et al., 1974). Stimulation of the MRF is associated with behavioral arousal and also with desynchronization of the electroencephalogram (EEG), a physiological measure of arousal (Moruzzi and Magoun, 1949). Unilateral stimulation induces greater EEG desynchronization in the ipsilateral than in the contralateral hemisphere (Moruzzi and Magoun, 1949). Arousal is a physiological state that prepares the organism for sensory and motor processing. Bilateral MRF lesions result in coma. Unilateral lesions result in contralateral neglect, which is probably due to unilateral hemispheric hypoarousal (Watson et al., 1974).

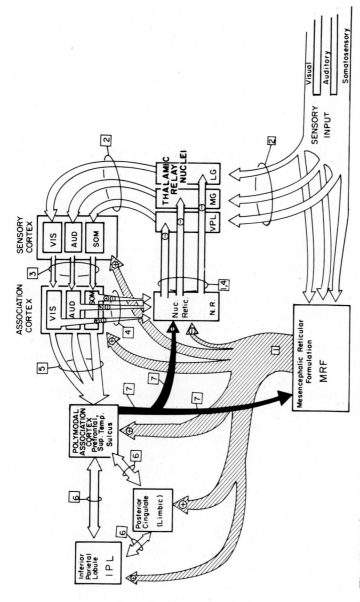

Fig. 10-8. Schematic representation of pathways important in sensory attention and tonic arousal. The pathways represent (1) arousal, (2) sensory transmission, (3) association cortex projections, (4) unimodal projections to nucleus reticularis thalami (NR), (5) sensory convergence to polymodal cortex, (6) supramodal cortex (inferior parietal lobule) and limbic connections, (7) cortical arousal through mesencephalic reticular formation (MRF) and NR. See text for details. STS indicates superior temporal sulcus; VIS, visual; AUD, auditory; SOM, somatosensory; MG, medial genic-ulate; LG, lateral geniculate; VPL, ventralis posterolateralis.

255

During the last 30 years there has been growing criticism of the mesencephalic reticular activating system–arousal theory (Vanderwolf and Robinson, 1981). Much of this criticism stemmed from the observation that under many circumstances EEG desynchronization correlates poorly with levels of arousal. For example, animals given drugs such as atropine may be behaviorally aroused but do not have low-voltage fast (desynchronized) EEG activity. These observations do not disprove the hypothesis, but only suggest that the EEG may not be a perfect correlate of arousal mediated by the mesencephalic reticular activating system.

It is not clear how the mesencephalic reticular activating system mediates its effects on the cortex. The recently defined major neurotransmitter pathways have been considered obvious candidates for this function, but no one system is clearly associated with arousal.

MRF influence on the cortex: major neurotransmitter pathways

Norepinephrine (noradrenaline.) Many neurons that ascend from the mesencephalic reticular activating system and its environs are monoaminergic. The locus coeruleus norepinephrine system projects diffusely to cortical structures. The area of the mesencephalon stimulated by Moruzzi and Magoun (1949) contains ascending catecholamine systems, including the noradrenergic system. Although this norepinephrine system would appear to be ideal for mediating cortical arousal (Jouvet, 1977), destruction of most of the locus coeruleus does not profoundly affect behavioral arousal, nor does it change EEG patterns (Jacobs and Jones, 1978). As mentioned above, Moruzzi and Magoun (1949) demonstrated that unilateral stimulation of the mesencephalic reticular activating system induced greater desynchronization ipsilaterally than contralaterally. We have shown that unilateral lesions in the region of the mesencephalic reticular formation induce EEG and behavioral changes suggestive of unilateral coma (Watson et al., 1974). Unilateral locus coeruleus lesions do not induce similar behavioral or EEG changes (Deuel, personal communication).

Dopamine. Although the dopaminergic system may be critical for mediating intention (see section below on intention), dopamine does not appear to be important in arousal because blockade of dopamine synthesis or of dopamine receptors does not appear to affect desynchronization (Robinson et al., 1977).

Acetylcholine. Acetylcholine appears to have a more promising role in the mediation of arousal. Shute and Lewis (1967) described an ascending cholinergic reticular formation. Stimulation of the midbrain mesencephalic reticular activating system not only induces the arousal response but also increases the rate of acetylcholine release from the neocortex (Kanai and Szerb, 1979). Cholinergic agonists induce neocortical desynchronization, while antagonists abolish desynchronization (Bradley, 1968). Unfortunately, however, while cholinergic blockers such as atropine interfere with EEG desynchronization, they do not dramatically affect behavioral arousal. Vanderwolf and Robinson (1981) suggested that there may be two types of cholinergic input to the neocortex from the reticular formation, only one of which is atropine sensitive. Therefore, the other cholinergic input may be responsible for behavioral arousal.

Polysynaptic MRF pathway to cortex via the thalamus. The mesencephalic reticular activating system probably projects to the cortex in a diffuse polysynaptic fashion

(Schiebel and Schiebel, 1967) (see Fig. 10-8, Pathway 1) and thereby influences cortical processing of sensory stimuli. Steriade and Glenn (1982) found that the centralis lateralis and paracentralis thalamic nuclei also project to widespread cortical regions. Other neurons from these thalamic areas project to the caudate. Thirteen percent of neurons with cortical or caudate projections could be activated by mesencephalic reticular activating system stimulation.

MRF influence on the nucleus reticularis of the thalamus. There is, however, an alternative means whereby the mesencephalic reticular activating system may affect cortical processing of sensory stimuli. Sensory information that reaches the cortex is relayed through specific thalamic nuclei: somatosensory information is transmitted from the ventralis posterolateralis (VPL) to the postcentral gyrus (Brodman's areas 3,1,2), auditory information is transmitted through the medial geniculate nucleus (MGN) to the supratemporal plane (Heschl's gyrus), and visual information is transmitted through the lateral geniculate nucleus (LGN) to the occipital lobe (area 17) (Fig. 10-8, Pathway 2). The nucleus reticularis thalami, a thin reticular nucleus enveloping the thalamus, projects to the thalamic relay nuclei and appears to inhibit thalamic relay to the cortex (Schiebel and Schiebel, 1966) (Fig. 10-8, Pathways 1,4). The mesencephalic reticular activating system also projects to the nucleus reticularis. Rapid mesencephalic reticular activating system stimulation or behavioral arousal inhibits the nucleus reticularis and is thereby associated with enhanced thalamic transmission to the cerebral cortex (Singer, 1977). Therefore, unilateral lesions of MRF may induce neglect not only because the cortex is not prepared for processing sensory stimuli in the absence of MRF-mediated arousal, but also because the thalamic sensory relay nuclei are being inhibited by the nucleus reticularis.

Unimodal sensory association cortex. Lesions of the thalamic relay nuclei or primary sensory cortex induce a sensory defect rather than neglect. Primary cortical sensory areas project to unimodal association cortex (see Fig. 10-8, Pathway 3). Association cortex synthesizes multiple features of a complex stimulus within a single sensory modality. Lesions of unimodal association cortex may induce perceptual deficits in a single modality (for example, apperceptive agnosia). Modality-specific association areas may also be detecting stimulus novelty (modeling) (Sokolov, 1963). When a stimulus is neither novel nor significant, corticofugal projections to the NR (nucleus reticularis) (Fig. 10-8, Pathway 4) may allow habituation to occur by selectively influencing thalamic relay. When a stimulus is novel or significant, corticofugal projections might inhibit the NR and thereby allow the thalamus to relay additional sensory input. This capacity for selective control of sensory input is supported by a study revealing that stimulation of specific areas within NR related to specific thalamic nuclei (e.g., NR lateral geniculate, NR medial geniculate, or NR ventrobasal complex) results in abolition of corresponding (visual, auditory, tactile) cortically evoked responses (Yingling and Skinner, 1977).

Polymodal and supramodal association areas. Unimodal association areas converge upon polymodal association areas (Fig. 10-8, Pathway 5). In the monkey these are the prefrontal cortex (periarcuate, prearcuate, orbitofrontal) and both banks of the supe-

rior temporal sulcus (STS) (Pandya and Kuypers, 1969). Unimodal association areas
may also project directly to the caudal inferior parietal lobule (IPL) or, alternatively,
may reach the IPL after a synapse in polymodal convergence areas (e.g., prefrontal
cortex and both banks of the STS) (See Fig. 10-8, Pathway 6) (Mesulam et al., 1977).
Polymodal convergence areas may subserve cross-modal associations and polymodal
sensory synthesis. Polymodal sensory synthesis may also be important in "modeling"
(detecting stimulus novelty) and detecting significance. In contrast to the unimodal
association cortex that projects to specific parts of the NR and thereby gates sensory
input in one modality, these multimodal convergence areas may have a more general
inhibitory action on NR and provide further arousal after cortical analysis. These convergence areas also may project directly to the MRF, which may either induce a
general state of arousal because of diffuse multisynaptic connections to the cortex, or
may increase thalamic transmission via connections with NR, as discussed above, or
both. Evidence that polymodal areas of cortex are important in arousal comes from
neurophysiological studies showing that stimulation of select cortical sites induces a
generalized arousal response. These sites include the prearcuate region and both banks
of the STS (Segundo et al., 1955). When similar sites are ablated there is EEG evidence of ipsilateral hypoarousal (Watson et al., 1978).

Limbic and frontal input.   Although determination of stimulus novelty may be
mediated by sensory association cortex, stimulus significance is determined in part by
the needs by the organism (motivational state). Limbic system input into brain regions
important for determining stimulus significance might provide information about biological needs. The frontal lobes might provide input about needs related to goals that
are neither directly stimulus-dependent nor motivated by an immediate biological
need, since the frontal lobes do play a critical role in goal-mediated behavior and in
developing sets (see Chap. 12).

   Polymodal (e.g, STS) and supramodal (IPL) areas have prominent limbic and frontal connections. The polymodal cortices project to the cingulate gyrus (a portion of
the limbic system), and the cingulate gyrus projects to the IPL (Fig. 10-8, Pathway
6). The prefrontal cortex, STS, and IPL have strong reciprocal connections. The posterior cingulate cortex (Brodmann's area 23) has more extensive connections with
polymodal association areas (prefrontal cortex, and exclusively for STS) and the IPL
than does the anterior cingulate cortex (Brodmann's area 24) (Vogt et al., 1979; Baleydier and Maugierre, 1980). These connections may provide an anatomic substrate
by which motivational states (e.g, biological needs, sets, and long-term goals) may
influence stimulus processing.

Physiological properties of neurons in the inferior parietal lobe (IPL).   In the past
decade investigators have been able to study the physiological function of specific
areas of the nervous system by recording from single neurons in awake animals. In
this experimental situation, the firing characteristics of individual neurons can be
measured in relation to specific sensory stimulation or motor behavior. For example,
a single neuron in the visual cortex may respond maximally to a contrast border in a
specific region of the visual field, sometimes in a specific orientation. By varying the
nature of the stimulus and by training the animal to respond in specific ways, the

characteristic patterns of firing of individual neurons can be defined in terms of the optimal stimulus and/or response parameters that cause a maximal change in firing rate. In this fashion, investigators have defined the properties of neurons in the inferior parietal lobule (area 7) of the monkey (Lynch, 1980; Motter and Mountcastle, 1981; Mountcastle et al., 1975; Mountcastle et al., 1981; Goldberg and Robinson, 1977; Robinson et al., 1978; Bushnell et al., 1981). Unlike single cells in primary sensory cortex, the activity of many neurons in the inferior parietal lobule correlates best with stimuli or responses of importance to the animal, while similar stimuli or responses that are unimportant are associated with either no change or a lesser change in neuronal activity. Several types of neurons have been described.

Projection neurons. Some neurons are active in relation to limb projection or hand manipulation. Projection neurons are active when an animal reaches toward an object of significance in immediate extrapersonal space, for example, food (when the animal is hungry) or water (when thirsty). Similar cells are found in the superior parietal lobule (area 5); but the cells in the IPL are more likely to be related to activity of both arms or of the ipsilateral arm, instead of only to the contralateral arm.

Visual fixation neurons. Visual fixation neurons are active when the animal fixates an object of interest within arm's reach. If the animal fixates a target which he must attend in order to perform for a reward, these neurons remain active until the animal is rewarded. Visual fixation cells are also active during smooth pursuit of moving visual stimuli, independent of direction. Most fixation cells are active only when the biologically significant target is placed in one half or one quarter of the visual field contralateral to the active cells. A minority of fixation cells are active when the stimulus is placed anywhere in the visual field. Eye position (direction of gaze) is also important: these partial fixation neurons are active when the direction of gaze is toward a specific half or quadrant of the visual field. To summarize, the activity of partial fixation cells depends on: (1) the biological significance of the stimulus, (2) the distance of the stimulus from the animal, (3) the region of the retina stimulated, and (4) the direction of gaze.

Visual tracking neurons. Visual tracking neurons do not discharge with fixation but only when the animal's eyes are smoothly pursuing an object of interest that is within arms reach and is moving in a given direction.

Saccade neurons. When a monkey makes a saccade, the activity of the fixation and tracking neurons abates. Saccade neurons have little activity during fixation or slow pursuit, but become active just (75 msec) before a saccade. Like fixation and tracking neurons, these cells become active with biologically significant stimuli: spontaneous saccades do not induce activity in these cells. Some saccade neurons become active with saccades in all directions, whereas others appear to be directionally dependent. Of these direction-dependent saccade neurons, most are more active before saccades in the contralateral hemifield.

Enhancement. Goldberg and Robinson (1977) and Robinson et al. (1978) have shown that the activity of some posterior parietal neurons is enhanced by motivationally significant visual stimuli independent of behavior. This enhancement is spatially selective. If an animal attends to a visual stimulus, then any response to that stimulus is enhanced, whether it be a saccade, reaching, or using the stimulus as a cue for behavior not requiring a targeted movement. These parietal neurons respond to aversive as well as rewarded stimuli and their activity may therefore be more dependent on selective attention than specific motivational significance, although motivational aspects are included in a general attentional mechanism.

Light-sensitive neurons. Mountcastle and co-workers (1981) have identified light-sensitive neurons (formerly called "visual space" neurons) of the monkey inferior parietal lobule having large response areas that do not include the fovea. The response areas may be distributed in both halves of the visual fields. These neurons are sensitive to stimulus direction and movement over a wide velocity range. A neuron with bilateral receptive fields will respond to movement in one direction in one visual field and will respond only to movement in the opposite direction in the other visual field, a property called opponent vector organization. During an act of attentive fixation, these neurons have an enhanced response to peripheral visual stimuli. These parietal neurons may play a role in the residual visual function of destriate primates and may be the projection target of the "second" visual system of retinocollicular origin. The facilitation of this system during foveal attention presumably allows the subject to be prepared to shift attention to novel, threatening, or aversive stimuli appearing in the periphery.

Nonvisual cells. The inattention to contralateral stimuli seen in humans and monkeys after lesions in the temporoparietal regions, however, is not limited to the visual modality. Meaningful somesthetic and auditory stimuli are also neglected. Hyvarinen and Poranen (1974) noted that the inferior parietal lobule also contained cells that exhibited enhanced activity when animals manipulated biologically significant objects. Some inferior parietal lobule cells seem to be activated by stimuli in both the visual and the somesthetic modalities.

Interpretation of physiological studies.   Mountcastle and co-workers have concluded that the posterior parietal cortex contains sets of neurons serving a command function for manual and visual exploration of immediate extrapersonal space. Deficits after lesions of this area would be explained by a lack of volition to explore with the hand and eye the contralateral side of space. Very few neurons were found that appeared to converge visual information with body position and movement—so few that it seemed unlikely that the posterior parietal cortex could be the region producing a neural model of the orientation and movement of the body in space. It was suggested that the region of the superior temporal sulcus might perform this function since it receives input from area 7.

Goldberg, Robinson, and co-workers have emphasized the importance of the inferior parietal lobule in directing attention. They saw no evidence that the parietal lobule contained cells that programmed responses. While this differs from the view of Mountcastle and co-workers who assign a command function to this area, there are more similarities than differences in the two interpretations, and an analysis of these studies provides insight into the role of the inferior parietal lobule in behavior. This area is not simply a sensory association region. It acts in parallel with the retinostriate system and functions as an interface between attention to, reception of, and response to significant events in extrapersonal space. The retinostriate system is important for discriminating shape, color, and size when a subject concentrates on foveal work. The light-sensitive neurons of the inferior parietal lobule provide continual updating of the neural image of extrapersonal space and therefore allow for the attraction of attention toward events in peripheral vision. Fixation neurons maintain attention on a significant fixated object. Oculomotor neurons, such as the saccade neurons described above, subserve the motor events of shifting visual attention. Projection and manipulation neurons are active during limb movements directed toward an object in extrapersonal space. Neurons in the inferior parietal lobule are movement-independent (Bushnell et al., 1981). They are probably not only subserving attention to extrapersonal space but also processing information to determine its emotional or motivational significance.

SUMMARY OF THE ATTENTIONAL MODEL

The attentional model we have discussed is summarized in Fig. 10-8. Unilateral inattention will follow unilateral mesencephalic reticular activating system lesions because loss of inhibition of the ipsilateral nucleus reticularis by the mesencephalic reticular activating system decreases thalamic transmission of sensory input to the cortex or because the mesencephalic reticular formation does not prepare the cortex for sensory processing, or both. Unilateral lesions of the primary or association cortices cause contralateral unimodal sensory loss or inabiltiy to synthesize contralateral unimodal sensory input. Corticothalamic collaterals from the association cortex to the nucleus reticularis may serve unimodal habituation and attention. Unilateral lesions of multimodal sensory convergence areas (e.g., the superior temporal sulcus) that project to mesencephalic reticular activating system and nucleus reticularis induce contralateral inattention because the subject cannot be aroused to, or process, multimodal contralateral stimuli. A lesion of the inferior parietal lobule, because of its reciprocal connections with polymodal areas (prefrontal lobes, superior temporal sulcus) and the limbic system, may impair the subject's ability to determine the significance of a stimulus.

Mechanisms Underlying Extinction

Extinction is said to occur when an organism is able to report or respond to a stimulus presented in isolation but unable to report this same stimulus presented simultaneously with another stimulus (usually on the other side of the body). Extinction also may be induced by stimuli in different modalities. The nature and complexity of a stimulus may also affect extinction.

Extinction can be seen in normal subjects as well as in patients with central nervous system lesions (Benton and Levin, 1972; Kimura, 1967). The lesions causing extinction are often in the same areas as lesions that cause inattention. However, certain forms of extinction may also occur after lesions of the corpus callosum (Sparks and Geschwind 1968; Milner et al. 1968), and left-sided extinction has even been reported to follow left hemisphere lesions (Schwartz et al., 1979). Extinction in normal subjects, extinction in patients with callosal lesions, and extinction in patients with hemisphere lesions may all differ. In this section we will mainly discuss the extinction seen after hemisphere lesions.

Patients with cerebral dysfunction, particularly in the temporoparietal region, may show extinction (Heilman et al., 1983). Multimodal extinction may also occur in monkeys with temporoparietal lesions (Heilman et al., 1970). Unlike the ipsilateral extinction reported by Schwartz et al. (1979) that only occurred with the use of complex stimuli, extinction after parietal lobe lesions can be demonstrated using simple stimuli.

In general, despite many published reports, especially about dichotic listening in normal subjects, the mechanisms underlying extinction are poorly understood. We will discuss several hypotheses that have been advanced to explain extinction.

SENSORY THEORIES

Extinction has been reported to be induced by lesions that affect purely sensory systems. Because patients with partial deafferentation may exhibit extinction, several authors have postulated a sensory mechanism to explain inattention and extinction. Psychophysical methods have been used to demonstrate that in normal subjects sensory threshold increases on one side when the opposite side is stimulated (obscuration). If this obscuration phenomenon (perhaps induced by reciprocal inhibition) occurs in patients with an elevated threshold from an afferent lesion, it would appear similar to extinction in patients without deafferentation.

SUPPRESSION AND RECIPROCAL INHIBITION

Nathan (1946) and Reider (1946) suggested that extinction results from suppression: the normal hemisphere inhibits the damaged hemisphere more than the damaged hemisphere inhibits the normal hemisphere. Consequently, stimuli contralateral to the damaged hemisphere are not perceived when the normal side is stimulated. The notion of transcallosal inhibition also has bearing on theories of inattention: Kinsbourne (1970) postulated that each hemisphere inhibits the other by callosal mechanisms but did not specify how and where this inhibition was being mediated. He proposed that neglect results from decreased inhibition of the normal hemisphere, which becomes hyperresponsive. We also believe that many symptoms of neglect can be induced by asymmetries of orientational tendencies; but unlike Kinsbourne, who believes that the imbalance is due to increased activity of the nonlesioned hemisphere, we believe that asymmetrical orientational tendencies are associated with decreased activity of the lesioned hemisphere (Heilman and Watson, 1978; Heilman, 1979).

Furmanski (1950) proposed a mechanism of extinction based on a model of attention in normal persons. In this model, cortical "suppressor areas" were proposed which inhibit thalamic relay nuclei so that unimportant afferent information would not be relayed to the cortex. Cortical suppressor areas were thought to be adjacent to, and to have input from, cortical sensory areas. They project to ipsilateral thalamic relay nuclei, and to contralateral suppressor areas. Unilateral stimuli that are deemed important diminish the activity of ipsilateral suppressor areas related to that particular sensory input, while suppressor activity related to other ipsilateral stimuli and to contralateral stimuli is increased. Furmanski proposed that parietal lesions destroy both thalamocortical sensory projections and parietal suppressor areas. Frontal, temporal, and occipital suppressor areas continue to suppress the thalamus, and thalamocortical damage prevents the intact suppressor areas from receiving thalamic input that would decrease their activity. If inhibition of thalamic relay nuclei is not complete, some sensory input will still be transmitted, and a stimulus given to the side opposite the lesion will still be reported. But if a simultaneous stimulus is given on the other side, the thalamus on the damaged side will be further suppressed and the stimulus opposite the damaged hemisphere may no longer be perceived (extinction).

There are several problems with Furmanski's model. First, there is little evidence that cortical suppressor areas exist. Second, neglect in humans and monkeys can be induced by lesions that do not disrupt thalamocortical projections but instead involve polymodal association cortex.

Many of the functions attributed to the suppressor areas have been postulated by Singer (1977) to be properties of the thalamic reticular nucleus—that is, portions of this nucleus can selectively inhibit various thalamic sensory nuclei. Ipsilateral cortical association areas have also been postulated to inhibit this inhibitor. (Please see the section on inattention, on pp. 255–257, for a full discussion of this mechanism). However, to explain extinction using this nucleus reticularis thalami model, we would have to theorize that each association cortex also projects to the contralateral thalamic reticular nucleus and facilitates rather than inhibits it. Therefore, even under normal conditions, a stimulus on one side would induce an increase of threshold for stimuli on the other side. With a lesion of association cortex there would be less inhibition of NR, which in turn would inhibit the thalamic sensory nuclei, thus making the thalamus less sensitive to contralateral stimuli. If the opposite side was also simultaneously stimulated, activated attentional cells would further increase contralateral NR activity, further inhibiting the thalamic sensory nuclei and thereby inducing extinction. The pathway by which one association cortex may influence the contralateral NR is not known.

INTERFERENCE THEORY

Birch et al. (1967) proposed that the damaged hemisphere processes information more slowly than the intact hemisphere. Because of this inertia the damaged side is more subject to interference from the normal side. To support their hypothesis the authors demonstrated that stimulating the abnormal side (contralesional side) before stimulating the normal side (ipsilateral side) reduced extinction; however, stimulating the normal side before the abnormal side had no effect on extinction.

LIMITED ATTENTION THEORY

According to the limited attention theory, under normal circumstances bilateral simultaneous stimuli are processed simultaneously, each hemisphere processing the contralateral stimulus. However, a damaged hemisphere may be unable to attend to contralateral stimuli, making the organism inattentive to those stimuli. As the organism recovers, it becomes capable of attending to contralateral stimuli. This improvement may be mediated by the normal, ipsilateral hemisphere. The normal hemisphere, however, may have a limited attentional capacity. Therefore, with bilateral simultaneous stimulation the normal hemisphere's attentional mechanism, occupied with the contralateral stimulus, may be unable to attend to an ipsilateral stimulus (Heilman, 1979).

We will briefly review studies which have some bearing on the various theories of extinction. We should note that these theories may not be mutually exclusive: because extinction can be caused by lesions in a variety of anatomically and functionally different areas, the reciprocal inhibition, limited attention, and interference theories could each be correct, but for different lesions.

Benton and Levin (1972) reported that in normal subjecs threshold is raised by presenting a simultaneous stimulus. Because normal persons do not have lesions inducing inertia, do not have to rely on weaker ipsilateral pathways, and have two intact hemispheres, Benton and Levin's findings cannot readily be explained by the limited attention or interference models. Their findings appear to support the reciprocal inhibition model. The findings of Birch et al. (1967) described above (that extinction is reduced when a contralateral stimulus precedes an ipsilateral stimulus, but not when an ipsilateral stimulus precedes a contralateral stimulus) are compatible with both the reciprocal inhibition and limited attention interference theories. Sevush and Heilman (1981) showed that a unilateral stimulus preceding a trial with simultaneous stimuli may alter the pattern of extinction. That is, when a bilateral trial is preceded by a contralateral (e.g., left) stimulus the subject is more likely to show extinction than when a bilateral trial is preceded by an ipsilateral (e.g., right) stimulus. These findings cannot be explained by the interference model.

Partial support for the limited attention theory comes from studying patients who exhibit extinction (Heilman et al., 1984). Subjects were asked to report where they were given a tactile stimulus: on the right, the left, both, or neither (in the "neither" situation, the subject was not stimulated, but was still asked to give a response). Subjects erred by reporting "both" when the arm ipsilateral to the damaged hemisphere was stimulated more than they reported "both" when the contralateral arm was stimulated. One interpretation of these results is that these patients were not sufficiently attentive to their contralesional extremities to realize when they had *not* been touched. Since the errors consisted of reporting a stimulation that did not occur rather than failing to report a stimulus, these results cannot be explained by the suppression, reciprocal inhibition, or interference theories and are most compatible with the limited attention theory.

Mechanisms Underlying Intentional Neglect and Akinesia

Unilateral neglect has been described following unilateral dorsolateral frontal lesions in monkeys (Bianchi, 1895; Kennard and Ectors, 1938; Welch and Stuteville, 1958) and man (Heilman and Valenstein, 1972). Watson et al. (1978) recognized that in most testing paradigms, the animal is required to respond to a stimulus contralateral to the lesion either by orienting to the stimulus or by moving the limbs on the side of the stimulus. Since these animals with frontal lobe lesions were not weak, when they failed to make the appropriate response, it was assumed that they had sensory neglect. Although this neglect was usually assumed to result from inattention to the sensory stimuli, Watson et al. (1978) suggested that it could be equally attributable to unilateral akinesia. They therefore trained monkeys to use the left hand in responding to a tactile stimulus on the right leg, and the right hand in responding to a left-sided tactile stimulus. After a unilateral frontal arcuate lesion the monkeys showed contralateral neglect, but when stimulated on their neglected side, they responded normally with the limb on the side of the lesion. When stimulated on the side ipsilateral to the lesion, however, they often failed to respond (with the limb on the neglected side), or responded by moving the limb ipsilateral to the lesion. These results cannot be explained by sensory or perceptual hypotheses and are thought to reflect a defect in intention to make a correct response.

ANATOMIC AND PHYSIOLOGICAL MECHANISMS

The region of the arcuate gyrus is also known as the frontal eye field. Stimulation of the frontal eye field elicits contralateral eye movement, head rotation, and pupillary dilation resembling attentive orienting (Wagman and Mehler, 1972).

Connections of the frontal eye fields (periarcuate cortex). The connections of the frontal eye field are important in understanding its possible role in attention and intention to multimodal sensory and limbic inputs. The periarcuate region has reciprocal connections with auditory, visual, and somesthetic association cortex (Chavis and Pandya, 1976). Evoked potential studies have confirmed this as an area of sensory convergence (Bignell and Imbert, 1969). The periarcuate region is also reciprocally connected with STS, another site of multimodal sensory convergence, and with the intraparietal sulcus, an area of somatosensory and visual convergence. There are also connections with prearcuate cortex. The periarcuate cortex has reciprocal connections with subcortical areas: the paralamellar portion of dorsomedial nucleus (DM) and the adjacent centromedian-parafascicularis (CM-Pf) complex (Kievet and Kuypers, 1977; Akert and Von Monakow, 1980). Just as the periarcuate region is transitional in architecture between agranular motor cortex and granular prefrontal cortex, the paralamellar-CM-Pf complex is situated between medial thalamus, which projects to granular cortex, and lateral thalamus, which projects to agranular cortex. Projections to MRF (Kuypers and Lawrence, 1967) as well as nonreciprocal projections to caudate also exist. Last, the periarcuate region also receives input from the limbic system, mainly from the anterior cingulate gyrus (Baleydier and Mauguiere, 1980).

We may speculate about the functions of these various connections. The neocortical sensory association and sensory convergence area connections may provide the frontal lobe with information about external stimuli that may call the individual to action. The limbic connections (anterior cingulate gyrus) may provide the frontal lobe with motivational information. Connections with the MRF may be important in arousal.

Physiological studies. Because the dorsolateral frontal lobe has sensory association cortex, limbic, and reticular formation connections, it would appear to be an ideal candidate for mediating a response to a stimulus that the subject is attending. There is evidence from physiological studies to support this hypothesis. Recordings from single cells in the posterior frontal arcuate gyrus reveal responses similar to those of superior colliculus, a structure also important in oculomotor control (Goldberg and Bushnell, 1981). These visually responsive neurons show enhanced activity time-locked to the onset of stimulus and preceding eye movements. The neurons are not enhanced by attending to an object without an associated eye or limb movement. This differs from IPL neurons that respond to visual input independent of behavior: an IPL neuron whose activity enhances in a task that requires a saccade also enhances with tasks that do not require a saccade. Therefore, the IPL neurons seem to be responsible for selective spatial attention, which is independent of behavior; and any neuron that is enhanced to one type of behavior will also be enhanced to others (Bushnell et al., 1981). The frontal eye field neurons, however, are linked to behavior, but only to movements that have motivational significance. Responses to other stimulus modalities (e.g., audition) may be controlled by another group of nearby neurons in the arcuate gyrus (Whittington and Hepp-Reymond, 1977).

The role of CM-Pf in behavior.　As mentioned above, the dorsolateral frontal lobe has extensive connections with CM-Pf, one of the "nonspecific" intralaminar thalamic nuclei. Nonsensory neglect has also been reported in monkeys after CM-Pf lesions (Watson et al., 1978), and an akinetic state (akinetic mutism) is seen with bilateral CM-Pf lesions in humans (Mills and Swanson, 1978). We have postulated a possible role for CM-Pf in behavior (Watson et al., 1981). This role is based on behavioral, anatomic, and physiological evidence that CM-Pf and periarcuate cortex are involved in mediating the response of an individual to meaningful stimuli.

Low-frequency stimulation of CM-Pf at 6–12 cps induces cortical recruiting responses (Jasper, 1949). This stimulation activates the inhibitory NR through a CM-Pf-frontocortical-NR system (Fig. 10-9, Pathway 2) (Yingling and Skinner, 1975). This NR activation elicits inhibitory postsynaptic potentials in the ventrolateral thalamic nucleus (VL), and thus blocks VL transmission to motor cortex (Fig. 10-9, Pathways 1 and 2) (Purpura, 1970). Transmission in VL has been shown to be inversely proportional to NR activity (Filion et al., 1971). VL projects to motor cortex, and may be important in the initiation of movements.

High-frequency stimulation of the CM-Pf or MRF induces inhibition of NR, EEG desynchronization, and behavioral arousal (Moruzzi and Magoun, 1949; Yingling and Skinner, 1975). These manifestations elicited by high-frequency CM-Pf stimulation are predominantly mediated via the MRF-NR system (Fig. 10-9, Pathway 1), since they are blocked by a lesion between the CM-Pf and MRF (Weinberger et al., 1965). A lesion of the CM-Pf-frontocortical-NR system also prevents inhibition of the NR response to rapid CM-Pf stimulation, whereas rapid MRF stimulation during this blockade will continue to inhibit the NR (Yingling and Skinner, 1977). This indicates that the NR can be inhibited by either an MRF-NR system or a CM-Pf frontocortical-NR system and suggests that different types of behavior may be mediated independently by these systems.

Novel or noxious stimuli, or anticipation of a response to a meaningful stimulus, produce inhibition of the NR and a negative surface potential over the frontal cortex (Yingling and Skinner, 1977). This surface-negative potential occurs if a stimulus has

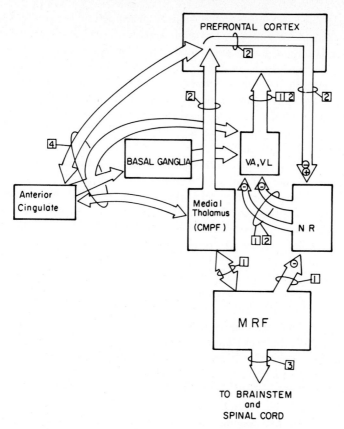

Fig. 10-9. Schematic representation of pathways important for motor activation and preparation to respond. The pathways represent (1) mesencephalic reticular formation (MRF)-nucleus reticularis thalami (RF) system (see Fig. 10-8), (2) medial thalamic-frontocortical-NR system, (3) MRF to brainstem and spinal cord for primitive orienting, and (4) limbic subcortical connections. See text for details. CMPF indicates centromedian parafascicularis thalamic nucleus; VA, ventral anterior thalamic nucleus; VL, ventrolateral thalamic nucleus.

acquired behavioral significance (Walter, 1973). Specifically, when a warning stimulus precedes a second stimulus that requires a motor response, a negative waveform appears between stimuli and has been called the "contingent negative variation" (CNV) and is thought to reflect motivation, attention, or expectancy.

Skinner and Yingling (1976) demonstrated that in a conditional tone/shock expectancy paradigm, both the frontal negative wave and inhibition of NR elicited by the tone were abolished by blockade of the CM-Pf-frontocortical-NR system, although primitive orienting persisted (Fig. 10-9, Pathway 3). Novel or noxious stimuli or rapid MRF stimulation continued to inhibit NR. In an operant task involving alternate bar press for reward, cooling of the CM-Pf-frontocortical-NR loop sufficient to block cortical recruitment induced incorrect responses to the previously reinforced bar press (i.e., perseveration) (Skinner and Yingling, 1977). Further cooling caused the subject to cease responding altogether. These behavioral observations demonstrated that an appropriate response to a meaningful stimulus in an aroused subject requires an intact CM-Pf-frontocortical-NR system, whereas primitive behavioral orienting elicited by novel or noxious stimuli depends on an intact MRF-NR system. Responding to basic survival stimuli (e.g., food when hungry) may also depend on an MRF-NR system.

Extensive connections exist from dorsolateral prefrontal cortex to anterior cingulate gyrus (Fig. 10-9, Pathway 4) and through hippocampal mechanisms to lateral hypothalamus and the MRF (Nauta, 1958). Single-cell recordings from these hypothalamic neurons reveal cells firing before a monkey's response to food but not firing to objects other than food (Rolls et al., 1979).

Skinner and Yingling (1977) interpreted their data as supporting a role for the MRF-NR system in tonic arousal and the CM-Pf-frontocortical-NR system in "selective" attention. We agree with the hypothesized role of the MRF-NR system in tonic arousal but suggest that the role of the CM-Pf-frontocortical-NR system is preparing the aroused organism to respond to a meaningful stimulus. The demonstration that intralaminar neurons have activity time-locked to *either* sensory or motor events, depending on the experimental condition, supports the pivotal role of this structure in sensory–motor integration (Schlag-Rey and Schlag, 1980).

The periarcuate region and thalamic zone around the lateral aspect of the dorsomedial nucleus and intralaminar nucleus share common anatomic features. In addition to reciprocal connections, there is a complex arc from periarcuate cortex, motor cortex, and CM-Pf to the neostriatum (caudate and putamen), from the neostriatum to globus pallidus, from globus pallidus to CM-Pf and VL, and from CM-Pf and VL back to premotor and motor cortex. Not surprisingly, lesions of structures within this loop, including arcuate gyrus (Watson et al., 1978), basal ganglia (Valenstein and Heilman, 1981), VL (Velasco and Velasco, 1979), and CM-Pf (Watson et al., 1978), have induced a deficit in responding to multimodal sensory stimuli.

NEUROPHARMACOLOGY OF INTENTIONAL DISORDERS

Dopamine.   There is much evidence to suggest the importance of dopaminergic neurons in the mediation of aspects of intention. Marked defects of intention have long been known to be prominent in patients with Parkinson's disease, which is characterized pathologically by degeneration of ascending dopaminergic neurons. In animals, unilateral lesions in these pathways cause unilateral neglect, while stimulation of dopamine pathways reinforces ongoing behavior (Olds and Milner, 1954; Corbett and Wise, 1980).

Three related pathways have been defined. The *nigrostriatal* pathway originates in the pars compacta of the substantia nigra (SN), and projects to the neostriatum (caudate and putamen). The *mesolimbic* and *mesocortical* pathways originate principally in the ventral tegmental area (VTA) of the midbrain, just medial to the SN, and terminate in the limbic areas of the basal forebrain (nucleus accumbens septi and olfactory tubercle) and the cerebral cortex (frontal and cingulate cortex), respectively (Ungerstedt, 1971a, Lindvall et al., 1974).

These dopaminergic (DA) fibers course through the lateral hypothalamus (LH) in the median forebrain bundle. Bilateral lesions in the lateral hypothalamus of rats induce an akinetic state (Teitelbaum and Epstein, 1962). Unilateral LH lesions cause unilateral neglect: these rats transiently circle toward the side of their lesion; after they recover to the point where spontaneous activity appears symmetrical, they still tend to turn toward their lesioned side when stimulated (e.g., by pinching their tails), and they fail to respond to sensory stimuli delivered to the contralateral side (Marshall et al., 1971). There is considerable evidence that LH lesions cause neglect by damaging DA fibers passing through the hypothalamus. Neglect occurs with 6-hydroxy-dopamine lesions of LH, that damage DA fibers relatively selectively (Marshall et al., 1974), but not with kainic acid lesions, that damage cell bodies but not fibers of passage (Grossman et al., 1978). Unilateral damage to the same DA fibers closer to their site of origin in the midbrain also cause unilateral neglect (Ljungberg and Ungerstedt, 1976; Marshall, 1979). Conversely, unilateral *stimulation* in the area of ascending DA fibers (Arbuthnott and Ungerstedt, 1975) or of the striatum (see Pycock, 1980) causes animals to turn away from the side of stimulation, as if they are orienting to the opposite side. Normal (nonlesioned) rats spontaneously turn more in one direction. They also have an asymmetry in striatal dopamine concentration and their direction of turning is generally away from the side of the brain with more dopamine (Glick et al., 1975).

Lesions of the ascending dopaminergic pathways affect the areas of termination of these pathways in at least two ways. First, degeneration of dopamine-containing axons depletes these areas of dopamine. Marshall (1979) has shown that the neglect induced in rats by ventral tegmental 6-OHDA lesions is proportional to the depletion of dopamine in the neostriatum, and, to a lesser extent, in the olfactory tubercle and nucleus accumbens. Second, the target areas attempt to compensate for the depletion of DA afferents by increasing their responsiveness to dopamine. This is mediated, at least in part, by an increase in the number of DA receptors (Heikkila et al., 1981), which correlates with behavioral recovery from neglect (Neve et al., 1982).

Changes in DA innervation and in DA receptor sensitivity can explain many effects of pharmacological manipulation in animals with unilateral lesions of the ascending DA pathways. Such lesions result in degeneration of DA axon terminals on the side of the lesion. Drugs such as L-dopa or amphetamines that increase the release of dopamine from normal DA terminals will therefore cause more dopamine to be released on the unlesioned side than on the lesioned side, resulting in orientation or turning toward the lesioned side (Ungerstedt, 1971b; 1974). Several days after the lesion is made, when DA receptor concentrations on the side of the lesion begin to increase, drugs such as apomorphine that directly stimulate DA receptors cause the animal to turn away from the side of the lesion (Ungerstedt, 1971b; 1974). This effect of apomorphine is blocked by prior administration of drugs such as spiroperidol that block DA receptors (Ungerstedt, 1971c). In rats without brain lesions, amphetamine increases spontaneous turning preference, while apomorphine may cause turning in the opposite direction (Jerussi and Glick, 1976). These effects are also blocked by DA-blocking drugs (haloperidol). It is of interest that even though amphetamine increases the release of both norepinephrine and dopamine in the brain, the major behavioral effects of amphetamine are not blocked by pharmacological or anatomic lesions of the noradrenergic systems, but are affected by drugs or lesions that reduce activity in the ascending DA systems.

Although rats have been used in most studies, lesions that probably involve the ascending DA systems have also induced unilateral neglect in cats (Hagamen et al., 1977) and monkeys (Deuel, 1980). As mentioned above, bilateral degeneration of the nigrostriatal fibers in humans is associated with Parkinsonism, in which hypokinesia is a prominent symptom. Ross and Stewart (1981) described a patient with akinetic mutism secondary to bilateral damage to the anterior hypothalamus. This patient responded to treatment with bromocriptine, a direct DA-receptor agonist. Since the lesion was probably anterior to the site at which nigrostriatal fibers diverge from the median forebrain bundle, the authors suggested that damage to the mesolimbic and mesocortical pathways was critical in causing their patient's hypokinesia.

The evidence summarized above indicates the importance of DA pathways in mediating intention. Although the neglect induced by LH or VTA lesions has been called "sensory" neglect or inattention, rats trained to respond to unilateral stimulation by turning toward the side opposite the side of stimulation respond well to stimulation of their "neglected" side (the side opposite the lesion) but fail to turn when stimulated on their "normal" side (Hoyman et al., 1979). This paradigm is similar to that used by Watson et al. (1978), and demonstrates that lesions in ascending DA pathways cause a defect of intention. (Some authors, however, have argued that the defect in orientation to sensory stimuli is not intentional—see Feeney and Weir, 1979.)

The mechanism by which the ascending DA systems produce their effect is not known, even though much has been learned about the circuitry of the DA projections to the striatum (Grofova, 1979; Fonnum and Walaas, 1979). The striatum projects strongly via the globus pallidus and thalamus to the motor cortex, but motor cortex lesions do not abolish drug-induced turning in animals with lesions in the ascending DA pathways (Crossman et al., 1977). The nucleus accumbens and striatum project via the globus pallidus to the intralaminar nuclei of the thalamus (Mehler, 1966). The striatum also projects to the substantia nigra, in part providing feedback to DA neurons, but also connecting the striatum with the targets of SN projections: the intralaminar nuclei of the thalamus, the superior colliculus, and portions of the reticular formation (Anderson and Yoshida, 1977; Dalsass and Krauthamer, 1981; Herkenham, 1979). These projections are thought to be important in mediating the drug-induced turning behavior seen after lesions in the ascending DA pathways (Morelli et al., 1981). The intralaminar thalamus, the superior colliculus, and the mesencephalic reticular formation are all areas that have been implicated in the mediation of attention, and in which lesions can induce unilateral neglect. It appears likely that striatal input into these areas, regulated in part by activity in the ascending DA pathways, provides information about the intentional state of the organism.

Other neurotransmitters.   Since relatively more is known about the relationship of DA systems to orienting behavior, the tendency has been to explain the effects of other neuropharmacological agents in terms of their influence on DA systems. Acetylcholine (ACh), for example, antagonizes the effect of dopamine on striatal neurons (Guyenet et al., 1977), and administration of ACh antagonists to animals with unilateral lesions of the ascending DA system will cause circling toward the side of the lesion, presumably by allowing greater DA activity in the normal striatum (Corrodi et al., 1972).

Opposite effects are obtained using ACh agonists (Iwamoto et al., 1976). The effects of drugs that affect other neurotransmitter systems (GABA, norepinephrine, and serotonin) on turning behavior are summarized by Pycock (1980). Injection of GABA into the pars compacta of the SN induces ipsilateral turning, presumably by inhibiting the ascending DA system on that side. Injections of GABA into the pars reticulata of the SN, however, causes contralateral turning, probably by stimulating nondopaminergic nigral projections (Olianas et al., 1978).

There is relatively little evidence to link the noradrenergic pathways to intentional behavior. Rats with bilateral lesions of the noradrenergic projections in the dorsal tegmental bundle fail to extinguish their behavior normally when not rewarded (Mason and Iversen, 1979). Underlying this behavioral deficit is an inability to learn to ignore or filter out irrelevant environmental stimuli; that is, an attentional disturbance. The effects of unilateral manipulation of norepinephrine or serotonin on turning behavior and neglect are not well understood.

Cortical lesions. The frontal neocortex and cingulate cortex receive DA input from the ventral tegmental area (Brown et al., 1979), and the entire neocortex projects strongly to the striatum.This corticostriatal projection is at least in part glutaminergic (Divac et al.. 1977). Stimulation in the motor or visual areas of the cat's cortex causes a release of dopamine in the striatum and substantia nigra (Nieoullon et al., 1978). But in rats 6-OHDA lesions of the mesial prefrontal cortex resulted, after thirty days, in an increase of both striatal dopamine content and of striatal DA receptor concentration (Pycock et al., 1980). The pharmacological effects of cortical lesions are not well described or understood. Several studies have shown that bilateral frontal cortical ablations in the rat increase locomotor response to amphetamine (Lynch et al., 1969; Iversen et al., 1971, Glick, 1972). Rats with unilateral frontal cortical ablations may turn toward the side of their lesion, and amphetamines initially increase this turning (Avemo et al., 1973). After one week, amphetamines induce contralateral turning, while apomorphine causes turning toward the side of the lesion (that is, the opposite of the pharmacological effects seen after unilateral lesions of the ascending DA pathways). Rats subjected to a previous unilateral 6-OHDA lesion of the ascending DA pathways and then a unilateral frontal lesion initially reverse their direction of spontaneous turning, but do not change their turning response to amphetamine or apomorphine (Crossman et al., 1977). Monkeys that have recovered from neglect induced by unilateral frontal arcuate lesions do not show asymmetrical behavior when given L-dopa, amphetamine, haloperidol, scopolamine, physostigmine, or bromocriptine, but do show dramatic turning toward the side of their lesion when given apomorphine (Valenstein et al., 1980). This turning is blocked by prior administration of haloperidol. These studies are difficult to reconcile with one another. They do serve to indicate that frontal lesions influence DA systems, but the site and mechanism of these effects are not known.

Mechanisms Underlying Hemispatial Neglect

Patients with hemispatial neglect fail to perform in the side of space opposite their lesion, even when using their "normal" (ipsilesional) hand. For example, they may draw only half of a clock or daisy, or bisect lines to one side (see Figs. 10-1, 2, and 3). Although hemianopia may enhance the symptoms of hemispatial neglect, hemianopia by itself cannot entirely account for the deficit, for two reasons. First, some patients with hemispatial neglect are not hemianopic (McFie, et al., 1950). Second, hemianopic patients without neglect do not perform differently from nonhemianopic patients in the visual discrimination of bisected lines (Rosenberger, 1974). The dramatic performance of patients with hemispatial neglect cannot therefore be attributed to a simple sensory deficit. The abnormal performance of patients in contralesional space suggests that brain mechanisms relating to the opposite hemispace have been disturbed. It suggests that each hemisphere is responsible not only for receiving stimuli from contralateral space, and for controlling the contralateral limbs, but also for attending and intending in contralateral hemispace independent of which hand is used (Heilman, 1979; Bowers and Heilman, 1980).

Hemispace is a complex concept, since it can be defined according to the visual half-field (eye position), head position, or trunk position. With the eyes and head facing directly ahead, the hemispaces defined in these three ways are congruent. But if the eyes are directed to the far right, for example, the left visual field falls in large part in right hemispace, as defined by the head and body midline. Similarly, if the head and eyes are turned far to the right, left head and eye hemispace can both be in body right hemispace. There is evidence to suggest that head and body hemispace are of importance in determining the symptoms of hemispatial neglect (Heilman and Valenstein, 1979; Bowers and Heilman, 1980; Coslett and Heilman, in preparation) (see below).

Experimental evidence in normal subjects supports the hypothesis that each hemisphere is organized at least in part to mediate activity in contralateral hemispace. If a subject fixes his gaze at a midline object, keeps his right arm in right hemispace and his left arm in left hemispace, and receives a stimulus delivered in his right visual half field, he will respond more rapidly with his right hand than with his left hand. Similarly, if a stimulus is delivered in his left visual half field, he will respond more rapidly with his left hand than with his right (Anzola et al., 1977). These results were traditionally explained by an anatomic pathway transmission model: the reaction time is longer when the hand opposite the stimulated field responds because in this situation information must be transmitted between hemispheres, and this takes more time than when information can remain in the same hemisphere. But if a choice reaction time paradigm is used, and the hands are crossed so that the left hand is in right hemispace and the right hand is in left hemispace, then the faster reaction times are made by the hand positioned in the same side of space as the stimulus (Anzola et al., 1977), even though in this situation the information must cross the corpus callosum. Clearly, these results cannot be explained by a pathway transmission model.

Cognitive theorists have attributed the stimulus–response compatibility in the crossed-hand studies to a "natural" tendency to respond to a lateralized stimulus with the hand that is in a corresponding spatial position (Simon et al., 1970). Alternatively, each hemisphere may be important for intending in the contralateral hemispatial field independent of which hand is used to respond (Heilman and Valenstein, 1979; Heilman, 1979).

If the cerebral hemispheres are organized hemispatially, a similar compatibiliy may exist between the visual half-field in which a stimulus is presented and the side of hemispace in which the visual half-field is aligned. Our group (Bowers et al., 1981) has found a hemispace–visual half-field compatibility suggesting that each hemisphere may not only be important for intending to the contralateral hemispatial field, independent of hand, but may also be important in attending or perceiving stimuli in contralateral hemispace independent of the visual field to which these stimuli are presented.

Microelectrode studies in alert monkeys support this hemispatial hypothesis. Researchers have identified cells with high-frequency activity while the monkey is looking at an interesting target (fixation cells). The activity of these cells depends not only on an appropriate motivational state, but also on an appropriate oculomotor state. That is, certain cells become active only when the animals are looking into contralateral hemispace (Lynch, 1980).

These studies support the hypothesis that each hemisphere mediates activity in contralateral hemispace independent of the sensory hemifield or the extremity used. The neural substrate underlying this hemispatial organization of the hemispheres remains unknown. One would think, however, that some sort of corollary discharge would be critical. For example, if one looks into right hemispace, there should be a corollary discharge to the "attentional" cells in the left hemisphere, so that even if a stimulus comes into the left visual half-field, the left hemisphere attentional cells would process these stimuli.

Distinguishing whether hemispatial neglect is induced by a hemifield defect or a hemispatial defect can be accomplished by certain procedures in patients with hemispatial neglect. If such patients with hemispatial neglect bisect lines incorrectly (e.g., to the right of midline) because a hemifield defect such as hemifield inattention prevents them from seeing how far the line extends to the neglected side, a strategy that ensures their seeing the left side of the line in their normal field should improve performance. If patients have a hemispatial defect, performance should be improved by moving the line toward the normal hemispace independent of visual field.

We required patients with left-sided neglect to identify a letter at either the right or left end of a line before bisecting the line. The task was given with the lines placed in either right, center, or left hemispace. When subjects were required to look to the left before bisecting a line, their performance did not differ from when they were required to look right. However, performance was significantly better when the line was placed in right hemispace rather than left hemispace (Heilman and Valenstein, 1979) (see Fig. 10-2). These observations indicate that patients with hemispatial neglect have a hemispatial defect rather than a hemifield defect.

There are several neuropsychological mechanisms that could account for the hemispatial defect associated with neglect.

REPRESENTATIONAL MAP HYPOTHESIS

Bisiach and Luzzatti, 1978, proposed a representational map hypothesis similar to Brain's body schema hypothesis. They asked two patients with right hemisphere damage to describe from memory a familiar scene (the main square in Milan) from two different spatial perspectives, one facing the cathedral and the other facing away from the cathedral. Regardless of the patients' orientation, left-sided details were omitted. On the basis of these findings and from a second study (Bisiach et al., 1979), these investigators postulated that the mental representation of the environment is structured topographically and is mapped across the brain. That is, the visual image of the environment conjured up by the mind may be split between the two hemispheres (like the projection of a real scene). With right hemisphere damage there is a representational disorder for the left half of this image. The representational map postulated by Bisiach may be hemispatially organized such that left hemispace is represented in the right hemisphere and right hemispace is represented in the left hemisphere.

GAZE DEFECT HYPOTHESIS

Neglect may be induced by a gaze defect. For example, in the line bisection task the subjects will have to move their eyes to the left of the line to read the letter, but they will then move their eyes to the right. It is possible that a gaze defect prevents them from fully reexploring the left side of the line. If the patient's decision about where to bisect the line is based on these latter explorations, he may "bisect" the line to the right of midline. Partial support for the gaze hypothesis is provided by De Renzi et al. (1982), who demonstrated that patients with right hemisphere lesions and neglect have eye deviation to the right.

HEMISPATIAL ATTENTIONAL DEFICIT HYPOTHESIS

Patients with hemispatial neglect could have a hemispatial attentional deficit. Although the line is "seen" in the normal visual field, it is not attended, and therefore is not processed fully. This prevents consolidation of the percept, and prevents the stimulus from affecting the patient's behavior.

UNILATERAL MEMORY DEFECT HYPOTHESIS

In our laboratory we demonstrated that patients with neglect have a unilateral memory defect. We randomly presented consonants via earphones to patients on either the neglected or non-neglected side. We asked the patients to report the stimulus either immediately or after a distraction-filled interval. We found that distraction induced more of a defect in the neglected ear than in the normal ear (Heilman et al., 1974).

Samuels et al. (1971) tested patients with right parietal lesions and found a similar phenomenon in the visual modality, though they did not evaluate their subjects for neglect. William James (1890) noted that "an object once attended will remain in the memory whilst one inattentively allowed to pass will leave no trace behind." In the line bisection task, although our subjects saw the full extent of the line, the part of the line in the left hemispatial field may not have formed a stable memory trace. As the subject explored the remainder of the line, he "forgot" the side of the line in the left hemispatial field.

HEMISPATIAL HYPOKINESIA HYPOTHESIS

Watson et al. (1978) demonstrated that monkeys with unilateral neglect from unilateral dorsolateral frontal or intralaminar thalamic lesions had unilateral hypokinesia (see page 264). They failed to use the limbs contralateral to the lesion to respond to a stimulus on their non-neglected (ipsilesional) side, while they responded normally with their ipsilesional limbs to a stimulus delivered to their neglected (contralesional) side. These findings suggest that in neglect the behavioral response in the neglected field, and not stimulus appreciation per se, is disrupted. Similar findings have also been observed in monkeys with parietotemporal lesions (Valenstein et al., 1982). It is possible that patients with hemispatial neglect have hemispatial or directional hypokinesia.

EVIDENCE BEARING ON THE MECHANISMS OF HEMISPATIAL NEGLECT

To determine whether hemispatial neglect was being induced by hemispatial visual inattention, a hemispatial memory defect, or a gaze defect, we performed a spatial task not requiring vision. Hemispatial neglect has already been demonstrated in a nonvisual modality (De Renzi et al., 1970), but because hemispatial inattention, memory defects, and exploratory defects may be multimodal, we also wanted a task that did not require sensory input from the neglected hemispace. We asked control subjects and patients with left-sided hemispatial neglect to close their eyes, point their right index finger to their sternum and then point to an imaginary spot in space that was midline with their chest. The patients with neglect pointed approximately 9 cm to the right of midline, whereas the controls pointed *slightly* to the left of midline (Heilman et al., 1983). Because this task did not require visual or somesthetic input from left hemispace, the defective performance could not be attributed to hemispatial inattention or to a defect in hemispatial visual or somesthetic memory. Similarly, because the patient did not need to explore left hemispace, this defect could not be explained by an exploratory or gaze defect. The findings of this study are most compatible with the hemispatial and directional hypokinesia or representational map hypotheses. This, of course, does not mean that patients with hemispatial neglect cannot also have hemispatial inattention, memory defects, and exploratory defects.

To learn if hemispatial akinesia and hypokinesia have a directional component, we tested the ability of patients with left-sided hemispatial neglect to move a lever toward or away from the side of their lesion. These subjects needed more time to initiate movement toward the neglected left hemispace than to initiate movement toward right hemispace, thus demonstrating a directional hypokinesia. These asymmetries were not found in brain-lesioned controls without neglect (Heilman et al., 1983). We concluded that each hemisphere may not only be important in mediating attention and intention in contralateral hemispace, but may also be important in mediating intention toward contralateral hemispace (directional intention). The directional hypokinesia demonstrated in this study cannot be explained by the representational map hypothesis.

If each hemisphere mediates sensorimotor processes of the contralateral extremities and also mediates intention toward and in contralateral hemispace independent of the sensory field or extremity used, both hemispheres must work in concert when an arm is used in or moved toward opposite hemispace. If both hemispheres did not work together, each extremity should err toward its own hemispace, giving the appearance of hemispatial neglect. To test this hypothesis, we examined a patient who had a partial callosal disconnection. In trying visually and somesthetically to bisect lines with her left hand in right hemispace, the patient made systematic errors to the left; in bisecting lines in left hemispace with her right hand, she made systematic errors to the right (Heilman et al., 1982). These results further support the hypothesis that each hemisphere mediates activities in contralateral hemispace independent of sensory field or extremity used.

Although these studies provide support for a directional and/or hemispatial akinesia, they do not refute the postulates that gaze defects and inattention may be associated with hemispatial neglect, nor do they refute the representational map hypothesis of Bisiach. It is possible, however, that the gaze defects reported by De Renzi et al., 1982 may be a manifestation of a directional intentional defect.

Attention, inattention, gaze, and memory (representational map) are probably all closely linked functions; however, observation of a patient we tested provides evidence that these processes may be dissociable. A patient with intermittent right parieto-occipital seizures was monitored by an EEG while he received right, left, and bilateral stimuli (Heilman and Howell, 1980). Interictally the patient did not have inattention or extinction; however, while the seizure focus was active, he had left-sided extinction and allesthesia. When asked to bisect lines immediately *after* a seizure, he tended to bisect the line to the right of midline, which suggested left hemispatial neglect. However, when asked to bisect lines *during* two focal seizures, the patient attempted to make a mark to the left of the entire sheet of paper. This case illustrates that attention to contralateral stimuli and intention to perform in the contralateral hemispatial field may be dissociable. The seizure-induced hyperintention to contralateral hemispace followed by postictal hemispatial neglect cannot be completely explained by the representational map hypothesis. However, the parietal lobe in man may contain attentional cells similar to those described by Lynch (1980), which may be important in helping to select significant stimuli; after a stimulus is detected these cells may activate intentional systems to prepare the individual for action. During a seizure when these cells are abnormally functioning, they may not be able to respond normally to stimuli, which may account for inattention and extinction. At the same time, however, these cells may be activating hemispheric intentional systems, thereby inducing a hyperintentional state.

Although the hemispatial and directional hypokinesia hypothesis is consistent with this patient's behavior, it is not clear how a hemispatial akinesia hypothesis may explain the findings of Bisiach and Luzzatti (1978). Bisiach and Luzzatti's patients were unable to recall left-side detail when imagining they faced the cathedral, but when asked to imagine that they were facing away from the cathedral, they could recall the details that had been on the left side and were now on the right. At least two explanations may explain these observations. The first is that offered by Bisiach—namely, a disorder in a representational map. However, for this hypothesis to be correct, when the patients were facing the cathedral they would have to have a representational map that was different and independent of the one they had when they were facing away from the cathedral. Since one can orient in any direction in the square, many representational maps would be needed to store a full scene.

When normal subjects are asked to recall a detail of a scene, they often move their eyes in the direction of the imagined detail: that is, if the detail was on the right, they move their eyes to the right. These observations suggest that when recalling the details of a scene, one must activate the image and then orient to a point within the iconic image. If this is the case, Bisiach and Luzzatti's patients might not have had defects in their representational maps but rather might have had defective activation or orientation (attention). The attentional-intentional defect in patients with neglect may not be just for external stimuli but also for internal images.

HEMISPHERIC ASYMMETRIES OF NEGLECT

Many early investigators noted that the neglect syndrome was more often associated with right than with left hemisphere lesions (Brain, 1941; McFie, et al., 1950; Critchley, 1966). Although Battersby et al. (1956) thought this preponderance of right hemisphere lesioned patients was the result of a sampling artifact caused by the exclusion of aphasic subjects, more recent studies confirm that lesions in the right hemisphere more often induce neglect and that the neglect induced by right hemisphere lesions is also more severe (Albert, 1973; Gainotti et al., 1972; Costa et al., 1969).

In previous sections we have reviewed evidence that the neglect syndrome may result from interference with normal brain mechanisms for attention and intention. The substantial asymmetry in hemispheric lesions causing neglect suggests that these brain mechanisms are asymmetrically distributed; specifically, that the right hemisphere is in some way more important for these functions than the left. There is evidence from work in both brain-damaged and normal persons that this is indeed the case.

Inattention

The attentional cells (or comparator neurons) found in the parietal lobe of monkeys by Lynch (1980) and Robinson et al. (1978) usually had contralateral receptive fields, but some of these neurons had bilateral receptive fields. That is, some responded to stimuli presented in the right or the left visual half-fields. To account for a hemispheric asymmetry of attention in humans, we would suggest that the temporoparietal regions of the human brain also have attentional or comparator neurons, but that the cells in the right hemisphere are more likely to have bilateral receptive fields than cells in the left hemisphere. Thus, cells in the left hemisphere would be activated predominantly by novel or significant stimuli in the right hemispace or hemifield, but cells in the right hemisphere would be activated by novel or significant stimuli in either visual field or either side of hemispace (or both). If this were the case, right hemisphere lesions would more often cause inattention than left hemisphere lesions. When the left hemisphere is damaged, the right can attend to ipsilateral stimuli, but the left hemisphere cannot attend to ipsilateral stimuli after right-sided damage. If activation of comparator neurons induces local EEG desynchronization (Sokolov,

1963) and if the right hemisphere is dominant for attention, the right hemisphere should desynchronize to stimuli presented in either field, whereas the left hemisphere should desynchronize only to right-side stimuli. We therefore gave lateralized visual stimuli to normal subjects while recording the electroencephalogram. We found that the right parietal lobe desynchronized equally to right- or left-sided stimuli while the left parietal lobe desynchronized mainly to right-sided stimuli. These observations are compatible with the hypothesis that the right hemisphere (parietal lobe) dominates the comparator, or attentional, processes (Heilman and Van Den Abell, 1980). A similar phenomenon was demonstrated using position emission tomography (Rosen et al., 1981), and regional cerebral blood flow (Prohovnik et al., 1981). These electrophysiological and isotope studies provide evidence for a special role of the right hemisphere in attention and may also help explain why inattention is more often caused by right hemisphere lesions.

Arousal

We have studied arousal in patients with right or left temporoparietal lesions, using the galvanic skin response to electrical stimulation of the hand ipsilateral to the lesion as a measure of arousal. Patients with right temporoparietal lesions responded poorly and those with left temporoparietal lesions responded well (Heilman et al., 1978). We also compared the EEG from the nonlesioned hemisphere of awake patients with right or left temporoparietal infarctions. Patients with right-sided lesions showed more theta and delta activity over their nonlesioned hemisphere than did the patients with left-side lesions (Heilman et al., in preparation). Both of these studies suggest that the right hemisphere may have a special role in attention and in mediating arousal.

Intention

Patients with right hemisphere lesions more often have contralateral limb akinesia than patients with left hemisphere lesions (Coslett and Heilman, 1984). Hypokinesia, however, is not always limited to the contralateral extremities. Although patients with cerebral lesions confined to a single hemisphere have slower reaction times with the hand contralateral to a lesion than with the hand ipsilateral to a lesion, they also have slower reaction times using the hand ipsilateral to the lesion than do nonlesioned controls using the same hand (Benton and Joynt, 1959). Lawrence and Kuypers (1968) showed that there is ipsilateral as well as contralateral motor control of an extremity. However, the ipsilateral control is limited mainly to the proximal musculature. Since reaction times are performed by distal musculature, the ipsilateral slowing revealed by Benton and Joynt's reaction task cannot be completely explained by a motor defect.

De Renzi and Faglioni (1965) also used a simple reaction time task to study patients with unilateral cerebral lesions. Although lesions of either hemisphere slowed the reaction times of the hand ipsilateral to the lesion, right hemisphere lesions caused greater slowing than left hemisphere lesions. De Renzi and Faglioni (1965) proposed that reaction time slowing is proportional to the extent and severity of a cerebral lesion, without respect to its focus. They thought that right hemisphere lesions would usually be larger than left hemisphere lesions, since the aphasia associated with small left hemisphere lesions would more likely bring the patient to medical attention. Subsequently, Howes and Boller (1975) confirmed that patients with right hemisphere lesions had slower reaction times, but found that the right hemisphere lesions associated with these deficits were not larger than the left hemisphere lesions. Although Howes and Boller alluded to a loss of topographical sense as perhaps being responsible, they did not draw any conclusions about why right hemisphere lesions produced slower reaction times. They did note, however, that the right parietal lobe lesions appeared to induce the most profound slowing. Unfortunately, they did not mention whether the patients with profound ipsilateral slowing had unilateral neglect.

In monkeys, no hemispheric asymmetries in the production of the neglect syndrome have been noted; however, we (Valenstein et al., in preparation) found that monkeys with lesions inducing neglect had slower ipsilateral reaction times than monkeys with equal-sized lesions that did not induce neglect.

It has been shown that warning stimuli may prepare an individual for action and thereby reduce reaction times (Lansing, et al., 1959). Pribram and McGuiness (1975) used the term "activation" to define the physiological readiness to respond to environmental stimuli. Because patients with right hemisphere lesions have been shown to have reduced behavioral evidence of activation (Howes and Boller, 1975), we have postulated that in humans the right hemisphere may dominate in mediating the activation process. That is, the left hemisphere prepares the right extremities for action and the right prepares both. Therefore, with left-sided lesions, left-side limb akinesia is minimal, but with right-sided lesions there is severe left-limb akinesia. In addition, because the right hemisphere is more involved than the left hemisphere in activating the right extremities with right hemisphere lesions, there will be more ipsilateral hypokinesia than with left hemisphere lesions.

If the right hemisphere dominates mediation of activation or intention (physiological readiness to respond), normal subjects may show more activation (measured behaviorally by the reaction time) with warning stimuli delivered to the right hemisphere than with warning stimuli delivered to the left hemisphere. We therefore gave normal subjects lateralized warning stimuli followed by central reaction time stimuli. Warning stimuli projected to the right hemisphere reduced reaction times of the right hand more than warning stimuli projected to the left hemisphere reduced left-hand reaction times. Warning stimuli projected to the right hemisphere reduced reaction times of the right hand even more than did warning stimuli projected directly to the left hemisphere. These results support the hypothesis that the right hemisphere dominates activation (Heilman and Van Den Abell, 1979).

Hemispatial Neglect

Gainotti et al. (1972), Albert (1973), and Costa et al. (1969) have shown that hemispatial neglect is more frequent or more severe or both with right-sided lesions than with left-sided lesions. In the preceding sections we have discussed some of the mechanisms that may underlie hemispatial neglect. It is difficult to understand how the representational map or body schema hypotheses, by themselves, can explain the asymmetries of hemispatial neglect. The right hemisphere has a special role in vis-uoperceptive, visuospatial, and visuoconstructive processes (see Chap. 8, for a review), and several authors (McFie et al., 1950; Albert, 1973) have proposed that the asymmetries of hemispatial neglect are related to disorders of these processes.

Kinsbourne (1970) proposed that language-induced left hemisphere activation makes neglect more evident with right than with left hemisphere lesions. Behavioral and psychophysiological studies have shown that language may induce left hemisphere activation (Kinsbourne, 1974; Bowers and Heilman, 1976). Patients are usually tested for hemispatial neglect using verbal instructions, and, not being aphasic, they usually think and communicate verbally. To test Kinsbourne's hypothesis, we (Heilman and Watson, 1978) presented patients with left-sided hemispatial neglect a crossing-out task in which the subject was asked either to cross out words or to cross out lines oriented in a specific direction (e.g., horizontal). In the verbal condition the target words were mixed with two others that were foils, and in the visuospatial condition the target lines were mixed with other lines (e.g., vertical and diagonal) that acted as foils. All the subjects tested crossed out more lines and went farther to the left on the paper in the nonverbal condition than in the verbal condition, thereby giving partial support to Kinsbourne's hypothesis.

One mechanism proposed to explain hemispatial neglect is that it could be induced by hemispatial or directional akinesia (see *Mechanisms Underlying Hemispatial Neglect*, page 271). In the preceding section, we postulated that the right hemisphere is dominant for intention—that is, it is capable of physiologically preparing both arms for action, whereas the left hemisphere can prepare only the right arm for action. That hemispatial neglect occurs more often after right hemisphere lesions may also be explained by a similar phenomenon, namely that the right hemisphere can physiologically prepare the extremities to work in (or toward) either right or left hemispace, but the left hemisphere can only activate the extremities to work in (or toward) right hemispace. Therefore, with left hemisphere lesions the right hemisphere can activate the extremities to work in (or toward) either hemispace, and hemispatial neglect is not a prominent symptom; however, with right hemisphere lesions the left hemisphere can only activate the extremities to work in (or toward) right hemispace; therefore, profound neglect occurs.

De Renzi et al. (1982) noted more frequent conjugate gaze paresis following right hemisphere lesions than left. He postulated that the oculomotor centers are more focal on the right than the left. This phenomenon, however, could also be explained by a mechanism similar to that which we postulated to explain asymmetries of hemispatial neglect.

NEUROPATHOLOGY OF NEGLECT

Neglect in man can accompany lesions in the following areas: (1) inferior parietal lobule (Critchley, 1966); (2) dorsolateral frontal lobe (Heilman and Valenstein, 1972); (3) cingulate gyrus (Heilman and Valenstein, 1972); (4) neostriatum (Heir et al., 1977); (5) thalamus (Watson and Heilman, 1978). On the basis of CT scan localization,

Heilman, Watson, and Valenstein (1983) concluded that neglect is probably seen most frequently after temporoparietal lesions.

The most common cause of neglect from cortical lesions is cerebral infarction (from either a thrombosis or embolus) and the most common cause of subcortical neglect is intracerebral hemorrhage. Neglect can also be seen with tumors. Rapidly growing malignant tumors (e.g., metastic or glioblastoma) are more likely to produce neglect than slowly growing tumors. It is unusual to see neglect as the result of a degenerative disease, because the degeneration is most often bilateral and insidious. However, the akinesia often seen with these diseases may be bilateral neglect (Heilman and Valenstein, 1972; Watson et al., 1973) which we believe is the cause of akinetic mutism. We have also seen a transient neglect syndrome as a postical phenomenon in a patient with idiopathic right temporal-lobe seizures, and the transient bilateral akinesia seen with other types of seizures may also be induced by similar mechanisms (Watson et al., 1974). Neglect may also be seen after unilateral (right) ECT (Sackeim, personal communication, 1983).

RECOVERY OF FUNCTION AND TREATMENT

Natural History

Some patients demonstrate a characteristic acute syndrome after a cerebral infarction: they have neglect of their extremities, limb akinesia, profound inattention or an allesthetic response, hemispatial neglect, head-and-eye deviation, and an explicit (verbal) denial of illness. In a period of weeks to months, profound inattention and allesthesia abate but extinction can be demonstrated with bilateral simultaneous stimulation. Hemispatial neglect also diminishes and, although an explicit denial of illness disappears, patients continue to show a flattening of affect and anosodiaphoria. Extinction, emotional flattening, and anosodiaphoria may persist for years. In our experience akinesia is the most persistent disabling aspect of neglect.

Unlike humans, who recover from the neglect syndrome slowly and often incompletely, monkeys rarely show evidence of neglect after one month. The neural mechanisms underlying this recovery are poorly understood. One hypothesis is that the undamaged hemisphere plays a role in recovery. It may receive sensory information from the side of the body opposite the lesion, either via ipsilateral sensory pathways, or from the damaged hemisphere via the corpus callosum. The uninjured hemisphere might also enhance the injured hemisphere's ability to attend to contralateral sensory information, and to initiate contralateral limb movements. If the uninjured hemisphere is processing sensorimotor information delivered from the injured hemisphere or enhancing the injured hemisphere's capacity to process sensorimotor activity, then a corpus callosum transection should worsen symptoms of neglect. Crowne et al. (1981) showed that neglect from frontal arcuate gyrus ablations was worse if the corpus callosum was simultaneously transected than if the callosum was intact. Watson et al. (1983) showed that monkeys receiving a frontal arcuate gyrus ablation several months after a corpus callosum transection also had worse neglect than animals with intact callosums. These results suggest that the hemispheres are mutually excitatory or compensatory through the corpus callosum.

Although callosal section worsened the severity of neglect, both groups of investigators found that it did not influence the rate of recovery. Subjects with callosal transections recovered completely. This suggests that recovery is an intrahemispheric process. If the intact hemisphere is responsible for the recovery, then a callosal transection after recovery should not reinstate neglect. Crowne et al. (1981) did reinstate neglect in three animals undergoing corpus callosum transections after recovering from neglect induced by frontal arcuate gyrus lesions. It is possible, however, that extra-callosal damage might be responsible for reinstating neglect. We have followed this order of lesions in one animal without inducing neglect. Furthermore, if the intact hemisphere is responsible for recovery in an animal with divided hemispheres then this recovery would have to be mediated through ipsilateral pathways. We have made a unilateral spinal cord lesion to interrupt ipsilateral sensory pathways in one of our recovered subjects without reinstating neglect. Our observations suggest that recovery is occurring within the injured hemisphere.

Hughlings Jackson (1932) postulated that certain functions could be mediated at several levels of the nervous system (hierarchical representation). Lesions of higher areas (e.g., cortex) would release phylogenetically more primitive areas which may take over the function of the lesioned cortical areas. Perhaps after cortical lesions disrupt the corticolimbic-reticular loop, a subcortical area takes over function and is responsible for mediating responses. Ideally, the area which substitutes for the lesioned area must have similar characteristics to the areas which, when lesioned, produce neglect. It must have multimodal afferent input, and must not only have reticular connections but also be capable of inducing activation with stimulation. Lastly, ablation of this area should induce the neglect syndrome, even if transient. The superior colliculus not only receives optic fibers but also receives somesthetic projections from the spinotectal tract (Sprague and Meikle, 1965) and fibers from the medial and lateral lemnisci and from the inferior colliculus (Truex and Carpenter, 1964). Sprague and Meikle believe that the colliculus is more than a reflex center controlling eye movements. They think it is a sensory integrative center. Tectoreticular fibers project to the mesencephalic reticular formation and ipsilateral fibers are more abundant than contralateral fibers (Truex and Carpenter, 1964). Stimulation of the colliculus (like stimulation of the arcuate gyrus or the inferior parietal lobe) produces an arousal response (Jefferson, 1958). Unilateral lesions of the superior colliculus produce a multimodal unilateral neglect syndrome, and combined cortical-collicular lesions produce a more profound disturbance regardless of the order of removal (Sprague and Meikle, 1965). Therefore, it is possible that in the absence of the corticoreticular loop, a collicular-reticular loop, or a similar subcortical system, takes over function.

Unlike cortical lesions in monkeys, some subcortical lesions of ascending dopamine projections in rats induce permanent neglect (Marshall, 1982). The severity and persistence of neglect induced by 6-hydroxydopamine injections into the ventral tegmental area (VTA) of rats is correlated with the amount of striatal dopamine depletion: those with more than 95% loss of striatal dopamine have a permanent deficit. The extent of recovery of these animals is also directly related to the quantity of neostriatal dopamine present at sacrifice. Nonrecovered rats show pronounced contralateral turning after injections of apomorphine, a dopamine receptor stimulant.

Recovered rats given methyl-*p*-tyrosine, a catecholamine synthesis inhibitor, or spiroperidol, a dopamine receptor blocking agent, had their deficits reappear. These results suggest that a restoration of dopaminergic activity in dopamine-depleted rats is sufficient to reinstate orientation (Marshall, 1979). Further investigation of these findings indicates that a proliferation of dopamine receptors may contribute to pharmacological supersensitivity and recovery of function (Neve et al., 1982). Finally, implanting dopaminergic neurons from the ventral tegmental area of fetal rats adjacent to the ipsilesional striatum will induce recovery in rats having unilateral neglect from a 6-hydroxydopamine lesion in the ascending dopamine tracts (Dunnett et al., 1981). This recovery is related to growth of dopamine-containing neurons into the partially denervated striatum.

(^{14}C) 2-deoxy-O-glucose (2-DG) incorporation permits a measure of metabolic activity. In rats with 6-OHDA lesions of the VTA that had shown no recovery from neglect, the uptake of (^{14}C)-2-DG into the neostriatum, nucleus accumbens septi, olfactory tubercle, and central amygdaloid nucleus was significantly less on the denervated side than on the normal side. Rats recovering by 6 weeks showed equivalent (^{14}C)-2-DG uptake in the neostriatum and central amygdaloid nucleus on the two sides. Recovery is therefore associated with normalization of neostriatal metabolic activity (Kozlowski and Marshall, 1981).

Similar results have been found in monkeys recovering from frontal arcuate gyrus induced neglect (Deuel et al., 1979). Animals with neglect showed depression of (^{14}C)-2-DG in ipsilateral subcortical structures including the thalamus and basal ganglia. Recovery from neglect occurred concomitantly with a reappearance of symmetrical metabolic activity.

It is possible that cortical lesions in animals induce only transient neglect because these lesions affect only a small portion of a critical neurotransmitter system. Critically placed small subcortical lesions, on the other hand, can virtually destroy all of a transmitter system, and can cause a permanent syndrome.

Recovery from cortically induced neglect might also depend on the influence of cortical lesions on subcortical structures. It is likely that just as certain homologous cortical structures are thought to be mutually inhibitory via the corpus callosum, certain pairs of subcortical structures may also be mutually inhibitory. For example, in the study of Watson et al. (1983) a prior corpus callosal lesion worsened neglect from a frontal arcuate lesion. Although this could be explained by loss of an excitatory or compensatory influence from the normal frontal arcuate region on the lesioned hemisphere, it could also be interpreted as a loss of excitation from cortex on a subcortical structure such as the basal ganglia, that in turn inhibits the contralateral basal ganglia. The latter is supported by a study showing that anterior callosal section in rats enhances the normal striatal dopamine asymmetry and increases amphetamine-induced turning (Glick et al., 1975). In addition, Sprague (1966) showed that the loss of visually guided behavior in the field contralateral to occipitotemporal lesions in cats could be restored by a contralateral superior colliculus removal or by transection of the collicular commissure. The only way to explain this observation is to assume that the superior colliculi are mutually inhibitory.

The two hemispheres are clearly cooperating in our daily activities. However, it appears that recovery from a central nervous system insult can occur within the injured hemisphere. For the neglect syndrome this may be secondary to alteration in dopamine systems. An understanding of interhemispheric cortical and subcortical interactions, and intrahemispheric cortical and subcortical interactions in the normal state and during recovery of function, is one of the most intriguing aspects of the neglect syndrome and holds great promise for pharmacological and possibly even surgical intervention in this syndrome.

Treatment

The neglect syndrome is a behavioral manifestation of underlying cerebral disease. The evaluation and treatment of the underlying disease is of primary importance.

There are several things that can be done to manage the symptoms of the neglect syndrome. The patient with neglect should have his bed placed so that his "good" side faces the area where interpersonal actions are most likely to take place. When he must interact with people or things, these interactions should take place on his good side. When discharged home, his environment should be adjusted in a similar manner. So long as a patient has the neglect syndrome, he should not be allowed to drive or work with anything that, if neglected, will induce injury to himself or others.

During the acute stages when patients have anosagnosia, rehabilitation is difficult; however, in most patients, this symptom is transient. In addition, because patients with neglect remain inattentive to their left side and in general are poorly motivated, training is laborious and in many cases nonrewarding; however, Diller and Weinberg (1977) were able to train patients with neglect to look to their neglected side.

It is hoped that in the future neuropharmacological or electrophysiological means may be used in treating these behavioral disorders; however, at present, operant conditioning and similar behavioral modification paradigms are the best hope of giving patients relief from this behaviorally devastating syndrome.

REFERENCES

Akert, K. and Von Monakow, K. H. (1980). Relationship of precentral, premotor, and prefrontal cortex to the mediodorsal and intralaminar nuclei of the monkey thalamus. *Acta Neurobiologiae Experimentalis (Warszawa)* 40:7–25.

Albert, M. C. (1973). A simple test of visual neglect. *Neurology* 23:658–664.

Anderson, M. and Yoshida, M. (1977). Electrophysiological evidence for branching nigral projections to the thalamus and the superior colliculus. *Brain Res.* 137:361–364.

Anzola, G. P., Bertoloni, A., Buchtel, H. A., and Rizzolatti, G. (1977). Spatial compatibility and anatomical factors in simple and choice reaction time. *Neuropsychologia* 15:295–302.

Arbuthnott, G. W. and Ungerstedt, U. (1975). Turning behavior induced by electircal stimulation of the nigro-striatal system of the rat. *Experimental Neurology* 47:162–172.

Avemo, A., Antelman, S., and Ungerstedt, U. (1973). Rotational behavior after unilateral frontal cortex lesions in the rat. *Acta Physiol. Scand. Suppl. (Abstr.)* 396:77

Babinski, J. (1914). Contribution à l'étude des troubles mentaux dans l'hémiplégie organique cerebrale (agnosognosie). *Rev. Neurol.* 27:845–847.

Baleydier, C. and Mauguiere, F. (1980). The duality of the cingulate gyrus in monkey—neuroanatomical study and functional hypothesis. *Brain 103*:525–554.

Battersby, W. S., Bender, M. B., and Pollack, M. (1956). Unilateral spatial agnosia (inattention) in patients with cerebral lesions. *Brain 79*:68–93.

Bender, M. B. (1952). *Disorders of Perception.* Springfield, Ill.: C. C. Thomas.

Bender, M. B. and Furlow, C. T. (1944). Phenomenon of visual extinction and binocular rivalry mechanism. *Trans. Am. Neurol. Assoc. 70*:87–93.

Bender, M. B. and Furlow, C. T. (1945). Phenomenon of visual extinction on homonymous fields and psychological principles involved. *Arch. Neurol. Psychiat. 53*:29–33.

Benson, F. and Geschwind, N. (1969). The alexias. In *Handbook of Neurology,* Vol. 4, P. J. Vinken and G. W. Bruyn (eds.) Amsterdam: North Holland.

Benton, A. L. and Joynt, R. J. (1959). Reaction times in unilateral cerebral disease. *Confinia Neurologica 19*:147–256.

Benton, A. L. and Levin, H. S. (1972). An experimental study of obscuration. *Neurology 22*:1176–1181.

Bianchi, L. (1895). The functions of the frontal lobes. *Brain 18*:497–522.

Bignall, K. E. and Imbert, M. (1969). Polysensory and cortico-cortical projections to frontal lobe of squirrel and rhesus monkey. *Electroenceph. Clin. Neurophys. 26*:206–215.

Birch, H. G., Belmont, I., and Karp, E. (1967). Delayed information processing and extinction following cerebral damage. *Brain 90*:113–130.

Bisiach, E. and Luzzatti, C. (1978). Unilateral neglect of representational space. *Cortex 14*:29–133.

Bisiach, E., Luzzatti, C., and Perani, D. (1979). Unilateral neglect, representational schema and consciousness. *Brain 102*:609–618.

Bowers, D. and Heilman, K. M. (1976). Material specific hemispheric arousal. *Neuropsychologia 14*:123–127.

Bowers, D., Heilman, K. M., and Van Den Abell, T. (1981). Hemispace-visual half field compatibility. *Neuropsychologia 19*:757–765.

Bowers, D. and Heilman, K. M. (1980). Effects of hemispace on tactile line bisection task. *Neuropsychologia 18*:491–498.

Bradley, P. B. (1968). The effect of atropine and related drugs on the EEG and behavior. *Progr. Brain Res. 28*:3–13.

Brain, W. R. (1941). Visual disorientation with special reference to lesions of the right cerebral hemisphere. *Brain 64*:224–272.

Brown, R. M., Crane, A. M., and Goldman, P. S. (1979). Regional distribution of monoamines in the cerebral cortex and subcortical structures of the rhesus monkey: concentrations and in vivo synthesis rates. *Brain Res. 168*:133–150.

Bushnell, M. C., Goldberg, M. E., and Robinson, D. L. (1981). Behavioral enhancement of visual responses in monkey cerebral cortex: I. Modulation in posterior parietal cortex related to selected visual attention. *J. Neurophys. 46*:755–772.

Chavis, D. A. and Pandya, D. N. (1976). Further observations on corticofrontal connections in the rhesus monkey. *Brain Res. 117*:369–386.

Corbett, D. and Wise, R. A. (1980). Intracranial self-stimulation in relation to the ascending dopaminergic systems of the midbrain: moveable electrode mapping study. *Brain Res. 185*:1–15.

Corrodi, H., Farnebo, L.-O., Fuxe, K., Hamberger, B., and Ungerstedt, U. (1972). ET495 and brain catecholamine mechanisms: evidence for stimulation of dopamine receptors. *Eur. Pharmacol. 20*:195–204.

Coslett, H. B. and Heilman, K. M. (1984). Hemihypokinesia following right hemisphere stroke. *Neurology 34*, Suppl. 1:190.

Costa, L. D., Vaughan, H. G., Horwitz, M., and Ritter, W. (1969). Patterns of behavior deficit asociated with visual spatial neglect. *Cortex* 5:242–263.

Critchley, M. (1966). *The Parietal Lobes.* New York: Hafner.

Crossman, A. R., Sambrook, M. A., Gergies, S. W., and Slater, P. (1977). The neurological basis of motor asymmetry following unilateral 6-hydroxydopamine lesions in the rat: the effect of motor decortication. *J. Neurol. Sci.* 34:407–414.

Crowe, D. P., Yeo, C H., and Russell, I. S. (1981). The effects of unilateral frontal eye field lesions in the monkey: visual-motor guidance and avoidance behavior. *Behav. Brain Res.* 2:165–185.

Dalsass, M. and Krauthamer, G. M. (1981). Behavioral alterations and loss of caudate modulation in the CM-PF complex of the cat after electrolytic lesions of the substantia nigra. *Brain Res.* 208:67–79.

De Renzi, E., Colombo, A., Faglioni, P., and Gilbertoni, M. (1982). Conjugate gaze paralysis in stroke patients with unilateral damage. *Arch. Neurol.* 39:482–486.

De Renzi, E., Faglioni, P., and Scotti, G. (1970). Hemispheric contribution to the exploration of space through the visual and tactile modality. *Cortex* 6:191–203.

De Renzi, E. and Faglioni, P. (1965). The comparative efficiency of intelligence and vigilance test detecting hemispheric change. *Cortex* 1:410–433.

Denny-Brown, D. and Banker, B. Q. (1954). Amorphosynthesis from left parietal lesions. *Arch. Neurol. Psychiat.* 71:302–313.

Deuel, R. K. (1980). Sensorimotor dysfunction after unilateral hypothalamic lesions in rhesus monkeys. *Neurology* 30:358.

Deuel, R. K., Collins, R. C., Dunlop, N., and Caston, T. V. (1979). Recovery from unilateral neglect: behavioral and functional anatomic correlations in monkeys. *Society of Neuroscience (Abstr.)* 5:624.

Diller, L. and Weinberg, J. (1977). Hemi-inattention in rehabilitation: the evolution of a rational remediation program. In *Advances in Neurology,* Vol. 18, E. A. Weinstein and R. P. Friedland (eds). New York: Raven Press.

Divac, I., Fonnum, F., and Storm-Mathisen, J. (1977). High affinity uptake of glutamate in terminals of corticostriatal axons. *Nature (London)* 266:377–378.

Dunnet, S. B., Bjorklund, A., Stenevi, U., and Iversen, S. D. (1981). Behavioral recovery following transplantation of substantia nigra in rats subjected to 6-OHDA lesions of the nigrostriatal pathway. I. Unilateral lesions. *Brain Res.* 215:147–161.

Eidelberg, E. and Schwartz, A. J. (1971). Eperimental analysis of the extinction phenomenon in monkeys. *Brain* 94:91–108.

Feeney, D. M. and Wier, C. S. (1979). Sensory neglect after lesions of substantia nigra or lateral hypothalamus: differential severity and recovery of function. *Brain Res.* 178:329–346.

Filion, M., Lamarre, Y., and Cordeau, J. P. (1971). Neuronal discharges of the ventrolateral nucleus of the thalamus during sleep and wakefulness in the cat. Evoked activity. *Exp. Brain Res.* 12:499–508.

Fonnum, F. and Walaas, I. (1979). Localization of neurotransmitter candidates in neostriatum. In *The Neostriatum,* I. Divac and R. G. E. Oberg (eds). Oxford: Pergamon Press, pp. 53–69.

Furmanski, A. R. (1950). The phenomena of sensory suppression. *AMA Arch. Neurol. Psychiat.* 63:205–217.

Gainotti, G. and Tiacci, C. (1971). The relationships between disorders of visual perception and unilateral spatial neglect. *Neuropsychologia* 9:451–458.

Gainotti, G. Messerli, P., and Tissot, R. (1972). Qualitative analysis of unilateral spatial neglect in relation to laterality of cerebral lesions. *J. Neurol. Neurosurg. Psychiat.* 35:545–550.

Glick, S. D. (1972). Changes in amphetamine sensitivity following frontal cortical damage in rats and mice. *Eur. J. Pharmacol. 20*:351–356.

Glick, S. D., Crane, A. M., Jerussi, T. P., Fleisher, L. N., and Green, J. P. (1975). Functional and neurochemical correlates of potentiation of striatal asymmetry by callosal section. *Nature 254*:616–617.

Goldberg, M. E. and Busnell, M. C. (1981). Behavioral enhancement of visual responses in monkey cerebral cortex: II. Modulation in frontal eye fields specifically related to saccades. *J. Neurophysiol. 46*:773–787.

Goldberg, M. E. and Robinson, D. C. (1977). Visual responses of neurons in monkey inferior parietal lobule. The physiological substrate of attention and neglect. *Neurology (Abstr.) 27*:350.

Grofova, I. (1979). Extrinsic connections of the neostriatum. In *The Neostriatum*, I. Divak and R. G. E. Oberg (eds). Oxford: Pergamon Press, pp. 37–51.

Grossman, S. P., Dacey, D., Halaris, A.E., Collier, T., and Routtenberg, A. (1978). Aphagia and adipsia after preferential destruction of nerve cell bodies in hypothalamus. *Science 202*:537–539.

Guyenet, P., Euvrard, C., Javoy, F., Hebet, A., and Glowinski, J. (1977). Regional differences in the sensitivity of cholinergic neurons to dopaminergic drugs and quipazine in the rat striatum. *Brain Res. 136*:487–500.

Hagamen, T. C., Greeley, H. P., Hagamen, W. D., and Reeves, A. G. (1977). Behavioral asymmetries following olfactory tubercle lesions in cats. *Brain Behav. Evol. 14*:241–250.

Heikkila, R. E., Shapiro, B. S., and Duvoisin, R. C. (1981). The relationship between loss of dopamine nerve terminals, striatal ^{3}H spiroperidol binding and rotational behavior in unilaterally 6-hydroxydopamine-lesioned rats. *Brain Res. 211*:285–292.

Heilman, K. M. (1979). Neglect and related disorders. In *Clinical Neuropsychology*, K. M. Heilman and E. Valenstein (eds). New York: Oxford University Press, pp. 268–307.

Heilman, K. M., Bowers, D., Coslett, H. B., and Watson, R. T. (1983). Directional hypokinesia in neglect. *Neurology Suppl. 2,33*:104.

Heilman, K. M., Bowers, D., Valenstein, E., and Watson, R. T. (1981). A nonvisual test for hemispatial neglect. *Neurology* (Abstr. Part 2) 83.

Heilman, K. M., Bowers, D., and Watson, R. T. (1982). Pseudoneglect in a callosally disconnected patient. *Ann. Neurol. 12*:96 (Abstract).

Heilman, K. M. and Howell, F. (1980). Seizure-induced neglect. *J. Neurol. Neurosurg. Psychiat. 43*:1035–1040.

Heilman, K. M., Odenheimer, G. L., Watson, R. T., and Valenstein, E. (1984). Extinction of non-touch. *Neurology 34*, Suppl. 1:188.

Heilman, K. M., Pandya, D. N., and Geschwind, N. (1970). Trimodal inattention following parietal lobe ablations. *Trans. Am. Neurol. Assoc. 95*:259–261.

Heilman, K. M., Schwartz, H. D., and Watson, R. T. (1978). Hypoarousal in patients with the neglect syndrome and emotional indifference. *Neurology 28*:229–232.

Heilman, K. M. and Valenstein, E. (1972). Frontal lobe neglect in man. *Neurology 22*:660–664.

Heilman, K. M. and Valenstein, E. (1979). Mechanisms underlying hemispatial neglect. *Ann. Neurol. 5*:166–170.

Heilman, K. M., Valenstein, E., and Watson, R. T. (1983). Localization of neglect. In *Localization in Neuropsychology*, A. Kertesz (ed). New York: Academic Press, pp. 471–492.

Heilman, K. M. and Van Den Abell, T. (1979). Right hemispheric dominance for mediating cerebral activation. *Neuropsychologia 17*:315–321.

Heilman, K. M. and Van Den Abell, T. (1980). Right hemisphere dominance for attention: the mechanisms underlying hemispheric asymmetries of inattention (neglect). *Neurology 30*:327–330.

Heilman, K. M. and Watson, R. T. (1978). Changes in the symptoms of neglect induced by changes in task strategy. *Arch. Neurol.* 35:47–49.

Heilman, K. M., Watson, R. T., and Schulman, H. (1974). A unilateral memory defect. *J. Neurol. Neurosurg. Psychiat.* 37:790–793.

Heir, D. B., Davis, K. R., Richardson, E. T. et al. (1977). Hypertensive putaminal hemorrhage. *Ann. Neurol.* 1:152–159.

Herkenham, M. (1979). The afferent and efferent connections of the ventromedial thalamic nucleus in the rat. *J. Comp. Neurol.* 183:487–518.

Holmes, G. (1918). Disturbances of vision of cerebral lesions. *Br. J. Ophthalmol.* 2:353–384.

Howes, D. and Boller, F. (1975). Evidence for focal impairment from lesions of the right hemisphere. *Bran* 98:317–332.

Hoyman, L., Weese, G. D., and Frommer, G. P. (1979). Tactile discrimination performance deficits following neglect-producing unilateral lateral hypothalamic lesions in the rat. *Physiol. Behav.* 22:139–147.

Hyvarinen, J. and Poranen, A. (1974). Function of the parietal associative area 7 as revealed from cellular discharge in alert monkeys. *Brain* 97:673–692.

Iverson, S. D., Wilkinson, S., and Simpson, B. (1971). Enhanced amphetamine responses after frontal cortex lesions in the rat. *Eur. J. Phrmacol.* 13:387–390.

Iwamoto, E. T., Loh, H. H., and Way, E. L. (1976). Circling behavior in rats with 6-hydroxy-dopamine or electrolytic nigral lesions. *Eur. J. Pharmacol.* 37:339–356.

Jackson, J. Hughlings (1932). *Selected Writings of John Hughlings Jackson*, J. Taylor (ed). London: Hodder and Stoughton.

Jacobs, B. L. and Jones, B. E. (1978). The role of central monoamine and acetylcholine systems in sleep wakefulness states. Mediation or modulation? In: *Cholinerigic-Monoaminergic Interactions of the Brain*, I. I. Butcher (ed). New York: Academic Press, pp. 271–290.

James, W. (1890) *The Principles of Psychology*, Vol. 2. New York: Holt.

Jasper, H. H. (1949). Diffuse projection systems: The integrative action of the thalamic reticular system. *Electroencephalography Clin. Neurophysiol.* 1:405–419.

Jefferson, G. (1958). Substrates for integrative patterns in the reticular core. In *Reticular Formation*, M. E. Scheibel and A. B. Scheibel (eds). Boston: Little, Brown.

Jerussi, T. P. and Glick, S. D. (1976). Drug-induced rotation in rats without lesions: behavioral and neurochemical indices of a normal asymmetry in nigrostriatal function. *Psychopharmacologia (Berlin)* 47:249–260.

Jouvet, M. (1977). Neuropharmacology of the sleep waking cycle. In: *Handbook of Psychopharmacology*, L. L. Iverson, S. D. Iverson and S. H. Snyder (eds). New York: Plenum Press, pp. 233–293.

Kanai, T. and Szerb, J. C. (1965). Mesencephalic reticular activating system and cortical acethylcholine output. *Nature* 205:80–82.

Kennard, M. A. and Ectors, L. (1938). Forced circling movements in monkeys following lesions of the frontal lobes. *J. Neurophys.* 1:45–54.

Kievet, J. and Kuypers, H. G. J. M. (1977). Organization of the thalamo-cortical connections to the frontal lobe in the rhesus monkey. *Exp. Brain Res.* 29:299–322.

Kimura, D. (1967). Function asymmetry of the brain in dichotic listening. *Cortex* 3:163–178.

Kinsbourne, M. (1970). A model for the mechanism of unilateral neglect of space. *Trans. Am. Neurol. Assoc.* 95:143.

Kinbourne, M. (1974). Direction of gaze and distribution of cerebral thought processes. *Neuropsychologia* 12:270–281.

Kozlowski, M. R. and Marshall, J. F. (1981). Plasticity of neostriatal metabolic activity and behavioral recovery from nigrostriatal injury. *Exp. Neurol.* 74:313–323.

Kuypers, H. G. J. M. and Lawrence, D. G. (1967). Cortical projections to the red nucleus and the brain stem in the rhesus monkey. *Brain Res.* 4:151–188.

Lansing, R. W., Schwartz, E., and Lindsley, D. B. (1959). Reaction time and EEG activation under alerted and nonalerted conditions. *J. Exp. Psychol.* 58:1–7.

Lindvall, O., Bjorklund, A., Morre, R. Y., and Stenevi, U. (1974). Mesencephalic dopamine-neurons projecting to neocortex. *Brain Res.* 81:325–331.

Ljungberg, T. and Ungerstedt, U. (1976). Sensory inattention produced by 6-hydroxydopamine-induced degeneration of ascending dopamine neurons in the brain. *Exp. Neurol.* 53:585–600.

Loeb, J. (1885). Die elementaren storunger eirfacher functionennach oberflachlicher umschriebener Verletzung des Grosshirns Pfluger's. *Arch f. Physiologie* 37:51–56.

Lynch, G. S., Ballantine, P., and Campbell, B. A. (1969). Potentiation of behavioral arousal after cortical damage and subsequent recovery. *Exp. Neurol.* 23:195–206.

Lynch, J. C. (1980). The functional organization of posterior parietal assocation cortex. *Behav. Brain Sci.* 3:485–534.

Marshall, J. F. (1979). Somatosensory inattention after dopamine-depleting intracerebral 6-OHDA injections: spontaneous recovery and pharmacological control. *Brain Res.* 177:311–324.

Marshall, J. F. (1982). Neurochemistry of attention and attentional disorders. Annual course 214, Behavioral Neurology. Presented at the American Academy of Neurology, April 27, 1982.

Marshall, J. F., Turner, B. H., and Teitelbaum, P. (1971). Sensory neglect produced by lateral hypothalamic damage. *Science* 174:523–525.

Marshall, J. F., Richardson, J. S., and Teitelbaum, P. (1974). Nigrostriatal bundle damage and the lateral hypothalamic syndrome. *J. Comp. Physiol. Psychol.* 87:808–830.

Mason, S. T. and Iverson, S. (1979). Theories of the dorsal bundle extinction effect. *Brain Res. Rev.* 1:107–137.

McFie, J., Piercy, M. F., and Zangwill, O. L. (1950). Visual spatial agnosia associated with lesions of the right hemisphere. *Brain* 73:167–190.

Mehler, W. R. (1966). Further notes of the center median nucleus of Luys. In *The Thalamus*, D. P. Purpura, and M. D. Yahr (eds). New York: Columbia University Press, pp. 109–122.

Mesulam, M., Van Hoesen, G. W., Pandya, D. N., and Geschwind, N. (1977). Limbic and sensory connections of the inferior parietal lobule (area PG) in the rhesus monkey: a study with a new method for horseradish peroxidase histochemistry. *Brain Res.* 136:393–414.

Mills, R. P. and Swanson, P. D. (1978). Vertical oculomotor apraxia and memory loss. *Ann. Neurol.* 4:149–153.

Milner, B., Taylor, L., and Sperry, R. W. (1968). Lateralized suppression of dichotically presented digits after commissural section in man. *Science* 161:184–186.

Morelli, M., Imperato, A., Porceddu, M. L., and DiChiara, G. (1981). Role of dorsal mesencephalic reticular formation and deep layers of the superior colliculus in turning behavior elicited from the striatum. *Brain Res.* 215:337–341.

Moruzzi, G. and Magoun, H. W. (1949). Brainstem reticular formation and activation of the EEG. *Electroencephal. Clin. Neurophys.* 1:455–473.

Motter, B. C. and Mountcastle, V. B. (1981). The functional properties of the light senstive neurons of the posterior parietal cortex studied in waking monkeys: foveal sparing and opponent vector organization. *J. Neurosci.* 1:3–26.

Mountcastle, V. B., Anderson, R. A., and Motter, B. C. (1981). The influence of attentive fixation upon the excitability of the light sensitive neurons of the posterior parietal cortex. *J. Neurosci.* 1:1218–1245.

Mountcastle, V. B., Lynch, J. C., Georgopoulos, A., Sakata, H., and Acuna, C. (1975). Posterior parietal association cortex of the monkey: command function from operations within extrapersonal space. *J. Neurophys.* 38:871–908.

Nathan, P. W. (1946). On simultaneous bilateral stimulation of the body in a lesion of the parietal lobe. *Brain* 69:325–334.

Nauta, W. J. H. (1958). Hippocampal projections and related neural pathways to the midbrain in cat. *Brain* 81:319–339.

Nauta, W. J. H. (1961). Fiber degeneration following lesions of the amygdaloid complex in the monkey. *J. Anat.* 95:515–531.

Neve, K. A., Kozlowski, M. R., and Marshall, J. F. (1982). Plasticity of neostriatal dopamine receptors after nigrostriatal injury: relationship to recovery of sensorimotor functions and behavioral supersensitivity. *Brain Res.* 244:33–44.

Nieoullon, A., Cheramy, A., and Glowinski, J. (1978). Release of dopamine evoked by electrical stimulation of the motor and visual areas of the cerebral cortex in both caudate nuclei and in the substantia nigra in the cat. *Brain Research* 15:69–83.

Obersteiner, H. (1882). On allochiria—a peculiar sensory disorder *Brain* 4:153–163.

Olds, J. and Milner, P. (1954). Positive reinforcement produced by electrical stimulation of septal area and other regions of the rat brain. *J. Comp. Physiol. Psychol.* 47:419–427.

Olianas, M. C., DeMontis, G. M., Mulas, G., and Tagliamonte, A. (1978). The striatal dopaminergic function is mediated by the inhibition of a nigral, nondopaminergic system via a strio-nigral GABAergic pathway. *Eur. J. Pharmacol.* 49:233–241.

Oppenheim, H. (1885). Ueber eine durch eine klinisch bisher nicht verwertete Untersuchungs-methode ermittelte Form der Sensibilitats-storung bei einseitigen Erkrankungen des Grosshirns. *Nerol. Centrabl* 4;529–533. Cited by A. L. Benton (1956). Jacques Loeb and the method of double stimulation. *J. Hist. Med. Allied Sci.* 11:47–53.

Pandya, D. M. and Kuypers, H. G. J. M. (1969). Cortico-cortical connections in the rhesus monkey. *Brain Res.* 13:13–36.

Paterson, A. and Zangwill, O. L. (1944). Disorders of visual space perception associated with lesions of the right cerebral hemisphere. *Brain* 67:331–358.

Poppelreuter, W. L. (1917). Die psychischen Schadigungen durch Kopfschuss Krieg im 1914–1916: Die Storungen der niederen und hoheren Leistungen durch Verletzungen des Oksipitalhirns. Vol. 1, Leipzig: Leopold Voss. Referred to by M. Critchley, (1949). *Brain* 72:540.

Pribram, K. H. and McGuinness, D. (1975). Arousal, activation and effort in the control of attention. *Psychol. Rev.* 182:116–149.

Prohovnik, I., Risberg, J., Hagstadius, S., and Maximilian, V. (1981). *Cortical activity during unilateral tactile stimulation: a regional cerebral blood flow study.* Presented at the meeting of the International Neuropsychological Society, Atlanta, Georgia, February.

Purpura, D. P. (1970). Operations and processes in thalamic and synaptically related neural subsystems. In *The neurosciences, second study program,* F. O. Schmitt (Ed.-in-Chief). New York: Rockefeller University Press, pp. 458–470.

Pycock, C. J. (1980). Turning behavior in animals. *Neuroscience* 5:461–514.

Pycock, C. J., Kerwin, R. W., and Carter, C. J. (1980). Effect of lesions of cortical dopamine terminals of subcortical dopamine receptors in rats. *Nature* 286:74–77.

Reeves, A. G. and Hagamen, W. D. (1971). Behavioral and EEG asymmetry following unilateral lesions of the forebrain and midbrain of cats. *Electroenceph. Clin. Neurophys.* 30:83–86.

Reider, N. (1946). Phenomena of sensory suppression. *Arch. Neurol. Psychiat.* 55:583–590.

Riddoch, G. (1935). Visual disorientation in homonymous half-fields. *Brain* 58:376–382.

Robinson, D. L., Goldberg, M. E., and Stanton, G. B. (1978). Parietal association cortex in the primate: sensory mechanisms and behavioral modulations. *J. Neurophys. 41*:910–932.

Robinson, T. E., Vanderwolf, C. H., and Pappas, B. A. (1977). Are the dorsal noradrenergic bundle projections from the locus coeruleus important for neocortical or hippocampal activation? *Brain Res. 8*:75–98.

Rolls, E. T., Sanghera, M. K., and Roper-Hall, A. (1979). The latency of activation of neurones in the lateral hypothalamus and substantia innominata during feeding in the monkey. *Brain Res. 164*:121–135.

Rosen, A. D., Gur, R. C., Reivich, M., Alavi, A., and Greenberg, J. (1981). *Preliminary observation of stimulus-related arousal and glucose metabolism.* Presented at the meetings of the International Neuropsychological Society, Atlanta, Georgia, February.

Rosenberger, P. (1974). Discriminative aspects of visual hemi-inattention. *Neurology 24*:17–23.

Ross, E. D. and Stewart, R. M. (1981). Akinetic mutism from hypothalamic damage: successful treatment with dopamine agonists. *Neurology 31*:1435–1439.

Samuels, I., Butters, N., and Goodglass, H. (1971). Visual memory defects following cortical-limbic lesions: effect of field of presentation. *Physiol. Behav. 6*:447–452.

Schiebel, M. E. and Schiebel, A. B. (1967). Structural organization of nonspecific thalamic nuclei and their projection toward cortex. *Brain 6*:60–94.

Schiebel, M. E. and Schiebel, A. B. (1966). The organization of the nucleus reticularis thalami: a Golgi study. *Brain Res. 1*:43–62.

Schlag-Rey, M. and Schlag, J. (1980). Eye movement neurons in the thalamus of monkey. *Invest. Ophthal. Vis. Sci.* ARVO Supplement, 176.

Schwartz, A. S., Marchok, P. L., Kreinick, C. J., and Flynn, R. E. (1979). The asymmetric lateralization of tactile extinction in patients with unilateral cerebral dysfunction. *Brain 102*:669–684.

Sevush, S. and Heilman, K. M. (1981). Attentional factors in tactile extinction. Presented at a meeting of the International Neuropsychological Society, Atlanta, Georgia, February.

Shute, C. C. D. and Lewis, P. R. (1967). The ascending cholinergic reticular system, neocortical, olfactory and subcortical projections. *Brain 90*:497–520.

Singer, W. (1977). Control of thalamic transmission by corticofugal and ascending reticular pathways in the visual system. *Physiol. Rev. 57*:386–420.

Skinner, J. E. and Yingling, C. D. (1976). Regulation of slow potential shifts in nucleus reticularis thalami by the mesencephalic reticular formation and the frontal granular cortex. *Electroencephalography Clin. Neurophys. 40*:288–296.

Skinner, J. E. and Yingling, C. D. (1977). Central gating mechanisms that regulate event-related potentials and behavior—a neural model for attention. In J. E. Desmedt (ed). *Progress in Clinical Neurophysiology*, Vol. 1, New York: S. Karger, 30–69.

Sokolov, Y. N. (1963). *Perception and the Conditioned Reflex.* Oxford: Pergmon Press.

Sparks, R. and Geschwind, N. (1968). Dichotic listening in man after section of the neocortical commissures. *Cortex 4*:3–16.

Sprague, J. M. (1966). Interaction of cortex and superior colliculus in mediation of visually guided behavior in the cat. *Science 153*:1544–1547.

Sprague, J. M. and Meikle, T. H. (1965). The role of the superior colliculus in visually guided behavior. *Exp. Neurol. 11*:115–146.

Sprague, J. M., Chambers, W. W., and Stellar, E. (1961). Attentive, affective and adaptive behavior in the cat. *Science 133*:165–173.

Steriade, M. and Glenn, L. (1982). Neocortical and caudate projections of intralaminar thalamic neurons and their synaptic excitation from the midbrain reticular core. *J. Neurophys. 48*:352–370.

Teitelbaum, P. and Epstein, A. N. (1962). The lateral hypothalamic syndrome: recovery of feeding and drinking after lateral hypothalamic lesions. *Psychol. Rev. 69:*74–90.

Truex, R. C. and Carpenter, M.B. (1964). *Human Neuroanatomy.* Baltimore: Williams and Wilkins.

Ungerstedt, U. (1971a). Striatal dopamine release after amphetamine or nerve degeneration revealed by rotational behavior. *Acta Physiol. Scand. (Suppl. 367) 82:*49–68.

Ungerstedt, U. (1971b). Post-synaptic supersensitivity of 6-hydroxydopamine induced degeneration of the nigro-striatal dopamine system in the rat brain. *Acta Physiol. Scand. (Suppl. 367) 82:*69–93.

Ungerstedt, U. (1974). Brain dopamine neurons and behavior. In *The Neurosciences*, Vol. 3, F. O. Schmidt and F. G. Woren (eds). Cambridge, Mass.: MIT Press, pp. 695–703.

Ungerstedt, U. (1981). Stereotaxic mapping of the monoamine pathway in the rat brain. *Acta Physiol. Scand. (Suppl. 367) 82:*1–48.

Valenstein, E. and Heilman, K. M. (1978). Apraxic agraphia with neglect induced paragraphia. *Arch. Neurol. 36:*506–508.

Valenstein, E. and Heilman, K. M. (1981). Unilateral hypokinesia and motor extinction. *Neurology 31:*445–448.

Valenstein, E., Van Den Abell, T., Tankle, R., and Heilman, K. M. (1980). Apomorphine-induced turning after recovery from neglect induced by cortical lesions. *Neurology 30:*358 (abstr.).

Valenstein, E., Van Den Abell, T., Watson, R. T., and Heilman, K. M. (1982). Nonsensory neglect from parietotemporal lesions in monkeys. *Neurology 32:*1198–1201.

Vanderwolf, C. H. and Robinson, T. E. (1981). Reticulo-cortical activity and behavior: a critique of arousal theory and a new synthesis. *Behav. Brain Sci. 4:*459–514.

Velasco, F. and Velasco, M. (1979). A reticulothalamic system mediating proprioceptive attention and tremor in man. *Neurosurgery 4:*30–36.

Vogt, B. A., Rosene, D. L., and Pandya, D. N. (1979). Thalamic and cortical afferents differentiate anterior from posterior cingulate cortex in the monkey. *Science 204:*205–207.

Wagman, I. H. and Mehler, W. R. (1972). Physiology and anatomy of the cortico-oculomotor mechanism. *Progr. Brain Res. 37:*619–635.

Walter, W. G. (1973). Human frontal lobe function in sensory-motor association. In *Psychophysiology of the Frontal Lobes*, K. H. Pribram and A. R. Luria (eds). New York: Academic Press, pp. 109–122.

Watson, R. T. and Heilman, K. M. (1979). Thalamic neglect. *Neurology 29:*690–694.

Watson, R. T., Andriola, M., and Heilman, K. M. (1977). The EEG in neglect. *J. Neurol. Sci. 34:*343–348.

Watson, R. T., Heilman, K. M., Cauthen, J. C., and King, F. A. (1973). Neglect after cingulectomy. *Neurology 23:*1003–1007.

Watson, R. T., Heilman, K. M., Miller, B. D., and King, F. A. (1974). Neglect after mesencephalic reticular formation lesions. *Neurology 24:*294–298.

Watson, R. T., Miller, B., and Heilman, K. M. (1977). Evoked potential in neglect. *Arch. Neurol. 34:*224–227.

Watson, R. T., Miller, B. D., and Heilman, K. M. (1978). Nonsensory neglect. *Ann. Neurol. 3:*505–508.

Watson, R. T., Valenstein, E., and Heilman, K. M. (181). Thalamic neglect: the possible role of the medial thalamus and nucleus reticularis thalami in behavior. *Arch. Nurol. 38:*501–507.

Weinberger, N. M., Velasco, M., and Lindsley, D. B. (1965). Effects of lesions upon thalamically induced electrocortical desynchronization and recruiting. *Electroenceph. Clin. Neurophys. 18:*369–377.

Welch, K. and Stuteville, P. (1958). Experimental production of neglect in monkeys. *Brain* *81*:341–347.

Whittington, D. A. and Hepp-Reymond, M.-C. (1977). Eye and head movements to auditory targets. *Neurosci. Abstr.* *3*:158. (Abstracts of the 7th Annual Meeting of the Society of Neuroscience, November 6–10, 1977, Anaheim, California).

Yingling, C. D. and Skinner, J. E. (1975). Regulation of unit activity in nucleus reticularis thalami by the mesencephalic reticular formation and the frontal granular cortex. *Electroenceph. Clin. Neurophys.* *39*:635–642.

Yingling, C. D. and Skinner, J. E. (1977). Gating of thalamic input to cerebral cortex by nucleus reticularis thalami. In *Progress in Clinical Neurophysiology*, Vol. 1, J. E. Desmedt (ed). New York: S. Karger, pp. 70–96.

11

The Callosal Syndromes

JOSEPH E. BOGEN

In spite of evidence affirming it, the callosal syndrome, whose principal elements
were magnificently described before 1908, has been discussed, forgotten, rediscovered, denied, proven, put in doubt; it continues a subject for argument in 1975.

Brion and Jedynak

The corpus callosum is by far the largest of those nerve fiber collections that directly
connect one cerebral hemisphere with the other and are called the cerebral commissures. These include the anterior commissure, the hippocampal commissure, and, for
some purposes, the massa intermedia. Not included are the posterior and the haben-
ular commissures (parts of the midbrain) as well as other commissures of the spinal
cord and brainstem.

When the cerebral commissures have been surgically divided (the "split-brain"
operation) and the patient has recovered from the acute effects of the operation, a
variety of deficits in interhemispheric communication can be demonstrated. These
make up "the syndrome of the cerebral commissures," also known as "the syndrome
of brain bisection" or "the syndrome of hemisphere disconnection" (Sperry et al.,
1969; Reeves, 1983). Many of these same deficits can occur with only a partial interruption of the commissures (for example, a portion of the corpus callosum) when this
partial disconnection occurs in a setting of acute, naturally occurring disease, such as
a thrombosis (Geschwind, 1965). Earlier cases were often described as examples of
"the anterior cerebral artery syndrome" (Foix and Hillemand, 1925a; Critchley, 1930;
Ethelberg, 1951).

Callosal lesions are often accompanied by damage to neighboring structures. As a
result, neighborhood signs may accompany signs of callosal disconnection. The situation may also be complicated by nonlocalizing signs, such as meningismus when the
callosal lesion is associated with hemorrhage from an anterior communicating aneurysm, or signs of increased intracranial pressure when the callosal lesion is a tumor.
Although any sign after cortical damage (in a region giving rise to callosal fibers)

could be suspected of being partially callosal in origin, small lesions of the callosum, as pointed out later, rarely can be reliably correlated with any behavioral deficit. This chapter will focus on signs of hemispheric disconnection and give some attention to neighborhood signs. A brief history of studies of the corpus callosum will help us to understand how the disconnection signs have come to be emphasized, and why we often take the trouble to speak of "the cerebral commissures," including the anterior commissure, rather than just the corpus callosum. After this historical account, the callosal syndromes will be described. The next section will focus on the clinical approach to naturally occurring lesions, and the concluding section will touch on three problems as examples of the ongoing controversy in this area.

HISTORICAL BACKGROUND

The history of studies of the corpus callosum can be considered to have five periods, each characterized by the views of leading contributors:

1. The humoral anatomists
2. The traffic anatomists
3. The classical neurologists
4. The critics
5. The two-brain theorists

Contributors not mentioned **here** are cited in the extensive reviews included in the bibliography.°

The Humoral Anatomists

By "humoral anatomists" I mean those writers of antiquity whose concepts of brain function emphasized the contents of the brain cavities and the flow of various fluids such as air, phlegm, CSF, blood, etc. For them, the corpus callosum seemed largely a supporting structure. Even that original genius, Vesalius, believed that the corpus callosum served mainly as a mechanical support, maintaining the integrity of the various cavities. In 1543 he wrote:

> There is a part [whose] external surface is gleaming white and harder than the substance on the remaining surface of the brain. It was for this reason that the ancient Greeks called this part "tyloeides" ["callosus" in Latin] and, following their example, in my discourse I have always referred to this part as the corpus callosum. If you look at the right and left brain . . . and also if you compare the front and rear, the corpus callosum is observed to be in the middle of the brain; . . . Indeed, it relates the right side of the cerebrum to the left; then it produces and supports the septum of the right and left ventricles; finally, through that septum it supports and

°Lévy-Valensi, 1910; Mingazzini, 1922; Bremer et al., 1956; Geschwind, 1965; Unterharnscheidt et al., 1968; Bogen and Bogen, 1969; Eliot, 1969; Kuhlenbeck, 1969; Cumming, 1970; Doty and Negrão, 1972; Berlucchi, 1972; Joynt, 1974; Selnes, 1974; Brion and Jedynak, 1975; Pandya, 1975; Rudel, 1978.

props the [fornix] so that it may not collapse and, to the great detriment of all the functions of the cerebrum, crush the cavity common to the two [lateral] ventricles of the cerebrum. [Clarke and O'Malley, 1968, p. 597]

The Traffic Anatomists

The "traffic anatomists" took a major step forward. As indicated by Joynt (1974), it was at about the time of Willis (1664) that anatomists began thinking more in terms of a traffic or communication between the more solid parts of the brain. This view became quite explicit in the statement of Viq d'Azyr who wrote in 1784:

It seems to me that the commissures are intended to establish sympathetic communications between different parts of the brain, just as the nerves do between different organs and the brain itself. . . . [Clarke and O'Malley, 1968, p. 592]

For over two centuries, beliefs about callosal function consisted almost solely of inferences from its central location, widespread connections, and large size (larger than all those descending and ascending tracts, taken together, which connect the cerebrum with the outside world). Willis, Lapeyronie, and Lancisi, among others, thought the corpus callosum a likely candidate for "the seat of the soul"; or they used some other expression intended to cover that highest or ultimate liaison which brings coherent, vital unity to a complex assemblage.

The observations of the early anatomists have been supported by subsequent anatomic observations, including the large number of callosal fibers, some 200 million of them, and the important fact that the callosal fibers myelinate quite late, indicating that they probably serve later-developing functions. It certainly seems reasonable to suppose that the cerebral commissures have to do with the "highest," most educable, and characteristically human functions of the cerebrum.

Inference of function from observable structure is time-honored and productive. On the other hand, such inference has its limitations. The physiological evidence has only partially sustained anatomic inference. We now know from various observations (notably the split-brain) that the corpus callosum does indeed serve as an important integrative structure; we also know it is neither sufficient nor crucial, providing only one of a number of integrative mechanisms. That it is not the exclusive "seat of the soul" is evident from the apparent normality of patients who have had complete cerebral commissurotomies. That it is an important integrating mehanism is clear from the peculiarities of such patients. These include, among other things, a unilateral tactile *anomia,* a left *hemialexia,* and a unilateral *apraxia.* That is, for the right-hander with complete cerebral commissurotomy, there is an inability to name aloud objects felt with the left hand, an inability to read aloud written material presented solely to the left half-field of vision, and an inability to execute with the left hand actions verbally named or described by the examiner. The apraxia usually recedes in a few months, whereas the hemialexia and unilateral anomia persist for years.

Such deficits are now easily and clearly demonstrable in individuals who have had surgical section of the cerebral commissures. But these deficits were first recognized, by a number of exceptionally astute clinicians, in patients with vascular disease causing very complex and evolving syndromes.

The Classical Neurologists

In the closing decades of the 19th century (or more broadly construed, in the period between the American Civil War and the First World War) there emerged that group of neurologists whose discoveries and formulations are still the core of current clinical knowledge; even the issues which they debated among themselves remain live issues today. Among them were several, including Wernicke, Liepmann, Dejerine, and Goldstein, who interpreted various neurological symptoms as resulting from disconnection, more specifically, interruption of information flow through the corpus callosum.

The concept of apraxia was developed by Liepmann expressly to describe a patient who could carry out commands with one of his hands but not with the other. Liepmann and Maas (1908) described a right-hander whose callosal lesion caused a left apraxia as well as a left-hand *agraphia*—an inability to write—in the absence of aphasia. These disabilities have subsequently been observed many times. Unilateral apraxia and the unilateral agraphia are not always present, and they may subside when a stroke victim progressively recovers, but they remain among the cardinal signs of hemisphere disconnection.

Among Leipmann's ideas were two which he considered to be necessarily connected, but whose acceptance, in fact, has waxed and waned independently. We can call them: (1) the concept of callosal motor mediation or "the callosal concept" and (2) the concept of left hemisphere motor dominance or "motor dominance."

According to the first concept, interruption of transcallosal interhemispheric communication results in apraxia. Liepmann considered the corpus callosum instrumental in left-hand responses to verbal command: the verbal instruction was comprehended only by the left hemisphere and the left hand followed instructions which were delivered not by a directly descending pathway (what we would now call "ipsilateral control") but by a route involving callosal interhemispheric transfer from left to right and then by way of what we now call "contralateral control," that is, by right hemisphere control of the left hand. Necessarily then, callosal interruption would result in an inability to follow verbal commands with the left hand although there would be no loss of comprehension (as expected from a left hemisphere lesion). And there would be no weakness or incoordination of the left hand (as would usually result from a right hemisphere lesion). This view was largely ignored or rejected (particularly in the English-speaking countries) for nearly half a century, although it is now thought to be essentially correct. Correspondingly, we now recognize the notion of spatial or pictorial instructions understood by the right hemisphere and requiring callosally mediated interhemispheric communication for correct right-hand execution. This right-to-left aspect of callosal function was not part of Liepmann's original callosal concept although, in retrospect, it seems a natural corollary.

Second, there was Liepmann's concept of the left hemisphere as the organizer of complex (particularly learned) motor behavior. Indeed, according to Goldstein (1953) it was Liepmann who made " . . . the important discovery of the dominance of the left hemisphere." Unlike the callosal concept, this idea of motor dominance was readily accepted, along with the already established concept of language dominance by the left hemisphere. Almost everyone came to think of the left hemisphere as *gen-*

erally "the dominant hemisphere" (Benton, 1977). The reemergence in the 1960's of interest in the corpus callosum (as described below) was coincidentally accompanied by a recognition of right hemisphere dominance for certain nonverbal processes, including their motor expression. Hence, while Liepmann's callosal concept was regaining popularity, his motor dominance concept was losing some of its appeal. This seems to be an example of how ideas thought by their inventor to be necessarily linked can be separated by the judgments of others. Whether, and in what way, the left hemisphere is dominant for skilled movements generally (and not just those linguistically related) is currently a matter of active controversy (Kimura and Archibald, 1974; Denckla, 1974; Geschwind, 1975; Albert et al., 1976; Zaidel and Sperry, 1977; Denckla and Rudel, 1978; Haaland and Delaney, 1981; Jason 1983 a, b; Kimura, 1983). For a further discussion of apraxia (including callosal apraxia) see Chapter 7.

Meanwhile, Liepmann's callosal concept is now hardly doubted. But this was not always so.

The Critics

Even during the time of Liepmann, there were critics and doubters; they became progressively more influential in the ensuing decades. In their extensive review, Ironside and Guttmacher (1929) concluded:

> Taking into account the completeness of the case records, our series of tumour cases would lead us to believe that apraxia is not a common symptom of tumours of the corpus callosum.
>
> The symptoms in corpus callosum tumours are largely of the "neighbourhood" type and arise from involvement of, or pressure on, adjacent structures by the growth.

In addition to the criticism of hemisphere disconnection as a cause of symptoms, the situation was clouded by certain distractions which we can consider briefly before returning to the central theme of disconnection.

MENTAL SYMPTOMS WERE DISPUTED

Distractions arose as the result of attempts to correlate lesions, especially tumors of the corpus callosum, with mental symptoms. For example, a mental callosal syndrome was formulated by Raymond et al., (1906) and their views were widely accepted for many years. They observed a certain loss of connectedness of ideas but no delirium, a difficulty with recent memory, a "bizarreness" of manner, and a lability of mood. One is impressed with the extent to which this resembles symptoms which are now commonly attributed to frontal lobe damage (Botez, 1974; Barbizet et al., 1977).

Alpers (1936) redescribed the callosal syndrome emphasizing "imperviousness": a certain indifference to stimuli as if the threshold were elevated, difficulties in concentration, and a lack of elaboration of thought.

After reviewing the relevant literature, and on the basis of personal cases, Brihaye agreed with the observation of Le Beau (1943) that, "There is a certain apathy, that is to say, a clouding without somnolence which is possibly very specific. . . ." (Bremer et al., 1956). When we actually read Le Beau, we find that the rest of his sentence is, " . . . but this, in any case, is insufficient to permit more than a clinical suspicion of localization in the corpus callosum. Most of the time, there is nothing of the sort." [page 1370] And on the very first page of his extensive article, Le Beau says, "The clinical diagnosis of these tumors is hardly possible, because there is no callosal syndrome." [page 1365] And in his summary, " . . . in particular there is no characteristic mental deficit and no apraxia." [page 1381]

In my experience, patients with anterior callosal lesions often *do* have "a certain apathy." This "imperviousness" occurs in patients with acute or progressive callosal lesions—especially the malignancy which is sometimes called a "butterfly glioma" because it spreads its wings into both frontal lobes. The patient who is impervious to instructions will eventually respond, and often appropriately (but sometimes incompletely), but only after repeated requests and considerable delay. We are now inclined to attribute this symptom not to involvement of the genu of the corpus callosum (which is, to be sure, involved) but rather to involvement of the medial aspects of the frontal lobes including the anterior cingulate gyri. And we suppose the imperviousness to be a milder form of akinesia, often approaching a mute immobility, of a patient who has what is sometimes called "the subfrontal syndrome" consequent to bleeding from an anterior cerebral artery aneurysm, or wth a third ventricle tumor. (Also see Chaps. 10 and 12 on the neglect syndrome and the frontal lobes, respectively.)

In any event, imperviousness can be a useful sign of anterior callosal lesions, although it is probably not a result of callosal interruption. This seems, in retrospect, a good example of anatomic relationships being important clinically, although misleading from the point of view of physiological theory.

Neighborhood signs have also been noted with posterior callosal lesions, with involvement of the hippocampi. Translating Escourolle et al. (1975):

> A certain number of our tumors of the splenium [twice as common as genu gliomas] were accompanied by memory dysfunction, whereas the anterior tumors were more often manifested by akinetic states with mutism, probably because of bilateral anterior cingulate involvement. [page 48]

DISCONNECTION SIGNS WERE NOT OFTEN SEEN

The demise of Liepmann's understanding of the corpus callosum was only partly attributable to clouding of the issue with neighborhood signs: mainly it was from an unwillingness to accept as meaningful such disconnection signs as unilateral apraxia, unilateral agraphia, and hemialexia. The objections which were raised included the following six points:

1. *Callosal lesions are rarely if ever isolated, so that deficits attributed to such lesions may well result, at least in part, from associated damage.*
This problem is real enough; the only solution is to obtain a sufficient variety of cases so that one can reasonably attribute to their common anatomic aspects those clinical

features which they also have in common. This is reminiscent of the generally accepted attitude among scientists that a belief becomes more secure through the convergence of widely differing lines of evidence.

2. *Signs attributable to callosal lesions often subside or disappear altogether.*
This criticism is correct, especially for younger patients with unimanual dyspraxia and unimanual dysgraphia. But it does not apply to all callosal signs, notably the unilateral anomia and the hemialexia following commissurotomy. Even if it did, subsidence does not mean that a sign was without significance, any more than the frequent subsidence of aphasia means that it is not a reliable sign (in right-handers) of a left hemisphere lesion. Progressive compensation following focal damage is one of the most characteristic features of the brain.

3. *In numerous cases of callosal disease the expected disconnection signs are not elicited.*
This included cases of toxic degeneration of the corpus callosum (such as Marchiafava-Bignami disease) as well as the far more common cases of callosal tumor or callosal infarction.

In retrospect, these negative findings can often be attributed to a lack of looking; it is not everyone's routine to look for dysgraphia in the left hand or even for an anomia; and hemialexia in the left half-field can be even more elusive, particularly if no precautions are taken to prevent shift of gaze (such as using a tachistoscope so that stimuli appear, in one visual half-field or the other, for only a fraction of a second). In addition, disconnection signs may not be demonstrable because patients wth callosal tumors or toxic degeneration are often too obtunded to be appropriately tested. When patients with toxic malfunction of the corpus callosum are testable, and appropriately tested, such signs as unilateral anomia and dyspraxia have been found (Lechevalier et al., 1975; Lhermitte et al., 1977; Barbizet et al., 1978).

4. *Patients with agenesis of the corpus callosum (and/or callosal lipoma) do not manifest most of the so-called callosal signs.*
Lévy-Valensi (1910) was an ardent admirer of Liepmann, gave him the credit for the concept of apraxia, and said, " . . . apraxia is part of the callosal syndrome." But he, like so many others, was particularly troubled by callosal agenesis and admitted, "The physiologist is no less embarrassed than the anatomist by these disconcerting cases." A sizable number of callosal agenesis patients have been seen in the past few years; and a few deficits in interhemispheric transfer have seemed to be present (Jeeves, 1965 a,b; Lehmann and Lampe, 1970; Dixon and Jeeves, 1970; Kinsbourne and Fisher, 1971; Sadowsky and Reeves, 1975; Milner and Jeeves, 1979; Lassonde et al., 1981; A. Milner, 1982).

But there has been no disconnection syndrome typical of the split-brain in such patients. This observation cannot be explained away on methodological grounds since it is true even with the most extensive, systematic testing (Saul and Sperry, 1968; Ettlinger et al., 1974; Ferriss and Dorsen, 1975; Reynolds and Jeeves, 1977; Gott and Saul, 1978; Jeeves, 1979).

The presence of interhemispheric transfer in spite of callosal agenesis has been attributed to various causes, most notably the use of other commissural systems such as the anterior commissure. There may also be a duplication of function (such as speech in each hemisphere) or the compensatory appearance, during brain development, of unusually effective ipsilateral fiber tracts.

The anterior commissure explanation is appealing because the available postmortem evidence indicates that individuals with callosal agenesis (if they reach an age sufficient for psychological testing) all have anterior commissures, sometimes larger than normal (Bruce, 1890; Segal, 1935; Kirschbaum, 1947; Slager et al., 1957, Loeser and Alvord, 1968; Bossy, 1970; Ito et al., 1972; Sheremata et al., 1973; Shoumura et al., 1975; Carleton et al., 1976).

The anterior commissure has been shown in animal experiments to serve visual transfer nearly as well as the splenium (Downer, 1962; Black and Myers, 1964; Gazzaniga, 1966; Doty and Overman, 1977; Sullivan and Hamilton, 1973). And it is now known that in the chronic, stabilized state, splenial remnants can effect sufficient interhemispheric exchange to avoid the usual signs of disconnection (Gordon, Bogen, and Sperry, 1971; Gazzaniga et al., 1975; Ozgur et al., 1977; Cobben et al., 1978; Benes, 1982; Apuzzo et al., 1982). This conclusion is based on cases having very extensive but not quite complete commissurotomy, that is, section of the anterior commissure and all of the corpus callosum except for a part (about one half) of the splenium. Later in this chapter an extensive list of deficits reliably found after a complete commissurotomy is presented; these deficits are not found after surgery if the splenium is spared (Greenblatt et al., 1980). Two points are important:

a. An apparent lack of callosal symptoms in cases of long-standing partial lesion (or of callosal agenesis) is largely due to the remarkable compensatory capabilities of the remaining fibers.
b. Partial lesions are not usually compensated immediately. Hence, disconnection symptoms are more likely to occur after a sudden partial lesion (such as a stroke), or in the presence of progressive lesions (such as tumors) where the deficit is increasing faster than it can be compensated.

The paucity of disconnection deficits in patients with callosal agenesis is not wholly explained by the presence of the anterior commissure. It should be kept in mind that compensation for loss of the splenium, by the anterior commissure, was not 100% in animal experiments. Nor does the anterior commissure compensate completely for splenial loss in humans, as is shown by the hemialexia usually persisting after splenial section (Trescher and Ford, 1937; Maspes, 1948; Gazzaniga and Freedman, 1973; Iwata et al., 1974; Sugishita et al., 1984).

Interhemispheric transfer via the anterior commissure seems to be, in surgical cases, incomplete (Goldstein and Joynt, 1969; Goldstein et al., 1975). When present, it is largely restricted to visual information (Risse et al., 1978). Even if the anterior commissure is responsible for visual transfer in cases of callosal agenesis, how are we to explain the somesthetic transfer in such cases? One consideration is that agenesis cases typically have a large longitudinal bundle of fibers along the medial aspect of each

hemisphere (the bundle of Probst). As pointed out by R. Saul (personal communication) this bundle might make available to the anterior commissure some types of
information which it does not ordinarily transfer. In any event, the presence of
Probst's bundle fits the view that brains with callosal agenesis differ from normal
brains in ways other than disconnection.

Also implying that such a brain is peculiar in its principles of operation is the notion
of increased function of ipsilaterally descending or ascending fiber tracts. In this
regard, Dennis (1976) confirmed that callosal agenesis is accompanied by deficits
within each hemisphere, appearing as a loss of finely differentiated tactile localization
and individual finger movements. This was attributed to a lack of inhibitory action
by the corpus callosum during early development of the brain. The corpus callosum,
she suggests, ordinarily suppresses information contained in uncrossed pathways.
Somewhat related are the suggestions: (a) that unilateralization of language (and other
engrams) depends on callosal inhibition active at the time of engram acquisition
(Doty et al., 1973); (b) that the development of hemispheric specialization depends
on competitive interaction between the hemispheres during early childhood (Galin,
1977).

Some reservation is necessary with respect to the interpretation of intrahemispheric
deficits in callosal agenesis, since the condition is so often associated with other anomalies. Hence, any deficit in intrahemispheric function might easily be coincidental,
not a direct result of the absence of commissures. Further evidence may be forthcoming from animal experiments in which the cerebral commissures are severed shortly
after birth (Jeeves and Wilson, 1969; Sechzer et al., 1976; Elberger, 1980; Ptito and
Lepore, 1983).

5. *Callosal section in animal experiments does not produce significant deficits.*
This includes the experiments of Zinn (1748), Magendie, Muratow, Roussy, Franck
and Pitres; Koranyi, Dotto, and Pusateri; Lo Monaco; and Baldi, all reviewed by
Lévy-Valensi (1910) whose own monkey experiments were (to his dismay) also negative. Also negative were the experiments (cited by Bremer et al., 1956) of Lafora
and Prados (1923), Hartmann and Trendelenberg (1927), Seletzky and Gilula (1928),
and Kennard and Watts (1934).

In retrospect, all of these negative results can be attributed to a lack of relevant
testing (as will be discussed in the following section). Besides, the more striking signs
and symptoms seen in human patients are attributable to hemispheric specialization
which is poorly developed in cats, dogs, or even monkeys (Warren and Nonneman,
1976; Doty and Overman, 1977; Hamilton, 1977; Stamm et al., 1977; Dewson, 1977;
Doty and Overman, 1982; Hamilton and Vermeire, 1983).

6. *Surgical section of the corpus callosum is often asymptomatc.*
Walter Dandy went so far as to say in 1936:

> The corpus callosum is sectioned longitudinally . . . no symptoms follow its division.
> This simple experiment puts an end to all of the extravagant hypotheses on the
> functions of the corpus callosum.

Even more persuasive was the negative testing by Akelaitis of patients who had callosal section. These results were admitted by Tomasch (1954, 1957) whose interest in the corpus callosum and anterior commissure led him to make the now widely accepted estimates of their fiber content. Of the Akelaitis results he wrote:

> They showed very clearly and in accordance with some earlier authors like Dandy, Foerster, Meagher and Barre, whose material however was not so extensive, that the corpus callosum is hardly connected with any psychological functions at all.

Ethelberg (1951), after an extensive review, concluded:

> It may be premature to consider the recent clinical, surgical, and experimental observations an obituary of Liepmann's concepts as to the role played by the corpus callosum in the development of "true" apraxia. But they certainly suggest the need of some hesitance in accepting them. [page 117]

About the same time, Fessard (1954) summarized the view which was then generally accepted:

> ... there is a great deal of data showing [that] section of important associative white tracts such as the corpus callosum does not seem to affect mental performances. Other similar observations in man or animals are now accumulated in great number and variety. These results are so disturbing that one may be tempted to admit the irrational statement that a heterogeneous system of activities in the nervous system could form a whole in the absence of any identified liaison.

We now realize that most of the negative findings resulted from two sources:

a. As already mentioned, when surgical section of the commissures is incomplete, a remarkable capacity for maintaining cross-communication between the hemispheres may be retained with quite small commissural remnants, particularly when the part remaining is at the posterior end of the corpus callosum (in other words, in the splenium).
b. Negative findings often result from the use of inappropriate or insensitive testing techniques. What one finds depends on what one looks for; whereas Dandy (1936) said that callosal section produces no observable deficits, among his own patients was the one reported by Trescher and Ford to have hemialexia.

The Two-Brain Theorists

A distinct reversal of opinion occurred during the 1960's, following publication of the "split-brain" experiments on cats and monkeys.

Current views on callosal function are attributable in large part to studies, under the aegis of R. W. Sperry, of our patients with surgical section of the cerebral commissures. These patients are indeed without, in Dandy's words, "any deficits" in the ordinary social situation, or even as determined by most of a routine neurological examination (Bogen and Vogel, 1975; Botez and Bogen, 1976). In specially devised testing situations, however, they can be shown to have a wide variety of deficits in interhemispheric communication (Gazzaniga, 1970; Gazzaniga et al., 1962, 1963, 1965, 1967; Gazzaniga and Sperry, 1970; Sperry, 1970, 1974; Sperry and Gazzaniga, 1967; Sperry et al., 1969; Zaidel, 1973).

The split-brain patients confirmed in a particularly dramatic way the importance of commissural fibers for interhemispheric communication. But the essential facts had already been described in animal experiments during the 1950's, initiated by Myers and Sperry (1953 and 1958; Myers, 1956). It was found that each hemisphere of a cat or monkey could learn solutions to a problem different from (even conflicting with) the solutions learned by the other hemisphere. This made it clear that effective functioning could occur independently in the two hemispheres. As Sperry (1961) put it:

> Callosum-sectioned cats and monkeys are virtually indistinguishable from their normal cagemates under most tests and training conditions. [But] if one studies such a "split-brain" monkey more carefully, under special training and testing conditions where the inflow of sensory information to the divided hemispheres can be separately restricted and controlled, one finds that each of the divided hemispheres now has its own independent mental sphere or cognitive system—that is, its own independent perceptual, learning, memory, and other mental processes . . . it is as if the animals had two separate brains. [page 1749]

It is important to understand that the duality of minds seen after hemisphere disconnection is not an inference solely from certain striking clinical cases, and a handful of surgical patients, as is sometimes said. Split-brain experiments have been carried out with many different species by hundreds of investigators around the world. They are virtually unanimous in concluding that each of the disconnected hemispheres can act independently of the other (Bogen, 1977). Let us consider two examples of variation on the basic idea of what has been called the "double-brain" (Dimond, 1972).

a. One of the most reliable signs of a bilateral prefrontal lobectomy in monkeys is their inability to do delayed-alternation tasks (Jacobsen and Nissen, 1937; Iversen and Mishkin, 1970; Pribram et al., 1977; Markowitsch et al., 1980). It was long supposed that this inability might be explained as the result of the hyperactivity and/or distractability which is also characteristic of such monkeys. This supposition can be tested in a split-brain monkey, where each hemisphere can function separately. If one hemisphere has a prefrontal lobectomy, it performs poorly on the delayed-alternation task. This poor performance by the lobectomized hemisphere is not accompanied by hyperactivity or distractability. Apparently, the remaining frontal lobe keeps the monkey quiet and attentive even though the intact hemisphere is not participating in the recognition of various stimuli or the evaluation of their significance (Glickstein et al., 1963).

b. A truly dramatic example occurs when only one hemisphere of a split-brain monkey has had a temporal lobectomy. A bitemporal monkey manifests the Klüver-Bucy syndrome, which includes difficulties in the visual identification of objects, orality (often mouthing inappropriate objects), hypersexuality, hypomotility, and tameness in the presence of humans. When the intact hemisphere can see, the split-brain rhesus monkey behaves in the usual rhesus manner, manifesting a fierce fear of humans. But if only the temporal lobectomized hemisphere receives the visual information, the split-brain animal acts like a Klüver-Bucy monkey, particularly as regards its relative tameness. When this was reported (Downer, 1961, 1962) it was so amazing that many of us doubted it, although we were already convinced of the duality of mind in the split-brain monkey. Little room for doubt remains because this finding has, in its essentials, been reported by a number of other investigators (Bossom et al., 1961; Horel and Keating, 1969, 1972; Doty et al., 1971, 1973; Doty and Overman, 1977).

It was knowledge of the split-brain experiments in laboratory animals that alerted Geschwind and Kaplan (1962) to the possibility of a hemisphere-disconnection syndrome in the human. This led them, when a likely patient appeared, to search in a deliberate way for the disconnection effects. From a complex, evolving picture, they expertly teased out the relevant phenomena.

One of the first things Geschwind and Kaplan found was that although the patient wrote clearly with his right hand, he wrote "aphasically" with his left (and was astonished by what he had written). Among other things they found that an object placed in the left hand was handled correctly and was corrected retrieved by feel, but it could not be named; nor could it be retrieved by feel with his right hand. In their words,

> he behaved as if his two cerebral hemispheres were functioning nearly autonomously. Thus, we found that so long as we confined stimulation and response within the same hemisphere, the patient showed correct performance.

In contrast, the patient performed incorrectly when the stimulus was provided to one hemisphere and the response required from the other. They concluded that the best explanation was to suppose that his hemispheres were disconnected by a lesion of the corpus callosum. Their anatomic prediction was eventually confirmed by autopsy. Their conclusions were soon amply confirmed by the surgical cases whose description we come to in the next section.

Liepmann's callosal concept has been resurrected. There is now widespread acceptance of an idea long ignored. It is an interesting example of what Kuhn (1962) called scientific "revolutions." Geschwind (1974) wrote,

> What was astonishing was the fact that this work had been so grossly neglected . . . that important confirmed scientific observations could almost be expunged from the knowledge of contemporary scientists.

Geschwind has suggested in correspondence that there was a widespread revulsion against attempts to link brain to behavior, associated with the rise of psychoanalysis; and he had another, sociological explanation:

> Henry Head had been shrewd enough to point out that much of the great German growth of neurology had been related to their victory in the Franco-Prussian war.

He was not shrewd enough to apply this valuable historical lesson to his own time and to realize that perhaps the decline of the vigor and influence of German neurology was strongly related to the defeat of Germany in World War I and the shift of the center of gravity of intellectual life to the English-speaking world, rather than necessarily to any defects in the ideas of German scholars. [Geschwind, 1964].

But there were other factors. One thing that was missing was a widespread conviction that the essential facts could be observed repeatedly in humans under controlled, prospective circumstances. Such observations are possible with persons who have had a complete cerebral commissurotomy.

THE SYNDROME FOLLOWING COMPLETE CEREBRAL COMMISSUROTOMY

Clarification and extensive confirmation of the callosal syndrome came from observations on patients whose forebrain commissures were sectioned to control severe intractable epilepsy. Results were favorable in our early patients (Bogen and Vogel, 1962; Bogen et al. 1965). These results led to continued application of the operation which included section of the entire corpus callosum and anterior and hippocampal commissures plus in some cases the massa intermedia—all in a single operation. The patients exhibit a wide spectrum of disconnection deficits. At one extreme, our first patient, who had grossly apparent right-frontal atrophy, was oldest at the time of brain injury (age 30), the oldest at time of operation (45), and subsequently showed the most severe apraxic and related symptoms. Least affected was a 13-year-old boy who had the smoothest postoperative course, relatively little brain damage before surgery, early date of brain injury (birth), was youngest at time of operation, and whose left-hand apraxia was minimal. Following a similar operation by others (Wilson et al., 1975, 1977; Holtzman et al., 1981) further variation has been encountered, but the crucial observations have been the same. The following briefly outlines some of the typical findings. (Left-handers are excluded.)

Overall Effects

Within a few months after operation, the symptoms of hemisphere disconnection tend to be compensated to a remarkable degree. In personality, and in social situations, the patient appears much as before. However, with appropriate tests the disconnected hemispheres can be shown to operate independently to a large extent. Each of the hemispheres appears to have its own learning processes and its own separate memories, all of which are largely inaccessible to the other hemisphere. This mutual inaccessibility, rather than neighborhood damage, is probably responsible for memory deficits present after commissural section (Zaidel and Sperry, 1974; Campbell et al., 1981; Milner, 1984; Gur et al., 1984).

Visual Effects

Visual material can be presented selectively to a single hemisphere by having the patient fix his gaze on a projection screen onto which pictures of objects or symbols are backprojected to either right, left, or both visual half-fields, using exposure times of ⅒ sec or less. The patients can read and describe material of various kinds in the right half-field at a level substantially the same as before surgery. When stimuli are presented to the left half-field, however, the patients usually report that they see "nothing" or at most "a flash of light."

Auditory Suppression

Following cerebral commissurotomy, the patient readily identifies single words (and other sounds) if they are presented to one ear at a time. The auditory effects of callosal lesions require special testing methods. That is, if *different* words are presented to the two ears simultaneously (so-called "dichotic listening") only the words presented to the right ear will be reliably reported (Milner et al., 1968; Sparks and Geschwind, 1968; Springer and Gazzaniga, 1975; Gordon, 1975; Cullen, 1975; Zaidel, 1976; Efron et al., 1977).

This large right-ear advantage is usually considered to be the result of two concurrent circumstances: (1) the ipsilateral pathway from the left ear (to the left, speaking, hemisphere) is suppressed by the presence of simultaneous but differing inputs, as it is in intact individuals during dichotic listening (Kimura, 1967). (2) The contralateral pathway from the left ear (to the right hemisphere) conveys information which ordinarily reaches the left (speaking) hemisphere by the callosal pathway, which has now been severed. Although left-ear words are rarely reported, their perception by the right hemisphere is occasionally evidenced by appropriate actions of the left hand (Gordon, 1973).

Motor Function

The degree of left-hand dyspraxia is subject to large individual differences. Immediately after surgery all the patients showed some left-sided apraxia to verbal commands such as "Wiggle your left toes," or "Make a fist with your left hand." This left-limb dyspraxia is attributable to the simultaneous presence of two deficits: poor comprehension by the right hemisphere (which has good control of the left hand), and poor ipsilateral control by the left hemisphere (which understands very well). Subsidence of the dyspraxia can therefore result from two compensatory mechanisms: increased right hemisphere comprehension of words, and increased left hemisphere control of the left hand. The extent of ipsilateral motor control can be tested by flashing to right or left visual half-field sketches of thumb and fingers in different postures, for the subject to mimic with one or the other hand. Responses are poor with the hand on the side opposite the visual input, simple postures such as closed fist or open hand being attainable after further recovery. As recovery proceeds, good ipsilateral control is first attained for responses carried out by the more proximal musculature. After several months, most of the patients can form a variety of hand and finger postures with either hand to verbal instructions, such as, "Make a circle with your thumb and little finger," and the like.

Subsidence of the apraxia continues so that eventually it is hardly in evidence. But even many years later, it can be demonstrated to some degree, (Zaidel and Sperry, 1977).

The capacity of either hemisphere, and particularly the left hemisphere, to control the ipsilateral hand varies from one patient to another both in the immediate post-operative period and many years later. This, together with variations in right hemisphere language, probably accounts for many of the discrepancies in descriptions of the callosal syndrome as presented by various authors.

Somesthetic Effects

The lack of interhemispheric transfer following brain bisection can be demonstrated with respect to somesthesis (including touch, pressure, and proprioception) in a variety of ways.

CROSS-RETRIEVAL OF SMALL TEST OBJECTS

Unseen objects in the right hand are handled, named, and described in normal fashion. In contrast, attempts to name or describe the same objects held out of sight in the left consistently fail. In spite of the patient's inability to name an unseen object in his left hand, identification of the object by the right hemisphere is evident from appropriate manipulation of the item showing how it is used, or by retrieval of the same object with the left hand from among a collection of other objects screened from sight. What distinguishes the split-brain patients from normal is that their excellent same-hand retrieval (with either hand) is *not* accompanied by ability to retrieve with one hand objects felt with the other.

CROSS-REPLICATION OF HAND POSTURES

Specific postures impressed on one (unseen) hand by the examiner cannot be mimicked in the opposite hand. Also, if a hand posture in outline form is flashed by tachistoscope to one visual half-field, it can be copied easily by the hand on that side but usually not by the other hand.

A convenient way to test for lack of interhemispheric transfer of proprioceptive information is as follows: the patient extends both hands beneath the opaque screen (or vision is otherwise excluded) and the examiner impresses a particular posture on one hand. For example, one can put the tip of the thumb against the tip of the little finger and have the other three fingers fully extended and separated (or the other three fingers can be kept close together, as the examiner wishes). The examiner then says, "Now make a fist—good—now put it back the way it was." Then the examiner says, "Keep your hand just the way it is and do exactly the same with your other hand." The patient with complete cerebral commissurotomy cannot mimic with the other hand a posture being held by the first hand. When confirming the presence of hemisphere disconnection, this procedure should be repeated with various postures and in both directions. In this way, one can establish quite clearly (in the absence of malingering) that there is a hemisphere disconnection.

CROSS-LOCALIZATION OF FINGERTIPS

After complete cerebral commissurotomy there is a partial loss of the ability to name exact points stimulated on the left side of the body. This defect is least apparent, if at all, on the face and it is most apparent on the distal parts, especially the fingertips. This is not a deficit dependent on language since it can be done in a nonverbal fashion and in both directions (right-to-left and vice versa). An easy way to demonstrate the defect is to have the subject's hands extended, palms up (again with vision excluded). One touches the tip of one of the four fingers with the point of a pencil, asking the patient to then touch the same point with the tip of the thumb of the same hand. Repeating this maneuver many times produces a numerical score, about 100% in normals for either hand. In the absence of a parietal lesion, identification of any of the four fingertips by putting the thumb tip upon the particular finger can be done with great reliability. It can be done at nearly 100% level by the split-brain patient.

One then changes the task so that the fingertip is to be indicated, not by touching it with the thumb of the same hand but by touching the *corresponding* fingertip of the other hand with the thumb of that (other) hand. Sometimes the procedure should be demonstrated with the patient's hand in full vision until the patient understands what is required. This cross-localization cannot be done by the split-brain patient at a level much better than chance (25%). Normal adults almost always do better than 90%.

It is of interest that an incompetence to cross-localize or cross-match has been found in young children (Galin et al., 1977, 1979) possibly because their commissures are not yet fully functioning (Yakovlev and Lecours, 1967). Immaturity of transcallosal inhibition has been suggested as the source of unnecessary duplication during simple reaching (Lehman, 1978).

Verbal Comprehension by the Right Hemisphere

Auditory comprehension of words by the disconnected right hemisphere is suggested by the subject's ability to retrieve with the left hand various objects if they are named aloud by the examiner. Visual comprehension of printed words by the right hemisphere is often present; after a printed word is flashed to the left visual half-field, the subjects are often able to retrieve with the left hand the designated item from among an array of hidden objects. Control by the left hemisphere in these tests is excluded because incorrect verbal descriptions given immediately after a correct response by the left hand show that only the right hemisphere knew the answer.

The language capabilities of the right hemisphere, including certain right hemisphere influences on linguistic processing by the left hemisphere, are of considerable theoretical interest.[°] Right hemisphere language capabilities are distinctly more in evidence when the left hemisphere has been removed. Indeed, if the left hemisphere

[°](Smith, 1966; Gazzaniga and Sperry, 1967, Gazzaniga and Hillyard, 1971; Levy et al., 1971 and Burklund and Smith, 1977; Bradshaw et al., 1977; Ssanuma et al., 1977, Kinsbourne, 1971; Zurif and Ramier, 1972; Caplan et al., 1974; Kinsbourne, 1975; Brown and Jaffe, 1975; Carmon et al., 1977; Moscovitch, 1976; Selnes, 1976; Bradshaw et al., 1977; Sasunuma et al., 1977; Rogers et al., 1977; Winner and Gardner, 1977; Ornstein et al., 1979; Lecours and Lhermitte, 1979; Ludlow, 1980; Lassen and Larsen, 1980; Cavalli et al., 1981; Roland et al., 1981; Kimura et al., 1982; Segalowitz, 1983).

is removed (or was severely incapacitated) in infancy, these capabilities may seem normal (Smith, 1974; Kohn and Dennis, 1974; Smith and Sugar, 1975; Dennis and Whitaker, 1976). But when the left hemisphere is present and relatively intact, they are largely absent, or suppressed. The disconnected right hemisphere's receptive vocabulary can grow considerably over the years, reaching levels comparable with the vocabulary of a 10 or even a 16 year old. But this impressive single-word comprehension is rarely accompanied by speech. In a broad spectrum of patients, the most extreme cases to date of right hemisphere language ability in right-handed (and left-hemisphere speaking) split-brain subjects are two with right hemisphere speech (both with anterior commissure uncut) (LeDoux et al., 1977; Sidtis et al., 1981; McKeever et al., 1982; Myers, 1984).

In addition to the rarity of speech, right hemisphere language in the split-brain subject has other limitations, syntactic ability being rudimentary at best (E. Zaidel, 1973, 1977, 1978 a, b). Studying a few cases in great depth for over ten years, Zaidel concluded:

> Whereas phonetic and syntactic analysis seem to specialize heavily in the left hemisphere, there is a rich lexical structure in the right hemisphere. The structure of the right hemisphere lexicon appears to be unique in that it has access to a severely limited short term verbal memory, and it has neither phonetic encoding nor grapheme-to-phoneme correspondence rules . . . [this] represents the limited linguistic competence that can be acquired by a nonlinguistic, more general purpose (or other purpose) cognitive apparatus. . . . [Zaidel, 1978a]

Right Hemisphere Dominance

Following commissurotomy, we can test each hemisphere separately. It is thus possible to demonstrate in a positive way those things which each hemisphere can do better than the other, rather than inferring what a hemisphere does from the loss of function when it is injured. Right hemisphere dominance for faces has already been discussed, and other aspects will be mentioned in the following section. For those particularly interested in right hemisphere dominance in the commissurotomized human, representative reviews are included in the bibliography (Bogen and Bogen, 1969; Milner and Taylor, 1972; Levy, 1974, Nebes, 1974; Sperry, 1974; Zaidel, 1983). There is an enormous and continually growing literature on hemispheric specialization, much of it well summarized by Bradshaw and Nettleton (1983).

CLINICAL TESTING FOR CALLOSAL SIGNS AND SYMPTOMS

Following are some abbreviated descriptions of what one can look for using simple maneuvers in the clinic, when hemisphere disconnection is suspected. The descriptions apply to right-handers. In left-handers the situation is rarely a simple reversal; usually it is quite complex, as can be seen in the case histories described in the literature (Liepmann, 1900; Hécaen and Ajuriaguerra, 1964; Gloning et al., 1966; Botez and Crighel, 1971; Tzavaras et al., 1971; Heilman et al., 1973; Schott et al., 1974;

Aptman et al., 1977; Hirose et al., 1977; Herron, 1980; Hécaen et al., 1981; Gur et al., 1982).

History

Discussions with the patient, relatives, or nursing personnel often disclose sensations or occurrences suggesting hemisphere disconnection. As usual, if one is aware of what can sometimes happen, one is more apt to elicit the relevant report.

DISSOCIATIVE PHENOMENA

If the extracallosal damage is small enough that each hemisphere can retain a capacity for integrative behavior (as distinguished from cases with dense hemiplegia, for example), conflicting actions may occur more or less simultaneously. The commonest of these (which is not very helpful because it often occurs in normal subjects) is a disparity between facial expression and verbalization. More meaningful is a dissociation between what the left hand is doing and what the patient is saying. Or there may be a dissociation between general bodily actions (rising, walking, etc.) and what is being done by either hand or what is being said.

One suspects a conversion hysteria when dissociative phenomena occur. But such dissociations have occurred sufficiently often following callosal section in animals (Trevarthen, 1965) and in humans with cerebral commissurotomy as well as in naturally occurring cases, that they should arouse suspicion of a hemisphere disconnection. Indeed, there may be some substance to the view that such conative or volitional ambivalence, when it occurs in normal subjects, might be attributable, on some occasions at least, to altered information transfer by anatomically intact commissures (Galin, 1974; Hoppe, 1977; Ross and Rush, 1981).

In contrast with volitional ambivalence, emotional ambivalence (such as the report by the patient of possessing two conflicting internal feelings simultaneously) has not been a symptom of commissurotomy nor of most reported natural cases. Indeed, individuals with cerebral commissurotomy are *less* apt than normal individuals to discuss their feelings, conflicting or otherwise (Hoppe and Bogen, 1977).

INTERMANUAL CONFLICT

The dissociative phenomenon most clearly identifiable with hemisphere disconnection is intermanual conflict, in which one hand is acting at cross purposes to the other. Almost all of our complete commissurotomy patients manifested some degree of intermanual conflict in the early postoperative period. For example, a few weeks after a certain patient (RY) underwent surgery, his physiotherapist said, "You should have seen Rocky yesterday—one hand was buttoning up his shirt and the other hand was coming along right behind it undoing the buttons!" The following example is excerpted from the follow-up examination in February 1973 of another patient (AM):

> The most interesting finding in the entire examination is the frequent occurrence
> of well-coordinated movements of the left arm which are at cross-purposes with

whatever else is going on. These sometimes seem to occur spontaneously, but on other occasions are clearly in conflict with the behavior of the right arm. For example, when attempting a Jendrassic reinforcement, the patient reached with his right hand to hold his left, but the left hand actually pushed his right hand away. While testing finger-to-nose test (with the patient sitting), his left hand suddenly started slapping his chest like Tarzan.

Similar phenomena were observed after commissurotomy by Wilson et al. (1977) and by Akelaitis (1944–45) who called it "diagonistic dyspraxia." And the phenomenon has been described in many individual case reports of callosal infarcts or tumors (Fisher, 1963; Schaltenbrand, 1964; Joynt, 1977; Barbizet et al., 1978; Beukelman et al., 1980; Sine et al., 1984; Watson and Heilman, 1983). Such behavior soon subsides after callosotomy, probably because of other integrative mechanisms supplementing or replacing commissural function. But when it occurs, the phenomenon is quite striking, and probably pathognomonic.

The Alien Hand

Possibly a lesser form of intermanual conflict is what Brion and Jedynak (1972) called, "la main étrangère." This is a circumstance in which one of the patient's hands, the left hand in the right-handed patient, behaves in a way which the patient finds "foreign," "alien," or at least uncooperative. Even our youngest patient, who had no long-term appreciable apraxia to verbal command, manifested this alienation three weeks after surgery: while doing the block design test unimanually with his right hand, his left hand came up from beneath the table and was reaching for the blocks when he slapped it with his right hand and said, "That will keep it quiet for a while." Among our patients it has been most persistent in a subject with a rather flamboyant personality which we believe contributed materially to her frequent complaints about "my little sister" in referring to whoever or whatever it was that made her left hand behave peculiarly. And it may be that when the "alien hand" accompanies callosal tumors or infarcts, some predisposing personality features play a part, particularly since so many patients with callosal lesions do not emphasize this problem. However, even Rocky, a rather stolid fellow, complained for several years of an inability to get his left foot to go in the same direction as the rest of him. This may be related to the surgical retraction in his case, since evidence has been adduced that the alien hand, especially if accompanied by a strong grasp reflex, may depend on mesial frontal cortical dysfunction (Goldberg et al., 1981).

AUTOCRITICISM

There is a related phenomenon, emphasized by Brion and Jedynak (1975), which they called "l'autocritique interhémisphérique." They refer to the fairly frequent expressions of astonishment by the patient with respect to the capacity of the left hand to behave independently of conscious volition. The patient may say, when the left hand makes some choice among objects, that "my hand did that," rather than taking the responsibility. A patient was described by Sweet (1945) as saying, "Now you want me to put my left index finger on my nose." She then put that finger into her mouth and said, "That's funny; why won't it go up to my nose?" [page 88].

Split-brain patients soon accept the idea that they have capacities of which they are not conscious, such as left-hand retrieval of objects not namable. They may quickly rationalize such acts, sometimes in a transparently erroneous way (Gazzaniga and LeDoux, 1978). But even many years after operation, the patients will occasionally be quite surprised when some well-coordinated or obviously well-informed act has just been carried out by the left hand. This is particularly common under conditions of continuously lateralized input (Zaidel, 1977, 1978b; Zaidel and Peters, 1981).

Examination

Most naturally occurring cases of hemisphere disconnection are in a process of recovery (as with a stroke) or are worsening (as with a tumor) or may be fluctuating (as with remitting vascular disease or fluctuating edema). Findings which are quite clear on one occasion may be doubtful later (or earlier). Hence, repeated examinations at different times are most informative.

Various *neighborhood signs* can prevent the demonstration of disconnection signs. The imperviousness from certain bifrontal lesions may render the patient insufficiently cooperative. Forced deviation of *gaze*, not uncommon with unilateral hemispheric involvement, can interfere. The *anterior cerebral artery syndrome* classically includes a unilateral crural (leg) weakness of the "pyramidal" type and/or a strong grasp reflex, uni- or bilateral. Such an abnormality (especially forced grasping) makes testing for disconnection quite difficult. Most neighborhood signs will eventually subside after a stroke, with the emergence of a period during which disconnection signs can be demonstrated for a time, before compensation supervenes.

UNILATERAL "VERBAL ANOSMIA"

Following complete cerebral commissurotomy, the patient is unable to name odors presented to the right nostril, even when they can be named quite readily when presented to the left nostril. This is not a defect of smell with the right nostril, since the patient can select, by feeling with the left hand, an object which corresponds to the odor, such as selecting a plastic banana or a plastic fish after having smelled the related odor (Gordon and Sperry, 1969). This has been confirmed in a case (including section of the anterior commissure) from a different surgical series (Gazzaniga et al., 1975). Callosotomy without section of the anterior commissure does not affect smell (Risse et al., 1978). Naturally occurring cases await investigation.

DOUBLE HEMIANOPIA

Most clinicians do not have routinely available a tachistoscope or other means for lateralizing visual information. But the disconnection (if it includes the splenium) can sometimes be demonstrated with simple confrontation testing of the visual field. The patient is allowed to have both eyes open but does not speak, and is allowed to use only one hand (sitting on the other hand, for example). Using the free hand, the subject indicates the onset of a stimulus, such as the wiggling of the examiner's fingers. With such testing there may appear to be an homonymous hemianopia contralateral to the indicating hand (the patient reliably points to the right half-field stimulus with the right hand but not to a left half-field stimulus). When the patient is tested with the *other* hand, there seems to be an homonymous hemianopia in the *other* half-field. Occasionally a stimulus in the apparently blind half-field (on the left when the right hand is being used) will produce turning of the head and eyes toward the stimulus and *then* the hand will point.

When the stimuli appear in both fields simultaneously, the patient, if free to do so, will often use both hands simultaneously. But if one hand is restrained, only one half-field will be indicated. This peculiar situation must be distinguished from the much more commonly occurring extinction or hemi-inattention deficits from a hemispheric lesion (commonly right parietal) such that the patient tends to indicate only one stimulus when the stimuli are in fact bilaterally present. An observable difference is that the double hemianopia is a symmetrical phenomenon (the deficit occurs on each side), whereas extinction or hemi-inattention is typically one-sided, more commonly for the left side. Another difference is that the double hemianopia is the result of a sharply defined projection system combined with the commissural disconnection. That is, it is thought to be a relatively primitive sensory loss. In contrast, the phenomenon of hemi-inattention is usually considered to be a higher-order derangement (Heilman and Watson, 1977; Weinstein and Friedland, 1977). For a further discussion of hemi-inattention, see Chapter 10 which covers the neglect syndrome.

Each hemisphere can exert a modicum of ipsilateral control, especially for gross arm movements. As a result, stimuli in the right half-field (seen only by the left hemisphere) may be pointed to when the patient is using only the left hand, and similarly for the left half-field stimuli when only the right hand is available. But such pointing is unreliable and inaccurate, as compared with the dependable response and precise localization possible when the patient is using the hand contralateral to the stimulated hemisphere.

When a patient has a left hemiplegia, one cannot prove that an apparent left hemianopia (when the patient is responding verbally or with right hand) is the result of a commissural lesion; but if threats in the left half-field produce wincing or flinching, failure to point to left half-field stimuli with the right hand is suggestive of a disconnection.

HEMIALEXIA

When the splenium is affected, it is sometimes possible to demonstrate a hemialexia by the brief presentations of cards, on which are printed letters or short words, in the left half-field. The patient is often unable to read a card presented this way, although he can readily read it when it is presented in the right half-field. Eye movements are usually too active for such simple testing methods; but hemialexia was, in fact, observed by such methods long before its demonstration by tachistoscopic presentation (Trescher and Ford, 1937).

It is necessary to show that the hemialexia is not merely a matter of a left hemianopia, for example by having the patient correctly retrieve objects which are briefly shown in the left half-field. Less reliable but suggestive is to see the patient point quickly (with the left hand) to stimuli (which cannot be read) when they appear in the left half-field. Sometimes a patient can name objects in the left half-field although hemialexic in that half-field and reading normally in the right.

Quite often the patient will manifest normal visual fields by perimetry and tangent screen examination (particularly if permitted to use both hands to indicate the appearance of the stimulus). There may be a partial homonymous defect in the left half-field caused by extension into the right hemisphere of the callosal lesion; but the defect would be insufficient to account for the hemialexia if it were not accompanied by a callosal lesion (Wechsler, 1972).

AUDITORY SUPPRESSION

Following cerebral commissurotomy, the right ear advantage for verbal stimuli present in most right-handers becomes so great as to be almost complete. Left ear suppression or extinction also appears after right hemispherectomy or other right hemisphere ablations or lesions (Curry, 1968; Schulhoff and Goodglass, 1969; Oxbury and Oxbury, 1970; Netley, 1972; Nebes and Nashold, 1980; Michel and Péronnet, 1982; Zaidel, 1983). Left ear extinction has also been found in patients with lesions of the left hemisphere, when the lesions are fairly deep (where they are apt to interrupt commissural fibers). Since there is usually suppression of the right ear by left hemisphere lesions, the suppression of the left ear by a left hemisphere lesion has been called "paradoxical ipsilateral extinction." Further observations have led to the conclusion that, whether the lesion is in the left or the right hemisphere, if it is close to the midline the suppression of left ear stimuli is probably attributable to interruption of interhemispheric pathways (Michel and Péronnet, 1975; Damasio and Damasio, 1979).

UNILATERAL (LEFT) IDEOMOTOR APRAXIA

Historically, the first described callosal symptom was unilateral ideomotor apraxia, by which we mean that in response to verbal command the right-handed subject is unable to carry out with the left hand some behavior which is readily executed with the right hand. This ready execution demonstrates that the failure is not ascribable to a lack of understanding. It is also necessary to demonstrate that the inability is not attributable to either weakness (paresis) or incoordination (ataxia) in the left hand (Wilson, 1908; Nielsen, 1936; Denny-Brown, 1958; Bogen, 1969 a and b; Geschwind, 1975; Poeck et al., 1982).

Strength and coordination in the left hand can be demonstrated in various ways. The main problem is not to confuse an ideomotor (also called "ideokinetic") apraxia with the much more commonly occurring loss of dexterity which is called "kinetic dyspraxia" or "limb-kinetic dyspraxia" or "innervatory apraxia" or "melokinetic dyspraxia." This occurs in the left hand as a result of various right hemisphere lesions, which can cause a mild weakness, or a release of excessive grasping or groping tendencies which interfere with function. In the words of K. Poeck (personal communication), "There is no apraxia at all!" What many of us, including Poeck, consider the hallmark of apraxia is the appearance of well-executed but incorrect movements.

These so-called *parapraxias* are analogous to the paraphasias (incorrect sounds or entire words) which are so characteristic of most aphasic speech. (For another view, see Chap. 7, *Apraxia*.)

Nor should ideomotor apraxia be confused with "ideational apraxia" in which a sequence of movements is ineffective to some overall purpose in spite of adequate performance of individual movements. Ideational apraxia can be seen in either or both hands, often in association with linguistic deficit. It can result from a left hemisphere lesion but usually is caused by diffuse brain disease. (For further discussion, see Chap. 7.)

The best way to demonstrate an absence of weakness or incoordination in the left hand is to see the patient carry out exactly the same behavior (which could not be carried out to verbal instruction) on some other occasion. This may either occur spontaneously or it may result from some difficult (nonverbal) instruction. The right-handed patient with callosal disconnection often cannot follow a verbal command such as "pretend you are turning a door knob" or "pretend you are combing your hair" while using the left hand. In contrast, the very same behavior will be readily executed when the patient is actually confronted with a real door knob to turn, or given (into the left hand) some article whose use is to be demonstrated.

Left-handed apraxia can sometimes be easily demonstrated simply by requesting a number of individual finger motions such as "stick out your little finger." When the patient is attempting to cooperate with the left hand, such a request may result in a parapraxis, or only in bewilderment on the patient's part; however the left little finger is adroitly extended when one silently demonstrates the desired action. In the most pronounced cases, the disability may include such relatively crude acts as opening or closing the fist, or even whole arm movements such as saluting, waving goodby, etc. when they are verbally requested.

A pronounced inability to perform certain movements in the left hand under the circumstances just described is strong evidence for a callosal lesion. One problem is that the dyspraxia is commonly accompanied by some weakness, because the naturally occurring callosal lesions often extend toward one or the other hemisphere. When the dyspraxia is accompanied by paresis or forced grasping, it can nonetheless be quite suggestive, especially if it is out of proportion to any weakness or incoordination simultaneously present.

UNILATERAL (LEFT) AGRAPHIA

Right-handers can write legibly, if not fluently, with the left hand. This ability is commonly lost with callosal lesions, especially (but not always) those which cause a unilateral apraxia (Gersh and Damasio, 1981). An inability to write to dictation is common with left hemisphere lesions, but these almost always affect the right hand at least as much as they affect the left. The left hand may be dysgraphic because it is affected by a right hemispheric lesion, such as a frontal lesion causing forced grasping. That the left dysgraphia is not simply attributable to an incoordination or paresis resulting from a right hemisphere lesion can be established if one can demonstrate some *other* ability in the left hand requiring as much control as would be required for writing. One cannot expect to see spontaneous left-handed writing, since the right hemisphere of most individuals rarely possesses sufficient language capacity for this (Gazzaniga and Sperry, 1967; Sperry and Gazzaniga, 1967; Gazzaniga and Hillyard, 1971; Levy et al., 1971; E. Zaidel, 1973; Gazzaniga et al., 1977), but one can some-times see the left hand doodling spontaneously or one can ask the patient to use the left hand to copy various designs or diagrams. Here, as elsewhere, it is not so much the presence of a deficit but rather the *contrast* between certain deficits and certain retained abilities that is most informative.

Simple or even complex geometric figures can often be copied by a left hand that cannot write or cannot even copy writing previously made with the patient's own right hand (Bogen and Gazzaniga, 1965; Bogen, 1969a; Kumar, 1977; D. Zaidel and Sperry, 1977). Copying of block letters may be present when the copying of cursive writing is not; this may be not an example of printing with the left hand but rather a copying of geometric figures that happen also to have linguistic content. (For a further discussion of agraphia, also see Chap. 4.)

UNıLATERAL (LEFT) TACTILE ANOMIA

One of the most convincing ways of demonstrating hemisphere disconnection is to ask the patient to feel with one hand and then to name various small, common objects, such as buttons, coins, and safety pins. When these are placed in the patient's hand, it is essential that vision be occluded. A blindfold is notoriously unreliable. It is better to have an assistant hold the patient's eyelids closed or to put a pillowcase over the patient's head for the brief testing session. For longer testing sessions, an opaque screen should be used.

Patients with hemisphere disconnection are generally unable to name or describe an object held in the left hand although they readily name objects held in the right hand. Sometimes a patient will be able to give a vague description of the object but be unable to name it; in this case there can still be a contrast with the ability to readily name the object when it is placed in the right hand.

To establish hemisphere disconnection, it is necessary to exclude other causes of unilateral anomia, particularly astereognosis (or even a gross sensory deficit), as may occur with a right parietal lesion. The best way to exclude astereognosis is to show that the object has in fact been recognized even though it cannot be verbally identi-fied or described. The most certain proof that the object has been identified is for the subject to retrieve it correctly from a collection of similar objects. Such a collection is most conveniently placed in a paper plate about 15 cm in diameter, around which the subject can shuffle the objects with one hand while exploring for the test object. Even without the evidence of correct retrieval, one can often reasonably exclude astereognosis by observing the rapid, facile, and appropriate manipulation of an object in spite of its unavailability to naming or verbal description.

In testing for anomia, one must be aware, in certain clever patients, of strategies for circumventing the defect. For example, the patient may drop an object or may manipulate it in some other way (such as running a fingernail down the teeth of a comb) to produce a characteristic noise by which the object can be identified. In the same vein, a subject may identify a pipe or some other object by a characteristic smell and thus circumvent the inability of the left hemisphere to identify, by palpation alone, an object in the left hand.

UNILATERAL (RIGHT) CONSTRUCTIONAL APRAXIA

By "constructional praxis" we mean the ability to put together a meaningful configuration. This can be an object (three dimensions) or a complex drawing (two dimensions). Constructional dyspraxia is the inability to organize several parts into a configuration despite a normal ability to handle or draw the individual parts (Benton, 1962, Benton and Fogel, 1962; Warrington, 1969; DeRenzi, 1982). Constructional dyspraxia can occur from lesions in either hemisphere; left lesions usually result in an absence of some of the parts and in simplified versions of a model, and right hemisphere lesions tend to result in inappropriate relationships among the parts, including a loss of perspective in drawings intended to represent three dimensions (Paterson and Zangwill, 1944; Warrington et al., 1966 Benton, 1967; Hécaen, 1969, Hécaen and Assal, 1970; Gainotti et al., 1977). (See Chap. 8.)

Constructional apraxia can be quite prominent in the right hand of right-handers with callosal lesions. The simplest way to test for this is to ask the patient to copy with one hand (and subsequently with the other) various geometric figures that can either be drawn right then by the examiner or prepared beforehand. It is usually better to proceed from simple squares and triangles to more complex figures, eventually including drawings that represent three-dimensional objects. Drawing with a felt pen is often easier than with a pencil.

Hemisphere disconnection (in a right-hander) is strongly suggested if the patient can copy designs better with the left hand. Of course, if a callosal lesion is accompanied by right hemisphere involvement, the left hand may be paretic or ataxic so that the patient does no better with the left hand than with the right.

SPATIAL ACALCULIA

Because hemisphere disconnection (or a right hemisphere lesion) can cause a right-hand disability for spatial forms, such a patient may have difficulties using pencil and paper to solve problems. This deficit may be mild and not noticeable unless the patient has an occupation in which sketching is regularly employed. Sometimes the deficit is so severe that it interferes with doing arithmetic problems (Dahmen et al., 1982). In our patients with complete cerebral commissurotomy, we usually observed some difficulty in doing written arithmetic following the operation, a deficit that progressively receded (Bogen, 1969a, p. 92). On a few occasions we were surprised to note that a patient would have difficulty in doing arithmetic on paper whereas comparable problems could be done by mental calculation. This was a rather elusive phenomenon and was never pursued; that it was, in fact, a sign of hemisphere disconnection is suggested by the report of a similar situation in the case of a 41-year-old woman with a callosal hematoma associated with an (operated) anterior cerebral aneurysm (Brion and Jedynak, 1975).

It is rare to find a patient who can do arithmetic to verbal instruction but cannot do similar problems presented on paper, despite adequate reading and writing skills;

but the phenomenon is sufficiently dramatic and is of sufficient scientific interest that looking for it, in appropriate circumstances, is probably worthwhile.

The foregoing signs of disconnection are all dependent on hemispheric dominance—either left or right, depending upon the particular task. Even more convincing are disconnection signs appearing with tests for which there is little, if any, dominance. These include the transfer of somesthetic information, whether tactile, proprioceptive, or stereognostic. How to test for these is described on p. 309.

THREE EXAMPLES OF REMAINING PROBLEMS

Postcommissurotomy Mutism

Following complete section of the cerebral commissures, there is a mutism of variable duration during which the patient does not talk even when she or he is quite cooperative and able to write. I first thought this was simply a neighborhood sign, a partial form of akinetic mutism (without the akinesia) that resulted from retraction around the anteror end of the third ventricle during section of the anterior commissure (Cairns, 1952; Ross and Stewart, 1981). However, it may be a disconnection sign, since I have now seen a number of patients with similar retraction whose commissural section spared the splenium and who did *not* have mutism. So I now favor the speculation that the mutism results either from some hemispheric conflict (possibly at a brainstem level) or from a bilateral diaschisis that affects speech much more than writing (Bogen, 1976; Bogen, 1983; Sussman et al., 1983). Whatever the speculative explanation for these postsurgical obsevations, clinical experience indicates that, when mutism occurs with naturally occurring callosal lesions, the disease process probably involves the anterior cingulate regions bilaterally (above the callosum) or the septal area (below the callosum). These patients, however, are usually also akinetic.

The Anterior Commissure

Among other unresolved problems is the role of the anterior commissure, both in the normal state and following callosal injury. Previously mentioned was the compensatory role of the anterior commissure in callosal agenesis and following splenial section. However, most of the syndrome seen after a complete cerebral commissurotomy is also seen (i.e., has *not* been compensated) after a callosotomy sparing the anterior and hippocampal commissures (Gazzaniga and LeDoux, 1978; McKeever et al., 1981). This is perhaps not surprising since the anterior commissure is only $\frac{1}{100}$ the size of the corpus callosum. On the other hand, we can appreciate how significant it might be when we consider the wealth of information conveyed over one optic nerve—the diameter of which is about the same as that of the anterior commissure. This question is complicated by the fact that the anterior commissure, with respect to size, seems to be one of the most variable structures in the brain; it may have as much as three or four times as great a diameter in some people as in others (Yamamoto et al. 1981). In addition to these individual differences, there are phylogenetic differences in the anterior commissure; it seems to play a much greater role in interhemispheric transmission in monkeys than in cats (Hamilton, 1982). And one might expect it to be even more important in humans. The discrepancy between monkeys (transfer of learning by the anterior commissure) and humans (inability to compensate for callosotomy) remains unexplained. It may reflect the artificial nature of the tasks used to test monkeys. It may also be related to persistent memory deficits noted after callosotomy in humans (Gur et al., in press;).

Alexia without Agraphia

Stroke patients who can write but are unable to read, even what they have just written correctly to dictation, are not extremely rare. This remarkable dissociation of reading from writing has been known for nearly a century (Dejerine, 1892). How can it be explained? A popular explanation is as follows. Since such a patient usually has a right homonymous hemianopia resulting from a left occipital lobe lesion, nothing can be seen, much less read, in the right half-field. Hence, visual information can reach the left hemisphere language zone only from the left half-field via the right occipital cortex and the splenium. In addition, another (or confluent) splenial lesion (usually present in such cases) has disconnected the right occipital cortex from the left hemisphere. On this explanation, the left hemisphere still retains a competence to write to dictation but no longer has access to information arriving in the right occipital lobe from the left visual half-field (Foix and Hillemand, 1925b; Geschwind and Fusillo, 1966; Benson and Geschwind, 1969; Geschwind, 1970; Cumming et al., 1970; Ajax et al., 1977; Benson, 1977; Damasio, 1977; Benson, 1979).

As its proponents have recognized, there are some difficulties with this explanation. For example, after surgical section of the splenium leaving the anterior commissure intact, patients can often name objects or pictures of objects in the left half-field, showing that information *can* reach the language zone from the left half-field (Iwata et al., 1974). In at least some cases of complete callosotomy with retained anterior commissure, there may be no alexia for the left half-field (Risse et al., 1978). Moreover, alexia without agraphia can sometimes occur without an accompanying loss of the right visual half-field (Ajax, 1967; Heilman et al., 1971; Goldstein et al., 1971; Greenblatt, 1973; Vincent et al., 1977). And there occur cases of alexia without agraphia in which the splenium is likely to be largely intact (Wechsler et al., 1972; Hécaen and Gruner, 1975; Greenblatt, 1976; Staller et al., 1978; R. N. N. Holtzman et al., 1978; Bigley and Sharp, 1983) as well as a personal (Bogen) post-traumatic case with CAT scan lesion in the left temporoparietal region.

Some of the problems in explaining alexia without agraphia can be seen in the very first, famous case of Dejerine (1892). This 68-year-old man, "of above-average intelligence and culture," suffered a left occipital infarct. He was followed for four years, during which time he continued to manage his business affairs. On a number of different testing sessions he could write without error entire pages, none of which he could read. An accomplished musician and sight-reader, he readily learned difficult passages by ear following his stroke, but he could no longer read "a single musical note." Nor could he name a single written letter, but he readily named written numbers as well as real objects, and he could do arithmetic problems written on paper. Moreover, his hemianopia was not terribly dense, objects being obscure and gray in his right visual half-field. His callosal (splenial) lesion was quite small and was dismissed by Dejerine as irrelevant to the behavioral deficit. (Also see Chap. 3.)

Alexia without agraphia has been argued for nearly a century; it is still a puzzle. Part of the answer may be, among other things, that reading is a multistage process that can be disturbed in a variety of ways (Hécaen and Kremin, 1976; Greenblatt, 1977; Landis et al., 1980). There is a good deal more to be learned about this striking condition in which the ability to read is disturbed far out of proportion to disturbance in other abilities.

In the past 25 years, our understanding of commissural function has been greatly enriched and clarified, but there remain many unresolved issues. Postcommissurotomy mutism, the compensatory capacity of the anterior commissure, and alexia without agraphia are but three of these issues.

REFERENCES

Ajax, E. T. (1967). Dyslexia without agraphia. *Arch. Neurol. 17*:645–652.

Ajaz, E. T., Schenkenberg, T., and Kosteljanetz, M. (1977). Alexia without agraphia and the inferior splenium. *Neurology 27*:685–688.

Akelaitis, A. J. (1944–45). Studies on the corpus callosum, IV: Diagnostic dyspraxia in epileptics following partial and complete section of the corpus callosum. *Am. J. Psychiat. 101*:594–599.

Akelaitis, A. J. (1944). A study of gnosis, praxis and language following section of the corpus collosum and anterior commissure. *J. Neurosurg. 1*:94–102.

Albert, M. L., Silverberg, R., Reches, A., and Berman, M. (1976). Cerebral dominance for consciousness. *Arch. Neurol. 33*:453–454.

Alpers, B. J. (1936). The mental syndrome of tumors of the corpus callosum. *Arch. Neurl. Psychiat. 35*:911–912.

Aptman, M., Levin, H., and Senelick, R. C. (1977). Alexia without agraphia in a left-handed patient with prosopagnosia. *Neurology 27*:533–536.

Apuzzo, M. L. J., Chikovani, O. K., Gott, P. S., Teng, E. L., Zee, C. S., Giannotta, S. L., and Weiss, M. H. (1982). Transcallosal, interfornicial approaches for lesions affecting the third ventricle: Surgical considerations and consequences. *Neurosurgery 10*:547–554.

Assal, G. (1969) Regression des troubles de la reconnaissance des physionomies et de la mémoire topographique chez un malade opéré d'un hématome intracérébral pariéto-temporal droit. *Rev. Neurol. 121*:184–185.

Bale, P. M., and Reye, R. D. K. (1976). Epignathus, double pituitary and agenesis of corpus callosum. *J. Pathol. 120*:161–164.

Barbizet, J., Degos, J. D., Duizabo, P., and Chartier, B. (1974). Syndrome de déconnexion interhémisphérique d'origine ischémique. *Rev. Neurol. 130*:127–142.

Barbizet, J., Degos, J. D., Leeune, A., and Leroy, A. (1978). Syndrome de dysconnection interhémisphérique avec dyspraxie diagonistique au cours d'une maladie de marchafava-bignami. *Rev. Neurol. 134*:781–789.

Barbizet, J., Duizabo, P., Bouchareine, A., Degos, J. D., and Poirier, J. (1977). *Abrégé de Neuropsychologie*. Paris: Masson.

Beneš, V. (1982). Sequelae of transcallosal surgery. *Child's Brain* 9:69–72.

Benson, D. F. (1977). The third alexia. *Arch. Neurol.* 34:327–331.

Benson, D. F. (1979). *Aphasia, Alexia and Agraphia.* New York: Churchill Livingstone.

Benson, D. F., and Geschwind, N. (1969). The alexias. *Handbook Clin. Neurol.* 4:112–140.

Benson, D. F., Segarra, J., and Albert, M. L. (1974). Visual agnosia-prosopagnosia. *Arch. Neurol.* 30:307–310.

Benton, A. L. (1962). The visual retention test as a constructional praxis task. *Confin. Neurol.* 22:141–155.

Benton, A. L. (1967). Constructional apraxia and the minor hemisphere. *Confin. Neurol.* 29:1–16.

Benton, A. L. (1977). Historical notes on hemispheric dominance. *Arch. Neurol.* 34:127–129.

Benton, A. L. (1980). The neuropsychology of facial recognition. *Am. Psychol.* 35:176–186.

Benton, A. L., and Fogel, M. L. (1962). Three-dimensional constructional praxis. *Arch. Neurol.* 7:347–354.

Benton, A. L., and Van Allen, M. W. (1972). Prosopagnosia and facial discrimination. *J. Neurol. Sci.* 15:167–172.

Berlucchi, G. (1972). Anatomical and physiological aspects of visual functions of corpus callosum. *Brain Res.* 37:371–392.

Berlucchi, G., Brizzolara, D., Marzi, C. A., Rizzolatti, G., and Umiltà, C. (1974). Can lateral asymmetries in attention explain interfield differences in visual perception? *Cortex* 10:177–185.

Beukelman, D. R., Flowers, C. R., and Swanson, P. D. (1980). Cerebral disconnection associated with anterior communicating artery aneurysm: Implications for evaluation of symptoms. *Arch. Phys. Med. Rehabil.* 61:18–23.

Bigley, G. K., and Sharp, F. R. (1983). Reversible alexia without agraphia due to migraine. *Arch. Neurol.* 40:114–115.

Black, P., and Myers, R. E. (1964). Visual function of the forebrain commissures in the chimpanzee. *Science* 146:799–800.

Bogen, J. E. (1969a). The other side of the brain. I: Dysgraphia and dyscopia following cerebral commissurotomy. *Bull. Los Angeles Neurol. Soc.* 34:73–105.

Bogen, J. E. (1969b). The other side of the brain. II: An appositional mind. *Bull. Los Angeles Neurol. Soc.* 34:135–162.

Bogen, J. E. (1976). Language function in the short term following cerebral commissurotomy. In *Current Trends in Neurolinguistics* (H. Avakian-Whitaker and H. A. Whitaker, eds.). New York: Academic Press.

Bogen, J. E. (1977). Further discussion on split-brains and hemispheric capabilities. *Br. J. Phil. Sci.* 28:281–286.

Bogen, J. (1983). Concluding overview. In *Epilepsy and the Corpus Callosum* (A. Reeves, ed.). New York: Plenum.

Bogen, J. E., and Bogen, G. M. (1969). The other side of the brain. III: The corpus callosum and creativity. *Bull. Los Angeles Neurol. Soc.* 34:191–220.

Bogen, J. E., and Gazzaniga, M. S. (1965). Cerebral commissurotomy in man: Minor hemisphere dominance for certain visuospatial functions. *J. Neurosurg.* 23:394–399.

Bogen, J. E., and Vogel, P. J. (1962). Cerebral commissurotomy in man. *Bull. Los Angeles Neurol. Soc.* 27 169–172.

Bogen, J. E., and Vogel, P. J. (1975) Neurologic status in the long term following cerebral commissurotomy. In *Les Syndromes de Disconnexion Calleuse chez L'Homme* (F. Michel and B. Schott, eds.). Lyon: Hopital Neurologique.

Bogen, J. E., Fisher, E. D., and Vogel, P. J. (1965). Cerebral commissurotomy: A second case report. *J. Am. Med. Assoc* 194:1328–1329.

Bogen, J. E., Sperry, R. W., and Vogel, P. J. (1969). Commissural section and the propagation of seizures. In *Basic Mechanisms of the Epilepsies* (H. H. Jasper, A. A. Ward, and A. Pope, eds.). Boston: Little, Brown.

Bornstein, B., Sroka, H., and Munitz, H. (1969). Prosopagnosia with animal face agnosia. *Cortex* 5:164–169.

Bossom, J., Sperry, R. W., and Arora, H. (1961). Division of emotional behavior patterns in split-brain monkeys. *Caltech. Biol. Ann. Rep.*, p. 127.

Bossy, J. G. (1970). Morphological study of a case of complete, isolated and asymptomatic agnesis of the corpus callosum. *Arch. Anat. Histol. and Embryol.* 53:289–340.

Botez, M. (1974). Frontal lobe tumours. *Handbook Clin. Neurol.* 17:234–280.

Botez, M. I., and Bogen, J. E. (1976). The grasp reflex of the foot and related phenomena in the absence of other reflex abnormalities following cerebral commissurotomy. *Acta Neurol. Scandinav.* 54:453–463.

Botez, M. I., and Crighel, E. (1971). Partial disconnexion syndrome in an ambidextrous patient. *Brain* 94:487–494.

Bradshaw, J. L., and Nettleton, N. C. (1983). *Human Cerebral Asymmetry.* Englewood Cliffs, N.J.: Prentice-Hall.

Bradshaw, J. L., Gates, A., and Nettleton, N. C. (1977). Bihemispheric involvement in lexical decisions: Handedness and a possible sex difference. *Neuropsychologia* 15:277–286.

Bremer, F., Brihaye, J., and André-Balisaux, G. (1956). Physiologie et pathologie du corps calleux. *Arch. Suisses Neurol. Psychiat.* 78:31–87.

Brion, S., and Jedynak, C. P. (1972). Troubles du transfert interhémisphérique (callosal disconnection) a propos de 3 observations de tumeurs du corps calleux: Le signe de la main étrangère. *Rev. Neurol.* 126:257–266.

Brion, S., and Jedynak, C. P. (1975). *Les Troubles du Transfert Interhémisphérique.* Paris: Masson.

Broman, M. (1979). Reaction-time differences between the right and left hemisphere for face and letter discrimination in children and adults. *Cortex* 14:578–591.

Brown, J. W., and Hécaen, H. (1976). Lateralization and language representation. *Neurology* 26:183–189.

Brown, J. W., and Jaffe, J. (1975). Hypothesis on cerebral dominance. *Neuropsychologia* 13:107–110.

Bruce, A. (1890). On the absence of corpus callosum in the human brain, with the description of a new case. *Brain* 12:171–190.

Burklund, C. W., and Smith, A. (1977). Language and the cerebral hemispheres. *Neurology* 27:627–633.

Butler, S. R., Glass, A., and Heffner, R. (1981). Asymmetries of the contingent negative variation (CNV) and its after positive wave (APW) related to differential hemispheric involvement in verbal and nonverbal tasks. *Biol. Psychol.* 13:157–171.

Cairns, H. R. (1952). Disturbances of consciousness with lesions of the brainstem and diencephalon. *Brain* 75:109–146.

Campbell, A. L., Bogen, J. E., and Smith, A. (1981). Disorganization and reorganization of cognitive and sensorimotor functions in cerebral commissurotomy. Compensatory roles of the forebrain commissues and cerebral hemispheres in man. *Brain* 104:493–511.

Caplan, D., Holmes, J. M., and Marshall, J. C. (1974). Word classes and hemispheric specialization. *Neuropsychologia* 12:331–337.

Carleton, C. C., Collins, G. H., and Schimpff, R. D. (1976). Subacute necrotizing encephalopathy (Leigh's disease): Two unusual cases. *South. Med. J.* 69:1301–1305.

Carmon, A., Gordon, H. W., Bental, E., and Harness, B. Z. (1977). Retraining in literal alexia: Substitution of a right hemisphere perceptual strategy for impaired left hemispheric processing. *Bull. L.A. Neurol. Soc. 42*:41–50.

Cavalli, M., De Renzi, E., Faglioni, P., and Vitale, A. (1981). Impairment of right brain-damaged patients on a linguistic cognitive task. *Cortex 17*:545–556.

Clarke, E., and O'Malley, C. D. (1968). *The Human Brain and Spinal Cord.* Berkeley: University of California Press.

Cobben, A., Seron, X., Gillet, J., and Bonnal, J. (1978). Absence de signe de déconnexion lors d'un examen neuro-psychologique différé dans quatre cas de lésions callosales antérieures et médianes partielles d'origine vasculaire et neurochirurgicale. *Acta Neurol. Belg. 78*:207–216.

Cohn, R., Neumann, M. A., and Wood, D. H. (1977). Prosopagnosia: A clinicopathological study. *Ann. Neurol. 1*:177–182.

Critchley, M. (1930). The anterior cerebral artery and its syndromes. *Brain 53*:120–165.

Cullen, J. K. (1975). *Tests of a model for speech information flow.* Ph.D. thesis, Louisiana State University.

Cumming, W. J. K., Hurwitz, L. J., and Perl, N. T. (1970). A study of a patient who had alexia without agraphia. *J. Neurol. Neurosurg. Psychiat. 33*:34–39.

Curry, F. K. W. (1968). A comparison of the performances of a right hemispherectomized subject and 25 normals on four dichotic listening tasks. *Cortex 4*:144–153.

Dahmen, W., Hartje, W., Bussing, A., and Sturm, W. (1982). Disorders of calculation in aphasic patients: Spatial and verbal components. *Neuropsychologia 20*:145–153.

Damasio, A. R. (1977). Varieties and significance of the alexias. *Arch. Neurol. 34:- 325–326.*

Damasio, A. R., Damasio, H., and Van Hoesen, G. W. (1982). Prosopagnosia: Anatomic basis and behavioral mechanisms. *Neurology 32*:331–341.

Damasio, H., and Damasio, A. (1979). "Paradoxic" ear extinction in dichotic listening: Possible anatomic significance. *Neurology 29*:644–653.

Dandy, W. E. (1936). Operative experience in cases of pineal tumor. *Arch. Surg. 33*:19–46.

Dejerine, J. (1892) Contribution a l'étude anatomo-pathologique et clinique des différentes variétés de cécité verbale. *Comptes rendus des séances et mémoires de la Soc. de Biol. Vol. 44 (vol. 4 of Series 9) (Second section-Mémoires)*:61–90.

Denckla, M. B. (1974). Development of motor coordination in normal children. *Dev. Med. Child Neurol. 16*:729–741.

Denckla, M. B., and Rudel, R. G. (1978). Anomalies of motor development in hyperactive boys. *Ann. Neurol. 3*:231–233.

Dennis, M. (1976). Impaired sensory and motor differentiation with corpus callosum agenesis: A lack of callosal inhibition during ontogeny? *Neuropsychologia 14*:455–469.

Dennis, M. and Whitaker, H. A. (1976). Language acquisition following hemidecortication: Linguistic superiority of the left over the right hemisphere *Brain and Language 3*:404–433.

Denny-Brown, D. (1958). The nature of apraxia. *J. Nervous Mental Dis. 126*:9–32.

De Renzi, E. (1982a). *Disorders of Space Exploration and Cognition.* New York: Wiley.

De Renzi, E. (1982b). Memory disorders folowing focal neocortical damage. *Phil. Trans. R. Soc. Lond. B298*:73–83.

De Renzi, E., Faglioni, P., and Spinnler, H. (1968). The performance of patients with unilateral brain damage on face recognition tasks. *Cortex 4*:17–34.

Dewson, J. H. III (1977). Preliminary evidence of hemispheric asymmetry of auditory function in monkeys. In *Lateralization in the Nervous System* (S. Harnad et al., eds.) New York: Academic Press.

Dimond, S. J. (1972). *The Double Brain*. London: Churchill-Livingsone.

Dixon, N. F., and Jeeves, M. A. (1970). The interhemispheric transfer of movement aftereffects: A comparison between acallosal and normal subjects. *Psychon. Sci. 20(4)*:201–203.

Doty, R. W., and Negrão, N. (1972). Forebrain commissures and vision. In *Handbook of Sensory Physiology VII/3* (R. Jung, ed.). Berlin: Springer-Verlag.

Doty, R. W., and Overman, W. H. (1977). Memonic role of forebrain commissures in macaques. In *Lateralization in the Nervous System*. (S. Harnad et al., eds.). New York: Academic Press.

Doty, R. W., Negrão, N., and Yamaga, K. (1973). The unilateral engram. *Acta Neurobiol. Exp. 33*:711–728.

Doty, R. W., Yamaga, K., and Negrão, N. (1971). Mediation of visual fear via the corpus callosum. *Proc. Soc. Neurosci. 1*:104.

Downer, J. L. de C. (1961). Changes in visual gnostic functions and emotional behavior following unilateral temporal pole damage in the split-brain monkey. *Nature 191*:50–51.

Downer, J. L. de C. (1962). Interhemispheric integration in the visual system. In *Interhemispheric Relations and Cerebral Dominance* (V. B. Mountcastle, ed.). Baltimore: Johns Hopkins University Press.

Dumas, R., and Morgan, A. (1975). EEG asymmetry as a function of occupation, task, and task difficulty. *Neuropsychologia 13*:219–228.

Efron, R., Bogen, J. E., and Yund, E. W. (1977). Perception of dichotic chords by normal and commissurotomized human subjects. *Cortex 13*:137–149.

Elberger, A. J. (1980). The effect of neonatal section of the corpus callosum on the development of depth perception in young cats. *Vis. Res. 20*:177–187.

Elliot, F. A. (1969). The corpus callosum, cingulate gyrus, septum pellucidum, septal area and fornix. *Handbook Clin. Neurol. 2*:758–775.

Escourolle, R., Hauw, J. J., Gray, F., and Henin, D. (1975). Aspects neuropathologiques des lésions du corps calleux. In *Les Syndromes de Disconnexion Calleuse Chez l'Homme* (F. Michel and B. Schott, eds.). Lyon: Hôpital Neurologique.

Ethelberg, S. (1951). Changes in circulation through the anterior cerebral artery. *Acta Psychiat. Neurol. Suppl. 75*:3–211.

Ettlinger, G., Blakemore, C. B., Milner, A. D., and Wilson, J. (1972). Agenesis of the corpus callosum: A behavioral investigation. *Brain 95*:327–346.

Ettlinger, G., Blakemore, C. B., Milner, A. D., and Wilson, J. (1974). Agenesis of the corpus callosum: A further behaviouralinvestigation. *Brain 97*:225–234.

Ferriss, G. D., and Dorsen, M. M. (1975). Agenesis of the corpus callosum: Neuropsychological studies. *Cortex 11*:95–122.

Fessard, A. E. (1954). Mechanisms of nervous integration and conscious experience. In *Brain Mechanisms and Consciousness* (J. F. Delafresnaye, ed.). Springfield, Ill.: C. C. Thomas.

Fisher, C. M. (1963). Symmetrical mirror movements and left ideomotor apraxia. *Trans. Amer. Neurol. Assoc. 88*:214–216.

Foix, C., and Hillemand, P. (1925a). Les syndromes de l'artère cérébrale antérieure. *Encéphale 20*:209–232.

Foix, C., and Hillemand, P. (1925b). Role vraisemblable du splenium dans la pathogénie de l'alexie pure par lésion de la artère cérébrale postérieure. *Bull. Mém. Soc. Méd. Hôp. 49*:393–395.

Gainotti, G., Miceli, G., and Caltagirone, C. (1977). Constructional apraxia in left brain-damaged patients: A planning disorder? *Cortex 13*:109–118.

Galin, D. (1974). Implications for psychiatry of left and right cerebral specialization. *Arch. Gen. Psychiat. 31*:572–583.

Galin, D. (1977). Lateral specialization and psychiatric issues: Speculations on development and the evolution of consciousness. *Ann. New York Acad. Sci. 299:*397–411.

Galin, D., Diamond, R., and Herron, J. (1977). Development of crossed and uncrossed tactile localization on the fingers. *Brain and Language 4:*588–590.

Galin, D., Johnstone, J., Nakell, L., and Herron J. (1979). Development of the capacity for tactile information transfer between hemispheres in normal children. *Science 204:*1330–1332.

Gardner, H., and Zurif, E. (1975). Bee but not be: Oral reading and single words in aphasia and alexia. *Neuropsychologia 13:*181–190.

Gazzaniga, M. S. (1966). Interhemispheric communication of visual learning. *Neuropsychologia 4:*183–189.

Gazzaniga, M. S. (1970). *The Bisected Brain.* New York: Appleton.

Gazzaniga, M. S., and Freedman, H. (1973). Observations on visual processes after posterior callosal section. *Neurology 23:*1126–1130

Gazzaniga, M. S., and Hillyard, S. A. (1971). Language and speech capacity of the right hemisphere. *Neuropsychologia 9:*273–280.

Gazzaniga, M. S., and LeDoux, J. E. (1978). *The Integrated Mind.* New York: Plenum.

Gazzaniga, M. S., and Sperry, R. W. (1967). Language after section of the cerebral commissures. *Brain 90:*131–148.

Gazzaniga, M. S., Bogen, J. E., and Sperry, R. W. (1962). Some functional effects of sectioning the cerebral commissures in man. *Proc. Nat. Acad. Sci. 48:*1765–9.

Gazzaniga, M. S., Bogen, J. E., and Sperry, R. W. (1963). Laterality effects in somesthesis following cerebral commissurotomy in man. *Neuropsychologia 1:*209–215.

Gazzaniga, M. S., Bogen, J. E., and Sperry, R. W. (1965). Observations on visual perception after disconnexion of the cerebral hemispheres in man. *Brain 88:*221–236.

Gazzaniga, M. S., Bogen, J. E., and Sperry, R. W. (1967). Dyspraxia following division of the cerebral commissures. *Arch. Neurol. 16:*606–612.

Gazzaniga, M. S., Risse, G. L., Springer, S. P., Clark, E., and Wilson, D. H. (1975). Psychologic and neurologic consequences of partial and complete cerebral commissurotomy. *Neurology 25:*10–15.

Geffen, G., Bradshaw, J., and Wallace, G. (1971). Interhemispheric effects on reaction time to verbal and non-verbal visual stimuli. *J. Exp. Psychol. 87:*415–422.

Gersh, F., and Damasio, A. R. (1981). Praxis and writing of the left hand may be served by different callosal pathways. *Arch. Neurol. 38:*634–636.

Geschwind, N. (1964). The development of the brain and the evolution of language. In *Monograph Series on Language and Linguistics,* Vol. 17 (C.I.J.M. Stuart, ed.). Washington: Georgetown University Press.

Geschwind, N. (1965). Disconnexion syndromes in animals and man. *Brain 88:*237–294, 585–644.

Geschwind, N. (1970). The organization of language and the brain. *Science 170:*940–944.

Geschwind, N. (1974). *Selected Papers on Language and the Brain.* Boston: Reidel.

Geschwind, N. (1975). The apraxias: neural mechanisms of disorders of learned movement. *Am. Sci. 63:*188–195.

Geschwind, N., and Fusillo, M. (1966). Colour-naming defects in association with alexia. *Arch. Neurol. 15:*137–146.

Geschwind, N., and Kaplan, E. (1962). A human cerebral deconnection syndrome: A preliminary report. *Neurology 12:*675–685.

Glass, A., Butler, S. R., and Heffner, R. (1975). Asymmetries in the CNV eliited by verbal and non-verbal stimuli. 10th Int. Cong. Anat., Tokyo.

Glickstein, M., Arora, H. A., and Sperry, R. W. (1963). Delayed/response performance following optic tract section, unilateral frontal lesion, and commissurotomy. *J. Comp. Physiol. Psychol.* 56:11–18.

Gloning, I., Gloning, K., Jellinger, K., and Quatember, R. (1970). A case of prosopagnosia with necropsy findings. *Neuropsychologia* 8:199–204.

Gloning, I., Gloning, K., and Tschabitscher, H. (1966). Zur dominanzfrage beim Syndrom: Reine wortblindheit-farbagnosie. *Neuropsychologia* 4:27–40.

Goldberg, G., Mayer, N. H., and Toglia, J. U. (1981). Medial frontal cortex infarction and the alien hand sign. *Arch. Neurol.* 38:683–686.

Goldstein, K. (1953). Hugo Karl Liepmann. In *The Founders of Neurology* (W. Haymaker, ed.). Springfield, Ill.: C. C. Thomas.

Goldstein, M., and Joynt, R. (1969). Long-term follow-up of a callosal-sectioned patient. *Arch. Neurol.* 20:96–102.

Goldstein, M., Joynt, R. J., and Goldblatt, D. (1971). Word blindness with intact central visual fields. *Neurology* 21:873–876.

Goldstein, M., Joynt, R., and Hartley, R. (1975). The long-term effects of callosal sectioning. *Arch. Neurol.* 32:52–53.

Gordon, H. W. (1973). *Verbal and Non-verbal Cerebral Processing in Man for Audition.* Thesis, California Institute of Technology.

Gordon, H. W. (1975). Comparison of ipsilateral and contralateral auditory pathways in callosum-sectioned patients by use of a response-time technique. *Neuropsychologia* 13:9–18.

Gordon, H. W., and Sperry, R. W. (1969). Lateralization of olfactory perception in the surgically separated hemispheres of man. *Neuropsychologia* 7:111–120.

Gordon, H. W., Bogen, J. E., and Sperry, R. W. (1971). Absence of deconnexion syndrome in two patients with partial section of the neocommissures. *Brain* 94:327–336.

Gott, P. S., and Saul, R. E. (1978). Agenesis of the corpus callosum: Limits of functional compensation. *Neurology* 28:1271–1279.

Greenblatt, S. (1973). Alexia without agraphia or hemianopsia. *Brain* 96:307–316.

Greenblatt, S. H. (1976). Subangular alexia without agraphia or hemianopsia. *Brain and Language* 3:229–245.

Greenblatt, S. H. (1977). Neurosurgery and the anatomy of reading: A practical review. *Neurosurgery* 1:6–15.

Greenblatt, S. H., Saunders, R. L., Culver, C. M., and Bogdanowicz, W. (1980). Normal interhemispheric transfer with incomplete section of the splenium. *Arch. Neurol.* 37:567–571.

Greenwood, P., Wilson, D H., and Gazzaniga, M. S. (1977). Dream report following commissurotomy. *Cortex* 13:311–316.

Gur, R. E. Sussman, N. M., O'Connor, M., Vey, M. M., and Gur, R. C. (1982). The effect of corpus callosotomy on writing in a left-hander with left hemisphere language. *Neurology* 32:A188.

Gur, R. C., Trope, I., Gur, R. E., Sussman, N. M., Saykin, A. J., and O'Connor, M. J. (in preparation). Memory before and after Callosotomy in Humans.

Haaland, K. Y., and Delaney, H. D. (1981). Motor deficits after left or right hemisphere damage due to stroke or tumor. *Neuropsychologia* 19:17–27.

Haaland, K. Y., Cleeland, C. S., and Carr, D (1977). Motor performance after unilateral hemisphere damage in patients with tumors. *Arch. Neurol.* 34:556–559.

Hamilton, C. R. (1977). Investigations of perceptual and mnemonic lateralization in monkeys. In *Lateralization in the Nervous System* (S. Harnad et al., eds.). New York: Academic Press.

Hamilton, C. R. (1982). Mechanisms of interocular equivalence. In *Advances in the Analysis of Visual Behavior* (D. Ingle, M. Goodale, and R. Mansfield, eds.). Cambridge, Mass.: MIT Press.

Hamilton, C. R., and Vermeire, B. A. (1982). Hemispheric differences in split-brain monkeys learning sequential comparisons. *Neuropsychologia 20*:691–698.

Hamilton, C. R., and Vermeire, B. A. (1984). Discrimination of monkey faces by split-brain monkeys. *Neuropsychologia* (in press).

Hamsher, K., Levin, H. S., and Benton, A. L. (1979). Facial recognition in patients with focal brain lesions. *Arch. Neurol. 36*:837–839.

Harnad, S., Doty, R. W., Goldstein, L., Jaynes, J., and Krauthamer, G. (1977). *Lateralization in the Nervous System*. New York: Academic Press.

Hécaen, H. (1969). Aphasic, apraxic and agnosic syndromes in right and left hemisphere lesions. *Handbook Clin. Neurol. 4*:291–311.

Hécaen, H. (1981). The neuropsychology of face recognition. in *Perceiving and Remembering Faces* (G. Davies, H. Ellis, and J. Shepherd, eds.), New York: Academic Press.

Hécaen, H., and Ajuriaguerra, J. (1964). *Left Handedness*. New York: Grune and Stratton.

Hécaen, H., and Angelergues, R. (1962). Agnosia for faces (prosopagnosia). *Arch. Neurol. 7*:92–100.

Hécaen, H., and Assal, G. (1970). A comparison of constructive deficits following right and left hemispheric lesons. *Neuropsychologia 8*:289–303.

Hécaen, H., and Gimeno Alava, A. (1960). L'apraxie idéo-motrice unilatérale gauche. *Rev. Neurol. 102*:648–653.

Hécaen, H., and Gruner, J. (1975). Alexie pure avec intégrité du corps calleux. In *Les Syndromes de Disconnexion Callese Chez l'Homme* (F. Michel and B. Schott, eds.). Lyon: Hôpital Neurologique.

Hécaen, H., and Kremin, H. (1976). Neurolinguistic research on reading disorders resulting from left hemisphere lesions: Aphasic and pure alexias. In *Studies in Neurolinguistics* (H. Whitaker and H. A. Whitaker, eds.). New York: Academic Press.

Hécaen, H., De Agostini, M., and Monzon-Montes, A. (1981). Cerebral organization in left-handers. *Brain and Language 12*:261–284.

Heilman, K. M., and Watson, R. T. (1977). The neglect syndrome: A unilateral defect of the orienting response. In *Lateralization in the Nervous System* (S. Harnad et al., eds.). New York: Academic Press.

Heilman, K. M., Coyle, J. M. Gonyea, E. F., and Geschwind, N. (1973). Apraxia and agraphia in a left-hander. *Brain 96*:21–28.

Heilman, K. M., Safran, A., and Geschwind, N. (1971). Closed head trauma and aphasia. *J. Neurol. Neurosurg. Psychiat. 34*:265–269.

Herron, J., ed. (1980). *Neuropsychology of Left-Handedness*. Academic Press: New York.

Hilliard, R. D. (1973). Hemispheric laterality effects on a facial recognition task in normal subjects. *Cortex 9*:246–259.

Hirose, G., Kin, T., and Murakami, E. (1977). Alexia without agraphia associated with right occipital lesion. *J. Neurol. Neurosurg. Psychiat. 40*:225–227.

Holtzman, J. D., Sidtis, J. J., Volpe, B. T., Wilson, D. H., and Gazzaniga, M. S. (1981). Dissociation of spatial information for stimulus localization and the control of attention. *Brain 104*:861–872.

Holtzman, R. N. N., Rudel, R. G., and Goldensohn, E. S. (1978). Paroxysmal alexia. *Cortex 14*:592–603.

Hoppe, K. D. (1977). Split brains and psychoanalysis. *Psychoanalytic Quart. 46*:220–244.

Hoppe, K., and Bogen, J. E. (1977). Alexithymia in 12 commissurotomized patients. *Psychother. Psychosom. 28*:148–155.

Horel, J. A., and Keating, E. G. (1969). Partial Klüver-Bucy syndrome produced by cortical disconnection. *Brain Res.* 16:281–284.

Horel, J. A., and Keating, E. G. (1972). Recovery from a partial Klüver-Bucy syndrome in the monkey produced by disconnection. *J. Comp. Physiol. Psychol.* 79:105–114.

Ironside, R., and Guttmacher, M. (1929). The corpus callosum and its tumours. *Brain* 52:442–483.

Ito, M., Yashiki, K., and Hirata, T. (1972). Agenesis of the corpus callosum in man. *Acta Anat. Nippon* 47:391–402.

Iversen, S. D., and Mishkin, M. (1970. Perseverative interference in monkeys following selective lesions of the inferior prefrontal convexity. *Exp. Brain Res.* 11:376–386.

Iwata, M., Sugishita, M., Toyokura, Y., Yamada, R., and Yoshioka, M. (1974). Étude sur le syndrome de disconnexion visuo-linguale après la transection du splénium du corps calleux. *J. Neurol. Sci.* 23:421–432.

Jacobsen, C. F., and Nissen, H. W. (1937). Studies of cerebral function in primates. IV: The effects of frontal lobe lesions on the delayed alternation habit in monkeys. *J. Comp. Physiol. Psychol.* 23:101–112.

Jason, G. W. (1983a). Hemispheric asymmetries in motor function. I: Left-hemisphere specialization for memory but not performance. *Neuosychologia* 21:35–45.

Jason, G. W. (1983b). Hemispheric asymmetries in motor function. II: Ordering does not contribute to left-hemispere specialization. *Neuropsychologia* 21:47–58.

Jeeves, M. A. (1965a). Agenesis of the corpus callosum-physiopathological and clinical aspects. *Proc. Austr. Assoc. Neurol.* 3:41–48.

Jeeves, M. A. (1965b). Psychological studies of three cases of congenital agenesis of the corpus callosum. In *Functions of the Corpus Callosum* (E. G. Ettlinger, ed.). London: Churchill.

Jeeves, M. A. (1979). Some limits to interhemispheric integration in cases of callosal agenesis and partial commissurotomy. In *Structure and Function of Cerebral Commssures* (I. S. Russell, M. W. van Hof, and G. Berlucchi, eds.). Baltimore: University Park Press.

Jeeves, M. A., and Wilson, A. F. (1969). Tactile transfer and neonatal callosal section in the cat. *Psychon. Sci. 16* (5):235–237.

Joynt, R. J. (194). The corpus callosum: History of thought regarding its function. In *Hemispheric Disconnection and Cerebral Function* (M. Kinsbourne and W. L. Smith, eds.). Springfield, Ill.: C. C. Thomas.

Joynt, R. J. (1977). Inattention syndromes in split-brain man. In *Hemi-Inattention and Hemisphere Specialization* (E. A. Weinstein and R. P. Friedland, eds.). New York: Raven Press.

Kimura, D. (1967). Functional asymmetry of the brain in dichotic listening. *Cortex* 3:163–178.

Kimura, D. (1983). Sex differences in cerebal organization for speech and praxic functions. *Can. J. Psychol.* 37:19–35.

Kimura, D., and Archibald Y. (1974). Motor functions of the left hemisphere. *Brain* 97:337–350.

Kimura, D., Battison, R., and Lubert, B. (1976). Impairment of nonlinguistic hand movements in a deaf aphasic. *Brain and Language* 3:566–571.

Kimura, D., Davidson, W., and McCormick, C. W. (1982). No impairment in sign language after right-hemisphere stroke. *Brain and Language* 17:359–362.

Kinsbourne, M. (1971). The minor cerebral hemisphere as a source of aphasic speech. *Arch. Nerol.* 25:302–306.

Kinsbourne, M. (1975). Minor hemisphere language and cerebral maturation. In *Foundations of Language Development* (H. Lenneberg and E. Lenneberg, ds.). New York: Academic Press.

Kinsbourne, M., and Fisher, M. (1971). Latency of uncrossed and of crossed reaction in callosal agenesis. *Neuropsychologia 9*:471–473.

Kinsbourne, M., and Smith, W. L. (1974). *Hemispheric Disconnection and Cerebral Function*. Springfield, Ill., C. C. Thomas.

Kirschbaum, W. R. (1947). Agenesis of the corpus callosum and associated malformations. *J. Neuropath. Exp. Neurol. 6*:78–94.

Klein, R., and Ingram, I. M. (1958). Functional disorganization of the left limbs in a tumour of the corpus callosum infiltrating the hemispheres. *J. Mental Sci. 104*:732–742.

Kling, A. and Steklis, H. D. (1976). A neural substrate for affiliative behavior in nonhuman primates. *Brain Behav. Evol. 13*:216–238.

Kohn, B., and Dennis, M. (1974). Patterns of hemispheric specialization after hemidecortication for infantile hemiplegia. In *Hemispheric Disconnection and Cerebral Function* (M. Kinsbourne and W. L. Smith, eds.). Springfield, Ill.: C. C. Thomas.

Krashen, S. D. (1976). Cerebral asymmetry. In *Studies in Neurolinguistics*. (H. Whitaker and H. A. Whitaker, eds.). New York: Academic Press.

Kuhlenbeck, H. (1969). Some comments on the development of the human corpus callosum and septum pellucidum. *Acta Anat. Nippon 44*:245–256.

Kuhn, T. S. (1962). *The Structure of Scientific Revolutions*. Chicago: University of Chicago Press.

Kumar, S. (1977). Short-term memory for a non-verbal tactual task after cerebral commissurotomy. *Cortex 13*:55–61.

Landis, T., Regard, M., and Serrat, A. (1980). Iconic reading in a case of alexia without agraphia caused by brain tumor: A tachistoscopic study. *Brain and Language 11*:45–53.

Lansdell, H. (1968). Effect of extent of temporal lobe ablations on two lateralized deficits. *Physiol. Behav. 3*:271–273.

Lassen, N. A., and Larsen, B. (1980). Cortical activity in the left and right hemispheres during language-related brain functions. *Phonetica 37*:27–37.

Lassonde, M. C., Lortie, J., Ptito, M., and Geoffroy, G. (1981). Hemispheric asymmetry in callosal agenesis as revealed by dichotic listening performance. *Neuropsychologia 19*:455–458.

Le Beau, J. (1943). Sur la chirurgie des tumeurs du corps calleux. *Union Med. Canada 72*:1365–1381.

Lechevalier, B., Andersson, J. C., Morin, P., and Poilpre, E. (1975). Syndrome de disconnexion calleuse avec trouble de la coordination visuomotice croisée (phénomène d'évitement croisé) au cours d'une maladie de Marchiafava-Bignami. in *Les Syndromes de Disconnexion Calleuse Chez l'Homme* (F. Michel and B. Schott, eds.). Lyon: Hôpital Neurologique.

Lecours, A. R., and Lhermitte, F. (1979). *L'Aphasie*. Paris: Flammarion.

LeDoux, J E.,Wlson, D. H., and Gazzaniga, M. S. (1977). A divided mind: Observations on the conscious properties of the separated hemispheres. *Ann. Neurol. 2*:417–421.

Lehman, R. A. W. (1978). The handedness of rhesus monkeys. II: Concurrent reaching. *Cortex 14*:190–196.

Lehmann, H. J., and Lampe, H. (1970). Observations on the interhemispheric transmission of information in nine patients with corpus callosum defect. *Europ. Neurol. 4*:129–147.

Levin, H. S., Hamsher, K. S., and Benton, A. L. (1975). A short form of the test of facial recognition for clinical use. *J. Psychol. 91*:223–228.

Levine, S. C., and Koch-Weser, M. P. (1982). Right hemisphere superiority in the recognition of famous faces. *Brain and Cognition 1*:10–22.

Levy, J. (1974). Cerebral asmmetries as manifested in split-brain man. In *Hemispheric Disconnection and Cerebral Function* (M. Kinsbourne and W. L. Smith eds.). Springfield, Ill., C. C. Thomas.

Levy, J., Nebes, R. D., and Sperry, R. W. (1971). Expressive language in the surgically separated minor hemisphere. *Cortex* 7:49–58.

Levy, J. Trevarthen, C., and Sperry, R. W. (1972). Perception of bilateral chimeric figures following hemispheric deconnexion. *Brain* 95:61–78.

Lévy-Valensi, J. (1910). *Le Corps. Calleux* (Paris theses 448). Paris: G. Steinheil.

Lhermitte, F., and Beauvois, M. F. (1973). A visual-speech disconnexion syndrome. *Brain* 96:695–714.

Lhermitte, F., Chain, F., and Chedru, F. (1975). Syndrome de déconnexion interhémisphérique: étude des performances visuelles. In *Les Syndromes de Disconnexion Calleuse Chez l'Homme* (F. Michel and B. Schott, eds.). Lyon: Hôpital Neurologique.

Lhermitte, F., Chain, F., Chedru, F., and Penet, C. (1974). Syndrome de deconnexion interhémisphérique: Étude des performances visuelles. *Rev. Neurol.* 130:247–250.

Lhermitte F., Chain, F., Chedru, F., and Penet C. (1976). A study of visual processes in a case of interhemispheric disconnexion. *J. Neurol. Sci.* 28:317–330.

Lhermitte, F., Chain, F., Escourolle, R., Ducarne, B., and Pillon, B. (1972). Etude anatomo-clinique d'un cas de prosopagnosie. *Rev. Neurol.* 126:329–346.

Lhermitte, F., Marteau, R., Serdaru, M., and Chedru, F. (1977). Signs of interhemispheric disconnection in Marchiafava-Bignami disease. *Arch. Neurol.* 34:254.

Liepmann, H. (1900). Das Krankheitsbild der Apraxie (motorische Asymbolie) auf Grund eines Falles von einseitiger Apraxie. *Monatasschr. Psychiat. Neurol.* 8:182–197.

Liepmann, H (1905, 1906). Der Weitere Krankheitsverlauf bei dem einseitig Apraktischen und der Gehirnbefund auf Grund von Serienschnitten. *Monatasschr. Psychiat. Neurol.* 17:289–311; 19:217–243

Liepman, H., and Mass, O. (1908). Fall von linksseitiger Agraphie und Apraxie bei rechssei-tiger Lähmung. *J. Psychol. Neurol.* 10:214–227.

Loeser, J. E., and Alvord, E. C. (1968). Agenesis of the corpus callosum. *Brain* 91:553–570.

Ludlow, C. L. (1980). Children's language disorders: Recent research advances. *Ann. Neurol.* 7:497–507.

Malone, D. R., Morris, H. H., Kay, M. C., and Levin, H. S. (1982). Prosopagnosia: A double dissociation between the recognition of familiar and unfamiliar faces. *J. Neurol. Neurosurg. Psychiat.* 8:820–822.

Markowitsch, H. J., Pritzel, M., Kessler, J., Guldin, W., and Freeman, R. B. (1980). Delayed alternation performance after selective lesions within the prefrontal cortex of the cat. *Behav. Brain. Res.* 1:67–91.

Maspes P. E. (1948). Le syndrome expérimental chez l'homme de la section du splénium du corps calleux: Alexie visuelle pure hémianopsique. *Rev. Neurol.* 80:100–113.

Mateer, C., and Kimura, D. (1977). Impairment of nonverbal oral movements in aphasia. *Brain and Language* 4:262–276.

McKever, W. F., Sullivan, K. F., Ferguson, S. M., and Rayport, M. (1981). Typical cerebral hemisphere disconnection deficits following corpus callosum section despite sparing of the anterior commissure. *Neuropsychologia* 19:745–755.

McKeever, W. F., Sullivan, K. F., Ferguson, S. M., and Rayport, M. (1982). Right hemisphere speech development in the anterior commissure-spared commissurotomy patient: A second case. *Clin. Neuropsychol.* 4:17–22.

Meadows, J. C. (1974). The anatomical basis of prosopagnosia. *J. Neurol. Neurosurg. Psychiat.* 37:489–501.

Michel, F., and Péronnet, F. (1975). Extinction gauche au test dichotique: Lesion hémisphérique ou lésion commissurale? In *Les Syndromes de Disconnexion Calleuse Chez L'Homme* (F. Michel and B. Schott, eds.). Lyon: Hôpital Neurologique.

Michel, F., and Péronnet, F. (1982). L'Hémianacousie, un déficit auditif dans un hémisphère. *Rev. Neurol.* 138:657–671.

Michel, F., and Schott, B., eds). (1975). *Les Syndromes de Disconnexion Calleuse Chez l'Homme.* Lyon: Hôpital Neurologique.

Milner, A. D. (1982). Simple reaction times to lateralized visual stimuli in a case of callosal agenesis. *Neurospchologia* 20:411–419.

Milner, A. D., and Jeeves, M. A. (1979). A review of behavioural studies of agenesis of the corpus callosum. In *Structure and Function of Cerebral Commissures* (I. S. Russell, M. W. van Hof, and G. Berlucchi, eds.). Baltimore: University Park Press.

Milner, B. (1968). Visual recogition and recall after right temporal lobe excision in man. *Neuropsychologia* 6:199–209.

Milner, B., ed. (1975). *Hemispheric Specialization and Interaction.* Cambridge, Mass.: MIT Press.

Milner, B. (1984). Analysis of memory disorder after cerebral commissurotomy. In *Essays in Honour of R. W. Sperry* (C. Trevarthen, ed.). Cambridge: Cambridge University Press.

Milner, B., and Taylor, L. (1972). Right-hemisphere superiority in tactile pattern-recognition after cerebral commissurotomy: Evidence for non-verbal memory. *Neuropsychologia* 10:1–15.

Milner, B., Taylor, L., and Sperry, R. W. (1968). Lateralized suppression of dichotically presented digits after commissural section in man. *Science* 161:184–186.

Mingazzini, G. (1922). *Der Balken.* Berlin: Springer.

Moscovitch, M. (1976). On the representation of language in the right hemisphere of right-handed people. *Brain and Language* 3:47–71; 3:590–599.

Myers, J. J. (1984). Right hemisphere language: Science of fiction? *Amer. Psychologist* 39:315–320.

Myers, R. E. (1956). Function of the corpus callosum in interocular transfer. *Brain* 79:358–363.

Myers, R. E., and Sperry, R. W. (1953). Interocular transfer of visual form discrimination habit in cats after section of the optic chiasma and corpus callosum. *Anat. Record.* 115:351–352.

Myers, R. E., and Sperry, R. W. (1958). Interhemispheric communication through the corpus callosum: Mnemonic carry-over between the hemispheres. *Arch. Neurol. Psychiat.* 80:298–303.

Nebes, R. D. (1974). Hemispheric specialization in commissurotomized man. *Psychol. Bull.* 81:1–14.

Nebes, R. D., and Nashold, B. S. (1980). A comparison of dichotic and visuo-acoustic competition in hemispherectomized patients. *Brain and Language* 9:246–254.

Netley, C. (1972). Dichotic listening performance of hemispherectomized patients. *Neuropsychologia* 10:233–240.

Newcombe, F., and Russell, W. R. (1969). Dissociated visual perceptual and spatial deficits in focal lesions of the right hemisphere. *J. Neurol. Neurosurg. Psychiat.* 32:73–81.

Nielsen, J. M. (1936). *Agnosia, Apraxia, Aphasia. Their Value in Cerebral Localization.* New York: Hoeber.

Ornstein, R., Herron, J., Johnstone, J., and Swencionis, C. (1979). Differential right hemisphere involvement in two reading tasks. *Psychophysiology* 16:398–401.

Overman, W. H.. and Doty, R. W. (1982). Hemispheric specialization displayed by man but not by macaques for analysis of faces. *Neuropsychologia* 20:113–128.

Oxbury, J. M., and Oxbury, S. M. (1970). Effects of temporal lobectomy on the report of dichotically presented digits. *Cortex* 5:3–14.

Ozgur, M. H., Johnson, T., Smith, A., and Bogen, J. E. (1977). Transcallosal approach to third ventricle tumor: Case report. *Bull. Los Angeles Neurol. Soc.* 42:57–62.

Pandya, D. N. (1975). Interhemispheric connections in primates. In *Les Syndromes de Disconnexion Calleuse Chez l'Homme* (F. Michel and B. Schott, eds.). Lyon: Hôpital Neurologique.

Paterson, A., and Zangwill, O. L. (1944). Disorders of visual space perception associated with lesions of the right cerebral heisphere. *Brain* 67:331–358.

Pevzner, S., Bornstein, B., and Loewental, M. (1962). Prosopagnosia. *J. Neurol. Neurosurg. Psychiat.* 25:336–338.

Pirozzolo, F. J., and Rayner, K. (1977). Hemispheric specialization in reading and word recognition. *Brain and Language* 4:248–261.

Poeck, K., Lehmkuhl, G., and Willmes, K. (1982). Axial movements in ideomotor apraxia. *J. Neurol. Neurosurg. Psychiat.* 45:1125–1129.

Preilowski, B. F. B. (1972). Possible contribution of the anterior forebrain commissures to bilateral motor coordination. *Neuropsychologia* 10:267–277.

Pribram, K. H., Plotkin, H. C., Anderson, R. M., and Leong, D. (1977). Information sources in the delayed alternation task for normal and frontal monkeys. *Neuropsychologia* 15:329–340.

Ptito, M., and Lepore, F. (1983). Interocular transfer in cats with early callosal transection. *Nature* 301:513–515.

Raymond, F., Lejonne, P., and Lhermitte, J. (1906). Tumeurs du corps calleux. *Encéphale.* 1:533–565.

Reeves, A., ed. (1984). *Epilepsy and the Corpus Callosum.* New York: Plenum.

Reeves, D. L., and Courville, C. B (1938). Complete agenesis of the corpus callosum. *Bull. Los Angeles Neurol. Soc.* 3:169–181.

Reynolds, D. McQ., and Jeeves, M. A. (1977). Further studies of tactile perception and motor coordination in agenesis of the corpus callosum. *Cortex* 13:257–272.

Risse, G. L., LeDoux, J., Springer, S. P., Wilson, D. H., and Gazzaniga, M. S. (1978). The anterior commisure in man: Functional variation in a multisensory system. *Neuropsychologia* 16:23–31.

Rizzolatti, G., and Buchtel, H. A. (1977). Hemispheric superiority in reaction time to faces: A sex difference. *Cortex* 13:300–305.

Rizzolatti, G., Umiltà, C., and Berlucchi, G. (1971). Oppostie superiorities of the right and left cerebral hemispheres in discriminative reaction time to physiognomical and alphabetical material. *Brain* 94:431–442.

Rogers, L., TenHouten, W., Kaplan, C. D., and Gardiner, M. (1977). Hemispheric specialization of language: An EEG study of bilingual Hopi Indian children. *Int. J. Neurosci.* 8:1–6.

Roland, P. E., Skinhoj, E., and Lassen, N. A. (1981). Focal activations of human cerebral cortex during auditory discrimination. *J. Neurophysiol.* 45:374–386.

Rondot, P., and Tzavaras, A. (1969). La prosopagnosie, apres vingt années d'études cliniques et neuropsychologiques. *J. Psycologie* 2:133–165.

Ross, E. D., and Rush, A. J. (1981). Diagnosis and neuroanatomical correlates of depression in brain-damaged patients. *Arch. Gen. Psychiat.* 38:1344–1354.

Ross, E. D., and Stewart, R. M. (1981). Akinetic mutism from hypothalamic damage: Successful treatment with dopamine agonists. *Neurology* 31; 1435–1439.

Rudel, R. G. (1978). Neuroplasticity: Implications for development and education. In *Education and the Brain.* (J. Chall and A. Mersky, eds.). New York: 77th NSSE Yearbook.

Sadowsky, C., and Reeves, A. G. (1975). Agenesis of the corpus callosum with hypothermia. *Arch. Neurol.* 32:744–776.

Sasanuma, S., Itoh, M., Mori, K., and Kobayashi, Y. (1977). Tachistoscopic recognition of kana and kanji words. *Neuropsychologia* 15:547–553.

Saul, R. E. (1969). Relearning following cerebral deconnection: A case report. *Excerpta Medica* 193:779.

Saul, R., and Sperry, R. W. (1968). Absence of commissurotomy symptoms with agenesis of the corpus callosum. *Neurology* 18:307.

Schaltenbrand, G. (1964). Discussion (p. 41) in *Cerebral Localization and Organization*. (G. Schaltenbrand and C. N. Woolsey, eds.). Madison: University of Wisconsin Press.

Schott, B., Michel, F., Michel, D., and Dumas, R. (1969). Apraxie idéomotrice unilatérale gauche avec main gauche anomique: Syndrome de déconnexion calleuse? *Rev. Neurol.* 12:359–365.

Schott, B., Trillet, M., Michel, F., and Tommasi, M. (1974). Le Syndrome de disconnexion calleuse chez l'ambidextre et le gaucher. In *Les Syndromes de Disconnexion Calleuse Chez l'Homme* (F. Michel and B. Schott, eds.). Lyon: Hôpital Neurologique.

Schulhoff, C., and Goodglass, H. (1969). Dichotic listening, side of brain injury and cerebral dominance. *Neuropsychologia* 7:149–160.

Sechzer, J. A., Folstein, S. E., Geiger, E. H., and Mervis, R. F. (1976). The split-brain neonate: A surgical method for corpus callosum section in newborn kittens. *Dev. Psychobiol.* 9:377–388.

Segal, M. (1935). Agenesis of the corpus callosum in man. *So. Afr. J. Med. Sci.* 1:65–74.

Segalowitz, S. J., ed. (1983). *Language Functions and Brain Organization*. New York: Academic Press.

Selnes, O. A. (1974). The corpus callosum: Some anatomical and functional considerations with special reference to language. *Brain and Language* 1:111–139.

Selnes, O. A. (1976). A note on "On the representation of language in the right hemisphere of right-handed people." *Brain and Language* 3:583–589.

Sheremata, W. A., Deonna, T. W., and Romanul, F. C. A. (1973). Agenesis of the corpus callosum and interhemispheric transfer of information. *Neurology* 23:390.

Shoumura, K., Ando, T., and Kato, K. (1975). Structural organization of callosal OBg in human corpus callosum agenesis *Brain Res.* 93:241–252.

Sidtis, J. J., Volpe, B. T., Wilson, D. H., Rayport, M., and Gazzaniga, M. S. (1981). Variability in right hemisphere language function after callosal section: Evidence for a continuum of generative capacity. *J. Neurosci.* 1:323–331.

Sine, R D., Soufi, A., and Shah, M. (1984). The callosal syndrome: Implications for stroke. *Arch. Phys. Med. (in press)*.

Slager, U. T., Kelly, A. B., and Wagner, J. A. (1957). congenital absence of the corpus callosum. *New Engl. J. Med.* 256:1171–1176.

Smith, A. (1966). Speech and other functions after left(dominant) hemispherectomy. *J. Neurol. Neurosurg. Psychiat.* 29:467–471.

Smith, A. (1974. Dominant and nondominant hemispherectomy. In *Hemispheric Disconnection and Cerebral Function* (M. Kinsbourne and . L. Smith eds.). Springfield, Ill.: C. C. Thomas.

Smith, A., and Sugar, O. (1975). Development of above-normal language and intelligence 21 years after left hemispherectomy. *Neurology* 25:813–818.

Sparks, R., and Geschwind, N. (1968). Dichotic listening in man after section of neocortical commissures. *Cortex* 4:3–16.

Speedie, L. J., and Heilman, K. M. (1981). Anterograde memory deficits for visuospatial material after infarction of the right thalamus. *Arch. Neurol.40*:183–186.

Sperry. R. W. (1961). Cerebral organization and behavior. *Science 133*:1749–1757.

Sperry, R. W. (1970). Perception in the absence of the neocortical commissures. *Assoc. Res. Nervous Mental Dis. 48*:123–138.

Sperry, R. W. (1974). Lateral specialization in the surgically separated hemispheres. In *Neuroscience 3rd Study Prog.*, (F. O. Schmitt and F. G. Worden, eds.). Cambridge, Mass.: MIT Press.

Sperry, R. W. (1982). Some effects of disconnecting the cerebral hemispheres. *Science 217*:1223–1226.

Sperry. R. W., and Gazzaniga, M. S. (1967). Language following surgical disconnection of the hemispheres. In *Brain Mechanisms Underlying Speech and Language*. New York: Grune and Stratton.

Sperry, R. W., Gazzaniga, M. S., and Bogen, J. E. (1969). Interhemispheric relationships: The neocortical commissures; syndromes of hemisphere disconnection. *Handbook Clin. Neurol. 4*:273–290.

Springer, S. P., and Gazzaniga, M. S. (1975). Dichotic testing of partial and complete split-brain subjects. *Neuropsychologia 13*:341–346.

Staller, J., Buchanan, D., Singer, M., Lappin, J., and Webb, W. (1978). Alexia without agraphia: An experimental case study. *Brain and Language 5*:378–387.

Stamm, J. S., Rosen, S. C., and Godotti, A. (1977). Lateralization of functions in the monkey's frontal cortex. In *Lateralization in the Nervous System* (S. Harnad, R. W. Doty, L. Goldstein, J. Jaynes, and G. Krauthamer, eds.). New York: Academic Press.

Sugishita, M., Shinohara, A. and Shimoji, T. (1984).Does a posterior lesion of the corpus callosum cause hemialexia. *Epilepsy and the Corpus Callosum* (Reeves, A. ed.). New York: Plenum.

Sullivan, M.C., and Hamilton, C. R. (1973a). Interocular transfer of reversed and non-reversed discriminations via the anterior commissure in monkeys. *Physiol. Behav. 10*:355–359.

Sullivan, M. C., and Hamilton, C. R. (1973b). Memory establishment via the anterior commissure in monkeys. *Physiol. Behav. 11*:873–879.

Sussman, N. M., Gur, R. C., Gur, R. E., and O'Connor, M. (1983). Mutism as a consequence of callosotomy. *J. Neurosurg. 59*:514–519.

Sweet, W. H. (1945). Seeping intracranial aneurysm simulating neoplasm: Syndrome of the corpus callosum. *Arch. Neurol. Psychiat. 45*:86–104.

Tomasch, J. (1954). Size, distribution, and number of fibres in the human corpus callosum. *Anat. Record 119;* 7–19.

Tomasch, J. (1957). A quantitative analysis of the human anterior commissure. *Acta Anat. 30*:902–906.

Trescher, H. H., and Ford, F. R. (1937). Colloid cyst of the third ventricle: Report of a case: operative removal with section of posterior half of corpus callosum. *Arch. Neurol. Psychiat.* 37:959–973.

Trevarthen, C. (1965). Motor responses in split-brain animals. In *Functions of the Corpus Callosum* (E. G. Ettlinger, ed.). London: Churchill.

Trevarthen, C. (1974). Functional relations of disconnected hemispheres with the brain stem, and with each other: Monkey and man. In *Hemispheric Disconnection and Cerebral Function* (M. Kinsbourne and W. L. Smith, eds.). Springfield, Ill.: C. C. Thomas.

Trevarthen, C.,and Sperry, R. W. (193). Perceptual unity of the ambient visual field in human commissurtomy patients. *Brain 96*:547–570.

Tzavaras, A., Hécaen, H., and Le Bras, H. (1971). Troubles de la reconnaissance du visage humain et latéralisation hémisphérique lésionnelle chez les sujets gauchers. *Neuropsychologia 9:*475–477.

Unterharnscheidt, F., Jalnik, D., and Gott, H. (1968). Der balkenmangel, in *Monographien a.d. gesamtgebiete Neurol. Psychiat. 128:*1–232. New York: Springer.

Van Lancker, D. R., and Canter, G. J. (1982). Impairment of voice and face recognition in patients with hemispheric damage. *Brain and Cognition 1:*185–195.

Vilkki, J., and Laitinen, L. V. (1974). Differential effects of left and right ventrolateral thalamotomy on receptive and expressive verbal performances and face-matching. *Neurosychologia 12;* 11–19.

Vincent, F. M., Sadowsky, C. H., Saunders, R. L. and Reeves, A. G. (1977). Alexia without agraphia, hemianopia, or color-naming defect: A disconnexion syndrome. *Neurology 27:*689–691.

Vincent, F. M., and Reeves, A. G. (1980). Alexia without agraphia: A reversible syndrome. *Ann. Neurol. 8:*206.

Warren, J. M., and Nonneman, A. J. (1976). The search for cerebral dominance in monkeys. *Ann. N.Y. Acad. Sci. 280:*732–744.

Warrington E. K. (1969). Constructional apraxia. *Handbook Clin. Neurol. 4:*67–83.

Warrington,E. K., and James, M. (1967). An experimental investigation of facial recognition in patients with unilateral cerebral lesions. *Cortex 3:*317–326.

Warrington, E. K., James, M., and Kinsbourne, M. (1966). Drawing disability in relation to laterality of cerebral lesion. *Brain 89:*53–82.

Watson, R. T. and Heilman, K. M. (1983). Callosal aprakia. *Brain 106:*391–403.

Wechsler, A. F. (1972). Transient left hemialexia. *Neurology 22:*628–633.

Wechsler, A. F., Weinstein, E. A., and Antin, S. P. (1972). Alexia without agraphia. *Bull. Los Angeles Neurol. Soc. 37:*1–11.

Weinstein, E. A., and Friedland, R. P., eds. (1977). *Hemi-Inattention and Hemisphere Specialization.* New York: Raven Press.

Whiteley, A. M., and Warrington, E. K. (1977). Prosopagnosia: A clinical, psychological, and anatomical study of three patients. *J. Neurol. Neurosurg. Psychiat. 40:*395–403.

Wilson, D. H., Culver, C., Waddington, M., and Gazzaniga, M. (1975). Disconnection of the cerebral hemispheres. *Neurology 25:*1149–1153.

Wilson, D. H., Reeves, A., Gazzaniga, M., and Culver, C. (1977). Cerebral commissurotomy for control of intractable seizures. *Neurology 27:*708–715.

Wilson, S. A. K. (1908). A contribution to the study of apraxia. *Brain 31:*164–216.

Winner, E., and Gardner, H. (1977). The comprehension of metaphor in brain-damaged patients. *Brain 100:*717–729.

Yakovlev, P. I., and Lecours, A. R. (1967). The myelogenetic cycles of regional maturation of the brain. In *Regional Development of the Brain in Early Life* (A. Minkowski, ed.). Edinburgh: Blackwell.

Yamamoto, I., Rhoton, A. L., and Peace, D.A. (1981). Microsurgery of the third ventricle: Part 1. *Neurosurgery 8:*334–356.

Yin, R. K. (1970). Face recognition by brain-injured patients: A dissociable ability? *Neuropsychologia 8:*395–402.

Zaidel, D., and Sperry, R. W. (1974). Memory impairment after commissurotomy in man. *Brain 97:*263–272.

Zaidel, D., and Sperry, R. W. (1977). Some long-term motor effects of cerebral commissurotomy in man. *Neuropsychologia 15:*193–204.

Zaidel, E. (1973). Linguistic competence and related functions in the right hemisphere of man following cerebral commissurotomy and hemispherectomy. Ph.D. thesis, California

Institute of Technology. *Dissertation Abstracts International* 34:2350B (University Microfilms 73–26, 481).

Zaidel, E. (1976). Language, dichotic listening, and the disconnected hemispheres. In *BIS Conference Report 42* (D. O. Walter, L. Rogers, and J. M. Finzi-Fried, eds.). Los Angeles: University of California.

Zaidel, E. (1977). Unilateral auditory language comprehension on the token test following cerebral commissurotomy and hemispherectomy. *Neuropsychologia* 15:1–18.

Zaidel, E. (1978a). Lexical organization in the right hemisphere. In *Cerebral Correlates of Conscious Experience* (P. Buser and A. Rougeul-Buser, eds.). Amsterdam: Elsevier.

Zaidel, E. (1978b). Concepts of cerebral dominance in the split-brain. In *Cerebral Correlates of Conscious Experience* (P. Buser and A. Rougeul-Buser, eds.). Amsterdam: Elsevier.

Zaidel, E. (1983). Disconnection syndrome as a model for laterality effects in the normal brain. In *Cerebral Hemisphere Asymmetry: Method, Theory and Application* (J. Hellige, ed.). Praeger: New York.

Zaidel, E., and Peters, A. M. (1981). Phonological encoding and ideographic reading by the disconnected right hemisphre: Two case studies. *Brain and Language* 14:205–234.

Zurif, E. B., and Ramier, A. M. (1972). Some effects of unilateral brain damage on the perception of dichotically presented phoneme sequences and digits. *Neuropsychologia* 10:103–110.

12

The Frontal Lobes

ANTONIO R. DAMASIO

Dysfunction of the frontal lobes is reflected in a number of relatively specific behavioral manifestations. The notion that frontal lobe lesions are associated with a single characteristic picture, the "frontal lobe syndrome," is not supported by clinical experience or by animal experiments. Yet a survey of the literature shows that the concept of a frontal lobe syndrome is commonly used, and that the frontal lobes have traditionally been regarded as a morphological unit.

The frontal lobes make up roughly half of the human cerebral cortex and have diverse anatomical units, each with distinct connections to other cortical and subcortical structures and to each other. Disregard for this heterogeneity has not helped to unravel the so-called riddle of the frontal lobe. As a consequence, attempts to shape significant syndromes out of the diverse manifestations of frontal lobe dysfunction have been somewhat unsatisfactory. Some useful clinicoanatomical correlations have been established, but it is clear that they are still imprecise.

Critical appraisal of clinical data indicates that the locus of a lesion is a crucial factor in the appearance of a given frontal lobe syndrome. Side of lesion, for instance, is important, as there is evidence that some lesions of the dominant frontal lobe interfere with verbal behavior more so than do corresponding nondominant lesions. Lack of fluency, disturbance of syntactic structure, and weakening of the drive to communicate verbally may be indexes of lateralized dominant involvement. Certain emotional changes may also be related to the left-right dichotomy, with nondominant frontal lesions causing the more significant alterations. On the other hand, there is evidence that bilateral lesions produce a different clinical picture, both quantitatively and qualitatively. The site of damage within a frontal lobe is also relevant to the development of a given syndrome. This regional effect may determine distinctive clinical configurations and allow the prediction of whether the involvement is predominantly mesial or dorsolateral or inferior orbital.

We thank Gary W. Van Hoesen, Hanna Damasio, Paul Eslinger, and Dan Tranel for their suggestions and Janis Carter for her preparation of the manuscript.

Analysis of the behavioral effects of different loci of damage must also take account of the nature of the lesion. The effects of infarction of the mesial portion of a frontal lobe may differ from gliomatous involvement of the connections of the same area, and hence the behavioral effects of one cannot be equated with those of the other. The discrepancies arising from such comparisons need not be treated as another riddle in the frontal-lobe mystery. As with any lesion of the CNS, the rate of development of damage is a crucial factor.

Depth of lesion is also an important variable, probably as much so as surface extent of damage. Many signs of frontal lobe dysfunction seem to be a consequence of severed subcortical connections, and a deep lesion has a better chance of destroying linking pathways.

The time elapsed after a lesion has fully developed is still another factor influencing the clinical picture. Often a patient with severe symptomatology will experience a remarkable remission within a period of weeks.

Another temporal factor is the age at which the dysfunction begins. There is evidence that the effects of lesions starting in childhood or adolescence are different from those caused by lesions starting in adulthood, particularly when they are extensive and bilateral. Level of education and acculturation are also pertinent. Characteristics of the premorbid personality are almost certainly of importance.

If these factors are not taken into account, it will not be possible to make an adequate clinical evaluation of patients and clinical research may produce paradoxical results. Even if all the rules are observed, however, there are other problems associated with the evaluation and investigation of the frontal lobe patient, since the signs and symptoms of frontal lobe dysfunction do not lend themselves easily to quantitative measurement. Unlike the impairment of the elementary instrumental abilities, which is the hallmark of lesions in the rolandic cortex or in the post-rolandic sensory cortices, frontal lobe dysfunction is more readily described as changes in quality. The contradiction between the claim that the frontal lobes control the highest forms of behavior in humans and the finding that intelligence test performance is not affected after extensive frontal damage is a manifestation of the problem of what to measure and how. Both claims are correct; they differ because they stem from types of analysis addressing different forms of frontal defect. Patients with frontal lobe dysfunction often fail to show quantifiable impairments when language and allied abilities are objectively assessed, but that hardly guarantees that the patient's personality has not been damaged. Even objective manifestations of frontal lobe dysfunction, such as bradykinesia or release of primitive reflexes, challenge quantification. The most telling signs are often subtle changes in alertness, affect, emotional response, and appropriate control of regulatory behaviors. The standard behavioral measurements available at the bedside or in the neuropsychology laboratory are simply not adequate to address these disturbances. The same can be said about impairment of high-level problem solving, one result of which is the inability to plan future actions appropriately. Current research on the anatomy and physiology of the frontal lobes in humans is likely to clarify many of the problems identified here.

ANATOMY

Knowledge of neuroanatomy is necessary to the comprehensive understanding of frontal lobe function and a prerequisite for the interpretation of research discussed later in this chapter. For that reason, a brief review of frontal lobe morphology is presented at this point.

Frontal Cortex

Inspection of the external surface of the lobe reveals three important natural borders—the rolandic sulcus, the sylvian fissure, and the corpus callosum—and three large expansions of cortex—in the lateral convexity, in the mesial flat aspect that faces the opposite lobe, and in the inferior concave aspect that covers the roof of the orbit. Traditional anatomy has divided this cortex in the following principal regions: the precentral cortex, the prefrontal cortex, and the limbic cortex (Fig. 12-1).

The precentral cortex corresponds to the long gyrus immediately anterior to the rolandic fissure, forming its anterior bank and depth. This area continues into the mesial portion of the lobe, ending in the cingulate sulcus. Histologically it is a region of agranular cortex and its function as the principal motor area is well known. The presence of Betz cells is a distinguishing feature. In Brodmann's map (Fig. 1-1), it corresponds to field 4. Anterior and parallel to this region lies the premotor cortex, which in humans corresponds to the posterior portion of the three horizontally placed frontal gyri. Histologically this is transitional cortex, the function of which is closely related to motor activity. For the most part, this is field 6 in Brodmann's map, but the lower region, which comprises a portion of the third (inferior) frontal gyrus, is referenced as field 44 and presumably corresponds to Broca's area. Field 45 is closely connected to 44, both anatomically and, in all probability, functionally. In the mesial prolongation of the premotor zone, which also terminates in the cingulate sulcus, lies the supplementary motor area. Anterior to both the precentral and premotor regions lies the prefrontal cortex, which makes up most of the frontal cortex and encompasses the pole of the lobe. Macroscopically, three major aspects may be distinguished: mesial, dorsolateral, and orbital. Histologically much of this is granular cortex that corresponds in Brodmann's map to fields 8, 9, 10, 11, 12, 47, and 46. This is the enigmatic area that most authors have in mind when they speak of the frontal lobe in relation to behavior. Little is known about the contribution of each of these separate areas, with the exception of field 8, the so-called eye field, which presumably serves a central role in relation to eye and head movements. Limbic system parts of the frontal lobe correspond to areas 24, 25, and 32 (the anterior and subgenual portions of the cingulate gyrus) and to areas 13 and 14 (the posterior parts of the orbitofrontal area and the gyrus rectus). Technically, these are agranular cortices; however, they are probably related in essential ways to both the granular and agranular cortices.

Frontal Lobe Connections

Understanding the prefrontal lobe depends upon knowledge of the company it keeps, that is, its afferent and efferent connections. Some of these connections are with other

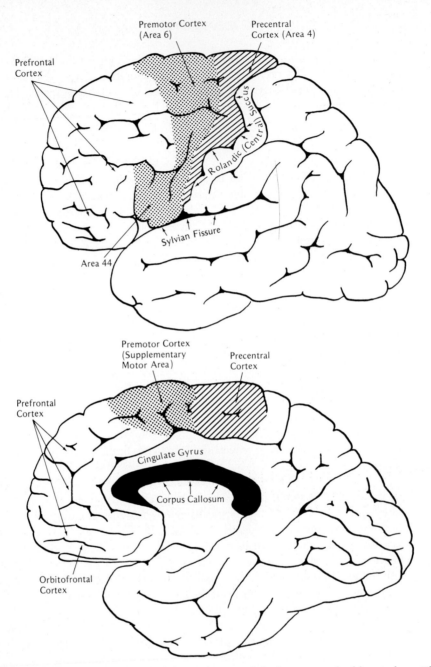

Fig. 12-1. Lateral (top) and medial (bottom) views of the human cerebral hemisphere. The diagonal hatching indicates the motor cortex (area 4), and the stippled area the pre-motor cortex, the inferior and anterior portion of which is area 44 (see Fig. 1-1).

neocortical structures, mainly from and to association areas in the temporal, parietal, and occipital lobes, including special areas of multimodal convergence. The prefrontal cortex is also connected to the premotor region and thus indirectly to motor cortex. There are significant connections with the limbic cortex of the cingulate gyrus and with limbic and motor subcortical structures. Some projections seem to be unidirectional, such as those to the caudate and putamen. Some seem to be bidirectional, such as those with the nucleus medialis dorsalis of the thalamus. The latter is a particularly important connection, so much so that some authors have defined the prefrontal cortex as that region which is coextensive with projections from the nucleus medialis dorsalis. The arrangement of projections is quite specific: the orbital aspect is linked with the pars magnocellularis, the dorsolateral cortex with the pars parvocellularis. Other major subcortical connections are with the hippocampus by way of the cingulate and hippocampal gyri, with the amygdala by way of the uncinate fasciculus, and with the hypothalamus, the septum, and the mesencephalon by direct pathways.

The prefrontal cortex thus receives input (by more than one channel) from the sensory association regions of the cortex, it is closely woven with the limbic system, and it can affect the motor system in multiple ways. The functionally central position of the frontal lobe can be made more clear by a brief review of its efferent and afferent connections in nonhuman primates. The frontal lobe of the monkey is roughly comparable to that of humans in shape, limits, connections, and cytoarchitecture (Fig. 12-2). Important differences, other than size, are apparent in the dorsolateral aspect

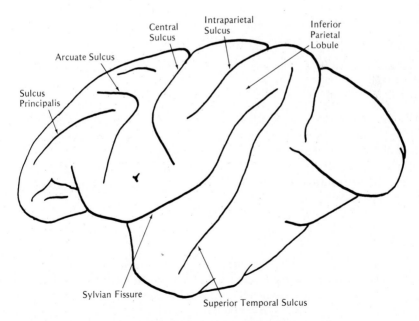

Fig. 12-2. Lateral view of the cerebral hemisphere of the rhesus monkey.

where instead of the three horizontally oriented gyri of the human frontal lobe, there are two fields placed in a dorsal and ventral position in relation to a single sulcus, the principalis (Fig. 12-2). One other major sulcus, the arcuate, arch-shaped and more or less vertically oriented, represents the seam between the monkey's prefrontal and premotor cortex. It is in this transition zone, particularly in the rostral bank of the sulcus, that Brodmann's field 8 is located. Sources used in the following description of subcortical and cortical projections are Ward and McCulloch, 1947; Bailey and Von Bonin, 1951; Pribram and MacLean, 1953; Pribram et al., 1953; Whitlock and Nauta, 1956; Crosby et al., 1962; Nauta, 1962; Akert, 1964; De Vito and Smith, 1964; Nauta, 1964; Kuypers et al., 1965; Powell, et al., 1965; Valverde, 1965; Johnson, et al., 1968; Nauta and Haymaker, 1969 Pandya et al., 1969; Pandya and Kuypers, 1969; Pandya and Vignolo, 1971; Pandya et al., 1971; Kievit and Kuypers, 1974; Chavis and Pandya, 1976; Rosene, et al., 1976; Goldman and Nauta, 1977; Yeterian and Van Hoesen, 1977; Goldman, 1978: Potter and Nauta, 1979; Damasio and Van Hoesen, 1980, Barbas and Mesulam, 1981; Porrino et al., 1981; Porrino, 1981; Goldman-Rakic Schwartz, 1982; Porrino and Goldman-Rakic, 1982.

Subcortical Connections

PROJECTIONS FROM THE HYPOTHALAMUS

Direct projections from the hypothalamus have not been as easy to identify as the ones in the opposite direction, which may possibly reflect a different functional significance. At any rate, there is some evidence that there are such projections to several regions above and below the arcuate sulcus and to the rostral part of the principal sulcus. These projections may be parallel to the monoaminergic projections arising in the mescencephalic tegmentum and may indeed be interwoven with them, since the latter are known to travel in the lateral hypothalamic region.

PROJECTIONS FROM THE AMYGDALA AND THE HIPPOCAMPUS

There are projections from the amygdala to the orbital cortex, particularly in its most posterior and medial region, but the amygdala also projects to the mesial aspect of the frontal lobe, particularly into areas such as the gyrus rectus and the subcallosal portion of the cingulate gyrus and the anterior parts of the cingulate gyrus (Brodmann's areas 25 and 24, respectively). The amygdala, as does the hippocampus, projects to areas of the diencephalon and mesencephalon to which the prefrontal lobe itself strongly projects.

PROJECTIONS FROM THE THALAMUS

The afferent projections from the thalamus originate mostly in the regions where the efferent projections from the prefrontal cortex terminate, that is, in both the medial and lateral aspects of the dorsomedial nucleus. The medial thalamus thus appears as a transforming station for inputs from the prefrontal regions. Projections of the medial pulvinar to area 8 have also been described, and it is likely that other projections from

the thalamic association nuclei exist. These receive important intrathalamic connection from the intralaminar nuclei and thereby link the frontal cortices to ascending
reticular systems.

PROJECTIONS TO AMYGDALA AND HIPPOCAMPUS

These arise mostly from the mesial and orbital aspects and partly from the inferior
ventral dorsolateral aspect and travel in the uncinate fasciculus. Many go directly to
the amygdala, although others go to rostral temporal cortex, which in turn projects to
the amygdala. Projection to the hippocampus is indirect via the limbic cortex of the
cingulate and hippocampal gyri.

PROJECTIONS TO THE HYPOTHALAMUS

Direct connections to various hypothalamic nuclei have been mentioned for a long
time. These, however. are poorly understood and in need of reinvestigation with modern neuroanatomical tracing procedures. Almost in continuum with the latter, there
are projections to the mesencephalic tegmentum, namely, to the anterior half of the
periaqueductal gray matter. These are areas to which both the hippocampus and the
amygdala send strong projections.

PROJECTIONS TO THE SEPTUM

In the monkey, these probably arise from the upper bank of the sulcus principalis. A
reciprocal connection is probably involved.

PROJECTIONS TO THE THALAMUS

Other than the well-known projections to the nucleus dorsalis medialis, fibers also
terminate in the intralaminar thalamic complex.

PROJECTIONS TO THE STRIATUM

Projections to the caudate and the putamen but not the pallidum have been identified.
The projections from the cingulate gyrus and supplementary motor area are especially strong. It was once thought that the frontocaudate projection was limited to the
head of the caudate, but it has recently been shown that the prefrontal cortex projects
to the whole caudate. Of particular interest is the fact that regions of the cortex with
which the frontal lobe is reciprocally innervated, e.g., the parietal lobe, seem to project to the caudate in approximately the same area.

PROJECTIONS TO CLAUSTRUM, SUBTHALAMIC REGION, AND MESENCEPHALON

Projections to the claustrum travel in the uncinate fasciculus and originate in the
orbital and inferior dorsolateral aspects. Projections to the regions of the subthalamic

nucleus and the red nucleus also seem to come primarily from the orbital aspects. Projections to the central grey seem to come from the convexity only.

Cortical Connections

PROJECTIONS FROM VISUAL, AUDITORY, AND SOMATOSENSORY CORTEX

Practically all areas of the association cortex project to the frontal lobe. In the rhesus monkey these projections have been studied in relation to two distinct regions: the periarcuate cortex, which surrounds the arcuate sulcus, and the prearcuate cortex, which includes all of the frontal pole lying anterior to the former region and which encompasses the region of the sulcus principalis.

Projections terminating in the periarcuate cortex arise from the caudal portion of the superior temporal gyrus, the lateral peristriate belt, the superior parietal lobule, and the anterior portion of the inferior parietal lobule. Projections terminating in the prearcuate cortex arise from the middle region of the superior temporal gyrus, the caudal and inferior temporal cortex, and the middle portion of the inferior bank of the intraparietal sulcus.

Direct projections to the orbital cortex come mainly from the anterior region of the superior temporal gyrus, but there are also indirect projections that reach this area by way of the mediodorsal thalamus; they originate in the middle and inferior temporal gyri and share the same route of projections from the olfactory cortex.

Considerable overlap takes place in relation to these connections, for instance, between the first-order visual and auditory projections in the periarcuate region and between second-order visual, auditory, and somatosensory projections in prearcuate cortex.

PROJECTIONS FROM OLFACTORY CORTEX

The pyriform cortex projects to the frontal lobe by way of the mediodorsal nucleus of the thalamus. In this way, olfactory information joins that of the other senses to create a convergence absent in the posterior sensory cortex.

PROJECTIONS TO TEMPORAL CORTEX

The temporal cortex receives projections from regions of the sulcus principalis in a well-organized fashion. The anterior third projects mainly to the anterior third of the superior temporal sulcus and the superior temporal gyrus. The middle third connects with both the anterior and the middle portions of the superior temporal sulcus. The posterior third projects mainly to the more caudal region of the superior temporal sulcus. The orbital aspect of the frontal lobe also projects to the rostral areas of the temporal lobe.

PROJECTIONS TO POSTERIOR SENSORY CORTEX

These are mainly directed to the inferior parietal lobule and originate in the posterior third of the sulcus principalis and in the arcuate sulcus.

PROJECTIONS TO LIMBIC CORTEX

Both the anterior and middle thirds of the sulcus principalis project to the cingulate gyrus, the latter in a more intense fashion, as do areas in the concavity of the arcuate sulcus. This is an interesting projection that courses all along the cingulate, distributing fibers to the overlying cortex but then continuing as a bundle to reach the hippocampal gyrus.

PROJECTIONS WITHIN THE FRONTAL LOBE

The lower bank of the sulcus principalis is connected to the orbital aspect of the frontal cortex. The region of the arcuate sulcus connects anteriorly to portions of the frontal pole. In general, however, the intrinsic connections of the frontal lobe are understood poorly in all species.

HUMAN INVESTIGATIONS

Individual Case Studies

The famous patient Gage, described by Harlow in the 1880's, provides the most solid early reference to specific injury of the frontal lobes and its relation to disturbances of complex behavior. Other important single-case observations were added in the first half of this century, and these, along with the results of prefrontal leucotomy and lobotomy, constitute the principal sources of information regarding the function of the frontal lobes. As would be expected, the cases and the circumstances in which the studies were carried out had little in common and were used as the basis for markedly divergent conclusions. These encompassed the opinion that the frontal lobe was indispensable for superior forms of human behavior as well as the claim that intellectual competence is not impaired by the absence of frontal lobe structures. Some of the more informative early case studies, such as those of Brickner (1934, 1936), Hebb and Penfield (1940), and Ackerly and Benton (1948), and one modern case study, that of Eslinger and Damasio (1984), will be reviewed.

Brickner's patient, known as A, was a 39-year-old New York stockbroker who, until one year before surgery, led a normal life. Slowly progressive headaches, which became more and more severe, and finally the sudden onset of mental obtundation brought him to medical attention. A diagnosis of a frontal mass was made, which, at surgery, proved to be a voluminous meningioma of the falx compressing both frontal lobes. The neurosurgeon, Walter Dandy, had to perform in two stages an extensive bilateral resection of frontal tissue. On the left side all the frontal tissue rostral to Broca's area was removed. On the right, the excision was even larger and included all the brain anterior to the motor area. The patient's condition gradually stabilized and no motor or sensory defect could be detected. For months there were frequent periods of restlessness, but akinesia or changes in tone were never noted, nor were there any signs of motor perseveration. Orientation to person, place, and time seemed intact as well as remote and recent memory. A was able to understand the circumstances of his illness and the surgical intervention to which he had been subject, and he was aware of the efforts of his family and physician to have him recover as much as possible. The range of his intellectual ability could be inferred from his capacity to play checkers, sometimes at a quick and expert pace, to explain the meaning of proverbs, and, occasionally, to discuss with lucidity the meaning of his predicament for himself, his relatives, and his friends. On the negative side, his behavior had undergone a marked deterioration in terms of ability to focus attention and to adjust his emotional reaction to almost any daily event. Furthermore, his affect was shallow. He became boastful, constantly insisting on his professional, physical, and sexual prowess, and showed little restraint, not only in describing his mythical adventures but in verbalizing judgments about people and circumstances surrounding him. His train of thought was often hypomanic, with facetious remarks to match, but he could suddenly become difficult and aggressive if frustrated. Frequently he tried to be witty, generally at the expense of others. He was particularly nasty toward his wife; prior to surgery he had always been kind to her, although not unusually considerate. His sex life, which his wife described as normal before the operation, changed radically. He became impotent and, after a few frustrated attempts at intercourse, never again sought her or indeed any other partner, although much of his conversation would revolve around his sexual exploits. Ability to plan meaningful daily activity had been clearly lost and so had his initiative and creativity. Although he constantly spoke of returning to work, he never made any effort to do so and continued living in close dependence on his relatives. Certain levels of learning ability, however, both verbal and nonverbal, seemed intact. For example, in the face of his constant distractability and lack of interest, he was taught how to operate proficiently a complex printing machine, on which he produced visiting cards. Moreover, when faced with strangers in a reasonably nondemanding situation, he would be charming, display impeccable manners, and be considerably restrained. Independent examiners, including neurologists, would then be unable to detect any abnormality even after fairly long conversations.

Brickner's painstaking description produced different impressions on the readers of the time. The overall view was that the intervention had had a crippling effect on A's mental ability, but for Egas Moniz, the enterprising pioneer of frontal leucotomy (1936), A's case was remarkable in that it proved bilateral frontal damage to be compatible with maintenance of major operational abilities and especially because it demonstrated a change in affect and emotional response with pronounced reduction of anxiety. This view is likely to have played a role in the theorization behind the leucotomy project.

The question of whether the changes reported in this case were due primarily to the frontal lobe resection should be considered. For the most part, we believe they were. Nonetheless, it is not possible to exclude preoperative damage produced by silent growth of the tumor and a period of sustained intracranial pressure. In view of the location and size of the tumor, damage to the septal and hypothalamic regions was a possibility, and although the autopsy report on this case (Brickner, 1952) mentioned no such evidence, there may have been microscopic basal forebrain changes. The report is clear in noting that the cortical territory of the anterior cerebral arteries was intact (which might have been predicted from the patient's lack of crural paresis). Nevertheless, the autopsy did becloud the issue by revealing several meningiomas, one of which was of significant size and located in the right occipital area. In retrospect, it seems clear that the latter tumor had not grown yet at the time of operation because the patient developed a new set of symptoms six to seven years after surgery. Such findings should not be used to minimize the significance of this case, as it is unlikely that they played any role in the patient's behavior.

Hebb and Penfield (1940) described an example of relatively successful bilateral removal of frontal tissue with a more straightforward possibility of a clinicoanatomical correlation. This patient had been normal until age 16 and had then sustained a compounded frontal fracture that damaged both frontal lobes, produced the formation of scar tissue, and resulted in a severe convulsive disorder. At age 28, the patient was operated on and the frontal lobes were extensively resected bilaterally, exposing both orbital plates back to the lesser wing of the sphenoid and transecting the frontal horns of the ventricles. The anterior cerebral arteries were spared. At least a third of the frontal lobes was removed. In terms of the anatomical result the intervention was not very different from that of Brickner's patient, but, unlike A, this patient's brain had not been distorted and edematous prior to resection and the ablation took place under optimal surgical circumstances. In the postoperative period, seizures practically stopped and the behavioral disturbances associated with interictal periods disappeared. The authors suggest that the patient's personality actually improved and that his intellectual ability was probably better than before the surgical intervention. We take this to mean that comparison with the period of convulsive disorder was favorable and bore out the lack of interictal behavior deviation. Comparison with the period prior to the initial damage would certainly not be as favorable, as we believe this patient's intellectual and emotional maturation had been considerably affected by his frontal lobe lesion. Even if he is described as relatively independent, socially adequate, and intellectually intact, some observers have felt that his personality development seemed arrested at the age of the accident and a certain resemblance with the patient of Ackerly and Benton has been indicated. In a later study, Hebb (1945) conceded that, in spite of the patient's apparently good adjustment, his long-term planning and initiative ability were impaired.

The patient of Ackerly and Benton (1948), on the other hand, sustained bilateral frontal lobe damage either at birth or during perinatal period. A neurosurgical exploration was performed at age 19 and revealed cystic degeneration of the left frontal lobe and absence of the right one, probably as a result of atrophy. This patient's history was marked throughout childhood and adolescence by severe behavioral problems, in school and at home. He could not hold a job, generally because after some days of being an obedient and even charming employee, he would suddenly show bursts of bad temper, lose interest in his activity, and often end up by stealing or being disorderly. He reacted badly to frustration, and departure from routine would easily frustrate him. Except for periods of frustration and catastrophic reaction, his docility, quietness, and polite manners were quite impressive. His general health seems to have been good. His sexual interests were apparently dim, and he never had an emotional involvement with any partner although, for a time, he did have occasional sex with prostitutes. As a whole, his behavior was described as stereotyped, unimaginative, and lacking in initiative. He never developed any particular professional skill or hobby, and this deficit never seemed to bother him. He also failed to

plan for the future, either immediate or long range, and previous reward and punishment did not seem to influence the course of his behavior. In keeping with this, his
memory was described as capricious, showing at times a remarkable capacity (such
as his ability to remember the makes of automobiles) and at other times an inaccurate
representation of events. There was no evidence of the common varieties of neurotic
disorder, of somatization or of deliberate antisocial behavior, or of addictive behavior.
Apparently he could not be described in terms of being joyful or happy, and it looked
like both pleasure and pain were short-lived and directly related to the presence or
absence of frustration.

When he was reevaluated 15 years later, there had been no remarkable personality
changes except for a higher frustration threshold. Intellectually, however, recent-
memory deficits were now noticeable and an inability to perform the Wisconsin Card
Sorting Test was recorded.

Eslinger and Damasio (1984) have described another significant example of frontal
lobe changes. Their patient, EVR, grew up happily, the oldest of five children, an
excellent student and a role model for many friends and siblings. After high school
he married and completed a business college degree in accounting. By age 30, he was
the father of two children and a church elder and had come through the ranks of his
company to the post of comptroller.

In 1973 his family and employers began to notice a variety of personality changes.
He became unreliable, could not seem to complete his usual work, and experienced
marital difficulties. He was suspended from his job. In 1975 a large orbitofrontal meningioma compressing both frontal lobes was removed. After his post operative recovery, EVR returned to accounting with a small home construction business. He soon
established a partnership with a man of questionable reputation and went into business, against sound advice. The venture proved catastrophic. EVR had to declare
bankruptcy and lost his entire personal investment. Next, he tried several different
jobs (warehouse laborer, apartment complex manager, accountant) but was consistently fired from all of them when it became clear that he could not keep reliable
standards. His wife left home with the children and filed for a divorce. When he was
reevaluated two years later, a CT excluded a recurrence of tumor and the neurological examination was normal except for slight incoordination in the left upper extremity and bilateral anosmia. Psychometric evaluation at that time revealed a verbal IQ
of 120 (91st percentile), a performance IQ of 108 (70th percentile) and a Wechsler
memory quotient of 140. A Minnesota Multiphasic Personality Inventory was valid
and entirely within the normal range.

EVR's problems persisted. He was fired from two additional jobs. The reasons given
included tardiness and lack of productivity. He remarried within a month after his
first divorce, against the advice of his relatives. The second marriage ended in divorce
two years later.

Further neurological and psychological evaluation of EVR at a private psychiatric
institution in September 1981 revealed "no evidence of organic brain syndrome or
frontal dysfunction." Assessment with the WAIS disclosed a verbal IQ of 125 (95th
percentile) and a performance IQ of 124 (94th percentile). His Wechsler memory
quotient was 143, and the Halstead-Reitan battery revealed average to superior ability on every subtest. An MMPI was once again valid with no evidence of psychopa-

thology on the clinical scales. The staff of the psychiatric hospital felt that his "problems are not the result of organic problems or neurological dysfunction. . . . Instead
they are reflective of emotional and psychological adjustment problems and therefore
are amenable to psychotherapy." They believed EVR could return to work by being
retrained for employment. The overall evaluation indicated adjustment and dys-
thymic disorders with a compulsive "personality style."

EVR is now a 42-year-old man whose neuropsychological test performances are
almost completely normal. CT shows clear evidence of bilateral damage of the frontal
lobes. The orbitofrontal surface and frontal polar cortex of both sides are almost
entirely missing as the consequence of an extensive ablation necessary to remove his
tumor. The dorsolateral sectors, the cingulate gyri, and the motor and supplementary
motor regions are intact. EVR is now considering a third marriage to a woman 14
years his senior and plans to establish a luxury travel business in which he would drive
vacationing persons around the country in a motor home.

Reflection on these cases is most rewarding. The patients of Hebb and Ackerly
shared a rigid, perseverative attitude in their approach to life, and both had the cour-
teous manner described as "English valet politeness," though in the judgment of several examiners Hebb and Penfield's patient led a clearly more productive, but not
fully independent, existence. The evolution of the personality in Hebb's patient seems
to have been somewhat arrested at the time of his accident, when he was 16, while
in Ackerly's patient the defect came early in development. Ackerly's case could thus
be viewed as an example of learning and personality development without the frontal
lobes, whereas Hebb's would represent an arrest of development in adolescence at an
age where some positive adaptation would still be possible. The patients of Brickner
and of Damasio and Eslinger, on the other hand, had a normal development and
sustained frontal lobe damage in adult life. The fact that their lesions were sustained
at an age when plasticity of the nervous system was limited may account for some
differences of outcome. Nonetheless, all patients share a number of features: inability
to organize future activity and hold gainful employment; tendency to present a favorable view of themselves; stereotyped but correct manners; diminished ability to experience pleasure and react to pain; diminished sexual and exploratory drives; lack of
motor, sensory, or communication defects; and overall intelligence within expectations based on educational and occupational background. With the exception of Eslinger and Damasio's patient, all patients showed lack of originality and creativity,
inability to focus attention, recent memory vulnerable to interference, and a tendency
to display inappropriate emotional reactions.

It seems probable that bilateral damage to the frontal lobes in infancy or childhood
produces a more devastating effect on personality and cognitive ability than the same
amount of damage sustained elsewhere in the brain at any time in the course of development. This point is illustrated by cases of early hemispherectomy on either side and
by cases of extensive unilateral or bilateral lesions of the parietal, occipital, and posterior temporal lobes, which demonstrate almost normal maturation of personality.
Few cases comparable to Ackerly and Benton's have been published, an exception
being that reported by Russell (1959), whose findings are in accord with this view.
We would surmise that early lesions of the frontal lobe are not compatible with normal development of intellectual abilities and affect and consequently are not com-

patible with normal maturation of personality. The same applies, in our view, to lesions of the anterior temporal lobe, the limbic system, and the anterior and dorso-medial thalami.

The results of prefrontal leucotomy and prefrontal lobotomy have been a constant source of controversy. Although Moniz (1936, 1949) was impressed by the lack of pronounced defects of motor, sensory, and communicative function in cases of frontal lobe lesion, it is clear that he attributed several important functions to the frontal lobe. He reasoned that in cases of schizophrenic thought disorder or of obsessive compulsive disease, "wrongly learned" thinking processes were dependent on frontal lobe function and based on reverberating circuitry connecting the frontal lobe to midline sub-cortical structures and to the posterior cortical areas. Such "repetitive linkages" called for surgical interruption. He also hypothesized a relation between the aberrant thought process and the accompanying emotional status of the patient and assumed that a lesion that altered one would also alter the other. He recalled the frequent observation of affective indifference in frontal lobe patients, as well as the remarkable affective changes shown in Jacobsen's chimpanzees (Fulton and Jacobsen, 1935) after frontal lobe surgery. As Jacobsen put it, "The animals had joined the happiness cult of the Elder Michaeux and had placed their burdens on the Lord" (Fulton, 1951). It is clear that Moniz conceived of the frontal lobes as important for cognitive matura-tion and for the regulation of emotion and that, far from designing an innocuous intervention, he was planning the active introduction of defects in patients whose previous abnormality might benefit from such diminution.

Objective assessment of the results of prefrontal surgery is extremely difficult. Sev-eral surgical methods have been devised involving various amounts of damage to dif-ferent structures, and these have been performed with more or less precision accord-ing to the technique. All cases suffered from preexisting psychiatric disease or intractable pain, generally of considerable severity and duration. Finally, the methods of behavioral assessment have been different in scope and quality (for a modern appraisal of the measurable neuropsychologic disturbances associated with leucotomy, see Stuss et al., 1981).

Nevertheless, several general conclusions may be drawn from a survey of the lit-erature in this area. The first is that bilateral, surgically controlled frontal lobe dam-age, particularly when it involves the mesial and inferior orbital cortices or their con-nections, causes modifications in the affective and emotional sphere. These changes may also appear as a result of dorsolateral lesions but seem less pronounced. On the other hand, measurable intellectual impairment more often follows dorsolateral involvement. Recent accounts supporting this view can be found in Hamlin (1970) and in Scoville and Bettis (1977) and are in keeping with the predictions that might have been formulated on the basis of studies such as those of Faust (1966). Changes related to higher levels of regulatory behavior are difficult to disentangle from the results of previous and ongoing psychiatric processes. These will probably be approachable as a result of the introduction of fractionated forms of psychosurgery, but possibly the most scientifically revealing trend in psychosurgery has been the attempt to produce behavior modification not by frontal lobe lesions but by direct approach to the hypothalamic centers, with which the frontal lobe has an intimate and possibly regulatory relationship (Dieckmann and Hassler, 1977; Nadvornick et al., 1977; Schneider, 1977).

Experimental Neuropsychological Studies

After World War II, new knowledge of neuroanatomy and neurophysiology led to neuropsychological studies of an experimental nature. In a pioneering study, Milner (1963) was able to demonstrate a measurable deficit as a result of frontal lobe lesions. Her subjects were epileptic patients undergoing frontal resections for treatment of convulsive disorder. There were no patients with tumors in the group. All patients had atrophic lesions, and most of them were studied before and after the operation. Measurement of IQ after the operation showed a mean loss of 7.2 points in the frontal lobe group; the left temporal and left parietal lobe groups and the general control group showed a mean loss of 8.4 points. Against this background, Milner then demonstrated the remarkable impairment her frontal patients showed in the Wisconsin Card Sorting Test.

The Wisconsin Card Sorting Test was first used by Berg (1948) and by Grant and Berg (1948). The subject is shown four cards whose figures are different in color, form, and number of elements (a red triangle, two green stars, three yellow crosses, and four blue circles). The subject is handed a pack of 128 cards that vary according to color, form, and number and is requested to sort each consecutive card from the pack (response cards) and place it in front of one of the four cards (stimulus cards) where she or he thinks it belongs. After a choice is made, the patient is told whether the approach is right or wrong and is asked to use that information in an attempt to make as many correct choices as possible. The first sorting criterion is color, and any other choice is called wrong. After the subject achieves ten consecutive correct color choices, the sorting criterion is changed without the subject being told so and color choices are then called wrong. A correct form choice is then called right, and after ten correct form choices, the criterion is again changed without warning, this time to number. The procedure is repeated until six changes have been completed using the order: color, form, number, color, form, number.

Milner found that all her frontal patients performed more poorly after the operation, in clear contrast to patients in her control group, which included several cases of resection of the left temporal lobe, left parietal lobe, and right temporoparietal-occipital and of combined orbitotemporal resections. Postoperatively, the frontal patients tended to stick to one choice and to perseverate throughout the test without shifting to other sorting categories. Milner described an additional group of patients tested only after the operation, and the results were so similar that she felt justified in combining the data into a final, larger group.

The findings were interpreted as strongly suggesting that the ability to shift from one strategy to another in a sorting task is more compromised by frontal lobe damage than by rolandic or posterior sensory-cortex damage. The manifest perseveration that made patients rigidly adhere to one criterion and ignore the examiner's guiding information was interpreted as an inability to overcome an established response set.

A complex question raised by this study relates to the difficulty of the Wisconsin Card Sorting Test. It is known that many normal subjects perform poorly on it, and one tends to expect a brain-damaged patient to do even worse. However, Milner's control group answers that comment fairly well by showing a clear difference between frontal and nonfrontal cases. Since the intelligence quotients were comparable and since the background conditions of all patients in terms of disease and production of lesion were similar, it is probable that the defect of performance was a consequence of frontal lobe damage. Further support for this view comes from the patient of Scoville and Milner (1957), who, in spite of bilateral lesions in the hippocampus and amygdala and a severe amnesia, performed the card sorting test remarkably well, achieving at least four categories.

Another question bears upon the correlation between these changes and the area of frontal lobe involvement. It is possible to say that the abnormal behavior of these patients was correlated with extensive and bilateral frontal lobe damage, predominantly prefrontal. Milner describes the pertinent lesions as dorsolateral. Although it appears that at least 15 of the 18 patients has significant mesial involvement, and that the extent of orbital involvement is not known except for one case, we believe that this is indeed the case. Milner's results were different from those of Teuber (1964), who pointed out that, although many of his frontal patients failed the Wisconsin Sorting Test, some did very well and individual variation was striking. This seems not to have been the case in Milner's study. On the other hand, Teuber's controls did not do as well as Milner's and thus the overall differences were minimized. The nature of the pathological process (gunshot wounds in Teuber's study) and the locus of lesion may be crucial factors, the probability being that Teuber's cases had lesser mesial involvement. One final point is that the procedure in the administration of the test was changed for Teuber's patients, in that they were informed that there would be changes in the sorting criteria, thus making the task easier.

Rosvold (1964) reported observing impairment in the Wisconsin Card Test in lobotomized patients. The defects were very pronounced one month after operation, but the patients subsequently improved and some recovered completely. His observation calls attention to the element of time after lesion as a factor in the disturbances related to frontal lobe damage. However, it is not possible to equate the results of the predominantly white-matter damage produced by lobotomy procedures with those from radical lobectomies.

Contrasting the effect of lesions in the frontal lobe with the effect of lesions in the temporal lobe has been tbe object of a recent study by Petrides and Milner (1982). The authors aimed at documenting changes, in the laboratory, of the type that can cause the diminished ability to plan short- and long-term activities that is so characteristic of frontal lobe patients. With that in mind, subjects were tested on four self-ordered tasks (sequential tasks in which the subject is free to choose his or her own order of response but is prevented from giving the same response twice) that required the organization of the sequence of pointing responses. As in Milner's previous study on the Wisconsin Card Sorting Test, the subjects were patients with circumscribed excisions of the frontal and temporal lobes. Patients with frontal lobe excisions had significant impairments in all four tasks, whereas the patients with temporal excisions either had no impairment or, when their lesions encompassed the hippocampus, exhibited material-specific deficits. It is of great interest that the patients with left frontal lobe excisions were impaired in both verbal and nonverbal tasks whereas the patients with right frontal lobe excisions were impaired only in nonverbal ones. Petrides and Milner (1982) pointed out how this disparity is compatible with the notion of left hemisphere dominance for the programming of voluntary actions.

Another important finding by Milner (1964) related to frontal lobe damage and verbal behavior. Using Thurstone's Word Fluency Test, she showed that patients with left frontal lobectomies that spared Broca's area scored very poorly in this test, despite there being no evidence of aphasia. The result was in keeping with traditional clinical observations of marked paucity of speech after frontal lobe damage, but Milner went one step further and demonstrated that right frontal lobe resections did not produce the defect. Controls with temporal lobectomies performed as well as patients with right frontal lobectomies. Interestingly, both left and right frontals performed at the same level in a task of verbal memory, suggesting the relative independence of the mechanism underlying fluency. The temporal lobe controls did poorly on the verbal memory task.

Benton (1968) arrived at the same conclusions studying a group of patients with left, right, and bilateral frontal damage. The task used to test fluency was an oral version of the Thurstone test, in which the patient is requested to say as many words beginning with a given letter of the alphabet as come to mind. Not only did the left hemisphere patients do remarkably worse than the right hemisphere ones, but bilaterally damaged patients also performed more poorly than those with right hemisphere damage only. The observations of Ramier and Hécaen (1970) were in essential accord with these results.

The findings of Milner and of Benton provide empirical confirmation of the classic views of Feuchtwanger (1923) and Kleist (1936), according to which "dominant" frontal lesions, but not "minor" frontal ones, interfere with verbal processes, particularly in respect to spontaneity and the ability to maintain a flow of verbal evocation, without actually producing one of the typical aphasias. They are in opposition to the views of Jefferson (1937) and Rylander (1940), who denied any lateralization of defect after frontal lobectomies.

As suggested by Milner's results in the task of verbal memory, the impairment in fluency seems to have an independent mechanism and is not necessarily associated with verbal learning defects. Benton noted that left hemisphere patients were not worse than right hemisphere ones in tasks of verbal paired-associate learning.

Benton's study also demonstrated that right-hemisphere-damaged subjects perform significantly worse than left-hemisphere-damaged subjects on visuoconstructive tasks. The findings confirm earlier results of Corkin (1964) and support the notion of lateralized differences in function. Along the same lines, Milner (1971) showed right frontal lobe patients to be defective in spatial learning and noted that those defects seemed dissociated from nonspatial learning.

Teuber's (1964, 1966) contribution to the problem of frontal lobe function is of special interest. At a time when researchers were primarily looking at the sensory aspect of the problem, he emphasized the motor end of the process and introduced the concept of corollary discharge. In brief, this is defined as the preparatory action that the motor system exerts on the sensory system to announce the intention of incoming movement, correct for displacement of perception, and assures smooth perceptual continuity once movement is carried out. Teuber viewed this mechanism as being dependent on frontal lobe structures and considered it to be a basic physiological function of the frontal lobe. In keeping with this idea, he hypothesized that most signs of frontal lobe dysfunction in animals and humans were derived from impairment of the corollary discharge mechanism. Indications of dysfunction as disparate as delayed response deficits in monkeys, perseveration, and the inability to handle sorting tasks were seen as resulting from the absence of a motor sensory alerting signal.

There is no doubt that some mechanism of corollary discharge exists and is essential for the continuity of perception, but it is not clear that frontal lobe structures are indispensable to corollary information processes. Nor does it seem probable that a single impaired mechanism can explain the variety of clinical and experimental signs of frontal lobe damage.

The observations that led Teuber to his concept of corollary discharge were made in patients with penetrating gunshot wounds involving the frontal lobes. In agreement with other authors, Teuber found no major deficit in intelligence or in performance on memory tests (Teuber and Weinstein, 1954, 1956; Weinstein and Teuber, 1957; Ghent et al., 1962), but he and his co-workers were unable to replicate Milner's findings on the Wisconsin Card Sorting Test. As noted, the discrepancy may have been due to the difference in type of lesions as well as to different procedures and experimental design (Teuber, 1964).

Objective evidence of dysfunction in Teuber's patients was reflected in impairment in a series of perceptuomotor tasks that included tests of visuopostural orientation, visual-search, body-orientation, and reversal-of-perspective ability. The visuopostural task (Teuber and Mishkin, 1954) called for the mechanial setting of a brightly luminous rod in the vertical position. The test was conducted in a dark room with the patient under different conditions of body tilt. Frontal lobe subjects did poorly in this task, but if the task was strictly visual and no visuoproprioceptive conflict was established, the subjects performed normally. The visual-search and body-orientation tasks involved active head and eye movement in the search for certain patterns or rapidly shifting left-to-right pointing responses on the patient's body. The reversal-of-perspective task was performed with two Necker cubes with the patient being requested to signify perception of left or right perspective reversal by pressing levers placed to the left and to the right. Since all of these tasks are difficult for a normal person and probably more so for a brain-damaged individual, the strength of the results lies in the verification that patients with nonfrontal brain damage perform consistently better than those with frontal disease. The preliminary results of Teuber and co-workers suggested that this was so.

Luria's contribution to the study of frontal lobe function encompasses many years of extensive investigation of patients and normals (Luria, 1966, 1969; Luria and Homskaya, 1964). As in so many other studies on the frontal lobe, the importance of the results is somewhat limited by the choice of the subjects for experimentation. Most of the patients studied by Luria and his co-workers had large frontal tumors, some intrinsic and some extrinsic. Some involved subcortical limbic-system structures, such as the septum. Some had associated hydrocephalus and some did not. Most patients had associated nonfrontal dysfunction, due to mass effect or compromise of vascular supply elsewhere in the brain. The location within the frontal lobe was also variable.

The limits of studies performed under such unsatisfactory conditions are obvious. Nevertheless, Luria's concept of frontal lobe function and dysfunction is quite stimulating.

His interpretation emphasizes the verbally mediated activating and regulatory role of the frontal lobes and the role of the frontal lobes in problem solving. He suggests that the orienting reaction, as measured by galvanic skin response or suppression of the alpha rhythm in the EEG, cannot be stabilized by verbal stimuli in patients with frontal lobe lesions. In normal subjects, the presentation of verbally meaningful instructions is expected to prevent habituation to stimuli and therefore prevent the orienting response from disappearing (Homskaya, 1966). Apparently nonaphasic patients with tumors, gunshot wounds, or stroke involving the posterior sensory cortex behave as normals in terms of verbal stabilization of the orienting responses even in the presence of praxic and gnosic defects. In patients with frontal lobe lesions, however, the verbal signal does not prevent habituation. Moreover, subjects with damage to the frontal poles and to the mesial and basal aspects of the frontal structures tend to be more affected than those with dorsolateral involvement.

Additional evidence for altered orienting responses in frontal-lobe patients comes from studies of visual potentials evoked by verbally tagged stimuli. Stimuli that would have increased the amplitude of visual evoked potentials in normals failed to do so in patients with frontal lobe damage (Simernitskaya and Homskaya, 1966; Simernitskaya, 1970).

Another aspect of frontal lobe function impaired by disease concerns the possibility of directing the execution of complex actions by verbal mediation. Several authors have pointed out that frontal lobe patients may be able to repeat correctly the instructions for a given task while making no use whatever of the information in performing a task. Thus, while performing a sorting task, subjects may make perseverative sorting errors even while verbalizing the correct strategy. The same has been said regarding the utilization of perceived error: patients will verbally admit the mistake but fail to correct it. Luria has repeatedly called attention to this type of defect and considers it one of the hallmarks of frontal lobe dysfunction. He attempted to objectify the defect in a series of experiments in which patients were requested to follow progressively more complex verbal instructions. He noted that patients were able to perform only the more direct and simple commands and would fail to carry out more complex instructions, particularly if they involved some change in principle or some conflict with additional cues provided by the examiner. Since the patient would still be able to repeat the initial verbal instruction, Luria concluded that the primary difficulty was one of verbal guidance of actions (Luria and Homskaya, 1964). Again, the weakness of these studies resides in the subjects used for the observations, i.e., patients with massive bilateral tumors of the frontal lobes. Attempts at replication have met with difficulties (Drewe, 1975). Some defects of the kind reported by Luria were found, but the dissociation between verbal and motor ability was not verified and the author considered it unlikely that a loss of verbal regulatory action was the mechanism underlying impaired performance.

A similar objection may be raised about Luria's description of the changes in problem-solving behavior that attend massive lesions of the frontal lobes. A state of confusion seems to underlie many of the disturbances of planning and calculation exhibited by his patients. Naturally, one can respond to this argument by stating that an element of confusion is part of some frontal lobe syndromes to begin with, but confusion can be caused by CNS changes that have little to do with frontal lobe dysfunction, although they may coincide with it and derive from a common cause. Also, confusion is not a necessary accompaniment of frontal lobe damage; it is associated with acute and massive damage of frontal tissue and clearly improves with time as adaptation to the pathological process occurs.

Nonetheless, Luria's observations are very suggestive and his proposals have heuristic value. The idea that patients have trouble in the choice of programs of action, that their strategy for gathering information necessary for the solution of the problem is impoverished, and that they seldom verify whether their actions meet the original intent are interesting interpretations of some of the defects that can be found, together or in isolation, in instances of frontal lobe damage. In addition, it is our impression that even when these defects cannot be demonstrated by an experimental task in the immediate and consistent manner claimed by Luria, one can still encounter them at more complex levels of behavior, for instance, in goal-oriented decision making during long-term planning operations.

Neurological and Clinical Neuropsychologic Studies

A variety of pathophysiological processes can cause damage to frontal lobe structures in humans, and the clinical presentation of some of those processes can be quite characteristic. The vascular syndromes are the most distinctive, particularly those related to the anterior cerebral artery. Bilateral as well as unilateral involvement is a common cause of mutism with or without akinesia. Personality changes are also frequently found, however, and a characteristic amnesic syndrome has recently been identified with lesions in this vascular distribution (Damesio et al., 1983). Damage is predominantly to the ventro-medial and mesial aspects of the frontal lobe. The most common cause of those abnormalities is rupture of an aneurysm of the anterior communicating artery or of the anterior cerebral artery itself. The frontal branches of the middle cerebral artery may also be involved, the more frequent causes being embolism and thrombosis. Damage is almost always unilateral and predominantly affects the dorsolateral aspect of the lobe, giving rise to nonfluent aphasias (Broca and transcortical motor) when the dominant hemisphere is involved and to aprosodia when the nondominant hemisphere is injured.

Tumor syndromes naturally vary with location and histological nature. Extrinsic tumors, such as meningiomas, are frequently located subfrontally or in the falx, where they involve the mesial aspect of the lobes and cause bilateral changes. They may also have a more lateral origin and compress the dorsolateral aspect of one frontal lobe only. Intrinsic tumors may also show up unilaterally or bilaterally. The distinction often depends on time, as an originally unilateral glioma may invade the corpus callosum and cross to the opposite side.

Not uncommonly, frontal lobe tumors present with major intellectual and affective impairment that justifies the use of the term "dementia," so pervasive is the disorganization of normal behavior. For this reason, the diagnosis of frontal lobe tumor should always be considered in the study of a dementia syndrome. Confusional states are also frequently associated with tumors in the frontal lobe, perhaps more so than with tumors anywhere else in the central nervous system (Hécaen, 1964). Disturbances of mood and character, although less frequent than confusion or dementia, were noted almost as frequently in Hécaen's study.

Other pathological processes may cause lesions in the frontal lobes. Wounds related to head injury—whose clinical pictures were vividly described by Kleist (1936) and Goldstein (1948)—infections such as syphilis, or degenerative processes such as Pick's disease may have a preponderant frontal involvement and present with a combination of frontal lobe signs.

The importance of the rate of development of the lesion, of time elapsed since peak development, and of the age and education of the patient when struck by disease have already been stressed and are indispensable to the evaluation of each frontal lobe case. Worsening, stabilization, or recovery, depend on the nature of the underlying pathological process. Most patients with cerebrovascular lesions tend to stabilize and then improve slowly, whereas the course of patients with tumors is a function of the degree of cytological and mechanical malignancy of the tumor and of the type of surgical or medical management adopted.

Detailed neurological examination often discloses few of the so-called hard signs. Nevertheless, a comprehensive neurological evaluation will reveal a variety of manifestations, most of which unmistakably suggest pathological involvement of the anterior areas of the brain. Some of the more significant ones are listed below under clinical headings.

CHANGES IN GOAL-ORIENTED BEHAVIOR

Impairments of cognitive ability, as measured by standard intelligence tests, are not striking in most patients with frontal lobe lesions, even when bilateral. With the exception of patients who present with confusion or dementia, studies have shown that patients with frontal lobe lesions may still perform at average levels of intelligence although their overall performance may be lower than expected. One need only recall Hebb's patient whose IQ was 98 or the very disturbed patient of Brickner who scored 80 one year after operation but 12 months later reached 99, or Eslinger and Damasio's patient with an IQ in the 120's and a memory quotient greater than 140. As Zangwill (1966) clearly pointed out, intelligence tests are unlikely to address the type of cognitive ability lost by frontal lobe patients. In reality, most forms of objective neuropsychological assessment could be covered by Zangwill's criticism, and, accordingly, few such tests disclose any abnormality. A partial exception to this rule is impairment in constructive ability, which requires visuomotor coordination to carry out a relatively complex building plan. Such impairment may be seen with some cases of bilateral or right frontal lobe damage.

Changes in the high-level cognitive ability that permits goal-oriented behavior are the most characteristic changes resulting from frontal lobe damage and certainly the most difficult to evaluate. The assessment of changes at this level of behavior implies a notion of the limits or normal variation of several aspects of human personality. Naturally, only a relative judgment is possible, taking into account the patient's age, educational level, social and cultural group, and previous achievements. Knowledge of the clinical pictures of the more frequent dementias as well as an acquaintance with the principal psychiatric entities is necessary for this aspect of diagnosis.

In spite of these difficulties, several relatively objective abnormalities can be detected. Lack of insight and lack of foresight are usually quite prominent. Even if able to act on their own, few patients see the significance of their decisions for themselves and for those around them. Often patients are unable to organize their daily activity, and planning of near and long-term future is not possible. As a consequence, during the acute phase of frontal lobe damage, patients are invariably dependent on relatives or guardians, even if perception and communication abilities are intact. In the more fortunate cases, moderate degrees of independence are achieved after recovery from major lesions. Few patients who sustain major frontal lobe lesions ever engage in creative endeavors or in the pursuit of meaningful interpersonal relationships. Taste, in the aesthetic and social sense, is a trait that the frontal-lobe-damaged patient will find difficult or impossible to cultivate.

Such impairments may result in an inability to assess the value of each new action, or lack of action, in terms of goals that are not overtly specified in the immediate environment. We presume that the disturbance of "abstract reasoning," of which so much has been made in analyses of frontal lobe dysfunction, really corresponds to this inability to reason according to a program not clearly expounded. One is tempted to hypothesize that either (a) the "master plan" is not readily available for continuous monitoring of the actions as they unfold or (b) the exact configuration of stimuli is not fully appreciated. In short, we see this impairment in goal-oriented behavior as the consequence of a high-level cognitive defect. We believe this set of behavioral abnormalities is strongly associated with lesions of the orbitofrontal region and not at all with more superior dorsolateral or mesial lesions.

CHANGES IN AFFECT AND REGULATION OF EMOTIONAL RESPONSE

The standard descriptions of affective and emotional changes in frontal lobe patients include witzelsucht, a term coined by Oppenheim (1889) to describe the facetiousness of these patients, and moria, a term coined by Jastrowitz (1888) to denote a sort of caustic euphoric state that is almost inseparable from witzelsucht. Phenomena resembling such descriptions are occasionally found, but it should be understood that in no patients are such changes a permanent feature. Indeed, a patient who appears facetious and boastful will look apathetic and indifferent at some later time or else may show a sudden burst of short-lived anger. The instability of humor also applies to the traditional and somewhat misleading descriptions of "tameness" and "bluntness" of emotion, which may be quite changeable and actually give way to unbridled aggressive behavior against a background of flat affect. External circumstances, particularly if they are stressful, as during an examining session, may "set" the patient's emotional tone. Frequently, the reaction will be found inappropriate to the circumstances but not necessarily in a consistent or predictable manner.

When present, facetiousness often has a sexual content, but this is kept within verbal limits and rarely, if ever, does a patient attempt to act according to the wishes or judgments expressed in his profane remarks. The lack of appreciation of social rules is usually quite evident, but even so there is no intentional viciousness associated with this type of behavior. Nor is there any indication that it produces pleasure: indeed, affect tends to be shallow. Inability to enjoy pleasurable stimulation, particularly if it involves social, intellectual, and aesthetic rewards, is probably characteristic of such patients and is in keeping with restricted response to pain. Both underscore the elementary disorder of affect.

Purely depressive or hypomanic states are not encountered. Frontal lobe patients rarely show the concern and preoccupation depressed patients do. They may appear psychopathic and show expansive, puerile behavior, but they lack the organization of the psychopathic personality. The same applies to the so-called hypomania of frontal lobe disease, which more often consists of an unstable state of exuberance occasionally interrupted by a flare-up of irritation. An interesting discussion of these distinctions is provided by Blumer and Benson (1975).

Primary regulatory behaviors associated with reward are markedly disturbed, and it is common to note the impairment of sexual drive and exploratory drive. Eating habits are commonly disturbed.

The association of changes in affect and in emotional control with predominant involvement of a specific region of the frontal lobe is still unsettled. Nonetheless, there is little doubt that the orbital aspect of the frontal lobe is especially involved in many patients presenting with emotional changes, particularly if the patient's conflicts are with society rather than intrapersonal. Also, patients with mesial frontal lobe lesions often appear to have blunted emotional responses, as if their affect had been neutralized (Damasio and Van Hoesen, 1983). It is too early to say whether lateralization of lesions may also be important, as has been suggested for interictal behavioral disorders (Bear and Fedio, 1977), or for the differences in discriminating affect (Heilman et al., 1975). Nevertheless, clinical experience indicates that bilateral or right frontal damage is probably more conducive to this type of disturbance than is left frontal damage.

CHANGES IN MEMORY

Most patients with frontal lobe damage fail to show memory disturbances. Nonetheless, lesions located in the most posterior aspect of the ventro-medial region of the frontal lobe can cause an amnesic syndrome (Damasio et al., 1983). These lesions, which can be unilateral or bilateral, are commonly caused by infarcts secondary to rupture of anterior communicating or anterior cerebral artery aneurysms. There is severe damage to the region of the basal forebrain, which contains the nucleus basalis of Meynert, among others, as well as its attending white-matter pathways. The syndrome is different from that caused by bilateral temporal damage and resembles that found in alcoholics with Korsakoff psychosis.

CHANGES IN SPEECH AND LANGUAGE

Broca's aphasia, transcortical motor aphasia, and the frontal apraxias are outside the scope of this chapter, but the disturbances of verbal fluency (in the sense of Thurstone's verbal association index) and the mutisms should be considered here.

Verbal fluency, as measured by verbal association tests, is often impaired. This may be noted in the absence of any detectable change in speech output. A curious instance is Brickner's patient A. He spoke fluent and well-articulated speech, often at a high rate, manifesting a free flow of verbal association of almost manic nature. However, when given a certain word, his ability to produce morphologically similar words by changing a letter or letter positions was impaired. This ability is also impaired in many cases of transcortical motor aphasia.

Mutism, generally associated with some degree of both akinesia and bradykinesia, is a frequent sign of frontal lobe dysfunction. It denotes involvement of the mesial cortex of the frontal lobe or of its connections, unilaterally or bilaterally. Current evidence indicates that lesions in the cingulate gyrus or the supplementary motor area (often in both) are crucial for the appearance of mutism and akinesia. Bilateral damage tends to cause longer-lasting changes. Unilateral damage, in vascular cases or in ablations, permits recovery in a matter of weeks. There is no evidence that side of lesion plays a major role here, and dominant as well as nondominant lesions cause much the same results, further evidence that the areas in question are related to affective and motor control but not to linguistic processing, thus being capable of interfering with speech (and all other movement, purposeful or automatic) but not language. The most frequent cause for the lesions that cause mutism is impairment in the blood supply of the anterior cerebral artery territories. Rupture of aneurysms of the anterior communicating or anterior cerebral artery is the usual antecedent event. The patient is mostly silent and motionless or nearly so, but tracking movements of the eyes and blinking are almost always preserved. The ability to walk is maintained in patients that do not have concomitant paraparesis from involvement of the mesial aspect of the motor areas. Often patients make many purposeful movements, such as those needed to adjust clothes or eat. The facial expression is empty, and the patient makes no effort to communicate verbally or by gesture. Rare isolated utterances may be produced, and repetition of single words and short sentences can occasionally be performed under coaxing. Whatever the amount of verbal output, patients do not produce paraphasias and have well-articulated though often hypophonic speech (Damasio and Van Hoesen, 1980, 1983).

The diagnosis of mutism should be made only after careful judgment of accompanying signs and of the whole context of the clinical presentation. Patients with mutism often evoke psychiatric disease, and if it were not for a clarifying previous history, a primarily neurological nature could go unnoticed. Mutism must be distinguished from anarthria and aphemia, conditions in which the inability to speak (or to speak without phonetic errors) is accompanied by a frustrated intent to communicate verbally and in which attempts to communicate by gesture or facial expression are often successful. These features also help distinguish mutism from the transcortical motor aphasias, in which speech is sparse and nonfluent, and in which word and sentence repetition are preserved.

CHANGES IN AROUSAL AND ORIENTING RESPONSE

Patients who move little or not at all often pay little or no attention to new stimuli. The possibility that akinesia associated with frontal lobe lesions goes pari passu with severe bilateral neglect is an interesting one. Thus, changes in motor and affective processing may be associated with changes in the mechanisms of arousal. The type of abnormality described by Fisher (1968) as "intermittent interruption of behavior" in cases of anterior cerebral artery infarction is another good example of the coexistence of such changes.

There is little doubt that orienting responses are impaired after dorsolateral and cingulate gyrus damage. The changes generally appear in the setting of neglect to stimuli arriving in the space contralateral to the lesion, with associated hypomobility of the neglected side (Heilman and Valenstein, 1972; Damasio et al., 1980). Lesions in the arcuate region in primates cause unilateral neglect (Kennard and Ectors, 1938; Welch and Stuteville, 1958), not unlike that determined by lesions of multimodal parietal association areas (Heilman et al., 1971), and the same applies to the cingulate gyrus (Watson et al., 1973). Lesions in non-frontal lobe structures—including the thalamus, hypothalamus, and midbrain—can also cause neglect in both humans and animals (Marshall and Teitelbaum, 1974; Marshall et al., 1971; Segarra and Angelo, 1971; Watson et al., 1974).

ABNORMAL REFLEXES

The more significant abnormal reflexes are the grasp reflex, the groping reflex, and the snout and sucking reflexes. Traditionally these abnormal responses have been termed "psychomotor signs," calling attention to the fact that they almost invariably appear in the setting of an abnormal mental status.

The most useful of the group is the grasp reflex (the prehension reflex of Kleist, the forced grasping of Adie and Critchley), which may appear unilaterally or bilaterally, in the hands or in the feet. It consists of a more or less forceful prehension of an object that has come into contact with the palm or the sole. It can be elicited by touching or by stroking the skin, particularly in the region between the thumb and index finger. Most maneuvers used to elicit the plantar reflex may produce a grasp reaction of the foot and may even mask an abnormal extensor response, which, in that case, may be obtained from stimulation of the lateral side of the foot. The degree of the grasp reflex varies from patient to patient and is generally more intense in cases with impaired mentation. In more alert states, it is characteristic that the patient cannot release the prehension even if told to do so and even if she or he wishes to do so. The reflex may extinguish after repeated stimulation and reappear after a period of rest. Classic descriptions used to refer to changes in lateralization induced by positioning of the head and body, but such changes are not reliable and should not be used for clinical localization.

The groping reflex is less frequent than the grasp reflex and generally appears in conjunction with the latter. The hand of the patient, as well as the eyes, tend to follow an object or the fingers of the examiner. For a brief period, the patient behaves as if stimulus-bound.

The sucking reflex is elicited by touching the lips of the patient with a cotton swab, and the snout reflex is obtained by tapping the skin of the upper perioral region with finger or hammer. These responses are often present in patients with disease confined to the frontal lobe, but, more so than the grasp reflex, they appear in a wide variety of demential syndromes associated with more wide-ranging damage. Furthermore, the snout reflex, just like the palmomental reflex, may appear in patients with basal ganglia disorders and even in normal older individuals.

Traditionally, these signs have been interpreted as an indication of release of primitive forms of reflex response, kept in abeyance by normal inhibitory function of frontal lobe structures. This view seems entirely valid.

ABNORMAL TONE

Patients with lesions in the prefrontal areas often show changes in muscle tone. These may be more closely associated with lesions in the dorsolateral aspect of the frontal lobes, particularly near the premotor regions. The most characteristic sign is Kleist's Gegenhalten, also referred to as counterpull, paratonia, opposition, or the Mayer-Reisch phenomenon. This is another of the so-called psychomotor signs and may be wrongly interpreted as a deliberate negative attitude on the part of the patient. When the examiner tries to assess tone by passively moving the arm, he or she may find a sudden resistance to the extension maneuver and note that the counteracting flexion movement actually increases in intensity in an attempt to neutralize the action. The patient may or may not be aware of this development and, as with the grasp reflex, will be unable to suppress the reflex even if desiring to do so. Rigidity may also be present, but since it is not associated with tremor, it will not have "cogwheel" characteristics. The degree of rigidity may show little consistency and may vary between observations. It is best described as plastic. Periodic hypotonia resembling cataplexy is quite rare (Ethelberg, 1949).

ABNORMAL GAIT AND POSTURE

Patients with severe frontal lobe damage often show abnormalities of gait. A wide range of characteristic changes may be present, including walking with short steps but without festination, loss of balance with retropulsion, or inability to walk (as in cases of gait apraxia). The latter may be seen in a variety of conditions, most frequently in the syndrome of normal-pressure hydrocephalus, which is, in effect, a frontal lobe syndrome consequent to periodically raised intraventricular pressure. In diagnosing gait apraxia, an effort should be made to demonstrate that the patient can execute while recumbent all the movements he or she is unable to perform while standing.

The designation "frontal ataxia" probably does not cover a manifestation typical of frontal lobe lesions, as even Bruns admitted when he coined the term. A tendency to fall backward rather than to the side and a predominance of deficits in the trunk rather than in the extremities are evident in some cases.

Abnormalities of posture are possible, though not pathogonomonic or frequent. In some cases, the examiner is able to place the arms of the patient in various bizarre positions and note the waxy flexibility with which the patient will remain in those unlikely positions. True catalepsy and sudden freezing of posture have also been described but seem rare.

CHANGES IN CONTROL OF EYE MOVEMENT

The control of eye and head movements is part of a highly developed system tuned to orient the organism toward possibly important stimuli and therefore aid perception of the environment. The role of the frontal eye fields, located bilaterally in area 8 of Brodmann, in the control of these movements is still a matter of controversy. The paucity of spontaneous head and eye movement toward new stimuli, which is commonly described in connection with the impairment of orienting responses of frontal lobe patients, is possibly related to eye field function. On the whole, however, the value of eye movement defects in the assessment of higher levels of behavior disturbance is limited.

Frontal seizures, originating in lesions in or near one eye field, may be characterized by a turning of the eye and head away from the side of the lesion. On the other hand, structural damage of one eye field, particularly if acute, produces a turning of eyes and head toward the side of lesion.

Clear anomalies of conjugate gaze mechanism have their greatest value in the assessment of the comatose patient, where their relation to a concomitant paresis may decide whether the damage is in the frontal lobe or in the brainstem.

OLFACTORY DISTURBANCES

Anatomical and electrophysiological studies in the monkey have suggested that the prefrontal cortex may be involved in *qualitative* olfactory discrimination (Tanabe et al., 1975a, 1975b; Potter and Nauta, 1979). Potter and Butters (1980) have reported that damage to the orbital region of the frontal lobe can lead to impaired odor-quality discrimination without a significant decrease in odor detection. Projections from the temporal lobe directly to orbitofrontal cortex as well as by way of the thalamus were hypothesized to carry olfactory information in a hierarchical system of "odor-quality analyzers." Damage to thalamic and prefrontal lobe structures has also been found to impair odor-quality discrimination in nonprimates without influencing odor detection (Eichenbaum et al., 1980; Sapolsky and Eichenbaum, 1980). The findings suggest that selective frontal lobe damage can be associated with deficits in a cognitive task of odor-quality discrimination without decreasing odor-detection ability.

CHANGES IN SPHINCTER CONTROL

It is often noted that patients with frontal lobe damage have disturbances of sphincter control. The patient shows little concern about urinating or even defecating in socially unacceptable situations. Bilateral involvement of the mesial aspect of the frontal lobe is the rule in these cases. Resection of an underlying tumor often improves sphincter disturbances, which tend to recover spontaneously in cases of stroke. Extensive lesions of the white matter may also produce incontinence, as the early techniques of frontal lobotomy demonstrated. This defect is probably the result of loss of the inhibitory action that the frontal lobe presumably exerts over the spinal detrusor reflex.

ANIMAL INVESTIGATIONS

A detailed review of animal experiments on frontal lobe function is outside the scope of this chapter. Nevertheless, consideration of some of the major results of animal research is in order because of their bearing on clinical issues.

The original findings of Jacobsen (1935; Jacobsen and Nissen, 1937) regarding the impairment in delayed responses in chimpanzees still dominate this area of study. During the past three decades an impressive number of researchers have replicated Jacobsen's results for both the delayed response and the delayed alternation tasks and extended the verification of the defects to rhesus monkeys, cats, dogs, and rats. Furthermore, within the prefrontal cortex, damage to the region of the sulcus principalis has been identified as the crucial region for the production of the defect (Blum, 1952). However, nobody has been able to reproduce the same delayed response defect in humans (Chorover and Cole, 1966).

The delayed response procedure consists of the presentation of two or more empty food wells, one of which is baited in front of the animal. The wells are then covered and hidden from view for at least 5 seconds, after which time the animal is again allowed to view the covered wells and requested to retrieve the bait. The number of errors the animal makes reaching for the food is the basis for the score. Jacobsen noted that animals with bilateral removals of the prefrontal lobes did very poorly in this task, unlike animals with bilateral lesions elsewhere in the brain. The initial interpretation was that of an immediate-memory defect, but this hypothesis was abandoned since the same animals that failed the delayed response task passed a visual discrimination procedure, which necessitates the use of immediate memory. If, for instance, one of the food wells was made different by the addition of a specific visual feature, the animal would make a correct choice after the delay. The fact that similar animals would perform normally if left in the dark during the delay suggested that retroactive erasing of traces was at stake. Also, if animals were allowed a rewarded response before the first trial, they would perform normally or with few errors, a finding that pointed to the obvious role of limbic reinforcement in the type of response (Finan, 1942; Malmo, 1942).

The delayed alternation tasks use the same setup, but the procedure is made more complicated by consecutive switching of the bait from one well to the other. Since delayed alternation naturally requires memory in a way that delayed response does not, performance in the two tasks may be dissociated by bilateral lesions of the hippocampus, which compromise delayed alternation but not delayed response (Orbach et al., 1960; Pribam et al., 1962). Destruction of the head of the caudate impairs both, however, in a manner similar to that produced by lesions in the region of the sulcus principalis, and electrical stimulation of the caudate during the trials also impairs the response (Rosvold and Delgado, 1956; Dean and Davis, 1959; Battig et al., 1960). Bilateral stimulation of the region of the sulcus principalis also impairs both tasks (Mishkin and Pribram, 1955, 1956; Pribram, 1961; Stamm, 1961). Furthermore, it has been shown that ablation or stimulation of the middle sector of the sulcus principalis disrupts delayed response or delayed alternation response, whereas ablation or stimulation of the anterior sector does not produce any impairment (Butters and Pandya, 1969; Stamm, 1969). Results of involvement of the posterior sector have been controversial. Finally, only lesions of both the upper and lower banks of the middle third (but not lesions of either upper or lower, in isolation) seem capable of producing the defects (Butters et al., 1971). The suggestion that lesions in the nucleus medialis dorsalis of the thalamus might impair delayed response (Schulman, 1969) has not been unquestionably verified.

The reason for the failure of nonhuman primates and other animals in the delayed response and delayed alternation tasks has not been unequivocally established. Lack of a so-called second signaling system does not explain the question entirely. Other factors that have been proposed are the impairment of processing of spatial and temporal cues and the effect of interference. Several studies tend to support the importance of these factors. For instance, Grueninger and Pribram (1969) showed that the performance of monkeys with dorsolateral lesions is impaired by distraction from the processing of spatial cues, which raises the possibility that changes in spatial information act as distractors in the delayed alternation task. This, in turn, suggests that the role of dorsolateral frontal lobe structures is that of an inhibitor of interference. That this inhibitory action might be more marked for spatial than nonspatial information is suggested by the better performance of monkeys with dorsolateral frontal lobe damage in nonspatial and go/no go problems (Mishkin, 1964).

Yet another cause for the delayed response defect may be the lack of limbic "tagging" of the stimuli, a circumstance that could arise from the destruction of a frontal region vital to the relay of sensory information into the limbic system. The facts that (a) the crucial area for delayed response impairment, the sulcus principalis, projects to the limbic system via the cingulate and from there to the hippocampus, (b) other areas of the anterior frontal cortex project to the caudate (from which similar defects may be obtained by stimulation), and, in addition, (c) delayed alternation defects can be obtained from almost anywhere in the limbic structures support the view that blocking the entry of input into this system is of importance in the determination of such defects. Both distractability and weakness of limbic marking are compatible with Konorski and Lawicka's (1964) interpretation of the defect on the basis of an abnormally rapid decay of the conditioning signal during the delay. In summary, it seems that delayed response defects result from the interaction of several factors, among which the limbic connection may be singled out as particularly important.

Animal studies have also addressed the idea that frontal lobe damage produces changes in the processing of information by altering the orienting response. Although it is not possible to draw a parallel with the human results, in which the changes seem to derive, at least in part, from lack of verbal control, animal studies have demonstrated the presence of abnormal orienting responses that fail to appear or appear inconsistently (Grueninger et al., 1965; Kimble et al., 1965).

If damage to the region of the sulcus principalis has been found to be crucial for the type of intellectual defects shown by Jacobsen's monkeys, damage to the orbital cortex seems to have been essential for their so-called bluntness of affect. Following their own observations that monkeys with orbital ablations showed marked and long-lasting changes in emotional behavior (Butter et al., 1963) that seemed to be related to an increase in aversive reactions and a concomitant decrease in aggressive reactions (Butter et al., 1968), Butter et al., (1970) made a careful study of aversive and aggressive behaviors in two groups of monkeys, one with oribtal lesions, the other with temporal lesions. The orbital lesions produced a clear reduction in aggressive behaviors, a change that was consistent and could still be seen after ten months. This reduction seemed to be situational, as there were noticeable differences in the way the animals reacted to different potentially threatening stimuli, and the animals could still demonstrate aggression when brought back to the colony where they had been dominant figures. This suggests that a regulatory mechanism of aggression had been impaired and that the capacity to display aggression had not been eliminated. The authors point out that the dependence on environmental configuration and the variety of possible emotional responses are not consistent with a permanent state of "bluntness of affect" used to describe similar changes in animals or in lobotomized patients, even if superficially the animals do look blunted and are indeed tame in many situations.

Anatomical study of the lesions indicated that the posteromedial region of the orbital aspect of the frontal lobe was closely associated with the reported changes. This in turn suggests involvement of that particular region in the regulation of aggressive behaviors. This area of the cortex is intimately connected to the amygdala, and furthermore, along with the dorsomedial nucleus of the thalamus, the amygdala and posteromedial orbital cortex project to roughly the same regions of the hypothalamus. The combination of behavioral and anatomical data supports the conjecture that these three structures form an integrated system capable of controlling certain types of emotional reaction.

It is clear that animal studies have made important contributions to the understanding of frontal lobe function. The most relevant results have been the unraveling of the anatomical connections referred to at the beginning of the chapter and the demonstration that monkeys with bilateral frontal damage are not able to utilize reinforcement properly and thus are prevented from guiding their behavior in terms of reward or punishment.

CONCLUSIONS

Reflecting on the variety of behavioral manifestations associated with frontal lobe damage and considering the localization of the responsible lesions, it is possible to arrive at some provisional conclusions regarding the function of these structures.

Damage to the motor and premotor cortices causes, in addition to well-known motor defects, a variety of language disorders when the lesion involves the dominant hemisphere and disturbances of prosody when the lesion involves the nondominant hemisphere.

Damage to the mesial sector of the frontal lobe is associated with a major disruption of the expression and experience of affect, an impairment of the drive toward motion, and, probably as a consequence of these, a major disturbance of communication. Akinesia, bradykinesia, and mutism are the principal signs of such involvement. Preliminary studies indicate that the position of the lesions is crucial for certain symptoms. For instance, the combined involvement of cingulate and supplementary motor area is probably necessary for the appearance of both mutism and akinesia. Mesial lesions inferior and anterior to cingulate and supplementary motor area may fail to cause akinesia but may be associated with mutism.

Damage to the orbital sector generates most of the disturbances generally associated with the concept of a "frontal lobe syndrome." Basic memory function and other intellectual abilities are preserved, provided the lesions spare the most posterior aspect of the ventromedial region of the frontal lobe, i. e., the basal forebrain. The clinical picture is dominated by a major disturbance of personality. We believe the orbital sector of the frontal lobe contains a variety of structures that "gate" diencephalic function. They can override a variety of primary hypothalamic mechanisms of response, substituting more elaborate forms of action suitable to complex social behaviors.

Damage to the dorso-lateral sector of the frontal lobe is associated with an impairment in high-level cognitive ability. There is severe impairment of the cognitive programs that permit the extraction of meaning from ongoing experience, that allow the coherent organization of mental contents on which creative thinking and language depend, and that permit, in general, artistic activities and the planning of future actions. The potential for multiple lines of cognitive activity—for instance, of the type that permits the planning of an elaborate verbal response to a complex question with a concommitant distractor—appears lost after lesions of the dorso-lateral frontal lobe.

The most dramatic and certainly the most permanent of the manifestations described above are related to bilateral lesions. Unilateral lesions, when extensive, may cause the same disturbances albeit less pronouncedly and with a better prognosis. The role of laterality in the appearance and recovery of these symptoms and signs has not yet been ascertained.

Research is likely to confirm the existence of a few consistent and frequent frontal lobe syndromes, caused, for instance, by the relatively stereotyped involvement of certain vascular territories, but the functional sectors outlined above are often compromised by pathological changes that overlap anatomical regions. Thus, there is real potential for the appearance of symptom clusters that derive manifestations from different structural sectors of the frontal lobe. Be that as it may, the notion of a single frontal lobe syndrome is just as absurd as the notion of a single frontal lobe function.

REFERENCES

Ackerly, S. S., and Benton, A. L. (1948). Report of a case of bilateral frontal lobe defect. *Research Publication of the Association for Research in Nervous and Mental Disease* 27:479–504.

Akert, K., (1964). Comparative anatomy of frontal cortex and thalamofrontal connections. In *The Frontal Granular Cortex and Behavior* (J. M. Warren and K. Akert, eds.). New York: McGraw-Hill, 1964.

Bailey, P., and Von Bonin, G. (1951). *The Isocortex of Man*. Urbana; University of Illiois Press.

Barbas, H., and Mesulam, M.M. (1981). Organization of afferent input of subdivisions of area 8 in the rhesus monkey. *J. Comp Neurol.* 200:407–431.

Battig, K., Rosvold, H. E., and Mishkin, M. (1960). Comparison of the effects of frontal and caudate lesions on delayed response and alternation in monkeys. *J. Comp. Psychol.* 53:400–404.

Bear, D. M., and Fedio, P. (1977). Quantitative analysis of interictal behavior in temporal lobe epilepsy. *Arch. Neurol.* 34:454–467.

Benton, A. L. (1968). Diferential behavioral effects in frontal lobe disease. *Neuropsychologia* 6:53–60.

Berg, E. A. (1948). A simple objective technique for measuring flexibility in thinking. *J. Genet. Psychol.* 39:15–22.

Blum, R. A. (1952). Effects of subtotal lesions of frontal granular cortex on delayed reaction in monkeys. *Arch. Neurol. Psychiat.* 67:375–386.

Blumer, D., and Benson, D. F. (1975). Personality changes with frontal and temporal lobe lesions. In *Psychiatric Aspects of Neurologic Disease* (D. F. Benson and D. Blumer, eds.). New York: Grune & Stratton.

Brickner, R. M. (1934). An interpretation of frontal lobe function based upon the study of a case of partial bilateral frontal lobectomy. Research Publication of the Association for Research in Nervous and Mental Disease 13:259–351.

Brickner, R. M. (1936). *The Intellectual Functions of the Frontal Lobes: Study Based upon Observation of a Man After Partial Bilateral Frontal Lobectomy.* New York: Macmillan.

Brickner, R. M. (1952). Brain of patient "A" after bilateral frontal lobectomy: Status of frontal lobe problem. *Arch. Neurol. Psychiat.* 68:293–313.

Butter, C. M., Mishkin,M., and Mirsky, A. F. (1968). Emotional responses toward humans in monkeys with selective frontal lesions. *Physiol. Behav.* 3:213–215.

Butter, C. M., Mishkin, M., and Rosvold, H. E. (1963). Conditioning and extinction of a food-rewarded response after selective ablations of frontal cortex in rhesus monkeys. *Exp. Neurol.* 7:65–75.

Butter, C. M., Snyder, D. R., and McDonald, J. A. (1970). Effects of orbital frontal lesions on aversive and aggressive behaviors in rhesus monkeys. *J. Comp. Physiol. Psychol.* 72:132–144.

Butters, N., and Pandya, D. (1969). Retention of delayed-alternation: Effect of selective lesions of sulcus principalis. *Science* 165:1271–1273.

Butters, N., Pandya, D., Sanders, K., and Dye, P. (1971). Behavioral deficits in monkeys after selective lesions within the middle third of sulcus principalis. *J. Comp. Physiol. Psychol.* 76:8–14.

Chavis, D. A., and Pandya, D. N. (1976). Further observations on corticofrontal connections in the rhesus monkey. *Brain Res.* 117:369–386.

Chorover, S. L., and Cole, M. (1966). Delayed alternation performance in patients with cerebral lesions. *Neuropsychologia* 4:1–7.

Corkin, S. H. (1964). Somesthetic function after focal cerebral damage in man. Unpublished doctoral thesis, McGill University.

Critchley, M. (1972). Interhemispheric partnership and interhemispheric rivalry. In *Scientific Foundations of Neurology* (M. Critchley, J. L. O'Leary, and B. Jennett, eds.). London: Heineman.

Crosby, E. C., Humphrey, T., and Lauer, E. W. (1962). *Correlative Anatomy of the Nervous System.* New York: Macmillan.

Damasio, A. R., Eslinger, P., Damasio, H., Van Hoesen, G. W., and Cornell, S. (1984). Multimodal amnesic syndrome following bilateral temporal and frontal damage: the case of patient DRB (Submitted).

Damasio, A. R., and Van Hoesen, G. W. (1980). Structure and function of the supplementary motor area. *Neurology 30:*359.

Damasio, A. R., and Van Hoesen, G. W. (1983). Emotional disturbances associated with focal lesions of the frontal lobe. In *The Neurophysiology of Human Emotion: Recent Advances* (K. Heilman and P. Satz, etd.). New York: Guilford Press.

Damasio, A. R., Damasio, H., and Chui, H. C. (1980). Neglect following damage to frontal lobe or basal ganglia. *Neuropsychologia 18:*123–132.

Damasio, A., Graff-Radford, N., Eslinger, P., and Kassell, N. (1983). Amnesia following ventromedial frontal lobe lesions. *Soc. Neurosci. 9:*29.

Dean, W. H., and Davis, G. D. (1959). Behavior following caudate lesions in rhesus monkey. *J. Neurophysiol. 22:*524–537.

DeVito, J. L., and Smith, O. E. (1964). Subcortical projections of the prefrontal lobe of the monkey. *J. Comp. Neurol. 123:*413.

Dieckmann, G., and Hassler, R. (1977) Treatment of sexual violence by stereotactive hypothalamatomy. In *Neurosurgical Treatment in Psychiatry, Pain, and Epilepsy* (W. H. Sweet, S. Obrador, and J. G. Martin-Rodriquez, eds.). Baltimore: Unviersity Park Press.

Drewe, E. A. (1975). An experimental investigation of Luria's theory on the effects of frontal lobe lesions in man. *Neuropsychologia 13:*421–429.

Eichenbaum, H., Shedlack, K. J., and Eckmann, K. W. (1980). Thalamocortical mechanisms in odor-guided behavior. I: Effects of lesions of the mediodorsal thalamic nucleus and frontal cortex on olfactory discrimination in the rat. *Brain Behavior and Evolution 17:*225–275.

Eslinger, P. J. and Damasio, A. R. (1984). Severe personality disturbance following bilateral prefrontal lobe ablation: patient EVR. (Submitted).

Ethelberg, S. (1949). On "cataplexy" in a case of frontal lobe tumour. *Acta Psychiat. Neurol. 24:*421–427.

Faust, C. I. (1966). Different psychological consequences due to superior frontal and orbitobasal lesions. *Intern. J. Neurol. 5:*3–4.

Feuchtwanger, E. (1923). Die funktionen des stirnhirns. In *Monographien aus dem Gesamtgebiete der Neurologie und Psychiatrie* (O. Förster and K. Willmanns, eds.). Berlin: Springer.

Finan, J. L. (1942). Delayed response with predelay reinforcement in monkeys after removal of the frontal lobes. *Am. J. Psychol. 55:*202–214.

Fisher, C. M. (1968). Intermittent interruption of behavior. *Trans. Am. Neurol. Assoc. 93:*209–210.

Fulton, J. F. (1951). *Frontal Lobotomy and Affective Behavior.* New York: Norton.

Fulton, J. F., and Jacobsen, C. F. (1935). The functions of the frontal lobes: A comparative study in monkeys, chimpanzees and man. *Advan. Mod. Biol. (Moscow) 4:*113–123.

Ghent, L., Mishkin, M., and Teuber, H. L. (1962). Short-term memory after frontal-lobe injury in man. *J. Comp. Physiol. Psychol. 55:*705–709.

Goldman, P. S. (1978). Neuronal plasticity in primate telencephalon: Anomalous projections induced by prenatal removal of frontal cortex. *Science 202:*768–770.

Goldman, P. S., and Nauta, W. J. H. (1977). An intricately patterned prefrontocaudate projection in the rhesus monkey. *J. Comp. Neurol. 171:*369–386.

Goldman-Rakic, P. S., and Schwartz, M. L. (1982). Interdigitation of contralateral and ipsilateral columnar projections to frontal association cortex in primates. *Science 216:*755–757.

Goldstein, K. (1948). *Aftereffects of Brain Injuries in War.* New York: Grune & Stratton.

Grant, D. A., and Berg, E. A. (1948). A behavioral analysis of degree of reinforcement and ease of shifting to new responses in a Weigl-type card-sorting problem. *J. Exp. Psychol.* 38:404–411.

Grueninger, W. E., and Pribram, K. H. (1969). The effects of spatial and nonspatial distractors on performance latency of monkeys with frontal lesions. *J. Comp. Physiol. Psychol.* 68:203–209.

Grueninger, W. E., Kimble, D. P., Grueninger, J., and Levine, S. E. (1965). GSR and corticosteroid response in monkeys with frontal ablations. *Neuropsychologia* 3:205–216.

Hamlin, R. M. (1970). Intellectual function 14 years after frontal lobe surgery. *Cortex* 6:299–307.

Hebb, D. O. (1945). Man's frontal lobes: A critical review. *Arch. Neurol. Psychiat.* 54:421–438.

Hebb, D. O., and Penfield, W. (1940). Human behavior after extensive bilateral removals from the frontal lobes. *Arch. Neurol. Psychiat.* 44:421–438.

Hecaen, H. (1964). Mental symptoms associated with tumors of the frontal lobe. In *The Frontal Granular Cortex and Behavior* (J. M. Warren and K. Akert, eds.). New York: McGraw-Hill.

Heilman, K. M., and Valenstein, E. (1972). Frontal lobe neglect in man. *Neurology* 22:660–664.

Heilman, K. M., Pandya, D. N., Karol, E. A., and Geschwind, N. (1971). Auditory inattention. *Arch. Neurol.* 24:323–325.

Heilman, K. M., Scholes, R., and Watson, R. T. (1975). Auditory affective agnosia: Disturbed comprehension of affective speech. *J. Neurol. Neurosurg. Psychiat.* 38:69–72.

Homskaya, E. D. (1966). Vegetative components of the orienting reflex to indifferent and significant stimuli in patients with lesions of the frontal lobes. In *Frontal Lobes and Regulation of Psychological Porcesses* (A. R. Luria and E. D. Homskaya, eds.). Moscow: Moscow University Press.

Jacobsen, C. F. (1935). Functions of the frontal association area in primates. *Arch. Neurol. Psychiat.* 33:558–569.

Jacobsen, C. F., and Nissen, H. W. (1937). Studies of cerebral function in primates. IV: The effects of frontal lobe lesion on the delayed alternation habit in monkeys. *J. Comp. Physiol. Psychol.* 23:101–112.

Jastrowitz, M. (1888). Beiträge zur Localisation im Grosshirn und über deren praktische Verwerthung. *Deutsche Medizinische Wochenschrift* 14:81.

Jefferson, G. (1937). Removal of right or left frontal lobes in man. *Br. Med. J.* 2:199.

Johnson, T. N., Rosvold, H. E., and Mishkin, M. (1968). Projections from behaviorally defined sectors of the prefrontal cortex to the basal ganglia, septum, and diencephalon of the monkey. *Exp. Neurol.* 21:20.

Kennard, M. A., and Ectors, L. (1938). Forced circling movements in monkeys following lesions of the frontal lobes. *J. Neurophysiol.* 1:45–54.

Kievit, J., and Kuypers, H. G. J. M. (1974). Basal forebrain and hypothalamic connections to frontal and parietal cortex in the rhesus mokey. *Science* 187:660–662.

Kimble, D. P., Bagshaw, M. H., and Pribram, K. H. (1965). The GSR of monkeys during orienting and habituation after selective partial ablations of the cingulate and frontal cortex. *Neuropsychologia* 3:121–128.

Kleist, K. (1936). *Gehirnpatholgie*. Leipzig: Barth.

Konorski, J., and Lawicka, W. (1964). Analysis of errors by prefrontal animals on the delayed-response test. In *The Frontal Granular Cortex and Behavior* (J. M. Warren and K. Akert, eds.). New York: McGraw-Hill.

Kuypers, H. G. J. M., Szwarobart, M. K., and Mishkin, M. (1965). Occipitotemporal cortico-cortical connections in the rhesus monkey. *Exp. Neurol.* 11:245.

Luria, A. R. (1966). *Human Brain and Psychological Processes.* New York: Harper & Row.

Luria, A. R. (1969). Frontal lobe syndrome. In *Handbook of Clinical Neurology*, vol. 2 (P. J. Vinken and G. W. Bruyn, eds.). Amsterdam: North-Holland.

Luria, A. R., and Homskaya, E. D. (194). Disturbances in the regulative role of speech with frontal lobe lesions. In *The Frontal Granular Cortex and Behavior* (J. M. Warren and K. Akert, eds.). New York: McGraw-Hill.

Malmo, R. B. (1942). Interference factors in delayed response in monkeys after removal of frontal lobes. *J. Neurophysiol.* 5:295–308.

Marshall, J. F., and Teitelbaum, P. (1974). Further analysis of sensory inattention ollowing lateral hypothalamic damage in rats. *J. Comp. Physiol. Psychol.* 86:375–395.

Marshall, J. F., Turner, B. H., and Teitelbaum, P. (1971). Sensory neglect produced by lateral hypothalamic damage. *Science* 174:523–525.

Milner, B. (1963). Effects of different brain lesions on card sorting. *Arch. Neurol.* 9:90–100.

Milner, B. (1964). Some effects of frontal lobectomy in man. In *The Frontal Granular Cortex and Behavior* (J. M. Warren and K. Akert, eds.). New York: McGraw-Hill.

Milner, B. (1971). Interhemispheric differences in the localisation of psychological processes in man. *Br. Med. Bull.* 27:272–277.

Mishkin, M. (1964). Perseveration of central sets after frontal lesions in monkeys. In *The Frontal Granular Cortex and Behavior* (J. M. Warren and K. Akert, eds.). New York: McGraw-Hill.

Mishkin, M., and Pribram, K. H. (1955). Analysis of the effects of frontal lesions in monkeys. I: Variations of delayed alternations. *J. Comp. Physiol. Psychol.* 48:492–495.

Mishkin, M., and Pribram, K. H. (1956). Analysis of the effects of frontal lesions in the monkey. II: Variations of delayed response. *J. Comp. Physiol. Psychol.* 49:36–40.

Moniz, E. (1936). *Tentatives Operatoires dans le Traitement de Certaines Psychoses.* Paris: Masson et Cie.

Moniz, E. (1949) Confidencias de um investigador cientifico. Lisbon: Livraria Atica.

Nadvornik, P., Sramka, M., and Patoprsta, G. (1977). Transventricular anterior hypothala-motomy in stereotactic treatment of hedonia. In *Neurosurgical Treatment in Psychiatry, Pain, and Epilepsy* (W. H. Sweet, S. Obrador, and J. G. Martin-Rodriquez, eds.). Baltimore: University Park Press.

Nauta, W. J. H. (1962). Neural associations of the amygdaloid complex in the monkey. *Brain* 85:505–520.

Nauta, W. J. H. (1964). Some efferent connections of the prefrontal cortex in the monkey. In *The Frontal Granular Cortex and Behavior* (J. M. Warren and K. Akert, ed.). New York: McGraw-Hill.

Nauta, W. J. H., and Haymaker, W. (1969). *The Hypothalamus.* Springfield, Ill.: Thomas.

Oppenheim, H. (1889). Zur pathologie der grosshirngeschwülste. *Arch Psychiat.* 21:560.

Orbach, J., Milner, B., and Rasmussen, T. (1960). Learning and retention in monkeys after amygdala-hippocampal resection. *Arch. Neurol.* 3:230–251.

Pandya, D. N., and Kuypers, H. G. J. M. (1969). Cortico-cortical connections in the rhesus monkey. *Brain Res.* 13:13.

Pandya, D. N., and Vignolo, L. A. (1971). Intra- and interhemispheric projections of the precentral, premotor and arcuate areas in the rhesus monkey. *Brain Res.* 26:217–233.

Pandya, D. N., Dye, P., and Butters, N. (1971). Efferent cortico-cortical projections of the prefrontal cortex in the rhesus monkey. *Brain Res.* 31:35–46.

Pandya, D. N., Hallett, M., and Mukherjee, S. K. (1969). Intra- and interhemispheric connections of the neocortical auditory system in the rhesus monkey. *Brain Res.* 13:49.

Penfield, W., and Roberts, L. (1959). *Speech and Brain Mechanisms*. Princeton: Princeton University Press.

Petrides, M., and Milner, B. (1982). Deficits on subject-ordered tasks after frontal- and temporal-lobe lesions in man. *Neuropsychologia 20*:249–262.

Porrino, J. J., and Goldman-Rakic, P. S. (1982). Brainstem innervation of prefrontal and anterior cingulate cortex in the rhesus monkey revealed by retrogrde transport of HRP. *J. Comp. Neurol. 205*:63–76.

Porrino, L. J., Crane, A. M., and Goldman-Rakic, P. S. (1981). Direct and indirect pathways from the amygdala to the frontal lobe in rhesus monkeys. *J. Comp. Neurol. 198*:121–136.

Potter, H., and Butters, N. (1980). An assessment of olfactory deficits in patients with damage to prefrontal cortex. *Neuropsychologia 18*:621–628.

Potter, H., and Nauta, W. J. H. (1979). A note on the problem of olfactory associations of the orbitofrontal cortex in the monkey. *Neuroscience 4*:316–367.

Powell, T. P. S., Cowan, W. M., and Raisman, G. (1965). The central olfactory connexions. *J. Anat. (London) 99*:791.

Pribram, K. H. (1961). A further experimental analysis of the behavioral deficit that follows injury to the primate frontal cortex. *Exp. Neurol. 3*:431–466.

Pribram, K. H., and MacLean, P. D. (1953). Neuronographic analysis of medial and basal cerebral cortex. II: Monkey. *J. Neurophysiol. 16*:324–340.

Pribram, K. H., Chow, K. L., and Semmes, J. (1953). Limit and organization of the cortical projection from the medial thalamic nucleus in monkey. *J. Comp. Neurol. 98*:433–448.

Pribram, K. H., Wilson, W. A., and Connors, J. (1962). Effects of lesions of the medial forebrain on alternation behavior of rhesus monkeys. *Exp. Neurol. 6*:36–47.

Ramier, A. M., and Hecaen, H. (1970). Rôle respectif des atteintes frontales et de la latéralisation lesionnelle dans les deficits de la "fluence verbale." *Rev. Neurol. 123*:17–22.

Rosene, D. L., Mesulam, M.-M., and Van Hoesen, G. W. (1976). Afferents to area FL of the medial frontal cortex from the amygdala and hippocampus of the rhesus monkey. In *Neuroscience Abstracts*, vol. 2, part 1. Bethesda, Md.: Society for Neuroscience.

Rosvold, H. E. (1964). In the discussion of B. Milner's presentation in *The Frontal Granular Cortex and Behavior* (J. M. Warren and K. Akert, eds.). New York: McGraw-Hill.

Rosvold, H. E., and Delgado, J. M. R. (1956). The effect on delayed-alternation test performance of stimulating or destroying electrically structures within the frontal lobes of the monkey's brain. *J. Comp. Physiol. Psychol. 49*:365–372.

Russell, W. R. (1959). *Brain, Memory and Learning*. New York: Oxford University Press.

Rylander, G. (1940). *Personality Changes After Operations on the Frontal Lobes*. Copenhagen: Munksgaard.

Sapolsky, R. M., and Eichenbaum, H. (1980). Thalamocortical mechanisms in odor-guided behavior. II: Effects of lesions of the mediodorsal thalamic nucleus and frontal cortex on odor preferences and sexual behavior in the hamster. *Brain, Behavior and Evolution 17*:276–290.

Schneider, H. (1977). Psychic changes in sexual delinquency after hypothalamotomy. In *Neurosurgical Treatment in Psychiatry, Pain, and Epilepsy* (W. H. Sweet, S. Obrador, and J. G. Martin-Rodriquez, eds.). Baltimore: University Park Press.

Schulman, J. S. (1969). Electrical stimulation of monkey's prefrontal cortex during delayed response performance. *J. Comp. Physiol. Psychol. 67*:535–546.

Scoville, W. B., and Bettis, D. B. (1977). Results of orbital undercutting today: A personal series. In *Neurosurgical Treatmnt in Psychiatry, Pain, and Epilepsy* (W. H. Sweet, S. Obrador, and J. G. Martin-Rodriquez, eds.). Baltimore: University Park Press.

Scoville, W. B., and Milner, B. (1957). Loss of recent memory after bilateral hippocampal lesions. *J. Neurol. Neurosurg. Psychiat.* 20:11–21.

Segarra, J., and Angelo, J. (1970). Anatomical determinants of behavioral change. In *Behavioral Change in Cerebrovascular Disease* (A. L. Benton, ed.). New York: Harper & Row.

Simernitskaya, E. G. (1970). *Evoked Potentials as an Indicator of the Active Process.* Moscow: Moscow University Press.

Simernitskaya, E. G., and Homskaya, E. D. (1966). Changes in evoked potentials to significant stimuli in normal subjects and in lesions of the frontal lobes.In *Frontal Lobes and Regulation of Psychological Precesses* (A. R. Luria and E. D. Homskaya, eds.). Moscow: Moscow University Press.

Stamm, J. S. (1961). Electrical stimulation of frontal cortex in monkeys during learning of an alternation task. *J. Neurophysiol.* 24:414–426.

Stamm, J. S. (1969). Electrical stimulation of monkeys' prefrontal cortex during delayed-response performance. *J. Comp. Physiol. Psychol.* 67:535–546.

Stuss, D. T., Kaplan, E. F., Benson, D. F., Weir, W. S., Naeser, M. A., Levine, H. L. (1981). Long-term effects of prefrontal leucotomy: An overview of neuropsychologic residuals. *J. Clin. Neuropsych.* 3:13–32.

Tanabe, T., Iino, M., and Takogi, S. F. (1975a). Discrimination of oders in olfactory bulb, pyriform-amygdaloid areas, and orbitofrontal cortex of the monkey. *J. Neurophysiol.* 38:1284–1296.

Tanabe, T., Yarita, H., Iino, M., Ooshima, Y., and Takagi, S. F. (1975b). An olfactory projection area in orbitofrontal cortex of the monkey. *J. Neurophysiol.* 38:1269–1283.

Teuber, H.-L.(1964). The riddle of frontal lobe function in man. In *The Frontal Granular Cortex and Behavior* (J. M. Warren and K. Akert, eds.). New York: McGraw-Hill.

Teuber, H.-L. (1966). The frontal lobes and their function: Further observations on rodents, carnivores, subhuman primates, and man. *Intern. J. Neurol.* 5:282–300.

Teuber, H.-L., and Mishkin, M. (1954). Judgment of visual and postural vertical after brain injury. *J. Psychol.* 38:161–175.

Teuber, H.-L., and Weinstein, S. (1954). Performance on a formboard task after penetrating brain injury. *J. Psychol.* 38:177–190.

Teuber, H.-L., and Weinstein, S. (1956). Ability to discover hidden figures after cerebral lesions. *Arch. Neurol. Psychiat.* 76:369–379.

Valverde, F. (1965). *Studies on the Piriform Lobe.* Cambridge, Mass.: Harvard University Press.

Ward, A. A., and McCulloch, W. S. (1947). The projection of the frontal lobe on the hypothalamus. *J. Neurophysiol.* 10:309–314.

Watson, R. T., Heilman, K. M., Cauthen, J. C., and King, F. A. (1973). Neglect after cingulectomy. *Neurology* 23:1003–1007.

Watson, R. T., Heilman, K. M., Miller, B. D., and King, F. A. (1974). Neglect after mesencephalic reticular formation lesions. *Neurology* 24:294–298.

Weinstein, S., and Teuber, H. L. (1957). Effects of penetrating brain injury on intelligence test socres. *Science* 125:1036–1037.

Welch, K., and Stuteville, P. (1958). Experimental production of neglect in monkeys. *Brain* 81:341–347.

Whitlock, D. C., and Nauta, W. J. H. (1956). Subcortical projections from the temporal neocortex in Macaca mulatta. *J. Comp. Neurol.* 106:183–212.

Yeterian, E. H., and Van Hoesen, G. W. (1977). Cortico-striate projections in the rhesus monkey: The organization of certain cortico-caudate connections. *Brain Res.* 139:43–63.

Zangwill, O. L. (1966). Psychological deficits associated with frontal lobe lesions. *Intern. J. Neurol.* 5:395–402.

13

Emotional Disorders Associated with
Neurological Diseases

KENNETH M. HEILMAN, DAWN BOWERS, AND EDWARD VALENSTEIN

Although everyone experiences emotions, emotion cannot be easily defined, and it is difficult to measure something that cannot be defined. However, a person can report emotional feelings verbally, and there are behavioral and psychophysiological changes associated with emotion that can be observed and measured. In general, emotions have at least two dimensions: intensity (e.g., strong, weak) and valence (e.g., sad, angry, happy). Both intensity and valence may be determined in part by observing and measuring overt behavior and physiological change; however, these behavioral variables do not fully reflect inner feelings.

Patients with neurological diseases may have an emotional response to their illness. Emotional states may enhance symptoms (e.g., anxiety may increase essential tremor) and may even induce neurological symptoms (e.g., headache). However, emotional response to a disease, emotion-induced enhancement of symptoms, and emotion-induced conditions are not unique to neurology and are not discussed in this chapter.

One of the major assumptions of neuropsychology is that behavior and experiential states are physically mediated. A corollary of this assumption is that emotions are physically mediated and that perturbations of critical physical processes may affect emotional experience and behavior. More specifically, since the central nervous system is critical for mediating emotional experiences and emotional behavior, diseases of the central nervous system may induce changes in emotional experience and behavior. This chapter discusses the effect of diseases of the central nervous system on emotional behavior and the pathophysiology underlying these changes.

Studies of the anatomical substrate of emotional behavior attest to the importance of the limbic system. This system receives input from many areas of the neocortex and in turn is extensively interconnected with hypothalamic centers important in regulating basic drives, such as hunger and thirst, as well as endocrine and autonomic function. (Endocrine and autonomic changes are prominent physiological features of emotional reactions.) While lesions in the limbic system and hypothalamus can have dramatic effects on emotional behavior, recent studies have demonstrated prominent and specific changes in emotional behavior after neocortical lesions in humans. In highly developed organisms and humans especially, survival depends on increasingly intricate patterns of behavior that require extensive neocortical analysis. It is therefore not surprising that hemispheric lesions in nonlimbic structures can lead to emotional changes. In addition, nonlimbic subcortical structures in the basal ganglia and thalamus are critical for the activation and modulation of cortical and limbic areas, at least in part through the mediation of specific neurotransmitter systems. Emotional symptoms can also be seen in diseases of the basal ganglia that cause defects in specific neurotransmitter systems.

In this chapter we first consider emotional changes that result from lesions in either the right or the left hemisphere. These changes may result from interference with specific neocortical emotional functions or with cognitive processes necessary for the production of emotions in response to certain circumstances or from disruption of cortical modulation of limbic or other subcortical regions. The frontal lobes have particularly strong limbic connections, and frontal lobe lesions can cause prominent emotional changes. These are discussed in Chap. 12 and not considered further here. After discussing emotional changes resulting from dysfunction of the right or left hemisphere, we consider changes associated with limbic and basal ganglia disorders. Finally, we discuss the pseudobulbar state, in which inappropriate emotional expression occurs despite appropriate emotional experience.

Throughout this chapter, we emphasize information gained from studies of humans with brain dysfunction, since most of our knowledge comes from the investigation of pathological states in humans. We also consider animal studies when they pertain to observations on humans, but we do not attempt to summarize the extensive literature on emotional states in animals.

HEMISPHERIC DYSFUNCTION

Right Hemisphere Dysfunction

Babinski (1914) noted that patients with right hemisphere disease often appeared indifferent or euphoric. Hécaen and associates (1951) and Denny-Brown and associates (1952) also noted that patients with right hemisphere lesions were often inappropriately indifferent. Gainotti's (1972) study of 160 patients with lateralized brain damage supported these earlier clinical observations: right hemisphere lesions were often associated with indifference. Terzian (1964) and Rossi and Rosadini (1967) studied the emotional reactions of patients recovering from barbiturate-induced hemispheric anesthesia produced by left or right carotid artery injections (Wada test). They observed that right carotid injections were associated with a euphoric-manic response. Milner (1974), however, was unable to replicate these findings.

Gainotti (1972) thought that the indifference reaction was an abnormal mood associated with denial of illness (anosognosia). Recent research has offered alternative hypotheses.

PERCEPTUAL AND COGNITIVE DEFECTS

Auditory-verbal processes.   Patients with right hemisphere lesions caused by cerebral infarction, trauma, or tumor might have a defect in the comprehension of affect or expression of affect or both. Developing an appropriate emotion depends in part on comprehension of speech. Speech carries at least two types of information: the linguistic content (what is said) and the affective content (how it is said). The linguistic content is conveyed by a complex code that requires semantic and phonemic decoding. Prosody—the pitch, tempo, and rhythm of speech—is also important in conveying the linguistic content, for example, in the differentiation of questions from statements. Prosody, however, is also important in conveying affective content (Paul, 1909). Affective intonation refers to those aspects of prosody important in conveying affective content.

In the vast majority of individuals (particularly right-handers), the left hemisphere is clearly more adept than the right in decoding the linguistic content of speech. Until several years ago, little was known about how affective intonations were mediated. We therefore attempted to determine whether the right hemisphere was more adept than the left in decoding the affective components of speech. In one study (Heilman et al., 1975b), sentences with semantically neutral content (e.g., "The boy went to the store.") were read in four different emotional intonations (happy, sad, angry, indifferent) to patients with right temporoparietal infarctions and to aphasic patients with left temporoparietal infarctions. The patients' task was to identify the emotional tone of the speaker. Patients with right hemisphere lesions performed worse on this task than those with left hemisphere lesions, suggesting that the right hemisphere is more critically involved in processing the affective intonations of speech.

Schlanger et al. (1976) performed a similar study on patients with right or left hemisphere damage. Although they found that brain-damaged subjects performed more poorly than did controls, these investigators did not find any differences between right- and left-hemisphere-damaged patients. However, only 3 of their 20 subjects with right hemisphere disease had temporoparietal lesions. Ross (1981) has confirmed our findings. Weintraub et al. (1981) demonstrated that right-hemisphere-damaged patients also had a defect in nonemotional prosody. Heilman et al. (1983) compared right- and left-hemisphere-damaged patients on the comprehension of filtered sentences that contained either emotional (happy, sad, angry) or nonemotional (interrogative, declarative, imperative) prosody. The right-hemisphere-damaged subjects performed no worse than the left-hemisphere-damaged subjects on the nonemotional prosody. However, the right-hemisphere-damaged subjects performed worse than the left-hemisphere-damaged subjects on the emotional prosody, suggesting that the right hemisphere plays a dominant role in comprehending affective intonation.

Further support for the role of the right hemisphere in processing affective intonation comes from the study of normal subjects. In dichotic listening tasks, two different auditory messages are simultaneously presented to the two ears and the subject is asked to recall what she or he has heard (Kimura, 1961, 1967). Stimuli are generally better recalled when presented to the ear contralateral to the hemisphere that is dominant for processing the stimuli. Using this technique, Haggard and Parkinson (1971) presented dichotic words spoken in different affective intonations to normal right-handed adults. When asked to indicate which words had been heard, subjects recalled more of the words presented to the right ear. However, when asked to indicate the emotional mood of the speaker, the subjects recalled more of the moods presented to the left ear. Ley (1980) has used a dichotic listening procedure with normal adults to replicate these findings. The dichotic stimuli were neutral sentences spoken with different affective intonations. Again, a left ear superiority was found for the judgment of emotional tone, which supported the hypothesis that the right hemisphere may be dominant for processing the affective components of speech stimuli.

The defect underlying the impaired ability of patients with right hemisphere disease to identify affective intonations in speech is not entirely clear. It may be related to a cognitive disability whereby these patients fail to denote and classify affective stimuli. It could also be related to an inability to discriminate perceptually between different affective intonations in speech. In a subsequent study, we (Tucker et al., 1977) replicated our previous findings and attempted to determine whether patients with right hemisphere disease could in fact discriminate between affective intonations of speech without having to classify or denote these intonations. Patients were required to listen to identical pairs of sentences spoken in either the same or different emotional tones. The patients did not have to identify the emotional intonation but had to tell whether the intonations associated with the sentences sounded the same or different. Patients with right hemisphere disease performed more poorly on this task than did patients with left hemisphere disease, which suggests that the perceptual discrimination between affectively intoned stimuli was impaired in the patients with right hemisphere damage. However, it remains unclear if this discrimination defect can entirely account for the comprehension defect.

Further evidence for the dominant role of the right hemisphere in comprehending affective intonation also comes from studies that demonstrate preserved abilities in patients with left hemisphere lesions. We examined a patient with pure word deafness (normal speech output and reading but impaired speech comprehension) from a left hemisphere lesion. In patients with pure word deafness the left auditory cortex is thought to be destroyed and the right auditory cortex is disconnected from Wernicke's area on the left; however, the right auditory area and its connections to the right hemisphere are intact. Although this patient comprehended speech very poorly, he had no difficulty recognizing either environmental sounds or emotional intonations of speech.

We presented the token test (a sensitive instrument for measuring language comprehension) to aphasic patients with left hemisphere disease (Heilman et al., 1975a). This test was administered in two conditions—one in the usual manner (normal speech) and one in which the intensity and prosody of the commands were varied and many of the commands affectively intoned. In the high prosody condition, comprehension was greatly improved. There are multiple possible explanations for this observation. The improved performance could have been due to the novelty rather than the emotional nature of the prosody. Emotional stmuli could have activated the right hemisphere and increased right hemisphere processing of affective stimuli.

We also studied five patients with global aphasia by giving them propositional commands like "point to the happy face" (Heilman et al., in preparation). These commands were either neutrally intoned or intoned with the appropriate affective intonation. In the happy condition, patients pointed to the correct face more often when the appropriate intonation was present than when the sentences were not intoned. In the sad and angry conditions, they were not aided by the affective intonation. Boller et al. (in press) presented sentences to eight patients with severe aphasia. These sentences had either neutral or emotional content. The sentences with emotional content produced a greater number of responses than did the neutral sentences.

Emotional messages may be conveyed by propositional speech. Graves and associates (1980) visually presented emotional and nonemotional words to aphasic patients with left hemisphere lesions. Their task was to read the words. Unlike speech, which can be affectively intoned, the written word carries no prosody. Nevertheless, Graves and co-workers found that emotional words were read better than nonemotional words. These authors also performed a study with normal adults in which emotional and nonemotional words were tachistoscopically presented to the left and right visual half-fields. In the left visual half-field, there was a relative superiority for the recognition of emotional words over nonemotional words. Unfortunately, Strauss (1983) was unable to confirm the findings of Graves et al. Therefore, it is not clear if the right hemisphere is important in processing only affective intonations or if it also processes emotional language and therefore mediates emotional comprehension independent of the nature of the stimulus.

Visual nonverbal processes. The development of an appropriate emotional state may depend not only on perceiving and comprehending auditory stimuli (e.g., intonations) but also on perceiving and comprehending visual stimuli, such as facial expressions, gestures, and scenes. Gardner and colleagues (1975) found that patients with right hemisphere disease and those with left hemisphere disease were equally impaired in selecting the most humorous of a group of cartoons. Patients with left hemisphere disease, however, performed better on cartoons without captions.

We gave affective tasks to patients with left or right hemisphere lesions, as well as to neurologic controls without hemispheric disease (DeKosky et al., 1980). We asked these patients to discriminate between a pair of neutral faces (e.g., "Are these two faces the same person or two different people"), to name the emotion expressed by a face (happy, sad, angry, indifferent), to select from a multiple choice array of faces a "target" emotion (e.g., "Point to the happy face"), and to determine whether two pictures of the same person's face expressed the same or a different emotion. Patients with right hemisphere disease were markedly impaired in their ability to discriminate between pairs of neutral faces, as previously reported by Benton and Van Allen (1968). Although both the right- and left-hemisphere-damaged patients had difficulty naming and selecting emotional faces, there was a trend for patients with right hemisphere disease to perform more poorly on these two tasks than patients with left hemisphere disease. In addition, patients with right hemisphere disease were more impaired in making same-different discriminations between emotional faces.

When performance across these various affect tasks was covaried for neutral facial discrimination (a visuospatial nonemotional task), differences between the two groups disappeared. Although this finding suggests that a facial discrimination defect may underlie right-hemisphere-damaged patients' inability to recognize and discriminate between emotional faces, the poor facial discrimination by the group with right hemisphere disease did not entirely correlate with their ability to recognize and discriminate between emotional faces. Retrospective review of the data revealed that about one third of the patients with right hemisphere disease performed poorly on both the neutral facial discrimination task and the emotional faces tasks, whereas about one third performed well on both. The remaining patients with right hemisphere disease, however, performed relatively well on neutral facial discrimination but poorly on the emotional faces tasks.

We therefore believe that the right hemisphere is important in perceiving both faces and facial expressions. These processes may be either interdependent (i.e., one must perceive faces before perceiving the emotions expressed by the face) or they may be independent but share the same or a contiguous anatomic locus. Cicone et al. (1980) also presented emotional faces to patients with right or left hemisphere damage and also found that right-hemisphere-damaged patients were impaired in recognizing emotional faces.

Tachistoscopic studies with normal adults have also implicated the right hemisphere in the processing of affective faces. Suberi and McKeever (1977) presented neutral and affective faces to the right and left visual half-fields of normal adult right-handers. They found that the left visual half-field was significantly superior in identifying emotional faces versus nonemotional faces. Similar findings have also been reported by Ley and Bryden (1979).

EXPRESSIVE DEFECTS

Verbal expression. We attempted to determine whether patients with right hemisphere disease can express emotionally intoned speech (Tucker et al., 1977). The patients were asked to say semantically neutral sentences (e.g., "The boy went to the store.") using a happy, sad, angry, or indifferent tone of voice. These patients were severely impaired. Typically, they spoke the sentences in a flat monotone and often denoted the target affect (e.g., "The boy went to the store and he was sad."). Ross and Mesulam (1979) described two patients who could not express affectively intoned speech but could comprehend affective speech. Ross (1981) also described patients who could not comprehend affective intonation but could repeat affectively intoned speech and postulated that right hemisphere lesions may disrupt the comprehension, repetition, or production of affective speech in the same manner that left hemisphere lesions disrupt propositional speech.

Facial expression. Buck and Duffy (1980) studied the ability of right- and left-hemisphere-damaged patients to make emotional faces in response to viewing slides such as those of familiar people, unpleasant scenes, and unusual pictures. The subjects' faces were videotaped as they viewed the slides and were later judged. The results showed that, compared with left-hemisphere-injured subjects, right-hemisphere-damaged patients were less facially expressive. Sackeim and coworkers (1978) demonstrated that in normal subjects emotions are expressed more intensely on the left side of the face.

MEMORY

In one of the few studies of affective memory, Wechsler (1973) presented right- and left-hemisphere-damaged patients with two stories—one designed to elicit an affective response, the other neutral. For example, the emotional story told of a king "who was very sick and the doctors were unable to cure him. He sent for his wise men who told him he would get well if he wore the shirt of a truly happy man." Immediately after the story was read to the patients, they were asked to reproduce it verbally. The score was based on the total units recalled (i.e., similar to the logical memory subtest of Wechsler Memory Scale). The patients with left hemisphere lesions made fewer errors on the emotionally charged story than did patients with right hemisphere disease; there were no differences in their performance on the neutral story.

UNDERLYING AFFECT

The studies reviewed thus far suggest that patients with right hemisphere disease have more difficulty than patients with left hemisphere disease in comprehending and expressing affectively intoned speech as well as comprehending and expressing emotional facial expressions. Patients with right hemisphere disease may also have more difficulty comprehending or remembering emotionally charged speech. These perceptual, cognitive, expressive, and mnemonic deficits might underlie and account for the flattened emotional reaction of patients with right hemisphere lesions (i.e., indifference reactions), as previously described by clinical investigators (Babinski, 1914; Hécaen et al., 1951; Denny-Brown et al., 1952; Gainotti, 1972). Alternatively, these perceptual, cognitive, expressive, and memory deficits may not reflect the patients' underlying mood.

To learn more about mood, we (Gasparrini et al., 1978) administered the Minnesota Multiphasic Inventory (MMPI) to patients with unilateral hemisphere lesions. The patients were matched for severity of cognitive (e.g., IQ) and motor defects (e.g., motor tapping). The MMPI has been widely used as an index of underlying affective experience, and the completion of this inventory does not require the perception or expression of affectively intoned speech or the perception of facial expression. Patients with left hemisphere disease showed a marked elevation on the depression scale of this inventory, whereas patients with right hemisphere disease did not. This finding suggests that the differences in emotional reactions of patients after right versus left hemisphere disease cannot be attributed entirely to difficulties in perceiving or expressing affective stimuli. Equally important, the difference in depression between the two groups appears unrelated to differences in the severity of cognitive or motor defects. Many patients with right hemisphere disease who have the indifference reaction may not appear depressed because they have anosognosia and do not recognize that they are disabled; that is, they have no reason to be depressed. In the clinic, however, we see patients who do not explicitly deny illness, in that they recognize that they have had a stroke, are in the hospital, and have a left hemiparesis, but nevertheless appear unconcerned (anosodiaphoria) (Critchley, 1953). Although a portion of this flattening and unconcern may be induced by a loss of ability to express affective intonations in speech or to use affective facial expressions, even when one uses propositional speech to assess affect, these patients still convey a lack of concern about their illness.

PATHOPHYSIOLOGY OF INDIFFERENCE REACTIONS

Cannon (1927) proposed that cortical activation induces the conscious emotional state. The visceral changes that occur simultaneously serve adaptive purposes. Cannon considered the thalamus an important central structure in the mediation of emotion, since the thalamus can be stimulated by either peripheral sensory input or central (visceral) impulses. Bard (1934) suggested that the hypothalamus is, in fact, the major effector of emotional expression, since it regulates both the endocrine system and the autonomic nervous system. Papez (1937) proposed that the limbic system, which has important connections with the hypothalamus, thalamus, and neocortex, is important in regulating emotion.

Cortical activation or arousal was central to Cannon's theory of emotion. Subsequent research led to a better understanding of the physiology of arousal. Berger (1933) noted that the electroencephalographic pattern decreased in amplitude and increased in frequency during behavioral arousal. This was termed "electroencephalographic desynchronization." Desynchronization also occurs during emotional states (Lindsley, 1970). Animals stimulated in the nonspecific thalamic nuclei or in the mesencephalic reticular formation also show behavioral indices of arousal and electroencephalographic desynchronization (Moruzzi and Magoun, 1949). In addition, stimulation of certain cortical areas, such as portions of the frontal or temporoparietal cortex, activates the mesencephalic reticular formation (French et al., 1955) and elicits an arousal response (Segundo et al., 1955). Areas in the limbic system have reciprocal connections with the cortex and strong input into the reticular formation. This is another pathway by which cortical stimulation can produce arousal (Heilman and Valenstein, 1972; Watson, et al., 1973).

The relationship between arousal and emotion was studied in 1924 by Maranon (see Fehr and Stern, 1970), who induced physiological arousal by administering sympathomimetic drugs to normal subjects. He reported that most of his subjects reported feeling "no emotions," although many reported that they experienced "as if" feelings. When Maranon induced an affective memory that was not strong enough to produce an emotion in the normal state, emotional reactions occurred if there was a concomitant pharmacological arousal. Schachter (1970) also pharmacologically aroused normal subjects, placed them in stressful situations, and found both subjective and objective evidence of emotional states. Pharmacological arousal alone did not produce emotional states. The stressful situation produced less emotion when the subjects were not pharmacologically aroused than when they were.

Maranon's (Fehr and Stern, 1970) and Schachter's (1970) studies suggest that the experiencing of emotion requires the appropriate cognitive state and arousal. Arousal is mediated by brainstem reticular formation, nonspecific thalamic nuclei, and certain regions of the neocortex. Emotions are accompanied by visceral changes mediated by the hypothalamus. The hypothalamus is strongly influenced by the limbic system, which in turn has considerable input from the neocortex (especially the frontal lobes). An emotion thus depends on varied anatomic structures, including cortical systems for producing the appropriate cognitive set, limbic structures for activating the brainstem and thalamic activating centers and for controlling the hypothalamic output, the hypothalamus for regulating endocrine and autonomic responses, and the brainstem and thalamic activating systems for producing cortical arousal.

Patients with right hemisphere disease have difficulty comprehending affectively intoned speech and recognizing affective facial expressions. These deficits may interfere with the development of an appropriate *cognitive state*. In addition, patients with right hemisphere disease and the indifference reaction might also be inadequately aroused. To determine whether such patients had normal arousal, we (Heilman et al., 1978) stimulated the normal side of patients with right or left hemisphere disease with an electrical stimulus and simultaneously recorded galvanic skin responses. The galvanic skin response is a measure of peripheral sympathetic activity that correlates well with other central measures of arousal, such as the electroencephalogram. We found that patients with right hemisphere disease and the indifference reaction had dramatically smaller galvanic skin responses than aphasic patients with left hemisphere disease or control patients without hemispheric lesions. Morrow and co-workers (in press) also found that the patients with right hemisphere disease had reduced galvanic skin responses to both neutral and emotional stimuli, providing further evidence that the indifference reaction is associated with hypoarousal.

Patients with the indifference reaction from right hemisphere disease typically have unilateral neglect (Denny-Brown et al., 1952; Gainotti, 1972; Heilman and Valenstein, 1972). We have proposed that unilateral neglect is an attention-arousal-activation defect caused by dysfunction in a corticolimbic-reticular loop (Heilman, 1979).

Supportive evidence for the importance of the right hemisphere in mediating attention and cerebral activation has been documented in our laboratory with normal right-handed adults (Heilman and Van den Abell, 1979). Because of the right hemisphere's dominant role in attention-arousal, the right hemisphere may also have a special role in mediating emotional behavior. Not only can the right hemisphere process affective stimuli and program emotional behavior, but it also appears to have a special relationship to those subcortical structures important for mediating cerebral arousal and activation.

Left Hemisphere Damage

PERCEPTUAL AND COGNITIVE DEFICITS

Verbal processes.   Left-hemisphere-damaged patients, especially those with word deafness or Wernicke's, global, transcortical sensory and mixed transcortical aphasia, may have defects in comprehending propositional speech. If the development of the appropriate cognitive state is dependent on propositional language, patients with these aphasias would not be able to develop the appropriate cognitive state. Patients with Broca's and conduction aphasia may have difficulty comprehending emotional messages conveyed by propositional speech if these messages contain complex syntax or require a large memory store.

Although left-hemisphere-damaged aphasic and word deaf patients may have difficulty comprehending propositional speech, some of these patients can comprehend emotional intonations, and their comprehension of propositional speech may be aided by these intonations (Heilman et al., 1975a, 1975b; Coslett et al., 1983).

Visual-nonverbal processes.   When patients with left hemisphere lesions were asked to match faces (a test of visuospatial skills), their performance was no different from that of brain damaged controls (DeKosky et al., 1980). However, when these patients were asked to name an emotional face or point to an emotional face, their performance, while not as poor as that of right-hemisphere-damaged patients, was worse than that of controls. Berent (1977) tested a group of depressed women before and after electroconvulsive therapy (ECT) to either the left or right hemisphere. ECT to the right hemisphere induced a deficit in recognizing faces, whereas ECT to the left hemisphere induced difficulty in naming the emotions expressed by the faces. Berent speculated that verbal mediation and verbal labeling might underlie the naming defect. Berent's hypothesis is compatible with the performance of the patients with left hemisphere disease in the study by DeKosky et al. (1980). With the exception of the neutral facial discrimination task, the test on which the aphasic patients with left hemisphere disease performed best (and significantly better than the group with right hemisphere disease) was matching emotional faces, a task that does not require verbal labeling or mediation.

EXPRESSIVE DEFECTS

Depending on the type of aphasia, patients with left hemisphere disease may have difficulty expressing emotions when these emotions are expressed as a spoken or written propositional message. However, Hughlings Jackson (1932) observed that even nonfluent aphasics could embue their simple utterances with emotional content by using affective intonation. In addition, some nonfluent aphasics may be very fluent when using expletives. Jackson postulated that the right hemisphere may be mediating these activities. Roeltgen et al. (1983) demonstrated that aphasic patients with agraphia were able to write emotional words better than nonemotional words; however, the role of the right hemisphere in these cases remains uncertain.

CATASTROPHIC REACTION

In contrast to the flattened emotional response or inappropriate euphoric mood associated with right hemisphere damage, Babinski (1914), Goldstein (1948), Hécaen et al. (1951), and Denny-Brown and co-workers (1952) noted that many patients with left hemisphere lesions and aphasia showed a profound depression which Goldstein called the "catastrophic reaction." Gainotti (1972) confirmed Goldstein's (1948) observations. Terzian (1964) and Rossi and Rosadini (1967) observed that barbiturate injections into the left carotid artery (Wada test) could induce a depressed or catastrophic reaction.

Although both Goldstein (1948) and Gainotti (1942) postulated that the catastrophic reaction was a normal response to a serious physical and cognitive defect, Gasparrini and co-workers (1978), using the MMPI, demonstrated that the difference in severity of depression between right- and left-hemisphere-damaged subjects could not be entirely explained by the severity of cognitive or motor deficits.

The pathophysiology of the depressive response is not entirely known. The depressive reaction is usually seen in nonfluent aphasic patients with anterior perisylvian lesions (Benson, 1979). As discussed, Hughlings Jackson (1932) noted that left hemisphere lesions induced deficits in propositional language. Nonfluent aphasics who could not express themselves with propositional speech could express feelings by using expletives and by intoning simple verbal utterances. Hughlings Jackson postulated that the right hemisphere may be mediating this activity. His postulate was supported by the observations of Tucker et al. (1977) and Ross and Mesulam (1979). Because left-hemisphere-damaged patients are unable to use propositional speech, they may rely more on right hemisphere nonpropositional affective systems by more heavily intoning their speech and by using more facial expression. As Gasparrini et al. (1978) showed, however, even left-hemisphere-damaged patients without aphasia, who did not have to rely on the right hemisphere to mediate expression, were more depressed than right-hemisphere-damaged patients. Therefore, increased reliance on right-hemisphere-mediated expression cannot be the entire explanation of the depressive response.

Several authors have proposed that the right hemisphere is more critically involved in processing negative emotions and the left hemisphere processes positive emotions (see Tucker, 1981). According to this postulate, the catastrophic reaction would result from left hemisphere damage because of the consequent predominance of right hemisphere "negative" emotion. The hypothesis that each hemisphere processes different aspects of emotion, however, has not been consistently substantiated (Ley, 1980).

In measuring arousal in patients with hemispheric lesions with the galvanic skin response, we found not only that patients with right hemisphere lesions were hypoaroused (Heilman et al., 1978) but also that patients with left hemisphere disease had a greater arousal response than normal controls. Trexler and Schmidt (1981) had similar findings. Because left-hemisphere-damaged patients are disabled, they have a cognitive state compatible with depression. The combination of this cognitive state with hyperarousal may be responsible for their profound depression and the catastrophic reaction.

INDIFFERENCE REACTIONS

Not all patients with left hemisphere dysfunction have the catastrophic reaction. Patients with fluent aphasia with poor comprehension from posterior lesions (i.e., Wernicke's aphasics) are often indifferent about their disability. However, these patients do demonstrate such affective states as frustration, anger, and fear and therefore are not similar to right-hemisphere-damaged patients, who demonstrate globally flattened affect. Their indifference may stem from unawareness of their deficit: often, they have no hemiparesis and their comprehension deficit may be associated with a defect in self-monitoring so that they are unaware of their language disturbance.

Patients with left-sided subcortical lesions (i.e., in the thalamus) may also be aphasic; however, unlike patients with cortical lesions, they frequently have a flattened affect (Watson and Heilman, 1982). Since many patients do not have a profound comprehension defect, their flattening cannot be attributed to an inappropriate cognitive state. Many of these patients have inattention that is thought to be associated with an arousal deficit (Heilman, 1979). Structures such as the thalamus are thought to play an important role in the mediation of arousal, and the flattening seen with these patients may be related to an arousal deficit.

Patients with any of the transcortical aphasias associated with mesial hemispheric lesions (in the distribution of the anterior cerebral artery) frequently have a flattened affect. Although in patients with comprehension deficits some of the flattening may be related to unawareness of the deficit, the areas injured in these cases are important modulators of arousal. In addition, Speedie and Heilman (1983) have demonstrated that, when mixed transcortical sensory aphasics are asked to repeat an emotionally intoned sentence, they repeat the propositional message devoid of intonations. It is possible that the brain lesions causing transcortical aphasias isolate the perisylvian speech region from the right hemisphere, which is dominant in programming emotional prosody.

Therapy for Affective Changes Induced by Hemispheric Disease

The four major goals of therapy are treatment of underlying disease (when possible), education, alternative strategies, and drug therapy. (The treatment of vascular disease, tumors, trauma, and other processes that may injure the hemisphere is not within the scope of this book.)

A major role of the therapist is educating patients and families. Although patients and families will attribute sensory, motor, and language disorders to brain injury, affective disorders are frequently incorrectly attributed to psychodynamic factors, even though there was a clear temporal relationship between the stroke and the affective changes. When patients and families learn that emotional changes may be related to brain injury, there is often a reduction of guilt, an improvement of interpersonal relations, and a refocusing on the appropriate problems.

In general, there are many alternative strategies available to patients with neurologically induced behavioral deficits. These strategies must be individually tailored. For example, if one has a patient with right temporoparietal injury who cannot comprehend affective intonations, the family should be instructed to use propositional speech to communicate affect. If a patient has a left temporoparietal lesion with decreased comprehension of propositional language, that person may still be able to comprehend affective intonation.

Drug therapy may also be helpful. For example, left hemisphere depressed patients may benefit from antidepressants.

LIMBIC SYSTEM DYSFUNCTION

Anatomy

In 1878, Broca designated a group of anatomically related structures on the medial wall of the cerebral hemisphere "le grand lobe limbique." Because these structures are in proximity to structures of the olfactory system, it was assumed that they all have olfactory or related functions. In 1901, Ramon y Cajal (1965) concluded on the basis of histological studies that portions of the limbic lobe (the hippocampal-fornix system) had no more than a neighborly relationship with the olfactory apparatus. Papez (1937) postulated that a "circuit" in the limbic lobe (cingulate—hippocampus—fornix—mammillary bodies—anterior thalamus—cingulate) was an important component of the central mechanism subserving emotional feeling and expression. Bard (1934) demonstrated that the hypothalamus was important in mediating the rage response, and Papez (1937) postulated that the hypothalamus was the effector of emotion. In 1948, Yakolev added the basolateral components (the orbitofrontal, insular, and anterior temporal lobe cortical regions, the amygdala, and the dorsomedial nucleus of the thalamus) to the medial system, and together these were designated as the limbic system (MacLean, 1952) (Fig. 13-1).

Experimental Observations in Animals

Myriad stimulation and ablation experiments in animals have attempted to define the role of the limbic system in regulating emotion (Valenstein, 1973). Many of these studies have provided confusing and contradictory results. Some of the difficulty undoubtedly results from the complex functional differentiation within each component of the limbic system (Isaacson, 1982). Adding to this is the difficulty of measuring affect in animals; most experiments use techniques such as active or passive avoidance and infer the emotional state from the animal's behavior. Finally, species differences may be significant, even in this phylogenetically older portion of the cerebral hemispheres.

One of the earliest and most important animal observations was that bilateral ablation of the anterior temporal lobe changes the aggressive rhesus monkey into a tame animal (Kluver and Bucy, 1937). Such animals also demonstrated hypersexuality and visual agnosia. Akert et al. (1961) demonstrated that the removal of the temporal lobe neocortex did not produce this tameness. Ursin (1960) stimulated the amygdaloid nucleus and produced a ragelike response and an increase in emotional behavior. Amygdala ablation (Woods, 1956) produced placid animals.

Septal lesions in animals, on the other hand, produced a ragelike state (Brady and Nauta, 1955), and septal stimulation produced an apparently pleasant state in which animals stimulated themselves without additional reward (Olds, 1958). Decortication in animals produces a state of pathological rage ("sham rage"). In a series of experiments, Bard (1934) demonstrated that the caudal hypothalamus was mediating this response. Both the amygdala (a component of the basolateral circuit) and the septal region (a portion of both limbic circuits) have great input into the hypothalamus (Yakolev, 1948). MacLean (1952) has proposed that the septal pathway is important for species preservation (that is, social-sexual behavior) and the amygdala circuit is more important for self preservation (fight and flight).

Limbic Dysfunction in Humans

DISCRETE LESIONS AND STIMULATION

Some of the findings in humans have been analogous to the results reported in animals. In humans, for example, tumors in the septal region have been reported to

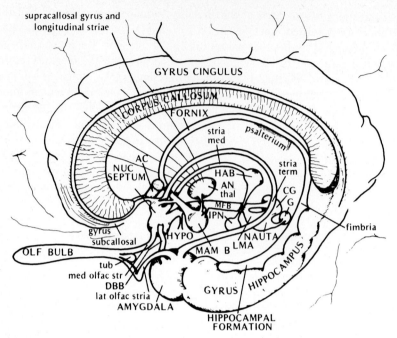

Fig. 13-1 A diagrammatic representation of the limbic system.

AC—Anterior commissure,
ANthal—Anterior Nucleus of the thalamus,
CG—Central gray matter of the midbrain,
DBB—Diagonal Band of Broca,
G—Gudden's deep tegmental nucleus,
HAB—Habenula,
HYPO—hypothalamus,
IPN—Interpeduncular nucleus,
LMA NAUTA—Lateral midbrain area of Nauta,
lat olf str—lateral olfactory stria,
med olf str—medial olfactory stria,
MFB—median forebrain bundle,
MAM B—mamillary bodies,
stria med—stria medullaris,
stria term—stria terminalis.

FIG. 13.1

produce ragelike attacks and increased irritability (Zeman and King, 1958; Poeck and Pilleri, 1961), and stimulation is reported to be pleasant and sexually arousing (Heath, 1964). Bilateral temporal lobe lesions in humans entailing the destruction of the amygdala, uncus, and hippocampal gyrus have been reported to produce placidity (Poeck, 1969). In aggressive patients, stereotactic amygdaloidectomy has been reported to reduce rage (Mark et al., 1972). Anterior temporal lobectomy for seizure disorders has been reported to increase sexuality (Blumer and Walker, 1975). Bilateral hippocampal removal produces a profound and permanent deficit in recent memory. (see Chap. 14).

INFLAMMATORY CONDITIONS

Several inflammatory and viral diseases have been known to affect the limbic system. Herpes simplex encephalitis has a predilection for the orbitofrontal and anterior temporal regions and thus selectively destroys much of the limbic system. Impulsivity, memory loss, and abnormalities of emotional behavior are frequently early manifestations of this infection. Limbic encephalitis may also be associated with carcinoma. There is degeneration and inflammation of amygdaloid nuclei, hippocampi, and cingulate gyri, as well as other structures. Clinically, the picture is similar to that of herpes infection, with memory loss and abnormalities of emotional behavior, including depression, agitation, and anxiety (Corsellis et al., 1968). Rabies, which also has a predilection for limbic structures, such as the hippocampus (as well as hypothalamic and brainstem regions), also has prominent emotional symptoms including profound anxiety and agitation.

TEMPORAL LOBE EPILEPSY

Partial (focal) seizures with complex symptomatology (temporal lobe epilepsy, psychomotor epilepsy) have long been known to produce emotional symptoms. These symptoms may be considered under three headings: ictal phenomena (phenomena directly related to the seizure discharge), postictal phenomena (occurring directly after a seizure), and interictal behavior (occurring between overt seizures).

Ictal phenomena.   One of the strongest arguments supporting the notion that the limbic system is important in mediating emotional behavior is the observation that emotional change as a manifestation of a seizure discharge is highly correlated with foci in or near the limbic system, particularly with foci in the anteromedial temporal lobes.

Sexuality.   Currier et al. (1971) described patients who had ictal behavior that resembled sexual intercourse. Undressing and exhibitionism have been described with temporal lobe seizures (Hooshmand and Brawley, 1969; Rodin, 1973). In one case reported to us a patient undressed and fondled another person during a temporal lobe seizure. In general, however, ictal sexual behavior is not purposeful. Remillard et al. (1983) reported 12 women with temporal lobe epilepsy who had sexual arousal or orgasm as part of their seizures, and they reviewed 14 other cases. Most cases had right-sided foci, and most were women. Spencer et al. (1983) reported sexual automatisms, in four patients with seizure foci in the orbitofrontal cortex. They proposed that sexual experiences were more likely to occur with temporal lobe foci whereas sexual automatisms occurred only with frontal foci.

Gelastic and dacrystic seizures.   Gelastic epilepsy refers to seizures in which laughter is a prominent ictal event (Daly and Mulder, 1957). Sackeim et al. (1982) reviewed 91 reported cases of gelastic epilepsy and found that, of 59 cases with lateralized foci, 40 were left-sided. Gascon and Lombroso (1971) described 10 patients with gelastic epilepsy: five had bilateral synchronous spike and wave abnormalities, and two of these had diencephalic pathology; the other five had right temporal lobe foci. Gascon and Lombroso thought they could differentiate two types of laughter: the diencephalic group appeared to have automatic laughter without affect and the temporal lobe group more affective components (including pleasurable auras).

Crying as an ictal manifestation, termed dacrystic epilepsy (Offen et al., 1976), is much less common than laughing. Of the six cases reviewed by Offen et al., four probably had right-sided pathology, one had left-sided pathology, and in one the site of pathology was uncertain.

Aggression.   Ictal aggression is rare. Ashford et al. (1980) documented nonpurposeful violent behavior as an ictal event. The relationship between epileptic seizures and directed, purposeful violence is controversial. Mark and Ervin (1970) are among the strongest proponents of such a relationship, finding a high incidence of epilepsy in a group of violent prisoners. Pincus (1980) reviewed other studies showing a similar relationship; however, Stevens and Hermann (1981) found that controlled studies did not support this view. Many neurologists who have cared for large numbers of temporal lobe epileptics have never seen directed, purposeful violence as an ictal phenomenon.

Fear and anxiety.   Fear is the affect most frequently associated with a temporal lobe seizure (Williams, 1956). Ictal fear may be found equally with right- and left-sided dysfunction (Williams, 1956; Strauss et al., 1982). A prolonged attack of fear has been associated with right-sided temporal lobe status (McLachlan and Blume, 1980).

Although fear responses are usually associated with temporal lobe seizures, they may also be associated with seizures emanating from the cingulate gyrus (Daly, 1958). The amygdala appears to be the critical structure in the induction of the fear response (Gloor, 1972).

Postictal phenomena.   Many patients are confused, restless, and combative after a seizure and apparently particularly after a temporal lobe seizure. Instances of aggression in this state are common but usually consist only of the patient's struggling with persons who are trying to restrain him or her.

Interictal phenomena.   This has proven to be the most difficult of issues and has yet to be resolved.

Anxiety, fear, and depression.   Currier et al. (1971) found that 44 per cent of patients with temporal lobe epilepsy had psychiatric complications. The most common were anxiety and depression. Men with left-sided foci reported more fear than men with right-sided foci. Patients with left-sided foci reported more fear of social and sexual situations (Strauss et al., 1982).

There is an increased risk of suicide in epileptics (Hawton et al., 1980). Flor-Henry (1969) found a relationship between right temporal lobe seizure foci and affective disorders. McIntyre et al. (1976) and Bear and Fedio (1977) also showed that patients with right hemisphere foci are more likely to show emotional tendencies.

Bear (1979) has suggested that a sensory-limbic hyperconnection may account for interictal behavioral aberrations. Hermann and Chhabria (1980) postulated that classical conditioning might mediate an overinvestment of affective significance. The unconditional stimulus is the firing of a limbic focus that induces an emotion (unconditioned response). The conditioned stimulus would be environmental stimuli.

Sexuality. Hyposexuality has been associated with temporal lobe epilepsy (Gastaut and Colomb, 1954). Taylor (1969) studied patients with temporal lobe seizures and found that 72 per cent had a decreased sexual drive. Pritchard (1980) was able to confirm that reduced libido and impotence were associated with temporal lobe seizures. The side of the epileptic focus, drug therapy, and seizure control did not seem to be related to the hyposexuality. The location of the locus did, however, appear important. The mesobasal area of the temporal lobe appears to be the critical area. Increased libido has also been reported (Cogen et al., 1979). The medial temporal lobe structures, including the amygdala, have a close anatomic and physiological relationship with the hypothalamus. Pritchard (1980) found that endocrine changes could be demonstrated, including eugonadotrophic, hypogonadotrophic, and hypergonadotrophic hypogonadism. Herzog et al. (1982) also demonstrated endocrine changes and suggested that hypothalamic-pituitary control of gonadotropin secretion may be altered in patients with temporal lobe epilepsy. Pritchard et al. (1981) found elevation of prolactin following complex partial seizures. Hyperprolactinemia may be associated with impotence in males.

Taylor (1969) and Cogen et al. (1979) noted that temporal lobectomy may restore normal sexual function.

Aggressiveness. Interictal aggressiveness, like ictal aggressiveness, remains controversial and has many medicolegal implications. Taylor (1969) found that about one third of patients with temporal lobe epilepsy were aggressive interictally. Williams (1969) reviewed the EEGs of aggressive criminals, many of whom had committed acts of violence. Abnormal EEGs were five times more common than in the general population. However, as mentioned, Stevens and Hermann (1981) note that this observation has not been validated by detailed controlled studies.

Other interictal changes. Patients with temporal-lobe epilepsy are said to have a dramatic, and possibly specific, disorder of personality (Blumer and Benson, 1975). Slater and Beard (1963) described "schizophreniform" psychosis in patients with temporal lobe epilepsy, but they described selected cases and could not comment on the incidence of this disorder in temporal lobe epileptics. Other studies (Currie et al., 1971) have failed to show a higher-than-expected incidence of psychosis in temporal lobe epileptics, but it can still be maintained that less severe psychiatric abnormalities could have eluded these investigators. Studies that claim to show no difference in emotional makeup between temporal lobe and other epileptics (Guerrant et al., 1962; Stevens, 1966) have been reinterpreted (Blumer, 1975) to indicate that there is, in fact, a difference: temporal lobe epileptics are more likely to have more serious forms of emotional disturbance.

The "typical personality" of the temporal lobe epileptic has been described in roughly similar terms over many years (Blumer and Benson, 1975; Geschwind, 1975, 1977). These patients are said to have a deepening of emotions; they ascribe great significance to commonplace events. This can be manifested as a tendency to take a cosmic view; hyper-religiosity (or intensely professed atheism) is said to be common. Concern with minor details results in slowness of thought and circumstantiality and can also be manifested by hypergraphia, a tendency of such patients to record in writing minute details of their lives (Waxman and Geschwind, 1974). In the extreme, psychosis, often with prominent paranoid qualities, can be seen (the schizophreniform psychosis noted above), but, unlike schizophrenics, these patients do not have a flat affect and tend to maintain interpersonal relationships better. McIntyre et al. (1976) demonstrated that, whereas patients with left temporal lobe foci demonstrate a reflective conceptual approach, patients with right temporal lobe foci are more impulsive.

Bear and Fedio (1977) designed a questionnaire specifically to detect personality features. They found that these personality changes are significantly more common among temporal lobe epileptics than among normal subjects. Patients with right hemisphere foci are more likely to show emotional tendencies and denial, and patients with left temporal lobe foci show ideational aberrations (paranoia, sense of personal destiny) and dissocial behavior. Since a control population with seizure foci in other sites was not used, the specificity of these changes to limbic regions can still be questioned.

BASAL GANGLIA DISORDERS

Basal ganglia disorders are commonly thought to be primarily motor disorders; however, patients with basal ganglia disorders frequently have intellectual and emotional disorders. Parkinson's disease and Huntington's disease are the two most common basal ganglia disorders associated with emotional changes.

Parkinson's Disease

Parkinson's disease is characterized by akinesia, rigidity, and resting tremor. There may be other associated signs and symptoms, including disorders of gait and intellectual deterioration. Parkinson (1938) noted that his patients were unhappy. Depression has subsequently been found to be a frequent part of the Parkinson's complex. Mayeux et al. (1981), for example, studied well-functioning outpatients. Using the Beck Depression Index, they found that 47 per cent of these patients were depressed. Other investigators have also found a high rate of depression (Warburton, 1967; Mindham, 1970; Celesia and Wanamaker, 1972).

The depression may be reactive or a part of the Parkinsonian syndrome or both. Support for the hypothesis that it is not entirely reactive comes from the observation that the motor impairment and the depression correlate poorly. Patients who are more severely disabled are often less depressed (Robins, 1976), and in many patients depression is noted prior to the onset of motor symptoms (Mindham, 1970; Mayeux et al., 1981).

As might be expected from the poor correlation between depression and motor impairment, the depression in Parkinsonism responds poorly to the drugs that help the motor symptoms. Many of the motor symptoms are primarily induced by deficits in the nigrostriatal dopaminergic system. Although L-dopa replacement therapy improves the motor symptoms, it may not reduce depression (Marsh and Markham, 1973; Mayeux et al., 1981).

Parkinson patients may also have pathological changes in regions such as the locus coeruleus and may have a reduction of norepinephrine and serotonin. Patients with endogenous depression may also have a change of these neurotransmitters (van Pragg and de Haan, 1979). Antidepressant therapy with agents such as nortriptyline seems to be effective in treating the depression associated with Parkinson's disease (Anderson et al., 1980).

Huntington's Disease

Huntington's disease, or Huntington's chorea, is characterized by involuntary movements and intellectual decline. Huntington (1872) noted that many patients with this disease have severe emotional disorders and that there is a tendency to suicide. Almost every patient who develops Huntington's disease has emotional or psychiatric signs and symptoms (Mayeux, 1983). Although it is possible that some of the emotional signs and symptoms are a reaction to the disease, in many cases they precede motor and cognitive dysfunction (Heathfield, 1967).

The emotional changes are variable and include mania and depression (Folstein et al., 1979), apathy, aggressiveness, irritability, promiscuity, and irresponsibility. Different emotional symptoms may be manifested at different times during the course of the disease. In general, however, the apathy is usually seen later in the course, when there are signs of intellectual deterioration.

The pathophysiology of the emotional disorders associated with Huntington's disease is unclear. In general, patients have cell loss in the neostriatum and especially in the caudate. There is also cortical cell loss. However, other areas of the brain may also show degenerative changes. Many of the signs displayed by patients with Huntington's disease are similar to those seen with frontal lobe dysfunction (e.g., apathy), and frontal lobe atrophy may be responsible for these signs (Chap. 12). However, there are profound neurochemical changes associated with Huntington's disease. For example, gamma-aminobutyric acid and acetylcholine levels are reduced in the basal ganglia. Unfortunately, it is not known how cellular degeneration and changes in neurotransmitters may account for the profound emotional changes seen in these patients.

SUBCORTICAL CONTROL OF EMOTIONAL EXPRESSION

Wilson (1924) postulated a pontobulbar area responsible for emotional facial expression. Lesions which interrupt the corticobulbar motor pathways bilaterally release reflex mechanisms for facial expression from cortical control.

The syndrome consists of involuntary laughing or crying (or both). As with many forms of release phenomena, this excess of emotional expression is stereotypic and does not show either a wide spectrum of emotions or different degrees of intensity of expression. It can be triggered by a wide variety of stimuli but cannot be initiated or stopped voluntarily. Examination usually shows weakness of voluntary facial movements and increase in the facial and jaw stretch reflexes.

The location of the centers for the control of facial expression is not known, and although Wilson postulated it to be in the lower brainstem, Poeck (1969) has postulated centers in the thalamus and hypothalamus. Although bilateral lesions are usually responsible, the syndrome has been described with unilateral lesions on either side (Bruyn and Gaithier, 1969). Patients with pseudobulbar palsy usually consistently either laugh or cry. Recently, Sackeim et al. (1982) noted that, although most patients with pseudobulbar crying or laughing have bilateral lesions, the larger lesion is usually in the right hemisphere when there is laughter and in the left when there is crying.

Patients with this syndrome report feeling normal emotions, despite the abnormality of expression. Commonly, their family and physicians speak of them as being emotionally labile, implying that they no longer have appropriate internal emotional feeling. It is important to make the distinction between true emotional lability (as may be seen with bilateral frontal lobe disturbance) and pseudobulbar lability of emotional expression (with normal inner emotions).

CONCLUSIONS

Schachter (1970) proposed that two conditions are necessary for the experiencing of emotion: the appropriate cognitive state and sufficient arousal. Although this may be applicable to normal persons, it is clear that brain-damaged individuals can show evidence of, and probably experience, strong emotions in the absence of the appropriate cognitive state. As discussed above, persons with temporal lobe epilepsy report varied emotions as ictal phenomena and persons with lesions in limbic and hypothalamic structures may show inappropriate rage or placidity.

It is likely, however, that the appropriate cognitive state, in the absence of arousal, is not sufficient for the experience of emotion. Patients with anosodiaphoria fail to evidence emotions despite verbally admitting their deficits, and patients with frontal lesions are often emotionally flat despite having relatively intact cognitive capacities. The evidence is strong that subcortical (brainstem, thalamic, basal ganglionic) as well as cortical regions are necessary for normal arousal responses. Furthermore, it is likely that limbic and hypothalamic areas are necessary to mediate the expression of particular emotions, with their characteristic motor, autonomic, and endocrine components. Cortical lesions may influence emotion in different ways. They may interfere with cognitive aspects of emotion. They may impair arousal mechanisms. They may disconnect intact cognitive capacities from the limbic-hypothalamic systems that provide information about basic needs and that probably mediate emotional expression. This disconnection may result in emotional flatness or in the release of emotions from higher control. In contrast to the psuedobulbar state, such released emotions may be associated with emotional feelings. Right hemisphere lesions interfere with emotions more than left hemisphere lesions at least in part because they reduce arousal. In addition, it is probable that the right hemisphere is specialized for cognitive processes necessary for the perception and expression of emotions (such as affective intonation). It is not known if the anatomic relationship of the right hemisphere with limbic system differs from that of the left hemisphere.

The final common pathway for the expression of emotions is not known. As discussed above (under subcortical control of emotional expression), the centers for facial expression of emotion are thought to be in the brainstem. Disconnection of these centers from higher control results in the spontaneous release of emotional expression divorced from emotional feeling.

REFERENCES

Akert, K., Greusen, R. A., Woolsey, C. N., and Meyer, D. R. (1961). Kluver-Bucy sundrome in monkeys with neocortical ablations of temporal lobe. *Brain 84*:480–498.

Anderson, J., Aabro, E., Gulmann, N., Hjelmsted, A., and Pedersen, H. E. (1980). Antidepressive treatment in Parkinson's Disease. *Acta Neurologica Scandinavia 62*:210–219.

Ashford, J. W., Schulz, S. C., and Walsh, G. O. (1980). Violent automatism in a complex partial seizure; Report of a case. *Arch. Neurol. 37*:120–122.

Babinski, J. (1914). Contribution à l'etude des troubles mentaux dans l'hemisplegie organique cerebrale (anosognosie). *Revue Neurologique 27*:845–848.

Bard, P. (1934). Emotion. I: The neuro-humoral basis of emotional reactions. In *Handbook of General Experimental Psychology* (C. Murchison, ed.). Worcester, Mass.: Clark University Press.

Bear, D. M. (1979). Temporal lobe, epilepsy: A syndrome of sensory-limbic hyperconnection. *Cortex 15*:357–384.

Bear, D. M., and Fedio, P. (1977). Quantitative analysis of interictal behavior in temporal lobe epilepsy. *Arch. Neurol. 34*:454–467.

Benson, D. F. (1979) Psychiatric aspects of aphasia. In *Aphasia, Alexia, and Agraphia.* (D. F. Benson, ed.) New York: Churchill Livingstone.

Benton, A. L., and Van Allen, M. W. (1968). Impairment in facial recognition in patients with cerebral disease. *Cortex 4*:344–358.

Berent, S. (1977) Functional asymmetry of the human brain in the recognition of faces. *Neuropsychologia 15*:829–831.

Berger, H. (1933). Uber das electroenkephalogram des menschen. *Archiv für Psychiatrie und Nervenkrankheiten 99*:555–574.

Blumer, D. (1975) Temporal lobe epilepsy and its psychiatric significance. In *Psychiatriac Aspects of Neurological Disease* (D. F. Benson and D. Blumer, eds). New York: Grune and Stratton.

Blumer, D., and Benson, D. F. (1975). Personality changes with frontal and temporal lobe lesions. In *Psychiatric Aspects of Neurological Disease* (D. F. Benson and D. Blumer, eds.). New York: Grune and Stratton.

Blumer, D., and Walker, A. E. (1975). The neural basis of sexual behavior. In *Psychiatric Aspects of Neurological Disease* (D. F. Benson and D. Blumer, eds.). New York: Grune and Stratton.

Brady, J. V., and Nauta, W. J. (1955). Subcortical mechanisms in control of behavior. *J. Comp. Physiol. Psychol. 48*:412–420.

Broca, P. (1878). Anatomie comparée des enconvolutions cérébrales: Le grand lobe limbique et al scissure limbique dans la série des mammiferes. *Rev. Anthrop. 1*:385–498.

Bruyn, G. W., and Gaither, J. C. (1969). The opercular syndrome. In *Handbook of Clinical Neurology*, Vol. 1, Chap. 5 (P. J. Vinken and G. W. Bruyn, eds.). Amsterdam: North Holland.

Buck, R., and Duffy, R. J. (1980). Nonverbal communication of affect in brain damaged patients. *Cortex* 16:351–362.

Cannon, W. B. (1927). The James-Lange theory of emotion: A critical examination and an alternative theory. *Am. J. Psychol.* 39:106–124.

Celesia, G. G., and Wanamaker, W. M. (1972) Psychiatric disturbances in Parkinson's disease. *Diseases Nerv. Sys.* 33:577–583.

Cicone, M., Waper, W., and Gardner, H. (1980). Sensitivity to emotional expressions and situation in organic patients. *Cortex* 16:145–158.

Cogen, P. H., Antunes, J. L., and Correll, J. W. (1979) Reproductive function in temporal lobe epilepsy: The effect of temporal lobectomy. *Surg. Neurol.* 12:243–246.

Corsellis, J. A. N., Goldberg, G. J., and Norton, A. R. (1968). Limbic encephalitis and its association with carcinoma. *Brain* 91:481–496.

Coslett, H. B., Brasher, H. R., and Heilman, K. M. (1983). Functional anatomy of the human auditory cortex: Evidence from pure word deafness. American Academy of Neurology, San Diego, April 1983 (abstract, *Neurology* 33:243, suppl. 2).

Critchley, M. (1953). *The Parietal Lobes*. London: E. Arnold.

Currie, S., Heathfield, K. W. G., Henson, R. A., and Scott, D. F. (1971). Clinical course and prognosis of temporal lobe epilepsy: A survey of 666 patients. *Brain* 94:173–190.

Currier, R. D., Little, S. C., Suess, J. F., and Andy, O. J. (1971). Sexual seizures. *Arch. Neurol.* 25:260–264.

Daly, D. (1958). Ictal affect. *Am. J. Psychiatry* 115:97–108.

Daly, D. D., and Mulder, D. W. (1957). Gelastic epilepsy. *Neurology* 7:189–192.

DeKosky, S., Heilman, K. M., Bowers, D., and Valenstein, E. (1980). Recognition and discrimination of emotional faces and pictures. *Brain and Language* 9:206–214.

Denny-Brown, D., Meyer, J. S., and Horenstein, S. (1952). The significance of perceptual rivalry resulting from parietal lesions. *Brain* 75:434–471.

Fehr, F. S., and Stern, J. A. (1970). Peripheral psychological variables and emotion: The James-Lange theory revisited. *Psychological Bull.* 74:411–424.

Flor-Henry, P. (1969). Psychosis and temporal lobe epilepsy: A controlled investigation. *Epilepsia* 10:363–395.

Folstein, S. E., Folstein, M. F., and McHugh, P. R. (1979). Psychiatric syndromes in Huntington's disease *Adv. Neurol.* 23:281–289.

French, J. E., Hernandez-Peon, R., and Livingston, R. (1955). Projections from the cortex to cephalic brainstem (reticular formation) in monkeys. *Brain* 18:74–95.

Gainotti, G. (1972) Emotional behavior and hemispheric side of lesion. *Cortex* 8:41–55.

Gardner, H., Ling, P. K., Flam, I., and Silverman J. (1975). Comprehension and appreciation of humorous material following brain damage. *Brain* 98:399–412.

Gascon, G. G., and Lombroso, C. T. (1971). Epileptic (gelastic) laughter. *Epilepsia* 12:63–76.

Gasparrini, W. G., Satz, P., Heilman, K. M., and Coolidge, F. L. (1978). Hemispheric asymmetries of affective processing as determined by the Minnesota multiphasic personality inventory. *J. Neurol. Neurosurg. Psychiatry* 41:470–473.

Gastaut, H., and Colomb, H. (1954) Etude du comportement sexuel chez les eipieptiques psychomoteurs. *Annales Medico-Psychologiques (Paris)* 112:659–696.

Geschwind, N. (1975). The clinical setting of aggression in temporal lobe epilepsy. In *The Neurobiology of Violence* (W. S. Fields and W. H. Sweet eds.). St. Louis: Warren H. Green.

Geschwind, N. (1977). Behavioral changes in temporal lobe epilepsy. *Arch. Neurol.* 34:453.

Gloor, P. (1972). Temporal lobe epilepsy. In *Advances in Behavioral Biology*, vol. 2, pp. 423–427 (B. Eleftheriou, ed.). New York: Plenum.

Goldstein, K. (1948). *Language and Language Disturbances*. New York: Grune and Stratton.

Graves, R., Landis, T., and Goodglass, H. (1980). Laterality and sex differences for visual recognition of emotional and nonemotional words. Paper presented before the Academy of Aphasia. Cape Cod, Mass.

Guerrant, J., Anderson, W. W., Fischer, A., Weinstein, M. R., Janos, R. M., and Deskins, A. (1962). *Personality in Epilepsy*. Springfield, Ill.: Charles C Thomas.

Haggard, M. P., and Parkinson, A. M. (1971). Stimulus and task factors as determinants of ear advantages. *Quart. J. Exp. Psychol. 23*:168–177.

Hawton, K., Fagg, J., and Marsack, P. (1980). Association between epilepsy and attempted suicide. *J. Neurol. Neurosurg. Psychiatry 43*:168–170.

Heath, R. G. (1964). Pleasure response of human subjects to direct stimulation of the brain: Physiologic and psychodynamic considerations. In *The Role of Pleasure in Behavior* (R. G. Heath, ed.). New York: Harper & Row.

Heathfield, K. W. G. (1967). Huntington's chorea. *Brain 90*:203-232.

Hécaen, H., Ajuriaguerra, J. de, Massonet, J. (1951). Les troubles visuoconstructifs par lesion parieto-occipitale droit. *Encephale 40*:122–179.

Heilman, K. M. (1979). Neglect and related syndromes. In: *Clinical Neuropsychology* (K. M. Heilman and E. Valenstein, eds.). New York: Oxford University Press.

Heilman, K. M., and Valenstein, E. (1972). Frontal lobe neglect. *Neurology* (Minneapolis) *22*:660–664.

Heilman, K. M., and Van den Abell, T. (1979). Right hemispheric dominance for mediating cerebral activation. *Neuropsychologia 17*:315–321.

Heilman, K. M., Bowers, D., Speedie, L. J., and Coslett, H. B. (1983). The comprehension of emotional and non-emotional prosody. *Neurology 33*:241, suppl. 2.

Heilman, K. M., Gold, M. S., and Tucker, D. M. (1975a). Improvement in aphasics' comprehension by use of novel stimuli. *Trans. Am. Neurological Assoc. 100*:201–202.

Heilman, K. M., Scholes, R., and Watson, R. T. (1975b). Auditory affective agnosia: Disturbed comprehension of affective speech. *J. Neurol. Neurosurg. Psychiatry 38*:69–72.

Heilman, K. M., Schwartz, H., and Watson, R. T. (1978). Hypoarousal in patients with the neglect syndrome and emotional indifference. *Neurology 28*:229-232.

Hermann, B. P., and Chhabria, S. (1980). Interictal psychopathology in patients with ictal fear: Examples of sensory-limbic hyperconnection? *Arch. Neurol. 37*:667–668.

Herzog, A. G., Russell, V., Vaitukatis, J. L., and Geschwind, N. (1982). Neuroendocrine dysfunction in temporal lobe epilepsy. *Arch. Neurol. 39*:133–135.

Hooshmand, H., and Brawley, B. W. (1969). Temporal lobe seizures and exhibitionism. *Neurology 19*:1119–1124.

Hughlings Jackson, J. (1932). In *Selected Writings of John Hughlings Jackson*, J. Taylor, (ed.). London: Hodder & Stoughton.

Huntington, G. W. (1872). On chorea. *Medical and Surgical Reports. 26*:317–321.

Isaacson, R. L., (1982). *The Limbic System* (2nd edn.) New York: Plenum Press.

Kimura, D. (1961). Cerebral dominance and the perception of verbal stimuli. *Canad. J. Psychol. 15*:166–171.

Kimura, D. (1967). Functional asymmetry of the brain in dichotic listening. *Cortex 3*:163–178.

Kluver, H., and Bucy, P. C. (1937). "Psychic blindness" and other symptoms following bilateral temporal lobectomy in rhesus monkeys. *Am. J. Physiol. 119*:352–353.

Ley, R. G. (1980). Emotion and the right hemisphere. Thesis, University of Florida.

Ley, R., and Bryden, M. (1979). Hemispheric differences in recognizing faces and emotions. *Brain and Language 1*:127–138.

Lindsley, D. (1970). The role of nonspecific reticulo-thalamo-cortical systems in emotion. In *Physiological Correlates of Emotion* (P. Black, ed.). New York: Academic Press.

MacLean, P. D. (1952) Some psychiatric implications of physiological studies on the fronto-temporal portion of the limbic system (visceral brain). *EEG Clin. Neurophysiol.* 4:407–418.

Mark, V. H., and Ervin, F. R. (1970). *Violence and the Brain.* New York: Harper & Row.

Mark, V. H., Sweet, W. H., and Ervin, F. R. (1972). The effect of amygdalectomy on violent behavior in patients with temporal lobe epilepsy. In *Psychosurgery* (E. Hitchcock, L. Laitinen, and K. Vernet, eds.). Springfield, Ill.: C. C. Thomas.

Marsh, G. G., and Markham, C. H. (1973). Does levodopa alter depression and psychopathology in parkinsonism patients? *J. Neurol. Neurosurg. Psychiatry* 36:925–935.

Mayeux, R. (1983). Emotional changes associated with basal ganglia disorders. In *Neuropsychology of Human Emotion* (K. M. Heilman and P. Satz, eds.). New York: Guilford Press.

Mayeux, R., Stern, Y., Rosen, J., and Leventhal, J. (1981). Depression, intellectual impairment, and Parkinson disease. *Neurology* 31:645–650.

McIntyre, M., Pritchard, P. B., and Lombroso, C. T. (1976). Left and right temporal lobe epileptics: A controlled investigation of some psychological differences. *Epilepsia* 17:377–386.

McLachlan, R. S., and Blume, W. T. (1980). Isolated fear in complex partial status epilepticus. *Ann. Neurol.* 8:639–641.

Milner, B. (1974) Hemispheric specialization: Scope and limits. In *The Neurosciences: Third Study Program* (F. O. Schmitt and F. G. Worden, eds.). Cambridge, Mass.: MIT Press.

Mindham, H. S. (1970). Psychiatric syndromes in Parkinsonism. *J. Neurol. Neurosurg. Psychiatry* 30:188–191.

Morrow, L., Urtunski, P. B., Kim, Y., and Boller, F. (In Press). Arousal responses to emotional stimuli and laterality of lesion. *Neuropsychologia.*

Moruzzi, G., and Magoun, H. W. (1949). Brainstem reticular formation and activation of the EEG. *EEG Clin. Neurophysiol.* 1:455–475.

Offen, M. L., Davidoff, R. A., Troost, B. T., and Richey, E. T. (1976). Dacrystic epilepsy. *J. Neurol. Neurosurg. Psychiatry* 39:829–834.

Olds. J. (1958). Self-stimulation of the brain. *Science* 127:315–324.

Papez, J. W. (1937). A proposed mechanism of emotion. *Arch. Neurol. Psychiatry* 38:725–743.

Parkinson, J. (1938). An essay of the shaking palsy, 1817. *Medical Classics* 2:964–997.

Paul, H. (1909). *Principien der Sprachgeschichte* (4th ed.). Niemeyer.

Pincus, J. H. (1980). Can violence be a manifestation of epilepsy? *Neurology* 30:304–307.

Poeck, K. (1969). Pathophysiology of emotional dosorders associated with brain damage. In *Handbook of Nuerology.* vol. 3 (P. J. Vinken and G. W. Bruyn, eds.). New York: American Elsevier.

Poeck, K., and Pilleri, G. (1961). Wutverhalten und pathologischer Schlaf bei Tumor der vorderen Mitellinie. *Arch. Psychiat. Nervenkr.* 201:593–604.

Pritchard, P. B. (1980). Hyposexuality: A complication of complex partial epilepsy. Trans. Am. Neurol. Assoc. 105:193–195.

Pritchard, P. B., Wannamaker, B. B., Sagel, J., and deVillier, C. (1981). Post-ictal hyperprolactinemia in complex partial epilepsy. *Ann. Neuro.* 10:81–82.

Ramon y Cajal, S. (1965). *Studies on the Cerebral Cortex (Limbic Structures)* (L. M. Kraft, translator). London: Lloyd-Luke.

Remillard, G. M., Andermann, F., Testa, G. F., Gloor, P., Aube, M., Martin, J. B., Feindel, W., Guberman, A., and Simpson, C. (1983). Sexual manifestations predominate in a woman with temporal lobe epilepsy: A finding suggesting sexual dimorphism in the human brain. *Neurology* 33:3–30.

Robins, A. H. (1976). Depression in patients with Parkinsomism. *Br. J. Psych.* 128:141–145.

Rodin, E. A. (1973). Psychomotor epilepsy and aggressive behavior. *Arch. Gen. Psych.* 28:210–213.

Roeltgen, D. P., Sevush, S., and Heilman, K. M. (In Press). Phonological agraphia: Writing by the lexical semantic route. *Neurology.*

Ross, E. D., (1981). The aprosodias: Functional-anatomic organization of the affective components of language in the right hemisphere. *Ann. Neurol.* 38:561–589.

Ross, E. D., and Mesulam, M. M. (1979). Dominant language functions of the right hemisphere? Prosody and emotional gesturing. *Arch. Neurol.* 36:144–148.

Rossi, G. S., and Rodadini, G. (1967). Experimental analysis of cerebral dominance in man. In *Brain Mechanisms Underlying Speech and Language* (C. Millikan and F. L. Darley, eds.). New York: Grune & Stratton.

Sackeim, H. A., Greenberg, M. S., Weiman, A. L., Gur, R. C., Hungerbuhler, J. P., and Geschwind, N. (1982). Hemispheric asymmetry in the expression of positive and negative emotions: Neurologic evidence. *Arch. Neurol.* 39:210–218.

Sackeim, H. A., Gur, R. C., and Saucy, M. C. (1978) Emotions are expressed more intensely on the left side of the face.

Schachter, S. (1970). The interaction of cognitive and physiological determinants of emotional state. In *Advances in Experimental Social Psychology,* vol. 1 (Berkowitz, ed.). New York: Academic Press.

Schlanger, B. B., Schlanger, P., and Gerstmann, L. J. (1976). The perception of emotionally toned sentences by right-hemisphere damaged and aphasic subjects. *Brain and Language* 3:396–403.

Segundo, J. P., Naguet, R., and Buser, P. (1955). Effects of cortical stimulation on electrocortical activity in monkeys. *J. Neurol. Neurosurg. Psychiatry* 18:236–245.

Slater, E., and Beard, A. W. (1963). The schizophrenia-like psychoses of epilepsy. *Br. J. Psychiat.* 109:95–150.

Speedie, L., and Heilman, K. M. (1983). Affective prosody in mixed transcortical aphasia. Presented before the International Neuropsychological Society, Mexico City.

Spencer, S. S., Spencer, D. D., Williamson, P. D., and Mattson, R. H. (1983). Sexual automatisms in complex partial seizures. *Neurology* 33:527–533.

Stevens, J. R. (1966). Psychiatric implications of psychomotor epilepsy. *Arch. Gen. Psychiat.* 14:461–471.

Stevens, J. R., and Hermann, B. P. (1981). Temporal lobe epilepsy, psychopathology and violence: The state of the evidence. *Neurology* 31:1127–1132.

Strauss, E. (1983). Perception of emotional words. *Neuropsychologia* 21:99–103.

Strauss, E., Risser, A., and Jones, M. W. (1982) Fear responses in patients with epilepsy. *Neurology* 39:626–630.

Suberi, M., and McKeever, W. (1977) Differential right hemisphere memory storage of emotional and nonemotional faces. *Neuropsychologia* 15:757–768.

Taylor, D. C. (1969). Aggression and epilepsy. *J. Psych. Res.* 13:229–236.

Terzian, H. (1964). Behavioral and EEG effects of intracarotid sodium amytal injections. *Acta Neurochirugica* (Vienna) 12:230–240.

Trexler, L. E., and Schmidt, N. D. (1981). Autonomic arousal associated with complex affective stimuli in lateralized brain injury. Paper presented before International Neuropsychological Society, Bergen, Norway.

Tucker, D. M. (1981). Lateral brain function, emotion, and conceptualization. *Psychological Bull.* 89:19–46.

Tucker, D. M., Watson, R. T., and Heilman, K. B. (1977). Affective discrimination and evocation in patients with right parietal disease. *Neurology* 17:947–950.

Ursin, H. (1960). The temporal lobe substrate of fear and anger. *Acta Psychiat. Scandinav.* 35:378–396.

Valenstein, E. S. (1973). *Brain Control: A Critical Examination of Brain Stimulation and Psychosurgery.* New York: Wiley-Interscience.

Van Pragg, H. M., and de Haan, S. (1979). Central serotonin metabolism and frequency of depression. *Psychiat. Res.* 1:219–224.

Warburton, J. W. (1967). Depressive symptoms in Parkinson patients referred for thalamotomy. *J. Neurol. Neurosurg. Psychiatry* 30:368–370.

Watson, R. T., and Heilman, K. M. (1982). Affect in subcortical aphasia (letter). *Neurology* 32:102–103.

Watson, R. T., Heilman, K. M., Cauthen, J. C., and King, F. A. (1973). Neglect after cingulectomy. *Neurology* 23:1003–1007.

Waxman, S. G., and Geschwind, N. (1974). Hypergraphia in temporal lobe epilepsy. *Neurology* 24:629–636.

Wechsler, A. F. (1973). The effect of organic brain disease on recall of emotionally charged versus neutral narrative texts. *Neurology* 23:130–135.

Weintraub, S., Mesulam, M. M., and Kramer, L. (1981). Disturbances in prosody. *Arch. Neurol.* 38:742–744.

Williams, D., (1956). The structure of emotions reflected in epileptic experiences. *Brain* 79:29–67.

Williams, D. (1969). Neural factors related to habitual aggression. *Brain* 92:503–520.

Wilson, S. A. K. (1924). Some problems in neurology. II: Pathological laughing and crying. *J. Neurol. Psychopathol.* 16:299–333.

Woods, J. W. (1956). Taming of the wild Norway rat by rhinocephalic lesions. *Nature* 170:869.

Yakovlev, P. I. (1948). Motility, behavior, and the brain: Stereodynamic organization and neural coordinates of behavior. J. Nervous Mental Dis. 107:313–335.

Zeman, W., and King, F. A. (1958). Tumors of the septum pellucidum and adjacent structures with abnormal affective behavior: An anterior midline structure syndrome. *J. Nervous Mental Dis.* 127:490–502.

14

Amnesic Disorders

NELSON BUTTERS AND PATTI MILIOTIS

GENERAL SYMPTOMS OF PERMANENT AMNESIA

Severe memory deficits are a common symptom following damage to a number of limbic system structures (Fig. 14-1). Difficulty in learning new material and in recalling remote events arises after hippocampal lesions, e.g., anoxia, herpes encephalitis, cerebrovascular accidents involving the posterior cerebral artery, closed head injuries, and surgical removal (Drachman and Arbit, 1966; Milner, 1970; Levin et al., 1982); atrophy or damage to medial diencephalic structures, including the dorsomedial nucleus of the thalamus and the mammillary bodies, e.g., alcoholic neurotoxicity, nutritional deficiencies, cerebrovascular accidents, trauma (Victor et al., 1971; Squire and Moore, 1979; Markowitsch, 1982; Speedie and Heilman, 1982, 1983); and lesions of the fornix, e.g., tumors (Heilman and Sypert, 1977).

Regardless of the locus of the lesion or the etiology of the disease, patients share four outstanding clinical characteristics. First, all amnesics have *anterograde amnesia*. This means that patients are unable to learn new verbal and nonverbal information from the time of onset of illness. They do not remember the names of physicians and nurses and will have difficulty learning the name of the hospital in which they are being treated. Events that occured only hours or even minutes before are lost to such patients. Not only do they fail to learn the names of important people and places but often do not remember previous encounters with these individuals. Experimentally, this severe learning deficit can be demonstrated by the great difficulty patients have in learning even short lists of paired associates (Ryan and Butters, 1980a). That is, when presented with a list of word pairs in which they must learn to associate the second word with the first, patients may require 70 or 80 trials to acquire the associations instead of the three or four needed by intact individuals.

The preparation of this chapter and some of the research cited were supported by funds from the Veterans Administration's Medical Research Service, by NIAAA grant AA-00187 to Boston University, and by NINCDS grant NS-16367 to Massachusetts General Hospital.

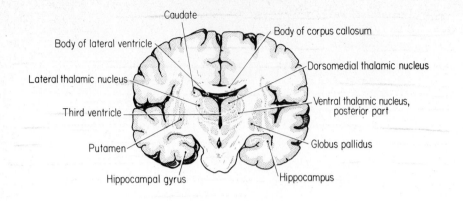

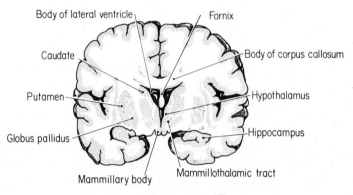

Fig. 14-1. Two coronal sections through the human brain. The dorsomedial nucleus of the thalamus, the mammillary bodies, the fornix, and the hippocampus have been frequently associated with amnesic syndromes. (From Butters and Cermak, 1980)

The second major symptom of amnesia is *retrograde amnesia*, in which patients have difficulty retrieving from long-term memory events that occurred before the onset of illness. When asked who was president of the United States before Reagan, the patient may answer "Johnson" or perhaps "Kennedy." If asked whether any other presidents held office between Reagan and Kennedy, patients may say no or at the very least be extremely uncertain as to the temporal ordering of the presidents they might ultimately recall. In general, this difficulty in retrieval of old memories is more pronounced for events just before the onset of the illness; remote events from childhood are often well remembered. For the alcoholic Korsakoff patient, this loss of remote memories is severe, extends over several decades, and is characterized by a temporal gradient in which memories for very remote events are relatively preserved (Seltzer and Benson, 1974; Marslen-Wilson and Teuber, 1975; Albert et al., 1979; Meudell et al., 1980; Cohen and Squire, 1981; Squire and Cohen, 1982). These features of the Korsakoff patient's retrograde amnesia have been demonstrated consistently with a number of remote memory tests involving the identification of famous faces (Albert et al., 1979) and voices (Meudell et al., 1980) and the recall and recognition of public events (Albert et al., 1979; Cohen and Squire, 1981). In contrast to the alcoholic Korsakoff patients' extensive losses, systematic assessments of the retrograde amnesias of other patient populations have reported temporally limited forgetting of old memories. The well-studied amnesic patients H. M. (Milner, 1966, 1970; Marslen-Wilson and Teuber, 1975) and N. A. (Squire and Slater, 1978; Squire and Moore, 1979; Cohen and Squire, 1981; Squire and Cohen, 1982), depressed patients receiving shock treatment (ECT) (Squire et al., 1975, 1976), and traumatic amnesics (Russell and Nathan, 1946; Benson and Geschwind, 1967; Levin et al., 1982) all have losses of remote memories limited to the 3 or 4 years immediately preceding illness or beginning of ECT. Recall of public events that occured prior to this circumscribed retrograde amnesia is normal, a finding consistent with the notion that old, very remote memories are more resistant to forgetting than are newly acquired engrams (Ribot, 1882).

Despite the consistency with which investigators have noted the relative or complete sparing of very remote memories, Sanders and Warrington (1971) have raised a serious methodological issue concerning the validity of the temporal gradient in retrograde amnesia. They administered public events questionnaires and a test of facial recognition to a group of amnesic patients of mixed etiology. With these tests, their amnesics were severely impaired with no relative sparing of very remote events. The patients had as much difficulty recalling and recognizing public events from the 1930's as they did events from the 1960's. Sanders and Warrington proposed that studies demonstrating sparing of remote memories may have failed to control for task difficulty. Faces from the 1930's and 1940's may be easier to recall than those from the 1960's and 1970's because they are of more lasting fame and have been overlearned, for example, pictures of Charlie Chaplin dressed as a tramp have been exposed to the public during every decade since the 1920's. Warrington and Weiskrantz (1973) have interpreted the demonstration of an extensive and "flat" retrograde amnesia as consistent with their interference-retrieval theory of amnesia. They believe that if all the memory difficulties of amnesic patients are related to an inability to retrieve information from long-term memory, there is no reason to expect memories from childhood, adolescence, and young adulthood to be spared.

Although Sanders and Warrington's (1971) empirical data were flawed by "floor" effects (i.e., their amnesics performed at chance levels on the recognition tests), their emphasis on the control of item difficulty and overlearning has face validity and has forced a reevaluation of retrograde amnesia with more carefully developed tests. Albert et al. (1979) constructed a retrograde amnesia test battery that statistically controlled for item difficulty. Their battery included a famous faces test, a recall questionnaire, and a multiple-choice recognition questionnaire. Each test consisted of items from the 1930's to the 1970's that had been assessed on a population of normal controls before inclusion in the final test battery. Half of the items were easy as judged by the performance of the standardization group; the other half were difficult judged by the same criterion. In addition, the famous faces test included photographs of some individuals early and late in their careers.

When this remote memory battery was administered to alcoholic Korsakoff patients and normal controls (Albert et al., 1979), little evidence supporting Sanders and Warrington's contentions was found. As shown in Fig. 14-2, the alcoholic Korsakoff patients identified more photographs from the 1930's and 1940's than from the 1960's. Furthermore, whereas the normal controls were more accurate identifying famous people later than earlier in their careers, the Korsakoff patients performed in the opposite manner. On the recall test of public events (Fig. 14-2), the same pattern emerged. For both easy and hard items, the Korsakoff patients recalled more information from the 1930's and 1940's than from the 1960's. Similar gradients were reported for the recognition test of public events.

Squire and Cohen (1982) have suggested that Albert et al.'s (1979) statistical approach to item difficulty may confound rather than solve the equivalence and over-

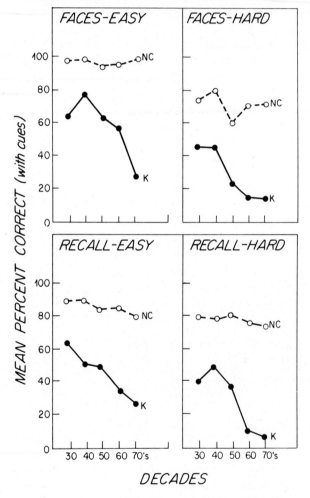

Fig. 14-2. Mean per cent of easy and hard items correctly recalled by alcoholic Korsakoff (K) and normal control (NC) subjects on famous faces test (top) and public events recall questionnaire (bottom). (From Albert et al., 1979)

learning issue. If two public events (or faces), one from the 1930's and one from the 1970's, are both remembered by 80 per cent of normal controls, can the two items be considered intrinsically equal in difficulty? Since one event occured 40 years prior to the other but is remembered as well, it seems likely that the more remote event is in fact more famous and overlearned than the more recent one. The mere passage of 30 years since original acquisition should have weakened the memory engram more than a five-year interval since original learning. From this viewpoint, statistical equality is simply a mask for an intrinsic inequality manifested by the temporal gradients of amnesic patients.

Butters and Albert (1982) have offered some additional empirical evidence for their statistical approach. They reanalyzed their original data on the famous faces test so that easy items from the recent past could be compared with hard items from the remote past. While normal controls, as expected, identified significantly fewer faces from the remote past than from the recent past, the alcoholic Korsakoff patients evidenced the opposite trend. That is, the amnesic Korsakoff patients correctly identified more "hard" faces from the remote past than "easy" faces from the recent past. Butters and Albert noted that this relative preservation of very remote memories under conditions of planned statistical inequality offers strong support that temporal gradients characterize the retrograde amnesia of alcoholic Korsakoff patients.

Albert et al.'s (1981) investigation of retrograde amnesia in demented patients with Huntington's disease (HD) is also relevant to Squire and Cohen's critique (Fig. 14-3). Huntington's disease is a genetically transmitted disorder in which the patient (usually at about 40 years of age) undergoes progressive motor and intellectual deterioration due to atrophy of the caudate nuclei and other basal ganglia. During the early and middle stages of the disease, HD patients complain of memory problems, but amnesic symptoms are only one aspect of their dementia, as witnessed by the loss of visuoperceptive and conceptual capacities. When Albert et al. administered their retrograde amnesia battery to a group of HD patients, they found that the demented HD patients, unlike the amnesic Korsakoff patients, showed equal forgetting of public events and famous faces across all decades from the 1930's to the 1970's (Fig. 14-3). Butters and Albert (1982) suggest that this equal loss of very remote and recent memories weakens any criticisms of the statistical approach to item difficulty. If the temporal gradients of Korsakoff patients were due to some intrinsic inequality in the difficulty of the faces and questions from the various decades, then the HD patients should have manifested a similar temporal gradient. Like the amnesic Korsakoff patients, the HD patients should have identified more of the easy (from the 1930's and 1940's) than hard (from the 1960's and 1970's) faces and public events. To simultaneously accept the flat gradients of the demented patients and dismiss the temporal gradients of the amnesic patients, one must explain why Albert et al.'s items from the 1930's and 1940's are not also intrinsically easy for demented individuals.

Like Albert and Butters, Squire and his colleagues have attempted to develop a remote memory test that circumvents the overlearning and overexposure problems noted by Sanders and Warrington (1971). To ensure limited but equivalent public exposure, Squire and Slater (1975) used titles of television programs that had been aired for one season or less in the construction of their recall and recognition tests. The individual items on these tests were matched for public exposure on the basis of

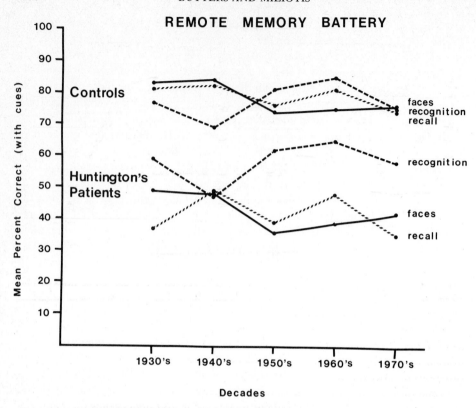

Fig. 14-3. Performance of Huntington's disease patients and normal control subjects on Albert et al.'s retrograde amnesia test battery. Results for the famous faces test and the public events recall and recognition questionnaires are shown. (From Albert et al., 1981)

known viewing histories, and since the items had a brief exposure, the time of learning could be specified. The fact that normal subjects who resided outside the United States were unable to recognize the titles of the one-season programs aired during their absence provided strong support for the investigators' claim that the programs queried on the test were not overexposed or publicized in the years following their limited broadcast (Squire and Slater, 1975). The recognition form of this television program test required subjects to select from several alternatives the title of an aired program. On the recall test, the subjects were asked to supply details about specified programs.

These tests of past television programs have been administered to depressed patients in the course of bilateral ECT. The results of these studies also support Ribot's (1882) hypothesis. As shown in Fig. 14-4, the retrograde amnesia following ECT is temporally limited. For both tests, the patients served as their own controls, with testing occurring prior to the first ECT and again one hour following the fifth administration of ECT. On the recognition form of the television test, the ECT patients were unable to recognize the titles of programs aired 1 to 3 years immediately prior to the ECT but had no difficulty recognizing titles of programs broadcast 4 to 17 years prior

TELEVISION PROGRAMS TEST

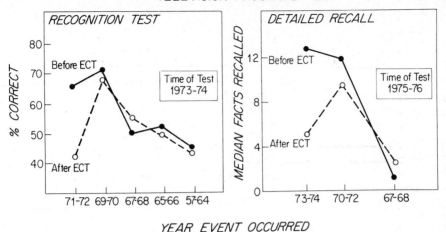

YEAR EVENT OCCURRED

Fig. 14-4. Retrograde amnesia following bilateral ECT; (left) recognition of titles of one-season television programs; (right) recall of details about one-season television programs. (From Squire et al., 1975; Squire and Cohen, 1979)

to ECT (Squire et al., 1975). For the detailed recall task, the patients were impaired in their recall of shows aired 1 to 2 years before ECT but had no difficulty recalling programs broadcast prior to that time (Squire and Cohen, 1979).

While the vast majority of the published research with amnesic patients confirms the differential sparing of very remote memories, it also underscores the heterogeneity of the retrograde amnesias exhibited by different patient populations. Of the various amnesic patients that have been studied systematically, only the alcoholic Korsakoff patients (and possibly postencephalitics; see Butters and Cermak, 1980) have remote memory losses that extend more than 10 years and involve all periods of the patients' lives. The alcoholic Korsakoff patients' memory of events that occurred during the 1940's is certainly superior to their recall of events in the 1960's, but their retention of information from the more remote decades is still significantly impaired in comparison to the recall of normal controls (Albert et al., 1979; Squire and Cohen, 1982). As noted previously, this extensive graded loss of old memories is much more evident and severe than the temporally limited retrograde amnesias (1 to 4 years) of depressed patients undergoing bilateral ECT, of patients with post-traumatic amnesia, and of the well-studied amnesic patients H. M. and N. A. More recently, Butters et al., (1983) have described the chronic amnesia of an electrical engineer (patient R. B.) following the clipping of an aneurysm of the anterior communicating artery. Despite an inordinate difficulty in retaining postsurgical life experiences and in learning verbal and digit-symbol paired associates, R. B.'s memory for events prior to his surgery seemed to be relatively intact.

This difference between the retrograde amnesias of alcoholic Korsakoff patients and of other amnesic populations has been addressed by Squire and Cohen (1982) and by Butters and Albert (1982). Both sets of investigators have suggested that the alcoholic Korsakoff patients' extensive loss of or access to remote memories may be secondary to a primary defect in establishing new memories (i.e., anterograde amnesia) during the 20 years of alcohol abuse that preceded the diagnosis of the amnesic syndrome. Although detoxified non-Korsakoff alcoholics have often been viewed as free of anterograde memory defects (Parsons and Prigatano, 1977), recent studies (Ryan and Butters, 1980a, 1980b) using complex verbal and nonverbal stimuli have shown that detoxified alcoholics are impaired on short-term memory and paired-associate learning tasks and that these deficits correlate positively with years of alcohol abuse. Consequently, if chronic alcoholics acquire less information each year due to a progressive anterograde memory deficit, then at the time an alcoholic patient is diagnosed as having Korsakoff's syndrome, one would expect to find a retrograde amnesia with a temporal gradient. From this viewpoint, the Korsakoff patients' loss of remote memories would be considered an artifact related to a primary defect in establishing new memories. A corollary of this hypothesis is that true retrograde amnesias, those uncontaminated by deficiencies in original learning and cognitive retrieval strategies, are temporally limited and are far less severe and devastating than the amnesic patients' anterograde memory problems (Squire and Cohen, 1982).

To evaluate this "chronic" explanation of the Korsakoff patients' retrograde amnesia, Albert et al. (1980) administered their remote memory battery to detoxified long-term (non-Korsakoff) alcoholics and nonalcoholic control subjects. They noted that if the learning deficit related to alcoholism was responsible for Korsakoff patients' difficulties in recalling past events, two predictions could be made. One, the alcoholics should be impaired in their identification of famous faces and public events. Two, since the detrimental effects of alcohol on the learning of new materials are related to years of alcohol abuse, the alcoholics' deficits in recalling past events should be most apparent for the years immediately preceding testing. The results partially confirmed these expectations. Although the alcoholics' mean recall scores for difficult famous faces from the 1960's and 1970's were considerably lower than the scores of the nonalcoholic controls, the differences did not attain statistical significance. However, on the recall questionnaire the alcoholics had a mild but significant impairment in their recall of difficult public events from the 1960's and 1970's, with the greatest loss associated with the immediately preceding decade. It was also important that this reported deficit in the recall of remote events from the last two decades was consonant with the length of the patients' alcohol abuse (Mean = 25.18 years). Recently, Cohen and Squire (1981) also reported mild-to-moderate remote memory deficits in chronic (non-Korsakoff) alcoholics.

Although the results of Albert et al.'s (1980) and Cohen and Squire's (1981) studies are not of a magnitude to allow the alcoholic Korsakoff patients' retrograde amnesia to be reduced to an anterograde memory problem, they do suggest that two separate etiological factors may be involved. One is the impact of chronic alcohol abuse on anterograde memory processes. Since long-term alcoholics may retain somewhat less information each year due to a chronic learning deficit, their store of remote memories for the recent past may be mildly or moderately deficient. The second factor may be a forgetting of or a loss of access to old memories that appears acutely during the Wernicke stage of the illness and results in a severe and equal loss for all time periods prior to the onset of the disease. When this acute loss of remote memories is superimposed on the patients' already deficient store, a severe retrograde amnesia with a temporal gradient is expected. Patients should be impaired with respect to controls across all time periods, but memory for recent events should be most severely affected since less had been learned initially during this period.

The most convincing evidence for this two-factor model of the alcoholic Korsakoff patients' retrograde amnesia emanates from an unpublished single-case study conducted by Butters and Cermak. Their patient (P. Z.), an eminent scientist and university professor who developed alcoholic Korsakoff's syndrome at the age of 65, had written and published an autobiography three years prior to the acute onset of his Wernicke's encephalopathy in 1982. Like all alcoholics with Korsakoff's syndrome, P. Z. had severe anterograde and retrograde amnesias as assessed by clinical and formal psychometric techniques. On Albert et al.'s famous faces test, P. Z.'s performance revealed significant impairment across all time periods, but with some relative sparing of his ability to recognize famous faces from the 1930's and 1940's. To determine whether P. Z. had also lost access to autobiographical material that was well known to him before his illness, a retrograde amnesia test based upon his autobiography was developed. The test consisted of questions about relatives, colleagues, collaborators, conferences, research assistants, research reports and books, all of which were prominently mentioned in the autobiography.

P. Z.'s recall of these autobiographical facts is shown in Fig. 14-5. Three points are evident. First, P. Z. has a very severe retrograde amnesia for autobiographical events, with considerable sparing of information from the very remote past. Second, P. Z.'s retrograde amnesia for autobiographical material cannot be secondary to a deficiency in original learning. The fact that all the questions were taken from his own autobiography eliminates the possibility that he had never acquired the information. Just three years prior to the onset of his Wernicke-Korsakoff's syndrome, P. Z. could

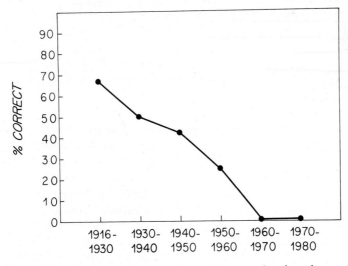

PATIENT P. Z.
RECALL OF AUTOBIOGRAPHICAL INFORMATION

Fig. 14-5. Patient P. Z.'s retrograde amnesia for information taken from his autobiography.

retrieve the information he considered most prominent in his professional and personal life. Clearly, P. Z.'s illness marked the acute onset of his inability to retrieve information that was once readily available to him. Three, the relatively severe impairment for the most recent decades suggests that autobiographical information acquired during those periods was not as stable (i.e., well consolidated) as that acquired earlier. Although it is customary to consider all material committed to long-term memory in a single stage of storage, there may in fact be several substages in long-term memory, with the temporally more recent substages more vulnerable to interruption by brain damage. An alternative explanation of P. Z.'s temporal gradient on his autobiography is that his encoding of personal events had become more deficient with the passage of time and therefore recent autobiographical material had become difficult to retrieve following damage to diencephalic brain structures.

The results of these remote memory studies also suggest that anterograde and retrograde amnesias can be dissociated from one another and may involve different neural circuits. Although alcoholic Korsakoff patients clearly demonstrate both types of amnesia, non-Korsakoff alcoholics can have substantial difficulty learning new information (Ryan and Butters, 1980a, 1980b; Brandt et al., 1983) but are often only mildly impaired in their recall of remote events (Albert et al., 1980; Cohen and Squire, 1981). The fact that alcoholic Korsakoff patients and other amnesic patients can be equally impaired in the learning of new information yet demonstrate retrograde amnesias of different duration and severity (Cohen and Squire, 1981; Butters et al., 1983) lends further support to the separability of anterograde and retrograde memory problems. It is not possible at this juncture to determine the exact neural circuits that mediate anterograde and retrograde memory processes, but a report based upon stimulation studies with epileptic patients (Fedio and Van Buren, 1974) has produced evidence for such an anatomical separation within the temporal lobes. Since the amnesia of alcoholic Korsakoff patients is often attributed to damage to the dorsomedial nucleus of the thalamus and to the mammillary bodies (Victor et al., 1971), it is also of interest that patient N. A., who is severely amnesic with regard to the learning of new verbal material but has a very limited retrograde amnesia, has been reported to have unilateral destruction of the dorsomedial nucleus of the thalamus and no other visible damage (Squire and Moore, 1979). Perhaps the alcoholic Korsakoff patients' severe anterograde amnesia develops slowly as a result of the gradual atrophy of the dorsomedial nucleus of the thalamus, while their loss of remote memories appears suddenly with acute damage to other subcortical brain structures.

Goldberg and his associates (1981) have also demonstrated, in an elegant case report of a patient with traumatic amnesia, the separation of anterograde and retrograde amnesic symptoms. Their 36-year-old male patient had an open skull fracture in the right temporoparietal region that resulted in extensive damage to the mesial and lateral surfaces of the right temporal lobe and to the ventral tegmental area of the upper mesencephalon. Although the patient had severe anterograde and retrograde amnesia immediately following his injury in 1977, his anterograde amnesia evidenced marked improvement during the next two years. In the 18 months separating his two evaluations, the patient's MQ improved from 86 to 106, and a corresponding increment was seen on a complex verbal recall test (Buschke's Selective Reminding Task), whereas his severely impaired performance on Albert et al's. (1979) retrograde amnesia battery remained almost unchanged. Thus, two years following his trauma and subsequent surgery, the patient was able to learn new information but was unable to recall public or personal events that occurred prior to his accident. Since damage to the right temporal lobe has not as yet been associated with a general loss of old memories, Goldberg et al. suggest that the tegmental lesion is responsible for their patient's inability to recall remote public events. They hypothesize that selective mesencephalic reticular activation of limbic structures is essential for retrieval of information from long-term storage.

The third characteristic of many amnesic patients is their tendency to *confabulate* when faced with questions they cannot answer. When asked to recall activities from the previous day, an alcoholic Korsakoff patient may "fill in" this gap in memory with a story concerning a trip or a sporting event that may have actually occurred many years ago. This confabulatory tendency is not a constant or necessarily permanent feature of all amnesic patients, and there are marked differences among amnesic populations. In general, confabulation is most marked during the acute stages of the illness and becomes progressively less noticeable as the patient adjusts to the disorder. For example, it is relatively easy to elicit confabulation from a patient in a Wernicke-Korsakoff confusional state but such responses are rare in chronic alcoholic Korsakoff patients who have had this disease for five or more years.

The fourth characteristic of amnesic patients is their relatively *intact intellectual functions* as measured by standardized intelligence tests. Except for the digit-symbol subtest, there are often no significant differences between amnesic patients and normal controls matched in terms of age, socioeconomic class, and educational background (Butters and Cermak, 1980). Special mention should be made of the amnesic patients' normal performance on the digit-span subtest of the WAIS, a task that is often considered a measure of immediate memory. Drachman and Arbit (1966) have demonstrated that postencephalitics, like normals, can repeat seven or eight numbers immediately after presentation but are severely impaired in attempting to learn supraspan lists of 12 numbers. Presumably, once the list has been lengthened to include 12 numbers, the first three or four numbers are no longer in immediate memory but rather in the patients' impaired short- or long-term storage.

Despite the amnesic patient's normal IQ, cognitive performance is not completely intact. A full neuropsychological evaluation usually reveals a number of secondary defects that may or may not contribute to the patient's severe memory problems. Among alcoholic Korsakoff patients, the most common deficits involve visuoperceptive and visuospatial capacities. Alcoholic Korsakoff patients are impaired on digit-symbol and symbol-digit substitution tasks (Glosser et al., 1977; Kapur and Butters, 1977), hidden or embedded figures tests (Talland, 1965; Kapur and Butters, 1977; Squire, 1982), and on various tests that require the sorting of complex visual stimuli (Oscar-Berman, 1973; Oscar-Berman and Samuels, 1977; Squire, 1982). Such visuoperceptive deficits should not be surprising since chronic alcoholics who are not clinically amnesic have been reported to have the same perceptual problems (Goldstein and Shelly, 1971; Parsons et al., 1971; Kleinknecht and Goldstein, 1972; Goodwin and Hill, 1975; Ryan and Butters, 1983).

Although there are some indications that these visuoperceptive deficits, like the memory disorder, may be due to damage to limbic structures surrounding the third ventricle (Jarho, 1973), many investigators have attributed such disorders to atrophy of frontal or parietal association cortex (Parsons et al., 1971; Parsons, 1975, Parsons and Farr, 1981; Moscovitch, 1982; Squire, 1982). Both Moscovitch (1982) and Squire (1982) caution that the presence of such visuoperceptive and conceptual deficits may confound the analysis of the amnesic syndrome. Whether these additional cognitive problems are independent of or contribute to some of the characteristics associated with the alcoholic Korsakoff amnesic syndrome must be considered by investigators concerned with the information processing deficits underlying the patient's retention problems.

While the secondary cognitive deficits of other types of amnesics have not been formally studied, their existence is obvious from clinical and neuropsychological evaluation. Patients who have survived herpes encephalitis are often left with some aphasic symptoms (e.g., anomia, paraphasia) as well as varying degrees of constructional apraxia, as noted by low performance IQ and difficulty with copying and drawing to command complex geometric figures. A similar combination of aphasic and constructional problems is usually associated with patients whose permanent amnesia is due to anoxia or trauma (Levin et al., 1982).

NEUROPSYCHOLOGICAL STUDIES OF AMNESIC STATES

Unfortunately for experimenters, brain damage in human populations is rarely limited to a single brain structure. In most cases the patient's disorder involves a combination of lesions that may or may not be confined to a single region. For example, alcoholic Korsakoff patients whose amnesia is related to alcohol intoxication and malnutrition have lesions involving the dorsomedial nucleus of the thalamus, the mammillary bodies, the vermis of the cerebellum, the oculomotor nucleus, and, in many cases, association cortex (Talland, 1965; Victor et al., 1971; Lishman, 1981; Wilkinson and Carlen, 1981). Similarly, patients with Alzheimer's disease whose amnesic symptoms are part of a general intellectual decline have progressive lesions of the hippocampus and of posterior and anterior association cortex (Tomlinson, 1977). Even postencephalitic patients whose amnesic symptoms are due to a herpes virus that directly attacks the hippocampus usually have considerable involvement of temporal and frontal neocortical areas (Drachman and Adams, 1962). When the multiplicity and variability of the patients' lesions are combined with a lack of postmortem verification of lesion sites, an assessment of what individual structures are contributing to a patient's amnesic symptoms becomes nearly impossible.

In addition to the problems with localization of lesions, the scientific inquiry into the memory of brain-damaged patients is handicapped by the lack of specificity and definition of the terms psychologists use to study memory. Constructs like "storage," "retrieval," and "encoding" are widely employed but poorly defined in the human memory literature. The havoc such lack of specificity produces for students of amnesia can be easily exemplified. Some amnesic patients perform better with cued than with free recall. They may be unable to recall the name of their doctor on direct inquiry but quickly supply the name when reminded that the physician's name begins with a "B" or is "something associated with bread." Such demonstrations of cueing have led investigators to propose that amnesia represents a problem with retrieval not storage (Warrington and Weiskrantz, 1970, 1973; Kinsbourne and Wood, 1975; McDowall, 1979). That is, the patient can and does store information normally but is impaired in the ability to retrieve. While this explanation seems plausible, it makes the implicit assumption that storage is all-or-none and not partial, an assumption that has little support in the literature on normal human memory. If, in fact, humans can partially store new information or store it in an inadequate form, then the cueing phenomenon becomes equally consistent with a storage or encoding hypothesis. Retrieval processes may be quite normal, although some form of phonemic or semantic cue may be required to retrieve a partially or inadequately stored (i.e., degraded) engram. Of course, the point of this example is that since storage is not fully understood in normal memory, attempts to separate storage and retrieval difficulties in amnesic patients have not been completely successful.

Meudell and Mayes (1981) have noted that many of the studies attempting to apply the concepts and methods of cognitive psychology to amnesia are difficult, if not impossible, to interpret because of floor and ceiling effects. Since amnesic patients invariably remember much less than their controls at any fixed retention interval, experimental manipulations (e.g., supplying the first two letters of the words, phonemic cues, semantic cues) that appear to have more beneficial effect upon the performance of amnesics than of control subjects may in fact reflect a significant interaction between the manipulation and the initial level of performance. Various cues and orientation tasks may have a greater effect upon amnesic patients not because of some special deficit in the patients' information processing but rather because any factor that aids retrieval may be more apparent the poorer the initial performance of the subjects. If the subjects are initially performing at a relatively high level, the beneficial effect of any manipulation will be limited by a performance ceiling. Furthermore, the interaction between initial level of performance and experimental manipulations may be seen even in normal controls when prolonged retention intervals are used to reduce retention scores. In such cases, the manipulations may tell us something about quantitative changes in the importance of certain cues over time but provide no information about the qualitative cognitive processes underlying the amnesics' memory disturbances.

Zola-Morgan and Oberg (1980) outlined a number of limitations of laboratory-based studies and suggested that a "naturalistic" approach to the amnesic patient can uncover phenomena not easily incorporable by current cognitive models of amnesia. On several occasions they guided an alcoholic Korsakoff patient (A. F.) through a section of Boston and then tested his memory for the trips periodically over two years. Memory was evaluated with free and cued recall techniques as well as with multiple-choice and true-false recognition tests. A number of findings are worth noting. One, the patient remembered more about the area than was anticipated from the severity of his retrograde amnesia. Two, some events were recalled consistently and accurately over the entire two-year period. Three, some events were remembered sporadically— i.e., total failure during one test session would be followed by full and accurate recall during a later session. Four, two years following the first guided tour, A. F. denied all recall of the first trip, yet his scores on the multiple-choice and true-false tests were far better than chance guessing and were almost identical to his scores from interviews that had occurred more than one year previously. The authors note quite accurately that a number of these observations would not have been predicted by current laboratory-based retrieval and encoding theories. Consequently, some important information concerning amnesia may be lost by restricting studies to the most currently popular experimental paradigms borrowed from cognitive-experimental psychology and ignoring how the patient's memory operates in a natural habitat.

Despite the lack of preciseness with regard to lesions and memory concepts and the methodological problems just described, there has been an increasing interest in the study of organic memory deficits during the past 20 years. Some of the neuropsychological studies have dealt with the localization and lateralization of memory functions, others with a description of the capacities and deficits of amnesic patients, and still others with the application of theories of information processing to the amnesic syndromes and milder forms of memory disturbances.

Amnesia Following Bilateral Lesions of the Mesial Region of the Temporal Lobes

The neuropsychological studies from the Montreal Neurological Institute (McGill University) have left little doubt that the mesial region of the temporal lobes is directly associated with memory processes in humans (Scoville and Milner, 1957; Penfield and Milner, 1958; Milner, 1966, 1970). Scoville and Milner described the severe memory disorder of a young man (H. M.) who had undergone bilateral mesial temporal lobe ablations to treat an uncontrolled form of epilepsy. This radical surgery was performed only after more conservative therapies had failed to control H. M.'s severe epileptic seizures. Upon recovering from surgery, H. M. manifested a severe inability to learn new information (anterograde amnesia) and was even unable to recall many events that had occurred prior to surgery (retrograde amnesia). In addition to H. M., Scoville and Milner described the memory disturbances of eight psychotic patients who had received bilateral mesial temporal removals as a treatment for their psychotic thought disorders. Severe anterograde amnesia was noted in those cases in which the lesions included the anterior sector of the hippocampus but was not evident when the lesion was limited to the uncus and the amygdala, sparing the hippocampus. On the basis of these nine patients, the investigators concluded that an intact hippocampus was necessary for the acquisition of new memories and the maintenance or retrieval of old traces.

H. M.'s surgery was successful in treating his seizures, but he was left with a permanent memory defect that has been extensively studied over 30 years by Brenda Milner, her colleagues, and her students. In the years immediately following surgery, H. M. showed a severe anterograde amnesia as evidenced by his inability to learn the names of friends and his new address. He had difficulty recalling events that had occurred just prior to his operation but was able to remember events from early childhood. His postoperative IQ was in the high-normal range and was somewhat improved over his preoperative score. He was reported to have been a placid individual before surgery, and there seemed to be no change in this personality evaluation after surgery.

In addition to this general clinical evaluation, a wide range of formal learning and cognitive tasks have been administered to H. M. Two investigations (Prisko, 1963; Sidman et al., 1968) have reported that H. M. is impaired on short-term memory tasks. In Prisko's study, H. M. was presented with two stimuli from the same modality separated by intervals ranging from zero to 60 seconds; he was then asked to indicate whether the second stimulus was identical to or different from the first. The stimuli were either nonverbal visual stimuli, such as light flashes and shades of red, or non-verbal auditory material, such as clicks and tones. The results were striking: although H. M. performed normally with very short delays between the two stimuli, his performance deteriorated as the delays increased. After a 60-second delay, his performance approached chance guessing. This short-term memory deficit stood in marked contrast to H. M.'s normal immediate memory span. If seven single-digit numbers were presented in succession, H. M. could recall all numbers in order if recall was attempted immediately following presentation. When, however, more than seven digits were presented or when a delay intervened between presentation and recall, H. M. was severely impaired on this task. H. M.'s performance on the digit-span task is typical of all amnesics and represents one of the features that distinguishes amnesia (a severe memory defect with no general intellectual decline) from dementia (a severe memory defect as part of a general intellectual decline). While the amnesic patient usually has a normal immediate memory span (about seven digits), the demented patient's span is often limited to four or five items.

H. M.'s ability to learn and retain motor and maze tasks has been evaluated (Milner, 1962; Milner et al., 1968). Although H. M. could learn and retain for several days mirror-drawing and pursuit rotor skills, his performance on visual and tactile mazes was grossly impaired. When Milner attempted to train H. M. on a visual stylus-maze (with 28 choice points), H. M. failed to show any progress in 215 trials. A subsequent study (Milner, 1968) indicated that H. M.'s failure on this test was because the 28 rights and lefts were well beyond his immediate memory span. When H. M. was tested on a shorter, seven-choice maze that was within his immediate span, he was able to attain criterion after 155 trials and 256 errors. What is more remarkable is that, when H. M. was tested on this shortened version of the visual maze two years later, he showed 75 percent savings despite the fact that he did not remember the previous testing session. Gardner (1975) noted a similar phenomenon in a patient with a traumatic amnesia (severe amnesic symptoms following a closed head injury in an automobile accident). This patient was taught to play a melody on the piano and retained this skill despite a total inability to remember the original learning sessions. Cohen and Squire (1980) reported that amnesic patients of various etiologies can learn and retain the general rules needed to read mirror-reflected words. The patients acquired this mirror-reading skill despite a severe amnesia for the training sessions as well as for the specific words they had read. It appears then that H. M., and other amnesics as well, may be able to acquire and retain general skills and rules but are unable to recognize specific pieces of data-based information despite numerous presentations.

Except for his severe and persistent memory defect, H. M. had few other cognitive deficits. Although he was unable to use visual imagery as a mnemonic to improve his verbal paired-associate learning (Jones, 1974), he performed normally on the Wisconsin card sorting task and on a number of visuoperceptual tasks such as the Mooney face perception task. Since these two tasks have been shown to be sensitive to frontal (Milner, 1963, 1964) and to temporal-parietal (Lansdell, 1968; Newcombe and Russell, 1969) cortical lesions, respectively, it was concluded that H. M.'s severe memory problems must be related to the mesial temporal ablations (probably the hippocampus) and not to any accessory cortical lesions.

In a recent series of brief abstracts, Corkin and her collaborators described the current status (28 years following surgery) of H. M.'s amnesic condition (Cohen and Corkin, 1981; Corkin et al., 1981; Eichenbaum et al., 1981; Hebben et al., 1981; Nissen et al., 1981). The most striking feature of H. M. is the stability of his anterograde amnesia. He still does not recall his most recent meal, the current year, and estimates his age to be 10 to 26 years less than it is. Like other amnesics, there are, however, islands of learning. According to Corkin et al., H. M. knows that an astronaut is someone who travels in outer space and that a public person named Kennedy was assassinated.

Despite the severity of his deficiencies in acquiring important declarative information since his operation, H. M. is capable of learning and retaining complex perceptual and cognitive skills that depend upon procedural knowledge. For example, Cohen and Corkin tested H. M. on the Tower of Hanoi puzzle, a rule-based problem involving a number of pegs and a number of blocks of differing sizes. At the beginning of the problem, all of the blocks are arranged on a "source" peg in order of size, with the smallest block at the top and the largest on the bottom. The subject is instructed to move the blocks, one at a time, onto a second ("goal") peg in such a sequence that the size order on the source peg is maintained. The subject is also told that she or he is not allowed to place a block onto one smaller than itself. H. M. was tested four times per day on four consecutive days and following a seven-day rest interval, for another four consecutive days. Despite his lack of memory for performing the task from day to day and his failure to recall particular moves, H. M., like normal controls, showed a systematic improvement within and over days in terms of the number of moves needed to solve the problem. "By the seventh and eighth days of training, despite near-perfect performance, his commentary during each trial always sounded as if he were solving the puzzle for the first time" (Cohen and Corkin, 1981). Clearly, in view of Cohen and Squire's (1980) and Cohen and Corkin's data, it appears that the learning and retention of general rules are not affected in amnesic patients and that this ability does not rely upon the limbic structures usally associated with learning and memory.

Other results of H. M.'s most recent assessment suggest the development of some general cognitive problems and the loss of some sensory capacities. Between 1977 and 1980 some decline was noted in verbal fluency, expressive and receptive language capacities, and overall IQ (WAIS) (Corkin et al., 1981). Hebben et al. (1981), using the methods of sensory decision theory, found that H. M. had significantly deficient thermal pain discriminability scores at several body sites. A similar deficit in discrimination was reported for H. M.'s ability to distinguish between feelings of satiation and hunger. Although he was able to discriminate normally the intensity of common odors, he was very impaired in identifying the odors and in making odor quality discriminations (Eichenbaum et al., 1981). The authors conclude that mesial temporal structures must play some role in mediating chemical and somesthetic senses and in the appreciation of internal states. Interestingly, the investigations of Jones and her collaborators (Jones et al., 1975a, 1975b, 1978) have suggested that damage to midline diencephalic structures may also disrupt a patient's olfactory capacities. It should be of more than passing interest to comparative neuroanatomists that those structures involved in human memory functions are also critical to the maintenance of the chemical senses.

Verbal and Nonverbal Memory Deficits
After Unilateral Temporal Lobectomies

While the case of H. M. and of other patients receiving bilateral mesial temporal lesions clearly established the importance of the mesial temporal region in memory, it has been the investigations of patients with unilateral temporal lobectomies that have pointed to the lateralized contributions of the two temporal regions to memory. Like H. M., patients with unilateral temporal lobectomies have had surgical intervention to treat uncontrolled epileptic seizures. In most cases, the surgery has been successful with regard to seizure activity and the patients have returned to productive lives without any obvious amnesic symptoms. However, close examination of these patients has uncovered subtle memory defects that are dependent on whether the left or right temporal lobe has been removed, and the severity of the memory problem seems to depend upon the amount of hippocampus ablated.

Removal of the left temporal lobe is followed by verbal memory deficits. Patients with left temporal lobectomies have more dfficulty learning and retaining verbal materials (both visually and auditorily presented) than do patients with right temporal lobectomies. For example, patients with left temporal lobectomies are impaired in the recall of prose passages, in verbal paired associate learning, and on Hebb's digit sequence task which assesses the patient's ability to learn a recurring sequence of numbers exceeding the patient's digit span (Milner, 1971; Gerner et al., 1972). On a short-term memory task that uses a distractor technique, left temporal patients show faster decay of consonant trigrams than do patients with right temporal lobectomies (Corsi, 1969). Some of these verbal learning deficits can be reduced by training patients with left temporal lesions to use the functions of their intact right hemispheres in a rehabilitative manner. Jones (1974) has shown that patients with left temporal lobectomies can use visual imagery as a mnemonic to diminish their deficits on a paired-associate task comprising 10 pairs of highly concrete words.

The results of these ablation studies have been supported and expanded by a study of the effects of electrical stimulation on language and memory processes (Fedio and Van Buren, 1974). The patients for this study were seven temporal lobe epileptics who were candidates for unilateral temporal lobectomies. Before such a patient undergoes neurosurgery, it is necessary to "map" via electrical stimulation the speech areas of the brain. The results of this procedure allow the surgeon to avoid ablating tissue that is crucial for the patient's language capacities. In the Fedio and Van Buren study, the patients were administered a naming and memory task as part of this mapping procedure. The task involved the presentation of a series of pictures of common objects with short delays between successive pictures. Patients were instructed to first name the object in the picture before them and then to recall the name of the object presented on the immediately preceding trial. As expected, electrical stimulation of the left temporal lobe led to a variety of anomic (dysphasic) naming errors but the new and important findings concerned the patients' memory (recall) performance during stimulation of the temporal lobes. Two distinct areas were found in the left temporal lobe: stimulation of the anterior sector of the left temporal lobe resulted in anterograde amnesia, and stimulation of the posterior (temporoparietal) region produced retrograde problems. If points in the anterior temporal region were stimulated while patients were correctly naming a picture, they often would be unable to recall this picture on a later trial when no stimulation was present. Somehow stimulation of this anterior point prevents the acquisition or consolidation of the picture's name. In contrast, electrical stimulation of points in the posterior left temporal region resulted in a failure to recall the picture exposed on the preceding trial despite the fact that at the time of original exposure and naming no stimulation was being applied to the brain. That is, electrical stimulation of the posterior region made it difficult for patients to recall events that occurred prior to the stimulation (i.e., retrograde amnesia). The investigators suggest that structures in the anterior portion of the left temporal lobe (e.g., the hippocampus) may play a role in the consolidation and storage of verbal materials, whereas sectors of the left posterior temporal region may be important in the retrieval of stored verbal stimuli. These findings offer further evidence for the separation of anterograde and retrograde memory losses.

While patients with right temporal lobectomies are unimpaired on verbal memory tasks, they are impaired relative to left lobectomy patients on tasks that require the processing of nonverbal patterned materials. Right temporal patients have difficulty remembering whether they have previously seen an unfamiliar geometric pattern (Kimura, 1963) and are impaired in the learning of visual and tactile mazes (Corkin, 1965; Milner, 1965). They have difficulty in the recognition of tonal patterns (Milner, 1967) and faces (Milner, 1968) after a short delay. Although patients with right temporal lobectomies have no difficulty in learning to associate pairs of abstract nouns, they are significantly impaired in forming associations between pairs of concrete nouns when visual imagery is encouraged for mnemonic purposes (Jones-Gotman and Milner, 1978).

Evidence that the right temporal region is also involved in the "automatic" encoding (i.e., incidental learning) of the spatial location of objects has recently been presented by Smith and Milner (1981). Patients with right or left temporal lobectomies and normal control subjects were asked to estimate the cost of 16 toys arranged randomly on a white board. Immediately following the estimation of cost, the subjects were asked to first recall the names of the objects presented (object recall) and then to indicate each object's original position on the board (spatial recall). Twenty-four hours later, object recall and spatial recall were repeated. While both temporal lobe groups evidenced some impairment in object recall, only the right temporal patients were impaired in spatial recall.

The temporal lobectomies performed on the McGill patients involved a number of neuroanatomical structures, such as the amygdala, uncus, hippocampus, anterior temporal neocortex, and parahippocampal gyrus, but there is now substantial evidence from Milner's laboratory that the ablation of the hippocampus is the critical factor in the patients' memory deficits. These studies were facilitated by the surgeons' care in recording the locus and extent of the temporal lobe lesions. When the left and right temporal groups were divided according to the amount of hippocampal involvement, it was found that the degree of behavioral deficit correlated with the amount of hippocampus removed. Corsi (1969) found that patients with left temporal ablations with extensive hippocampal damage were more impaired on short-term memory tasks and in the learning of supraspan digit sequences (Hebb's digit sequence task) than were patients with little or no involvement of the hippocampus. On the other hand, maze learning (Milner, 1965; Corkin, 1965), recognition of faces from photographs (Milner, 1968), image-mediated verbal learning (Jones-Gotman and Milner, 1978), and incidental spatial learning (Smith and Milner, 1981) were impaired only with extensive lesions of the right hippocampus. However, the impairments of right temporal patients on visual memory tasks involving unfamiliar geometric forms, such as the Rey-Osterrieth figure (Taylor, 1969) and recurring nonsense figures (Kimura, 1963), have not been found to correlate with amount of hippocampal damage. Milner (1970) suggested that such tasks involve extensive visuoperceptual analysis as well as memory and thus may depend on the integrity of both the temporal neocortex and the hippocampus.

For those studies that have shown a correlation between hippocampal damage and behavior deficits, it should be stressed that temporal lobe lesions that involved the amygdala, uncus, and cortex but left the hippocampus relatively intact produced no noticeable deficits on performance of verbal and nonverbal memory tasks. On the basis of these studies, it seems fair to conclude that H. M.'s severe amnesic syndrome, which involves both verbal and nonverbal skills, is due primarily to the bilateral and extensive ablation of the hippocampus. Since all of the patients with hippocampal damage also had extensive removal of the amygdala and uncus, the behavioral consequences of hippocampal lesions by themselves could not be evaluated in the McGill patient population.

Experimental Studies of Anterograde Amnesia

While Milner and her colleagues have established the importance of an intact hippocampus for normal memory, the vast majority of studies of the information processing deficits underlying anterograde amnesia have utilized alcoholic Korsakoff patients, whose severe memory disorders have been attributed to mesial diencephalic brain structures (dorsomedial nucleus of the thalamus and/or the mammillary bodies). The popularity of this alcoholic population is due primarily to its ubiquity as well as to the rarity of patients with lesions limited to the hippocampus. The essential clinical symptoms of Korsakoff's syndrome have been known for approximately 100 years (Talland, 1965; Victor et al., 1971; Butters and Cermak, 1980). The patient has combined chronic alcoholism and thiamine deficiency into a neurological syndrome characterized by changes in motor, sensory, cognitive, and personality processes. In the acute stage the patient presents with ataxia, nystagmus, confusion with regard to time and place, and peripheral neuropathy. If the patient is treated with large doses of thiamine, the motor and sensory abnormalities slowly improve over four to eight weeks, but in most cases the patient is left with a severe amnesia and striking personality alterations. In the chronic Korsakoff state, the patient is extremely passive, malleable, and otherwise emotionally flat, regardless of premorbid personality. The memory disorder is severe and permanent and closely resembles that of H. M.

Until recently, hippocampal lesions were believed to be responsible for the Korsakoff patients' memory problems (Talland, 1965; Victor et al., 1971; Mair et al., 1979), but the neuropathological analysis of an extensive series of alcoholic Korsakoff brains (Victor et al., 1971) has shown that the critical lesions involve mesial thalamic structures. In Victor et al.'s study, every Korsakoff patient who had an amnesic syndrome also showed atrophy of the dorsal medial nucleus of the thalamus and of the mammillary bodies of the hypothalamus, but lesions of the hippocampus were not found consistently. Mair et al. (1979) examined the brains of two alcoholic Korsakoff patients whose memory disorders had been carefully documented. In both cases, atrophy of the medial nuclei of the mammillary bodies and a thin band of gliosis between the wall of the third ventricle and the dorsomedial nucleus of the thalamus were the most striking neuropathological findings. Case studies demonstrating that tumors (Kahn and Crosby, 1972) and shrapnel wounds (Jarho, 1973) of the midline diencephalic region result in amnesic problems also point to thalamic and hypothalamic (mammillary bodies) involvement in memory. Teuber et al., (1968) have reported a single case (N. A.) of amnesia for verbal materials resulting from a stab wound that damaged sectors of the rostral midbrain. Squire and Slater (1978) and Squire and Moore (1979) confirmed N. A.'s anterograde and retrograde verbal memory deficits, and with the use of CT scans demonstrated that his brain damage is localized in the dorsomedial nucleus of the thalamus of the left (dominant) hemisphere. Most recently, Speedie and Heilman (1982, 1983) have described two patients with discrete lesions of the left or right dorsomedial thalamus. As anticipated, the patient with the discrete left dorsomedial thalamic lesion was impaired on verbal memory tasks and the patient with the damage limited to the right hemisphere had difficulty learning and retaining nonverbal patterned materials.

Coinciding with the recent neuropathological and neuroradiological findings, there have been a number of extensive experimental studies of the difficulty alcoholic Korsakoff patients have in acquiring new information (Cermak and Butters, 1973; Butters and Cermak, 1975, 1980; Piercy, 1977; Hirst, 1982). These studies have focused on the patients' short-term memory (STM) capacities and the role of interference, encoding, and contextual analysis in storage and retrieval problems.

With two notable exceptions (Baddeley and Warrington, 1970; Mair et al., 1979), all of the studies concerned with the STM of alcoholic Korsakoff patients reported severe deficits in these patients (Cermak et al., 1971; Samuels et al., 1971a; Goodglass and Peck, 1972; Butters et al., 1973; Squire and Cohen, 1982). Most of these studies used the Brown-Peterson distractor technique (Brown, 1958; Peterson and Peterson, 1959) with delays ranging between 0 and 18 seconds. With this procedure, the patients see or hear a stimulus (verbal or nonverbal) and immediately start to count backward by twos or threes. When the patient has counted for a predetermined interval, the examiner says "Stop" and the patient attempts to recall or to recognize the stimulus. The counting prevents the patients from rehearsing during the delay interval.

Figure 14-6 shows the performance of a group of alcoholic Korsakoff patients on the Brown-Peterson distractor task with word triads as the stimulus. The patients show normal performance with zero-second delays, but their decay functions are much steeper than those of control subjects. This deficit is apparent regardless of whether the stimulus is visual, auditory, or tactile (Butters et al., 1973) and of the verbalizability of the stimulus (DeLuca et al., 1975).

Squire and Slater (1978) administered a Brown-Peterson distractor task to patient N. A. (described previously) and found severe impairments in his ability to retain verbal information beyond a few seconds. Given the highly localized nature of N. A.'s lesion (i.e., n. medialis dorsalis in the left hemisphere), it would appear that damage to the midline diencephalic region is sufficient to produce significant impairments in STM. However, significant deficits on Brown-Peterson distractor tasks have also been reported in brain-damaged patients without amnesic syndromes. Patients with lesions involving the right parietal lobe show rapid loss of visually presented verbal and nonverbal materials (Samuels et al., 1971a, 1971b), especially if the stimuli are exposed initially to the patients' left visual field. Samuels et al. (1972) reported that both right and left temporal lobectomies (with relatively little involvement of the hippocampus) are followed by deficits on Brown-Peterson tasks in which verbal stimuli are presented orally.

Warrington and her colleagues (Warrington and Shallice, 1969, 1972; Shallice and Warrington, 1970; Warrington et al., 1972) described auditory verbal STM deficits in three nonamnesic patients with damage to the posterior parietal cortex of the left hemisphere. These patients had a reduced auditory (but not visual) immediate-memory span for letters and numbers that could not be reduced to a motor speech impairment or a problem with auditory perception. When the patients' STM was assessed with the Brown-Peterson technique, strings of one, two, or three letters were forgotten

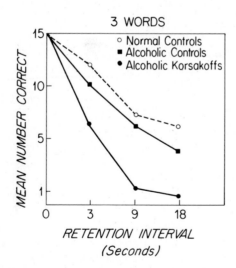

Fig. 14-6. Mean number of words recalled by alcoholic Korsakoff patients, alcoholics, and normal controls on the Brown-Peterson distractor task with word triads as the stimulus. (From Butters and Cermak, 1980)

more rapidly after auditory than after visual presentation. Despite this severe impairment in immediate and STM, these patients' long-term memory (LTM) appeared intact, as evidenced by their normal performance on verbal paired-associate and recall tasks. In view of this evidence that cortical lesions can be associated with stimulus-specific STM deficits, the attribution of all of the Korsakoff patients' problems on distractor tasks to diencephalic lesions remains problematical. The mounting neuroradiological evidence (Lishman, 1981; Wilkinson and Carlen, 1981) that alcoholic Korsakoff patients, as well as nonamnesic long-term alcoholics, often have extensive anterior and posterior cortical atrophy reinforces this conservative position.

The alcoholic Korsakoff patients' difficulties with the Brown-Peterson distractor task exemplify one of the most prominent features of their anterograde amnesia, i.e., increased sensitivity to proactive interference (PI). Previously learned materials interfere with attempts to acquire new information. There are three sources of evidence for this interference phenomenon: (1) the type of errors made by Korsakoff patients on learning tasks (Meudell et al., 1978), (2) demonstrations of normal performance when partial information is provided at the time of retrieval (Warrington and Weiskrantz, 1970, 1973), and (3) improved learning and retention when the experimental conditions are structured to reduce PI (Cermak and Butters, 1972; Butters et al., 1976). Although the Korsakoff patients' overall performance on a STM distractor task is severely impaired, the deficit is not manifested equivalently throughout the test session. On the first few trials the patients often perform within normal limits, but performance deteriorates rapidly on subsequent trials. Cermak et al. (1974) noted that alcoholic Korsakoff patients may accurately recall as much as 90 percent of presented verbal material on the first two trials but less than 50 percent on the fifth trial. On Trial 5 the patient is still recalling the material presented on Trials 1 and 2.

Meudell et al. (1978) compared the types of errors manifested on a Brown-Peterson distractor task by alcoholic Korsakoff patients and by patients with Huntington's disease. They found that both groups were significantly impaired but that the types of errors differentiated the two patient populations. The Korsakoff patients' errors were primarily intrusions from prior lists, whereas the demented patients made many omission errors. These results suggested that PI may not be a crucial factor in the memory disorders of all brain-damaged patients.

With methods of retrieval that reduce interference, the performance of amnesic patients may not differ from that of intact normal controls. Warrington and Weiskrantz (1970) have shown that, while amnesics are severely impaired on unaided recall or recognition tests, they do retrieve normally when partial information is provided. Warrington and Weiskrantz (1973) suggest that the superiority of the partial information method stems from the limitations it places on interference from previously learned information. If the first two letters of the to-be-recalled word are "st," the number of words that can possibly interfere with the recall of the target word "stamp" are greatly limited. According to Warrington and Weiskrantz (1973), free recall and recognition procedures do not limit PI to the same degree.

It is well known from the literature on normal human memory that PI may be reduced by specific manipulations of the conditions under which learning is attempted. For example, distributed presentation results in less interference than does massed presentation. When the Peterson distractor task was administered with distributed (one-minute rest between successive trials) rather than massed (six seconds between trials) presentation to alcoholic Korsakoff patients, Huntington's disease patients, and alcoholic control subjects, the Korsakoff patients and the controls showed significant improvements in performance (Butters et al., 1976). In fact, the Korsakoff patients recalled as many items with distributed presentation as the controls did with massed presentation. However, this reduction in interference (via distribution of trials) had no effect upon the memory deficits of the HD patients; they performed as poorly with distributed as with massed presentation.

The amnesic patients' increased sensitivity to PI has led Warrington and Weiskrantz (1970, 1973) to propose a retrieval-interference theory of amnesia. According to this view, amnesic patients encode and store information normally but are unable to retrieve specific material from LTM because of interference. Although amnesics may use normal retrieval strategies, they seem to be highly sensitive to interference from competing information and to have great difficulty in inhibiting this irrelevant material. This theory proposes that items in storage are poorly insulated from one another and are in constant competition during retrieval. Thus, when alcoholic Korsakoff or other amnesic patients are asked the name of their physician for the fifth or sixth time, they continue to provide an incorrect answer because they cannot differentiate the physician's name from all the other names held in LTM.

Despite the elegance of the retrieval-interference theory, a number of investigators (including Warrington and Weiskrantz) have noted empirical and theoretical difficulties with this approach. Woods and Piercy (1974) reported that the partial information phenomenon was not peculiar to amnesics and was actually characteristic of normal memory when traces were weak or poorly stored. Normal subjects were presented with lists of words and tested for retention of half the material one minute later and for the other half one week later. The differences between the one-minute and one-week retentions paralleled the differences between the normals and the amnesics reported by Warrington and Weiskrantz (1970). Although yes-no recognition was significantly poorer after one week than after one minute, the partial information technique did not yield significantly different performances with the two delay intervals. It appears, then, that if an intact individual's memories are weakened by the passage of time, his or her retrieval can also be facilitated by the use of partial information. This finding questions whether partial information experiments have uncovered any special processing problems of amnesic patients. As noted previously, this point also has been emphasized by Meudell and Mayes (1981).

Warrington and Weiskrantz (1978) also reported a series of experiments that necessitate modification of their original retrieval interference theory. In the main experiment, the effect of prior-list learning on the learning of a second list was evaluated. High PI was assured by the use of word pairs that were the only two words having the first three letters in common. For instance, the word "cyclone" appeared on one list and the word "cycle" on the other. Each word on list one was presented once visually, and retention was tested immediately by presenting the first three letters of each word on the list (cued recall). Immediately following this test of list 1 retention, list 2 was shown to the subjects and a cued retention of it followed without delay. In all, four presentation and cued retention trials of list 2 were administered.

The results indicated that, although the amnesic patients performed more poorly overall than did the normal control group, this difference became progressively greater as the testing proceeded. On list 1 and the first trial for list 2, no significant differences in retention were noted between the two groups. Both groups performed more poorly on the first retention trial of list 2 than on the single list 1 trial, but this decrement was equal for both groups. Differences between the amnesics and normal subjects appeared on the second, third, and fourth retention trials of list 2, and these differences increased with each succeeding retention trial.

As the investigators note, list 1 words were expected to interfere with the learning of list 2, but the effect of this PI should have been greater for the amnesic patients than for the normal subjects. Also, interference theory predicts that differences between amnesic and normal individuals should be greatest on the first retention trial of list 2 and should decrease with each successive presentation of list 2. As the results of this experiment are the opposite of those predicted, Warrington and Weiskrantz seem justified in concluding that the amnesics' retrieval difficulties cannot be accounted for by a simple interference model.

In addition to the noted empirical problems, interference retrieval theory has been viewed as primarily descriptive rather than explanatory (Piercy, 1977), and other hypotheses have been offered to account for the amnesic patients' retention and interference problems. Butters and Cermak (1974, 1975, 1980) suggested that the alcoholic Korsakoff patients' verbal memory impairment is related to a failure to encode, at the time of storage, all of the attributes of the stimulus. According to this hypothesis, patients may fully categorize verbal information according to its phonemic and associative attributes but may be inadequate in their analysis of the semantic features of the materials. Information that is not fully analyzed (encoded) may be stored in a degraded fashion and thus be more sensitive to interference. The initial evidence for this theory emanated from a series of cueing experiments in which phonemic and semantic cues were compared in terms of their ability to facilitate recall (Cermak and Butters, 1972; Cermak et al., 1973). In general, phonemic cues worked as well for Korsakoff patients as for controls but semantic cues aided the recall of only the control subjects.

Cermak et al.'s (1976) investigation of the rehearsal strategies manifested during list learning also provided evidence that Korsakoff patients do not facilitate their learning by utilizing the semantic features of words. Alcoholic Korsakoff patients, alcoholic controls, and normal controls were asked to learn three 20-word lists. One list consisted of semantically unrelated words, one of related words presented in random order, and one of related words presented in a blocked fashion. Each word in each list was presented visually for five seconds, and the subjects were instructed to rehearse aloud. Two findings are of special relevance to the semantic encoding hypothesis. One, although recall improved as a function of the relatedness of the lists, normal and alcoholic controls were able to take more advantage of the increasing salience of list organization than were the amnesic Korsakoff patients. The Korsakoff patients' recall on the related-blocked list was not appreciably better than their performance on the unrelated list. Two, while the two control groups used a semantic rehearsal strategy to aid their recall, the Korsakoff patients approached the rehearsal task in a concrete, limited fashion. On the two organized lists, the control groups produced many words per reharsal set belonging to the category of the presented word, whereas the Korsakoff patients simply repeated on each rehearsal set the single word that had just been presented. The authors concluded that the Korsakoff patients' inability to improve with related-organized lists could be traced to their passive rehearsal strategy, which seemed to ignore the semantic associations among the words.

While numerous studies have shown that alcoholic Korsakoff patients are sensitive to PI and engage in limited semantic encoding, there has been a lack of convincing demonstrations of a link between these two phenomena. Starting with the premise that deficits in semantic encoding lead to degraded engrams highly sensitive to PI, Cermak et al. (1974) adapted Wickens's (1970) release from PI technique for use with alcoholic Korsakoff patients. With a modification of the Brown-Peterson distractor technique, Wickens had discovered that the PI generated by the presentations of material from the same class of information on several consecutive trials can be released by the introduction of material from a new class of information. This finding was interpreted to mean that the extent of interference during STM recall is largely a function of the subject's ability to differentiate words in memory on the basis of their semantic features. When a subject encodes material differentially, this material is stored independently and does not interfere with the retrieval of other types of material. If the Korsakoff patients' increased sensitivity to interference is related to their lack of semantic encoding, then the amount of PI release shown by these patients should vary with the encoding requirements of the verbal materials. Cermak et al. (1974) anticipated that alcoholic Korsakoff patients would demonstrate normal PI release when the verbal materials involved only rudimentary categorizations (e.g., letters versus numbers) but would evidence far less PI release when the stimulus materials involved more abstract semantic differences (e.g., taxonomic differences such as animals versus vegetables).

Cermak et al.'s (1974) results are presented in Figs. 14-7 and 14-8. The alcoholic control subjects (Fig. 14-7) demonstrated release from PI for both alphanumeric and taxonomic materials, whereas the alcoholic Korsakoff patients (Fig. 14-8) released only when the relatively simple alphanumeric materials were used. The alcoholic Korsakoffs' failure to release with taxonomic materials was interpreted as reflecting inadequate semantic analyses. If the Korsakoff patients did not encode along such semantic dimensions, then the PI accumulating during the block of five trials would probably not be specific to any one category, and therefore a shift of categories would have no effect.

Although Cermak et al.'s (1974) findings seem to integrate the patients' retentive and encoding difficulties, Moscovitch (1982) has demonstrated that the failure to release from PI can occur in patients who are not clinically amnesic and consequently that this deficiency is not inextricably tied to memory deficits. Patients with left frontal, left temporal (with and without hippocampal involvement) right frontal, and right temporal lesions participated in this study. Five different lists of 12 words each were read to subjects who were instructed to recall each list immediately after presentation. The words on the first four lists were all drawn from the same taxonomic category, and the words for the fifth list from a different category. As anticipated, the buildup of PI, evidenced by a progressive decline in recall with each successive list,

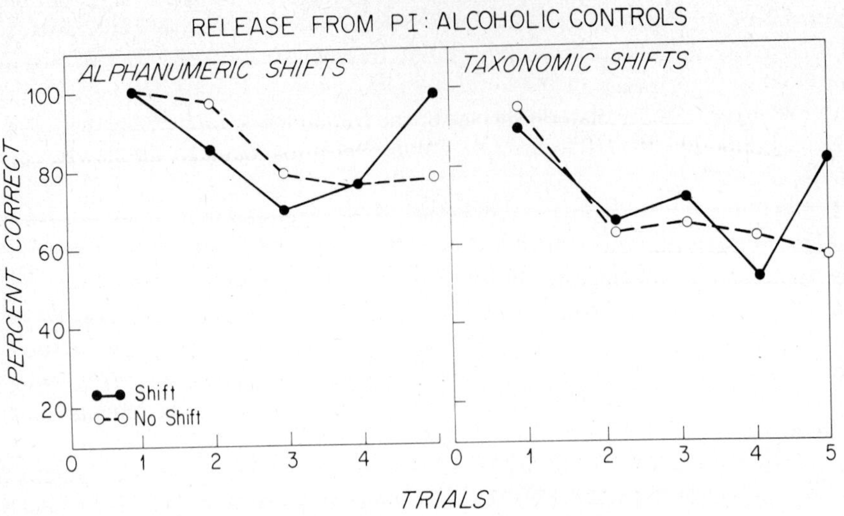

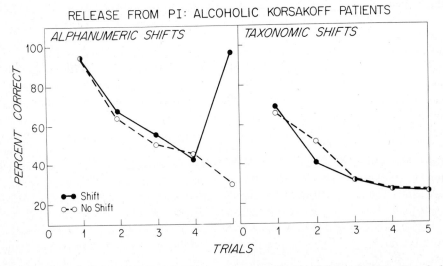

Fig. 14-7. Release from PI. Percentage of words correctly recalled by alcoholic control subjects after alphanumeric and taxonomic shifts. (From Cermak et al., 1974)

Fig. 14-8. Release from PI. Percentage of words correctly recalled by alcoholic Korsakoff patients after alphanumeric and taxonomic shifts. (From Cermak et al., 1974)

was apparent for all patient groups, but there were significant group differences in their tendencies to release from PI when a taxonomic shift occurred on the fifth recall trial. Despite the fact that the left temporal patients with hippocampal involvement had documented verbal learning deficits, these patients manifested normal release from PI. In contrast, the patients with left frontal damage, whose learning capacities were not obviously compromised, performed like alcoholic Korsakoff patients in that many of them failed to evidence release on the fifth trial. Of further interest was the finding that release from PI in the left frontal group was positively correlated with performance on a concept formation task (Wisconsin Card Sorting Test) known to be sensitive to long-term alcohol abuse (Tarter and Parsons, 1971; Tarter, 1973) as well as to damage to the dorsolateral surface of the frontal lobes (Milner, 1964). The other patient groups, like the left temporals with hippocampal damage, all showed normal release from PI.

In interpreting these results, Moscovitch (1982) suggested that amnesic patients of various etiologies may have numerous cognitive impairments that are independent of their anterograde memory problems. The evidence that nonamnesic frontal lobe patients do not release when categories of words are shifted indicates that this phenomenon, and perhaps other encoding deficits as well, may not contribute to the Korsakoff patients' anterograde amnesia. As Moscovitch noted, the Korsakoff patients' failure to release from PI may be more a symptom of frontal lobe damage than an indicator of an information processing deficit responsible for their inability to acquire new verbal materials. The neuroradiological evidence that long-term alcohol abuse is associated with extensive atrophy of the frontal lobes is consistent with this suggestion (Lishman, 1981; Wilkinson and Carlen, 1981).

Moscovitch's conclusions concerning the relationship between frontal lobe dysfunction and failure to release from PI have been echoed by Squire (1982), who found that, although alcoholic Korsakoff patients failed to release from PI, patient N. A. (who is amnesic for verbal materials) and depressed patients receiving bilateral ECT did so. Furthermore, although the Korsakoff patients, N. A., and the ECT patients were equally impaired on a sentence recognition task, the Korsakoff patients were significantly more impaired than the others in making temporal recency judgments about the same verbal materials. That is, when the alcoholic Korsakoff patients were successful at recognizing a previously presented sentence, they were usually unable to state from which of two lists, separated temporally by a few minutes, the familiar sentence had originated. Since impairments in recency judgments have been reported in nonamnesic frontal lobe patients (Milner, 1971), Squire suggested that alcoholic Korsakoff patients may have a number of cognitive deficits attributable to frontal lobe dysfunction. The fact that patient N. A. and ECT patients did not evidence these same problems with release from PI or with recency judgments indicates that these cognitive deficits may be separable and independent of the patients' amnesia.

In their search for evidence that deficits in semantic encoding play a vital role in the amnesic patients' anterograde amnesia, investigators have borrowed other experimental paradigms from the normal human learning literature. Cermak and Reale (1978), utilizing a technique developed by Craik and Tulving (1975), attempted to ameliorate the alcoholic Korsakoff patients' verbal learning performance with orientation tasks that forced their subjects to analyze and judge the semantic attributes of words. Subjects were not told that they would have to remember anything; rather they were simply instructed to analyze each word on the basis of the particular characteristic suggested by the examiner's question. The basic premise is that, the higher the level of encoding the subject is required to perform on a word, the greater the probability that she or he will remember the word on a subsequent but unnanounced recognition test. The questions were designed to necessitate processing on one of three levels: (a) a shallow orthographic level (e.g., "Is this word printed in upper case letters?"); (b) a phonemic level (e.g., "Does this word rhyme with *fat?*"); and (c) a semantic level (e.g., Does this word fit into the following sentence: _____ ?"). For each question the subject had to make a *yes* or *no* response by pressing an appropriate response key. Following the presentation of the entire series of questions, the patients were administered a recognition test to determine how many of the exposed words could be correctly identified.

In an initial experiment, Cermak and Reale (1978) presented their alcoholic Korsakoff patients and alcoholic control subjects with 60 words and required them to answer one question about each word. Twenty of the questions dealt with the orthographic features of the words, 20 with the phonemic features, and 20 with the semantic characteristics. After presentation of the last word, the subjects were given a typewritten sheet with 180 words (the 60 presented words and 120 filler nouns) and asked to circle those that had just been presented to them.

The results indicated that the alcoholic Korsakoff patients, unlike the control subjects, were unaffected by the level of processing performed upon the words. The alcoholic controls' recognition of semantic words was significantly better than their recognition of words orthographically or phonemically analyzed, and their recognition of orthographic words was the poorest of the three encoding conditions. The alcoholic Korsakoff patients, however, recognized few words overall, and there were no significant differences in their recognition of semantic, phonemic, and orthographic words. Recently, Squire (1982) repeated Cermak and Reale's procedures and found that Korsakoff patients' recognition memory was differentially aided by the semantic processing procedure. The difference between the two sets of data remains unexplained, although the severity of the patients' amnesia may be an important determinant in the success of any orienting task.

In a second experiment, Cermak and Reale (1978) investigated the possibility that the failure of alcoholic Korsakoff patients to benefit from a semantic orientation task may have been due to the magnitude of the word list and recognition task. They divided the 60-word stimulus list and the 180-word recognition test into a series of shorter encoding and recognition tasks. The patients were asked just 12 questions about 12 words, followed by a 36-word recognition test. This procedure was repeated five times until 60 words had been exposed and tested for recognition. Each of the 12-item lists contained four words that were analyzed orthographically, four that were analyzed phonemically, and four that were analyzed semantically.

The alcoholic Korsakoff patients' recognition performance with these abbreviated lists was at least partially consistent with the semantic encoding hypothesis. The Korsakoff patients were still impaired under all encoding conditions in comparison to the alcoholic controls, but they did benefit from the semantic orientation task. The Korsakoff patients' best recognition occurred for the semantic words, their poorest recognition for the words that had been associated with orthographic questions. While these results suggest that the alcoholic Korsakoff patients' memory performance can be manipulated by orientation tasks that encourage or discourage semantic analysis, they provide no evidence that the patients' anterograde amnesia may be eliminated by semantic analysis. In fact, Cermak and Reale's experiments fail to demonstrate that semantic orientation tasks have a greater effect upon Korsakoff patients than upon control subjects. This latter finding is necessary if one is to conclude that semantic encoding plays a special role in the memory disorders of amnesic patients.

McDowall (1979) also assessed the semantic encoding hypothesis with orientation tasks and, ironically, found stronger evidence for this theoretical position than did Cermak and his colleagues. Three conditions were employed in the McDowall experiments: (1) a baseline condition in which no specific instructions were provided, (2) a phonemic orientation task in which the subjects had to determine whether each word in a list contained the letter "e," and (3) a semantic orientation task that required the subjects to declare to which of four taxonomic categories each word belonged. For each condition, 20 words consisting of 5 nouns from each of 4 taxonomic categories were presented to alcoholic Korsakoff patients and to alcoholic controls. Immediately following two presentations of the 20-word list, the subjects were asked to recall as many of the words as possible.

The results yielded a significant group by condition interaction. The Korsakoff patients recalled many more words following the semantic orientation task than following the phonemic encoding and baseline conditions, and their performance on the latter two conditions did not differ. In contrast, the alcoholic controls recalled more words after the semantic and baseline conditions than after the phonemic orientation task, and their performance on the former two conditions could not be distinguished (Fig. 14-9).

These results suggest that, although intact subjects spontaneously encode the semantic features of words without formal instructions to do so, amnesic Korsakoff patients can utilize and benefit from such an encoding strategy only when forced to analyze the semantic attributes. Left to their own devices, as in the baseline condition, the alcoholic Korsakoff patients tend to rely upon very superficial and ineffective

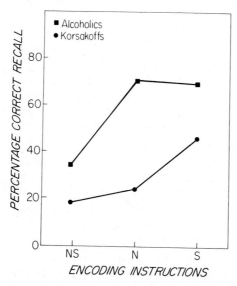

Fig. 14-9. Percentage of words correctly recalled by alcoholic Korsakoff patients and alcoholic control subjects after an undirected study (N) condition and nonsemantic (NS) and semantic (S) orientation tasks. (From McDowall, 1979).

encoding processes. This apparent support for the semantic encoding hypothesis is somewhat muted by McDowall's (1979) additional finding that supplying taxonomic cues at the time of retrieval was sufficient to significantly improve the recall of words presented with no special encoding instructions. He concluded subsequently that alcoholic Korsakoff patients may encode information normally at the time of storage but cannot generate the appropriate semantic retrieval strategies when attempting to recall previously presented verbal materials.

In recent years, Butters, Cermak, and their colleagues have proposed that the alcoholic Korsakoff patients' deficiency in semantic encoding is only a single exemplar of a general limitation in the patients' ability to analyze all of the dimensions of any complex stimulus, verbal or nonverbal. Glosser et al. (1976) used a modified version of the dichotic listening technique with alcoholic Korsakoff patients, chronic alcoholics, and normal controls. Their dichotic technique involved a simultaneous presentation of two single digits, one to the subject's right ear and one to the left, at the rate of one pair every 1.2 seconds. The subject was instructed to press a response key whenever the digit pairs had certain preselected spatial and/or identity features. Four conditions of dichotic presentation that made progressively greater demands with regard to stimulus analysis were administered to each subject.

The results showed that as the demands for stimulus analysis became greater, the alcoholic Korsakoff patients became increasingly impaired relative to the normal control group and made numerous commission errors, indicating an incomplete or partial stimulus analysis. It appeared that, under conditions requiring complex decision processes, the alcoholic Korsakoff patients did not fully analyze or attend to all of the incoming information. Glosser et al. (1976) provided some evidence that this deficit was time-dependent. When the interval was increased from 1.2 to 2.0 seconds, the number of commission errors committed by the Korsakoff patients was significantly reduced.

The limited encoding hypothesis has also been used to analyze the alcoholic Korsakoff patients' difficulties in analyzing and retaining complex visuoperceptive materials. It has been shown that alcoholic Korsakoff patients are impaired in their STM for random geometric forms (DeLuca et al., 1975), on digit-symbol substitution tasks (Talland, 1965; Glosser et al., 1977; Kapur and Butters, 1977), and on visual card-sorting tasks (Oscar-Berman, 1973; Oscar-Berman and Samuels, 1977). Oscar-Berman and Samuels reported that the alcoholic Korsakoff patients' perceptual problems may be indicative of a limited, partial analysis of all the attributes of visual stimuli. Their patients were trained to discriminate between complex visual stimuli differing on a number of relevant dimensions and then were administered transfer tasks to assess which of the relevant stimulus dimensions had been noted. While the intact controls showed transfer to all relevant stimulus dimensions, the Korsakoff patients' discriminations were based upon only one or two relevant features of the stimuli.

Dricker et al. (1978) used a series of facial recognition and matching tasks to determine whether the alcoholic Korsakoff patients' amnesia for faces is attributable to a general limitation in their analyses of nonverbal stimuli. On an initial task, they found that the Korsakoff patients not only were unable to recognize 12 photographs of faces after a 90-second delay but also made numerous errors on a simple facial matching task when a single target photograph and 25 comparison faces were exposed simultaneously. On a second test, the Korsakoff patients and control subjects were administered a facial matching task (developed by Diamond and Carey, 1977) that compared their tendency to use superficial, piecemeal cues (i.e., paraphernalia and expression) and more advanced configurational cues (i.e., the spatial relationships between the eyes, nose, and mouth) in their analysis. On each trial, the subjects were presented simultaneously with a target face and two comparison faces and had to indicate which of the two comparison faces was the same as the target. Under two conditions, paraphernalia was used to fool the subject; under two other conditions, facial expression was used for this purpose. For instance, the target face and the incorrect comparison face might be wearing the same hat or might be smiling in a similar manner. To select the correct comparison face on such trials, the subject had to reject superficial, peicemeal similarities and extend the analysis to the configurational features of the three faces.

The findings demonstrated that alcoholic Korsakoff patients were often fooled both by paraphernalia and by facial expression, although paraphernalia seemed to be the most distracting of the two cues. Dricker et al. (1978) concluded that, just as Korsakoff patients fail to encode all of the attributes of verbal material, they also incompletely and superficially analyze nonverbal visual stimuli. If this limited perceptual analysis is a general cognitive characteristic of the amnesic Korsakoff patient, it might at least partially explain the difficulties in learning, remembering, and perceiving nonverbal patterned materials.

With orientation tasks analogous to those used by Cermak and Reale (1978) and by McDowall (1979), two sets of investigators have evaluated the applicability of the limited analysis hypothesis to the Korsakoff patients' deficits in face perception. Mayes et al. (1980) compared alcoholic Korsakoff patients and normal controls on a face recognition task in which the subjects performed a high-level orientation task, a low-level orientation task, or received no specific instructions while examining the photographs. The high-level task was chosen because it presumably encouraged configurational analysis of faces, whereas the low-level task focused the subject's attention on the superficial features of faces. If the Korsakoff patients' impairments on face recognition tests are due to their lack of configurational analysis, they should benefit more than normal controls from the high-level procedure. The results did not substantiate this prediction. While both the Korsakoff patients and normal controls recognized more faces with high-level instructions than faces assigned to the other two experimental conditions, the two groups did not differ in the degree to which their recognition was facilitated. In view of these results, Mayes et al. dismissed deficiencies in perceptual encoding as the primary factor contributing to Korsakoff patients' nonverbal memory problems.

Another study (Biber et al., 1981) using an orientation procedure in an attempt to improve face recognition reported evidence that is consistent with the limited encoding hypothesis. Patients with alcoholic Korsakoff's syndrome, patients with Huntington's disease, patients with right hemisphere damage, and normal control subjects were administered a face recognition task under three experimental conditions that presumably induced different levels of analysis. The recognition scores of the Korsakoff patients, but not those of the other two patient groups, improved significantly following a high-level orientation task requiring the subjects to judge the "likeability" of the faces. Under baseline conditions (i.e., no orientation task), normal controls appeared to spontaneously encode faces in a manner induced by the high-level task, whereas the Korsakoff patients used strategies consistent with the low-level orientation task. These findings, shown in Fig. 14-10, closely parallel those reported by McDowall (1979) using verbal material and a semantic orientation task.

Although Biber et al.'s (1981) results suggest that faulty stimulus analysis plays an important and special role in the alcoholic Korsakoff patients' inability to recognize faces, their findings can also be explained by motivational-arousal concepts. Several investigators have remarked on the passivity and the lack of initiative of alcoholic Korsakoff patients (Talland, 1965; Victor et al., 1971; Oscar-Berman, 1980) and have suggested that reduced motivation may contribute to the patients' severe learning and memory problems. Adapting methods borrowed from animal learning studies, Oscar-Berman and her collaborators (1976, 1980) found that alcoholic Korsakoff patients evidence reduced responsiveness to the effects of positive reinforcement. When confronted with a two-choice spatial probability learning test in which the two spatial alternatives were reinforced on a 70:30 or a 30:70 ratio, normal controls altered their response tendencies to match the reinforcement contingencies. In marked contrast to the malleability of the normals' behavior, the alcoholic Korsakoff patients continued to respond to each spatial alternative 50 percent of the time and seemed totally unaffected by the prevailing reinforcement contingencies (Oscar-Berman et al., 1976). In a second experiment (Oscar-Berman et al., 1980), Korsakoff patients and normal controls were placed on a complex concurrent variable schedule of reinforcement. As with the spatial probability learning test, the responses of the normal controls, but not those of the Korsakoff patients, matched the reinforcement contingencies present in the experimental situation. In view of such demonstrations of motivational anomalies

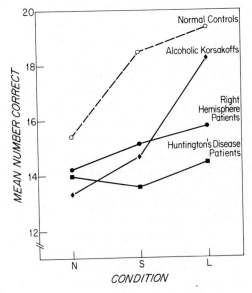

Fig. 14-10. Number of faces correctly identified by four subject groups after free study (S), nose judgements (N), and likeability judgments (L). (From Biber et al., 1981)

in Korsakoff patients, Oscar-Berman (1980) urged caution in explaining all of the Korsakoff patients' memory deficits strictly from a cognitive perspective. In Biber et al.'s (1981) study, the process of making a likeability judgment (high-level orientation task) may have motivational as well as cognitive consequences and the significant improvement in the memory of the alcoholic Korsakoff patients following these judgements may reflect some form of affective-motivational arousal.

Payne and Butters (1983) have presented additional evidence for the role of motivational-arousal factors in the memory disorders of alcoholic Korsakoff patients. They found that the Korsakoff patients' overall recall of short passages (similar to those used on the Wechsler Memory Scale) was greatly enhanced by embedding a single sexual reference within the story. Not only did the Korsakoff patients recall the sexual segment, but they also demonstrated significant improvement in the recall of neutral story segments that preceded and followed the sexual reference. When the same stories were read to normal controls and to demented patients with severe memory defects, the sexual segments did not lead to improved recall.

While interference-retrieval and stimulus encoding theories have dominated the amnesia literature during the past 12 years, other investigators (Kinsbourne and Wood, 1975; Huppert and Piercy, 1976; Winocur and Kinsbourne, 1976, 1978; Winocur et al., 1981) have suggested that amnesic memory deficits reflect a specific failure to retrieve the contextual attributes of verbal materials. That is, Korsakoff patients may be able to encode many of the specific physical or semantic attributes of stimuli but fail to discriminate the unique spatial and temporal contexts in which the stimuli were encountered. As a result of this deficit, the patients may later recognize the stimulus as familiar but cannot "recall" when or where they experienced the stimulus. It is important to note that these context theories focus on retrieval rather than on storage processes. Although Korsakoff patients are viewed as having normal encoding processes, it is believed that they are severely impaired in generating efficient temporal and spatial retrieval strategies to search their memory stores.

Kinsbourne and Wood (1975) tied their context-retrieval theory to Tulving's (1972) distinction between episodic and semantic memory and suggested that the amnesic syndrome represents a loss of episodic memory. The fact that amnesics do not forget the meaning of words, the rules of syntax, and basic arithmetical procedures is considered by Kinsbourne and Wood as evidence of an intact semantic memory. Weingartner et al. (1983) expanded this episodic-semantic distinction to encompass patients with progressive dementias as well as patients with relatively pure amnesic syndromes. According to these investigators, amnesia represents a loss of episodic memory whereas dementia involves a failure in both episodic and semantic memory. While this proposal with regard to amnesic patients is an intriguing one, it fails to account for the amnesic patients' severe retrograde amnesia discussed earlier in this chapter. It is difficult to understand how the Korsakoff patients' failure to identify photographs of Harry Truman or Elvis Presley can be viewed as an inability to retrieve specific episodic experiences. In addition, labeling a memory disorder as "episodic" or "semantic" may be purely descriptive and relate little about the mechanisms underlying the disorder.

Empirical evidence supporting context theories of amnesia can be found in an experiment by Huppert and Piercy (1976). These investigators showed 80 pictures to alcoholic Korsakoff patients and normal controls on day 1 and then 80 more on day 2. Day 2 pictures consisted of 40 new pictures and 40 repeats from day 1. Ten minutes after the exposure of the 80th picture on day 2, the subjects were presented with 160 pictures and asked to respond to the questions "Did you ever see this picture before?" and "Was it presented today?" Of the 160 pictures, 120 had been exposed previously (on day 1 and/or day 2) and 40 were "fillers" that had not been used on either day. Of the 120 that had been exposed previously, 40 had been shown only on day 1, 40 only on day 2, and 40 on both day 1 and day 2. The alcoholic Korsakoff patients had no difficulty determining whether they had or had not seen a picture previously but made false positive responses in answering the second question. In other words, the patients were able to recognize that they had viewed a picture but could not place this experience in a particular temporal context.

Two investigations by Winocur and Kinsbourne (1976, 1978) showed that the verbal learning of alcoholic Korsakoff patients can be improved by increasing the saliency of contextual cues. In their first investigation, amnesic patients and controls were required to learn two lists of verbal paired associates under conditions that maximized the interference between the lists (i.e., both lists contained the same stimulus but different response elements). In one condition, greater discriminability between the lists was achieved by printing the stimulus materials from list 1 and list 2 on cards of different colors. In another procedure, the stimulus and response elements from list 1 were combined and then served as the stimulus elements for list 2. For example, "battle-soldier" in list 1 became "battle, soldier-army" in list 2. Winocur and Kinsbourne postulated that this manipulation would eliminate interference by circumventing any tendency to emit the list 1 response during list 2 learning. Both procedures led to a reduction in intrusion errors in the learning of list 2, and with the latter manipulation the Korsakoff patients' rate of learning was significantly improved. In their second investigation, Winocur and Kinsbourne reported two additional methods of increasing the saliency of contextual cues for the alcoholic Korsakoff patients. Introducing a three-minute walk between the learning of the two lists and changing the room illumination for each list were manipulations sufficient to reduce PI from list 1 during the Korsakoff patients' attempts to learn list 2.

Winocur et al. (1981) suggested that the Korsakoff patients' ability to discriminate contexts also affects their performance on release from PI tasks. Alcoholic Korsakoff patients and normal subjects were asked to recall successive lists of nine nouns drawn from the same taxonomic category. In the no-shift (control) condition, the same category of nouns was used for five successive lists; in the shift (experimental) condition, a new taxonomic category was introduced on the fifth list after a single category had been used on the first four lists. Both groups demonstrated progressive decrements in performance over the five lists in the no-shift condition. When no effort was made to increase the contextual saliency of the fourth and fifth lists in the shift condition, only the normal control subjects evidenced a significant improvement in performance on the fifth list. However, if the subjects were provided with an instructional set warning them of the impending taxonomic change, or if the words making up the fourth and fifth lists were printed in inks of different colors, the Korsakoff patients also recalled more words on the fifth than on the fourth list (i.e., release from PI). On the basis of these findings, Winocur et al. concluded that the alcoholic Korsakoff patients' failure to release from PI was due not to a deficit in semantic encoding (Cermak et al., 1974) but rather to an inability to contextually discriminate the words of the fourth and fifth lists.

At this point, it is important to recall Moscovitch's (1982) and Squire's (1982) evidence that the alcoholic Korsakoff patients' failure to release from PI may be an indicator of possible frontal lobe damage rather than a phenomenon closely linked to their amnesic syndrome. When this finding is combined with Winocur et al.'s demonstration of the importance of contextual factors in release from PI, it follows that impairments in the retrieval of contextual cues may be more characteristic of the cognitive problems of frontal lobe patients than of the amnesic syndromes of hippocampal or diencephalic patients. Milner (1971), reporting an unpublished study by Corsi, provided empirical evidence that the left and right frontal lobes are involved in the "time-tagging" and temporal ordering of verbal and nonverbal materials, respectively. Patients with frontal, temporal, or combined fronto-temporal lobectomies were presented with a series of 184 cards with two words (or reproductions of abstract art for the nonverbal test) printed on each card. On recognition test trials, the patients had to indicate which of the two words (or pictures of art) had been presented previously during the test. On recency test trials, the patients had to judge which of the two stimuli had been exposed more recently (i.e., a contextual judgment). Whereas patients with combined fronto-temporal lobectomies performed poorly on both recognition and recency judgments (with left hemisphere patients impaired on the verbal test and the right hemisphere patients on the nonverbal task), the patients with lesions limited to one lobe or the other could be dissociated on the basis of their performance on the two judgment tasks. Patients with left temporal lobectomies were impaired only on verbal recognition judgments, and left frontal patients performed at chance levels only on the verbal recency problems. A similar dissociation between right-frontal and right-temporal patients was found with the nonverbal materials. Milner emphasizes that, despite their difficulty in making contextual judgments, none of her frontal-lobe patients were amnesic by conventional clinical criteria. It would appear then that the inability to retrieve the temporal and spatial contexts in which material is presented may be pronounced and enduring but still be unrelated causally to the anterograde memory deficits of amnesic patients.

Another weakness of context-retrieval theories of amnesia should be mentioned. Despite the emphasis investigators have placed on the retrieval process (Kinsbourne and Wood, 1975), the patients' failure to discriminate contexts may have its origin during the storage stage. Context is just one of the many attributes intact individuals encode in memorizing verbal and nonverbal materials. If alcoholic Korsakoff patients have a general limitation in stimulus analysis (Butters and Cermak, 1980), then an impairment in contextual encoding, like the aforementioned problems in semantic analysis, may be a single exemplar of a more pervasive processing problem. The fact that increments in contextual saliency reduced but did not eliminate the alcoholic Korsakoff patients' impairment in verbal learning (Winocur and Kinsbourne, 1976, 1978) is consistent with the possibility that a combination of encoding deficiencies is involved.

Other studies bearing directly upon the nature of the amnesic patients' anterograde amnesias have focused upon the forgetting of newly acquired pictorial information by patients with hippocampal (e.g., patient H. M.) or diencephalic (e.g., patient N. A., alcoholic Korsakoff patients) lesions. Huppert and Piercy (1977, 1978, 1979) reported that when H. M., alcoholic Korsakoff patients, and normal control subjects attain the same level of initial learning, important differences emerge in their rates of forgetting over seven days. To ensure that all subjects would attain approximately the same level of learning after a 10-minute delay, exposure time during the initial presentation of the pictures was manipulated to ensure a performance level of at least 75 per cent correct.

Huppert and Piercy's studies showed that, although patient H. M., normal subjects, and alcoholic Korsakoff patients all performed more poorly on recognition tasks with increasing retention intervals (one day, seven days), patient H. M.'s performance evidenced a much steeper rate of forgetting than did the scores of the other two groups. Huppert and Piercy suggest that the anterograde amnesias of H. M. and the alcoholic Korsakoff patients involve different deficits in information processing. The Korsakoff patients' difficulties may emanate from a lack of stimulus analysis or encoding. When provided with sufficient time to fully analyze a complex stimulus, these patients are capable of learning and demonstrate normal recognition over an extended period of time. H. M.'s rapid decline cannot, however, be accounted for by such a cognitive deficit. Huppert and Piercy postulate that H. M.'s difficulty in learning new materials may also reflect a deficit in stimulus analysis but that his inability to retain newly learned material may be an indicator of an additional problem with consolidation and storage.

Squire (1981) evaluated patient N. A., alcoholic Korsakoff patients, and depressed patients receiving bilateral ECT on pictorial and verbal forgetting tasks in which recognition was assessed after 10-minute, 2-hour, and 32-hour delays. His results were consistent with those of Huppert and Piercy. Patient N. A. and the alcoholic Korsakoff patients forgot at normal rates over the 32-hour period, whereas patients receiving ECT evidenced an accelerated decay of pictorial and verbal material during the same time period. Based upon his data and those of Huppert and Piercy, Squire proposes that ECT affects memory by disrupting hippocampal mechanisms used in consolidation. He also concludes that amnesic symptoms associated with diencephalic and hippocampal dysfunction are dissociable in terms of the stage of information processing adversely affected.

By this time readers should be convinced that the application of information processing concepts to neuropsychological studies of amnesia is a relatively new venture and that a solid empirical base upon which to develop theories is just beginning to emerge. Few should be surprised, then, that all the currently popular theories of amnesia are deficient in their explanations of the myriad symptoms associated with the disorder. Retrograde amnesia, in particular, represents a most difficult symptom for interference-retrieval, encoding, and context-retrieval theories to explain, and it is therefore not by accident that theorists have focused their empirical efforts on the patients' deficits in the acquisition and retention of new materials (i.e., anterograde amnesia). Ultimately, it may prove more beneficial for cognitive theorists to accept the independence of anterograde and retrograde amnesia and to develop separate models to explain these two symptoms.

Similarities and Differences Among Amnesic Patients

Since amnesia has been associated with a number of etiologies (vascular, alcohol, viral, trauma) and brain sites (hippocampus, mammillary bodies, midline thalamic nuclei), it is important to determine whether or not all amnesias reflect the same underlying impairments. The previously reviewed data concerning retrograde amnesia certainly suggest that important differences exist. The retrograde amnesias of H. M., N. A., and depressed patients receiving bilateral ECT were significantly more limited temporally than those of alcoholic Korsakoff patients (Albert et al., 1979; Cohen and Squire, 1981; Squire and Cohen, 1982). Furthermore, the retrograde amnesia of alcoholic Korsakoff patients has been reported to differ from that of patients with progressive degenerative dementias (Albert et al., 1981; Wilson et al., 1981). In contrast to the Korsakoff's relative sparing of very remote memories, patients with Huntington's disease (Albert et al., 1981) and patients with Alzheimer's disease (Wilson et al., 1981) display an equivalent loss of remote memories from all periods of their lives.

Despite this evidence for the heterogeneity of amnesic syndromes, Warrington and her collaborators have championed the position that amnesia is a unitary disorder regardless of the etiology or locus of the lesion (e.g., Baddeley and Warrington, 1970; Warrington and Weiskrantz, 1973). Their investigations of amnesia have included patients with alcoholic, viral, anoxic, and surgical etiologies, and they report that all these patients performed similarly on various learning and cognitive tasks. All appeared to perform normally on Brown-Peterson STM tasks, to be highly sensitive to PI, and to exhibit similar encoding strategies.

Other investigators have addressed the issue of the heterogeneity of amnesic syndromes by comparing the performances of alcoholic Korsakoff patients and postencephalitic (herpes simplex encephalitis) patients. Zangwill (1966) observed on the basis of clinical observations that these two groups were quite different. He noted that alcoholic Korsakoff patients, but not the postencephalitics, manifested cognitive changes that included an increased tendency to confabulate and a lack of insight into the nature of their illness. Lhermitte and Signoret (1972) compared these two groups on four tasks that involved the memorizing of a spatial array, a verbal sequence, a logical arrangement, and a code. On the first task, the alcoholic Korsakoff patients showed better retention than did the postencephalitic patients. However, on the other three tasks, not only were the postencephalitics superior to the Korsakoff patients, but they also did not differ from normal controls. Mattis et al. (1978) have also reported different patterns of memory deficits in alcoholic Korsakoff and postencephalitic patients with tests using recall, recognition, and d' measures of learning and retention. In this study, the postencephalitic patients showed little evidence of encoding and storage of any information whereas the recognition memory of Korsakoff and normal control subjects was similar for novel information. Consistent with predictions derived from semantic encoding theory (Butters and Cermak, 1980), recognition memory for English words was significantly impaired for alcoholic Korsakoff patients and worsened with increased semantic organization of the material. Mattis et al. concluded that their results are consistent with Lhermitte and Signoret's (1972) findings that postencephalitic and alcoholic Korsakoff patients have qualitatively distinct memory disorders.

Butters and Cermak (1980) compared 11 alcoholic Korsakoff patients and 4 post-encephalitic patients on Brown-Peterson distractor tasks. All four postencephalitic patients performed within the normal range, and as a group they recalled significantly more items than did the alcoholic Korsakoff patients. One of these patients (S. S.), a middle-aged optical engineer with a postgraduate education, has been described in detail by Cermak (1976; Cermak and O'Connor, 1983) and by Butters et al. (1983). Despite a total inability to retain new verbal information for more than a few minutes and to learn even simple verbal paired associates over many trials, S. S.'s scores on the Brown-Peterson task were superior to those of the vast majority of normal control subjects that these investigators tested. Interestingly, S. S. demonstrated normal release from PI when Wickens' technique was used (Cermak, 1976).

Although postencephalitic patients are usually normal on tests of STM, their performance on tests of retrograde amnesia is often worse than that of alcoholic Korsakoff patients and does not demonstrate the same degree of sparing of very remote memories. When Albert et al.'s (1979) retrograde amnesia battery was administered to both alcoholic Korsakoff and postencephalitic patients, Butters and Cermak (1980) found that postencephalitic patients performed more poorly than did alcoholic Korsakoff patients and did not evidence the same temporal gradient. For example, on the hard items drawn from Albert et al.'s famous faces test, the postencephalitic patients not only demonstrated an extensive retrograde amnesia encompassing a 20-to-40 year period of their lives but also evidenced little sparing of memories from the very remote past. Cermak and O'Connor (1983) and Butters et al. (1983) recently reevaluated S. S.'s retrograde amnesia 10 years following the acute onset of his encephalitis and found the severity and extent of his impairment unchanged. His ability to access or search for major public events and personal episodes that occurred prior to 1970 is very limited.

This dissociation of performance on Brown-Peterson distractor and remote memory tasks is exemplified in Figs. 14-11 and 14-12, which depict graphically the amnesia of an 18-year-old woman (L. D.) who suffered a severe attack of herpes simplex encephalitis during the summer of 1981. Although she evidenced both aphasic and amnesic symptoms initially, the former had resolved itself by the time the present authors evaluated her seven months after the onset of symptoms. At the time of testing, her major complaints dealt with her inability to recall past events and to remember new information for more than a few minutes. As seen in Fig. 14-11, L. D., like all amnesic patients, was unable to learn paired associates. Despite this severe impairment in associative learning, L. D. did perform at, or close to, normal levels on several Brown-Peterson tasks using consonant trigrams or word triads as the material to be recalled. Figure 14-12 shows L. D.'s severe impairment on a famous faces test and a public events recall questionnaire covering 1970 to 1982. Although this testing of retrograde amnesia was limited to 12 years because of the patient's age, two points are evident when her performance and those of eight control subjects are compared. One, L. D.'s retrograde amnesia is severe, and two, it encompasses the entire 12-year period tested without any hint of sparing of even the most remote memories. Clinical evaluation of her autobiographical remote memory indicated that she could not recall her parent's divorce, her high school graduation, or any social episodes involving close friends or even the young man she had been dating prior to her illness.

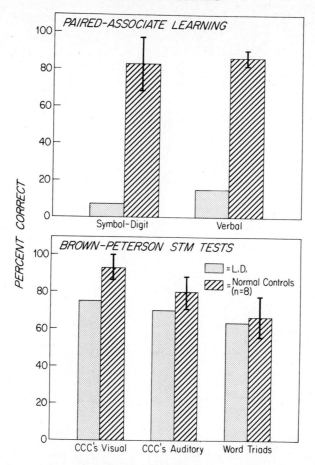

Fig. 14-11. Performance of postencephalitic patient L. D. on two paired associate learning tasks (top) and on three Brown-Peterson distractor tasks (bottom). Also shown are the performances of eight normal control subjects. The vertical lines indicate the 98 per cent confidence limits for the means of the normal control subjects.

The extensive retrograde amnesia manifested by S. S., L. D., and other postencephalitic patients poses two problems for clinicians and experimenters concerned with amnesic syndromes. If one accepts the premise that retrograde amnesia, in its pure form (e.g., patients H. M. and N. A.), is usually very brief, how do we explain the extended and severe losses of alcoholic Korsakoff and of postencephalitic patients? As noted previously, it has been suggested (Butters and Albert, 1982; Squire and Cohen, 1982) that some of the alcoholic Korsakoff patients' loss of remote memory may be artifactual. Since long-term alcoholics may retain somewhat less information each year due to a chronic learning deficit and to disinterest, their store of remote memories for the recent past may be mildly or moderately deficient. If some acute "forgetting" appears during the Wernicke stage of the illness (as with patient P. Z.) and is superimposed on the alcoholic patients' already deficient store, a severe retrograde amnesia with a steep temporal gradient might be expected. There is some evidence

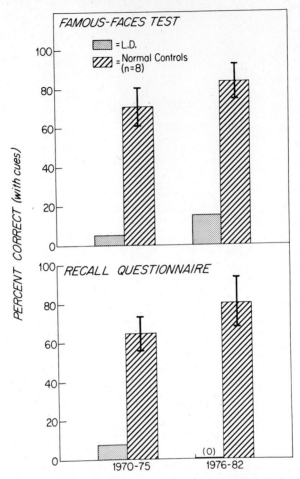

Fig. 14-12. Performance of postencephalitic patient L. D. and eight normal control subjects on famous faces test (top) and public events recall questionnaire (bottom). Because of L. D.'s age, only the period between 1970 and 1982 was tested. The vertical lines indicate the 98 per cent confidence limits for the means of the normal control subjects.

that this model may have some validity for the alcoholic Korsakoff patient (Albert et al., 1980; Cohen and Squire, 1981), but it obviously cannot account for the severe memory loss of patients like S. S. Since postencephalitic patients do not approach the acute onset of their disorder with a deficient store of information, their retrograde amnesia must reflect a general retrieval difficulty or a pervasive degrading and loss of old memories. Cermak and O'Connor (1983), in their extensive reevaluation of S. S., reported some evidence that favors some form of retrieval impairment.

A second unresolved issue is the remarkable contrast between the retrograde amnesias of postencephalitic patients like S. S. and L. D. and of patient H. M. (who had bilateral temporal lobectomies for epilepsy). Because the memory problems of both H. M. and postencephalitic patients have been attributed to bilateral destruction of the hippocampi in the mesial temporal region (Scoville and Milner, 1957; Drachman

and Adams, 1962; Drachman and Arbit, 1966; Milner, 1966, 1970), one might anticipate that their memory disorders would be quantitatively and qualitatively similar.
However, unlike the limited loss of remote memories reported for H. M., all of the
postencephalitic patients evaluated with Albert et al.'s (1979) famous faces test and
public events questionnaire were found to have severe retrograde amnesias involving
several decades of their lives (Butters and Cermak, 1980). One possible explanation
for this difference may involve the extent of hippocampal and temporal lobe damage.
If anterograde and retrograde amnesias are separable along the anterior-posterior axis
of the temporal lobes (Fedio and Van Buren, 1974), then it is possible that S. S. and
other postencephalitic patients have more extensive (and posterior) temporal lobe
damage than does H. M. The fact that postencephalitic patients often have mild
aphasic disorders certainly suggests that their lesions extend more posteriorly and lat-
erally than H. M.'s anterior and mesial surgical ablation. Presumably, the more posterior the lesion, the more severe the patient's retrograde amnesia may be. What are
needed are some animal studies comparing the effects of anterior and posterior hippocampal ablations on the retention of information learned prior to the surgical
procedure.

It was noted previously that patients with Huntington's disease differ markedly
from Korsakoff patients in the nature of their retrograde amnesia, and further differences between these groups have emerged from comparisons of their anterograde
amnesia. Butters and Cermak (1976, 1980) have reported that, although alcoholic
Korsakoff and HD patients are severely impaired on STM tasks, the HD patients'
disturbances seem relatively unrelated to PI. Korsakoff patients' recall improves when
low-interference (e.g., distributed rather than massed presentation trials) conditions
are used, but such manipulations of interference have little or no effect upon the
performance of HD patients. Caine et al. (1977) and Weingartner et al. (1979) successfully demonstrated verbal encoding difficulties in HD patients, but the similarities
and differences between these cognitive deficits and those reported for Korsakoff
patients (Butters and Cermak, 1980) have not been elucidated. Most recently, Butters
et al. (1983) have shown that, although both Korsakoff and HD patients are severely
impaired in their memory for pictorial material, the HD patients can utilize verbal
mediators (i.e., elaborators) to significantly improve retention. This finding provides
legitimacy for other dissociations between Korsakoff and HD patients. Although the
studies of patients' STM, retrograde amnesia, and memory for faces (Biber et al.,
1981) suggested significant differences between HD and Korsakoff patients, none of
them provided the elusive double dissociation needed to firmly establish the claim for
qualitative differences in the memory disorders of the two groups.

Oscar-Berman and Zola-Morgan (1980a, 1980b) compared alcoholic Korsakoff and
HD patients on visual and spatial discrimination tasks. In an initial experiment
(Oscar-Berman and Zola-Morgan, 1980a), visual and spatial reversal learning tests
were administered. Korsakoff patients were impaired on both types of reversal problems, and HD patients had difficulty only with the visual reversals. An inspection of
the types of errors compiled on the visual reversal tasks suggested that the HD and
Korsakoff patients' deficiencies involved different learning, cognitive, and motivational mechanisms. In a second experiment (Oscar-Berman and Zola-Morgan, 1980b),
both groups learned a series of two-choice simultaneous and concurrent pattern dis-

criminations. Again both groups were impaired, but they differed in the nature of their deficits. The HD patients were equally impaired on simultaneous and concurrent discriminations, whereas the Korsakoff patients encountered more difficulty with the concurrent than with the simultaneous tests. In summarizing their findings, Oscar-Berman and Zola-Morgan (1980b) suggested that, although both groups are deficient in their ability to form stimulus-reinforcement associations, the deficiency in Korsakoff patients also involves an increased sensitivity to PI and a lack of sensitivity to reinforcement contingencies.

While the exact processing deficits involved in the amnesic symptoms of various brain-damaged groups remain largely unknown, the evidence does suggest that the amnesic disorders manifested by patients with differing disease etiologies may not be identical on neuropsychological tests. Damage to the hippocampus, lesions of the mammillary bodies and the mesial thalamus, and perhaps even damage to other subcortical and cortical structures may all produce memory disturbances, but the specific processes underlying these deficits may vary depending on the lesion site. Intact memory may depend on an intact limbic-diencephalic-cortical circuit, but damage at different points in the circuit does not necessarily result in the same pattern of neuropsychological deficits.

REFERENCES

Albert, M. S., Butters, N., and Brandt, J. (1980). Memory for remote events in alcoholics. *J. Stud. Alcohol* 41:1071–1081.

Albert, M. S., Butters, N., and Brandt, J. (1981). Patterns of remote memory in amnesic and demented patients. *Arch. Neurol.* 38:495–500.

Albert, M. S., Butters, N., and Levin, J. (1979). Temporal gradients in the retrograde amnesia of patients with alcoholic Korsakoff's disease. *Arch. Neurol.* 36:211–216.

Baddeley, A. D., and Warrington, E. K. (1970). Amnesia and the distinction between long- and short-term memory. *J. Verbal Learning Verbal Behav.* 9:176–189.

Benson, D. F., and Geschwind, N. (1967). Shrinking retrograde amnesia. *J. Neurol. Neurosurg. Psychiat.* 30:539–544.

Biber, C., Butters, N., Rosen, J., Gerstmann, L., and Mattis, S. (1981). Encoding strategies and recognition of faces by alcoholic Korsakoff and other brain-damaged patients. *J. Clin. Neuropsychol.* 3:315–330.

Brandt, J., Butters, N., Ryan, C., and Bayog, R. (1983). Cognitive loss and recovery in chronic alcohol abusers. *Arch. Gen. Psychiat.* 40:435–442.

Brown, J. (1958). Some tests of the decay theory of immediate memory. *Quart. J. Exp. Psychol.* 10:12–21.

Butters, N., and Albert, M. S. (1982). Processes underlying failures to recall remote events. In *Human Memory and Amnesia* (L. S. Cermak, ed.). Hillsdale, N.J.: Erlbaum.

Butters, N., and Cermak, L. S. (1974). The role of cognitive factors in the memory disorder of alcoholic patients with the Korsakoff syndrome. *Ann. N. Y. Acad. Sci.* 233:61–75.

Butters, N., and Cermak, L. S. (1975). Some analyses of amnesic syndromes in brain-damaged patients. In *The Hippocampus* (K. Pribram and R. Isaacson, eds.). New York: Plenum Press.

Butters, N., and Cermak, L. S. (1976). Neuropsychological studies of alcoholic Korsakoff patients. In *Empirical Studies of Alcoholism* (G. Goldstein and C. Neuringer, eds.). Cambridge, Mass: Ballinger Press.

Butters, N., and Cermak, L. S. (1980). *Alcoholic Korsakoff's Syndrome: An Information Processing Approach to Amnesia.* New York: Academic Press.

Butters, N., Lewis, R., Cermak, L. S., and Goodglass, H. (1973). Material-specific memory deficits in alcoholic Korsakoff patients. *Neuropsychologia 11:*291–299.

Butters, N., Miliotis, P., Albert, M. S., and Sax, D. S. (1983). Memory assessment: Evidence of the heterogeneity of amnesic symptoms. In *Advances in Clinical Neuropsychology,* vol. I, (G. Goldstein, ed.). New York: Plenum Press (in press).

Butters, N., Tarlow, S., Cermak, L. S., and Sax, D. (1976). A comparison of the information processing deficits of patients with Huntington's chorea and Korsakoff's syndrome. *Cortex 12:*134–144.

Caine, E. D., Ebert, M. H., and Weingartner, H. (1977). An outline for the analysis of dementia: The memory disorder of Huntington's Disease. *Neurology 27:*1087–1092.

Cermak, L. S. (1976). The encoding capacity of a patient with amnesia due to encephalitis. *Neuropsychologia 14:*311–326.

Cermak, L. S., and Butters, N. (1972). The role of interference and encoding in the short-term memory deficits of Korsakoff patients. *Neuropsychologia 10:*89–96.

Cermak, L. S., and Butters, N. (1973). Information processing deficits of alcoholic Korsakoff patients. *Quart. J. Studies Alcohol 34:*1110–1132.

Cermak, L. S., and O'Connor, M. (1983). The anterograde and retrograde retrieval capacity of a patient with amnesia due to encephalitis. *Neuropsychologia* (in press).

Cermak, L. S., and Reale, L. (1978). Depth of processing and retention of words by alcoholic Korsakoff patients. *J. Exp. Psychol.: Human Learning and Memory 4:*165–174.

Cermak, L. S., Butters, N., and Gerrein, J. (1973). The extent of the verbal encoding ability of Korsakoff patients. *Neuropsychologia 11:*85–94.

Cermak, L. S., Butters, N., and Goodglass, H. (1971). The extent of memory loss in Korsakoff patients. *Neuropsychologia 9:*307–315.

Cermak, L. S., Butters, N., and Moreines, J. (1974). Some analyses of the verbal encoding deficit of alcoholic Korsakoff patients. *Brain and Language 1:*141–150.

Cermak, L. S., Naus, M. J., and Reale, L. (1976). Rehearsal and organizational strategies of alcoholic Korsakoff patients. *Brain and Language 3:*375–385.

Cohen, N. J., and Corkin, S. (1981). The amnesic patient H. M.: Learning and retention of a cognitive skill. *Abstr. Soc. Neurosci. 80.2:*235.

Cohen, N. J., and Squire, L. R. (1980). Preserved learning and retention of pattern-analyzing skills in amnesia: Dissociation of knowing how and knowing that. *Science 210:*207–210.

Cohen, N. J., and Squire, L. R. (1981). Retrograde amnesia and remote memory impairment. *Neuropsychologia 19:*337–356.

Corkin, S. (1965). Tactually guided maze-learning in man: Effects of unilateral cortical excisions and bilateral hippocampal lesions. *Neuropsychologia 3:*339–351.

Corkin, S., Sullivan, E., Twitchell, T., and Grove, E. (1981). The amnesic patient H. M.: Clinical observations and test performance 28 years after operation. *Abstr. Soc. Neurosci. 80.1:*235.

Corsi, P. M. (1969). Verbal memory impairment after unilateral hippocampal excision. Paper presented at the 40th annual meeting of the Eastern Psychological Association, Philadelphia.

Craik, F. I. M., and Tulving, E. (1975). Depth of processing and retention of words in episodic memory. *J. Exp. Psychol.: General 104:*268–294.

DeLuca, D., Cermak, L. S., and Butters, N. (1975). An analysis of Korsakoff patients' recall following varying types of distractor activity. *Neuropsychologia 13:*271–279.

Diamond, R., and Carey, S. (1977). Developmental changes in the representation of faces. *J. Exp. Child Psychol. 23:*1–22.

Drachman, D. A., and Adams, R. D. (1962). Herpes simplex and acute inclusion body encephalitis. *Arch. Neurol. 7:*45–63.

Drachman, D. A., and Arbit, J. (1966). Memory and the hippocampal complex. *Arch. Neurol.*
*15:*52–61.

Dricker, J., Butters, N., Berman, G., Samuels, I., and Carey, S. (1978). Recognition and encoding of faces by alcoholic Korsakoff and right hemisphere patients. *Neuropsychologia*
*16:*683–695.

Eichenbaum, H., Potter, H., and Corkin, S. (1981). The amnesic patient H. M.: Severe selective olfactory discrimination deficit following bilateral temporal lobectomy. *Abstr. Soc.*
*Neurosci. 80.5:*236.

Fedio, P., and Van Buren, J. M. (1974). Memory deficits during electrical stimulation in the
speech cortex of conscious man. *Brain and Language 1:*29–42.

Gardner, H. (1975). *The Shattered Mind.* New York: Knopf.

Gerner, P., Ommaya, A., and Fedio, P. (1972). A study of visual memory: Verbal and nonverbal mechanisms in patients with unilateral lobectomy. *Intern. J. Neurosci. 4:*231–
238.

Glosser, G., Butters, N., and Kaplan, E. (1977). Visuoperceptual processes in brain-damaged
patients on the digit-symbol substitution tests. *Intern. J. Neurosci. 7:*59–66.

Glosser, G., Butters, N., and Samuels, I. (1976). Failures in information processing in patients
with Korsakoff's syndrome. *Neuropsychologia 14:*327–334.

Goldberg, E., Antin, S. P., Bilder, R. M. Jr., Hughes, J. E. O., and Mattis, S. (1981). Retrograde
amnesia: Possible role of mesencephalic reticular activation in long-term memory. *Science 213:*1392–1394.

Goldstein, G., and Shelly, C. H. (1971). Field dependence and cognitive, perceptual and
motor skills in alcoholics. *Quart. J. Studies Alcohol 32:*29–40.

Goodglass, H., and Peck, E. A. (1972). Dichotic ear order effects in Korsakoff and normal
subjects. *Neuropsychologia 10:*211–217.

Goodwin, D. W., and Hill, S. Y. (1975). Chronic effects of alcohol and other psychoactive
drugs on intellect, learning and memory. In *Alcohol, Drugs, and Brain Damage* (J. Ran-
kin, ed.). Ontario: Addiction Research Foundation.

Hebben, N., Shedlack, K., Eichenbaum, H., and Corkin, S. (1981). The amnesic patient H.
M.: Diminished ability to interpret and report internal states. *Abstr. Soc. Neurosci.*
*80.4:*235.

Heilman, K. M., an Sypert, G. W. (1977). Korsakoff's syndrome resulting from bilateral fornix
lesions. *Neurology 27:*490–493.

Hirst, W. (1982). The amnesic syndrome: Descriptions and explanations. *Psychological Bull.*
*91:*435–460.

Huppert, F. A., and Piercy, M. (1976). Recognition memory in amnesic patients: Effect of
temporal context and familiarity of material. *Cortex 12:*3–20.

Huppert, F. A., and Piercy, M. (1977). Recognition memory in amnesic patients: A defect of
acquisition? *Neuropsychologia 15:*643–652.

Huppert, F. A., and Piercy, M. (1978). Dissociation between learning and remembering in
organic amnesia. *Nature 275:*317–318.

Huppert, F. A., and Piercy, M. (1979). Normal and abnormal forgetting in organic amnesia:
Effect of locus of lesion. *Cortex 15:*385–390.

Jarho, L. (1973). *Korsakoff-like Amnesic Syndrome in Penetrating Brain Injury.* Helsinki:
Rehabilitation Institute for Brain Injured Veterans in Finland.

Jones, B. P., Butters, N., Moskowitz, H. R., and Montgomery, K. (1978). Olfactory and gustatory capacities of alcoholic Korsakoff patients. *Neuropsychologia 16:*323–337.

Jones, B. P., Moskowitz, H. R., and Butters, N. (1975a). Olfactory discrimination in alcoholic Korsakoff patients. *Neuropsychologia* 13:173–179.

Jones, B. P., Moskowitz, H. R., Butters, N., and Glosser, G. (1975b). Psychophysical scaling of olfactory, visual, and auditory stimuli by alcoholic Korsakoff patients. *Neuropsychologia* 13:387–393.

Jones, M. K. (1974). Imagery as a mnemonic aid after left temporal lobectomy; Contrast between material-specific and generalized memory disorders. *Neuropsychologia* 12:21–30.

Jones-Gotman, M., and Milner, B. (1978). Right temporal-lobe contribution to image-mediated verbal learning. *Neuropsychologia* 16:61–71.

Kahn, E. A., and Crosby, E. (1972). Korsakoff's syndrome associated with surgical lesions involving the mammilary bodies. *Neurology* 22:317–325.

Kapur, N., and Butters, N. (1977). Visuoperceptive deficits in long-term alcoholics with Korsakoff's psychosis. *J. Stud. Alcohol* 38:2025–2035.

Kimura, D. (1963). Right temporal lobe damage: Perception of unfamiliar stimuli after damage. *Arch. Neurol. (Chicago)* 8:264–271.

Kinsbourne, M., and Wood, F. (1975). Short-term memory processes and the amnesic syndrome. In *Short-Term Memory* (D. Deutsch and J. A. Deutsch, eds.). New York: Academic Press.

Kleinknecht, R. A., and Goldstein, S. G. (1972). Neuropsychological deficits associated with alcoholism. *Quart. J. Stud. Alcohol* 33:999–1019.

Lansdell, H. (1968). Effects of extent of temporal lobe ablations on two lateralized deficits. *Physiology of Behavior* 3:271–273.

Levin, H., Benton, A., and Grossman, R. (1982). *Neurobehavioral Consequences of Closed Head Injury.* New York: Oxford University Press.

Lhermitte, F., and Signoret, J.-L. (1972). Neuropsychological analysis and differentiation of amnesic syndromes. *Rev. Neurol.* 126:161–178.

Lishman, W. A. (1981). Cerebral disorder in alcoholism: Syndromes of impairment. *Brain* 104:1–20.

Mair, G. P., Warrington, E. K., and Weiskrantz, L. (1979). Memory disorder in Korsakoff's psychosis: A neurological and neuropsychological investigation of two cases. *Brain* 102:749–783.

Markowitsch, H. J. (1982). Thalamic mediodorsal nucleus and memory: A critical evaluation of studies in animals and man. *Neuroscience Biobehavioral Rev.* 6:351–380.

Marslen-Wilson, W. D., and Teuber, H.-L. (1975). Memory for remote events in anterograde amnesia: Recognition of public figures from news photographs. *Neuropsychologia* 13:347–352.

Mattis, S., Kovner, R., and Goldmeier, E. (1978). Different patterns of mnemonic deficits in two organic amnesic syndromes. *Brain and Language* 6:179–191.

Mayes, A., Meudell, P., and Neary, D. (1980). Do amnesics adopt inefficient encoding strategies with faces and random shapes? *Neuropsychologia* 18:527–540.

McDowall, J. (1979). Effects of encoding instructions and retrieval cueing on recall in Korsakoff patients. *Memory and Cognition* 7:232–239.

Meudell, P., and Mayes, A. (1981). Normal and abnormal forgetting: Some comments on the human amnesic syndrome. In *Normality and Pathology in Cognitive Function* (A. Ellis, Ed.). London: Academic Press.

Meudell, P. R., Butters, N., and Montgomey, K. (1978). Role of rehearsal in the short-term memory performance of patients with Korsakoff's and Huntington's disease. *Neuropsychologia* 16:507–510.

Meudell, P. R., Northern, B., Snowden, J. S., and Neary, D. (1980). Long-term memory for famous voices in amnesic and normal subjects. *Neuropsychologia 18:*133–139.

Milner, B. (1962). Les troubles de la memoire accompagnant des lesions hippocampiques bilaterales. In *Physiologies de l'Hippoampe*. Paris: C.N.R.S. English translation in *Cognitive Processes and the Brain* (P. M. Milner and S. Glickman, eds.), Princeton, N.J.: Van Nostrand.

Milner, B. (1963). Effects of different brain lesions on card sorting. *Arch. Neurol. 9:*90–100.

Milner, B. (1964). Some effects of frontal lobectomy in man. In *The Frontal Granular Cortex and Behavior* (J. M. Warren and K. Akert, eds.). New York: McGraw-Hill.

Milner, B. (1965). Visually-guided maze learning in man: Effects of bilateral hippocampal, bilateral frontal and unilateral cerebral lesions. *Neuropsychologia 3:*317–338.

Milner, B. (1966). Amnesia following operation on the temporal lobes. In *Amnesia* (C.W.M. Whitty and O. L. Zangwill, eds.). London: Butterworths.

Milner, B. (1967). Brain mechanisms suggested by studies of temporal lobes. In *Brain Mechanisms Underlying Speech and Language* (F. L. Darley, ed.). New York: Grune and Stratton.

Milner, B. (1968). Visual recognition and recall after right temporal-lobe excision in man. *Neuropsychologia 6:*191–210.

Milner, B. (1970). Memory and the medial temporal regions of the brain. In *Biology of Memory* (K. H. Pribram and D. E. Broadbent, eds.). New York: Academic Press.

Milner, B. (1971). Interhemispheric differences in the localization of psychological processes in man. *Br. Med. Bull. 27:*272–275.

Milner, B., Corkin, S., and Teuber, H.-L. (1968). Further analysis of the hippocampal amnesic syndrome: A 14-year follow-up study of H. M. *Neuropsychologia 6:*215–234.

Moscovitch, M. (1982). Multiple dissociations of functions in amnesia. In *Human Memory and Amnesia* (L. S. Cermak, ed.). Hillsdale, N.J.: Erlbaum.

Newcombe, F., and Russell, W. R. (1969). Dissociated visual perceptual and spatial deficits in focal lesions of the right hemisphere. *J. Neurol. Neurosurg. Psychiat. 32:*73–81.

Nissen, M., Cohen, N., and Corkin, S. (1981). The amnesic patient H. M.: Learning and retention of perceptual skills. *Abstr. Soc. Neurosci. 80.3:*235.

Oscar-Berman, M. (1973). Hypothesis testing and focusing behavior during concept formation by amnesic Korsakoff patients. *Neuropsychologia 11:*191–198.

Oscar-Berman, M. (1980). Neuropsychological consequences of long-term chronic alcoholism. *Am. Scientist 68:*410–419.

Oscar-Berman, M., and Samuels, I. (1977). Stimulus preference and memory factors in Korsakoff's syndrome. *Neuropsychologia 15:*99–106.

Oscar-Berman, M., and Zola-Morgan, S. M. (1980a). Comparative neuropsychology and Korsakoff's syndrome. I: Spatial and visual reversal learning. *Neuropsychologia 18:*499–512.

Oscar-Berman, M., and Zola-Morgan, S. M. (1980b). Comparative neuropsychology and Korsakoff's syndrome. II: Two-choice visual discrimination learning. *Neuropsychologia 18:*513–525.

Oscar-Berman, M., Heyman, G. M., Bonner, R. T., and Ryder, J. (1980). Human neuropsychology: Some differences between Korsakoff and normal operant performance. *Psychol. Res. 41:*235–247.

Oscar-Berman, M., Sahakian, B. J., and Wikmark, G. (1976). Spatial probability learning by alcoholic Korsakoff patients. *J. Exp. Psychol.: Human Learning and Memory 2:*215–222.

Parsons, O. A. (1975). Brain damage in alcoholics: Altered states of unconsciousness. In *Alcohol Intoxication and Withdrawal II* (M. Gross, ed.). New York: Plenum Press.

Parsons, O. A., and Farr, S. P. (1981). The neuropsychology of alcohol and drug abuse. In *Handbook of Clinical Neuropsychology* (S. B. Filskov and T. J. Boll, eds.). New York: Wiley.

Parsons, O. A., and Prigatano, G. P. (1977). Memory functioning in alcoholics. In *Alcohol and Human Memory* (I. M. Birnbaum and E. S. Parker, eds.). Hillsdale, N.J.: Erlbaum.

Parsons, O. A., Tarter, R. E., and Jones, B. (1971). Cognitive deficits in chronic alcoholics. *Il Lavoro Neuro Psichiatrico 49:*5–14.

Payne, M. A., and Butters, N. (1983). Motivational factors affecting immediate recall for prose: A comparison of amnesic and dementing patients. Paper presented at the International Neuropsychological Society Meeting, Mexico City.

Penfield, W., and Milner, B. (1958). Memory deficit produced by bilateral lesions in the hippocampal zone. *A.M.A. Arch. Neurol. Psychiat. 79:*475–497.

Peterson, L. R., and Peterson, M. J. (1959). Short-term retention of individual verbal items. *J. Exp. Psychol. 58:*193–198.

Piercy, M. F. (1977). Experimental studies of the organic amnesic syndrome. In *Amnesia*, 2d edn. (C. W. M. Whitty and O. L. Zangwill, eds.). London: Butterworths.

Prisko, L. (1963). Short-term memory in focal cerebral damage. Unpublished doctoral disseration, McGill University.

Ribot, T. (1882). *Diseases of Memory.* New York: Appleton.

Russell, W. R., and Nathan, P. W. (1946). Traumatic amnesia. *Brain 69:*280–300.

Ryan, C., and Butters, N. (1980a). Further evidence for a continuum of impairment encompassing male alcoholic Korsakoff patients and chronic alcoholic men. *Alcoholism: Clinical and Experimental Research 4:*190–197.

Ryan, C., and Butters, N. (1980b). Learning and memory impairments in young and old alcoholics: Evidence for the premature-aging hypothesis. *Alcoholism: Clinical and Experimental Research 4:*288–293.

Ryan, C., and Butters, N. (1983). Cognitive deficits in alcoholics. In *The Pathogenesis of Alcoholism*, vol. 7 (B. Kissin and H. Begleiter, eds.). New York: Plenum Press.

Samuels, I., Butters, N., and Fedio, P. (1972). Short-term memory disorders following temporal lobe removals in humans. *Cortex 8:*283–298.

Samuels, I., Butters, N., and Goodglass, H. (1971a). Visual memory deficits following cortical and limbic lesions: Effect of field of presentation. *Physiol. Behav. 6:*447–452.

Samuels, I., Butters, N., Goodglass, H., and Brody, B. (1971b). A comparison of subcortical and cortical damage in short-term visual and auditory memory. *Neuropsychologia 9:*293–306.

Sanders, H. I., and Warrington, E. K. (1971). Memory for remote events in amnesic patients. *Brain 94:*661–668.

Scoville, W. B., and Milner, B. (1957). Loss of recent memory after bilateral hippocampal lesions. *J. Neurol. Neurosurg. Psychiat. 20:*11–21.

Seltzer, B., and Benson, D. F. (1974). The temporal pattern of retrograde amnesia in Korsakoff's disease. *Neurology 24:*527–530.

Shallice, T., and Warrington, E. K. (1970). The independent functioning of verbal memory stores: A neuropsychological study. *Quart. J. Exp. Psychol. 22:*261–273.

Sidman, M., Stoddard, L. T., and Mohr, J. P. (1968). Some additional quantitative observations of immediate memory in a patient with bilateral hippocampal lesions. *Neuropsychologia 6:*245–254.

Smith, M. L., and Milner, B. (1981). The role of the right hippocampus in the recall of spatial location. *Neuropsychologia 19:*781–793.

Speedie, L., and Heilman, K. (1982). Amnesic disturbance following infarction of the left dorsomedial nucleus of the thalamus. *Neuropsychologia 20:*597–604.

Speedie, L., and Heilman, K. (1983). Anterograde memory deficits for visuospatial material after infarction of the right thalamus. *Arch. Neurol.* 40:183–186.

Squire, L. R. (1981). Two forms of human amnesia: An analysis of forgetting. *J. Neurosci.* 1:635–640.

Squire, L. R. (1982). Comparisons between forms of amnesia: Some deficits are unique to Korsakoff's syndrome. *J. Exp. Psychol.: Learning, Memory and Cognition* 8:560–571.

Squire, L. R., and Cohen, N. (1979). Memory and amnesia: Resistance to disruption develops for years after learning. *Behavioral Neural Biol.* 25:115–125.

Squire, L. R., and Cohen, N. J. (1982). Remote memory, retrograde amnesia, and the neuropsychology of memory. In *Human Memory and Amnesia* (L. S. Cermak, ed.). Hillsdale, N.J.: Erlbaum.

Squire, L. R., and Moore, R. Y. (1979). Dorsal thalamic lesions in a noted case of chronic memory dysfunction. *Ann. Neurol.* 6:503–506.

Squire, L. R., and Slater, P. C. (1975). Forgetting in very-long-term memory as assessed by an improved questionnaire technique. *J. Exp. Psychol.: Human Learning and Memory* 104:50–54.

Squire, L. R., and Slater, P. C. (1978). Anterograde and retrograde memory impairment in chronic amnesia. *Neuropsychologia* 16:313–322.

Squire, L. R., Chace, P. M., and Slater, P. C. (1976). Retrograde amnesia following electroconvulsive thereapy. *Nature (London)* 260:775–777.

Squire, L. R., Slater, P. C., and Chace, P. M. (1975). Retrograde amnesia: Temporal gradient in very-long-term memory following electroconvulsive therapy. *Science* 187:77–79.

Talland, G. A. (1965). *Deranged Memory.* New York: Academic Press.

Tarter, R. E. (1973). An analysis of cognitive deficits in chronic alcoholics. *J. Nerv. Mental Dis.* 157:138.

Tarter, R. E., and Parson, O. A. (1971). Conceptual shifting in chronic alcoholics. *J. Abnorm. Psychol.* 77:71–75.

Taylor, R. L. (1969). Comparison of short-term memory and visual sensory analysis as sources of information. *J. Exp. Psychol* 81:515–522.

Teuber, H.-L., Milner, B., and Vaughan, H. G., Jr. (1968). Persistent anterograde amnesia after stab wound of the basal brain. *Neuropsychologia* 6:267–282.

Tomlinson, E. (1977). Pathology of dementia. In *Dementia* 2d ed. (C. Wells, ed.). Philadelphia: Davis.

Tulving, E. (1972). Episodic and semantic memory. In *Organization of Memory* (E. Tulving and W. Donaldson, eds.). New York: Academic Press.

Victor, M., Adams, R. D., and Collins, G. H. (1971). *The Wernicke-Korsakoff Syndrome.* Philadelphia: Davis.

Warrington, E. K., and Shallice, T. (1969). The selective impairment of auditory verbal short-term memory. *Brain* 92:885–896.

Warrington, E. K., and Shallice, T. (1972). Neuropsychological evidence of visual storage in short-term memory tasks. *Quart. J. Exp. Psychol.* 24:30–40.

Warrington, E. K., and Weiskrantz, L. (1970). Amnesic syndrome: Consolidation or retrieval? *Nature* 228:628–630.

Warrington, E. K., and Weiskrantz, L. (1973). An analysis of short-term and long-term memory defects in man. In *The Physiological Basis of Memory* (J. A. Deutsch, ed.). New York: Academic Press.

Warrington, E. K., and Weiskrantz, L. (1978). Further analysis of the prior learning effect in amnesic patients. *Neuropsychologia* 16:169–176.

Warrington, E. K., Logue, V., and Pratt, R. T. C. (1972). The anatomical localization of selective impairment of auditory verbal short-term memory. *Neuropsychologia* 9:377–387.

Weingartner, H., Caine, E., and Ebert, M. (1979). Encoding processes, learning and recall in Huntington's Disease. In *Advances in Neurology*, vol. 23, *Huntington's Disease* (T. Chase, N. Wexler, and A. Barbeau, eds.). New York: Raven Press.

Weingartner, H., Grafman, J., Boutelle, W., Kaye, W., and Martin, P. (1983). Forms of memory failure. *Science 221*:380–382.

Wickens, D. D. (1970). Encoding categories of words: An empirical approach to meaning. *Psychological Rev. 77*:1–15.

Wilkinson, D. A., and Carlen, P. L. (1981). Chronic organic brain syndromes associated with alcoholism: Neuropsychological and other aspects. In *Research Advances in Alcohol and Drug Problems*, vol. 6 (Y. Israel, F. Glaser, H. Kalant, R. Popham, W. Schmidt, and R. Smart, eds.). New York: Plenum Press.

Wilson, R. S., Kaszniak, A. W., and Fox, J. H. (1981). Remote memory in senile dementia. *Cortex 17*:41–48.

Winocur, G., and Kinsbourne, M. (1976). Transfer of learning in brain-damaged patients. Paper presented at the International Neuropsychological Society Meeting, Toronto.

Winocur, G., and Kinsbourne, M. (1978). Contextual cueing as an aid to Korsakoff amnesics. *Neuropsychologia 16*:671–682.

Winocur, G., Kinsbourne, M., and Moscovitch, M. (1981). The effect of cueing on release from proactive interference in Korsakoff amnesic patients. *J. Exp. Psychol.: Human Learning and Memory 7*:56–65.

Woods, R., and Piercy, M. (1974). A similarity between amnesic memory and normal forgetting. *Neuropsychologia 12*:437.

Zangwill, O. L. (1966). The amnesic syndrome. In *Amnesia* (C. W. M. Whitty and O. L. Zangwill, eds.). London: Butterworths.

Zola-Morgan, S. M., and Öberg, R. (1980). Recall of life experiences in an alcoholic Korsakoff patient: A naturalistic approach. *Neuropsychologia 18*:549–557.

15
Dementia

ROBERT J. JOYNT AND IRA SHOULSON

Dementia has been called the "disease of the century" (Thomas, 1981). There are several reasons for renewed interest in dementia. First, it is evident that dementia is one of our most pressing public health problems since the increasing age of our population puts more people in the at-risk population. Interest in dementia has also been prompted by research into its pathogenesis. Advanced technology has increased knowledge in the area of neuotransmitters. It is not clear to what extent the causes of dementia relate to neurotransmitter disturbances, but these investigations have opened up new approaches that have already resulted in more rational attempts at therapy. Finally, and most pertinent to this chapter, there has been increased interest in behavioral neurology and neuropsychology that has resulted in the development of new techniques for looking at the deficits of demented patients.

DEFINITION

Dementia is a loss of intellectual function. Because the term is loosely used, qualification is necessary. It means an *unusual* loss of intellectual function, as there is normally an inexorable, noticeable decline in certain mental powers with advancing age. The normal loss of cognitive and mnemonic ability with age has been called "benign senescent forgetfulness" (Kral, 1962). Dementia is also usually interpreted as an *acquired* loss, as opposed to mental retardation, in which the intellect was never normal. It does not necessarily mean a gradual loss of these functions, for it may be of sudden onset, as, for example, following an episode of anoxia or a cerebrovascular accident.

Intellectual function covers a variety of mental operations; however, isolated neurological defects, such as aphasia, are not usually classified as dementia. This is controversial, since some investigators believe that aphasic patients have lost internal speech and have defects in intelligence. In clinical practice, however, language disorders, such as aphasia, alexia, and agraphia, are usually excluded from the general classification of dementia. Similarly, defects such as denial of illness, denial of body parts, or the Gerstmann's syndrome are not included. Some would even exclude circumscribed memory disorders such as Wernicke-Korsakoff syndrome since in these cases mental operations seem to function well on what memories the patient can use. Generally, however, memory disorders are included among the dementias. Disorders of attention and arousal may cause confusion and delirium. Delirious and confused patients may have impaired intellectual function, and therefore these patients may also be considered to be demented.

Two important admonitions about the problem of dementia must be stated. The first is that dementia is a symptom of many disorders and not a disease entity. Symptoms are a function of the locus and not the type of disease. For example, atrophy affecting the frontal lobes and tumors invading the same region may present in similar fashion. *The second point follows from the first: since dementia has different etiologies, some cases are remediable.* This places a great deal of responsibility on the clinician. The specter of dementia, a failing mind in a healthy body, is so dreadful that a missed chance for treatment has immense implications for both patient and family.

EPIDEMIOLOGY

It is estimated that about 5 per cent of the population over age 65 have severe dementia and about 10 per cent have mild to moderate dementia. This population group will triple by the year 2050. In pointing out this prevalence, Katzman (1976) estimated that senile dementias are likely the fourth or fifth most common cause of death in this country, as the presence of dementia in elderly patients considerably shortens their expected life span. There is evidence that this is likely an underestimation. One report quoted by Arie (1973) estimates that more than 80 per cent of moderate to severely demented patients were not known to be so by their family physician.

CLASSIFICATION

Dementias may be classified in a number of ways, as, for example, by age of onset, etiology, underlying pathlogy (e.g., degenerative, metabolic, vascular), accompanying neurological signs, or response to therapy. From a diagnostic standpoint it is most useful to classify them on the basis of their localization because the signs and symptoms are dependent on this and not, for example, on their etiology.

Classification on the basis of localization has several drawbacks. Although in some dementias we are dealing with pathology restricted to specific regions (as, for example, with dementia caused by a tumor or strokes), in others neuronal systems or specific neurochemical systems may be involved. Although classical neuropsychology related behavioral alterations to discrete lesions, we now have to think of how behavioral abnormalities relate to alteration of one or more neurotransmitter systems. For example, there is a propensity for Alzheimer's disease to selectively affect association areas early in the disease, but recent findings indicate that Alzheimer's disease may preferentially affect cholinergic neurotransmitter systems with cell bodies in the basal nuclei (Rossor, 1981) that project to many cortical areas. These neurotransmitter systems often blur the anatomical distinctions that we use as the basis of our classification.

Another problem with such a classification is the varied behavioral pattern with which any of the dementias may present. Geschwind (1975) has emphasized the variable nature of brain diseases, pointing out any one feature, such as memory disorder, may be prominent in one patient and lacking in another. It is possible, as well, that symptoms may relate in part to the *amount* of brain damage as well as to its location. Chapman and Wolff (1955) found that if less than 120 grams of cortical tissue was removed, memory and orientation were intact but certain adaptive responses were impaired. However, to measure accurately or even to define such abstruse concepts as adaptation or drive is almost an insurmountable task. When the behavioral task, no matter how complex, is broken down into its basic components, it is possible to make more accurate anatomical and clinical correlations. The view that certain mental functions are not assignable to specific brain areas is likely to be mainly a condemnation of our inadequate observation and testing. Finally, the classification of dementia on the basis of localization becomes difficult in advanced cases, since many of the dementias progressively involve more and more of the brain.

Recognizing these drawbacks, we shall use the following classification system:

I. Localized dementia
    A. Cortical
    A. Frontal-subcortical
    C. Axial
II. Mixed dementia

Cortical dementias are characterized by cognitive defects. These patients have disorders that affect association areas subserving language, skilled movements, and perception and result in aphasia, apraxia, and agnosia. Early in the disease, signs and symptoms may be subtle. Since in many cortical dementias the loss of brain tissue is gradual, the dramatic syndromes of aphasia, apraxia, and agnosia seen with vascular disease (where there is sudden, complete, and circumscribed brain loss) may not be seen.

With *subcortical dementia* there is a gradual decline in cognitive powers. However, the posterior cortical association areas are usually not affected, and therefore aphasia, apraxia, and agnosia are absent. McHugh and Folstein (1975) emphasize that the lack of specific posterior cortical cognitive deficits along with a profound apathy constitute the "subcortical dementia syndrome."

Axial dementias are so designated because they involve the "axial" structures of the brain, such as the medial portion of the temporal lobes, hippocampus, fornix, mammillary bodies, and hypothalamus. These areas are in part concerned with the registration of memory, as documented by Victor and his coworkers (1971). The prominent feature of these dementias is marked disturbance in recent memory, making the learning of new tasks almost impossible. Equally striking is the relative absence of cognitive disturbances (see also Chap. 14).

In our discussion of the categories of dementias, we shall consider one disease that typifies each category and more briefly discuss other diseases. For example, we shall discuss Alzheimer's disease as an example of cortical dementia, Huntington's disease as an example of frontal-subcortical dementia, and Wernicke-Korsakoff syndrome as an example of axial dementia. As noted above, the classification is only approximate: there are axial and subcortical changes in Alzheimer's disease, and there is cortical involvement in Huntington's disease and in many alcoholic patients with Wernicke-Korsakoff syndrome.

CORTICAL DEMENTIAS

Alzheimer's Disease

Alzheimer's disease and senile dementia were formerly distinguished by their age of onset, but behavioral and neuropathological studies indicate that they are probably the same disease. In this discussion, the terms *Alzheimer's disease* and *senile dementia* are used synonymously.

Alzheimer's disease is the most common form of dementia, accounting for about half of all cases of dementia in most series. Its prevalence increases with increasing age. It is therefore one of the most prominent public health problems today.

PRESENTATION

Patients with Alzheimer's disease rarely refer themselves because there is a concomitant loss of insight. The patients are therefore often insensitive to their own shortcomings. In contrast, active people in their 40s or 50s, many of whom normally perform at a high intellectual level, may refer themselves for diagnostic evaluation when they become concerned that they cannot maintain this performance. Most turn out to be depressed. Only a few turn out to have progressive dementia.

Although Alzheimer's disease is usually insidiously progressive, patients are often referred emergently, at which time they are found to already be grossly demented. Characteristic patterns of referral were noted by Arie (1973). He noted the "Monday morning syndrome," in which family members who infrequently visit their aging parents or parent find one weekend that the patient is not doing well. Because of the infrequent contact, there appears to be a worsening, and the doctor is called "first thing" after the weekend. Another type is the "Friday afternoon crisis," in which the family taking care of the demented parent has need of respite and arrives at the hospital prior to a short vacation. Many of these referrals are caused by some change in the patient's health or living situation. Elderly patients with moderate dementia may do quite well living alone in familiar surroundings and with a regular routine. However, some mild illness or the initiation of or change in medication of almost any type may cause them to become confused. Changes in routine, such as a move to a nursing home or the closing of a neighborhood grocery store, may make their underlying dementia more obvious. Also, many families can cope with a demented parent as long as they can get a good night's sleep. When this is disrupted, the family can no longer manage as before.

PERSONALITY CHANGES

Personality change may be prominent early in the course of the illness, and it is this rather than loss of memory or cognitive function that often alerts the family to the problem of dementia. Three prominent personality changes are commonly encountered: (1) accentuation of prior personality traits to the point of eccentricity, (2) an apathetic attitude that precludes taking on novel ventures, and (3) marked distractibility, especially when fatigued.

Accentuation of previous personality traits is very common. While it can generally be said that many of the social graces and neatness of dress eventually disappear in senile dementias, it is not unusual for a housewife noted for her cleanliness to become obsessive about household tasks. Patients who are secretive and suspicious become frankly paranoid and make severe recriminations about the behavior of close friends, family, and spouses. Individuals who have been sexually active may pursue this activity indiscriminately.

Novel undertakings of any type are very difficult for patients with dementia. The urging of a concerned family or spouse that a change of scenery is necessary may often precipitate disastrous worsening. As the dementia progresses, this reluctance to take on new things evolves into a marked apathy. With this the patient may fail to wash, comb the hair, or dress properly.

Many patients with dementia can carry on with their work or hobbies if they are not called upon to handle more than a few operations at a time. The shopkeeper may handle one customer without difficulty, but the appearance of a few more people waiting to be served may precipitate a temper outburst.

Another less frequent but prominent feature is the loss of a sense of humor. This has been stressed as an early sign of intellectual loss. Unfortunately, many people, including some examining physicians, may not have a particularly well-developed sense of humor. Thus, it may be difficult to quantitate the loss.

The vacillation of emotional reponse with wide mood swings is not, in our experience, as common as stated. It does occur but usually represents an exaggeration of a previously unstable temperament.

The personality abnormalities discussed above, as well as the patient's intellectual capabilities, are subject to fatigue. After a night of rest many patients are quite lucid, but as the day goes on, their ability to cope with intellectual material lessens and behavior disintegrates. Therefore, mental status testing and behavioral observations are necessary throughout the day to assess accurately the degree of impairment.

INTELLECTUAL CHANGES

The earliest sign of intellectual deficit in most patients is the impairment of memory. Immediate ("scratch-pad") memory is characteristically preserved, but it may be impossible to hold material in memory for several minutes. Patients often use *aide-memoires* like writing notes to themselves, but even these may be misplaced. Frequently a spouse will report that there are literally hundreds of notes in various places in the home. Items of apparel may be forgotten or put on improperly, pots may boil dry on the stove, and familiar friends may be misnamed.

Defects in abstract thinking are more difficult to detect. These defects blunt the insight of the patient, who may continue on in a position of authority and responsibility. It is frightening to find patients with major intellectual deficits who are responsible for decisions affecting the lives and fortunes of others. Two essays on this subject point out the difficulties in dealing with brain failure in public life (Goody, 1979; Joynt, 1981): it is the people in power who make the decisions about whether or not they are themselves fit to continue.

As Alzheimer's disease progresses, mental operations, such as language and perception, become affected. As noted earlier, these are usually partial defects since the loss of brain cells is gradual and diffuse. Eventually, well-developed aphasic, apraxic, and agnostic syndromes may emerge. Early language problems are usually manifested by word-finding difficulties and gradual attrition of complex language capabilities, both in expression and in comprehension. Items are misnamed and phonemic substitutions are made. Subtleties of language, such as subjunctive and complex sentence forms, disappear. More and more jargon is uttered when the patient is stimulated to speak. Intrusions, or the inappropriate placement of previously used words, are commonly encountered in Alzheimer patients (Fuld et al., 1982). Other forms of communication, such as reading and writing, suffer along with the deterioration in speech.

Perceptual disorders are usually manifested by problems with spatial perception and route finding. Patients may get lost even in familiar surroundings. This is particularly true if they also suffer from defective vision or hearing. Confusion at night is common because sensory input is lessened. Most perceptual defects are negative symptoms, but positive symptoms, such as visual and auditory hallucinations, may occur. Medications that sedate and depress awareness may precipitate hallucinations.

Praxic disorders are usually present in advanced cases. Mild clumsiness may increase to marked confusion about the sequence of motor acts. Taking a match from a book and striking it may tax the patients' abilities so they sit dumbfounded when asked to do this. On the other hand, overlearned motor behavior, such as eating, may persist undisturbed even when other functions have severely deteriorated.

CRANIAL NERVE, MOTOR, AND SENSORY ABNORMALITIES

Early in Alzheimer's disease the signs are restricted to decline of intellectual function. However, with gradual decrease in the population of nerve cells, other neurological signs appear. They consist of loss of inhibition of rudimentary reflexes (the so-called frontal release signs—the snout reflex, grasp reflex, and palmomental reflex) along with a general increase in muscle stretch reflexes. In advanced stages, Babinski responses may appear. Rarely, there are positive signs of cerebral involvement with myoclonic, focal, and generalized seizures. Liston (1979a) notes that various investigators have observed different degrees of involvement of the abnormal signs in dementia. However, in most surveys at least one half of the patients had some abnormal finding. In the more advanced cases this figure was higher. Paulson and Gottlieb (1968) noted at least one release reflex in their group of severely demented patients. It should be stressed, however, that until the disease is advanced, the typical patient with Alzheimer's disease looks entirely normal to the casual observer and has a normal elementary neurological examination. Only when the mental status is examined do deficits appear.

LABORATORY STUDIES

Laboratory studies contribute to the diagnosis principally by excluding other causes of dementia, such as neoplasm, metabolic, infectious, or deficiency diseases. Cortical atrophy can now be assessed by the CT scan, but the correlation between cortical atrophy and dementia is still inexact. In addition to the CT scan and lumbar puncture, serological tests for syphilis (e.g., FTA), thyroid function, serum B_{12}, serum lipids and chemistries should be performed in all patients with dementia. The EEG can be normal, but varying amounts of slowing are often seen. This, however, is not diagnostic. Late evoked potentials (P_{300}) may be markedly delayed in Alzheimer's disease (Goodin et al., 1978).

COURSE

The clinical course can be varied. This fact has led some investigators to propose that we are dealing with more than one disease. However, at autopsy the findings are remarkably uniform. It may be that the early signs and symptoms of dementia reflect differences in the areas or systems of the brain first affected. Unfortunately, as the disease progresses, the clinical picture is much more stereotypic and the pathological correlations that may have reflected early differences may not be apparent by the time the autopsy is done.

A fairly typical staging of Alzheimer's disease reported by most workers consists of three phases (Liston, 1979a, 1979b; Schneck et al., 1982). The first is the "forgetful" phase. As noted before, some degree of memory loss is experienced by most aging people. Indeed, this is so common it may be passed off by the family. Personality disturbances, however, are usually noted by the family; this likely accounts for the observation that the age of contact is lower when complaints are psychiatric rather than neurological (Liston, 1979b).

The next stage is "confusional." The patient gets lost in familiar surroundings and has more severe memory impairment and inappropriate social behavior.

In the final, or "dementia" stage there are language problems, incontinence, and severe disorientation and patients are unable to care for themselves.

Any one of the above stages may last for varying periods of time. Also, one phase may overlap with another so that language problems, for example, may appear early in some and late in others. Social awareness and standards of personal cleanliness may persist in some.

The capricious course of this illness, particularly in the early stages, constitutes a real diagnostic challenge for the examiner. Laboratory studies are not diagnostic. The examination and testing require time. If the clinician is unable to provide this, then others should be given this responsibility.

PATHOLOGY AND PATHOPHYSIOLOGY

The brain weight is often less than 1000 grams. Cortical atrophy, when present, is mainly in the association areas. Subcortical white matter may also be reduced.

Histologically there is nerve cell loss. In addition, neurons demonstrate neurofibrillary degeneration, argyrophilic (amyloid) plaques, and granulovacuolar degeneration. The severity of the dementia correlates with the number of plaques (Blessed et al., 1968).

Postmortem neurochemical studies of Alzheimer's disease have demonstrated a reduction of choline acetyltransferase (ChAT), the enzyme responsible for the synthesis of acetylcholine (Coyle et al., 1983). The reduction of ChAT activity in the cortex correlates with the severity of the behavioral disorder (Perry et al., 1978). The reduction of ChAT also correlates with the density of senile plaques (Perry et al, 1978). In normals, anticholinergic drugs temporarily interfere with memory (Drachman and Leavitt, 1974).

The cholinergic projections to the cortex and hippocampus arise mainly from the basal forebrain and septal areas (Mesulam and Van Hoesen, 1976). The reduction of ChAT activity in Alzheimer's disease is related to loss of these cholinergic neurons. The clinical and pathological hallmarks of Alzheimer's disease closely correlate with the loss of cholinergic neurons (Whitehouse et al., 1981, 1982, 1983). Other neurotransmitters systems may also be impaired in Alzheimer's disease (e.g., norepinephrine); however, the significance of these changes is unknown.

TREATMENT

A variety of treatments have been attempted based on the cholinergic hypothesis, including the use of acetylcholine precursors (choline, lecithin), antiacetylcholinesterase drugs to retard the degradation of acetylcholine (physostigmine), and choline agonists (arecoline). The results of cholinergic therapy have been inconsistent (Bartus et al., 1982). Naloxone has also been reported to be beneficial. No therapy has been shown to arrest the progression of the disease.

Pick's Disease

CLINICAL FEATURES

Pick's disease is a progressive dementia that is difficult clinically to distinguish from Alzheimer's disease. Some authors have claimed, however, that there are clinical differences. Pick's disease is said to affect personality before affecting memory, whereas in Alzheimer's disease, memory is affected early. Elements of the Kluver-Bucy syndrome may be seen early in the course of Pick's disease. Finally, presentation with language abnormalities with relatively spared memory may also favor Pick's disease over Alzheimer's disease.

LABORATORY STUDIES

Computed tomography may show frontal and anterior temporal lobe atrophy. The EEG in Pick's disease may show less slowing than in Alzheimer's disease, but since the EEG is sometimes normal in Alzheimer's disease, and can be abnormal in Pick's, this is not very helpful in differentiating these diseases.

In most cases, the brain weight is below 1000 grams. Atrophy is most impressive in the frontal lobes and in the anterior portion of the temporal lobes. In addition to cell loss and gliosis in the affected areas, cells may be swollen and contain argyrophilic inclusions (Pick cells) that are diagnostic.

Other Degenerative Dementias

In 1910 Kraeplin described a form of dementia characterized by emotional changes, such as anxiety and depression, along with language disorders. Sometimes catatonia was associated. The neuropathology revealed nerve cell damage and loss but was otherwise nonspecific (Corsellis, 1976). Schaumberg and Suzuki (1968) described a familial dementia characterized by disturbances in memory and cognition (poor calculations, right/left confusion, aphasia, and alexia), again without specific pathological changes. Most recently, Mesulam (1982) described six patients with slowly progressive expressive aphasia and other cognitive defects (e.g., acalculia and apraxia). One patient developed akinesia (perhaps similar to what Kraeplin called catatonia). Several patients had emotional changes. One patient had a cortical biopsy demonstrating nonspecific degenerative changes but no abnormalities consistent with Alzheimer's or Pick's diseases. There thus remain to be better defined degenerative dementias that appear to differ from Alzheimer's or Pick's disease pathologically and perhaps clinically.

Angular Gyrus Syndrome

Alzheimer's disease may be associated with aphasia, apraxia, alexia, and elements of the Gerstmann's syndrome (right/left confusion, finger agnosia, agraphia, acalculia). Focal lesions in the posterior aspect of the left hemisphere (including the angular gyrus) can also cause these symptoms. Benson and his colleagues (1982) described three patients with posterior left hemisphere lesions who were thought originally to have Alzheimer's disease. Clinically, they differed from Alzheimer's patients in that they did not have memory loss or impaired topographical orientation.

FRONTAL-SUBCORTICAL DEMENTIAS

The term *frontal-subcortical dementia* is used to designate the dementia seen mainly with disease of subcortical regions. However, disease of the frontal lobe may be behaviorally similar. The most prominent examples are Huntington's disease, variants of Parkinson's disease, progressive supranuclear palsy, hydrocephalus, thalamic surgery, a variety of vascular diseases including multi-infarct dementia, Binswanger's disease, vasculitis induced by infectious agents (e.g., syphilis and fungi), and autoimmune disorders (e.g., systemic lupus). Thalamic, basal ganglia, and frontal-subcortical tumors (e.g., gliomas) may also produce similar symptoms. These diseases are not identical in location or extent of lesion, as evidenced by the different patterns of neurological deficit present in each. Albert and his coworkers (1974) pointed out certain common features of the dementia present in these diseases. There are defects in timing and activation, with slowing of memory, thought, and motor performance. Although these patients may have memory defects, they do not have aphasia, apraxia, agnosia, or related cortical cognitive disorders. The clinical picture of a patient with Huntington's disease is characteristic of frontal-subcortical dementia.

Huntington's Disease

PERSONALITY CHANGES

The hereditary nature of Huntington's disease presents special psychological problems for family members at risk for the disease as well as for patients with early disease. The specter of progressive dilapidation of mental function and a distressing movement disorder colors their lives. Thus, marked anxiety and preoccupation with health are common. This occasionally culminates in major depressive symptoms with suicide as one outcome. This issue is complicated, however, by the fact that depression can itself be a symptom of Huntington's disease (see below). In families where one parent has Huntington's disease, there is a larger incidence of conduct disorders in the children likely relating to family disruption (Folstein et al., 1983).

Patients with Huntington's disease can also demonstrate behavioral features common to all the subcortical dementias. Marked apathy and slowing of thinking and memory can lead to gradual withdrawal from former activites and severing of old friendships. Attention to work, interpersonal relationships, and personal appearance wanes. As with many patients with frontal-lobe disease, there is disinhibition of emotional responses, so that outbursts of temper and violent behavior may occur.

Prominent psychotic changes may be seen in patients with Huntington's disease. McHugh and Folstein (1975) describe two types: mood disorders resembling manic-depressive psychosis and delusionary-hallucinatory states resembling schizophrenia.

INTELLECTUAL CHANGES

Many of the cognitive changes seen in the cortical dementias are not seen in subcortical dementia or are not as severe. Nearly all aspects of language function are preserved, including reading, writing, speaking, and comprehension. There may be mild word-finding difficulties, but the prominent jargon seen in patients with Alzheimer's disease, for example, is not seen in the subcortical dementias. Speech may be dysarthric because of motor deficits (such as chorea). Other cortical functions also escape so that major apraxias and agnosias are not prominent. Occasionally, there are some problems with spatial perception in patients with Huntington's disease. A prominent finding on testing is the inability of these patients to maintain a cognitive set and to organize cognitive operations. This is also manifest in the ability to switch from one modality to another. This shows up particularly in the Stroop test (Fisher et al., 1983).

Memory function is usually affected after the cognitive defects appear. In memory testing, these patients are easily distracted. The deficit in memory is usually not present early in the disease and never approaches the severity seen in axial dementia.

However, it is difficult for them to learn extensive new material. We noted that patients cognizant of their susceptibility to distraction would take great pains to shut out competing stimuli while being tested. They would turn off radios and television sets and shut doors prior to memory testing (also, see Chap. 14).

The intellectual defects progress much more slowly in patients with Huntington's disease than in patients with Alzheimer's disease. The end result may appear similar in both except for the relative preservation of language in Huntington's disease.

CRANIAL NERVE, MOTOR, AND SENSORY ABNORMALITIES

In Huntington's disease, there is generalized chorea accompanied by dystonic posturing of the extremities and the trunk. The neurological abnormalities may precede or follow the onset of intellectual dysfunction.

LABORATORY STUDIES

Computed tomography or pneumoencephalography can be normal early in the illness but later may demonstrate atrophy of the caudate nucleus and cortex. The EEG may show nonspecific abnormalities (low voltage with slowing to theta and delta range).

PATHOLOGY AND PATHOPHYSIOLOGY

Postmortem examination of the brain may demonstrate loss of small neurons in the neostriatum and cortex, expecially in the frontal lobes and head of caudate.

Although decreased concentrations of gamma aminobutyric acid (GABA) have been reported in Huntington's disease (Perry et al., 1973), other neurochemical defects have also been reported, and the relationship between the GABA deficiencies and the abnormal behavior seen in the disease is not clear.

In animals, injection of kainic acid into the striatum reproduces many of the biochemical changes seen in Huntington's disease (Coyle and Schwarcz, 1976). Kainic acid destroys cell bodies in the striatum and may selectively destroy cells with glutaminergic input. There is an extensive glutamatergic neocortical projection to the striatum.

TREATMENT

Although the choreiform movements and some of the mood changes can be symptomatically treated, there is no treatment that affects the dementia or the progression of the disease.

Parkinson's Disease

PERSONALITY AND INTELLECTUAL CHANGES

Approximately 30 to 50 per cent of patients with Parkinson's disease have depression (Mayeux, 1983). Parkinson's disease may also be associated with anxiety. Psychotic behavior reported to be associated with Parkinson's disease is usually related to the drugs used in treatment.

There are two forms of intellectual change that may accompany Parkinson's disease. Although in his original description of this disease, Parkinson did not refer to dementia, patients with Parkinson's disease may have many of the intellectual changes seen with other forms of frontal-subcortical dementia, including apathy and inertia. However, more recently it has been demonstrated that many patients with Parkinson's disease develop signs of cortical dementia that are very similar to Alzheimer's disease (Boller et al., 1980).

CRANIAL NERVE, SENSORY, AND MOTOR ABNORMALITIES

The major findings of Parkinson's disease are akinesia, bradykinesia, plastic and cogwheel rigidity, and a resting tremor. There may be gait abnormalities similar to those seen with atherosclerotic dementia (see below). Patients may have masklike faces with hyperactive blink reflexes and a loss of smooth ocular pursuit.

LABORATORY STUDIES

There are no specific abnormal tests.

PATHOLOGY AND PATHOPHYSIOLOGY

Parkinson's disease is characterized by loss of dopaminergic cells in the mesencephalon (substantia nigra and the neighboring ventral tegmental area). There also may be loss of noradrenergic cells in the locus coeruleus. In addition, there may be intracytoplasmic inclusions in the affected cells (Lewy bodies).

The subgroup of Parkinson's disease patients who develop signs of Alzheimer's disease also have the pathological changes of Alzheimer's disease (see above).

Many frontal-subcortical and motor signs associated with Parkinson's disease may be related to loss of dopaminergic and noradrenergic neuons. Recently, Mayeux (1983) provided evidence that a defect in serotonergic neurons may be related to signs of depression in Parkinson's disease.

TREATMENT

Depression may be treated with tricyclic antidepressants, and frontal-subcortical and motor signs may be treated with dopaminergic replacement (L-DOPA) or dopamine agonists (bromocriptine). The dementias of Parkinson's disease usually do not respond well to these treatments.

Arteriosclerotic or Multi-Infarct Dementia

For many years it was assumed that senile dementia was caused by atherosclerosis ("hardening of the arteries"), but we now know that most (at least 50 per cent) of patients with senile dementia have Alzheimer's disease. Nevertheless, vascular disease remains the second leading cause of dementia, accounting for about 20 per cent of cases in most series.

PERSONALITY AND INTELLECTUAL CHANGES

Personality changes can be dramatic and include flattening of affect, inappropriate moods, irritability, and poor hygiene. As with other frontal-subcortical dementias, apathy, including a decrease in goal-oriented behavior, is prominent. There may be memory defects, but these are usually related to the loss of goal-oriented behavior. There is intellectual inertia, a loss of creativity, and an inability to manipulate knowledge. There is also an inability to deal with new or complex problems or environments.

CRANIAL NERVE, SENSORY, AND MOTOR ABNORMALITIES

The patient may have a loss of smooth ocular pursuit. There may also be "frontal" release signs, including suck, root, and grasp reflexes. Paratonic rigidity and increased reflexes with positive extensor plantar responses are common. The gait may be abnormal with loss of righting reflexes (resulting in retropulsion), small steps (petit pas), and inertia (slipping clutch). The patient may also have urgency incontinence.

Hachinski and his coworkers (1975) have devised an index for differentiation between vascular and degenerative dementias. Some of the factors favoring multi-infarct dementia include abrupt onset, stepwise deterioration, emotional incontinence, focal signs, and a fluctuating course.

LABORATORY STUDIES

These patients are usually hypertensive. CT scan may show enlarged ventricles with cortical atrophy. In some patients multiple infarctions, including subcortical and basal ganglia lacunes, may be seen. There may also be extensive areas of white matter that are hypodense, particularly at the corners of the lateral ventricles.

The EEG may show focal abnormalities. Other laboratory tests are nonspecific.

PATHOLOGY

The brains of patients with multi-infarct dementia show small (lacunar) or large areas of ischemic infarction. Atherosclerosis of medium and large vessels may lead to large areas of infarction by reducing blood flow or by providing a source of emboli. In addition, hypertension may cause lipohyalinosis of smaller vessels. There may be softening of subcortical white matter without discrete infarction (Binswanger's disease). These changes may be related to prolonged hypertension; however, emboli from large vessels in the neck or from the heart may induce multi-infarct dementia. There are also a large variety of diseases that can cause an inflammatory response in blood vessels (vasculitis) that may lead to multi-infarct dementia.

TREATMENT

The treatment of hypertension helps prevent the occurrence or progression of this disease. There is continued debate as to whether carotid artery stenosis may induce a hypoperfusion state and hence a dementia. There have been claims that endarterectomy and bypass surgery can improve dementia, but there appears to be no consensus. The role of anticoagulant therapy also remains controversial.

It is now uncommon to see a vasculitis with syphilis; however, other infectious diseases may induce vasculitis (for example, rickettsial diseases, chronic granulomatous meningitis). These are treated with the appropriate antibiotic agents. Vasculitis may also be induced by autoimmune disease, and these may be treated with the appropriate immune suppressive treatments.

Progressive Supranuclear Palsy

Steele et al. (1964) described a progressive disorder characterized by gaze disorders, such as inability to look down or up, pseudobulbar palsy, rigidity, gait disorder, and akinesia. The associated dementia, like other frontal-subcortical dementias, is characterized by apathy, inertia, inability to manipulate acquired knowledge, and slowness of thought.

The CT scan may demonstrate atrophy of the mesencephalon and cerebellum, but other laboratory studies are nonspecific. Pathological examination of the brain reveals neuronal loss, neurofibrillary tangles, and granulovacuolar degeneration in the basal ganglia, brainstem, and cerebellum.

Patients with progressive supranuclear palsy have been treated with dopaminergic agents, such as bromocriptine and L-DOPA: the results of these medications are not dramatic. Whipple's disease may also present with supranuclear palsy and can be treated with antibiotics.

AXIAL DEMENTIA

The axial structures of the brain are essential for the proper registration and retention of new material. The most important structures for mediation of recent memory are the dorsomedial nucleus of the thalamus, the mammillary bodies of the hypothalamus, the medial aspect of the temporal lobes, and possibly the fornices. Also, as discussed above, lesions in the basal forebrain (basal nucleus of Meynert) may also cause memory disturbance. The most flagrant example of this disorder is Wernicke-Korsakoff syndrome. Other conditions that may cause similar memory disturbances are head injury, normal-pressure hydrocephalus, hypoxia and hypoglycemia, encephalitis (particularly those varieties with a propensity for medial temporal-lobe involvement like herpes simplex encephalitis), infarctions (medial thalamus or medial temporal lobe), hermorrhage (thalamic hemorrhage and hemorrhage from anterior communicating artery aneurysms), tumors (in the diencephalon or temporal lobes), seizures, and degenerative disease (Alzheimer's).

Wernicke-Korsakoff Syndrome

This disorder is caused by vitamin B_1 (thiamine) deficiency and is probably selective for those patients who have vulnerable enzyme systems that are particularly dependent on thiamine. Acute thiamine deficiency causes Wernicke's encephalopathy, characterized by confusion, eye movement disorders, and ataxia. Untreated, this can be fatal. Resolution of Wernicke's encephalopathy often leaves residual mental changes, i.e., Wernicke-Korsakoff syndrome.

PERSONALITY CHANGES

The behavior of a patient with Wernicke-Korsakoff syndrome secondary to alcoholism may be complicated by other mental changes seen in chronic alcoholics. The patients lack initiative and are generally unaware of, or are not disturbed by, their profound memory loss. The swings in mood seen with other types of dementia are not a feature of the axial dementias. In fact, most of the patients appear placid and cooperative. The social amenities are ordinarily preserved, and most patients are mindful of their personal appearance.

INTELLECTUAL CHANGES

The most striking change is in memory. There is some retrograde memory loss, which may extend back for weeks or years. This is usually a discontinuous loss with some islands of preserved memories. Immediate memory is commonly intact: series of numbers may be parroted back, but anything delayed for more than several seconds is lost. Tests of abstraction may be performed if patients are working on old retained information or if they are capable of quickly thinking through the problem before forgetting the new information. Language problems are not encountered. Confabulation is not a *sine qua non* for the diagnosis of this disorder but is frequently present.

Some argue that Wernicke-Korsakoff syndrome is not a dementia because patients often function quite adequately with the information they have retained. However, they often seem to be unaware of their disturbance, a characteristic that is out of keeping with the statement that all functions except memory are intact.

CRANIAL NERVE, MOTOR, AND SENSORY ABNORMALITIES

In the acute stages of Wernicke's encephalopathy, there may be eye movement disorders and ataxia. With thiamine treatment, confusion and eye movement disorders subside but the gait disorder may remain (ataxia).

PATHOLOGY

In Wernicke's encephalopathy, cellular necrosis, petechial hemorrhages, and glosis can be seen in the diencephalon, including the thalamus (especially the dorsomedial nucleus) and the hypothalamus (mammillary bodies), and surrounding the aqueduct of Sylvius in the brainstem. Lesions in the dorsomedial nucleus of the thalamus are most reliably associated with memory loss in Wernicke-Korsakoff's disease. (See Chap. 14 for a detailed description of these disorders.)

TREATMENT

Wernicke-Korsakoff syndrome is treated with parenteral thiamine and avoidance of alcohol.

Transient Global Amnesia

Fisher and Adams (1964) described patients who had periods of disorientation lasting hours. During this time, they act as if they have forgotten events of their recent past (days to years) and they cannot acquire new information. Unlike patients with Wernicke-Korsakoff dementia, these patients appear concerned and characteristically ask a series of questions repeatedly as if to try to orient themselves. Following an attack, the examination is normal. Although the prognosis is generally good, recurrent attacks and even residual neuropsychological deficits (Mazzucchi et al., 1980) have been described. The localization is uncertain, but EEG recording sometimes demonstrates focal temporal abnormalities. Vascular insufficiency or focal seizures are thought to account for most cases.

MIXED DEMENTIAS

Dementias that, early in their course, have prominent symptoms reflecting dysfunction in more than one of the three major regions (cortical, subcortical, or axial) discussed above are called mixed dementias. Although many cortical or subcortical or axial dementias evolve into mixed dementias, this classification gives a basis for diagnosis, further investigation, and treatment early in the course of these illnesses. The following diseases are examples of mixed dementias.

Post-Traumatic Dementia

Many clinicians believe that intellectual failure is an unusual sequel of closed head injury; however, the results of psychological testing do not support this viewpoint. Meticulous assessment of memory and learning skills following head injury has demonstrated personality and cognitive deficits in a substantial proportion of patients.

Following head injury, psychosis has been reported, including both affective disorders and schizophrenic-like activity. The affective psychosis is characterized by euphoria, poor insight, and delusions of grandeur. There may be hypermania or depression. The schizophrenia-like psychosis may be associated with hallucinations, poor associations, and inappropriate thought content. However, a reactive depression is the most common affective change. In some cases, there is profound apathy. Following head injury, there may be an inability to inhibit emotions, especially anger and frustration.

Depending on the nature and severity of the head injury, almost any type of cognitive disorder may be seen. Anterograde and retrograde amnesia are frequently seen and are frequently associated with loss of goal-oriented behavior. Language disturbances are usually not prominent; however, patients with severe injuries may have anomic, conduction, or Wernicke's aphasia. There may also be evidence of parietal dysfunction, including right-left confusion, acalculia, finger agnosia, agraphia, alexia, constructional apraxia, and visuospatial disorders. Rarely, callosal disconnection may be seen.

CT scan may reveal subdural hematoma, intracerebral and subarachnoid hemorrhage, hydrocephalus, or atrophy. The EEG may be slow or show evidence of seizure activity. Pathological examination may reveal contusions at the site of the injury, as well as "contrecoup" injuries at a distance (sometimes in the opposite hemisphere). Contusions are particularly common in the anterior temporal lobes and in the undersurface of the frontal lobes. The frontal and temporal lesions may account for the prominent frontal-subcortical signs (apathy) and axial signs (amnesia) frequently seen with head trauma. Lacerations may be seen, especially with depressed skull fractures. Head trauma may also be associated with epidural, subdural, and intracerebral hemorrhage. Hydrocephalus may also be seen. Microscopically there is frequently evidence of widespread shearing of nerve fibers.

Patients with repeated head trauma, such as boxers, may develop a dementia (dementia pugilistica) that can progress even after the head injuries have stopped. This syndrome is characterized pathologically by typical and widespread neurofibrillary tangles, as seen in Alzheimer's disease. Unlike Alzheimer's disease, however, senile (neuritic) plaques are not prominent in dementia pugilistica.

Infectious Dementias

Many infectious agents can cause dementia. Mental changes are sometimes seen after meningitis and commonly follow viral encephalitis (as mentioned above, herpes simplex encephalitis may result in an axial dementia). While these diseases usually present with signs of acute infection (headache, fever, etc.), some infections present as progressive dementias. Among these are chronic fungal meningitis, syphilis (general paresis of the insane), and several slow virus infections.

JACOB-CREUTZFELDT DISEASE

Jacob-Creutzfeldt disease is a slow-virus infection of the brain that usually presents with dementia. Early in the disease there may be personality and emotional changes, including anxiety, depression, and inappropriate euphoria. The presence of hallucinations and delusions may even suggest a functional psychosis. Language difficulties, visuospatial disorders, and memory disorders are often seen. Later in the disease frontal-subcortical signs become predominant. The patient eventually becomes akinetic and mute.

There are multiple cranial nerve and motor signs that accompany this disease, including visual disorders, involuntary movements (such as myoclonic jerks), ataxia, frontal release signs (suck, grasp, gegenhalten), spasticity, and extensor plantar responses. There may also be extrapyramidal signs.

The EEG may show bursts of high-voltage slow activity. Other laboratory studies are usually unrewarding. The CSF is usually normal.

Pathological examination reveals widespread atrophy, including the cortex, basal ganglia, thalamus, and cerebellum. Histologically status spongiosus is seen.

This disease has been transmitted to monkeys and to humans. A virus-like agent is thought to be responsible. Antiviral therapy may be of some use in the treatment of this disease.

Nutritional, Endocrine, and Metabolic Dementias

The dementing disorders resulting from nutritional deficiencies (vitamin and protein depletion) and endocrine-metabolic disturbances (thyroid/adrenal/parathyroid disease, carbohydrate and lipoprotein disturbances) deserve their accorded emphasis because they are frequently remediable. They are, however, relatively rare. Screening batteries have heightened attention to unsuspected endocrine-metabolic disorders, particularly calcium, magnesium, and phosphorus disturbances. The protein deficiency states and hypovitaminoses deserve re-emphasis because of the advent of intravenous hyperalimentation and of renal dialysis.

Toxic Dementias

Central nervous system toxins may be exogenous or endogenous. Iatrogenic or surreptitious drug exposure appears to be a more common cause of dementia than do the combined nutritional-endocrine-metabolic disorders. The published data are probably a conservative estimate of the numbers of patients whose intellectual performance improves after discontinuation or dose reduction of existing medication. The anticholinergics, antipsychotics, and sedative-hypnotics account for a substantial proportion of drug-related dementias. These observations suggest that "drug holidays" be considered in the evaluation of dementia. Recent evidence suggests that aluminum may play a role in the pathogenesis of dialysis dementia. The contribution of environmental toxins to dementia has gained some popular attention, and prospective investigative approaches are clearly needed.

The most common diseases induced by endogenous toxins are uremia (renal failure) and hepatic encephalopathy.

ALCOHOLIC DEMENTIAS

Although the relatively abrupt onset of severe memory disturbance and oculomotor impairment is usually recognized as Wernicke-Korsakoff syndrome, a more global type of dementia may actually be more common in those who chronically abuse alcohol. In the more global form, psychometric testing may show a profile of slow cerebration, circumstantiality, perseveration, and frank confusion in addition to prominent memory disturbance. These patients do not show the usual periventricular pathology of Wernicke-Korsakoff syndrome (Lishman, 1981). In the more global form of dementia, the head CT scan characteristically shows prominent cerebral atrophy and ventricular enlargement. Interestingly, abstinence from alcohol may reverse some of these radiographic findings. In general, gradual-onset patients with more global alcoholic dementia are able to function at a higher level than those with Korsakoff syndrome.

Alcoholic patients are also prone to get several diseases that may also cause dementia. These include head injury, infections, and degenerative conditions (Marchiafava-Bignami disease).

Normal Pressure Hydrocephalus

Patients with normal pressure hydrocephalus (NPH) may have evidence of both frontal-subcortical dysfunction, such as apathy and loss of goal-oriented behavior, and axial dementia. Along with these, gait apraxia and bladder and bowel incontinence are the cardinal features associated with NPH. This syndrome represents a constellation of clinical features in the setting of disproportionately enlarged ventricles and impaired absorption of cerebrospinal fluid. The head CT scan and radioisotope cisternography are essential diagnostic procedures in those patients in whom ventricular shunting is considered. It is important to emphasize that the constellation of clinical and radiographic features of NPH can be secondary to diverse etiologies, such as infection, head trauma, and subarachnoid hemorrhage. Unfortunately, therapeutic response to surgical shunting procedures is unpredictable, and favorable responses may not be sustained.

Pseudodementia

In recent years it has been better appreciated that cognitive impairment may result from well-delineated psychiatric disorders, including affective disturbances and schizophrenia. The term *pseudodementia* has been applied to this category of cognitive impairment. In general, the intellectual profile in pseudodementia most closely resembles that of a subcortical dementia with prominent slowing of responses and apathy. Depressive pseudodementia is seen only in persons over 60 years old, suggesting an interaction between the effects of depression and aging processes in the brain. Recognition of this entity is obviously important because of potential reversibility with antidepressant medication or antipsychotic therapies.

Dementias Associated with Neurodegenerative or Demyelinating Disorders

This category of dementias includes those neurological diseases where intellectual failure is a recognized feature or sequelae of the disorder. Additional classifications in this category may be made according to the type of neurological disease (e.g., extrapyramidal, spinocerebellar, demyelinating, epileptic, hereditary, systemic). Clarification of an underlying neurological disease is of obvious importance in formulating therapy and in clinical investigation.

DIAGNOSTIC EVALUATION

The vast majority of patients who experience a loss of intellectual function can be reliably classified into clinical categories that correlate suprisingly well with postmortem studies (Constantinidis, 1978; Sulkava et al., 1983). Seltzer and Sherwin (1978) were able to arrive at a specific diagnosis in 96 per cent of patients with previously unclassified dementia. Of course, a proper diagnostic evaluation is not often accomplished with ease. Historical information is usually incomplete, and patients may be less than cooperative during the examination and laboratory investigation. Because dementia implies intellectual decline over time, repeated assessment is usually required. However, these obstacles should not prevent a skilled and experienced clinician from establishing a specific diagnosis. Of greatest importance, Seltzer and Sherwin found that identification of the underlying disease had direct therapeutic importance in the treatment of approximately 50 per cent of patients with previously unclassified dementia. In all cases, the evaluation process may help to focus on the needs and concerns of patients and their families. The skill and experience required in the assessment of the patient with dementia preclude the use of simple algorithmic approaches in the evaluation process. We offer the basic precept that all patients with presumed intellectual decline undergo a comprehensive clinical appraisal, based on a systematic and comprehensive history, examination, and laboratory investigation.

History

The history must usually be taken from a relative or friend, but the manner in which the patient attempts to relate the history can provide information about the nature and severity of the disorder. It is unusual for the demented patient to initiate clinical contact. As noted above, the patient who spontaneously complains of a memory disorder is usually depressed.

The onset and course of the dementia provide diagnostically important information. A sudden onset is associated with infarction, head trauma, infection, or toxic exposure. A more insidious evolution of symptoms suggests neurodegenerative processes, nutritional depletion, or endocrinological disturbance. A rapid, progressive course is typically seen in the dementia associated with Jakob-Creutzfeldt disease or mass lesions. A relatively slow course usually characterizes Alzheimer's or Huntington's disease. Some dementias, such as multi-infarct dementia, may progress slowly but show episodic stepwise deterioration.

The history should document the types of mental operations that appear to be most involved and the order of appearance of these symptoms. Particular inquiries should be made into drug, toxic, or infectious exposure, nutritional status, previous psychiatric illness, education and vocational status, and family history. A complete family pedigree is important in the consideration of some eminently treatable disorders, such as Wilson's disease.

Examination

The examination of the patient should include full mental status, cranial nerve, motor, sensory, and general physical examination.

Patients should be observed for attention and responsiveness. Their responses to stimuli should be recorded.

Mental status.   Many brief and standardized tests have been formulated and validated to aid in the systematic assessment of mental status (Folstein et al., 1975; Katzman et al., 1983). To give a quick appraisal of mental status, the following are tested: orientation, memory, abstraction, judgment, perception, and language.

Orientation is assessed by questions about persons, places, and time. It is rare that a person does not know who she or he is, but this does occur in advanced dementias. Place disorientation is common, but here consideration must be given to the state of the patient's alertness when brought to the hospital. Time information includes the day, date, month, year, hour, and season. The date is often off a few days when a patient has been in the hospital for several days. However, patients with dementia are frequently unable to recall the precise year or may reverse numerals.

Memory is broken down into immediate, recent, and remote. Immediate memory is tested by recall of digit sequences (digit span). Most patients can parrot back five or more digits. Reversing digits is more difficult because the patient has to retain and manipulate these. An excellent test of recent memory, concentration, and attention is to have the patient learn and repeat a 10-digit sequence. Ten trials are given and the numbers of trials and errors noted. Most patients succeed after three to five trials if the numbers are slowly repeated to them after each trial. Another useful test of recent memory is to have the subject retain three items for five minutes. Remote memory is tested by referring to past events, keeping in mind that events relating to early life need to be confirmed by a spouse or relative. For additional discussion of memory, see Chap. 14.

Abstraction is usually tested by proverb interpretation. One must be careful because certain cultures do not employ proverbs and young patients not exposed to McGuffey' reader or to the early teachings of proverbs conveying moral concepts do not use or understand proverbs. Another way to approach this is to pick a terse newspaper headline and ask what it means and what are the implications of the information.

Judgment can best be assessed by information from relatives. In most instances of intellectual failure they can cite examples of poor judgment. A standard question is to ask the patient what should be done if he or she finds a stamped, addressed envelope on the sidewalk, but this actually tests the ability to manipulate knowledge rather than judgment. A good assessment of judgment is to note the patient's attitude in the testing. The unimpaired patient will recognize the significance and object of the examination. Those with impaired judgment will question, resent, or ignore the examination or answer with absurdities or in poor taste.

Perception is most easily tested by visual response. Copying figures or constructing simple geometric designs tests both perception and constructional ability. Spatial orientation should also be tested by asking the patient to draw a map and identify specific areas on the map. If there are defects, more extensive testing can be done (see discussion of visuospatial disorders in Chap. 8).

Language testing is treated in Chap. 2. A quick survey can be done in the course of the conversation. Observations should be made regarding spontaneous production of speech, complexity of speech, use of correct names, and comprehension. Object naming should be tested, since the patient who seems to have normal speech may fail in this test. The examiner should be cognizant of potential intrusion errors involving the inappropriate recurrence of a response from a preceding conversation or test procedure. Such word intrusions are commonly seen in patients with Alzheimer's dementia (Fuld et al., 1982).

As a simple test of *frontal lobe dysfunction* in nonaphasic persons, patients are asked to name as many words beginning with a single letter as they can (excluding proper names). Normal patients can recite nine or more words per minute using one of the letters "F," "A," or "S."

More extensive testing can be done during hospitalization. Testing should be performed at different times of the day. Many patients who are depressed and anxious do much better when they become more familiar with the examiner or after a few days of rest. A formal review of psychiatric behavioral features during the mental status examination is frequently overlooked. The need to examine mood, emotional status, reality testing, and thought content of the patient is as compelling as the evaluation of cognitive functions.

Cranial nerve, motor, and sensory examination.   The critical appraisal of the neurological examination of the elderly patient has provided some needed reference standards, as pointed out by Klawans et al. (1971) and Critchley (1956). Specific cranial nerve, motor, and sensory disorders are mentioned above in our discussion of specific illnesses causing dementia. In addition, a group of complex, polysynaptic reflexes may indicate diffuse or focal cortical involvement. They include the nuchocephalic reflex, motor impersistence, perseveration, tonic foot responses, glabellar blink, and a variety of oral responses, as noted by Jenkyn et al. (1977), Paulson (1977), and Joynt et al. (1962). The sensitivity and specificity of these so-called release signs suggest that they may be of limited value. A comprehensive eye examination should not be overlooked. The uniquely responsive pupillary patterns of Argyll-Robertson may provide the only physical clue to neurosyphilis. Impairment in gaze, visual tracking, and eye-head coordination may be important indicators of cortical disease, as emphasized by Herman and Atkin (1976) and Hurwitz (1968).

GENERAL PHYSICAL EXAMINATION

The general physical examination is an essential part of the patient's evaluation. An accurate assessment and recording of vital signs, cardiovascular condition, pulmonary status, and hepatic/renal functions is needed in all patients. Many of the readily remediable diseases producing dementia may surface as a result of the general physical examination. These include the metabolic encephalopathies, endocrine disturbances, hyperlipidemic disorders, nutritional deficiencies and dementia resulting from cerebral emboli, cardiac failure, and pulmonary insufficiency.

Laboratory Examination

The laboratory evaluation of the patient with dementia has been greatly enhanced by the introduction and application of computerized tomography. We consider the head CT scan to be an integral part of the laboratory evaluation of all patients with dementia. Of course, it should not be implied that the CT scan is a screen for dementia; rather, it serves as an aid in assessing the particular types of diseases that produce recognizable morphological changes (Menzer et al., 1975, Huckman et al., 1977, Naeser et al., 1980), such as vascular causes of dementia, mass lesions, normal-pressure hydrocephalus, basal ganglia calcifications, and the caudate atrophy that eventually develops in patients with Huntington's disease. To date, reliable indices of cortical atrophy have not been validated. Accordingly, the presence or extent of cortical atrophy may correlate imprecisely with the degree of dementia.

Other tests considered essential in the laboratory investigation of the patient with dementia are serological tests for syphilis; metabolic screens for electrolytes, calcium, serum magnesium, serum lipids, and cholesterol; tests of hepatic and renal function; urinalysis; electrocardiogram; chest x-ray; and screening tests for endocrine dysfunction, drug and heavy metal exposure, and vitamin deficiencies. A determination of arterial blood gases may aid in the evaluation of patients with suspected pulmonary insufficiency. A drug holiday may be indicated for those patients receiving drugs at the time of evaluation. Isotope cisternography or angiography may occasionally be required in special circumstances. With the advent of newer technologies, the value of the electroencephalogram has been underemphasized. The EEG may assist in the recognition of metabolic disorders or the identification of focal or regional types of dementing diseases (Wilson et al., 1977).

Psychological Tests

Formal and systematic neuropsychological testing has gained wider application in the evaluation of patients with dementia. Although the systematic process of a comprehensive mental status examination may suffice for the formulation of a specific diagnosis, formal neuropsychological testing may be helpful in delineating certain profiles of cognitive and behavioral impairment. Neuropsychological testing may also be important in establishing a baseline for the follow-up evaluation of patients with dementia. Several brief ratings scales of intellectual performance have been formulated in recent years and may prove useful to the clinician in follow-up evaluations (Coblentz et al., 1973; Folstein et al., 1975; Jacobs et al., 1977; Strub and Black, 1977; Wells, 1977; Katzman et al., 1983). From an investigative standpoint, formal neuropsychological testing is important in the objective quantification of cognitive performance and in the evaluation of therapeutic efficacy.

TREATMENT

The recent empirically derived data of clinical investigations do not support the widespread therapeutic nihilism regarding treatment of patients with dementia. Conservative estimates from the Seltzer and Sherwin (1978) study show that 10 per cent of their patients with unclassified dementia had readily remediable conditions. An additional 35 per cent had diseases that existing therapy could ameliorate considerably or retard. These data are strikingly similar to those of Marsden and Harrison (1972), Katzman (1976), Freemon (1976), Wells (1977), and Smith and Kiloh (1981), where various selected groups of individuals with unclassified dementia were systematically evaluated. All of these studies support the critical need for a systematic, comprehensive evaluation of patients, not only for investigative purposes but because of the therapeutic implications for patients and their families.

As discussed above, certain dementing disorders may be readily remediable. Common examples include the endocrine disorders, nutritional deprivation states, drug-induced dementias, and pseudodementia. The progression of some disorders may be aborted or reversed if the disease is properly recognized. Examples include multi-infarct dementia and normal pressure hydrocephalus. Some dementias may require specific care, such as family and genetic counseling, as in Huntington's disease (Shoulson, 1982). Some diseases, such as the dementias produced by transmissible virus-like agents, may require special precautions in the handling of materials from patients (Brown et al., 1982). Finally, the diagnosis of inexorably progressive dementing diseases is important for patients and families. It is our contention that the proper care of all patients is critically dependent on comprehensive and systematic clinical evaluation. Even home care can be improved on the basis of proper recognition of the underlying state.

There are certain guidelines for treating all patients with dementia. Obviously, specific therapy is given when available. In addition, any general medical condition should be corrected if possible. The correction of cardiac failure, for example, may help reduce confusion. Insofar as possible, the fewest and simplest drugs should be used. Because relatives of patients with dementia, in their frustration, seek help from many sources, patients may end up on multiple drugs. In most instances a greater service is done for the patient by withdrawal and not addition of drugs. Patients should be kept in familiar surroundings if possible. Many elderly patients with mild dementia can carry on very well in their own home. Often the family with good intentions wishes to move a patient to a more comfortable retirement or nursing home. They are fearful that the patient may fall or become ill without their notice. In general, taking the chance is better than displacing such persons from their surroundings.

Hazlitt said in the nineteenth century, "The worst old age is that of the mind." The challenge is there, but the efforts to meet it are still woefully inadequate.

REFERENCES

Albert, M. L., Feldman, R. G., and Willis, A. L. (1974). The subcortical dementia of progressive supranuclear palsy. *J. Neurol. Neurosurg. Psychiat.* 37:121.

Arie, T. (1973). Dementia in the elderly: Diagnosis and assessment. *Br. Med. J.* 4:540.

Bartus, R. T., Dean, R. L., Beer, B., and Lippa, A. S. 1982). The cholinergic hypothesis of geriatric memory dysfunction. *Science 217:*408.

Benson, D. F., Cummings, J. L., and Tsai, S. Y. (1982). Angular gyrus syndrome simulating Alzheimer's disease. *Arch. Neurol. 39:*616–620.

Blessed, G., Tomlinson, B. E., and Roth, M. (1968). The association between quantitative measurements of dementia and of senile changes in the cerebral grey matter of elderly subjects. *Br. J. Psychiatry 14:*797–811.

Boller, F., Mizutani, T., Roessmann, U., and Gambett, P. (1980). Parkinson disease, dementia, and Alzheimer disease: Clinicopathological correlations. *Ann Neurol. 7:*329–335.

Brown, P., Gibbs, C. J., Amyx, H. L., Kingsbury, D. T., Rohwer, R. G., Sulima, M. P., and Gajdusek, D. C. (1982). Chemical disinfection of Creutzfeldt-Jakob disease virus. *N. Engl. J. Med. 306:*1279.

Chapman, L. F., and Wolff, H. G. (1959). The cerebral hemispheres and the highest integrative functions of man. *Arch. Neurol. 1:*357.

Coblentz, J. M., Mattis, S., Zingesser, L. H., Kasoff, S. S., Wisniewski, H. M., and Katzman, R. (1973). Presenile dementia. *Arch. Neurol. 29:*299.

Constantinidis, J. (1978). Is Alzheimer's disease a major form of senile dementia? Clinical, anatomical, and genetic data. In *Alzheimer's Disease: Senile Dementia and Related Disorders (Aging,* vol. 7), R. Katzman, R. D. Terry, and K. L. Bick, (eds). New York: Raven Press.

Corsellis, J.A.N. (1976). Aging and dementia. In *Greenfield's Neuropathology.* Chicago: Yearbook Medical, p. 833.

Coyle, J. T., and Schwarcz, R. (1976). Lesion of striatal neurons with kainic acid provides a model for Huntington's chorea. *Nature* (London) *263:*244–246.

Coyle, J. T., Price, D. L., and DeLong, M. R. (1983). Alzheimer's disease: A disorder of cortical cholinergic innervation. *Science 219:*1184.

Critchley, M. (1956). Neurologic changes in the aged. *J. Chron. Dis. 3:*459.

Drachman, D. A., and Leavitt, J. (1974). Human memory and the cholinergic system. *Arch. Neurol. 30:*113–131.

Fisher, C. M., and Adams, R. D. (1964). Transient global amnesia. *Acta. Neurol. Scand. 40* (suppl. 9):1.

Fisher, J. M., Kennedy, J. L., Caine, E. D., and Shoulson, I. (1983). Dementia in Huntington's disease: A cross-sectionl analysis of intellectual decline. In *The Dementias* (R. Mayeux and W. G. Rosen, eds. New York: Raven Press.

Folstein, M. F., Folstein, S. E, and McHugh, P. R. (1975). "Mini-mental state": A practical method for grading the cognitive state of patients for the clinician. *J. Psychiat. Res. 12:*189.

Folstein, S. E.,Franz, M. L., Fensen, B. A. Chase, G. A., and Folstein, M. F. (1983). Conduct disorder and affective disorder among the offspring of patients with Huntington's disease. *Psychol. Med. 13:*45.

Freemon, F. R. (1976). Evaluation of patients with progressive intellectual deterioration. *Arch. Neurol. 33:*658.

Fuld, P. A., Katzman, R., Davies, P., and Terry, R. D. (1982). Intrusions as a sign of Alzheimer dementia: Chemical and pathological verification. *Ann. Neurol. 11:*155.

Geschwind, N. (1975). The borderland of neurology and psychiatry: Some common misconceptions. In *Psychiatric Aspects of Neurological Disease* (R. Benson and D. Blumer, eds. New York: Grune and Stratton.

Goodin, D. C., Squires, K. C., and Starr, A. (1978). Long latency event-related components of the auditory evoked potential in dementia. *Brain 101:*635–648.

Goody, W. (1979). Brain failure in private and public life. *Br. Med. J. 1:*591.

Hachinski, V. C., Iliff. L. D., Zelkha, E., du Boulay, G.H.D., McAlister, V. L., Marshall, J., Russell, R.W.R., and Symon, L. (1975). Cerebral blood flow in dementia. *Arch. Neurol.* 32:632.

Herman, P., and Atkin, A. (1976). A modification of eye-head coordination by CNS disease. *J. Neurol. Sci.* 28:301.

Huckman, M. S., Fox, H. H., and Ramsey, R. G. (1977). Computed tomography in the diagnosis of degenerative diseases of the brain. *Sem. Roentgenol.* 12:63.

Hurwitz, L. J. (1968). Neurological aspects of old age and capacity. *Gerentol. Clinica* 10:146.

Jacobs, J. E., Bernhard, M. R., Delgado, A., and Strain, J. J. (1977). Screening for organic mental syndromes in the medically ill. *Ann. Intern. Med.* 86:40.

Jenkyn, L. R., Walsh, D. B., Culver, C. M., and Reeves, A. G. (1977). Clinical signs in diffuse cerebral dysfunction. *J. Neurol. Neurosurg. Psychiat.* 40:956.

Joynt, R. J. (1981). Senility: A look at your future. *Sm. Neurol.* 1:1.

Joynt, R. J., Benton, A. L., and Fogel, M. L. (1962). Behavioral and pathological correlates of motor impersistence. *Neurology* 12:876.

Katzman, R. (1976). The prevalence and malignancy of Alzheimer disease: A major killer. *Arch. Neurol.* 33:217.

Katzman, R., Brown, T., Fuld, P., Peck, A., Schechter, R., and Schimmel, H. (1983). Validation of a short orientation-memory-concentration test of cognitive impairment. *Am. J. Psych.* 140:6.

Klawans, H., L., Tufo, H. M., Ostfeld, A. M., Shekelle, R. B., and Kilbridge, J. A. (1971). Neurological examination in an elderly population. *Dis. Nerv. Sys.* 32:274.

Kral, V. A. (1962). Senescent forgetfulness: Benign and malignant. *Canad. Med. Assoc. J.* 86:257.

Lishman, W. A. (1981). Cerebral disorders in alcoholism: Syndromes of impairment. *Brain* 104:1.

Liston, E. H. (1979a). Clinical findings in presenile dementia: A report of 500 cases. *J. Nerv. Ment. Dis.* 167:337.

Liston, E. H. (1979b). The clinical phenomelogy of presenile dementia: A critical review of the literature. *J. Nerv. Ment. Dis.* 167:329.

Marsden, C. D., and Harrison, M.J.G. (1972). Outcome of investigation of patients with presenile dementia. *Br. Med. J.* 2:249.

Mayeux, R. (1983). Emotional changes associated with basal ganglia disorders. In *Neuropsychology of Human Emotion.* K. M. Heilman and P. Satz, eds. New York: Guilford, pp. 141–164.

Mazzucchi, A., Moretti, G., Caffara, P., and Parma, M. (1980). Neuropsychological functions in the follow-up of transient global amnesia. *Brain* 103:161–178.

McHugh, P. R., and Folstein, M. F. (1975). Psychiatric syndromes of Huntingdon's chorea: A clinical and phenomenologic study. In *Psychiatric Aspects of Neurological Disease* (F. Benson and D. Blumer, eds.). New York: Grune and Stratton.

Menzer, L., Sabin, T., and Mark, V. H. (1975). Computerized axial tomography: Use in the diagnosis of dementia. *J.A.M.A.* 234:754.

Mesulam M. M., and Van Hoesen, G. W. (1976). Acetylcholinesterase-rich projections from the basal forebrain of the rhesus monkey to neocortex. *Brain Res.* 109:152–157.

Naeser, M. A., Gebhardt, C., and Levine, H. L. (1980). Decreased computerized tomography numbers in patients with presenile dementia. *Arch. Neurol.* 37:401.

Paulson, G. W. (1977). The neurological examination in dementia, In *Dementia* (C. Wells, ed.). Philadelphia: Davis.

Paulson, G., and Gottlieb, G. (1968). Developmental reflexes: The reappearance of foetal and neonatal reflexes in aged patients. *Brain 91*:37.

Perry, E. K., Tomlinson, B. E., Blessed, G., Bergman, K., Gibson, P. H., and Perry, R. H. (1978): Correlation of cholinergic abnormalities with senile plaques and mental test scores in senile dementia. *Br. Med. J. 2*:1457–1459.

Perry, T., Hansen, S., and Kloster, M. (1973). Huntington's chorea. Deficiency of gamma-aminobutyric acid in brain. *N. Engl. J. Med. 288*:337.

Rosser, M. N. (1981). Parkinson's disease and Alzheimer's disease as disorders of the isodendritic core. *Br. Med. J. 283*:1588.

Schaumberg, H. H., and Suzuki, K. L. (1968). Non-specific familial pre-senile dementia. *J. Neurol. Neurosurg. Psychiat. 31*:479.

Schneck, M. K., Reisberg, B., and Ferris, S. H. (1982). An overview of current concepts of Alzheimer's disease. *Am. J. Psychiat. 139*:165.

Selzer, B., and Sherwin, I. (1978). "Organic brain syndromes": An empirical study and critical review. *Am. J. Psychiat. 135*:13.

Shoulson, I. (1982). Care of patients and families with Huntington's disease. In *Movement Disorders* (C. D. Marsden and S. Fahn, eds.) London: Butterworths.

Smith, J. S., and Kiloh, L. G. (1981). The investigation of dementia: Results in 200 consecutive admissions. *Lancet 1*:824.

Steele, J. C., Richardson, J. C., and Olszewski, J. (1964). Progressive supranuclear palsy. *Arch. Neurol. 10*:333–359.

Strub, R. L., and Black, F. W. (1977). Composite mental status examination. In *The Mental Status Examination in Neurology*, App. 2, p. 163. Philadelphia: Davis.

Sulkava, R., Haltia, M., Paetau, A., Wikstrom, J., and Palo, J. (1983). Accuracy of clinical diagnosis in primary degenerative dementia: Correlation with neuropathological findings. *J. Neurol. Neurosurg. 46*:9.

Thomas, L. (1981). On the problem of dementia. *Discover*, August, p. 34.

Victor, M., Adams, R. D., and Collins, G. H. (1971). *The Wernicke-Korsakoff Syndrome*. Philadelphia: Davis.

Wells, C. E. (1977). Diagnostic evaluation and treatment in dementia. In *Dementia* (C. Wells, ed.). Philadelphia: Davis.

Whitehouse, P. J., Hedreen, J. C., White, C. L., and Price, D. L. (1983). Basal forebrain neurons in the dementia of Parkinson disease. *Ann. Neurol. 13*:243.

Whitehouse, P. J., Price, D. L., Clark, A. W., Coyle, J. T., and DeLong, M. R. (1981). Alzheimer disease: Evidence for selective loss of cholinergic neurons in the nucleus basalis. *Ann. Neurol. 10*:122–126.

Whitehouse, P. J., Price, D. L., Struble, R. G., Clark, A. W., Coyle, J. T., and DeLong, M. R. (1982). Alzheimer's disease and senile dementia: Loss of neurons in the basal forebrain. *Science 215*:1237.

Wilson, W. P., Musella, L., and Short, M. J. (1977). The electroencephalogram in dementia. In *Dementia* (C. Wells, ed.). Philadelphia: Davis.

16

Recovery and Treatment

ANDREW KERTESZ

The study of recovery from CNS lesions has been difficult since it requires that patients be followed for months or years. Clinicians observing patients in the acute state often do not have the opportunity to follow them this long, and rehabilitation specialists rarely see them during the early stages of their illness. Compounding this difficulty is the tendency for rehabilitation therapists to attribute recovery to treatment, thus underestimating the extent of spontaneous recovery. Those interested primarily in clinical and pathological diagnosis, on the other hand, tend to disregard changes in performance or in the clinical pattern of deficits and thus view the neuropsychological deficit as stable. Despite these difficulties, a considerable body of information is accumulating on recovery of function and there are several recent reviews of its various aspects (Stein et al., 1974; CIBA Foundation Symposium, 1975; Lebrun and Hoops, 1976; Sullivan and Kommers, 1977; Finger, 1978).

The mechanisms underlying recovery of function are incompletely understood. Before discussing the patterns of recovery in specific clinical situations, I review the major theories proposed to explain recovery of function, as well as some of the experimental evidence supporting these theories.

THEORETICAL AND EXPERIMENTAL CORRELATES OF RECOVERY

Acute Changes

Some of the recovery occurring in the first one to three weeks after an acute lesion can be ascribed to the reversal of early physiological abnormalities. Blood flow may increase to areas not irreversibly damaged (Kohlmeyer, 1976), edema may subside, cellular infiltrates may resolve, and pressure associated with hemorrhage or dynamic changes in the flow of cerebrospinal fluid may return to normal.

Long-term Improvement

Recovery often continues after the first one to three weeks. The rate of recovery is maximal for two to three months after an acute lesion and then slows. Beyond one year, recovery is less likely. Many mechanisms have been proposed to explain the second phase of recovery.

THEORY OF EQUIPOTENTIALITY

It can be argued that since destruction of a particular area of brain does not result in permanent loss of function, a particular function cannot be localized to the destroyed portion of the brain. In other words, according to this view, rigid localization of function in the nervous system cannot be reconciled with the repeated observation that recovery does occur. One of the earliest opponents of phrenological localization was Flourens (1824), who demonstrated recovery after ablative experiments in pigeons. Lashley (1938) based his well-known theory of equipotentiality on similar extensive ablations. He also found 18 cases in the clinical literature in which he could correlate the degree of recovery from motor aphasia with the estimated magnitude of lesions in the frontal lobe. The correlation was negative (-0.9). He considered this analogous to the finding that learning in brain-lesioned animals was positively correlated with the amount of remaining intact cortical tissue.

SUBSTITUTIONIST THEORIES

Fritsch and Hitzig (1870) observed dogs with motor system dysfunction from unilateral cortical lesions and proposed that the opposite hemisphere was taking over motor function for the injured hemisphere. In adult animals, however, destruction of an analogous area in the opposite hemisphere did not interrupt recovery. In humans, observations of patients with hemispherectomies (Smith, 1966) and callosal sections (Gazzaniga, 1970) provided evidence that the right hemisphere is capable of assuming some speech functions, such as comprehension (nouns better than verbs) and automatic nonpropositional speech. Kinsbourne (1971) argued that the right hemisphere may be the source of some aphasic speech. In the adult, however, the extent to which this recovery occurs is finite, both in cases of hemispherectomy and in global aphasics. In fact, the behavior of hemispherectomized patients is very similar to the behavior of global aphasics with extensive perisylvian infarction. This indicates that the remaining language function of global aphasics is probably subserved entirely by the right hemisphere. That the restitution of speech is often due to the activity of the opposite hemisphere is known as Henschen's axiom. Henschen (1922) gave credit to Wernicke and other contemporaries for this principle. Nielsen (1946) further advocated the idea that recovery occurs to a large extent by the variable capacity of the right hemisphere to develop speech. Geschwind (1969) also believes there is a considerable amount of individual variation in hemispheric substitution. Some people can make use of certain commissural connections and can activate some cortical mechanisms in the right hemisphere more than others. Munk (1881) thought that regions of the brain previously "not occupied" could assume certain functions (vicarious functioning). Lashley (1938), on the other hand, thought that preservation of part of a system concerned with the same function is necessary. Bucy (1934), however, performed "reverse ablations," which indicated that areas needed for recovery do not necessarily contribute to normal function. Clinically, it is evident that right hemisphere lesions do not cause aphasia in most people, even though the right hemisphere subserves some language functions.

HIERARCHICAL RE-REPRESENTATION

Jackson (1873) proposed that the nervous system is organized hierarchically, with higher centers controlling lower ones. Damage at a higher level releases lower ones from inhibition and leads to "compensation." Geschwind (1974) cited examples of neuronal systems that could take over function when released by destruction of higher centers: the spinal cord innervation of the diaphragm is one such system.

DIASCHISIS

Von Monakow (1914) postulated that damage to one part of the nervous system deprives other areas of normal stimulation and thereby creates a state of shock. He coined the term "diaschisis" for this phenomenon, which occurs during recovery from the initial deficit. Eventually, the undamaged portions of the brain resume normal functioning. Physiological changes that may be related to diaschisis have been found. Following unilateral cerebral infarction, there is bilateral reduction of cerebral blood flow (Meyer et al., 1970) which can persist for up to two months. Release of catecholamines has also been demonstrated during this period (Meyer et al., 1974). It is not known, however, whether these changes cause diaschisis or whether they are merely associated phenomena. Recent studies indicate that recovery does not correlate well with cerebral blood flow changes (Demeurisse et al., 1983). Diaschisis is more marked after acute lesions, such as infarcts or trauma, than it is with lesions that progress slowly, e.g., slowly growing tumors. This may be one reason why animals tolerate two-stage removal of a particular brain area better than one-stage removal (Ades and Raab, 1946), a phenomenon called the "serial lesion effect." Clinically, it is not unusual to see patients who have no language deficits despite large, slowly growing tumors in the speech areas.

Factors Influencing Recovery

Several factors help to explain the variability of behavioral effects among patients who suffer similar lesions and the variability in rate and completeness of recovery.

PLASTICITY

Transfer of function occurs more easily in the immature nervous system. Kennard and McCulloch (1943) demonstrated that unilateral precentral lesions in immature animals have minimal effects when compared with similar lesions in adults. In children, recovery from aphasia acquired before the age of 10 to 12 is excellent (Basser, 1962; Hécaen, 1976). Maturation of the left hemisphere appears to inhibit the language abilities of the right hemisphere. Lesions in the left speech area early in life release this inhibition and enable recovery to occur (Milner, 1974). It has been proposed that the functional plasticity of the young may depend on the adaptability of

Golgi type II cells (Hirsch and Jacobson, 1974). These cells remain adaptive, whereas cells with long axons responsible for the major transmission of information in and out of the CNS are under early and exacting genetic specification and control. In humans, the flexibility of these neurons may be terminated in the teens by hormonal changes. This may explain the age limit on the relocalization of language. It is of interest that acquisition of a foreign language without an accent also appears to be limited by puberty (personal observations). Although comparisons between species are risky, there appears to be an analogous effect of hormone levels on bird song acquisition (Nottebohm, 1970).

ANATOMICAL AND FUNCTIONAL VARIATIONS

The anatomy of the speech areas is variable, so that lesions of similar size may affect language differently in different patients. In addition, there is some variability in the degree to which language is lateralized: in particular, left-handers are more likely to have language function in both hemispheres. Consequently, aphasias in left-handers are more common, less severe, and more likely to improve than aphasias in right-handers (Gloning et al., 1969; Geschwind, 1974). Anatomical asymmetries as measured on CT scans were suggested to correlate with recovery (Pieniadz et al., 1983). Global aphasics who had atypical occipital-frontal torques and width, indicating more bilateral or reverse distribution of language function, appeared to recover better.

THE NATURE OF THE LESION

The nature of the injury may provide another variable. Rubens (1977) explained the dramatic recovery from thalamic hemorrhage in one patient by the fact that dysfunction was caused by the distortion of neural structures by the hemorrhage rather than by their destruction.

Physiological Changes Underlying Recovery of Function

The physiological mechanisms underlying recovery of function from CNS lesions are not well understood. The physiological changes that may accompany diaschisis and the possible importance of Golgi type II neurons in explaining plasticity were mentioned. In addition, other physiological mechanisms have been proposed as being important in recovery of function.

REGENERATION

Although for quite some time it was thought that regeneration occurred only in the peripheral nervous system, it is now known to occur in the CNS. Axonal regrowth has been demonstrated in ascending catecholaminergic fibers; growing zones tend to invade vacant terminal spaces (Schneider, 1973). In addition, neighboring neurons may sprout and send fibers to synapse on vacant terminals (collateral sprouting) (Liu and Chambers, 1958). Both regenerative and collateral sprouting have been demonstrated by Moore (1974). Collateral sprouting appears to be more important, whether from intact axons or from collaterals of the damaged axons.

CENTRAL DENERVATION HYPERSENSITIVITY

Denervation hypersensitivity (Stavraky, 1961) may explain why some central structures become more responsive to stimulation after damage. The remaining fibers from the damaged area may produce a greater effect on the denervated region, thereby promoting recovery. The opposite effect, however, has also been argued. The initial hypersensitivity could induce inhibition of function (diaschisis), and the appearance of collateral sprouting might reduce the denervation and the accompanying inhibition (Goldberger, 1974).

PHARMACOLOGICAL ASPECTS

Pharmacological aspects of recovery are most complex. Cholinergic agents (Ward and Kennard, 1942), anticholinesterases (Luria et al., 1969), and amphetamines (Braun et al., 1966) accelerate recovery, whereas barbiturates slow recovery (Watson and Kennard, 1945). Catecholamines may inhibit recovery (Meyer et al., 1974), and bicuculline may facilitate recovery (Duffy et al, 1976).

Functional Compensation

Functional compensation explains recovery with a behavioral rather than a neural model. Instead of rerouting connections, the brain-damaged organism develops new solutions to problems using residual structures. Substitute maneuvers or tricks have been described and documented by Sperry (1947). Luria et al. (1969) formulated the theory of retraining, which claims that the dynamic reorganization of the nervous system is promoted by specific therapy.

Motivational Factors

Motivational factors, which have been shown to affect postlesion behavior in animals, have been demonstrated to be important in humans. Lashley illustrates this in a poignant anecdote. He bet a patient who had not learned the alphabet after 900 repetitions that he could not learn it in a week—the prize being 100 cigarettes. "After ten trials, he was letter perfect and remembered it until the debt was paid." Many patients develop functional disorders superimposed on their organic deficit. A passive attitude and depression are particularly likely to impede recovery. Increasing motivation enhances recovery. The experiments of Franz and Odin (1917), where subjects were forced to use paralyzed limbs, provided evidence that intense motivation is effective. Stoicheff (1960) demonstrated the effect of positive and negative verbal comments on the performance of aphasics. Improvement was promoted by positive reinforcement, and worsening was observed with negative reinforcement.

RECOVERY FROM APHASIA

Factors Affecting the Natural History of Recovery

Until recently, most long-term studies of aphasic patients concerned speech therapy. Vignolo (1964) was the first to include the objective assessment of untreated patients at various intervals. Subsequent studies of spontaneous recovery have been performed by Culton (1969), Sarno et al. (1970a, 1970b), Sarno and Levita (1971), Hagen (1973), Basso et al. (1975), and Kertesz and McCabe (1977). These studies are difficult to compare. The methods of evaluation differed. The patient populations were not comparable, since some authors restricted their study to severe aphasics (Sarno et al., 1970a, 1970b; Sarno and Levita, 1971) but others did not (Kertesz and McCabe, 1977). Finally, different classification systems were used: Hagen (1973), for example, used Schuell's system (Schuell et al., 1964), whereas Basso et al. (1975) divided their patients into only two categories—Broca's and Wernicke's aphasics (see Chap. 2 for definitions of aphasic syndromes.)

In spite of these diversities, several important factors in the recovery of treated and untreated patients emerge.

ETIOLOGY

Recovery and prognosis depend to some extent on etiology. Patients with post-traumatic aphasia recover better than patients with aphasia following stroke (Butfield and Zangwill, 1946; Wepman, 1951; Marks et al., 1957; Godfrey and Douglass, 1959; Luria, 1970). Complete recovery was seen in more than half of our post-traumatic cases (Kertesz and McCabe, 1977). Dramatic spontaneous recovery, such as global aphasia improving to a mild anomic state, occurred after closed head injury but not in patients with vascular lesions with a similar degree of initial impairment (Fig. 16-1). Age and extent of lesion were confounding variables: many of the patients with traumatic aphasia were younger (although the age scatter was considerable), and the extent and severity of lesions in our motor vehicle accident population was variable (most had closed head injuries, but a few had contusion or subdural hemorrhage).

Aphasias resulting from subarachnoid hemorrhage showed a wide variation in rate of recovery. This variability was presumably related to the extent of hemorrhage and to the variable presence of infarction or tissue destruction (Fig. 16-2). To some extent, the prognosis was predictable from the initial severity of the aphasia. It is of interest that some of the worst jargon and global aphasias were seen following ruptured middle-cerebral-artery aneurysms.

APHASIA TYPE

Head (1926) recognized that some types of aphasia improve more rapidly than others. Weisenburg and McBride (1935), Butfield and Zangwill (1946), Messerli et al. (1976), and Kertesz and McCabe (1977) considered Broca's, or "expressive," aphasics to improve most, Vignolo (1964) considered expressive disorders to have a poor prognosis, and Basso et al. (1975) did not find any difference between the recovery of

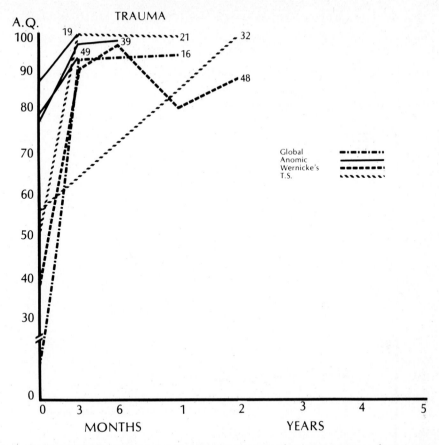

Fig. 16-1. Individual recovery graphs of various types of post-traumatic aphasics. AQ = overall score out of 100. Ages of patients are at the ends of the graph lines.

fluent and nonfluent aphasic patients. The variability of conclusions in part reflects problems in classification. For example, an expressive disorder is found in many different kinds of aphasias.

We assessed the prognosis of 47 patients with aphasia following stroke who had both an initial examination in the acute stages of illness and a follow-up test performed at least one year later (Kertesz and McCabe, 1977). The outcome after this long-term follow-up (average 28.6 months) was categorized on the basis of the aphasia quotient (AQ), a summary of the Western Aphasia Battery (Kertesz and Poole, 1974) (Table 16-1). Almost all of the global aphasics remained impaired. Broca's and Wernicke's aphasics showed a wider range of outcome (Figs. 16-3 and 16-4). Some patients with Wernicke's aphasia retain fluent jargon for many months. After a while, however, they lose their phonemic paraphasias and their language deficit consists of verbal substitutions and anomia. Broca's aphasics have an intermediate outlook, just about evenly divided between fair and good recovery. Anomic, conduction, and transcortical aphasics have a uniformly good prognosis, the majority of cases showing excellent spontaneous recovery. Some of the completely recovered patients were not

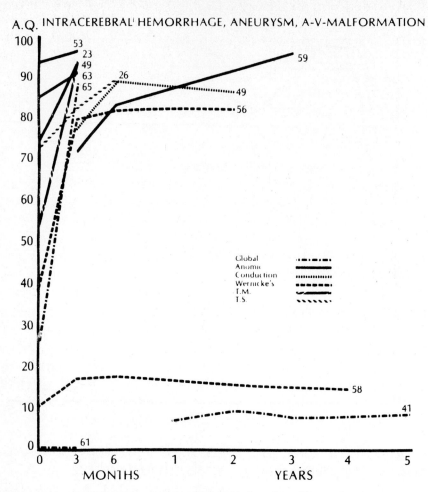

Fig. 16-2. Recovery graphs after intracerebral and subarachnoid hemorrhage. AQ = overall score (aphasia quotient).

Table 16-1. Final Outcome of Aphasia

Percentile Group	N	0–25 (poor)	25–50 (fair)	50–75 (good)	75–100 (very good)
Global	16	13	2	0	1
Broca's	12	0	6	6	1
Conduction	6	0	1	1	4
Wernicke's	13	4	6	3	0
Isolation	1	0	1	0	0
Transcortical motor	2	0	0	2	0
Transcortical sensory	3	0	0	1	2
Anomic	13	0	0	3	10
Total	67	17 (25.4%)	16 (23.9%)	16 (23.9%)	18 (26.9%)

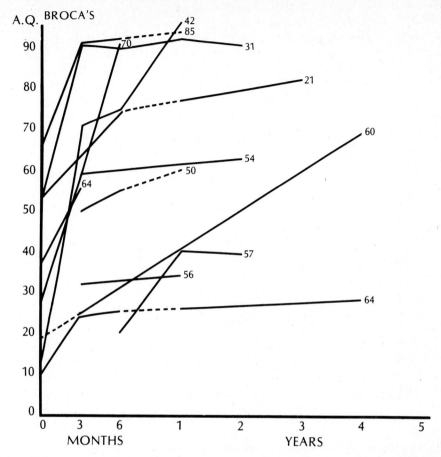

Fig. 16-3. Recovery from Broca's aphasia. Interrupted lines indicate duration of speech therapy. AQ = overall score.

even included in this analysis because they were not tested again after their three months' repeat scores were normal (as were almost half of the anomic aphasia patients' scores). The overall prognosis, regardless of aphasia type, for these 47 patients was as follows: poor for 28 per cent, fair for 19 per cent, good for 13 per cent, and excellent for 40 per cent.

The determination of complete recovery from aphasia depends on the definition of normal language function. We used an arbitrary cutoff AQ of 93.8. This was the actual mean score of a standardization group of brain-damaged patients who were judged clinically not to be aphasic (Kertesz and Poole, 1974). Final AQs indicated that 12 anomic, 5 conduction, 2 transcortical sensory, and 1 transcortical motor aphasic reached this criterion of recovery. Although this represents only 21 per cent of the 93 patients having aphasias with various etiologies (Kertesz and McCabe, 1977), it represents 62.5 per cent of the conduction, 50 per cent of the transcortical, and 48 per cent of the anomic patients (Table 16-2).

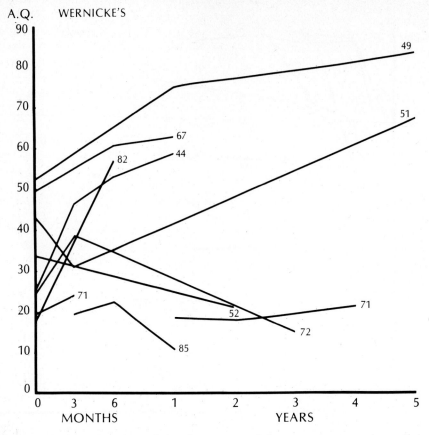

Fig. 16-4. Recovery from Wernicke's aphasia. None of these patients received speech therapy. AQ = overall score.

SEVERITY

The initial severity of the aphasia is closely tied in with the type of aphasia, and it is considered to be highly predictive of outcome (Godfrey and Douglass, 1959; Schuell et al., 1964; Sands et al., 1969; Sarno et al., 1970a, 1970b; Gloning et al., 1976; Kertesz and McCabe, 1977). Unfortunately, it is not always considered in studies of recovery. The most severely affected patients show little gain, whether treated or not (Sarno et al., 1970a), even though they have the most room for improvement. Mildly affected patients, on the other hand, more often recover completely (Kertesz and McCabe, 1977).

AGE

The influence of age is controversial. There is a clinical impression that younger patients recover better (Eisenson, 1949; Wepman, 1951; Vignolo, 1964). We demonstrated an inverse correlation between age and initial recovery rates (from 0 to 3

Table 16-2. Evolution of Aphasia from Initial to Endstage Classification and Percentages of Complete Recovery

Classification		%Recovered
Initial	Endstage	Completely
Globals (22)	2 Broca	
	1 Transcortical motor	
	1 Conduction	
	1 Anomic	
Broca's (17)	1 Transcortical motor	
	3 Anomic	
Conduction (8)	2 Anomic	
	5 Nonaphasic ----------------------- (62.5%)	
Wernicke's (13)	1 Global	
	1 Transcortical sensory	
	4 Anomic	
Isolation (2)	1 Anomic	
Transcortical 3 motor ⎱ (6)	2 Anomic	
	1 Nonaphasic ⎱	
Transcortical 3 sensory ⎰	2 Nonaphasic ⎰ ----------------- (50%)	
	1 Anomic	
Anomic (25)	12 Nonaphasic ------------------------- (48%)	
Total 93		21%

months), but when we excluded the post-traumatic group whose mean age was well below that of the patients with infarction, the trend just missed being significant (Kertesz and McCabe, 1977). Others have failed to show any correlation between age and recovery (Culton, 1971; Sarno and Levita, 1971; Smith et al., 1972). Clinicians also observe remarkable improvement in some elderly patients and lack of recovery in some young patients.

SEX

McGlone and Kertesz (1973) suggest that language and visuospatial functions are organized differently in men and women. The more bilateral representation in women would predict better recovery from aphasia; however, this is not substantiated by our data (Kertesz and McCabe, 1977; Shewan and Kertesz, 1981), which demonstrate no significant sex differences in rates of recovery from aphasia.

HANDEDNESS

The data from Subirana (1969) and Gloning et al. (1969) indicate that left-handers recover better from aphasias than right-handers. Gloning et al. (1969) also suggested that left-handers are likely to become aphasic regardless of which hemisphere is damaged. Interestingly, right-handers with a history of left-handedness among parents, siblings, or children recover, on the average, better than right-handers without such a family history (Geschwind, 1974).

OTHER FACTORS

Darley (1972) considered premorbid intelligence, health, and social milieu to have significant influence on recovery. Although intellectual and educational level influence what the patient and the family consider recovery to be, Kennan and Brassel's (1974) study indicated that health, employment, and age had little if any prognostic value when compared with factors such as listening and motor speech (comprehension and fluency). Sarno et al. (1970b) similarly showed that recovery in severe aphasia was not influenced by age, sex, education, occupational status, pre-illness language proficiency, or current living environment.

Time Course of Recovery

There is a surprising amount of agreement about the time course of recovery. A large number of stroke patients recover a great deal in the first two weeks (Kohlmeyer, 1976). The greatest amount of improvement occurs in the first two or three months after onset (Vignolo, 1964; Culton, 1969; Sarno and Levita, 1971; Basso et al., 1975; Kertesz and McCabe, 1977). After six months, the rate of recovery significantly drops (Butfield and Zangwill, 1946; Vignolo, 1964; Sand et al., 1969; Kertesz and McCabe, 1977). In the majority of cases, spontaneous recovery does not seem to occur after a year (Culton, 1969; Kertesz and McCabe, 1977); however, there are reports of improvement in cases under therapy many years after the stroke (Marks et al., 1957; Schuell et al., 1964; Smith et al., 1972; Broida, 1977).

Linguistic Features of Recovery

Not only do the various types of aphasia recover differently, but the various components of language do also. Of course, types of aphasia and language components are interdependent, a fact that is sometimes ignored. Kreindler and Fradis (1968) found that naming, oral imitation, and comprehension of nouns showed the most improvement. In the study of Broca's aphasics by Kenin and Swisher (1972), gains were greater in comprehension than in expressive language but no such difference was found by Sarno and Levita (1971). Hagen (1973) found improvement in language formulation, auditory retention, visual comprehension, and visual motor abilities in a three- to six-month period after the onset of symptoms. Ludlow (1977) found the greatest improvement in digit repetition reverse, identification by sentence, and word fluency in fluent aphasics; while digit repetition forward, sentence comprehension, and tactile naming improved most in Broca's aphasics. We studied various language components in four groups of 31 untreated aphasics (Lomas and Kertesz, 1978). Comprehension (as examined by yes-no questions), sequential commands, and repitition were the most improved components, and word fluency improved least. In fact, word fluency remained impaired while all other language factors improved, indicating that word fluency measures a nonlanguage factor in addition to language-related factors. This is corroborated by the observation that word fluency is often impaired in nonaphasic brain-damaged subjects. The highest overall recovery scores were attained by the low-fluency high-comprehension group. The groups with low initial comprehension showed recovery in yes-no comprehension and repetition tasks, and patients with high comprehension recovered in all tasks except word fluency.

Other linguistic features have also been studied. Ludlow (1977) studied mean sentence length, grammaticability index, and sentence production index as measures of recovery in Broca's and fluent aphasics. Both groups showed the greatest gains in the second month after onset of symptoms. Alajouanine (1956) distinguished four stages of recovery in severe expressive aphasia: (1) differentiation by intonation, (2) decreased automatic utterances, (3) less-rigid stereotypic utterances, and (4) volitional, slow, agrammatical speech. Kertesz and Benson (1970) pointed out the predictable pattern of linguistic recovery in jargon aphasia. Copious neologistic or phonemic jargon is replaced by verbal paraphasias or semantic jargon, and eventually anomia, or more rarely a "pure" word deafness, develops. The fact that overproduction of jargon is replaced by anomic gaps or circumlocutions indicates that there is recovery of regulatory or inhibitory systems.

We have also studied the evolution of aphasic syndromes, documenting the patterns of transformation from one clinically distinct aphasic type into another, as defined by subscores on subsequent examinations using the Western Aphasia Battery (Kertesz and McCabe, 1977). We found that anomic aphasia is a common end-stage of evolution, in addition to being a common aphasic syndrome de novo (Table 16-2). Four of 13 Wernicke's, 4 of 8 transcortical, 4 of 17 Broca's, 2 of 8 conduction, and 1 of 22 global aphasias evolved into anomic aphasia. Reversal of the usual direction of evolution of aphasic patterns (Table 16-2) should make the clinician suspect that a new lesion has appeared, as from an extension of a stroke or a tumor. Thus, for example, an anomic aphasic should not in the course of recovery become nonfluent, nor should he or she develop fluent paraphasic or neologistic jargon. Leischner (1976) also studied the transformation of aphasic syndromes three months after stroke. A significant number of patients with total aphasia and mixed aphasia evolved toward motor-amnestic aphasia.

Recovery from Alexia

Recovery from alexia is scantily documented. Newcombe et al. (1976) drew recovery curves for the performance of two patients who were followed—one for six months and one for four years—after removal of occipital lesions (abscess and meningioma). Without language therapy, the rate of recovery of the ability to read word lists was maximal initially and decelerated until eight to ten weeks after surgery, at which time a lower rate was achieved. Object naming curves showed that the patient with an abscess recovered more slowly and retained more residual errors than a post-traumatic patient, who exhibited better recovery of naming. Newcombe et al. classified linguistic errors as (1) visual confusions (beg → leg), (2) failure of grapheme-phoneme translation (of → off), (3) semantic substitutions (berry → grape), and (4) combinations of these. "Pure dyslexics" tended to make visual errors, and patients with dysphasic symptoms showed more grapheme-phoneme mistranslations; semantic errors were rare. Mixed errors were numerous initially, with many neologistic errors. In the residual phase the visual errors seemed independent of the syntactic class of words, but in cases of persistent aphasia, syntax had a marked effect; nouns were easier to read than verbs or adjectives.

RECOVERY OF NONVERBAL FUNCTION

In contrast to the increasingly large literature on recovery and treatment of aphasias, there is very little information available concerning recovery of nonverbal function in either aphasic or nonaphasic brain-damaged patients.

Recovery of Nonverbal Function in Aphasics

Studies of aphasic patients have shown that performance on Raven's Colored Progressive Matrices (RCPM), a nonverbal intelligence test, is impaired, with some exceptions. Culton (1969) used Raven's Standard Progressive Matrices in testing aphasics and found that considerable recovery of nonverbal performance occurred after 2 months and no further recovery occurred after 11 months. Our own analysis of RCPM performance in aphasic patients suggested that, of all the subtests in the aphasia battery, language comprehension correlated best with performance on the RCPM (Kertesz and McCabe, 1975). If the neuropsychological functions underlying language comprehension and nonverbal performance on the RCPM are related, recovery of language comprehension should parallel recovery of performance on the RCPM. At present, we are studying recovery in aphasic and nonaphasic (right-hemisphere-damaged) patients using the RCPM and various language tests. The initial portion of the study included 44 aphasic patients studied with the RCPM and the Western Aphasia Battery within a month of their stroke and three months later. Twenty aphasics were studied for 3 to 6 months, and 19 were studied for 6 to 12 months. Correlations were made between the recovery rates of RCPM performance and AQ, as well as other verbal and nonverbal performance subtests. Recovery of language function significantly correlated with performance on the RCPM during the first six months. Significant correlations were also obtained between recovery of RCPM scores and such subtests as auditory word discrimination (comprehension), object naming, sentence completion, responsive speech, and repetition. Correlation was poor with recovery of sentence comprehension, fluency, information content, calculation and praxis and, surprisingly, with other nonverbal performance tasks, such as drawing and block design. Recovery curves for the RCPM in various aphasic groups indicated that performance on the RCPM recovers in excess of language function in global aphasics, but there is less-than-expected recovery of RCPM and more scatter of initial RCPM performance among Broca's, Wernicke's, conduction, and anomic aphasics.

In conclusion, although recovery of nonverbal function as measured by the RCPM seems to correlate in a general way with recovery of language function, more severely affected global aphasics seem to recover more from this nonverbal impairment than others. Recovery of some language functions, such as comprehension of words, naming, and repetition, seems to correlate better than recovery of other language functions with nonverbal recovery. The results suggest that recovery of language and non-language function are not always parallel.

Recovery of Function in Nonaphasic Brain-Damaged Patients

NEGLECT

Lawson (1962) emphasized that unawareness of left unilateral neglect retards recovery and that active treatment is needed to overcome it. Campbell and Oxbury (1976) examined the performance of right-hemisphere-damaged patients three to four weeks (and then six months) after a stroke, on verbal and nonverbal tasks, including block design and matrices. Those who demonstrated neglect on the initial drawing tests remained impaired on visuospatial tests six months later, in spite of the resolution of neglect. Other reports describe unilateral neglect remaining up to 12 years after onset. (For further discussion of recovery from neglect, see Chap. 10.)

BILATERAL INJURY FROM TRAUMA

Performance skills on the Wechsler Adult Intelligence Scale took longer to recover than verbal intelligence in patients with traumatic brain injuries (Bond, 1975). The most rapid recovery occurred during the first six months; recovery then slowly reached a maximum at 24 months. Psychosocial outcome, which was affected by intellectual and personality changes, correlated negatively with the duration of post-traumatic amnesia.

CORTICAL BLINDNESS AND VISUAL AGNOSIA

Recovery from cortical blindness and related syndromes of the parietal and occipital lobes has been described by Gloning et al. (1968). There appear to be regular stages of progression from cortical blindness through visual agnosia and partially impaired perceptual function to recovery. (For further discussion of visual agnosia, see Chap. 9.)

RECOVERY OF MEMORY

The etiology of the most frequently studied memory loss is trauma. The prognosis of post-traumatic memory impairment has been correlated with the duration of post-traumatic amnesia by Russell (1971): 82 per cent of his patients returned to full duty, 92 per cent of these in less than three weeks. Learning capacity may continue to be impaired after the acute amnesia has subsided (the postconcussional syndrome). The phenomenon of shrinking retrograde amnesia, seen with head trauma (Russell and Nathan, 1946; Benson and Geschwind, 1967), suggests that during the amnestic period memories are not lost but rather cannot be activated (retrieved).

Memory loss secondary to alcoholic, postinfectious, and toxic causes, when severe, tends to persist (Talland, 1965), whereas ECT-induced memory loss is rarely permanent (Williams, 1966). The acute amnestic confabulatory syndrome (Wernicke's encephalopathy) often subsides within weeks, becoming a more chronic state of Korsakoff psychosis. Korsakoff himself was optimistic about the prognosis but did not have reliable reports beyond the acute stage. Later clinicians denied seeing complete remissions. Victor and Adams (1953) arrived at a more hopeful conclusion but noted that "complete restoration of memory is . . . unusual when the defect is severe." Amnestic symptoms from unilateral infarctions subside in a few months, but more lasting deficit occurs with bilateral posterior cerebral artery involvement (Benson et al., 1975). (For a further discussion of memory disorders, see Chap. 10.)

RECOVERY FROM HEMIPLEGIA

Even though hemiplegia is not a subject covered by this book, the parallels between recovery of neuropsychological function and motor function cannot be ignored. There is an extensive body of information on this subject. The testing of hemiplegia is a more uniform procedure than the testing of neuropsychological disorders, and in spite of the variability of recovery, there is general agreement about many aspects. For example, the recovery of the upper extremity is not as good as that of the lower extremity. Motion begins proximally and then occurs in the more distal portions of the arm. The initial motion occurs from one to six weeks following the stroke. A study by Van Buskirk (1954) concluded that restitution of function occurs chiefly in the first two months and appears to be a spontaneous process. When full recovery occurs, initial motion begins within two weeks and full motion occurs within three months. About 45 per cent recover full motion, 40 per cent partial motion, and 15 per cent do not recover function of the upper extremity (when followed for more than seven months). The role of cerebral dominance was examined in the recovery of ambulation. Right hemiplegics recovered independent ambulation more often and faster than left hemiplegics. The spatial-perceptual deficiencies of left hemiplegics were considered to be more resistant to recovery and hampered recovery of ambulation (Cassvan et al., 1976). The influence of impaired sensory feedback was investigated by Van Buskirk (1955). Newman (1972) suggested that much of the early recovery (especially in the upper limb) could be due to return of circulation to ischemic areas. Transfer of function to undamaged neurons is suggested as the mechanism underlying late recovery (especially in the lower limbs). (For a discussion of the recovery from apraxia, see Chap. 7.)

LANGUAGE THERAPY

The treatment of aphasics is an established practice, even though only a few studies have considered spontaneous recovery in assessing the efficacy of therapy. The first systematic study of treatment (Butfield and Zangwill, 1946) did not use untreated controls, but an attempt was made to describe the method of therapy—mainly the use of oral drills and transmodal cues. Gains after six months were attributed to therapy, assuming that further spontaneous recovery was not significant at that time. Vignolo (1964) studied treated and untreated patients and did not find a significant difference between these groups; nevertheless, he suggested that therapy between the second and sixth months may be beneficial. Sarno et al. (1970a) compared global aphasics who underwent stimulation therapy and programmed instruction with untreated controls and found no significant difference.

A few studies that use untreated controls present evidence that therapy is effective. Hagen (1973) compared ten treated aphasics matched for severity and type (sensorimotor type III of Schuell) with ten untreated aphasics and found significantly better recovery in language formulation, speech production, reading comprehension, spelling, and arithmetic in the treated group. Most improvement occurred during the first six months of treatment. Auditory comprehension, auditory retention, visual comprehension, and visuomotor abilities improved equally in the treated and control group. All patients were included in the study at three months, and treatment began at six months after the stroke. Basso et al. (1975) studied 91 treated aphasics and 94 controls who could not come for therapy for personal or logistic reasons. The control group was significantly older than the treated group. The etiologies were said to be the same for the two groups, but no data were published to support this statement, although it is crucial to control for etiology in a study of recovery. A minimum of six months of therapy was shown to significantly affect the oral expression of aphasics; the longer the duration of aphasia before therapy was begun, the less effective the therapy. Unfortunately, the experimental design lumped all aphasics into two categories, possibly allowing more global or severe-jargon aphasics to be included in the untreated sample. This is bound to occur in everyday therapy situations, as therapists are much less likely to persist with global or severe-jargon patients who do not improve. Another important problem of this retrospective study is that, instead of controlling the time of inclusion after the onset, it examined the "effect of this variable" in improvement. This, in fact, allowed patients seen soon after their stroke, who would be expected to have more spontaneous recovery, to be overrepresented in the treated group and patients seen longer after their stroke, when recovery is less likely to occur, to be overrepresented in the untreated group. To design a study of treatment of aphasia, it is essential to match patients for initial severity, type, etiology, and time from onset.

A comparison of language-oriented, stimulation therapy by speech therapists and supportive therapy by untrained therapists revealed no significant differences (Shewan and Kertesz, 1981). Patients were admitted to treatment at two weeks poststroke and had at least three hours of therapy per week, if possible, for one year. Because of attrition the average duration of treatment was about 20 weeks. The Western Aphasia Battery was used to follow patients on entry at 3, 6, 12, and 18 months poststroke. A nonrandomized, untreated group (less severely affected) showed less recovery in writing and other performance scores than the treated groups. The oral language scores also showed less improvement in this untreated (by default) group, but the difference did not reach significance.

David et al. (1982) reported a multicenter trial comparing therapy for 155 stroke patients by either speech therapists or untrained volunteers. They used the Functional Communication Profile as a basic measure. Patients were entered any time after three weeks post-onset and were randomized to the two treatment groups. Treatment was only for 30 hours over 15 to 20 weeks. A group of nine late referrals also showed improvement. This was taken as a period beyond spontaneous recovery and therefore attributable to treatment. The study concluded that there was no significant difference between the treatment groups. These workers felt that the improvement was the result of the support and stimulation provided by speech therapist and volunteer alike.

Therapy itself is most complex and difficult to standardize. It is said that there are as many varieties of aphasia treatment as there are aphasics. Therapists, pointing out the need to tailor therapy to the needs of the individual, are reluctant to follow rigidly prescribed treatment programs. The content of therapy, as well as the methods, differs considerably, creating overlapping categories. Lately, the contribution of psycholinguistic principles to the content of therapy has been increasing.

A cooperative study of aphasia therapy, by Wertz et al. (1981), followed stroke patients undergoing stimulus-response speech therapy and compared them with the results of "social interaction" group therapy. The results showed significant gains, as measured by the PICA, in both groups, with individually treated patients doing slightly better. Other measures, such as RCPM, showed less overall improvement. Maximum improvement occurred in the first three months. Significant improvement occurred in the language performance between 26 and 48 weeks in both groups, and it was assumed that spontaneous recovery was not operational at that time. This allowed the authors only to speculate about the efficacy of therapy, since no true control group was studied. If, however, one assumes that the social interaction group was, in effect, a control group, one might interpret their data as indicating that more structured speech therapy did not contribute much to recovery.

The following methods of therapy are in use at present. The first two are used by most therapists (Darley, 1975).

Stimulation Approach

Wepman (1951) recognized that aphasics are, in fact, stimulated rather than educated during treatment. Familiar materials relevant to the patient are used. The patient is not pressured: every response is accepted and reinforced.

Schuell et al.'s (1964) approach is similar; (1) use intensive *auditory stimulation,* i.e., meaningful patterns and high-frequency words, adjusting the rate, loudness, and length of presentation to the needs of each patient, (2) use highly repetitive stimulation, (3) elicit, rather than force, some response to every stimulus, (4) stimulate more responses rather than correct errors, and (5) use different language modalities for facilitation: spelling aloud to help writing, writing to help auditory retention, etc. Various forms of the specific stimulation approach were defined by Taylor (1964): (1) association approach: attempting to elicit associated words by structuring sessions around families of words, using the maximum possible word environments for each target word; (2) situational approach: everyday situations are acted out, facilitating learning functionally useful vocabulary or statements; and (3) minimal differences approach: similarly sounding words and similar-looking written material are used as stimuli for teaching.

Other varieties of stimulation are less structured. These are variously called (1) environmental stimulation: everybody talks to the patient as much as possible; (2) rapport approach: a warm relationship is established between the clinician and the patient without regard to the content and method of contact; (3) socialization approach: individual or group sessions include informal "fun" activities; (4) interest approach: subjects related to the patient's previous group or individual work activities and interests are discussed; and (5) psychotherapeutic approach: problems of anxiety and loss of self-esteem are focused upon.

Programmed Instruction

The desired language behavior is defined and programs to reach it are constructed. Martha Taylor Sarno and associates defined and developed this approach (Taylor, 1964). Many individual steps, from preverbal programs to practicing syntax, are used to achieve the desired language behavior (Sarno et al., 1970a). Although repeatable and quantifiable, it is very difficult to design and persist in such a program. This is also called the psycholinguistic approach when careful attention is directed to the rules of language and the language deficit itself. Goda (1962) advocated using the patient's own spontaneous speech to design programs and drill material. Language-oriented therapy, as described by Shewan (personal communication), also uses an operant paradigm while the content is based on knowledge about language impairment in aphasics. It considers the language modalities of training and the level at which the patient should be trained. Criteria for moving from one level to another are predetermined. The purpose is to teach strategies rather than responses.

Other Therapies

Various other more or less distinct therapeutic approaches can be identified from the literature. What follows is far from a complete catalog.

DEBLOCKING METHOD

Weigl (1968) described a special kind of stimulation that uses an intact channel to eliminate a block in understanding or expression via other channels. A response is evoked in an intact channel (e.g., recognition of a printed word) just before presenting the same stimulus to a blocked channel (auditory comprehension). This is similar to Schuell's intermodality facilitation.

PREVENTIVE METHOD

This is a specific application of a linguistic theory by Beyn and Shokhor-Trotskaya (1966). Instead of object naming, patients work on expressions as a whole, preventing the occurrence of telegraphic speech.

COMPENSATORY APPROACH

This encourages patients to use their own compensatory strategies (e.g., the patient who needs repetition to understand is encouraged to ask for it). Patients with word-finding difficulty are encouraged to circumlocute (Holland, 1977).

OPERANT CONDITIONING WITH AUTOMATIC TEACHING MACHINES

These have been described by Keith and Darley (1967). Patients universally and understandably prefer human contact! Microcomputers, however, have been used with increasing frequency. There is no scientific evidence for or against their use.

MELODIC INTONATION THERAPY

This has been tried for global aphasics (Sparks et al., 1974) based on evidence that many severely affected aphasics can sing words better than they speak and that musical, tonal abilities are subserved by the right hemisphere. The patient intones a melody for simple statements.

VISUAL COMMUNICATION

Nonverbal symbols are used to train global aphasics to express themselves, since there has been a successful demonstration that chimpanzees can be taught a nonverbal communication system (Glass et al., 1973). Gardner et al. (1976) taught patients to recognize and manipulate symbols in order to respond to commands, answer questions, describe their actions, and express desires and feelings. A similar approach is the use of hand signals to teach global aphasics basic communication (Eagleson et al., 1970).

DRUG TREATMENT

Drugs used to treat aphasia include dexamethasone, sodium amytal, priscol, meprobamate, and hyperbaric oxygen—with unimpressive results (Darley, 1975).

DIRECT PSYCHOTHERAPY AND HYPNOSIS

These have at times been considered useful in reducing the emotional problems of aphasics and in facilitating recovery.

SPECIAL THERAPIES

Therapies for various modalities have been suggested, for example, therapies for correcting "verbal apraxia" (Rosenbeck et al., 1973) or for retraining of writing (Hatfield and Weddell, 1976).

Brookshire (1977) attempted to analyze the relationship between clinician behavior and patient behavior. He is developing a system for recording and coding events during therapy. He has aptly stated that "a definite study of the effects of treatment on recovery from aphasia will be impossible without some means of describing objectively and unambiguously the exact nature of the treatment program or programs employed in the study."

REFEFENCES

Ades, H. W., and Raab, D. H. (1946). Recovery of motor function after two-stage extirpation of area 4 in monkeys. *J. Neurophsyiol.* 9:55–60.

Alajouanine, T. (1956). Verbal realization in aphasia. *Brain* 79:1–28.

Basser, L. S. (1962). Hemiplegia of early onset and the faculty of speech with special reference to the effects of hemispherectomy. *Brain* 85:427–460.

Basso, A., Faglioni, P., and Vignolo, L. A. (1975). Etude controlee de la reeducation du langage dans l'aphasie: Comparaison entre aphasiques traites et non-traitee. *Rev. Neurol* 131:607–614.

Benson, D. F., and Geschwind, N. (1967). Shrinking retrograde amnesia. *J. Neurol. Neurosurg. Psychiat.* 30:539–544.

Benson, D. F., Marsden, C. D., and Meadows, J. C. (1975). The amnesic syndrome of posterior cerebral artery occlusion. *Acta Neurol. Scandinav.* 50:133–145.

Beyn, E. S., and Shokhor-Trotskaya (1966). The preventive method of speech rehabilitation in aphasia. *Cortex* 2:96–108.

Bond, M. R. (1975). Assessment of psychosocial outcome after severe head injury. In *Outcome of Severe Damage to the Central Nervous System*. Amsterdam: Elsevier.

Brookshire, R. H. (1977). A system for recording events in patient-clinician interactions during aphasia treatment sessions. In *Rationale for Adult Aphasia Therapy*. Univ. of Nebraska Medical Centre.

Braun, J. J., Meyer, P. M., and Meyer, D. R. (1966). Sparing of a brightness habit in rats following visual decortication. *J. Comp. Physiol. Psychol.* 61:79–82.

Broida, H. (1977). Language therapy effects in long term aphasia. *Arch. Phys. Med. Rehabil.* 58:248–253.

Bucy, P. C. (1934). The relation of the premotor cortex to motor activity. *J. Nervous Mental Dis* 79:621–630.

Butfield, E., and Zangwill, O. L. (1946). Re-education in aphasia: A review of 70 cases. *J. Neurol. Neurosurg. Psychiat.* 9:75–79.

Campbell, D. C., and Oxbury, J. M. (1976). Recovery from unilateral visuospatial neglect. *Cortex* 12:303–312.

Cassvan, A., Ross, P. L., Dyer, P. R., and Zane, L. (1976). Lateralization in stroke syndromes as a factor in ambulation. *Arch. Phys. Med. Rehab.* 57:583–587.

CIBA Foundation Symposium (1975). *Outcome of Severe Damage to the Nervous System*. Amsterdam: Elsevier.

Culton, G. L. (1969). Spontaneous recovery from aphasia. *J. Speech Hearing Res.* 12:825–832.

Culton, G. L. (1971). Reaction to age as a factor in chronic aphasia in stroke patients. *J. Speech Hearing Disorders* 36:563–564.

Darley, F. L. (1972). The efficacy of language rehabilitation in aphasia. *J. Speech Hearing Disorders* 30:3–22.

Darley, F. L. (1975). Treatment of acquired aphasia. In *Advances in Neurology*, vol. 7, *Current Reviews of Higher Nervous System Dysfunction* (W. S. Friedlander, ed.). New York: Raven.

David, R., Enderby, P., and Bainton, D. (1982). Treatment of acquired aphasia: Speech therapists and volunteers compared. *J. Neurol. Neurosurg. Psychiatry* 45:957–961.

Demeurisse, G., Verhas, M., Capon, A., and Paternot, J. (1983). Lack of evolution of the cerebral blood flow during clinical recovery of a stroke. *Stroke* 14:77–81.

Duffy, F., et al. (1976). Pharmacological reversal of deprivation amblyopia in the cat. Paper presented at 28th annual meeting of American Academy of Neurology, Toronto.

Eagleson, H. M., Vaughn, G. R., and Knudson, A.B.C. (1970). Hand signals for dysphasia. *Arch. Phys. Med.* 51:111–113.

Eisenson, J. (1949). Prognostic factors related to language rehabilitation in aphasic patients. *J. of Speech Hearing Disorders,* 14:262–264.

Finger, S. (1978). *Recovery from Brain Damage*. New York: Plenum.

Flourens, P. (1824). Recherches Experimentales sur les Proprietes et les Fonctions du Systeme Nerveux dans les Animaux Vertebres. Paris: Crevot.

Franz, S. I., and Oden, R. (1917). On cerebral motor control: The recovery from experimentally produced hemiplegia. *Psychobiol. 1*:3–18.

Fritsch, G. and Hitzig, E. (1870). Über die elektrische Erregbarkeit des Grosshirns. *Arch. Anat. Physiol., Leipzig 37*:300–332.

Gardner, H., Zurif, E. B., Berry, T., and Baker, E. (1976). Visual communication in aphasia. *Neuropsychologia 14*:275–292.

Gazzaniga, M. S. (1970). *The Bisected Brain*. New York: Appleton.

Geschwind, N. (1969). Problems in the anatomical understanding of the aphasias. In *Contributions to Clinical Neuropsychology* (A. Benton, ed.). Chicago: Aldine.

Geschwind, N. (1974). Late changes in the nervous system: An overview. In *Plasticity and Recovery of Function in the Central Nervous System* (D. Stein, J. Rosen, and N. Butters, eds.). New York: Academic Press.

Glass, A. V., Gazzaniga, M. S., and Premack, D. (1973). Artificial language training in global aphasics. *Neuropsychologia 11*:95–103.

Gloning, I., Gloning, K., and Haff, H. (1968). *Neuropsychological symptoms and syndromes in lesions of the occipital lobes and adjacent areas*. Paris: Gauthier-Villars.

Gloning, I., Gloning, K., Haub, G., and Quatember, R. (1969). Comparison of verbal behavior in right-handed and non-right-handed patients with anatomically verified lesion of one hemisphere. *Cortex 5*:43–52.

Gloning, K. Trappl, R., Heiss, W. D., and Quatember, R. (1976). *Prognosis and Speech Therapy in Aphasia in Neurolinguistics. 4. Recovery in Aphasics*. Amsterdam: Swets & Zeitlinger, B.V.

Goda, S. (1962). Spontaneous speech: A primary source of therapy material. *J. Speech Hearing Disorders 27*:190–192.

Godfrey, C. M., and Douglass, E. (1959). The recovery process in aphasia. *Can. Med. Assoc. J. 80*:618–624.

Goldberger, M. E. (1974). Recovery of movement after CNS lesions in monkeys. In *Plasticity and Recovery of Function in the Central Nervous System* (D. Stein, J. Rosen, and N. Butters, eds.). New York: Academic Press.

Hagen, C. (1973). Communication abilities in hemiplegia: Effect of speech therapy. *Arch. Phys. Med. Rehab. 54*:454–463.

Hatfield, F., and Weddell, R. (1976). Re-training in writing in severe aphasia. In *Neurolinguistics. 4. Recovery in Aphasics*. Amsterdam: Swets & Zeitlinger, B.V.

Head, H. (1926). *Aphasia and Kindred Disorders of Speech*. Cambridge: Cambridge University Press.

Hécaen, H. (1976). Acquired aphasia in children and the ontogenesis of hemispheric functional specialization. *Brain and Language 3*:114–134.

Henschen, S. E. (1922). *Klinische und anatomishe Beitrage zur Pathologie des Gehirns*, vols. 5, 6, 7. Stockholm: Nordiska Bokhandelin.

Hirsch, H.V.B., and Jacobson, M. (1974). The perfect brain. In *Fundamentals of Psychobiology* (M. S. Gazzaniga and C. B. Blakemore, eds.). New York: Academic Press.

Holland, A. L. (1977). Some practical considerations in aphasia rehabilitation. In *Rationale for Adult Aphasia Therapy* (M. Sullivan and M. S. Kommers, eds.). University of Nebraska Medical Center.

Jackson, J. H. (1873). On the anatomical and physiological localization of movements in the brain. *Lancet 1*:84–85, 162–164, 232–234.

Keenan, S. S., and Brassel, E. G. (1974). A study of factors related to prognosis for individual aphasic patients. *J. Speech Hearing Disorders*. 39:257–269.

Keith, R. L., and Darley, F. L. (1967). The use of a specific electric board in rehabilitation of the aphasic patient. *J. Speech Hearing Disorders* 32:148–153.

Kenin, M., and Swisher, L. (1972). A study of pattern of recovery in aphasia. *Cortex* 8:56–68.

Kennard, M. A., and McCulloch, W. S. (1943). Motor response to stimulation of cerebral cortex in absence of areas 4 and 6 *(Macaca mulatta)*. *J. Neurophysiol.* 6:181–190.

Kertesz, A., and Benson, D. F. (1970). Neologistic jargon: A clinicopahological study. *Cortex* 6:362–387.

Kertesz, A., and McCabe, P. (1975). Intelligence and aphasia: Performance of aphasics on Raven's Coloured Progressive Matrices. *Brain and Language* 2:387–395.

Kertesz, A., and McCabe, P. (1977). Recovery patterns and prognosis in aphasia. *Brain* 100:1–18.

Kertesz, A., and Poole, E. (1974). The aphasia quotient: The taxonomic approach to measurement of aphasic disability. *Can. J. Neurol. Sci.* 1:7–16.

Kinsbourne, M. (1971). The minor cerebral hemisphere as a source of aphasic speech. *Arch. Neurol.* 25:302–306.

Kohlmeyer, K. (1976). Aphasia due to focal disorders of cerebral circulation: Some aspects of localization and of spontaneous recovery. In *Neurolinguistics. 4. Recovery in Aphasics.* Amsterdam: Swets & Zeitlinger B. V.

Kreindler, A., and Fradis, A. (1968). *Performances in Aphasia: A Neurodynamical, Diagnostic and Psychological Study.* Paris: Gauthier-Villars.

Lashley, K. S. (1938). Factors limiting recovery after central nervous lesions. *J. Nerv. Mental Diseases* 88:733–755.

Lawson, I. R. (1962). Visual-spatial neglect in lesions of the right cerebral hemisphere: A study in recovery. *Neurology* 12:23–33.

Lebrun, Y., and Hoops, R. (1976). *Neurolinguistics. 4. Recovery in Aphasics.* Amsterdam: Swets & Zeitlinger, B.V.

Leischner, A. (1976). Aptitude of aphasics for language treatment. In *Neurolinguistics. 4. Recovery in Aphasics.* Amsterdam: Swets & Zeitlinger B.V.

Liu, C. N., and Chambers, W. W. (1958). Intraspinal sprouting of dorsal root axons. *Arch. Neurol. (Chicago)* 79:46–61.

Lomas, J., and Kertesz, A. (1978). Patterns of spontaneous recovery in aphasic groups: A study of adult stroke patients. *Brain and Language* 5:388–401.

Ludlow, C. (1977). Recovery from aphasia: A foundation for treatment. In *Rationale for Adult Aphasia Therapy* (M. A. Sullivan and M. S. Kommers, eds.). University of Nebraska Medical Center.

Luria, A. R. (1970). *Traumatic Aphasia.* Hague: Mouton.

Luria, A. R., Naydin, V. L., Tsvetkova, L. S., and Vinarskaya, E. N. (1969). Restoration of higher cortical function following local brain damage. In *Handbook of Clinical Neurology,* vol. 3 (R. J. Vinken and G. W. Bruyn, eds.). Amsterdam: North Holland.

Marks, M. M., Taylor, M. L., and Rusk, L. A. (1957). Rehabilitation of the aphasic patient: A survey of three years' experience in a rehabilitation setting. *Neurology* 7:837–843.

McGlone, J., and Kertesz, A. (1973). Sex differences in cerebral processing of visuospatial tasks. *Cortex* 9:313–320.

Messerli, P., Tissot, A., and Rodriguez, J. (1976). Recovery from aphasia: Some factors of prognosis. In *Neurolinguistics. 4. Recovery in Aphasics.* Amsterdam: Swets & Zeitlinger, B.V.

Meyer, J. S., et al. (1970). Diaschisis result from acute unilateral cerebral infarction. *Arch. Neurol.* 23:241–247.

Meyer, J. S., et al. (1974). Disordered neurotransmitter function. *Brain* 97:655–64.

Milner, B. (1974). Hemispheric specialization: Scope and limits, in *The Neurosciences: Third Study Program* (F. O. Schmitt and F. G. Worden, eds.). Cambridge, Mass.: MIT Press.

Moore, R. Y (1974). Central regeneration and recovery of function: The problem of collateral reinnervation. In *Plasticity and Recovery of Function in the Central Nervous System*. New York: Academic Press.

Munk, H. (1881). *Ueber die funktionen der Grosshirnrinde, Gesammelte Mitteilungen aus den Jahren 1877–1880*. Berlin: August Hirshwald.

Newcombe, F., Hions, R. W., and Marshall, J. C. (1976). Acquired dyslexia: Recovery and Retraining. In *Neurolinguistics. 4. Recovery in Aphasics*. Amsterdam: Swet & Zeitlinger B.V.

Newman, M. (1972). The process of recovery after hemiplegia. *Stroke* 3:702–710.

Nielsen, J. M. (1946). *Agnosia, Apraxia, Aphasia*. New York: Hoeber.

Nottebohm, F. (1970). Ontogeny of bird song. *Science* 167:950–956.

Pieniadz, J. M., Naeser, M. A., Koff, E., and Levine, H. L. (1983). CT scan cerebral hemispheric asymmetry mesurements in stroke cases with global asphasia: atypical asymmetries associated with improved recovery. *Cortex* 19:371–391.

Rosenbeck, J. C., Lemme, M. L., Ahern, M. B., Harris, E. H., and Wertz, R. T. (1973). A treatment for apraxia of speech in adults. *J. Speech Hearing Disorders* 38:462–472.

Rubens, A. (1977). The role of changes within the central nervous system during recovery from aphasia. In *Rationale for Adult Aphasia Therapy* (M. A. Sullivan and M. S. Kommers, eds.). University of Nebraska Medical Center.

Russell, W. R. (1971). *The Traumatic Amnesias*. London: Oxford University Press.

Russell, W. R., and Nathan, P. W. (1946). Traumatic amnesia. *Brain* 69:280–300.

Sands, E., Sarno, M. T., and Sankweiler, D. (1969). Long-term assessment of language function in aphasia due to stroke. *Arch. Phys. Med. Rehab.* 50:202–222.

Sarno, M. T., and Levita, E. (1971). Natural course of recovery in severe aphasia. *Arch. Phys. Med. Rehab.* 52:175–179.

Sarno, M. T., Silverman, M., and Levita, E. (1970b). Psychosocial factors and recovery in geriatric patients with severe aphasia. *J. Am. Geriatr. Soc.* 18:405–409.

Sarno, M. T., Silverman, M., and Sands, E. (1970a). Speech therapy and language recovery in severe aphasia. *J. Speech Hearing Res.* 13:607–623.

Schneider, G. E. (1973). Early lesions of superior colliculus: Factors affecting the formation of abnormal retinal projections. *Brain Behav. Evol.* 8:73–109.

Schuell, A., Jenkins, J. J., and Jimenez-Pabon (1964). *Aphasia in Adults*. New York: Harper & Row.

Shewan, C. M., and Kertesz, A. (1981). Effects of speech and language treatment on recovery from aphasia. Paper presented at Academy of Aphasia meeting, London, Ontario.

Smith, A. (1966). Speech and other functions after left (dominant) hemispherectomy. *J. Neurol. Neurosurg. Psychiat.* 29:467–471.

Smith, A. Chamoux, R., Leri, J., London, R., and Muraski, A. (1972). *Diagnosis, Intelligence and Rehabilitation of Chronic Aphasics*. Ann Arbor: University of Michigan Department of Physical Medicine and Rehabilitation.

Sparks, R., Helm, N., and Albert, M. (1974). Aphasia rehabilitation resulting from melodic intonation therapy. *Cortex* 10:303–316.

Sperry, R. W. (1947). Effect of crossing nerves to antagonistic limb muscles in the monkey. *Arch. Neurol. Psychiat.* 58:452–473.

Stavraky, G. W. (1961). Supersensitivity following lesions of the nervous system. Toronto: University of Toronto Press.

Stein, D. G., Rosen, J. J., and Butters, N. (1974). *Plasticity and Recovery of Function in the Central Nervous System*. New York: Academic Press.

Stoicheff, M. L. (1960). Motivating instructions and language performance of dysphasic subjects. *J. Speech Hearing Res.* 3:75–85.

Subirana A. (1969). Handedness and cerebral dominance. In *Handbook of Clinical Neurology* (P. J. Vinken and G. W. Bruyn, eds.). Amsterdam: North Holland.

Sullivan, M., and Kommers, M. S. (1977). *Rationale for Adult Aphasia Therapy*. University of Nebraska Medical Center.

Talland, G. A. (1965). *Deranged Memory*. New York: Academic Press.

Taylor, M. L. (1964). Language therapy. In *The Aphasic Adult: Evaluation and Rehabilitation* (H. G. Burr, ed.). Charlottesville: Wayside Press.

Van Buskirk, C. (1954). Return of motor function in hemiplegia *Neurology* 4:919–928.

Van Buskirk, C. (1955). Prognostic value of sensory defect in rehabilitation of hemiplegics. *Neurology (Minneap.)* 6:407–411.

Von Monakow, C. (1914). *Die Lokalisation im Grosshirnrinde und der Abbau der Funktion durch korticale Herde.*Wiesbaden: J. F. Bergmann.

Victor, M., and Adams, R. D. (1958). The effect of alcohol on the nervous system. *Proc. Assoc. Res. Nervous Mental Disorders* 32:526–573.

Vignolo, L. A. (1964). Evolution of aphasia and language rehabilitation: A retrospective exploratory study. *Cortex* 1:344–367.

Ward, A. A. Jr., and Kennard, M. A. (1942). Effect of cholinergic drugs on recovery of function following lesions of the central nervous system. *Yale J. Biol. Med.* 15:189–229.

Watson, C. W., and Kennard, M. A. (1945). The effect of anticonvulsant drugs on recovery of function following cerebral cortical lesions. *J. Neurophysiol* 8:221–231.

Weigl, E. (1968). On the problem of cortical syndromes. In *The Reach of Mind* (M. L. Simmel, ed.). New York: Springer.

Weisenburg, T., and McBride, K. E. (1935). *Aphasia: A Clinical and Psychological Study*. New York: Commonwealth Fund.

Wepman, J. M. (1951). *Recovery from Aphasia*. New York: Ronald Press.

Wertz, R. T., Collins, M. J., Brookshire, R. H., Friden, T., Kurtzke, J., Pierce, J., and Weiss, D. (1978). The Veterans Administration Cooperative Study on Aphasia: A Comparison of Individual and Group Treatment. Presentation to the Academy of Aphasia Meeting, Chicago.

Williams, M. (1966). Memory disorders associated with electroconvulsive therapy. In *Amnesia* (C.W.M. Whitby and O. L. Zangweill, eds.). London: Butterworths.

Wood, B. T., and Teuber, H.-L. (1978). Changing patterns of childhood aphasia. *Ann. Neurol.* 3:273–280.

Index of Authors Cited

507

Subject Index

Page numbers in *italics* indicate illustrations. Page numbers followed by *t* indicate tables.